Creating Web Sites Bible

Third Edition

Creating Web Sites Bible

Third Edition

Philip Crowder with David A. Crowder

Wiley Publishing, Inc.

Creating Web Sites Bible, Third Edition

Published by
Wiley Publishing, Inc.
10475 Crosspoint Boulevard
Indianapolis, IN 46256
www.wiley.com

Published by Wiley Publishing, Inc., Indianapolis, Indiana

Published simultaneously in Canada

ISBN: 978-0-4702-2363-5

Manufactured in the United States of America

10 9 8 7 6 5 4 3 2 1

For general information on our other products and services or to obtain technical support, please contact our Customer Care Department within the U.S. at (800) 762-2974, outside the U.S. at (317) 572-3993 or fax (317) 572-4002.

Library of Congress Cataloging-in-Publication Data:

Crowder, Philip.
Creating web sites bible / Philip Crowder with David Crowder. — 3rd ed.
p. cm.
Includes index.
ISBN 978-0-470-22363-5 (paper/website)
1. Web site development. 2. Web sites — Design. I. Crowder, David A.
II. Title.
TK5105.8888.C76 2008
006.7 — dc22
2008004976

About the Authors

Philip Crowder of Bristol, Tennessee, is the director of the Computer and Information Management (CIM) program at Virginia Intermont College where he teaches future Web designers and programmers the ins and outs of HTML, XHTML, XML, CSS, JavaScript, and a variety of other Web languages and technologies. He has also done funded research into computer-based human language translation systems.

David A. Crowder is a professional Web developer, and the author or coauthor of more than 20 books on Web design and development. He has been involved in the online community for more than a decade, and has helped to teach hundreds of thousands of readers to create their own cutting-edge Web sites.

Credits

Executive Editor
Chris Webb

Development Editor
Kevin Shafer

Technical Editor
Auri Rahimzadeh

Production Editor
Debra Banninger

Copy Editor
Foxxe Editorial Services

Editorial Manager
Mary Beth Wakefield

Production Manager
Tim Tate

Vice President and Executive Group Publisher
Richard Swadley

Vice President and Executive Publisher
Joseph B. Wikert

Project Coordinator, Cover
Lynsey Stanford

Proofreader
David Parise (Word One)

Indexer
Jack Lewis

Acknowledgments

From Philip Crowder (Third Edition):

Christ Jesus is my personal Savior and all that is done is done through God's saving Grace and abiding love.

I should acknowledge my editors above all others, for it was through their strenuous efforts that this book was brought about. They were always professional and gentlemanly, and wonderful exemplars of the highest ideals of publishing. I should wish to especially single out Mr. Chris Webb, the Executive editor, for his excellence, followed closely by the very, very patient Mr. Kevin Shafer for his brilliant editorial work, and the very astute technical editor, Mr. Auri Rahimzadeh, whom I should one day soon hope to see write a book himself. Mr. Robert Diforio, my literary agent and patient tutor, is the man who guided me, with lively humor and wisdom, from the beginning to the successful conclusion of this book, and I thank him very much for all he has done.

To my brother, the bold and brave, who early took his way and will always be one of the flag bearers and great heralds of the Information Age. He is erudite, educated, hard-working, has led a great life of the mind and is a tremendous writer... and is a generous, loving, and inspiring brother.

Parents: This book is in honor of my father, the greatest man I have ever met, and my mother, who shared in his vision and worked with him every step of the way to achieve it. His success is equally hers. One could not ask for finer parents and one may only strive to be as good, as wise, and as loving as they are.

To my wife, HuRim, whose life and faith have touched millions, who could have had so much more in her life, and yet who, in her boundless love, took me (as I was) and made me as I am, I joyously and lovingly dedicate this book.

To my daughters Etosha and Elysha whom I once carried so lightly and lovingly in my arms: may God ever bless you with your mother's faith, wisdom, love, courage, and strength.

And God bless Jordan and precious Aaiden, too.

To Gene Wine (Godfather), who imparted without measure equal amounts of love and wisdom. To the extent that the world is better, it is so because you have uncompromisingly fought to make it so.

Acknowledgments

To Rainer Rackl, Karl Pilger and Eric Harmsen, I have never had greater friends than you. God bless you in all you do.

To Ahn Byong Man, hyungnim, and Ma Young Sam, Kim Man Bok, and Park Dong Sun, my students, in whose shadows I will ever stand. It has been a blessing to have had you in our lives and may God continue to bless Korea and continue to provide her sincere servants of your unequalled excellence: of faithfulness, honor, integrity, insight, and wisdom.

To my students: Abdullah Lubwana, American, (serving now with honor on the far frontiers of freedom), to Alex, Codie, Moogy, Mary, Jesse, Josh, Justin, Jean, Ishmael, Oz, Johnny, Chad, Andron, Shawn, Brandon, and so many others of my remarkable and wonderful computer students who over the years have proven the truth of the adage that in teaching I have been taught, I give thanks.

For their patience and quiet support I also thank President Mike Puglisi and Provost Anne Shumaker of Virginia Intermont (VI) College. And to my friends at VI, especially Gary Akers, Jim and Mary, and all the wonderful people of that school. And last, though I should put this first, to all my brothers and sisters in faith (especially those of Yun-ae-in and Onnuri, Westminister and Walnut Hill), and to all those who have loved my wife in her labor of the Lord, I dedicate this book.

From David Crowder (Second Edition):

Thanks are due to Chris Webb and Sharon Nash, my fine editors, who were there for me every step of the way. Also Carol Sheehan, Laura Brown, Valerie Perry, Carmen Krikorian, Eric Butow, Matthew David, Patricia Hartman, Stephanie Cottrell Bryant, Wendy Willard, Chris Stone, Doug Sahlin, Bud Smith, and Andy Bailey, without whom this book would not be in your hands right now. All helped to make this the best book we could all put together for you. And they're just the tip of the iceberg: about a zillion people work their tails off anonymously and behind the scenes at Wiley to bring you the finest books they can possibly produce. My hat is off to all of them, from the top editors to the humblest laborer on the loading dock. Last, but by no means least, I'd like to say how much I appreciate all the hard work done by my literary agent, Robert G. Diforio, without whose help I would be lost in the intricacies of the publishing world.

Contents
at a Glance

Part VIII Keeping Your Site Fresh

Contents

Part IV Making It Look Professional

Part V Transitioning to the Future: XHTML, XML, and Ajax

Part VI Images on the Web

Part VII Cashing in on eCommerce

Introduction

Welcome to the *Creating Web Sites Bible, Third Edition*. Like all books in the Bible series, you can expect to find hands-on tutorials, real-world practical application information, and reference and background information that provides a context for what you are learning. This book is a comprehensive resource on how to develop your Web page using HTML. It guides you through the process of placing it on the Web, getting it noticed, and driving business your way. By the time you have completed reading the *Creating Web Sites Bible, Third Edition*, you will be well-prepared to design and publish your own Web site.

What is new in this third edition of the book is expanded coverage on developing your Web site using HTML with numerous examples per chapter that can used as a model for your own site. We show you how to set up Web links and hotspots, as well as how to navigate your Web site. We also extensively cover the use of tables in your Web site, as well as the use of frames, and provide examples of how to develop interactive forms. We also review Cascading Style Sheets (CSS).

Additionally, there is now coverage of Adobe Creative Suite 3 (CS3), Corel, Xara, and other image application programs.

We have significantly revised the chapter on JavaScript and added new chapters on XHTML, XML, RSS, and Ajax to reflect ongoing developments in Web design.

We have left largely intact the chapters regarding eCommerce. Where necessary, we have updated the changes in site references, statistics, and figures. We have, however, made revisions in setting up your online store to reflect the rapid advancement of PayPal to allow secure transactions online, and tried to keep current with the developments in blogging and Web forums.

Finally, throughout the course of this book, we have scattered answers to those questions about the development of the Information Age, and provided brief vignettes on the unsung (and largely unknown) geniuses behind the decades-long development of the Internet and Web technologies such as TCP/IP, the Ethernet, and e-mail.

Who Should Read This Book

If you are new to Web design and want to learn how to design a Web page using HTML, this book is for you. If you are an old hand at Web design who wants to drive more business to your site, this book is for you. If you want a quick reference on Web design, this book is for you. In short, this book is designed to show you step-by-step how to develop your Web page using HTML, and then guide you through the process of placing it on the Web, getting it noticed, and driving business your way.

If you are new to Web site design, you could run through the tutorials sequentially from Chapters 4 through 13 (HTML building blocks through JavaScript) to develop some programs of your own in increasing complexity.

If you are an old hand at Web design using HTML, but are interested in improving access to your site and increasing sales as traffic increases, you may want to go straight into Parts VII and VIII. If you want to catch up on the newer technologies, you may want to look at Part V to see how screen refreshes can be done faster and more efficiently through `XMLhttpRequest` object. And you might want to look over any of the chapters in Parts II and III to work through the examples in these chapters (or to refresh your memory) to learn how to create tables, forms, or frames. You could also learn interactivity through incorporating JavaScript into your forms.

Additionally, you can review and learn about Web graphics and image manipulation in Chapters 2, 6, and 18.

How This Book Is Organized

Learn the basics of what goes into Web design and you will be able to use your knowledge to develop fairly sophisticated Web pages that are interactive and have the sort of foundation to enable you to go on learning, and applying to your Web site, new Web-based technologies as they continue to emerge. Again, this book is organized in a way that enables you to start off at the very beginning with HTML, but still allows you to grow to the point where you can get going with some new and powerful programming applications.

Part I: Laying the Foundation

This is a typical introductory section.

- **Chapter 1: The Basics of Building Web Pages and Sites** — This chapter simply introduces you (in a general way) to the Internet, types of Web pages, and some of the uses of Web design.
- **Chapter 2: Popular Web Design Tools** — This chapter introduces you to some of the most powerful and popular programs used in Web design.

Part II: The Basics

In the second section, you learn more specifically about the development and background of the Internet in the context of the development of the World Wide Web, and then you start learning (hands-on) the design and development of your own Web pages.

- **Chapter 3: History and Development of the Internet and HTML** — This chapter introduces you to the fascinating history of the Web, and concludes with a discussion on Web browsers.
- **Chapter 4: HTML Building Blocks** — This chapter introduces you to standard block-level elements, discusses the similarities and differences of logical and physical elements, and ends up relating the role of ASCII and Unicode in Web design.
- **Chapter 5: Links, Hotspots, and Web Site Navigation** — This chapter shows you how to work with internal and external links, and shows you how to reference through relative and absolute addressing.
- **Chapter 6: The Elements of Color and Images in Web Pages** — This chapter is all about color for your site. It discusses both color mixing the major image type formats (JPG, GIF, and PNG), and how to work with images and backgrounds on your site.
- **Chapter 7: Text Formatting** — This chapter introduces you to text manipulation, resizing images, and customizing fonts.

Part III: Advanced Design Features

This section takes you to a higher level of formatting and structuring your site, and also introduces forms.

- **Chapter 8: Harnessing the Power of Tables** — This chapter allows you to develop your Web layouts through tables. It guides you through the various features of tables (such as creating, spanning, aligning, resizing, borders, and so forth).
- **Chapter 9: Organizing Your Site with Frames** — This chapter shows you how to create framesets and nest frames, how to use the `base:target` command, and how to create expanding/collapsing lists.
- **Chapter 10: Getting Input with Forms** — This chapter shows you how to create a form and its elements for user input. It introduces labels and text boxes, option buttons, check boxes, hidden fields, password protection, and data submittal through the Submit button.

Part IV: Making It Look Professional

This section has more than one focus.

- **Chapter 11: Adding Multimedia and Other Objects** — This chapter is concerned with the multimedia aspect of the Web site. It discusses embedded audio and video, as well as animated objects.
- **Chapter 12: Styling Web Pages with Cascading Style Sheets** — This chapter covers the topic of Cascading Style Sheets (CSS), which are used to easily manipulate the elements of multiple pages of a site from a single location.

- **Chapter 13: Making Dynamic Pages with JavaScript** — This chapter gets into JavaScript with discussion and illustrations of events, event triggers, and event handlers.
- **Chapter 14: Putting It on the Web** — This chapter talks about ways of putting your site on the Web through researching Web hosting providers (what to look for... and look out for), uploading, working with search engines, and Web directories.

Part V: Transitioning to the Future: XHTML, XML, and Ajax

This section examines the newer versions of Web languages and the rationale for them.

- **Chapter 15: XHTML** — This chapter first discusses some of the shortcomings of earlier HTML versions by way of contrast with newer XHTML. It discusses valid and invalid documents, and introduces the three types of Document Type Defintions (DTDs), and what functions they serve in Web design validation.
- **Chapter 16: Designing with XML** — This chapter looks at XML, SML, and CSS integration; XML
schemas; and XML and wireless communications.
- **Chapter 17: Ajax** — This chapter introduces Ajax and the `XMLHttpRequest` object. It also gives an overview of the DOM, and relates the importance of `XMLHttpRequest` object to the Mobile Web.

Part VII: Images on the Web

This section contains a single but vital chapter concerning creating and enhancing images on the Web.

- **Chapter 18: Finding, Creating, and Enhancing Images on the Web** — This chapter explores the three main graphics types (JPG, GIF, and PNG), looks at various image-editing tools, and examines how to use them to modify images. You also learn how to obtain images off the Web and some legal implications.

Part VII: Cashing in on eCommerce

This section addresses the topic of eCommerce.

- **Chapter 19: Setting Up Your Store** — This chapter provides a practical how-to guide on setting up your store. This chapter discusses appropriate setups for your site and the ways to take payments over the Internet. It also points out ways to keep your site fresh and interesting (RSS feeds, for example).
- **Chapter 20: Using Advertising** — This chapter goes a bit into the types of advertising used in eCommerce. It also examines banner exchanges.
- **Chapter 21: Covering All the Bases** — This chapter rounds off the section with a generic review of eCommerce.

Part II: Keeping Your Site Fresh

This section provides insights on how to keep your site alive after you have created it.

- **Chapter 22: Maintaining Your Site** — This chapter adds more information on how to maintain viewer interest in your site and, most importantly, gives you suggestions on testing your site for ease of use and sturdiness (the "Mom" test), and how to check for ways to prevent users from inadvertently making alterations to your site.
- **Chapter 23: RSS** — This chapter is actually a quick walk-through of the hierarchy and origins of Real Simple Syndication (RSS) with illustrations of some NASA feeds and links to additional RSS resources.
- **Chapter 24: Blogging** — This final chapter discusses the continually evolving area of blogging.

Conventions and Features

There are many different organizational and typographical features throughout this book designed to help you get the most out of the information.

Whenever the authors want to bring something important to your attention the information will appear in a Tip, Note, or Caution.

CAUTION **This information is important and is set off in a separate paragraph with a special icon. Cautions provide information about things to watch out for, whether simply inconvenient or potentially hazardous to your data or systems.**

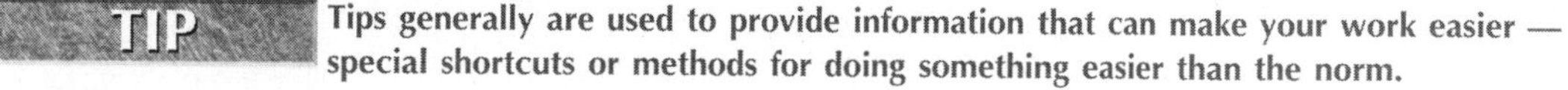

TIP **Tips generally are used to provide information that can make your work easier — special shortcuts or methods for doing something easier than the norm.**

NOTE **Notes provide additional, ancillary information that is helpful but somewhat outside of the current presentation of information.**

Coding is set apart from the text and is presented as follows:

```
This is an illustration of code.
```

As for styles in the text:

- We *highlight* important words when we introduce them
- We show keyboard strokes like this: Ctrl + A
- We show file names, URLs, and code within the text like this: `persistence.properties`

What's on the Companion Web Site/CD

On the companion Web site, you will find the following:

- **Sample code** — Each chapter has its own subfolder on the Web site, and you'll find all the code output that was discussed in each chapter organized accordingly.
- **CSS Templates for the tutorials in Chapters 4 through 10** — As mentioned in the chapters, you'll find the Web sites we designed for most of the illustrations in those chapters.

Minimum Requirements

Minimum requirements for this book would be Windows 2000 or later (preferably XP or Vista, either Home or Professional), a text editor program such as Microsoft Notepad (preferably an HTML editor), some commercial graphics program (the newer the better), a browser (preferably Internet Explorer 6.0 or above — or some equivalent such as Apple's Safari or Mozilla's Firefox), and a machine with at least 512 MB memory, 1 GHz CPU, and 233 FSB up. Of course, you will also need an Internet connection.

Where to Go from Here

You may expect to take away from this book a very good foundational knowledge of how to design interactive Web pages using HTML, XHTML, and JavaScript. You should be able to use links, multimedia, tables, frames, forms, and CSS. After reading this book, you should know how to put a site on the Web and market it using a variety of tools. And you should know how to maintain the Web site.

On the companion Web site, you may access most of the programs and documents used in the course of the book.

We would direct you to the Wiley Web site (`www.wiley.com`) for further research into any of the topics we have discussed in this book. Wiley has a number of very fine technical writers and subject area experts to cover every topic discussed in *Creating Web Sites Bible, Third Edition*, and we heartily encourage you to avail yourself of them.

Part I

Laying the Foundation

IN THIS PART

Chapter 1

The Basics of Building Web Pages and Sites

IN THIS CHAPTER

Web browsers

Web pages

Web sites

Analyzing Web site types

Understanding Internet demographics

Determining your approach

Dos and don'ts of Web site development

If you have a completely solid, totally clear idea of exactly what you want to do on the Web, you can safely skip this chapter — maybe.

Are you absolutely certain that you have considered all the details? How does your site compare to other similar ones? Where does it fit in? What are the differences between them? Are those differences enough to distinguish your Web site, to attract visitors away from competing sites? Have you covered everything from setting a budget to grasping current Internet demographics? Has it occurred to you that you might want to avoid some apparently useful technologies?

If your answer to any of these questions isn't a resounding "yes," you should start right here and read this chapter before you do anything else.

Starting here really means stepping back and taking a look at the origins of the technologies we use today and that ubiquitously govern our communications, our transports, our trade, our military, our education, our medicine, our understanding of ourselves, and the direction of our society to come. These are astounding transformations, and we must spend a bit of time looking at the roots and vines to better understand the fruit of the Information Age. The future cannot be predicated from a present that has no past.

Therefore, this chapter begins with a discussion of the origin of Web browsers so that you may understand why browsers do what they do, which will allow you, the user, to determine what is the best browser for you. Similarly, when building your site, you must understand not only its infrastructure but also the workings of the audience (clientele) that will be utilizing your Web site so that you will be in a better position to efficiently deliver services. A better understanding of how to structure the delivery method allows more effective delivery of the content itself. This chapter discusses the structure of a Web page using HTML to help you understand what coding a Web page is like.

Web Browsers

In the last few decades of the last century of the last millennium, small groups of men and women of genius and vision working at European and American research and academic locales developed the technologies that would result in the radical growth of the Internet worldwide. Although the development and growth of the Internet will be covered in some detail in Chapter 3, a bit of the background of the Internet is provided here in the context of the development of the Web browser.

The Web browser is a technological tool that allows access to networked Web pages. You may think that all the knowledge of the world lies just a few finger strokes away, but a good portion of all the Web pages created are inaccessible because of restrictions on their access. By one estimate, only 20 percent of all Web pages are freely accessed via the Internet. In short, a *Web browser* is a software application used to locate and display Web pages. Not all of these pages are on the Internet. Most corporations have extensive intranets with their own Web pages created and/or maintained by employees and departments.

The earliest graphical user interface (GUI) Web browser (actually called *WorldWideWeb*) was developed by Sir Tim Berners-Lee in 1990 at *Organisation européenne pour la recherche nucléaire (CERN)*. The World Wide Web was so named by Berners-Lee after a lunchtime discussion with another CERN colleague, Robert Cailliau, who was a systems engineer and a strong proponent of a hypertext transfer program.

NOTE **CERN was established in 1954 as an initial consortium of 11 European nations, to do fundamental research in physics. Today, about half of the fundamental research experiments are conducted at CERN. Its association with the Internet arose because, one of its researchers, Berners-Lee, sought (and created) a way to access hypertext documents on other sites. This discovery led him to create the first Web browser. Almost by default, he became creator of the first Web server. He also managed to create the protocol by which Web page content is sent across the Web (Hypertext Transfer Protocol, or HTTP). Of course, he also unavoidably created the first version of Hypertext Markup Language (HTML).**

NOTE **A graphical user interface (GUI) is icon-driven. Prior to GUIs, users would use a text-based process to gain access to their desired files, folders, and Web locations by typing in the destination. Today, we still have text-based Web browsers such as Lynx. An advantage of text-based browsers is that they allow much faster loading of Web page content over slow connections.**

Berners-Lee also developed an addressing scheme (described later in this chapter) so that Web content could be reached, retrieved, and rendered. This first Web browser ran on a NeXT computer platform. The content of this first browser, WorldWideWeb, was rendered in grayscale and, because the art of placing images inline had not yet been mastered, images and icons were shown in separate windows. Figure 1-1 shows the first graphical browser created by Berners-Lee at CERN.

WorldWideWeb had significant font-manipulation capabilities. Users could adjust the font size, select from a range of font types, align elements, work with tables, lists, and so forth, and generally implement the features associated with HTML 1.0 — which was the dominant version of HTML from 1989 to approximately 1994. WorldWideWeb was the first browser to incorporate a basic HTML editor to allow users to work with and edit Web pages.

At almost the same time, a graduate student at University of California, Berkley named Pei Wei had independently developed a Web browser that was, in many respects, almost identical to WorldWideWeb. It also possessed a few features that were more advanced than the Berners-Lee model. It incorporated such advanced features as inline graphics, embedded stylesheets, tables, and scripts, as shown in Figure 1-2. It was, in the words of James Gillies and Robert Cailliau in their book, *How the Web Was Born: The Story of the World Wide Web* (Oxford University Press, 2000), "the most feature rich browser at that time" and "was to set the standard for everything to follow it. . . ." Certainly the *violaWWW* browser was good enough for CERN, which used it as the main browser for its lab units until the development of Mosaic.

FIGURE 1-1

WorldWideWeb was the first graphical browser.

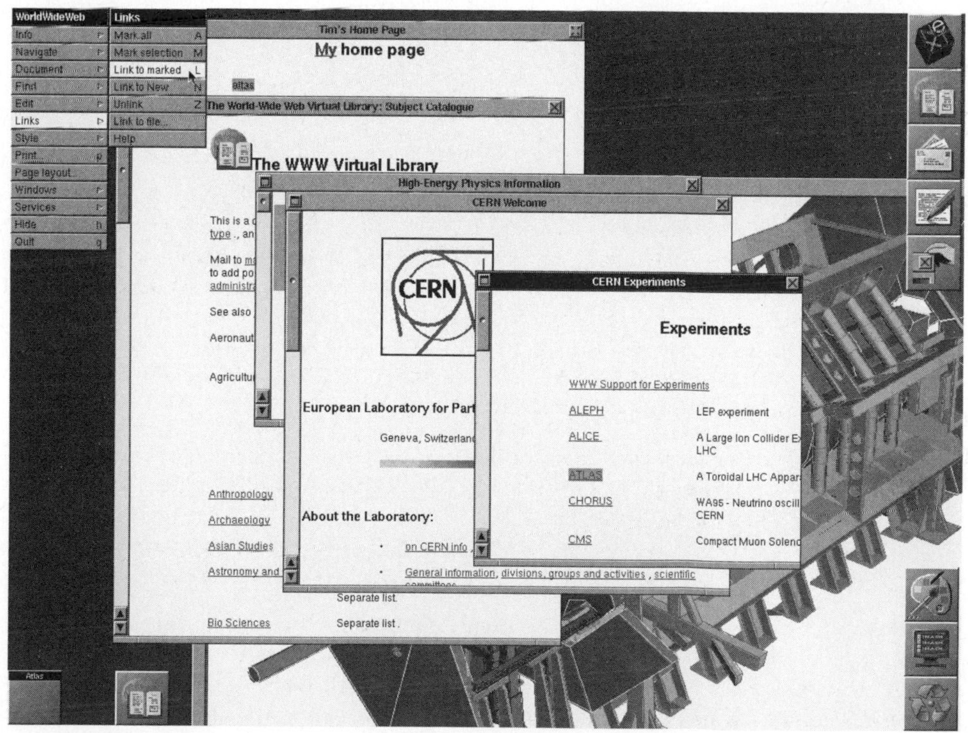

FIGURE 1-2

The violaWWW browser was used by CERN before the arrival of Mosaic.

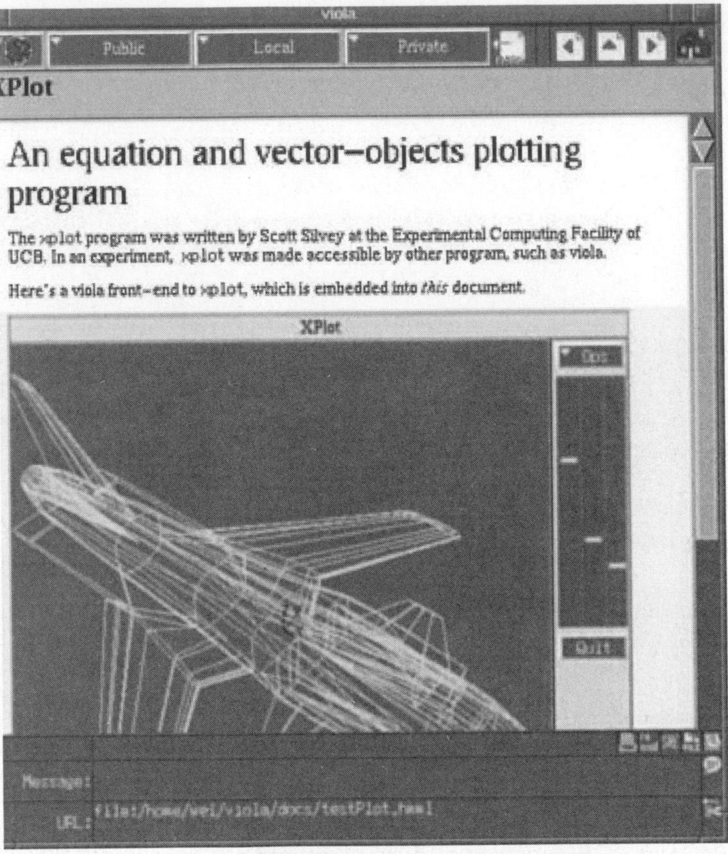

NOTE **Perhaps it was limited by only running on *Unix X-Windows* when the world was facing a looming showdown of Mac versus PC, or perhaps it was just too advanced for its time. Regardless of the reason, in this same time period, there was a mad rush to cash in on the Berners-Lee open source Web browser, WorldWideWeb, and commercialize it.**

The *Mosaic* browser, shown in Figure 1-3, may be considered the first great commercial and popular success. Marc Andreessen and Eric Bina of the University of Illinois' National Center for Supercomputer Applications (NCSA) created and then heavily promoted this new commercially available portable browser. Mosaic improved upon the open source code of the noncommercial Web browser in a number of significant ways:

- It was user-focused, being relatively easy to install and use.
- It was cross-platform compatible with Unix and Apple (Macintosh).

- It was the first commonly available browser to have inline images.
- It offered support for a number of graphics formats.
- It was able to render both video and audio formats.
- It introduced as add-ons the features of history (which allowed the tracking of sites visited) and bookmarks.

The Mosaic browser was aggressively marketed with a hitherto unknown 24-hour technical support for its client base. Problems were efficiently monitored, tagged, and resolved. In a matter of months, Bina improved Mosaic, and it became known as *Netscape*. Ultimately, NCSA asserted its rights over Mosaic and the innovations developed in Mosaic were licensed to Microsoft (among several other companies). Hence, the *Internet Explorer* (*IE*) browser was originally built around the Mosaic core. Development work on Mosaic officially ceased in 1997.

FIGURE 1-3

The Mosaic browser introduced a number of new features.

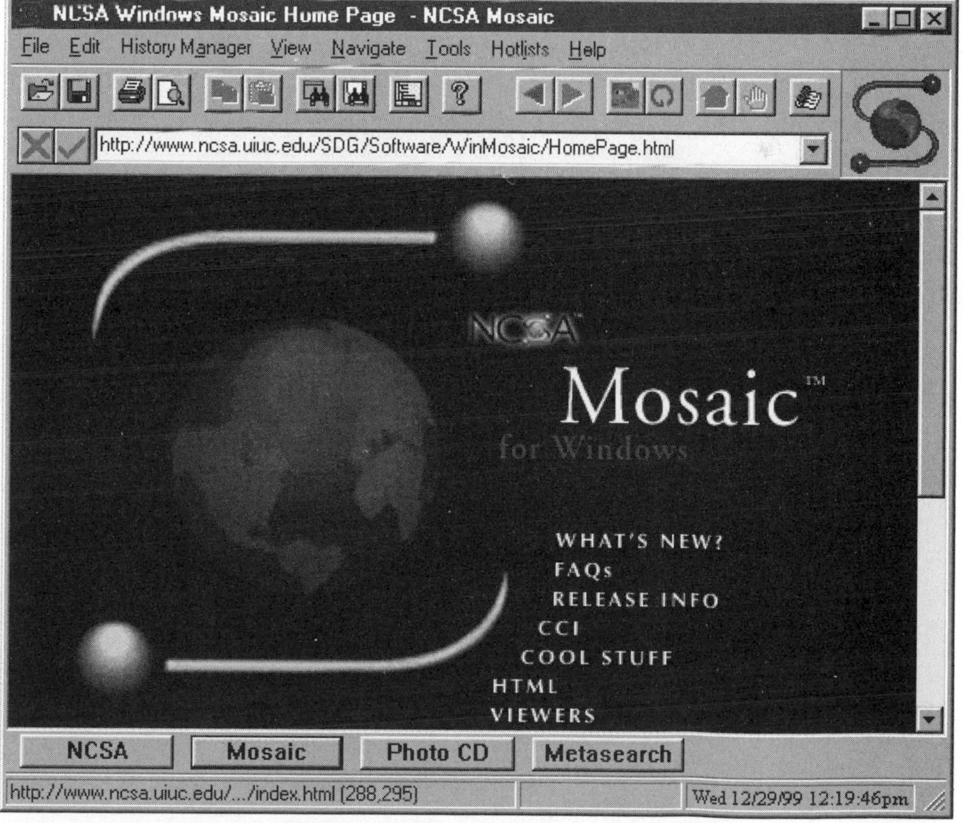

Other browsers were also being rapidly developed by other academic or government institutions, using different operating systems and using different ways of developing and executing what was evolving as the standard core of browser features:

- Fetching
- Decoding
- Faithfully rendering Web pages, history, and bookmarks
- Cross-platform compatibilities
- Scripts
- Embedded objects
- Interactive forms

For more in-depth information on various browsers, see the support tables at `http://en.wikipedia.org/wiki/Comparison_of_web_browsers`**.**

These days, the search for the best (the fastest, most secure, and most feature-rich) browser continues, and some of the newer players (upon close inspection) seem eerily familiar. For example, Firefox (2004) from Mozilla (see Figure 1-4) is actually a direct descendant of open source Netscape (2002) — known an even earlier time as Mosaic.

FIGURE 1-4

The Mozilla browser is a descendant of Netscape.

NOTE **There is, as Paul Harvey would say, the rest of the story. It may concern an Easter egg. Those who have Firefox let them see... about:Mozilla. *Book of Mozilla 7:15.***

As for the best of the best, about two years ago extensive tests were run by a very committed, highly organized, and methodical programmer named Mark Wilton-Jones in the United Kingdom. His subsequent tables of results were endlessly copied in both print and electronic media. If you are curious (and it is quite interesting material), you should visit his Web site at `www.howtocreate.co.uk/browserSpeed.html` to see his rigorously tested results.

Web Pages

A *Web page* is a document that is written in (or convertible to) HTML and that is accessible to Web browsers so that they can upload or download content. The Web page, if online, is found by an address. The address is in the format of `http://www.goto.com/goinggoing/gone` and is frequently referred to as a *Uniform Resource Locator* (*URL*).

NOTE **This chapter does not delve into a technical discussion regarding the differences between *URL, URI,* and *URN.* Berners-Lee (the creator of the above address schema), uses universal resource identifier (URI) when referring to an Internet address. The reference to the address of the Web page is URL for academics and for the rest of us. For more information on the differences in terminology, see `http://gbiv.com/protocols/uri/rfc/rfc3986.html#RFC1630`, which provides a thorough explanation of the reasoning behind the development of specific features of Web addresses.**

URLs (or addresses) are broken down into three parts:

- *Protocol* — This is the name of the "language" that is used to transport the data across the network from source address to destination address. The language used to transfer document content is Hypertext Transport Protocol (HTTP). Recall that the format of the Web page is Hypertext Markup Language (HTML), so it is easy enough to associate the transport method (HTTP) with what is being transported (HTML), since both are *hypertext*. The two forward slashes following the protocol essentially indicate to the Web browser, "this is where you start your business and ignore anything to the left of the //."
- *Domain* — This is a two-part name separated by a dot (.) that identifies a particular institution or group. The first section before the dot is some specific corporate entity, and the part following the dot is a suffix that defines the top-level domain of the cited entity. For example, `yahoo.com` indicates an organization referenced by the domain name. `Yahoo` belongs to the top-level domain, and `com` further defines `yahoo` as a commercial business. Other top-level domains with which you are probably already familiar include `gov` for government sites, `org` for nonprofits, `mil` for military sites, `net` for network organizations, `mobi` for mobile, and `edu` for educational sites.
- *Web page (file or folder)* — After the domain name comes the forward slash (/) or multiple slashes that define the path to the specific Web page. The addressing scheme is hierarchical, and the address goes from the general to the specific. The Web page the

user is fetching could be located directly on the domain, or within a folder within the domain. For example, if you have a Web page called `Crowder`, stored directly on the `wiley` site, the format of the address would be `http://wiley.com/Crowder` If the Web page, however, were stored within a folder called, say, `CWSB`, the file (or Web page) reference would be: `http://www.wiley.com/CWSB/Crowder`. The Web page `Crowder` is stored within the folder `CWSB`, which itself is part of the `wiley.com` domain.

The `www` prefixing the domain name indicates that the user is referencing a networked Internet server that is hosting a specially formatted document — in other words, a Web page. This page is formatted in the markup language, HTML, a simplified subset of *Standard Generalized Markup Language* (*SGML*). HTML is a (more or less) standardized system for manipulating, labeling, and "accessorizing" document content and structure. Chapter 4 goes into more detail about the structure of the Web page using element tags.

IP addresses and domain names

Actually, the addressing scheme is a tad more complicated than the way it is represented here because all addresses are actually numbers and not names at all. Therefore, when you type in `yahoo.com`, this is converted by a *domain name server* (*DNS*) into its numeric equivalent of 209.191.93.52, which would most likely be the address of one of Yahoo's numerous servers.

IP addresses, also known as *network addresses*, are used by the Internet to locate and retrieve data from specific hosts within a specified network. Most Internet users access the Internet through an Internet service provider (ISP) that has a range of IP address available. These are assigned by the nonprofit corporation *Internet Corporation for Assigned Names and Numbers* (*ICANN*). These addresses are portals or doorways to the Internet, and are used by multiple users for varying lengths of time. If they checked their IP addresses, users might note that addresses dynamically change each time they log off and log on to the Internet. If their IP number is, for example, a 172.16.x.x network number, that address is internal to the ISP and not a routable Internet address — even though, through it, users have access to the Internet features to which they have subscribed. `run ipconfig` is one of several ways to check the user IP address and default gateway. The *subnet mask*, which also appears in the data about IP addresses, is for another book.

NOTE **Another great way to learn your IP address on the Internet, rather than your potentially internal address, is `www.whatismyip.com`.**

Use of HTTP and FTP

There may be some confusion regarding the use of HTTP and File Transfer Protocol (FTP) as Web *transport protocols* because both transfer files. The distinction would be that HTTP is used to transfer Web page content to a browser from a Web server and the service is one way: from server

continued

continued
to browser. FTP is used to upload and download files to and from a workstation to a file server. Another way to remember the distinction is that HTTP uses port 80, whereas FTP uses ports 21 and 20 (command and data).

A Web page is written in HTML or *Extensible HTML* (*XHTML*). There are various versions of HTML, each of which gives greater flexibility to the developer of the Web site to add features such as interactive forms, embedded scripts, stylesheets, accessibility features and so on. HTML v1.0 provided support for inline images and font manipulation. HTML v2.0 gave interactive elements to forms (for example, submit, exit, and clear buttons; text boxes or areas; labels; check boxes; radio buttons; and so on). Most browsers have this level of Web page support. HTML v3.0 features were never widely used, and the latest version, v4.02, added support for scripting, multimedia, and stylesheets.

The common features of a simple Web page consist of the following:

- *Head* — This section holds information about the Web page. Comment lines within this section typically provide information on the programmer and program purpose. These also contain metatags that are used by search engines. These are used to set the title, load page scripts, and set special tags (such as `META` tags) to help other browsers and systems use the page. Though there may be executable calls to *functions* contained in the head, none of the content of the head section appears directly on the Web page.
- *Body* — This is where the content is formatted, and it is from the body that the content is displayed. Typical tags in the body would be `<p>` for paragraph (where text and inline images would appear), `<ul>` for a list that is unordered ("ul" meaning "unordered list") with a line-by-line column of each item in the list, `<li>` for a horizontal line to attractively divide the sections of the Web page, and `<para>` for an address.

CROSS-REF **Chapter 4 provides much more detail about HTML and its basic elements. This discussion provides an introductory examination.**

Elements are colloquially referred to as *tags*, (as in *tagging* an item such as clothes for sale). Note that all elements (except for two) appear in pairs, indicating an opening tag and a closing tag:

- `<html></html>`
- `<p></p>`
- `<ul></ul>`
- `<li></li>`
- `<p></p>`

Within each tag pair is the content to be displayed on the Web page.

`<br />` and `<hr />` are both examples are what are called *empty tags* because they relate to the appearance or format of the Web page but include no content themselves.

A simple setup for a Web page would be as follows:

```
<HTML>
<HEAd>
<title>  A simple web page</title>
</head>
<body>
<P>This is paragraph one.</p>
<p>This is paragraph two.</p>
<p>and this is paragraph three.</p>
<ul>
<li>Item 1</li>
<li>Item 2</li>
<li>Item 3</li>
</ul>
<br>
<hr>
<address>street, city, state</address>
</body>
</html>
```

Note that HTML is not case-sensitive and does not care what is uppercase and/or lowercase in these elements. To the thousands of users challenged by pressing the Shift key correctly every time, count your blessings. However, the content in between the tags won't be automatically corrected, so make sure that you capitalize words where necessary in the content you want to display to the user of your Web page. In more advanced coding that deals with attributes, you will learn that case does occasionally matter.

You will also note that every element in this example appears in a straight line against the left margin. This formatting may provide for easier reading, but it is not necessary to produce effective HTML code. Because HTML is totally insensitive to whitespaces, you could also enter the previous example as follows:

```
<HTML><HEAd><title>A simple web page</title></head><body>
<P>This is paragraph one.</p><p>This is paragraph two</p>
<p>and this is paragraph three.</p>
<ul><li>Item 1</li><li>Item 2</li><li>Item 3</li></ul>
<br><hr>

<address>street, city, state</address></body>
</html>
```

NOTE **Many Web browsers will fix small HTML errors automatically, since there are so many different ways of interpreting HTML and all its different versions. This is sometimes known as "promiscuous" or "dirty rendering" mode.**

You can see how annoying this would be trying to read, however, especially if you were trying to find where you made a typo. So, by convention, HTML is printed nicely, line by line, one command per line, and sometimes indented to distinguish related sections (such as when using nesting in `if-else` command structures).

You'll see many examples of this (and do it yourself) later in this book as you are developing your own pages.

XHTML (which came out in 2001) was designed to provide a strict structure currently lacking in HTML coding. The reason for some of the strict structure may be obvious, but some of it may be needlessly complicated.

NOTE **One reason for XHTML is so that we know how to detect a properly formatted page. By requiring end tags, and setting more-strict formatting requirements, the browsers can better render the pages.**

Back in the "good old days," capitalization of elements didn't matter — `<heaD>`, `hEaD>`, `<Head>`, `<head>`, and `<HEAD>` were all the same. Size now matters, and tags must all be lowercase. The format of the single-sided tags has changed, as has the closing of tags. Some elements have absolute requirements that were optional in the past. Some commands (in the interest of consistency to the object-oriented paradigm) have been made more attribute-heavy. The command for embedding a video clip, for example, changed from the simple `<embed src = "url">`to `<object data = "url"type = "media spec"width = "x"height = "y"> </object>`. Another issue is that a number of commonly used tags are no longer compatible with strict XHTML (such as `label`, `map`, `span`, `input`, `img`, `fieldset`, `iframe`, `button`, `cite`, `em`, and `form`). You should be aware that there would be compatibility issues with earlier versions of HTML.

It is very important to also be aware that a Web page will appear differently on different computers. Some computers may have different screen resolutions than the one used by the designer. A user may have a browser (remember that there are easily 50 or more of them available) that may not have the capacity to render all features of the Web page. The latest version of *Cascading Style Sheets (CSS)*, the range of acceptable colors, or fonts may not be available. All this boils down to is this: a Web page developer must test the Web page on different browsers to verify the correctness of their appearances, and the designer may also want to design with a version of HTML that is acceptable to the largest possible audience. This might even mean forgoing some multimedia or interactive features.

CROSS-REF **See Chapter 13 for more information on Cascading Style Sheets.**

Web Sites

There is no single accepted typology of Web sites. Web sites may be divided into several types and subtypes, such as the following:

- Static and dynamic
- Individual or group
- Domain types (such as `gov`, `mil`, `co`, `com`, `net`, `edu`, `mobi`) grouped by shared interests (such as download or humor sites, review sites, news sites, or search sites)

And there are numerous extended classifications. Later in this chapter, you will see one breakdown of Web sites, and others will be presented throughout this book as appropriate to the topic. This section offers a brief overview of links, which are the single most critical shared feature of all Web sites. Other important technologies for Web site functions (including scripts, multimedia tools, and stylesheets) are examined in separate chapters throughout the book.

A *Web site* consists of a number of associated Web pages for an entity that share a common theme. The most critical part of a Web site is its linking structure. A Web site cannot exist without a way of linking together the Web pages of which it consists. These linked Web pages are, hopefully, related in a logical fashion that allows intuitive and speedy access to any of the other pages in the Web site from any location within the site. Depending on the number of linked pages and the number of levels of pages in each of those links on the home page, Web pages may be linked *linearly, hierarchically*, or a mixture of both (sometimes called an *augmented linear structure*).

NOTE **Hidebound traditionalists prefer links the plain, old-fashioned way: in blue and underlined. A designer might even go so far as to change colors for a visited link. But the truth is that you can do all sorts of funky stuff with links: you can change colors, or sizes, or fonts; you can make them look like ordinary text in the Web page; you can use images as links; you can even use multiple links within an image (known as *hotspots*). The details of how to do all this are reserved for later chapters in this book, but be aware that what you can do with links is only limited by your sense of the creative.**

Sites with a large number of pages (for example, seven or more) use a full or modified hierarchical structure that incorporates the linear structure at specific levels. A hierarchical structure moves in layers from the general to the specific. It is very much like an inverted tree structure in which the branches spring from the trunk, and from them spring smaller limbs and then twigs and then leaves. This allows the user to get to an area of interest by using a few mouse clicks, or to move rapidly to another area or areas within the site.

At the top would be the single point of entry into the Web site: the *home page*. The purpose of the home page is to provide an overview of the organization or individual presenting the site, generate consumer interest, and allow quick and useful access into the site. There are several formats for offering links, and numerous good examples exist on the Web. One of the most helpful navigation features of a home page is a drop-down list of most frequently accessed links (*quick links*). Navigation within the site should be intuitive, and entry in and out of a page should be easy. Fundamentally, the successful home page allows access to site info in small structured bites.

Figure 1-5 shows an example of such a well-designed home page for Emory and Henry College. In this example, the home screen acts as a portal to its various divisions.

Click on any of the sections and you will be conveyed to a Web page on that selection, and the Web page will have a quite similar layout to the home page. Consider the pages of a printed book, where each page is formatted exactly like every other page, and only what is written (the content) distinguishes the pages. (The page number would be the navigation tool for getting back and forth.) Similarly, for a Web site, the formatting would be a faithful copy of the main (or home) screen. The background would be the same, as would the font styles and colors, the layout of the screen, and its dimensions.

FIGURE 1-5

Home page of Emory and Henry College.

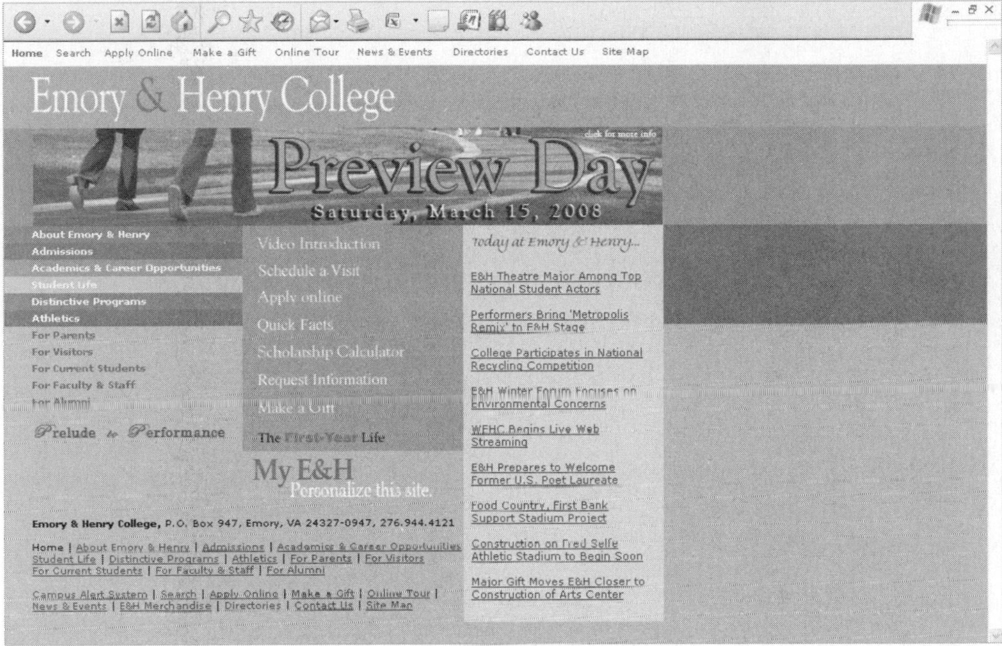

CROSS-REF **Chapter 4 provides more information about designing the structure of the Web site. At this point, however, you should at least appreciate the criticality of sitting down and drawing out your site before doing the fun stuff (the content).**

Though it is tempting to try to create the latest "gee whiz" site utilizing all sorts of bells and whistles to dazzle your peers, the plain truth is that Web sites are not only as good as their designers; they are also only as good as their users' connection to the Internet, their users' Web browsers, their users' screen resolution, and their users' general level of comfort with navigating the Web.

So, plan wisely — and well.

Analyzing Web Site Types

You could argue endlessly about how to categorize the overwhelming variety of sites on the World Wide Web. For all practical purposes, however, there are only five basic types of sites:

- Personal
- Informational

- Organizational
- Political
- Commercial

As with any attempt at *taxonomy* (that is, the art of lumping disparate entities into categories based on similarities), there are gray areas, fuzzy situations, and downright overlaps. What do you make of a personal home page that's largely political? In the system discussed here, it's still a personal home page. What about a genealogy site? Is that an extension of a personal home page, or is it an informational site? We vote for it being informational, and labeling a site "personal" only if its focus is limited to an individual and his or her immediate family and friends.

To categorize sites, the basic method we use is to try to determine the intent of the Web site. If it's to make money, then it's a commercial site, no matter what other angles there are to it. If it's to promote a particular candidate in an election, then it's a political site, even if it's made by one individual.

Personal home pages

Personal home pages exist for the purpose of introducing individuals to the world. Despite the phrase "personal home page" (which has become generically accepted as a description of this type of Web site), some personal sites involve many different Web pages and can be as elaborate as a corporate Web site. Generally speaking, the information in them is somewhat limited in scope, appealing mainly to the close friends and immediate family of the person involved. This isn't to say that some of them aren't very interesting, indeed. As with any other type of site, a carefully designed and well-written production is a real joy to explore and experience.

Just as when talking to strangers at a party you'd find some people are fascinating and have great stories to tell, whereas others send you running from the room (yawning from the boredom), personal Web sites can be a similar experience. Some home pages grab you, and others make you wish you had never clicked that link.

When putting together a personal site, it's a good idea to open up yourself as much as possible within your comfort level. The best personal sites enable you to get to know the people who created them. By the time you're done browsing these sites, you feel as if you could sit down to dinner with their authors and talk as if old friends. This isn't to say that you must spill your guts about every detail of your personal life, but the site *is* about you — and if *you* aren't really in it, what's the point of creating it?

Informational sites

Sites that are dedicated to providing information on a particular topic are common on the Web. If they weren't, it would be a pretty boring place. In fact, most people use the Web primarily to find the answer to some sort of question. Many of the informational Web sites are run by public-minded organizations whose goal is simply to make the public aware of particular issues.

The Daily Kos political blog, for example, provides much needed clarification about the confusing political situation within the Democratic party and the state of our nation at `www.dailykos.com`.

Search engines, on the other hand, are a perfect example of the kind of gray area discussed earlier, where it's difficult to slot many of them into one category. The vast majority of them are commercial operations designed to generate advertising revenue. Some of them even rank the results by how much they're paid instead of by true relevance. But the only interest that Web surfers have in them is to find information. The same is true of news sites.

Another type of informational site is one that offers a limited amount of information at no charge but that provides a greater amount for a fee. Spanish Learning Resources (`www.studyspanish.com`) is a prime example of this. The site, shown in Figure 1-7, provides about as much training as you would get in a typical first-year Spanish language course for free. If you simply need to understand such niceties as why *ser* and *estar* both mean "to be" or need a basic grasp of Spanish vocabulary and grammar, visit this site at `www.studyspanish.com`. (You should still pick up a copy of *Spanish for Dummies*, though — you never know when your Internet connection might go down.)

FIGURE 1-6

Political blogs can increase public awareness on civic concerns.

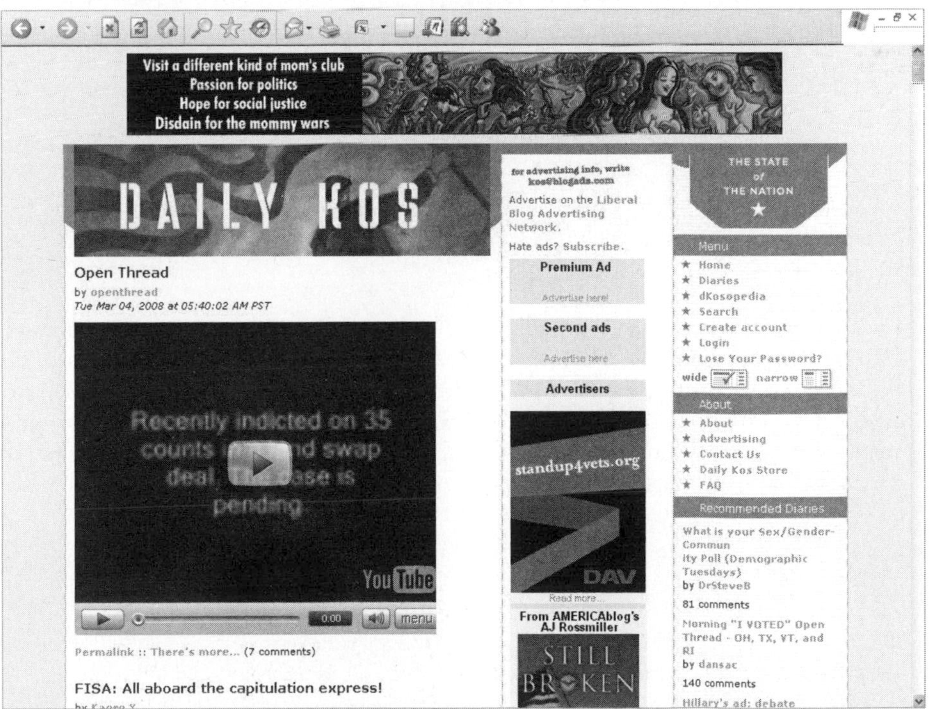

FIGURE 1-7

Spanish Learning Resources provides both free and premium information services.

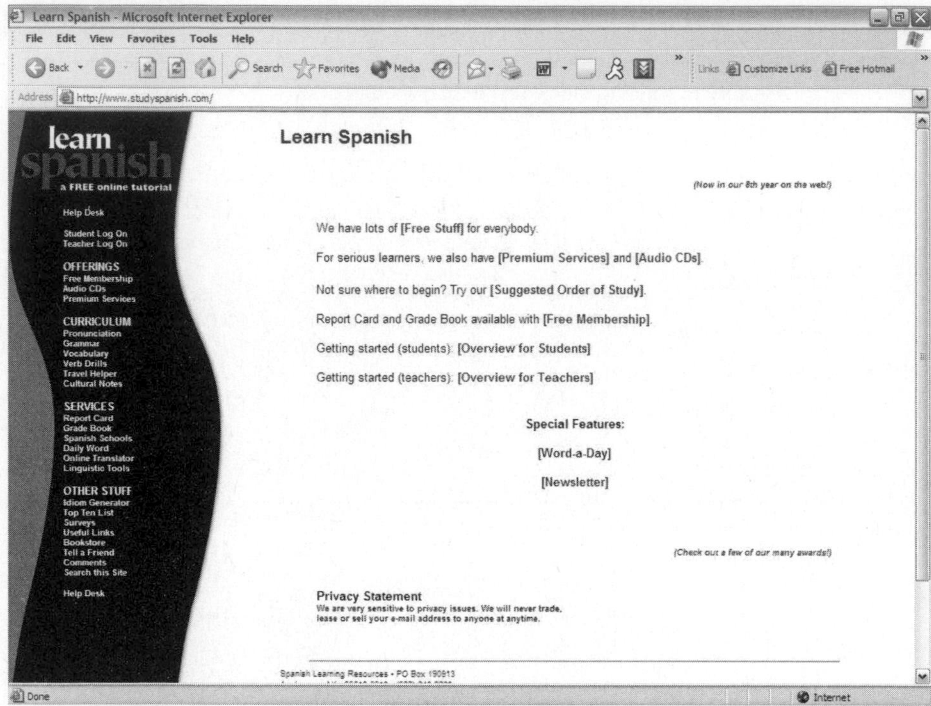

Table 1-1 lists the URLs of several informational sites that you can browse and study.

Organizational sites

Organizational Web sites are concerned with presenting information about — you guessed it — a particular organization. The reason these are distinguished from pure informational sites is their narrow focus. Their sole function is to describe the work of a particular organization, its structure, its personnel, and history. These sites don't diverge from their function at any point — no sidetracks to outside issues or topics exist, except for occasional links to other sites that partner with or support the goals and purposes of the organization.

As shown in Figure 1-8, the Internet Engineering Task Force (IETF) site, located at `ietf.cnri.reston.va.us`, is a classic example of an organizational site. It covers everything from the structure of the organization to the process for joining it.

Table 1-2 gives the addresses of some organizational sites on the World Wide Web.

TABLE 1-1

Informational Web Sites

Site	URL
AcqWeb's Directory of Book Reviews on the Web	acqweb.library.vanderbilt.edu/acqweb/bookrev.html
AnyWho	www.tollfree.att.net
Catalog of Solar Eclipses	sunearth.gsfc.nasa.gov/eclipse/SEcat/SEcatalog.html
CIA World Factbook	odci.gov/cia/publications/factbook
CIAC	ciac.llnl.gov/ciac/index.html
Dead People Server	www.dpsinfo.com/dps/
Indiana Department of Agriculture	ai.org/oca
Internet Traffic Report	InternetTrafficReport.com
King Arthur and the Matter of Britain	legends.dm.net/kingarthur
Letters and Dispatches of Horatio Nelson	wtj.com/archives/nelson
Sir Francis Drake	www.mcn.org/2/oseeler/drake.htm
Veterinary Information Network	vin.com

Political sites

Sites that have a political agenda to push aren't limited to dealing with particular candidates for certain offices in election years. Politics isn't all about elections. In our definition, such sites also include those with any social agenda that would be furthered by the passing of appropriate legislation. Thus, Web sites covering issues such as gun control, the medical usage of marijuana, development of wetland areas, or the control of personal information on the Internet — regardless of whether the site's editorial thrust is for or against — would qualify as political sites.

Figure 1-9 shows the Web site for the Democratic National Committee (DNC) at `www.democrats.org`. It could be argued that it is, in fact, an organizational Web site, representing as it does the DNC, its views, and activities. Because those activities are strictly political, however, it belongs here.

Table 1-3 provides the URLs of several political Web sites.

Commercial sites

This is the one simple, unambiguous area in the taxonomy — if the site is created strictly out of a profit motive, then it's a commercial site. Period. Other sites — particularly political sites — often engage in some kind of fund-raising activity that is secondary to their main purpose. With purely commercial sites, there is never any doubt — the main thrust is simply "Buy our product or service" or "Support our sponsors."

The Barnes & Noble Web site (`www.bn.com`), shown in Figure 1-10, goes straight to the point. It's there for one thing and one thing only — to enable you to find and buy books and music.

Simply accepting advertising or tossing in a few links to a bookstore doesn't magically transform another kind of site into a commercial Web site. There are few sites in any category that do not attempt to raise some money (often unsuccessfully) by a half-hearted foray into banner ads.

Sometimes, especially for sponsored sites or those which are participants in an affiliates program, the "buy" message is so subtle that the commercial nature of the site isn't obvious to the casual visitor. Many times, there is no mention at all of any sales intent, but the site's links lead to sponsored pages.

CROSS-REF **See Chapter 24 for more information on affiliates programs and advertising.**

FIGURE 1-8

The Internet Engineering Task Force (IETF) Web site has a full explanation of the structure, goals, and functions of the organization.

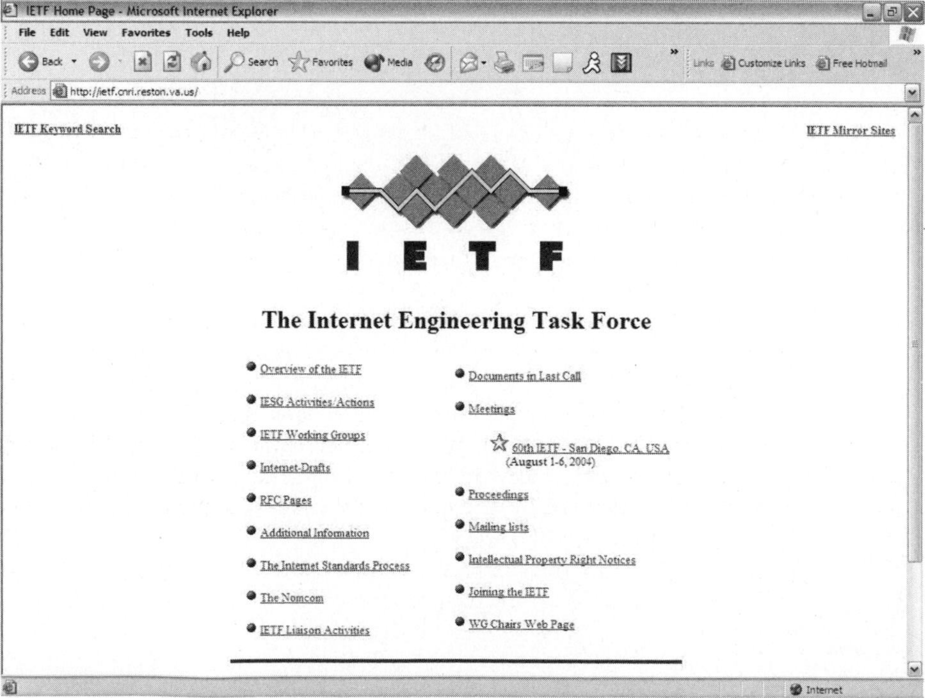

TABLE 1-2

Organizational Web Sites

Site	URL
International Center for Reiki Training	reiki.org
JustLinux	justlinux.com
National Weather Service	www.nws.noaa.gov
Nautical Research Guild	naut-res-guild.org
Nicholas Roerich Museum	roerich.org
Small Business Administration	www.sba.gov
State Library of New South Wales	www.sl.nsw.gov.au
The Naval Dockyards Society	www.hants.gov.uk/navaldockyard
The Royal Society	www.royalsoc.ac.uk
The Society for Creative Anachronism	sca.org
World Wide Web Consortium	w3.org

Table 1-4 guides you to a number of commercial Web sites.

We have just reviewed the five generally accepted categories of Web sites. The success of a Web site is dependent upon how well it defines its potential clientele. There is no monolithic client base, and much research has allowed potential users to be divided into so called B2B (business to business), B2C (business to consumer), C2C (consumer to consumer), and C2B (consumer to business) business categories. Ninety-seven percent of the online market is B2B.

The purpose of the following section is to introduce you to how these online markets are defined so that the categories of Web sites may match the services required of each particular category of user. For example, B2B would be likely to handle services and products that go into the production of a final product. Let's say the construction of this book is an illustration of B2B. We have an author who provides the raw material. We have a development editor and technical editor(s) who refine the raw material and process it into something. The general editor reviews our work and adds the polish. All of that is B2B. The book, when it finally appears at bookstores, is a B2C.

The way you relate to (or market) B2B would be different than the way the book would be presented to you by a bookseller. You structure your online Web site according to the type of clientele you market to.

That is why you need to understand the demographics of the online marketplace.

FIGURE 1-9

The Democratic National Committee site is a prime example of a political Web site.

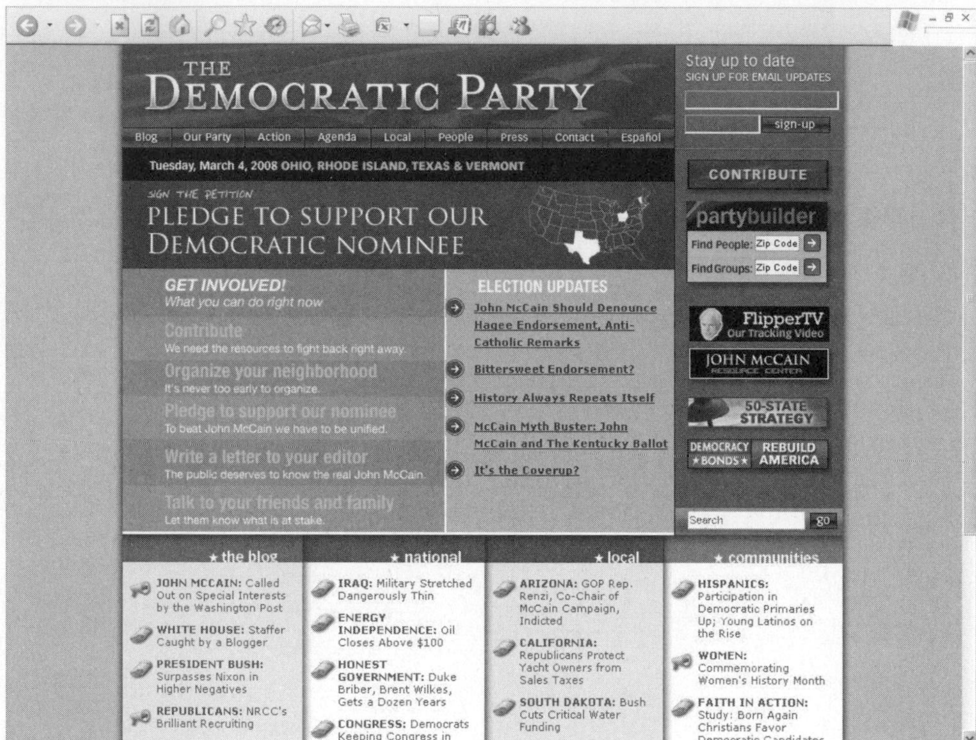

TABLE 1-3

Political Web Sites

Site	URL
Australian Politics Online	www.ozpolitics.com.au
Chinese Politics Online	www.politics.unimelb.edu.au/cpo
Conservative Party Website	www.conservatives.com/home.cfm
Labour Party Website	www.labour.org.uk
Republican National Committee	rnc.org
Southeast European Politics Online	www.seep.ceu.hu
Washington Center for Politics & Journalism	wcpj.org

FIGURE 1-10

The Barnes & Noble Web site is a prime example of a well-designed and successful commercial Web site.

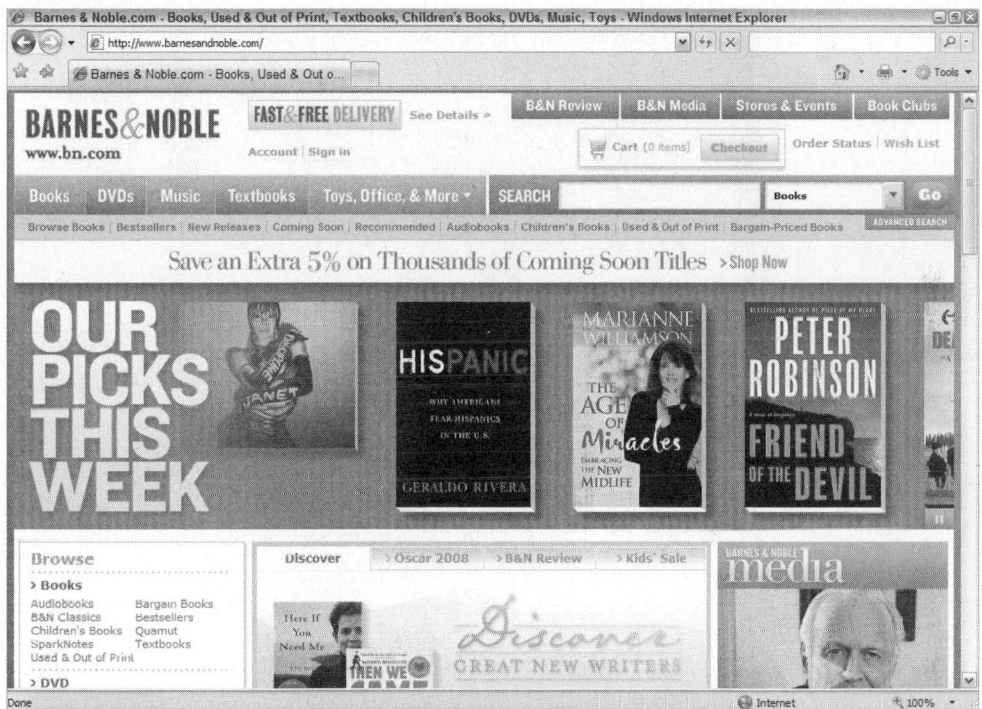

Understanding Internet Demographics

There are tons of "facts" available about the Internet. Unfortunately, most of these statistics can be classified by one of Mark Twain's most famous quips, "There are lies, damned lies, and statistics." As with so many of the greatest American writer's sayings, the truth of this rides into our present and, doubtless, our future as well.

Finding good information

It's easy to find anything you want to know about the Internet — just look on the Internet. But how do you know if you can trust what you find? One of the simplest ways is also one of the best — know the reputation of the source. If someone's Web site says that there are 8 billion people with Internet access, you might want to know who the source is and how many planets the source thinks are hooked up to the Internet.

TABLE 1-4

Commercial Web Sites

Site	URL
Australian Bush Flower Essences	www.ausflowers.com.au
Gibson Research Corporation	grc.com
Jagex Software	jagex.com
Janes Information Group	www.janes.com
Magix Entertainment Software	www.magix.net
Ptaah	www.ptaah.com/home.html
Staples Office Supplies	staples.com
The History Channel	www.historychannel.com/ontv/index.html
TV Guide	tvguide.com

The same is true, however, of even less obviously suspect figures. News stories are, unfortunately, one of the least reliable of all statistical sources, because they are generally written in a hurry by people who do not really understand statistics. They also often fall prey to the fault of accepting statistics from yet other news stories. This can easily lead to the kind of situation where one reporter gets something wrong, but the story is published in a major publication. Because another reporter believes that anything in *The Wall Street Journal* or *The New York Times* must be true, the figure is incorporated into yet another article, which is taken as gospel by someone else, creating a chain that perpetuates a number that is far removed from its original source.

We'd be inclined to trust (without more than a reflexive professional doubt) a report from companies such as comScore (see Figure 1-11), Nielsen, or WebSideStory, all of which are professional outfits that have proved reliable in the past.

Table 1-5 lists the URLs of some of the top Internet research firms.

You can never really trust any statistics, no matter what the source, unless you know how those figures were arrived at — not if you're going to bet your future on them. Any reputable research company is glad to provide you with the details of the methodology they used in arriving at certain figures.

NOTE **Neither the numbers nor the methodology is necessarily free. Most of these companies do issue some public reports, but they make their livings conducting custom research projects or selling the results of their own initiated studies. Often, the publicly released figures are only the tip of the iceberg. You can sometimes cut down on the cost of conducting a study by participating in an *omnibus study*, in which a group of companies each pay part of the costs, while all share in the results.**

FIGURE 1-11

comScore is one of the best sources of Internet facts.

Surveying site visitors

When it comes to learning about your particular site's visitors — or what they like — there's not much of a substitute for simply asking them. There are drawbacks, however, to the survey concept. The biggest problem is that people don't always respond truthfully for a variety of reasons, sometimes with the best of intentions, sometimes out of plain vanity. If you ask people whether they read tabloids or intellectual magazines, for example, the vast majority of them say that they don't read tabloids. While this has proved to be true in many different surveys, tabloids outsell intellectual magazines by millions of copies, so someone's not telling the truth. Remember, when devising your survey questions, that any time you ask people to admit something that's less than flattering to his or her self-image, you are asking those people to respond less than truthfully.

This phenomenon is widely recognized in the consumer research field, and a common (and simple) way around it was developed long ago. The trick is to ask other questions that help qualify the responses. The confirmatory questions should not be close to the sensitive one, but later, and scattered about within the survey. For example, you might ask visitors to choose their favorite

TABLE 1-5

Internet Research Firms

Company	Web Address
comScore Networks	`www.comscore.com`
Forrester Research	`www.forrester.com`
Harris Interactive	`www.harrisinteractive.com`
Jupiter Communications	`jupitercommunications.com`
Nielsen//NetRatings	`nielsennetratings.com`
Nua Internet Surveys	`www.nua.ie/surveys`
Statistical Research, Inc.	`statisticalresearch.com`
WebSideStory	`websidestory.com`
Zandl Group	`zandlgroup.com`

columnists from a list. If they fail to select a single one from the intellectual magazines, you have a red flag on their previous answer — why would they read those magazines if they didn't enjoy any of their writers? In that case, you should probably exclude that respondent's answers from your tally.

When designing a form for your Web site, however, you should bear in mind that you don't want to make it too long. People — especially Web surfers — do not have endless patience for answering zillions of questions, which limits your ability to mix in confirmatory questions.

CAUTION **If at all possible, resist the tremendous temptation to force your site visitors to fill out endless forms in order to access your site. You will drive away more people than you'll attract, if you don't avoid this temptation. You may think that you have the upper hand because you can withhold access, but visitors have the upper hand because they can refuse to participate.**

Determining Your Approach

Before you take the first step toward actually putting your Web site together, you have to determine how you are going to approach your intended audience. You must first set your goals, decide how complex your site's technology will be, and, armed with that knowledge, set a realistic budget.

Focusing on goals

Every Web site, in order to be successful, must fulfill some sort of need for its visitors. The word "need" doesn't have to be interpreted too strictly. After all, how many people really *need* a $400 leather jacket? Or a handcrafted miniature car? Yet, there are sites that are successfully selling such items.

Your goals must be set by one key rule: *The average person visiting your site should walk away happy*. The key to making your visitors happy — and making them want to come back again and again — is to satisfy people's desires. Most Web site designers make the mistake of assuming that people only come for what they really have to have — or, more accurately, what the designer *thinks* people really need. That's a fatal error to make. On the Internet, people are still people and, as in the outside world, people are driven more by emotions than by logic.

Put yourself in the shoes of your potential site visitors and take a look at what you're offering. Does your site solve their problems (or, more accurately, their *perceived* problems)? Does it provide them with the information or products they're looking for? Does it do it all that easily, without making your visitors work too hard to get what they want?

Deciding on complexity levels

How deeply are you going to get involved in Internet technology? When we're talking "technology" here, we mean both the hardware and the software — not just on your end, but on your site visitors' end, too.

Living and dying on the edge

Internet technology is constantly changing, and this means that you need to make one specific choice — whether or not to keep your Web site on the leading edge of that change. The leading edge is often sardonically referred to as "the bleeding edge," because lots of people and companies have suffered tremendously by trying to stay up with it.

The reasons for this are twofold. First, leading-edge technology has much higher expenses. Second, no one can guarantee which of several competing approaches will end up becoming the standard. What looks as if it's the most promising approach to accomplishing something can turn out to be unpopular in the end, regardless of its technical merits.

Our best recommendation is to hang back a little bit and not join the latest rush to the New Hot Internet Thing. But just for a little while — just long enough to be sure it's the real thing, and not just some fad that won't pan out in the end. As soon as you're sure that the change is permanent and the technology is here to stay, move ahead with it. Let some other company do the bleeding, then move in fast enough to reap the rewards — if there are any to be had.

Staying deliberately obsolete

That said, there are good and solid reasons to deliberately ignore even a well-established Internet technology in favor of still older approaches. And those reasons are stability and demographic reach. As new standards for Web design and applications emerge, anyone on the leading edge of implementing them will quickly find that the latest Web browsers (despite anything their makers say) only partially support the standards when they are first introduced.

To further confuse the situation, the average Web surfer doesn't keep up to date with the latest Web browser. Thus, even if the newest versions of browsers finally get around to supporting the latest advance in its entirety, you'll still lose the audience share that uses old browsers if your site uses the latest ideas. If you have committed to following hot on the heels of the standards committees, your site had better be an experimental one and not meant to serve any practical purpose.

The basic question you need to consider is whether or not you want to reach the vast majority of Web surfers — those who are using Web browsers that are, at least to some degree, obsolete. If so, you should consider using the lowest level of Internet technology that still achieves your basic goals.

On the other hand, if your target audience is users of higher-level technology — you run a Web site that has nothing but tutorials on Macromedia Flash, for example — you can confidently expect that the only low-tech visitors to your site will have wandered in by accident.

Establishing a budget

How much are you willing to spend on your site? This question (more than any other one) sets the practical limitations on what you're able to do.

If you're whipping up a personal site, the odds are pretty good that all you need to invest is nothing more than the amount that you have already put into getting online in the first place. All your needs are probably thoroughly covered by the basic amount of Web space that your ISP supplies as a basic part of their service. If the amount of Web space your ISP provides is inadequate, you can doubtless find plenty more available for little or no further investment.

You need to sit down and figure out exactly how much money you're willing to commit to your project if you're going for anything beyond that rock-bottom minimum. If the money's going to come out of your own pocket, you have to take a hard look at how much you're willing to lose, because every Internet startup is a gamble. Unless you're very rich or planning on a really small operation, you may have to put a substantial percentage of your wealth into the first year of your site's operation. Are you willing to risk giving up all your disposable income to try to make your dream come true? Half of it? Ten percent?

Whether or not your site is designed to generate an income, it still costs money to run. And, while there are exceptions to the rule, the best sites tend to cost the most money. Are you passionate enough about what you want to do on the Web to divert that money from all the other things you could do with it? If the answer is "yes," then you stand a better chance of success. But if you're hesitant about committing, you may want to think twice — maybe even thrice.

Dos and Don'ts of Web Site Development

The reasons for good Web site design are obvious. You want visitors to your site to have a pleasant productive experience when they do business with you. You not only want them to like what you have to offer but also to appreciate the ease and convenience with which their online shopping is done. You want customers to come back.

Tips for good Web sites

Here are ways to develop customer-friendly Web sites:

- *Take a minimalist approach* — Customers come to your site for the content, not the clutter. Limit the distracting eye candy.
- *Make navigation easy to use and understand* — This means providing rapid access to desired content within a few clicks.
- *Make the Web site fast-loading* — Many people still use a dial-up connection to the Internet. Too much animation can slow down the rendering of a Web page.
- *Skip the sticky advertisements that follow the cursor around like a lost pup* — They interfere with the reading of content and break the user's train of thought. Many users may soon remember those sites and avoid them. There are always others.
- *Skip the counters* — Why broadcast this information? What do they add to your site? In fact, some amounts could be quite small and convince the visitor that your site is not popular.
- *Keep the information on your site current* — This is not a Web-specific issue, but it is implicit in the Information Age that information should be accurate and up to date.
- *Be grammatically correct* — There are potential customers out there who believe that if you can't spell, you can't be very good at your business, either. They will go elsewhere.
- *Do not assume your Web designers can spell or write a grammatically correct sentence* — Check your Web sites. Without being specific, there was actually an academic institution's Web site in Statesville, North Carolina (state-funded, of course), that had mindless grammatical and spelling errors.
- *Be very sparing of sound effects or music* — Not all people have the same tastes. Not all people have the same audio cards or speakers. Also, keep in mind your visitors may be browsing to your site at work and may annoy their coworkers.
- *Use thumbnails as a good aid to site content and navigation* — Make certain that all thumbnails are clickable, that they're relevant to the content, and that the images they link to load fast. Do not clutter the page with them.
- *Make contact info obvious* — Even on a home page, include contact info such as business name, address, e-mail address, fax number, and phone number — maybe even two or three, such as generic office number, technical support number, and customer support number. This saves clients a lot of time, and they do not need to guess which

of three or more possible links actually contains the phone number they are so desperately seeking.

- *Make fonts readable* — Have high contrast with the background and, if you use them at all, do not put significant amounts of light-colored fonts against dark backgrounds.
- *Be conscious of backgrounds* — Consider white to be the background of choice. Notice the use of white backgrounds in some very high-traffic sites such as Google, Yahoo! and Drudge Report. White backgrounds make the content easier to read and enable graphics to stand out.
- *Be conscious of* your user's *screen resolution* — Screen resolutions can run from 640 x 480 on up. Therefore, when developing sites, be sure to make table widths flexible, not fixed.
- *Field-test the site using real, live, honest-to-goodness people who know nothing about your business* — Of course, people who designed the site or use it daily are not going to find it user-unfriendly.

The following are some sources for good Web-site design, advice, and techniques:

- `www.webreference.com`
- `websitesforgood.com`
- `www.lib.berkeley.edu/TeachingLib/Guides/Internet/Evaluate.html`

Top ways to have bad sites

On the other side of the coin, here are ways to develop customer-unfriendly (that is, bad) Web sites:

- Have links that don't work.
- Have messages that a Flash Macromedia advertisement is loading when you click on a company's URL and omit the Skip Intro button.
- Have a form completely clear if a customer makes any mistake anywhere in inputting information into the form.
- Have shipping charges appear on the very last screen of an online order.
- Do not specify the date, Social Security card, or phone number formats required for input.
- Have rapid, repetitive animation or video shorts, and use lots of them.
- Have short segments of loud annoying music — and loop them.
- Use lots of different colors, themes, and unrelated images and motifs on your home page and throughout the site.
- Use font colors that are practically indistinguishable from the background.
- Have your home page cluttered with countless links using different fonts and backgrounds.

- Have links unrelated to the main purpose(s) of the Web site.
- Do not use a spellchecker.

All of these faux pas have occurred, countless times, on real Web sites. Several examples of bad Web sites may currently be found at such locations as:

- `www.webpagesthatsuck.com`
- `www.worstoftheweb.com`
- `http://www.bad-websites.com/`

Summary

This chapter has explained the background and development of Web browsers and reviewed their various features. This chapter also touched upon Web protocols and gave a very basic outline of a Web page using HTML tags.

The purpose of a Web browser is to fetch, decode, and display content from hypertext documents. As the content of Web sites became more sophisticated as the result of the development of more complex audio and graphics programs, the Web browser technologies become equally sophisticated to be able to fetch, decode, and display the contents rapidly, accurately, and securely. The development of one fed upon the other technologies.

Chapter 2 briefly reviews some popular Web design applications, discusses designing for the mobile Web, and makes suggestions for additional freeware/shareware graphics applications.

Chapter 2

Popular Web Design Tools

IN THIS CHAPTER

Adobe Creative Suite 3

Freeware and shareware

Designing for the Mobile Web

The purpose of this chapter is to provide a brief look at some of the tools available for use in Web site design, and point you to where there is more in-depth coverage of each technology highlighted in later chapters. For readers working within the constraints of a variety of budgets, this chapter describes a range of image-editing tools that are available on the Web either as freeware, shareware, or trial versions of commercial software. This chapter also provides an overview of the next wave of Internet applications for the Mobile Web, and discusses the problems and opportunities associated with the so-called Web 2.0.

CROSS-REF **The topics touched upon in the following section, "Adobe Creative Suite 3 (CS3)," are extensively covered in Parts IV and VI of this book.**

Adobe Creative Suite 3 (CS3)

Adobe's Creative Suite 3 (CS3) is a collection of applications that provide Web designers with important tools. CS3 is available in the following six versions:

- *Design Premium* — Includes tools for print, Web, interactive, and mobile design
- *Design Standard* — Includes tools for professional print design
- *Web Premium* — Includes an enhanced collection of tools for Web design and development

- *Web Standard* — Includes a standard collection of tools for Web developers
- *Production Premium* — Includes tools for video professionals
- *Master Collection* — Includes design tools for a variety of media, including print, Web, interactive, mobile, video, and film

Both the Standard and Premium edition of CS3 offer a toolkit for designing, implementing, and maintaining Web sites. Both editions contain full versions of the latest Adobe Flash Professional, Adobe Dreamweaver, Adobe Contribute, Adobe Fireworks, Adobe Bridge, Adobe Version Cue, Adobe Stock Photos, Adobe Device Central, and Adobe Acrobat Connect.

The Premium version also includes Adobe Photoshop CS3 Extended, Adobe Illustrator, and Adobe Acrobat 8.0 Professional. You may think of the Premium edition as the top of the line because it offers every tool available in the Adobe arsenal for both Web 1.0 and Mobile Web, while the Standard edition is lower end. While both will help you reach your Web design goals, if you are a serious designer, you'll need those tools only contained in the Premium pack.

This chapter concentrates on the Web Premium edition of CS3. Included in this edition are the following applications:

- Photoshop
- Dreamweaver
- Illustrator
- Flash Professional
- Photoshop Extended
- Fireworks
- Acrobat
- Contribute

Let's take a look at each of these in a bit more detail.

Photoshop

This section discusses Photoshop in its latest Creative Suite 3 (CS3) configuration (see Figure 2-1) — though we should mention there are several other excellent image-editing applications such as CorelDraw, GIMP, PaintShopPro, and Xara with similar features. You can even use other image-editing applications (such as CorelDraw, as shown in Figure 2-2) to design an image before using Photoshop to edit it.

Photoshop is part of a suite of Adobe applications, CS3, that are related to graphics creation, manipulation, and presentation in print, mobile, and Web media formats. Adobe Photoshop is classified as an *image editor*, which you can use to alter photos or other image sources (including animations and movies) to meet a particular need (such as advertising a product, providing a newsworthy photo, creating illustrations for a children's book of poems, or even putting a church program on YouTube).

FIGURE 2-1

Photoshop comes in several versions.

Adobe has been implementing many additional design tools in the Photoshop application. Photoshop is primarily used for the manipulation of bitmap images, while Illustrator is for vector images.

All graphics fall into one of two categories: bitmap and vector.

NOTE **Bitmap images generally have 72, 96, or 120 dots per square inch (dpi). Of course, you can also customize that setting, and you can actually check to see what your dpi is. Click Display in the Control Panel, then the Settings tab, and, finally, the Advanced button.**

As shown in Figure 2-3, *bitmapped images* are represented using pixels (but are not pixelated). There are generally 72 pixels to an inch of screen space. All pixel-based graphics are resolution-dependent. This means that the larger you blow up an image, the more unpleasant it is to the eye. The images on the edges are a bit sawtoothed, and a review of the image itself will reveal a grid-like series of rectangles side by side, as shown in Figure 2-4.

FIGURE 2-2

You can use CorelDraw to design an image before using Photoshop to edit it.

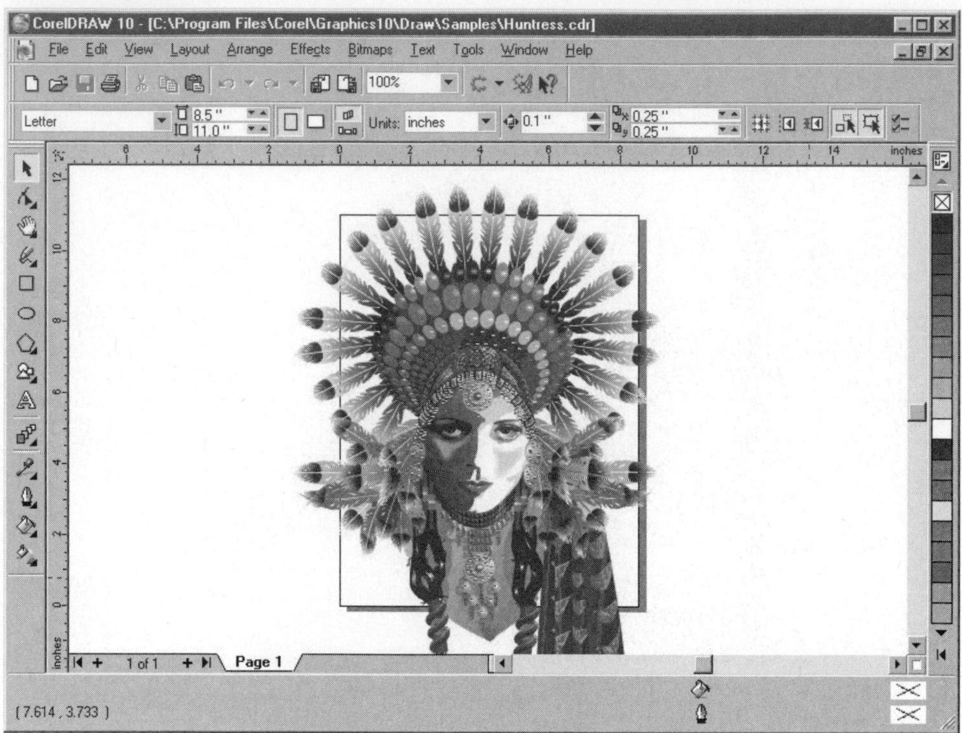

The larger an image is made, the more the pixels that must be inserted into it to keep the image coherent, but the colors assigned to the new pixels must be interpolated from the surrounding milieu, leading to a fading (or washed-out appearance) of the original colors and a fuzziness to the initial clarity of the picture.

NOTE ***Interpolate* means to introduce additional pixels into the new, larger image to have them blend in with the colors of the adjacent or surrounding pixels.**

However, the great thing about bitmaps is that, though they do not scale well, they are able to finely reproduce the enormous range of colors, harmonies, and textures that come through in the finest photographs and finely detailed portraits at normal sizes.

Some typical bitmap file formats are Bitmap (BMP), JPEG (JPG), Portable Network Graphics (PNG), Tagged Image File Format (TIFF), Graphics Interchange Format (GIF), and PICTure (PICT) (for the little bit of Mac in all of us).

FIGURE 2-3

This bitmap image of jelly beans shows both normal and magnified aspects. Notice the sawtoothed edges of the handle on the magnifying glass.

FIGURE 2-4

In this magnified bitmap image, notice the jagged edges and the rectangular structure of each pixel.

As shown in Figure 2-5, *vector images* are objects created by algorithms. (An *algorithm* is just a mathematical formula such as $e = mc^2$.) These objects may be lines, curves, or other shapes, and are infinitely elastic. They show up distinctly, unmarred by jagged edges, irrespective of degree of resizing or scaling. Note that there is no loss of clarity when the picture is enlarged several times from the original.

NOTE **Although crisp, clear, and attractive, the vector graphic lacks the succulent realism of the same image in bitmap format.**

Vector graphics are also sometimes referred to as *object-based graphics* because they are software-created objects (curves, outlines, and shapes) appearing in palettes such as the one shown in Figure 2-6. They are infinitely adjustable, and their cartoon-like appearance makes them ideal for representing objects in video games, or animations depicting historical re-creations. However, that is also their limitation. Object-based graphics are incapable of reproducing the rich and subtle tones of a photograph, although such imagery can now be embedded within existing containers of vector graphic outlines to achieve greater photorealism. This hybridization is called a metafile.

FIGURE 2-5

In this vector image, notice the almost lifelike fineness of detail of the thumb and fingers of the hand holding the cartoon crustacean.

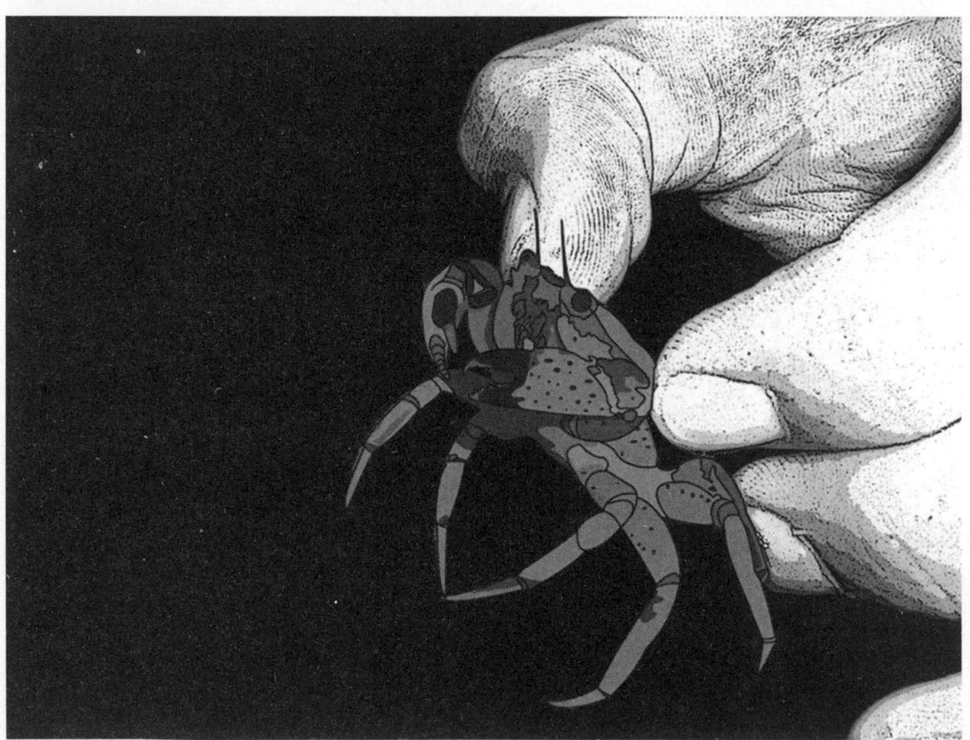

FIGURE 2-6

Tool palettes for vector images allow precise adjustments.

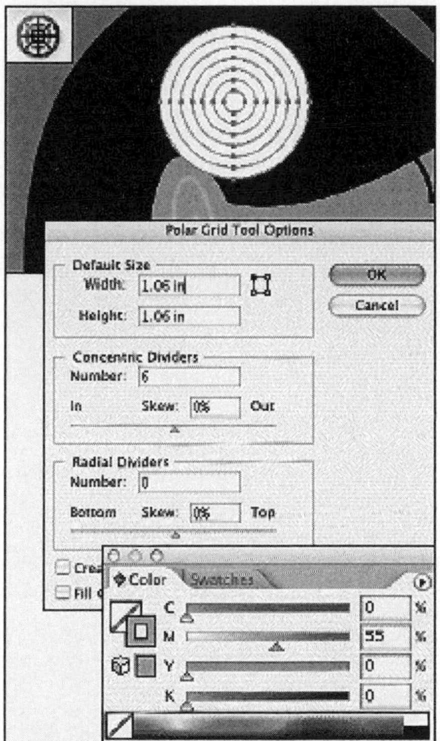

Dreamweaver

Dreamweaver is a full-featured, user-friendly application used to design and develop Web sites in an *integrated development environment* (*IDE*). In the same way, Visual Studio is an IDE for Visual Basic and other languages, while HTML-kit is an editor for generating HTML code. In the CS3 iteration of Dreamweaver, the developer can use the Spry framework for Ajax to develop sites that, according to the Adobe advertising promo, "will leave your competition standing still."

A lot of the development toolbars in Dreamweaver may seem familiar because they follow Windows conventions long established by Microsoft. As shown in Figure 2-7, the top menu bar of the Dreamweaver main screen includes File, Edit, View, and so on, all the way over to the Help menu on the far right. These all appear in Microsoft's recommended sequence.

Like many such applications, Dreamweaver is menu- and icon-driven with the menu bar and standard toolbar for such tasks as printing, copying, adjusting fonts, drawing, and the like. In addition, specialty toolbars appear at the top, such as the Insert toolbar shown in Figure 2-8.

FIGURE 2-7

A typical Dreamweaver document shows standard menus on the toolbar.

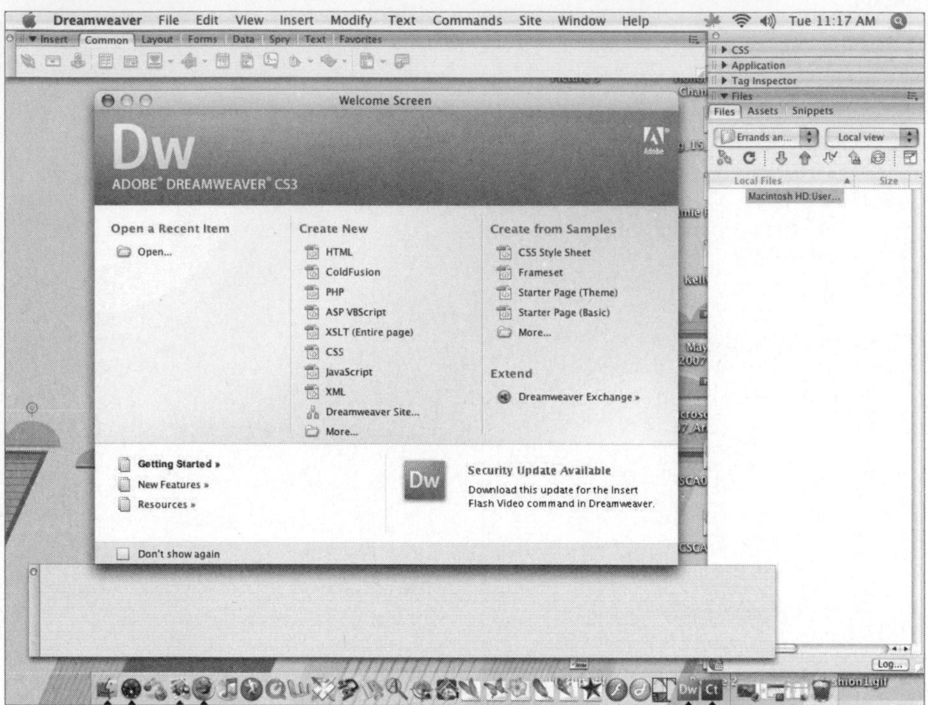

As with most applications, these toolbars can be resized, dragged, docked, minimized, added to, or subtracted from, and their associated icons are accessible via keyboard shortcuts (see Figure 2-9), mouse clicks, tabs, panels, and the taskbar. The *workspace* (the blank area surrounded by menus, panels, and other options) is the area where you develop the Web pages for a site. The easily accessible panels to the right of the workspace contain additional functionality (such as a CSS or properties). And, of course, the developer is able to modify the workspace to suit his or her individual needs.

Dreamweaver uses the standard tools of Web development: HTML code, JavaScript code for interactive functions, links, layout templates, tables, frames, interactive forms, and Cascading Style Sheets (CSS). In short, it is a comprehensive Web authoring tool that allows the developer to create, manage, maintain, and edit the site, even after it has been set up at its remote location (which is called a *Web server*). The developer can automatically use drag-and-drop techniques to select templates (for page layouts and for forms design, for example) or to query technologies, all while generating the associated HTML code.

FIGURE 2-8

Dreamweaver's Insert toolbar is a specialty item appearing as a drop-down menu on the main screen.

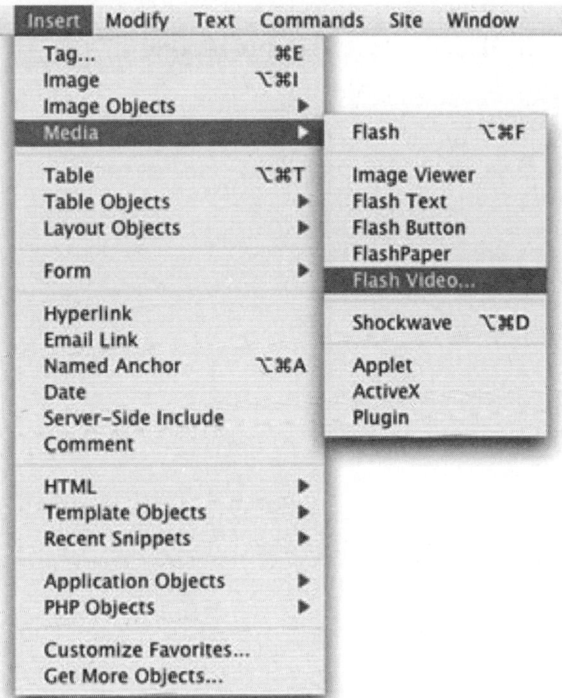

Dreamweaver has several admirable features dealing with *concurrency*. These features enable a designer who is working as part of a team of programmers to work on any particular Web page while the rest of the team is working on other multiple Web pages of a site. The concurrency features ensure that no duplicate versions of a file can be created by programmers who might otherwise unknowingly be working separately on the same file.

An associated application, Fireworks (discussed in greater detail later in this chapter), offers several options in its tool palettes for the modification of images — which provides a good companionship with Dreamweaver. For example, as shown in Figure 2-10, tables can be created simply by selecting an icon from the Insert bar and picking from the options offered.

Dreamweaver is a *WYSIWYG* ("what you see is what you get") development environment. The idea underlying a WYSIWYG is that, as a developer develops the page, he or she can literally see the page come to life as "a work in progress." As the page is created, modifications can be promptly made and/or discarded according to the judgment of the designer. To monitor the progress of the Web page development, the developer can switch between design and code view, or see both using the split screen feature shown in Figure 2-11.

FIGURE 2-9

Developers can use a variety of keyboard shortcuts in Dreamweaver.

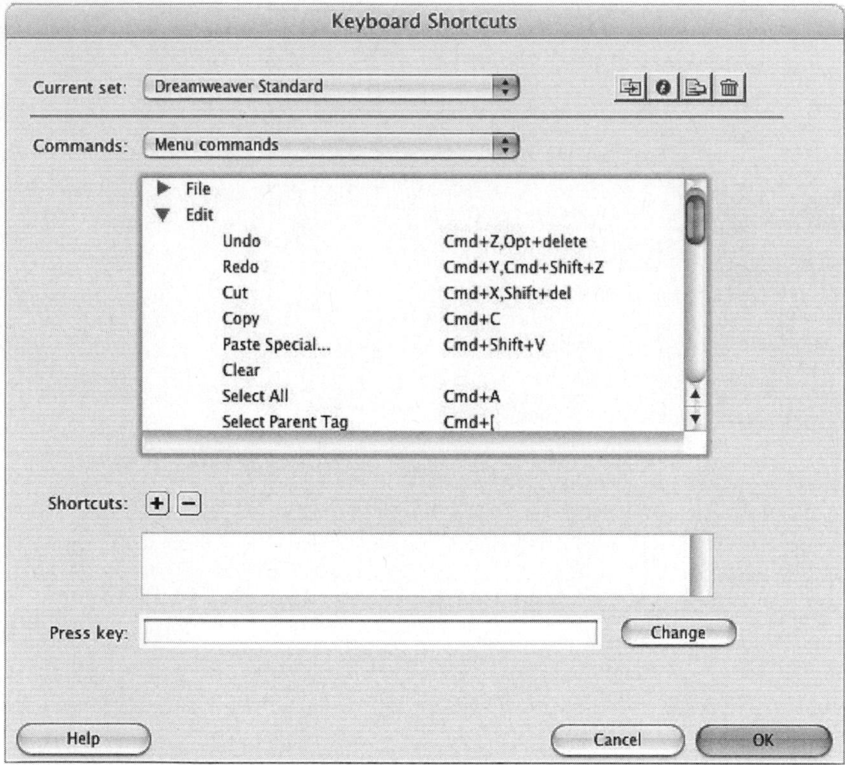

Bear in mind that the final product seen on the developer's screen will not necessarily be rendered the same way on all users' screens. There are going to be the adjustments to browser types, screen resolutions, graphics capabilities, and connection speed that will affect how (and when) the Web page is rendered on a viewer's device. For example, using the features available in Dreamweaver, the developer can provide multiple versions of each of the Web pages loaded on the site by creating and referencing multiple versions, and testing each type of browser that might try to access the site. The Dreamweaver developer must also be aware of not only different browsers but also different screen resolutions and sizes. The Internet is capable of servicing many device types, such as desktop computers and laptops, as well as handheld devices and *microbrowsers*, also known as *mobile browsers*, such as the one shown in Figure 2-12.

FIGURE 2-10

Using the point-and-click Table options can save significant amounts of time.

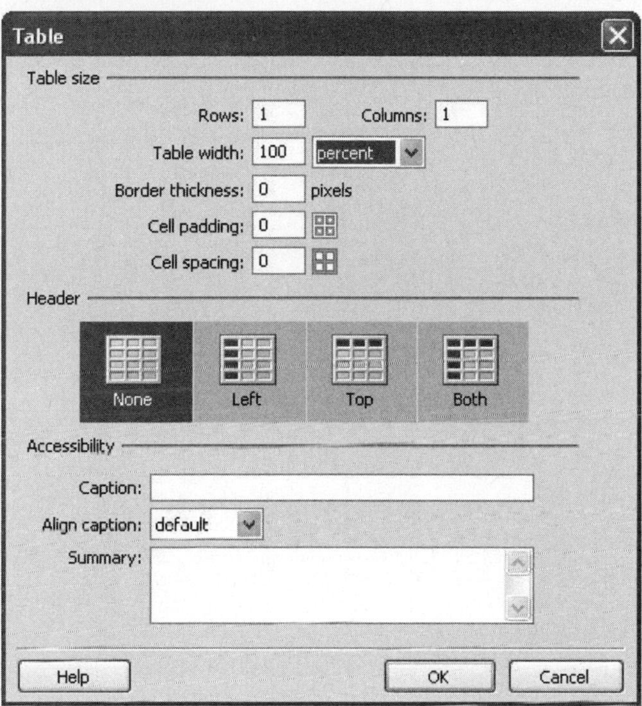

Professionals also understand that not all people on the Internet use dedicated T3 or even T1 lines for communication, and good developers minimize the eye candy to speed up delivery of content. Most of what developers cannot control directly, they can anticipate and plan for.

In addition to the now-standard features of line numbering and automatic color coding to help in resolving coding issues, Dreamweaver has sophisticated diagnostics for troubleshooting related problems.

Though it may seem difficult at first, learning how to use these Dreamweaver development tools makes coding for Web pages a breeze. However, it was not always this convenient. Many developers' first Web page code was written using Microsoft Notepad. If we made logical or syntactical errors in that nice little text application, they would be very difficult to find because there would be no pointers to where a glitch might be while running the program. The program would just run — or it just wouldn't. Of course, you could comment out sections you were suspicious of and run the program again, but sometimes the easiest troubleshooting methodology would be to just press the Delete key. Coding in plain text was no way to get home to dinner on time.

FIGURE 2-11

Dreamweaver offers a split view to help monitor Web page development.

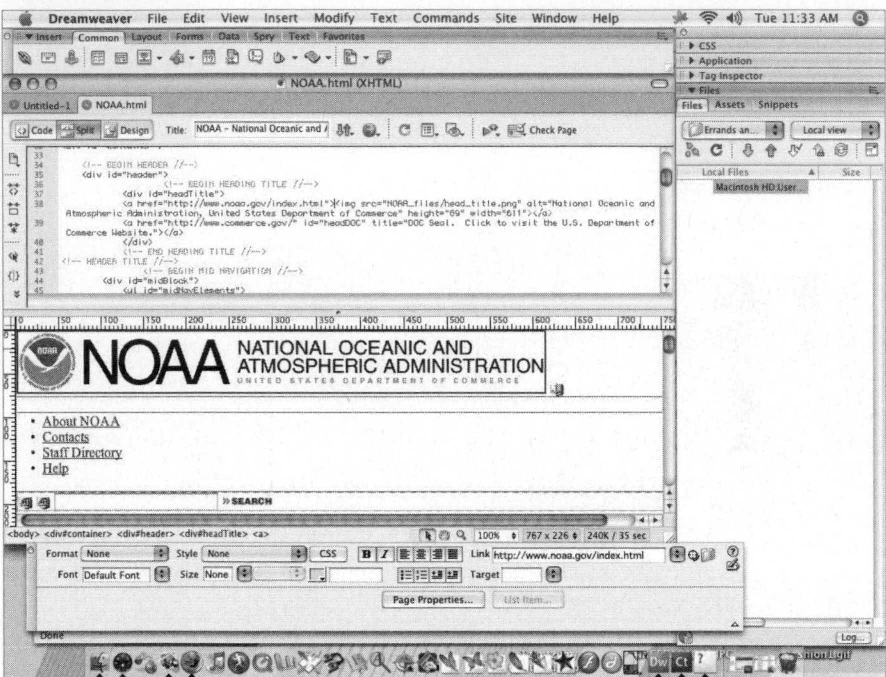

Plain text had no WYSIWYG, no split screens, no quick-and-easy back and forth between code and pages to aid in design and problem diagnosis. A developer did not have much of an idea of what the final site would look like until he or she ran the program. This meant a lot of tedious back and forth between the code and the unfinished page, and there would always be occasions when the screen would render nothing after a seemingly trivial change.

But no more coding drudgery!

Like all such applications, Dreamweaver has significant advantages and some drawbacks, but it is a premier Web site development and management tool.

Dreamweaver is included in many versions of CS3 for use by both the professional and casual users (it has very sophisticated design features, or is "feature-rich", as techies say). The Design Premium or Master Collection versions are designed for use by Web professionals, and consequently those versions can be rather pricey. In addition to the above CS3 versions, Dreamweaver is also available in a Web Standard edition (without a lot of the high-end tools), which may be more appropriate for use by occasional designers.

FIGURE 2-12

Google can be displayed in a handheld's microbrowser.

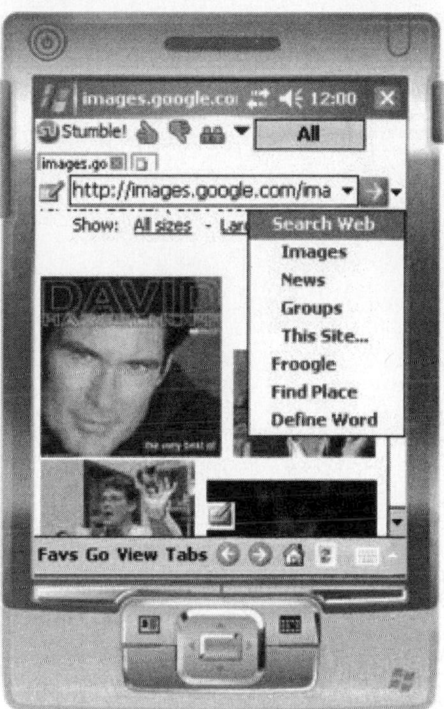

Learning new technologies

Learning anything can be a time-consuming, error-filled, and overall frustrating experience. It's like trying to climb up a greased pole for the prize on top. But this is because the novice user's world view, mindset, vocabulary, and certainly experience is different from that of a skilled designer. Beyond the basics, there is a steep and strange learning curve. As new patterns of hand-eye coordination are established, and these new patterns of behavior are being programmed into our brains, we will fall automatically back into our previous habits.

This is normal and expected. It is not a result of being slow or stupid. It is a result of being human. We have been hardwired (as a successful survival strategy) to apply previous successful behaviors to new situations that seem similar to those we have surmounted.

continued

continued

New users see new technology as an extension of something they are already familiar with, and it is naturally a shock to see that traditional learning strategies will sometimes not sustain them.

Remember that the confluence of radical new technologies at the end of the 1800s led to the development of the automobile which, in its first versions, was called the horseless carriage and perhaps not treated far differently from the horse-drawn kind.

Therefore, the learning process for beginners can be discouraging and time-consuming. Errors could be the result of neglecting a step, mistyping a formula, or making a simple alteration in the associated code of the page. In that event, the Undo button would be the instinctive choice, but would probably not work (How can you undo what you have done if you do not know what you have done wrong — if anything?). If you cannot fix a problem, you dispose of it or walk away from it (in other words, fight or flight) — the Web equivalent to pressing the Delete key and starting over — and this is really a rather sad result.

Illustrator

The Illustrator application allows the user to efficiently create vector graphics, and then seamlessly use the result with other applications included in CS3. The developer can prepare content for Web, mobile, and print media.

The interface of the CS3 version has been modified to provide more efficient utilization of the workspace. For example, the Tools palette has been streamlined from two columns to one that docks inconspicuously along the borders of the screen. Simultaneously, more options have been added (such as New Document Profiles, where designs for Illustrator video documents may be created and forwarded for display).

Some of the powerful new tools available include LiveColor (which allows the developer to dive into the intricacies of color harmonies and have fine alignment control), and an improved Erase Tool (which allows you complete control over the shape and smoothness of the erasure). This will surely be a boon to the many of us who do not have the hands of an old-fashioned watchmaker. The venerable Crop Tool now also has presets that can be used for video or still images, making the setting of those marks more intuitive.

Flash Professional

The next upgrade from Flash MX, Flash CS3 includes significant improvements over the older Macromedia product. One of the most notable features is the seamless integration with other CS3 applications. Adobe established a uniformity of menus, icons, and palettes that are identical in all applications. Importing vector graphics from Illustrator is now much easier. The user can copy and paste directly from one application to another without the loss of many of the associated properties of the graphic (an issue in previous versions).

The former pre-integration method had needless duplication through the use of similar functions that were configured just a bit differently — or had a feature that the almost identical button in the other program didn't have, which was time-consuming and cost-inefficient if you were paying someone to have this fun. Integration saves both time and money. Even many of the drawing components and palettes (or *panels*, as they are presently called) have a uniformity of formatting, docking, tabbing, and resizing features.

ActionScript, one of the programming languages Flash supports for advanced interactivity, has also been improved by allowing programmers to copy and preserve the properties of motion in Flash video clips, and then apply the selected properties to other images. Additional improvements allow greater ease in exporting video clips to QuickTime. Similarly, QuickTime media formats can now be more easily converted to Flash using Flash Video Encoder. Flash also has editing features that allow cropping and resizing to be done on the fly.

Properties and attributes

A *property* or *attribute* is a characteristic of an object. If we were discussing English grammar, a property would be the equivalent of an adjective, and the object would be equivalent to the noun. For example, say we had as the object of an illustration a drawing of Donald Duck. We color the duck's bill yellow. Therefore, the color property associated with the image of the bill would have the value of yellow. In English, this would be the equivalent of saying, "The duck's bill is the color yellow." Let's say that before the integration of the related applications, the object could be transferred (but not easily) and that the value of yellow could not easily be transferred, even though the property *color* could be. This might result in a rather colorless Donald Duck representation, though the bill could still be made triumphantly yellow again in the new resident program.

Other notable features of Flash Professional include the following:

- The Channel Mixer, which controls the conversion of color images to black and white
- The Curves dialog box, which allows for adjusting image tonality using a slider
- Camera Raw 4 (regarded by many in the photo industry as the best of its type on the market), in which filters are now less destructive, and it is easier to maintain the integrity of the original in photo touchups, tonal changes, and scaling

In summary, integration with Illustrator and Photoshop is the key feature of Flash. The standardization of panels and shortcuts, as well as tools such as Pen and Copy, improve productivity because a designer no longer has to learn/unlearn the placement and identity of the same tools differently represented in each application. Other improvements are those in easing the coding process for animations and those in the format conversion processes.

Lastly, Flash is a cross-platform application.

Photoshop Extended

Photoshop Extended is for professional developers. It has all the features of the standard version — and more. For example, the Vanishing Point feature for two-dimensional (2D) and three-dimensional (3D) perspectives (which debuted in CS2) now works for 3D imports from other applications (such as KMZ, COLLADA, and Acrobat 3D).

There are also significantly improved viewing and manipulation capabilities of the model using the Camera Tool and the Object Tool.

The Camera Tool moves in relation to the static object being viewed to provide the user with various angles of perspective. It is as if the user were able to do a walk-through of a home, or a subdivision layout, or walk around (and through) the Statue of Liberty.

The Object Tool is used to move the object and view it from any angle, as well as from top to bottom, while the observer remains static. These features are contained in specific 3D modeling programs, but having them now available in Photoshop Extended greatly enhances the capability of importing from another application.

Photoshop Extended requires at least a gigabyte of RAM to run, and runs much faster at twice that. It is an excellent tool to use for terrain mapping, and also has applicability in medical fields. Photoshop can import and export Digital Imaging and Communications in Medicine (DICOM) files. These images from magnetic resonance imaging (MRIs), computed axial tomography scans (CT scans), and ultrasounds can be resized, cloned, scaled, rotated, sliced into sections, and sequenced in a grid format for ease of review by specialists.

Another time-saving feature is the ability to rapidly edit movie frames using Duplicate Frame, or clone single or multiple frames (or even edit one frame at a time) using the Animation palette. A frame, as you may know, is one in a sequence of pictures.

Fireworks

Fireworks is an application that is designed to allow fast prototyping of Web designs by offering a large library of templates (called *presets*) to select from and the tools to quickly design special effects, process them, and then populate them site wide. The changes can be prototyped throughout the site, and any changes can be instantly applied using the Global command. An important and distinctive feature of Fireworks is that it can work with both vector and bitmap graphics.

The prototypes may also contain active links and coding that are done in one application and then transferred to another without losing functionality. There are several tools used to ensure image optimization, even while exporting in a wide variety of formats. Multiple pages can be created in a single document using the new Pages panel, and each page can contain its own tables, frames, layers, and slices. The application has hierarchical layer structure and is well integrated with both Dreamweaver and Flash. Figure 2-13 shows an example of Fireworks.

FIGURE 2-13

Fireworks allows fast prototyping of Web designs.

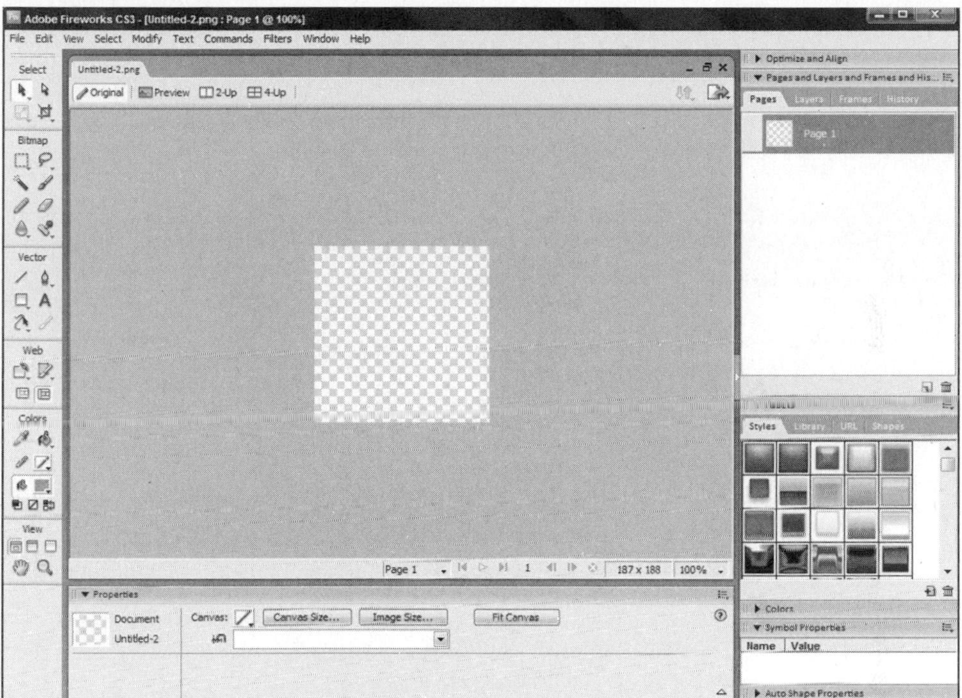

Acrobat

Most computer users have, at one time or another, used the Acrobat Reader part of the Adobe Acrobat family of products. New versions keep getting better and easier to use. Using Acrobat, a user can create a PDF file of documents from basically any application with a print function. One shortcoming, however, is that it's not interactive. For example, you can't first print into a PDF and then send it as an email attachment. But, you can export data to a spreadsheet.

Contribute

According to Adobe, Contribute (see Figure 2-14) allows users with even a minor level of experience to update blogs and Web sites, and have them appear professional. They can maintain site integrity and consistency of appearance. For any sites created with Dreamweaver, Contribute preserves the code quality and formats for the entirety of the update process. Through Contribute, content can be published directly to the Web from the site or directly from other applications such as Word, Excel, or Outlook. Site consistency can be maintained whether single or multiple

FIGURE 2-14

Contribute enables novice users to update blogs and Web sites.

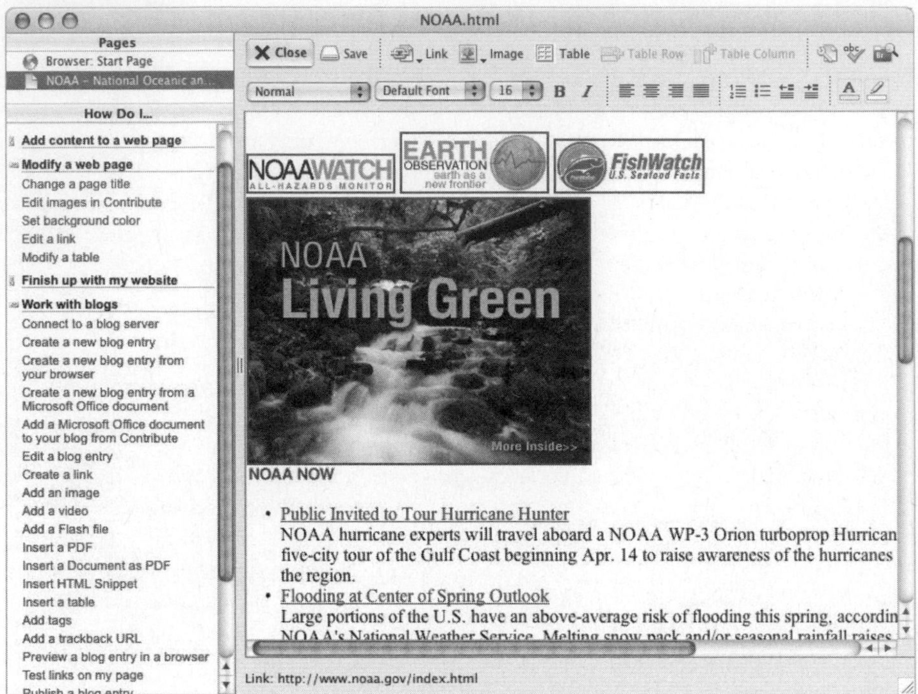

contributors are making updates to the Web site. The site administrator has a high degree of control for allowing access to the site, or particular parts, and establishing or changing the level of permissions for that access. Additionally, the administrator can publish to multiple Web sites and blogs from a single application.

Other features in Contribute allow the insertion of Flash video simply by dragging and dropping the files into the site or blog. There are WYSIWYG blog templates and Web templates. Pages may be edited from both IE 7 and Firefox 2, and all standard protocols for file transfer are supported.

Freeware and Shareware

Although we do use *freeware* (software that is available as a free download on the Internet), we are quintessentially aware that the nature of the beast is like a hunt for treasure in the flea market. On occasion during that treasure hunt, you'll find something that catches your eye. But, like that treasure you discover at the flea market, even though it was such a good bargain, you'll wonder why you bought it when you take it home (though you might brag about it to your friends) and seldom use it. And one nice spring day when you clear the clutter from your cabinets, you'll find it and it will inspire you to hold a garage sale to get rid of it.

We have several freeware programs lurking around hard drives that we thought we might just give a try, did, and then never bothered to use again. There are several freeware utilities that work just about as well as the utilities already part of the operating systems on our computers. There are several graphics freeware programs and several free security programs, but these have fancier names, cooler icons, or more eye-catching slider bars than the ones included with our operating systems. While there are many good sites featuring freeware, shareware, and/or trial versions of commercial software (for example, CS3), a couple of good, reliable sources for them are `tucows.com` and CNET's `download.com`.

NOTE `download.com` **advertises that it won't allow spyware or adware applications on its site. Also, "freeware" isn't always free — adware, spyware, and so forth, could be included.**

You should understand that some of these programs are fairly good and perform according to spec. That is why, after a certain number of days (or tries), these tend to migrate from freeware to shareware (software that is available for use, sometimes after a small fee is paid). Within this broad classification also fall trial versions of commercial software. There are some excellent programs offered by software businesses that are free for personal use, and there are also a number of programs that have achieved great popular success.

In this section, we will list the programs broadly according to the following categories:

- Image-editing programs
- Image making (drawing) programs
- Others that do not clearly fall into one of these categories, but are nonetheless related to Web-based graphic design and development

This examination will list programs according to familiarity and popularity, and we will point you to additional Web sites as potential sources for additional graphics. The descriptions included here do not distinguish between freeware, shareware, and trial versions of commercial software, but do provide sources where you can check out the applications on the Web for more information.

CAUTION **While this discussion does provide previews of freeware and shareware applications, the intent here is not to make any representation as to the quality or reliability of the applications. We do not examine application compatibilities, level of support, functionality, or anything else about the software, but do want to make you aware of some of the software that is available.**

Image-editing programs

Following are some popular image-editing applications:

- *The trial edition of Adobe Photoshop CS3* — This download is rated highly by users and ranked first in image-editing downloads with more than 8 million to date. This download requires site registration before use. There is also a shareware version available for Apple users.
- *PhotoImpact X3* (Figure 2-15) — This is a user-friendly image editor that actually has most of the editing tools that most people would need and use for greeting cards, DVD labels, retouching artwork, and the like. This is a large download. For more information, visit `www.ulead.com`.
- *Adobe Fireworks MX* — This is an older version of Fireworks, but it is still great for image editing and Web work.
- *Photo Pos Pro 1.37* — This is a great little program for working with photos and computer graphics. For more information, visit `www.softpedia.com`.

FIGURE 2-15

PhotoImpact contains many image-editing tools.

- *iPhoto* — This is another imaging-editing tool for Mac users that allows you to organize your photos, enhance their appearance, and put them on the Web. The application is good.
- *Microsoft Paint* — This simple graphics program is used to manipulate images and photos. Many of the images in this book were formatted using Paint.
- *Windows Photo Gallery (Vista Home Premium or Ultimate)* — This is a photo-manipulation and editing program.
- *GNU Image Manipulation Program (GIMP)* — This is often used as a open source alternative to Adobe Photoshop. Its logo is a fox named Wilber.

Image-creation programs

Following are some popular image-creation applications:

- *Page Focus Pro 6.85* (Figure 2-16) — This is used to create drawings, forms, and links. For more information, visit www.pagefocus.com.

FIGURE 2-16

Page Focus Pro enables you to create drawings, forms, and links.

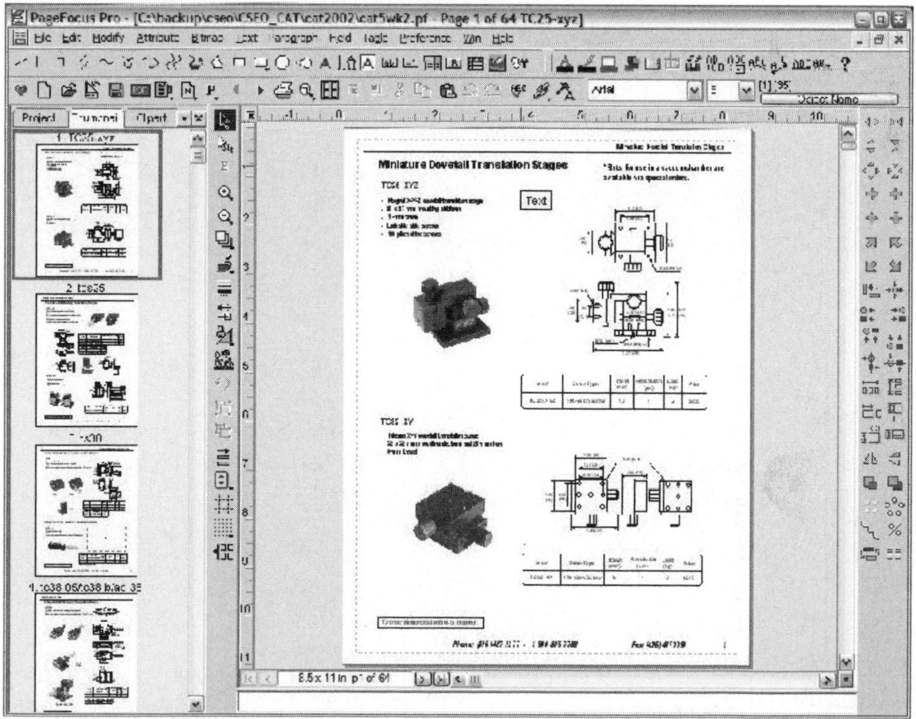

- *Polar Draw Component 3* — This does vector drawing and raster imaging, and is useful for drawing flowcharts. For more information, visit `www.polarsoftware.com/download`.
- *Avax Vector Active X* — Using this application, the developer can quickly view, create, edit, print, and manage 2D vector drawings. For more information, visit `www.topshareware.com`.
- *Aurigma Graphics Processor* — This is used to create images for use in Web page development. For more information, visit `www.aurigma.com`.
- *ConceptDraw* — This is used to create technical and business diagrams.

Other graphics-related applications

Following are some other graphics-related applications:

- *Okoker All Video Converter and Burner Pro 3.6* — This will convert videos to different video formats. For more information, visit `www.download.com/Okoker`.

FIGURE 2-17

PaintStar offers several image-processing functions.

- *ManyCam Virtual Webcam 2.1* — This application allows graphics and special effects to be added to Web broadcasts. For more information, visit `www.download.com/ManyCam-Virtual-Webcam`.
- *PaintStar* — This is handy, multifunction image-processing software (see Figure 2-17). For more information, visit `www.freewarefiles.com/program_3_36_19504.html`.
- *ForceVision* — This is a bitmap image viewer with advanced graphics capabilities. For more information, visit `www.softpedia.com`.
- *Rasterbator* — This application is used to create large poster-like images. For more information, visit `www.snapfiles.com`.

Designing for the Mobile Web

There are more than 50 companies producing mobile telephones in significant and marketable quantities. By 2009, projections indicate there will be 3 billion mobile phone users worldwide. The market for the delivery of Web content to these mobile device users dwarfs the market for desktops. There is theoretically unlimited potential for expansion of the Web (or Web 2.0) into these devices, and we are now on the cutting edge of Web site design for Mobile Web (or the "Ubiquitous Web," as it is also becoming known).

NOTE **Mobile Web, Web 2.0, and Ubiquitous Web all express the concept of a boisterous, erratically developing electronic frontier.**

The mobile device market is huge, but the very small screen sizes, relatively slow and weak processors, stripped down (simplified) operating systems, and limited memory and storage make it difficult to use the Web as efficiently as you can with static desktop computers. As an example, in growing acknowledgment of the importance of the handheld mobile market, and to help develop content specific to that environment, Adobe has reworked its Device Central development module to allow for previewing of Web content on such devices as cell phones and PDAs early in the Web page development cycle.

The discussion in this section begins with an overview of Web design for the Mobile Web. We will discuss the World Wide Web Consortium (W3C) Mobile Web Initiative (MWI) and review common difficulties hindering Web development (such as the lack of standardization, lack of new technology, network connectivity, hardware, and human factors). We will explore problems unique to developing and delivering Web content to the Mobile Web, look at current Web development and content tools (what role will scalable vector graphics play in content delivery, for example), look at Mobile Web browsers, and hazard a guess as to future technologies for Web site authoring for the Mobile Web.

NOTE **For more information on the MWI, see** `http://www.w3.org/Mobile/`.

Background for Mobile Web design

The Web is designed for physically static devices over a network, using tried-and-true technologies to access, store, and transmit data so that the process of sending and storing the data is entirely transparent to the user. The data transferred over the Web is the entire Web page (including the content), rather than content only. The underpinning of the Web protocols is that they are vendor-neutral and can used by any machine to upload/download content.

Some Mobile device providers would appear to take the view that, in order for the Web to function reliably, the coding must be device-dependent. However, the lack of standardization actually hinders the spread of Web technologies to mobile devices because each mobile device has its own proprietary coding scheme that will work on a particular device, but will not be rendered in a similar way on other devices. Therefore, W3C has established the Mobile Web Initiative (MWI) to establish a common set of standards that all communications companies can adopt (but are not required to) and work from so that there would be interoperability, cross-platform support, and common display configurations.

Even though we do discuss Wireless Access Protocol (WAP) again in the text, we can point out that, here-and-now, there are no standards. However, because WAP has been used for years, it has become the default standard. Many high-end handheld devices (such as the iPhone, the Sprint Blackberry 8830, Verizon Palm Treo, Samsung SCH-i760, Motorola Q Black, or even the SmartPhone) are coming out with much more capable browsers (for example, Windows Mobile Pocket Internet Explorer and Safari for iPhone).

As in the early days of network chaos (before standardization brought about by common reference to the OSI model), there are a plethora of platforms and physical sizes and types.

Screen sizes and resolutions vary, and a prime objective of MWI has been to bring forth standardized data formats that would be accessible by all Mobile Web devices. The MWI is developing a technology analogous to device drivers (called the *Device Description Repository*) to cope with the great variety of devices out in the worldwide market. These standards (or guidelines) are available to Web developers in W3Cs Best Practices Software Checker Tool.

One of the questions MWI dealt with was the type of content that was to be displayed on mobile devices (such as mobile phones and derivative smartphones, as well as pagers and PDAs, as shown in Figure 2-18), and other handheld devices utilizing Internet access on demand from any location and the tools required to develop that content.

As of July 2007, the *Device Independent Authoring Language* (*DIAL*) for the Web authoring tools was still officially a work in progress of the W3C. The purpose of DIAL is to provide a uniform coding structure and syntax that will allow content to be displayed on all handheld devices subscribing to the standard. DIAL is designed to allow the development and display of the typical formatting elements of a Web page, including lists, text, links, objects (images) tables, and forms. Objects would include both images and plug-ins, and forms would be interactive. Coding would conform to the XHTML 2.0 standard.

FIGURE 2-18

Pocket PDAs can now display Web content.

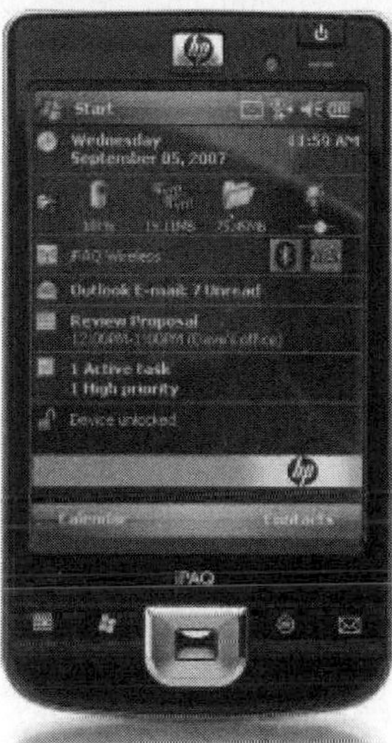

The 800-pound gorilla in the room is the issue of backward compatibility. No entirely satisfactory technological solution (hardware or software) has yet been reached for accessing the millions of existing Web sites in the Web 2.0 environment.

There are a number of minibrowsers available, but most are stripped down WAP versions of existing full-featured Web browsers (to compensate for the limited bandwidth and simplistic operating systems used in many handhelds). WAP browsers are used throughout most of the world (Japan has its own indigenous standard) to provide all of the basic services of a computer-based Web browser. Examples would be Opera Mobile and Pocket Internet Explorer. Nokia also has its separate (but proprietary) *microbrowsers* (see Figure 2-19). As of late 2006, a few began to incorporate more advanced Web authoring technologies such as CSS and Ajax.

Current difficulties with Web usage on mobile devices

Mobile devices were primarily used for sending brief messages, checking the weather, getting lists from the Web, getting stock quotes, placing orders on forms, reviewing documents, graphics development, or editing. The explosive growth of cell phones was powered by the revolutionary capability to provide (and receive) timely information anytime, anyplace reliably. This allowed, for example, the immediate updating of inventory through handheld devices, making plane or hotel reservations online from a cab in the middle of the George Washington Bridge, checking sports scores, updating forms, broadcasting messages — all interacting with the Web world when physically away from a computer. The promise of the devices was increased productivity at times and in places that had hitherto been considered unavoidable dead spots in a worker's day.

FIGURE 2-19

The T-Mobile cell phone is an example of a microbrowser.

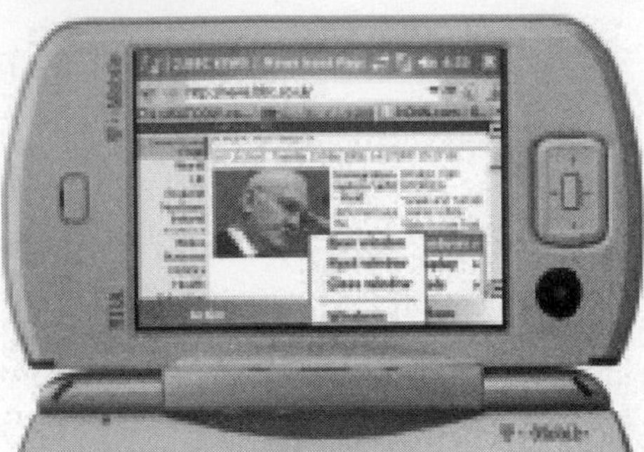

But, there are difficulties both in the transmission of data and the receipt and rendering of data. In the transmission of data, access to the Internet is not universal from every location. In addition, because of the different media involved, WAP is merely one in a long and varied chain of links from Point A to Point B, or Point A to Points B, QZ, and FFI. If a link goes down and connectivity is lost, that translates into time and labor lost because the information must be reentered and retransmitted. Network quality is not universal.

The needs of mobile users were found to be different from static Web users in that the devices were mobile and needed to have continuous Web access wherever the user might be. This would mean that in a warehouse where a worker was using a handheld device to check inventory, there could be no dead spots, or weak or intermittent access to the Web, or an intermediary server.

Reliability and network connectivity are issues. Limited bandwidth is an issue. And there are human factors. Ease of use is continually proving to be an issue. There are not only physical limitations in the design of mobile devices, small screens, and keypads, but most users of handheld devices are less computer literate than their more sedate desktop-bound types. Last, better filtering and compression algorithms must be put in place to streamline content delivery.

Future of the Mobile Web

No one can predict the future of the Mobile Web. And we have no Edward Bellamy of the Information Age to come forth and offer utopian prognostications. But it would not be unreasonable to anticipate the following:

- There will be standardization of Web content delivery systems.
- There will be an abrupt reduction in the number cell phone manufacturers.
- There will emerge a few dominant wireless network technologies.
- The giants of today (such as Sprint, Verizon, and AT&T) will be knocked out by some unknown kids currently working out of their garages.

- There will be less of an issue with accessibility as wireless connectivity spreads.
- As network infrastructure develops, the slowness of Web access experienced by Blackberry users will cease to be a problem.
- Device capabilities will improve to match the needs of the industry.

In short, what the future holds for mobile devices is that the variety and number of services will continue to improve, bandwidth will increase, and costs will decrease as Web 2.0 comes to flourish.

Summary

This chapter examined current Web design applications and suites, with particular focus on Adobe Creative Suite 3 (which is made up of a variety of tools, including Photoshop, Dreamweaver, Flash Professional, Illustrator, and Fireworks). The discussion highlighted some of the new features of each program (such as the toolbars, panels, and the drive toward uniformity and seamless integration). This chapter further defined the several program components within each application, and also noted new features within each program. You learned about the differences between vector and bitmap graphics, and how they are used within Web pages.

You learned about the differences between image-editing and image-creation (drawing) programs. The examination provided a list of several high-traffic freeware and shareware image-editing and image-drawing programs.

And finally, you learned about the largest potential market for Web designers and developers: handheld or mobile devices. The discussion explained some of the design challenges unique to this market.

Chapter 3 provides some background information about the Internet, as well as taking a look at HTML and the creation of Web pages.

Part II

The Basics

IN THIS PART

Chapter 3

History and Development of the Internet and HTML

IN THIS CHAPTER

- Origins of the Internet
- Development and evolution of HTML

The purpose of this chapter is to give you some context for the work you will be doing with Internet technologies. The Internet can be pretty intimidating, and this chapter takes a look at its development, some of the people and organizations that were in on its development, as well as the different parts of the Internet.

The Internet is a big thing that took decades to develop, but it's not monolithic. We will be looking at the origins of the Internet from the first tentative steps to the worldwide phenomenon it has become. We will look at why it is so difficult to understand, and explain it so that it makes better sense why certain things are the way they are.

We will be looking at the origins of Hypertext Markup Language (HTML) because it is the language of the Web and pretty much has been since the beginning of hypertext. But it wasn't born full-blown either. We owe a great deal to people who toiled long stubborn hours in obscurity, such as Dave Raggert, who has inspired us by working to make Web pages possible through his extensive rewrite of HTML.

Eric Bina, a man with burning vision, leads the browser revolution with Mosaic and has demonstrated how it can serve the business and customer base (B2B and B2C).

Origins of the Internet

One of the first ideas to get out of your mind (if it is there) is that the Internet is a monolithic creation that came about at a single point in time and at a single location.

The Internet is a conglomerate of overlapping and mutually reinforcing technologies from computer science, data storage and retrieval sciences (the once lowly data processing), and communications that have been developed (and are still being developed) over the past half century. From inception in the Department of Defense (DoD) and the research centers of premier universities, the Internet has been radically transformed time and time again as new hardware and software technologies that are continually developed stream into the global information matrix, mature, and are made obsolete in a seemingly endless evolution.

Rather than a single, static entity, the Internet is a living, pulsating, vibrant, multifaceted creation that is still rapidly evolving and changing our world in ways unimagined. Just like our grandparents and great-grandparents at the onset of the Age of the Automobile, we have not fathomed the societal changes the Internet will bring about.

Perhaps by watching our children in their eager embrace of cell phones, portable computers, iPods, instant messaging (IM), MySpace, and YouTube, our generation may gain insight into the near-term transformations of our society — that is, if we are not already too mentally numbed by earlier society-shattering discoveries to take account of them.

The Internet had its origins more than 40 years ago in 1962 during ongoing research into the possibility of using packets for communication as opposed to switched circuits. One of the early researchers (and most successful proponents of packet-switched circuits) was Leonard Kleinrock of the Massachusetts Institute of Technology (MIT). The concept of a network, however, over which to send the packets of information belongs to J. C. R. Licklider, also of MIT, who presciently wrote about the Galactic Network that could be used by anyone to access information contained in any connected computer.

Emergence of packet switching and ARPANET

All communication takes place from sender to receiver over a communications channel. Ever since the telephone era began, communications have taken place over copper lines, called *circuits*. You may recall seeing early twentieth or late nineteenth century photos of women in long skirts plugging lines into a switchboard. They were actually connecting a sender and a receiver using the phone lines. When one line (or *channel*) was being used, no other person or machine could use it. So, if there were three lines connecting Wichita to Omaha, and four people wanted to use them, one person was out of luck until one of the other three people decided to hang up. Then, for example, a person in Wichita could make a call.

Some of these calls could be very long (during which time no one else could contact anyone else on that line) and costly (the funds from which went into improving services and research into newer technologies). One of the motivating forces behind the development of packet-switching technology was to make more efficient (and, therefore, cheaper) use of the communications infrastructure. The idea was to take conversations from several different people, put these conversations into separate boxes, address them, and then send those boxes across a single circuit at the same time.

The advantage was efficiency because you could use one line to send lots of conversations across the same line at practically the same moment. Conversations from Cousin Sue, Preacher Paulsen, Freda the Librarian, Farmer Phil, and dozens of others, for example, could all be put in their boxes and shipped across the same single line to Omaha at the same time.

Packet switching meant that only one line was needed to carry multiple conversations, whereas *circuit switching* required one entire line to be used for each conversation, as shown in Figure 3-1. What this meant to the nascent Internet Age was that there was the potential to send greater amounts of data quicker and much more cheaply.

In the mid-to-late 1960s, research continued into a packet-switched network that would allow access to remote computers on multiple networks for data processing and the transfer of data files. Now, this is not to say that you could not access separate networks already. You could. It was just very clumsy. For each network to which you wanted to be connected, you would need a different computer that was physically connected to that one network. This is the same as you having to carry around a different phone for each of your friends you might wish to give you a ring.

FIGURE 3-1

When viewed together, the concepts of circuit switching and packet switching are quite different.

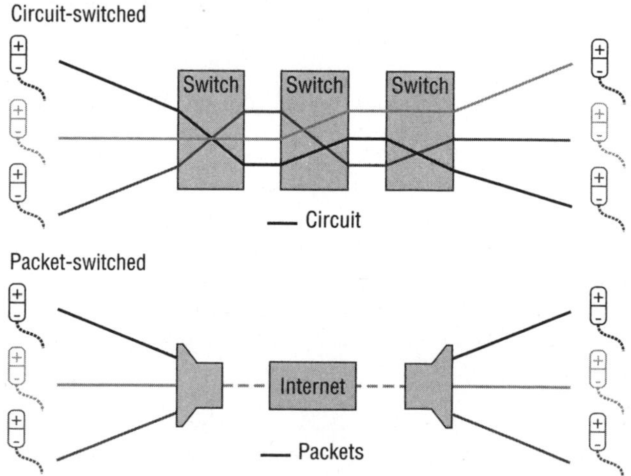

FIGURE 3-2

Interface Message Processor

In 1964, initial funding for what would become such a system, the DoD's Advanced Research Projects Agency (ARPA) network (ARPANET), was provided to research ways to network separate systems together. Under the directorship of Larry Roberts, what eventually became (at the end of the decade) ARPANET consisted of four nodes connected to each other via phone lines leased from the telephone company.

Located at the University of California at Los Angeles (UCLA), University of California at Santa Barbara (UCSB), Stanford Research Institute (SRI), and the University of Utah, the four nodes were connected by Interface Message Processors (IMPs) shown in Figure 3-2. These were the world's first routers. The creation of ARPANET in 1969, also the year of the first landing on the moon, passed without much public notice.

NOTE **See the sidebar, "How a router routes," for an explanation of a router.**

The simple and revolutionary IMP provided a common interface for all the disparate machines operating on several different operating systems to communicate across a common channel. This is the equivalent of having a universal language translator today. The protocol to route data from node to node (or host to host) was called the *Network Control Protocol* (*NCP*). Developed by the Networking Work Group, NCP was made obsolete only in 1983 when it was replaced by the *Transmission Control Protocol/Internet Protocol* (*TCP/IP*).

How a router routes

A *router* is actually a small computer used to route communications from source to destination. How it does this is rather complex in actuality, but conceptually it's simple.

An analogy often used to illustrate the concept is that of a post office delivering a letter. When you use "snail mail," you place the letter in an envelope and write on the envelope two addresses: one is yours (the sender), and the other is address of the place and person you wish to send it to (the destination or receiver). You then put the envelope in the mailbox for the postal carrier to pick up (or you drop it off at the local post office). After addressing and dropping it off, you are finished with it. (If you can see parallels to this and e-mailing by typing in an address, say, `myfriend@neighborhood.org`, and then clicking the Send button, good for you. You know where we are going with this.) However, your local post office or mailbox is not the final destination of the envelope. It is the first of many intermediary stops.

A letter usually, goes from a local post office in a neighborhood district or small town that feeds into a larger regional office that accepts mail from smaller surrounding stations. At this central post office (CPO), the mail is sorted and packed into bags. These sacks of mail are then sent to other regional and/or local offices. Eventually, after passing through these regional intermediaries, the letter is sent to the local destination office and, from there, delivered to the recipient.

Now, a router functions the same way. It accepts incoming mail (data packets) and looks at the address of the destination. Then it looks at its list of linked router addresses it keeps in its routing table. The router selects the best route to the destination and forwards the mail to it. That intermediary router in turn looks at its routing tables to select the correct port to send the mail out to reach its ultimate destination, and sends it on. The number of intermediate stops (or *hops*, as they are called) varies depending upon the location of the recipient on the Internet (just as the number of intermediate stations a letter goes to depends upon its geographic location in relation to the sender). If you were to send a letter to Chicago from Fairfax, Virginia, it might go to intermediate post offices in Knoxville, Lexington, Indianapolis, and then on to Chicago — a total of four hops, using networking lingo. Just mentally substitute routers for the local and intermediate post offices, and you know how a router works and what a router is.

Just like the post office, a router reads addresses and, based upon the destination address, forwards the packets and selects the most efficient path from sender to receiver.

Standard or protocol

Though they seem the same and are often used interchangeably, there is a distinction between the two terms "standard" and "protocol." *Standards* are guidelines provided by nationally and internationally accepted agencies (such as IEEE, ANSI, ITU) that govern the standardized (or interchangeable) development of protocols. In other words, standards are the benchmarks by which protocols are developed. *Protocols* are the formatting of data packets that allow the packets to be encoded (properly boxed) for transmittal across the Internet.

Evolution of Ethernet

In the early 1970s, ARPANET continued to be incrementally developed and, by 1973, evolved to include 30 institutions in its network. That same year, e-mail was developed to run over the existing ARPANET system by Ray Tomlison of BBN (the same company that initially developed IMP).

Also in the early 1970s, application protocols such as File Transfer Protocol (FTP), Telnet, and Simple Mail Transfer Protocol (SMTP) were being developed and tested by being run over ARPANET.

These developments (in conjunction with the growth of networks and their interconnectivity) began to ignite the utilization of ARPANET by academic, military, government, and private institutions. The explosive growth of a number of networks was a repeat of the problem of the last decade — connecting nodes together within one network. Both Robert Kahn and Vint Cerf worked on developing a common protocol to allow differing networks to communicate with each other. The result of their successful collaboration in 1973 was TCP/IP. Like so many of the technologies of that time (Unix and the C programming language just happen to come to mind), we still use it today — bigger, better, and stronger than ever.

Ethernet was also invented and tested in this same time period by Robert Metcalfe and his assistant David Boggs, although it was not officially designated as such in the 1980 codification of IEEE 802.3. There were also subsequent standards to emerge from IEEE in response to the phenomenal growth of wireless technology. Wireless Ethernet specifications are in 802.11b and 802.11g.

As shown in Figure 3-3, Ethernet is a local area network (LAN) technology that allows communication between devices such as printers, scanners, and computers on a shared physical network. A LAN is a small network that could be used in one building, one department or section, or one lab. Basically, when the devices need to communicate with each other, they encapsulate their data in an Ethernet frame and send their data down the shared wires to the destination.

The Ethernet *frame* has standardized fields for addressing, holding data, and checking to see that the data arrived safely at its destination. If it does not arrive safely, the data is usually resent, depending on the transmission protocol used. If a computer needs to send data to another device on another LAN, it sends its data packet to the switch or router attached to that local LAN, and the LAN router or switch forwards the data across the Internet to the device on the other network.

FIGURE 3-3

The three topologies of Ethernet allow communications on a LAN.

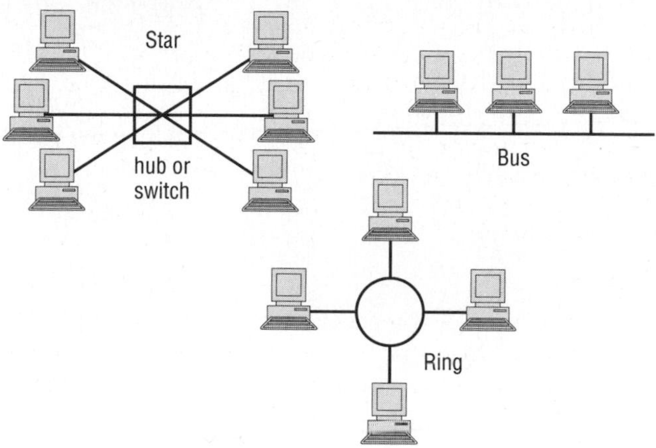

From Computer Desktop Encyclopedia, ©1998, The Computer Language Co. Inc.

Although when Ethernet was first devised in the mid-1970s when the physical media being used was coaxial cable running over what was called a *bus topology* (see Figure 3-3), Ethernet has proved enduring and astoundingly flexible as it has evolved to run over twisted-pair cabling at speeds of 10 Megabits per second (Mbps), 100 Mbps, 1 gigabit, and even 10 gigabits. It runs at the same range of speeds today over fiber, and the growing wireless (mobile and fixed) network infrastructures with remarkably little change in its underlying encapsulation and delivery structure.

Again, the structure of this frame has hardly changed since 1980, although the physical media that uses it (the cabling, the switches, repeaters, routers, and bridges) have undergone several significant evolutions. Like so much out of the 1980s, the creators of the protocols and the languages built far better products than those invented today. Much of what they have created (such as Ethernet) has proved fantastically scalable and portable.

Bytes and bits

If you ever wondered why the basic unit of datum representation (a *byte*) is 8 binary digits (*bits*) long, you may credit IBM. The 1964 introduction of its phenomenally successful 360 series of machines with complementary operating system wiped out the competing computers, which used 6-bit and 12-bit systems on their machines. The IBM 360 ran on an 8-bit system. Hence, the 8-bit byte became the standard. A byte is also sometimes referred to as a *word*, or *octet*, and a 4-bit byte is called a *nibble*.

Public emergence of the Internet

Time magazine was on target when it selected "the computer" as "Man of the Year" during the 1980s, but the magazine had no idea of the immensity of the transformation in our lives that the decade brought about. From the mid-1980s onward, huge numbers of entrepreneurs jumped into the extraordinary ocean of opportunity that was emerging from the cloistered halls of research. Some were like fireflies that barely lasted the decade, offering impossible *Star Trek* solutions to worldly workaday problems of office drudgery and persistently unfulfilled promises of a technological utopia. But there also arose the enduring giants of our age (such as Apple, Compaq, IBM, Gateway, TI, Microsoft, Intel, and AMD) from this siren dawn of the Internet Era, as if Aphrodite had risen again from the mists of the sea.

The 1980s witnessed the remarkable growth and acceptance of these new technologies in the public and commercial markets, as the underlying technologies continued to evolve and the backbone infrastructure was developed, funded, and put into place.

A lot of the funding was initially provided by the National Science Foundation (NSF) to set up and link networks for a university system called CSNET. NASA became involved, and soon there was a whole host of government entities funding the growth. Along with government participation, IBM introduced the personal computer (PC) in 1981 (with DOS) and Adam Osborne released the first portable computer (a 24-pound behemoth). As mentioned, NCP was replaced by TCP/IP in 1983 as the protocol for communication between networks across the Internet, and was incorporated into newer machines. Bill Joy added TCP/IP to his Unix package and soon founded Sun Microsystems. Newcomers to the world of business began to emerge. Novell got its start. Apple Computer released its IIE then the big one, the Mac. After IBM PCs were released, IBM clones began to emerge. Compaq developed a computer and began to rival IBM. CPM, developed by Digital Research as an operating system, was briefly popular, but then was overtaken in the market when PC clones were built with MS-DOS.

Telecommunications giant AT&T (once derisively referred to in that decade as "All Talk and no Tech") began to sense an opportunity and moved in response to the onset of rivals. MCI is one of many telecommunications firms that got its start in the 1980s.

Bill English of Xerox's famous Palo Alto Research Center (PARC) invented the trackball mouse in 1981 and shipped it with Xerox's Star computer. Mice are the predominate interface with computers to this day. Try to imagine the growth of the computer industry (and GUIs) if everything were keyboard-only. Where would the gaming industry be?

Because the Internet was growing so rapidly, the Domain Name System (DNS) was developed to keep clear nodes and their addresses. It has the now-familiar classifications of `.com`, `.net`, `.org`, `.gov`, and `.edu`. A generic International suffix (`.int`) was rejected in favor of two-letter country names. A way to manage the unwieldy Internet was developed, SMTP, as another interim solution.

In 1984, Orwellian though it might have been, Congress provided funding through the NSF to establish regional supercomputing centers throughout the nation with open access to all universities via the Internet (see Figure 3-4). These backbones quickly progressed from T-1 with a transmission capacity of 1.544 Mbps to T-3 pipes with the capacity of 28 T-1 lines (48 Mbps).

FIGURE 3-4

Regional supercomputing centers made up the Internet backbone in 1986.

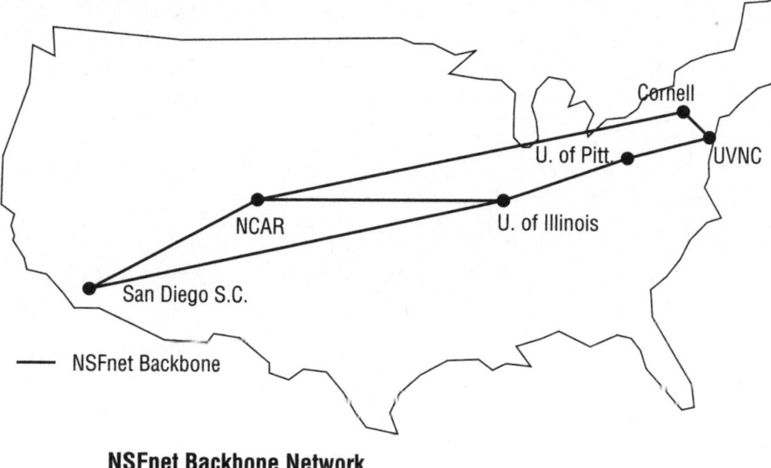

Courtesy of National Center for Atmospheric Research

By the end of 1985, there were 2,000 networks. By the end of 1987, there were nearly 30,000, and almost 10,000 were connected to the Internet (see Figure 3-5). To address the connectivity issues of these networks, yet another host of companies emerged (Synoptics, Banyan, Cabletron, Wellfleet, and Cisco) to service an industry that did not exist a few years earlier. Usenet emerged as a popular alternative to what was being offered, and bulletin board systems (BBS) enjoyed their brief day in the sun (arguably to emerge most recently in the guise of blogs).

By 1988, the first known virus, the Morris worm, led to the creation of the Computer Emergency Response Team (CERT), and with it, yet a new genus of Internet businesses to fight viruses branched out from the Internet tree of life.

By the end of the 1980s, more than 50 other nations had become associated with the Internet, thus changing it from a national to an international revolution.

Emergence of hypertext

The 1990s could be defined by the word *hypertext*, and by the man who created the technology for bringing it into reality, Sir Tim Berners-Lee. Without the successful implementation of HTML and its transfer protocol, the Web and so much industry, technology, and personal fulfillment associated with its instant graphical communication would simply be unknown.

CROSS-REF **Much of the history surrounding the Berners-Lee creation is covered in Chapter 1.**

FIGURE 3-5

The Internet backbone changed in 1988.

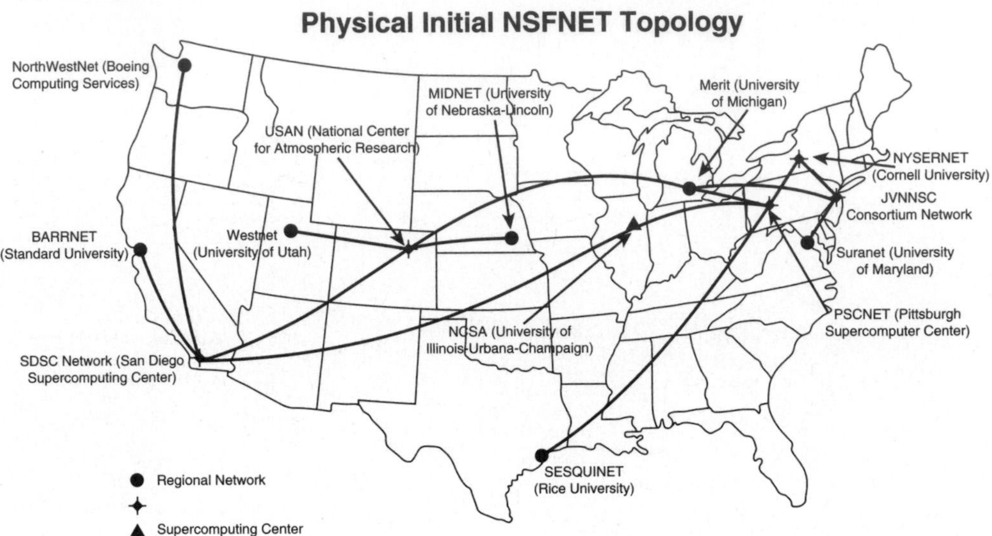

Other significant events of that decade could be summed up as growth. In a period of weeks, it would seem that entire industries would suddenly spring forth that were urgently seeking people for hundreds to thousands of new positions, and computer "experts" appeared from every bush and brush pile. Breathless entrepreneurs appeared almost overnight in their mighty pursuit of empire. Enormous fortunes were made in weeks or months. So many ISPs emerged (such as Microsoft, AOL, CompuServe, Earthlink, Yahoo!, and so many others) that the mind is dizzied trying to remember even a portion of them.

Hypercard (similar to HTML) use was at its height from the mid-1980s on. Gopher, WAIS, ARCHIE, and other early search engines entered the Internet landscape. Dow Jones even went online! Indeed, a mind-boggling array of new services became available — all dot-this and dot-that — and offered every imaginable bit of information to every conceivable interest.

After reaching more than 300,000 hosts (from just 4 nearly a decade earlier), ARPANET was officially retired.

The Age of the Internet had been ushered in (see Figure 3-6).

FIGURE 3-6

The Internet backbone changed again in the 1990s.

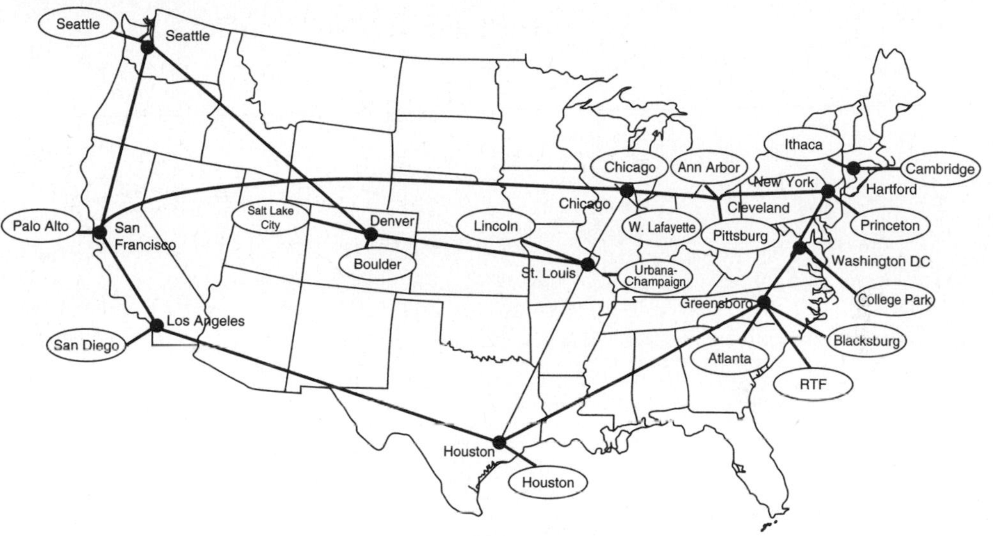

Development and Evolution of HTML

You might try a fun little experiment to see how pervasive Web pages have become. Pick any dictionary. Pick any word, even at random. Type it in your search engine. You will very, very, very likely find a Web site devoted to that word.

The Internet is not synonymous with the World Wide Web, but the Internet drove it, and then it drove the Internet as use synergistically increased the demand for network bandwidth, servers, software technologies, and hardware. The mantra for the 1990s would be "bigger, better, cheaper, faster." And the gurus of the Web and the Internet delivered, every year: better, faster, cheaper, but not, in vindication of Moore's Law, necessarily bigger.

But definitely better.

NOTE Gordon Moore, an engineer and one of the founders of Intel (along with Robert Noyce), observed that each year the number of transistors on a board doubled at the same price every 18 months. That observation has since become known as Moore's Law, and it has been applied to the idea that computer CPU capacity doubles every 18 months, while the price remains steady.

One of the earliest lessons of the Internet Age was that software drives hardware development, or, as one professor more delectably phrased it, "Software makes hardware happen."

Hypercard

Hypertext (that is, text that can be used as links to other data, or that responds in some way to a mouse click or hover — such as having a caption appear above an icon explaining its function — had been around for a while in theory and in practice. Apple came out with Hypercard in 1986. Hypercard was based on earlier concepts out of the 1940s, which had "cards" that held fields holding unique data. These cards were almost like early iterations of forms that could be used to store and manipulate data.

These cards were linked to other cards and kept in a stack that could be accessed by a previous/next feature. Think of your standard 3 × 5 index card or Rolodex card. The cards all look the same, but the information each card contains is unique. You can put these cards in any order. You can toss them if you want, and write data on a new card, or you can just cross out old data and write new data on the old card.

Suppose you have a CD game collection and you decide to keep information on each of your CDs on index cards that you keep in a small box on your desk (next to your desktop). The cards all have the same format: Name of CD, Group, Game type, Year, and Company. Each of those items of information is located on a separate line. The values input to those fields (CD, Group, Game type, Year, Company) would be unique (unless your had two or more copies of the same CD), but the format of the cards would be identical.

This foreshadowed the format/content dichotomy central to HTML. The technology of Hypercards, or hypertext, was naturally applied to the links that were developed within HTML coding.

HTML

The coding that drives the Web is HTML, and even though we are moving toward more general implementation of HTML version 4.01 and XHTML, the most browser-safe version is still HTML 2.0, because almost all graphical browsers support it. HTML 4.01 includes enhanced scripting support, stylesheet support, better multimedia support for streaming elements, and additional control over layout of the page.

Even though the latest HTML is version 4, it did not really have four generations; it actually had just three (including this latest evolution. 4.01 and 4.02). The first standardized (emphasis on *standardized*) version was HTML 2.0. It incorporated support for interactive form elements, including text boxes, labels, Option and Submit buttons, clear and exit, and table structure.

Leading up to 2.0 was a series of rapid developments regarding design features for Web implementation scattered around so much that, until 1993, no one really thought to put together. While the father of HTML (and HTTP and the browser) was Berners-Lee, his creation was rooted in some fertile soil.

His innovations were twofold:

- The concept of linking documents so that a user could look at documents from several different sources on his or her computer
- Modeling HTML on an existing worldwide standardized markup language — *Standardized General Markup Language (SGML)*.

From SGML, Berners-Lee borrowed several of the tags we will use in Chapter 4 to make a Web page. From SGML also came the concepts of a document, of separating a document into blocks of data, and of tagging (or marking up) the blocks of data and the elements contained therein.

The genius of Berners-Lee was to visualize and then create connections where none had existed before. He took hypertext and married it to a linking technology to give people the ability to bring blocks of data from various referenced sources on the screen. They had never been able to do this before.

So, in a manner of speaking, Berners-Lee could be seen as the link that made HTML the phenomenally successful Web design language it is today. In other words, succinctly put, he invented the link.

It might be argued, however, that David Raggett of Hewlett-Packard was a cofounder, for he so much improved upon this basic structure after a visit with Berners-Lee in 1992. Though we won't go into it the story of his lonely efforts at home night after night to create what would amount to a new language (HTML+) on a crowded dining room table, his dogged pursuit to present a language that addressed Web developers' common needs should be inspiring to all who stubbornly labor long hours in obscurity to bring to completion the fruit of a great idea.

So, by 1992 we have the second iteration (or first codification) of HTML, HTML+, which contained the following features:

- The capability to flow text around images and forms with captions
- The resizing of tables
- The creation of image backgrounds
- The use of arithmetical and logical relational operators

Figure 3-7 shows an example of these features. Raggert demonstrated all of these features in 1993 at the first WWW Conference by using the Arena browser he had developed to showcase HTML+.

One of the significant results of the WWW Conference was the decision to have one platform-independent version of HTML that could be used by any browser. At the conference, it was agreed that the work on HTML+ should be carried forward to lead to the development of an HTML 3 standard. Unfortunately, the rush of time and technology would not allow standardization to take effect, and the growth and acceptance of later versions of HTML was somewhat hindered by the competing browsers used to render Web pages.

This is why you have compatibility issues and must test for appearance of your Web page in multiple browsers. The big two, until quite recently, were Netscape versus IE. IE appears to have won the majority of market share. However, a successor to the Netscape browser, FireFox, is quickly gaining market share, and Apple's Safari browser is the default for the resurgent Macintosh market. The point is this: Test on the most popular browsers before you deploy your Web site, or users will complain.

Some of Raggett's planned features were scooped by the talented team from NCSA Mosaic led by Eric Bina. They were the first to present added images, nested lists, and interactive forms. And sometimes being first is enough, though some in academia and development circles have never ceased complaining that these features eventually incorporated into the corpus of HTML by version 3 weren't all that great.

FIGURE 3-7

A Web page from Wiley demonstrates the use of tables, text wrap, and captions.

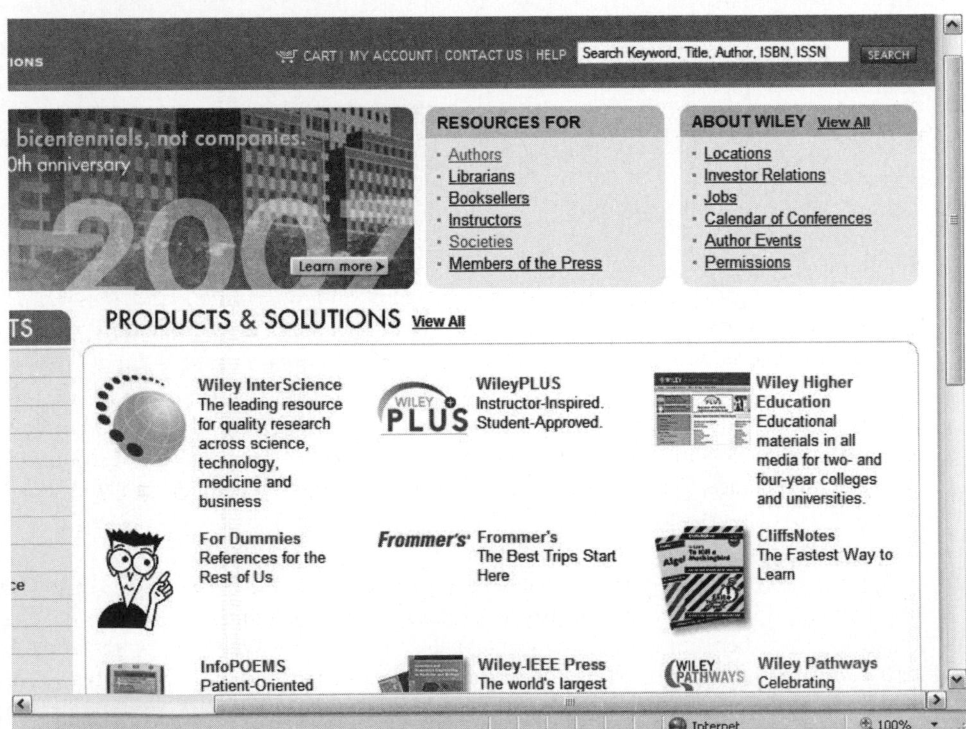

Because of the lack of cohesive development structure (that is, a standards body presenting a template of development for Web authors to follow), the support for HTML has been historically uneven. We have seen the addition of features (generically called *extensions*) that competing browsers put out that would work only on their own browsers. The use of Layers in Netscape is one illustration, and the coding differences in 3D shading for borders is another.

Cascading Style Sheets (CSS), used to simplify and standardize the formatting of Web sites and integrated into HTML 4.01, actually got its start as an extension. It would take years for popular code changes to percolate through browser versions and be widely accepted. Others would gradually pick up popular scripts, say, useful to sending data to a printer, and then someone else would write a piece of code that was useful and it would also filter into the user community. By the mid-1990s, you had an amorphous mass of programs that would flow in and out of a programmer's toolkit, and no real standardized set of tools that everyone could use all the time to accomplish set tasks.

The 1996 effort at standardization, HTML 3.0, just never really took off. Yet, in 1997, a newer implementation of the standards set forth in HTML 3.0 was again offered. HTML 3.2 offered increased support for tables, and gave more elements to interactive forms. But what may have underlain its importance (and acceptance) was the definition of the language allowing the incorporation of scripts as a Web authoring tool, not to mention backward compatibility.

Future trends in HTML

HTML v 4.01 kept pace with the dizzying developments in Information Technology (IT), and provided for additional support of stylesheets, enhancements to tables and interactive forms, expanded scripting capabilities, and increased support for multimedia.

There was always a drive to keep up to the market demands, and never really an opportunity to get ahead of the game. The driving forces of HTML and its various enhancements could be typed as *dynamism* and *interactivity*. These twins underlie the very rapid incorporation of scripts, forms, frames, and objects into the HTML platform.

However, some would complain that these developments hindered the broader acceptance of HTML. Developers who had just mastered one iteration of the language would complain because the rapid acceptance of these extensions made the language too cumbersome and "needlessly complex."

There was also the problem that bedeviled every earlier version: cross-platform compatibility. Not all browsers could support a common set of features, and sometimes had competing features so that a lot of the benefits of 4.01 went untapped. As usual, any Web page to get to the broadest user audience had to be backward compatible, and designers had to either design for multiple browsers (and even different versions of them) or design for the lowest common denominator, HTML 2.0.

The Arrival of XHTML

The solution was a newer version of HTML. Thus, HTML 4.02 and XHTML 1.0 co-emerged in 2001, combining the strengths of HTML 4.01 with the special benefits of Extensible Markup Language (XML) with the aim of creating a language that worked on a broad range of browser platforms and was also simpler to design with.

One of the apparent advantages of XHTML was now the capability to define and manipulate the types of content expressed within a Web page. This meant you could now reach into a block of data containing information about a date and make changes to one of the elements of the date object, such as the year or day or month.

XHTML also was more rigorous than any previous version of HTML in that all tags and attributes had to adhere to one of the following three XML document type definitions (DTDs) to be considered a well-formed executable document:

- *Strict* — As its name certainly implies, this DTD is strict. It does not allow any deprecated elements or attributes and does not support frames.
- *Transitional* — This is the very forgiving one. It accepts deprecated elements and attributes. It is for the old hands among us who are quite comfortable with HTML and who are willing to try something new, but not if it's going to be that difficult.
- *Frameset* — This is used for Web pages designed for frames.

Needless to say, XHTML is not supported among all browser types, though all modern browsers support XHTML to some extent. Firefox 2 and IE7 are XHTML-friendly. However, Microsoft's own validators inside the Visual Studio IDE validate against XHTML.

XHTML 2.0 came out in 2004 and was designed to transform into a Web design language that has left behind most of the presentational elements of HTML. Its current use in the Web design community is not extensive.

Even in 2007, with XHTML 2.0 designed for Web design, the implementation that developers can be certain almost all browsers would support is only HTML 2.0, which, again, was codified more than a dozen years ago.

For fun, just to see how close we (as Web developers) are to conforming to the new (and upcoming) standards that have been so hyped as the cure-all for staid limitations of HTML, we used the code checker `validator.w3.org/check/referrer` on a pretty good site: `www.google.com`. It came up with 178 noncompliance issues with the newest version of XHTML and, if you take a look at the source code, it's pretty standard HTML 4.01.

Now, even with the issue of backward compatibility when designing for the future, you simply come to the issue of need. Despite all the hyperbole regarding the advantages of XHTML, it just isn't happening in real life. This isn't to say that XHTML won't eventually supplant HTML, but history in the industry is against it.

Networking still uses TCP/IP, Unix is the foundation of Mac OSX, and millions upon millions of Web pages have been created using HTML. In other words, HTML in any form won't be going away, and any improvements to it will not be coming from a standards-making body. Rather, they will come about the way HTML has always improved: via a codification of existing practice.

Summary

This chapter introduced the Internet as a way to provide context (or framework or infrastructure, if you prefer) for the origin and direction of development of Web pages. We looked at the development decade by decade with special emphasis on technologies that fed into the growth of Web-related technologies. We noted again the pivotal importance of a single man, or a small group of men, creatively combining, or synthesizing, existing technologies to bring about revolutionary development of new technologies. We also noted, as Thomas Edison once observed, success is 99 percent perspiration and 1 percent inspiration. So, the development of the Internet was also a slow, sprawling process with some failures and blind alleys, but in the end it birthed a giant.

This chapter also discussed the history and future of HTML and its offshoots.

Chapter 4 takes you into basic HTML Web creation and design using Notepad. There you will learn to create and view a couple of your own Web pages.

Chapter 4

HTML Building Blocks

This chapter provides you with a basic introduction to the building blocks of Web page design. We review the structure of a basic Web page by introducing the head and body block elements and explaining what each part does. In the head block, we present and discuss metatags, comments tags, title tags, and functions. We next present the body section, where we explain the purpose and function of the tags used to mark up document content. We then introduce some commonly used body tags and explain how they are used to contain and format the document content. Some of the tags used to do this are paragraph tags, heading tags, list tags, inline tags (such as image tags), and empty tags (such as those used to create horizontal lines).

This chapter also discusses the difference between virtual and physical tags.

We conclude the chapter with a discussion of ASCII and Unicode.

IN THIS CHAPTER

Creating a Web Page Using HTML

The image shown in Figure 4-1 is a Web page. If you want to see "what it is made of," you may do either of the following. Go to the View menu on the standard toolbar in Internet Explorer, click on it, and then select source from the drop-down menu, as shown in Figure 4-2. Note that in Internet Explorer 7 you may need to first press the Alt key in order to display the standard toolbar.

FIGURE 4-1

Wiley's home page is a sample of a Web page.

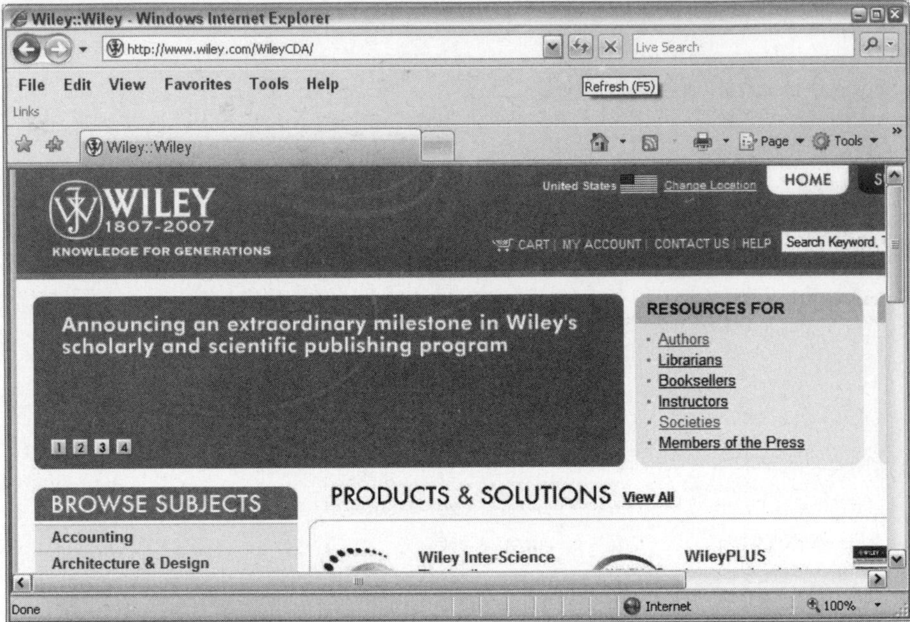

You may also select an empty area of the Web page you are viewing, right-click on it, and then select View Source from the list of options in the context menu, as shown in Figure 4-3. If you right-click on the mouse and the context menu does not have View Source as an option, select another area and try again, or simply go to the View menu to bring up the code that way.

NOTE **The *context menu* (so-called because it brings up menu options based on the surrounding context) is what appears when you right-click the mouse.**

Both methods will bring the underlying code into view in the Notepad application. Notepad is a simple text program from Microsoft, and may be accessed by clicking Accessories in the All Programs category of the Start menu, and then clicking on the Notepad icon, as shown in Figure 4-4.

FIGURE 4-2

You can view the source code for a Web page from the View menu on the standard toolbar.

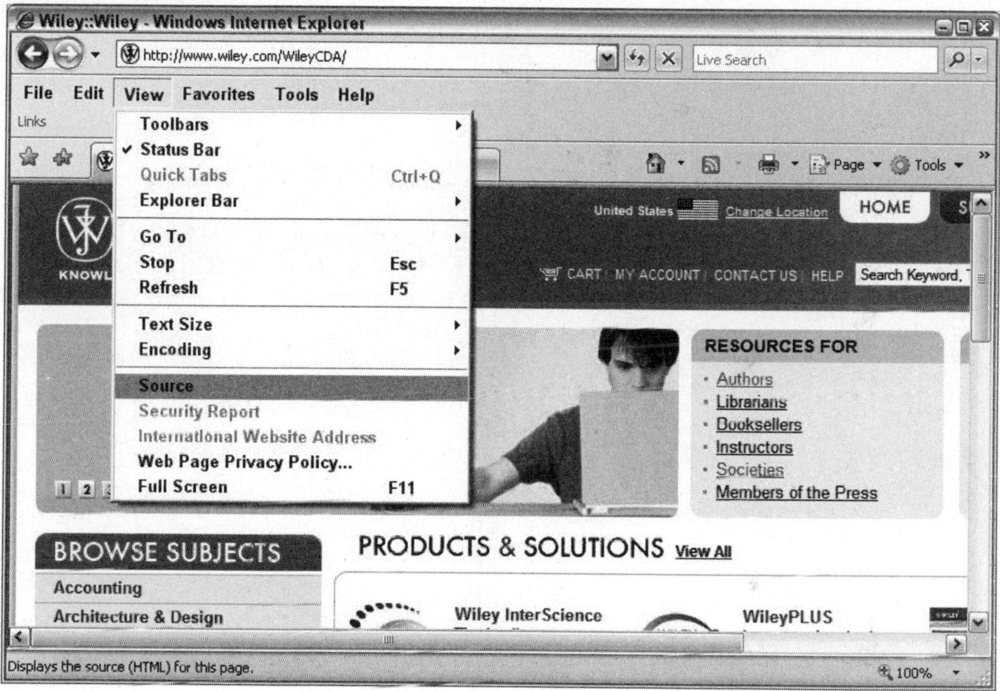

You may also view the page source in Firefox by clicking on View and then Page Source.

Either method you use results in something similar to Figure 4-5. This is the HTML code upon which all Web pages are based. You may think of this as the framework for a building upon which the sheetrock is installed, the walls are painted, and the pictures hung. Or, you may think of this as a skeleton to which the sinews and tendons are attached and then articulated, by which movements are defined, and to which the skin with its subtle shades and textures is applied.

In the example Web site shown in Figure 4-5, the following is the complete underlying code that is used to render the page:

```
DOCTYPE HTML PUBLIC "-//W3C//DTD HTML 4.01 Transitional//EN"
        "http://www.w3.org/TR/html4/loose.dtd">
<!-- Build: R12B015 -->
<!-- Strand Id: 0114864306 -->

<!-- layout( Wiley Homepage ) -->
 <html>
  <head>
  <link href="/WileyCDA/site/wiley2/include/style.css"
type="text/css"rel="stylesheet">
   <title>
Wiley::Wiley

   </title>
   <script language="javascript" src="/WileyCDA/site/shared/
form_validation.js" type="text/javascript">
   </script>
   <!--[if lt IE 7]>
    <link href="/WileyCDA/site/wiley2/include/style-ie.css"
rel="stylesheet" type="text/css">
   <![endif]-->
  </head>




  <body>
   <div id="page">
    <!-- dynamicFeature ( ref:SITE_SPECIFIC_NAV ) -->





    <!-- BEGIN HEADER -->

    <script language="JavaScript">
        function do_check (form) {
            if (form.query.value=="") {
                alert('Please make an entry in the product search
field.');
                return false;
            } else {
```

```
                return true;
            }
        }
    </script>
    <div id="top-nav">
        <a href="/WileyCDA/Section/id-300002.html"><img
src="http://media.wiley.com/spa_assets/site/wiley2/cvo/images/wiley-
logo-2007.gif" alt="wiley-logo-2007.gif" width="230" height="90"
/></a>
        <div>


            <p>
                <b>United States</b>
                <img
src="http://media.wiley.com/spa_assets/spa_images/flags/US.gif"
width="32" height="16">

                <a href="/WileyCDA/Section/id-
301023.html?&nocache=true" style="text-decoration:underline;">Change
Location</a>

            </p>


            <ul>

                <li id="home-btn"><a href="/WileyCDA/Section/id
300002.html" class="active"><b>Home</b></a></li>



                <li id="subjects-btn"><a href="/WileyCDA/Section/id-
302371.html"><b>Subjects</b></a></li>



                <li id="about-btn"><a href="/WileyCDA/Section/id-
301827.html"><b>About Wiley</b></a></li>


            </ul>
        </div>

</body>
</html>
```

FIGURE 4-3

You can right-click the mouse in a blank area of a Web page to view the source code.

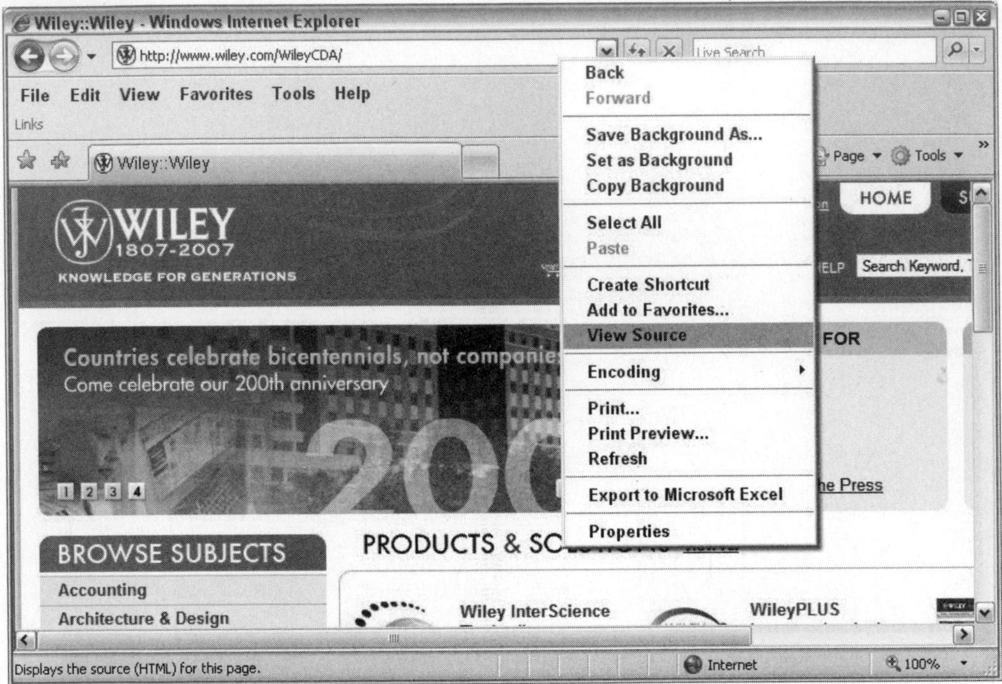

This particular Web site, by and large, is made up of HTML code — specifically HTML 4.01 Transitional code. Later in this chapter, you will be using this segment of code as a template for designing your own simple page. This example shows all of the types of tags (head, title, body, paragraph, unordered list, inline image, and comment) we will be examining in this chapter as we step through the design of a Web page. It also has some elements that we will be spending more time with later in this book when we look at object-oriented programming, data structures, JavaScript, and Java.

Note that the commands relating to the structure of the page and the formatting of the content are enclosed in `< and >`. These are sometimes referred to as *angle brackets* or *angled braces*, or you might see references to the *greater than* (>) and *less than* (<) *symbols*. But these have nothing to do with math. They are called *tags* or *elements*, and they are used to signal to the Web browser that they contain HTML commands that the Web browser is to follow when displaying the contents of the page. The content between the tags may also be referred to as *attributes*.

FIGURE 4-4

You can select Notepad from the Accessories icon on the All Programs menu.

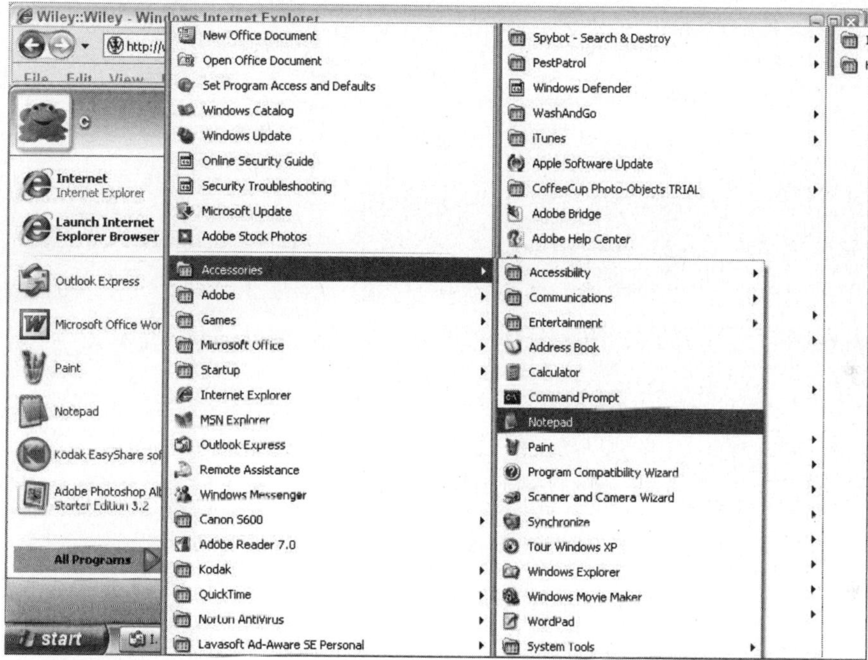

Content is what appears on the Web page in the browser and formatting is *how* it appears. The paragraph tag `<p></p>`, for example, will cause a blank line to appear between blocks of data, as shown in Figure 4-6. The paragraph tag formats the inner content as a paragraph.

Tags may be two-sided or one-sided. *Two-sided tags* have content between them, as shown here:

```
<p>This is a two-sided tag</p>.
```

Similar to how a light switch works, two-sided tags turn on and turn off a specific feature. Following are some examples of two-sided tags:

- `<b>BOLD</b>` — Here, `<b>` means turn on bold and `</b>` means turn off bold
- `<i>Italicize</i>` — Here, `<i>` means turn on italics and `</i>` means turn off italics

NOTE **You should be aware that XHTML is moving toward requiring all tags to be two-sided, except for certain tags that cannot be two-sided, such as line breaks.**

FIGURE 4-5

Using either the right-click method or selecting Notepad enables you to view the source code from a Web site.

```
WileyCDA[1] - Notepad
File  Edit  Format  View  Help
<!DOCTYPE HTML PUBLIC "-//W3C//DTD HTML 4.01 Transitional//EN"
        "http://www.w3.org/TR/html4/loose.dtd">
<!-- Build: R12B017 -->
<!-- Strand Id: 0499842701 -->

<!-- layout( Wiley Homepage ) -->
 <html>
  <head>
  <link href="/WileyCDA/site/wiley2/include/style.css" type="text/css" rel="stylesheet">
   <title>
Wiley::Wiley

   </title>
   <script language="javascript" src="/WileyCDA/site/shared/form_validation.js"
type="text/javascript">
   </script>
   <!--[if lt IE 7]>
    <link href="/WileyCDA/site/wiley2/include/style-ie.css" rel="stylesheet" type="text/css">
   <![endif]-->
  </head>
  <body>
   <div id="page">
    <!-- dynamicFeature ( ref:SITE_SPECIFIC_NAV ) -->




    <!-- BEGIN HEADER -->

    <script language="JavaScript">
        function do_check (form) {
            if (form.query.value=="") {
                alert('Please make an entry in the product search field.');
                return false;
            } else {
                return true;
            }
        }
    </script>
    <div id="top-nav">
        <a href="/WileyCDA/Section/id-300002.html"><img
```

FIGURE 4-6

The use of paragraph tags causes a blank line to appear between blocks of data.

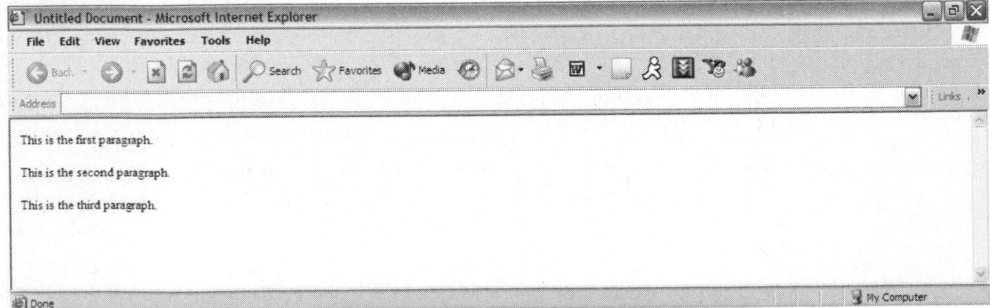

One sided tags do not, by the very nature of their being, have content. For this reason, they are also sometimes referred to as *empty tags*. Following are examples of one-sided (empty) tags:

- `<br>` — This tag will cause a line break to appear in a document. So, if you were to insert, for example, `<br><br>` in your code, you would cause two blank lines to appear. Guess what `<br><br><br>` will do?
- `<hr>` — This tag will cause a horizontal line to appear. Now, you can manipulate this horizontal line in a number of ways, but it carries no content. For example, the following line increases the size of the horizontal line:

```
<hr align="right" color="black" size="3" width="50%">
```

- `<img>` — This tag is used to specify the location, or URL, of an image. You could use this tag inside a block element to, for example, create a link to a photograph that you want to display on a Web page, as shown here:

```
<p><img src=<char:code last Char>"photograph.jpg"></p>
```

- `<meta>` — Metatags contain information regarding keywords for search engines

CROSS-REF **We will be working a lot with the image tag in Chapter 5.**

Search engines

A search engine uses a *Web crawler* to obtain a list of information about Web page contents. A Web crawler is just a computer program that obtains a standard set of information from each site it visits. This information includes keywords in metatags and lists of links to other sites that the Web crawler will, eventually, also visit. The information gathered is then processed using an indexer to group together related sites, and then put into a database for access by a query processor.

You should be familiar with the query process. It's what you type in the query or search box of `google.com`, `yahoo.com`, `msn.com`, `aol.com`, `ask.com`, and others. Sites are typically catalogued in terms of keywords, as well as the number and frequency by which the site has access to other popular Web sites. The list of sites returned may differ per search engine, even though the same terms are used in each search engine. This is because each search engine catalogues differ, and their search algorithms are not identical.

One of the promises of XHTML and XML is to allow much finer control over defining document content. This would benefit search engines because they could then search the actual content of a Web page to pull up specific information, rather than attempt to determine document content by the keywords contained in the page header.

You could pinpoint the location of the information you are looking for quite precisely.

All two-sided tags are closed (or turned off) using a forward slash (/). This can sometimes be confusing because forward slashes are also used in directory references to separate the elements of directory paths (for example, `http://hecda.wiley.com/WileyCDA/HigherEdCourse/cd-SI0000.html`). And this explains why you like to put quotes around directory paths. Otherwise, you might be telling the logic of the program to turn something off, and the machine, of course, would have no earthly idea what it is you are referring to.

If you inadvertently use the backslash (\) in place of a forward slash in a closing tag, the browser won't recognize the ending tag. This means that if you were to use the following, everything in program from that point on would be in bold: <b>BOLD<\b>.

NOTE **As discussed in Chapter 1 and Chapter 3, there are three major versions or iterations of HTML. Unless otherwise noted, the tags and conventions that we will use in this chapter are based on version 4.01 or 4.02. In the HTML version we are using here, the closing forward slash is optional for single-sided elements, but good practice also dictates its inclusion, such as in `<br/>`.**

All Web pages designed using HTML have a beginning and an ending tag that define for the browser the type of document to be rendered, as well as tags that define different page sections and must come in a particular order. Therefore, the first line (tag) to be used in the Web page is `<html>`. The `<head>`tag is used next to encapsulate header information, and finally the `<body>` tag is used to hold the actual content to display on the page.

Several of the terms we use in this chapter's discussions are on the *deprecated list*, which means that eventually they will be phased out — maybe. In our experience, this seldom happens. The new terms come out, the old ones are proclaimed dead, and 10 years later they're still around and the new ones still haven't quite caught on (or been superseded by a half dozen other new-and-improved widgets that no one bothers with anymore).

In any event, this means that we're fairly casual about the uppercase/lowercase dichotomy that is significant in newer (last three or four years) offshoots/hybrids of HTML. We are referring to strict XHTML or XML. The more astute among you will have already noticed that the flavor of HTML being used in the example site shown earlier in this chapter is 4.01, and that its Data Type Definitions (DTDs) are transitional. These definitions will be discussed later in more detail throughout this book and have absolutely no impact on what is being presented in this chapter.

Now, when you open a document in HTML, you must also close it. The command for doing so is `</html>`. The forward slash in the tag signifies for the browser that the particular element in use is now closed. Most elements (except for empty elements) have both open `<p>` and closed `</p>` tags. In the older versions of HTML, it was no big deal if you left off a closed tag. At the next occurrence of an open paragraph tag `<p>`, for example, upon encountering the occurrence of the new paragraph tag the browser would "understand" that the previous paragraph element should be closed.

Head and Body Sections

The basic block components of a Web page are `<head>` and `<body>`.

<head> section

Within the <head> tags are the nonprintable elements of the Web page. These would be the description of the Web page, including statement of purpose, date, last created/modified version, programmer information set off by comment tags, and any associated meta tags (metadata). Comment tags are set off by using the following format:

```
<!-- This is where you make a comment -->
```

Comments

Comments may be multi-line and only cease when the end tag --> is inserted. The program does not read or interpret comments as executable code. It simply skips over the commented lines. Here is an example of a comment section giving info about the program and programmer:

```
<!--This web page was constructed by John Q. Programmer on July 4,
2007.   Its purpose is to demonstrate the use of the following
common tags: <hr>, <p>, <ol>, <ul>, <li>, <address>  -->
```

Here is a section of actual comment code from the head of the example Web site (Figure 4-1):

```
<!--[if lt IE 7]>
    <link href="/WileyCDA/site/wiley2/include/style-ie.css"
rel="stylesheet" type="text/css">
   <!--[endif]-->
```

What this says in English is that if this Web browser trying to access the site is less than IE 7.0, then link it to the Internet Explorer styles page located at the address listed in the `href`. That's all (`endif`).

Comments may also appear in the <body> block of the document where they would be used to briefly explain the purpose of a subsection of the program (such as a subroutine, subprogram, submodule, and so on). Comments may also explain the next iteration or the setting of flags for a decision structure, or explain the values of a multivalued variable in a case structure. The following is an illustration of a comment regarding a function call:

```
<!--This case structure is to allow users to input which direction
they want to move player on a map -->

<script>
/* This is a JavaScript function and the commented section uses this
comments tag */

switch(direction)
{
  case 'n':
    go_north();
```

```
    break;
  case 'e':
    go_east();
    break;
  case 's':
    go_south();
    break;
  case 'w':
    go_west();
    break;
  default: exit ();
    break;}

</script>
```

NOTE **A *case structure* is a simpler way to set up a series of selection structures (`if/then/else` statements).**

Comments may also be used as a way to isolate a problem when troubleshooting nonfunctioning code. Putting a code within comment tags deactivates it, which is a technique used by programmers to determine the source of the code malfunction while watching to see if the flow of the program logic passes right over the commented out section.

In HTML comments open in the format `<!--` and close with `-->`. Multiple lines of text may be entered between these two sections. Everything between the beginning and end section of the one-sided tag is commented out. Often, for beginners, an error occurs when the programmer fails to close a comment tag with the result that nothing is executed. In the HTML editors, such errors are easy to spot because the comments are represented in different colors within the code itself.

If you are using JavaScript, as in the previous illustration, you comment using `/*` and `*/` to begin and end comments.

Titles, Metatags, and Functions

Other element tags appearing within the `<head>` section are, typically, titles, metatags, and Javascript functions. However, none of the information available in the `<head>` block is content that appears on the actual Web page. The one exception to this is the title of the site, which appears in the title bar across the top of the screen, as shown in Figure 4-7.

As shown in Figure 4-8, metatags (which are one-sided tags) normally contain information about the document type, encoding information, and keywords used by search engines to find documents.

FIGURE 4-7

"A first demonstration of tags" appears in the Web page's title bar.

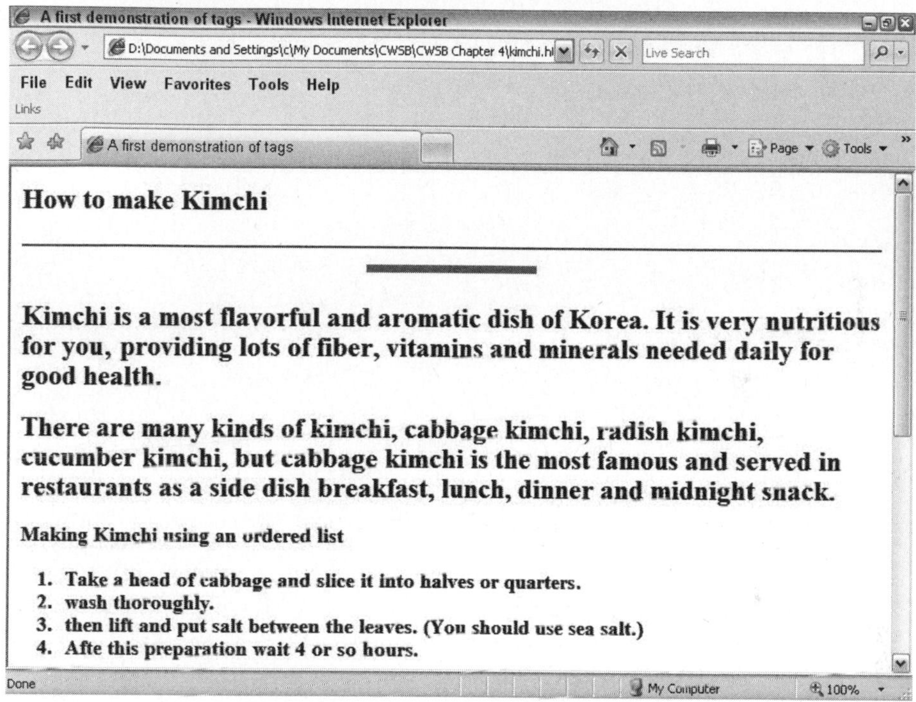

Functions are executable code that return a value or change a state. In good programming practice, it is desirable that they are called from the `<body>` section, but are written in the `<head>` section. Consequently, in such well-written code, functions do not appear in the actual, visible Web page, but the actions of functions do. Following is an example of a function in the `<head>` section of a document:

```
function MM_reloadPage(init) {  //reloads the window if Nav4 resized
```

NOTE **Javascript functions can be included in both the** `body` **and the header sections, or even externally referenced from the header and body sections using** `<script src = ''url''></script>`.

To better understand the concept of functions, let's take a look at two examples.

FIGURE 4-8

Metatags contain information about the Web page.

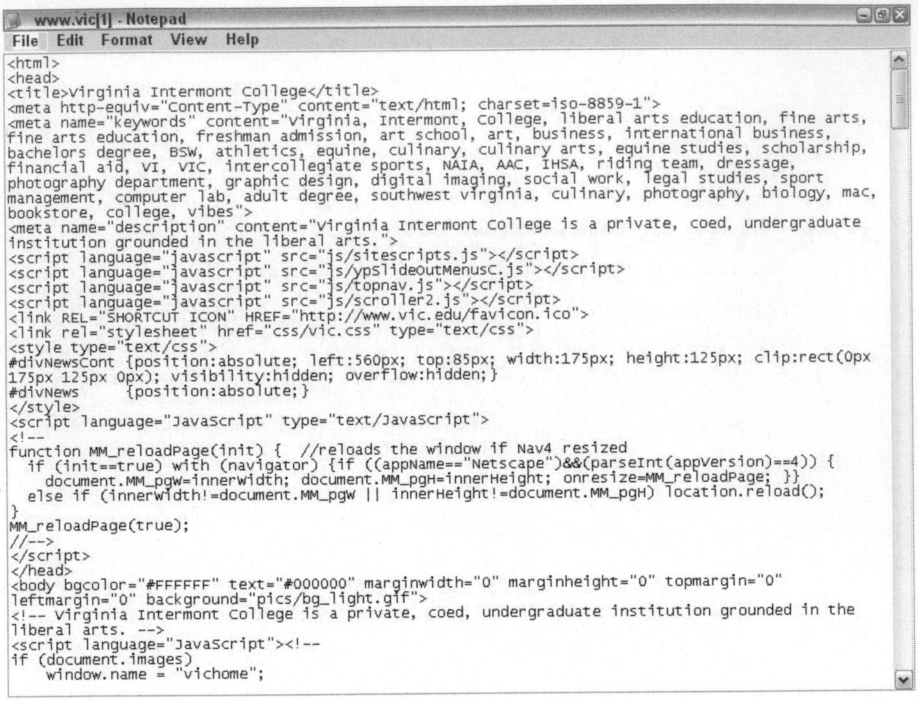

www.vic[1] - Notepad

File Edit Format View Help

```
<html>
<head>
<title>Virginia Intermont College</title>
<meta http-equiv="Content-Type" content="text/html; charset=iso-8859-1">
<meta name="keywords" content="Virginia, Intermont, College, liberal arts education, fine arts,
fine arts education, freshman admission, art school, art, business, international business,
bachelors degree, BSW, athletics, equine, culinary, culinary arts, equine studies, scholarship,
financial aid, VI, VIC, intercollegiate sports, NAIA, AAC, IHSA, riding team, dressage,
photography department, graphic design, digital imaging, social work, legal studies, sport
management, computer lab, adult degree, southwest virginia, culinary, photography, biology, mac,
bookstore, college, vibes">
<meta name="description" content="Virginia Intermont College is a private, coed, undergraduate
institution grounded in the liberal arts.">
<script language="javascript" src="js/sitescripts.js"></script>
<script language="javascript" src="js/ypSlideOutMenusC.js"></script>
<script language="javascript" src="js/topnav.js"></script>
<script language="javascript" src="js/scroller2.js"></script>
<link REL="SHORTCUT ICON" HREF="http://www.vic.edu/favicon.ico">
<link rel="stylesheet" href="css/vic.css" type="text/css">
<style type="text/css">
#divNewsCont {position:absolute; left:560px; top:85px; width:175px; height:125px; clip:rect(0px
175px 125px 0px); visibility:hidden; overflow:hidden;}
#divNews     {position:absolute;}
</style>
<script language="JavaScript" type="text/JavaScript">
<!--
function MM_reloadPage(init) {  //reloads the window if Nav4 resized
  if (init==true) with (navigator) {if ((appName=="Netscape")&&(parseInt(appVersion)==4)) {
    document.MM_pgW=innerWidth; document.MM_pgH=innerHeight; onresize=MM_reloadPage; }}
  else if (innerWidth!=document.MM_pgW || innerHeight!=document.MM_pgH) location.reload();
}
MM_reloadPage(true);
//-->
</script>
</head>
<body bgcolor="#FFFFFF" text="#000000" marginwidth="0" marginheight="0" topmargin="0"
leftmargin="0" background="pics/bg_light.gif">
<!-- Virginia Intermont College is a private, coed, undergraduate institution grounded in the
liberal arts. -->
<script language="JavaScript"><!--
if (document.images)
    window.name = "vichome";
```

Suppose that you have a checkbook, and it has $5,000 in it. If you write a check for $45 to buy this book, you will have $4,955 left. You know that. You can do that in your head. If you were using a computer, however, that calculation ($5,000 less $45) would be calculated by a function, and the result ($4,955) would be sent to appear on your screen in a little box saying something to the effect of "current balance: 4955." Hence, the action of the function — the result of the calculation — appears on the Web page, but the code handling the calculation does not.

When a function changes a state, it simply responds to a request from the user. Suppose that you have a Web page that is an electric blue background. But the Web designer, suspecting that not everyone may appreciate that blinding blue, has put a button to change the color to white. If a visitor to the site clicks the button, the background will change to white. Thus, through user intervention, the state of the background can be changed from blue to white. That process to change the color occurs by using a function in the `<head>` section of an HTML document.

<body> section

The `<body>` section contains the displayed content of the page as formatted by the Web designer. Succinctly put, anything that is not the title (or that are not metatags, scripts to external links, or functions) is contained in the `<body>`.

With a basic understanding of the `<head>` and `<body>` sections, let's now explore some of the more common tags used to develop a simple Web page.

Block-Level Elements

Block level means that content of the same type is put separately from other different blocks of content on the Web page. In other words, text within a set of paragraph tags is all one block (and there can be several blocks of paragraphs), address text is a different block; lists would constitute another block; and the head element is a different block from body element.

For example, the following code defines blocks that appear in Figure 4-9:

```
<h2>Headings</h2>
<table>Tables</table>
<p>Paragraphs like this and Horizontal Rules like the ones below:</p>
<hr>
<hr>
```

This section examines the following block-level elements used in creating the example Web page shown in Figure 4-1, and it will also be used by you to create a simple Web page:

- Head
- Comments
- Title
- Body
- Line break
- Inline element
- Heading
- Paragraph
- Unordered and ordered list
- Horizontal line

FIGURE 4-9

Block levels define blocks of data on Web pages.

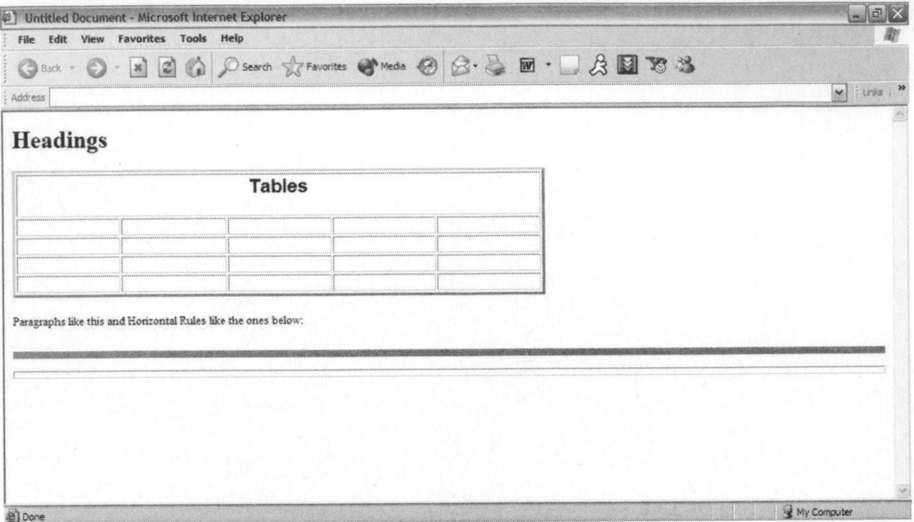

Head

The following, simplified source code of the example Web site (www.wiley.com) shows the <head> element:

```
<head>
   <title>
Wiley::Wiley
   </title>
</head>
```

Once the info contained in the head is complete, the head section also closes with </head>.

Title

The <title> tag will have Wiley appear in the title bar of the page. It is a two-sided tag surrounding the title and must end with the </title> closing tag.

Body

Within the <body> element, you can include the following tags:

- *Inline elements* — <img src>
- *Paragraph tag* — <p> content </p>
- *Unordered list* — <ul> content </ul>

- *Ordered list* — <ol> content </ol>
- *Definition lists* — <dl> content </dl>
- *Heading tags* — <h1> through <h6>

Following is an example of a <body> section showing some of these elements:

```
<body>
  <img src="goldilocksandthethreebears.jpg">
  <p>
    <b>Books for a Lifetime! <i>Goldilocks is a story of a little
girl lost in a forest and what she encounters when she wanders into
an empty house.</i></b>

</p>

  <ul>
    <li><h6>Goldilocks said this heading was too small</h6></li>

    <li><h1>and this heading was too large</h1></li>    <li>
<h3>but that this heading was just right</h3></li>
  </ul></body>
```

Inline elements

Inline elements (such as inline photos or inline styles) are displayed within the same block as the surrounding text. For example, the following code is for an inline image, named goldilocksandthethreebears.jpg:

```
<img src="goldilocksandthethreebears.jpg">
```

Any image type may be referenced as an image-sourced document (img src). In the previous example, we referenced a black and white drawing in jpg format. In referencing for images, you must be especially careful to have the correct path stated to the location of the picture. If you type in an incorrect path, the image will not display on the page; it will be replaced by a small icon of an "x" in an IE browser as shown in the upper-right corner of Figure 4-10.

To reduce the possibility of error in developing your Web page, it is helpful to place all documents and images that you will be referencing on your page within one folder along with your code, as shown in Figure 4-11. In that case, writing the path to the image is very simple — just the name of the image in quotation marks, as shown here:

```
<img src="goldilocksandthethreebears" alt="waiting for a picture
of the three bears to load" />
```

If the image is still an "x," then most likely you have mistyped the name of the file, or have actually placed it in a different location than the rest of the files for the page. In such cases, you may need to search to find it.

FIGURE 4-10

When an image is incorrectly linked, an ''x'' will appear where the image should appear.

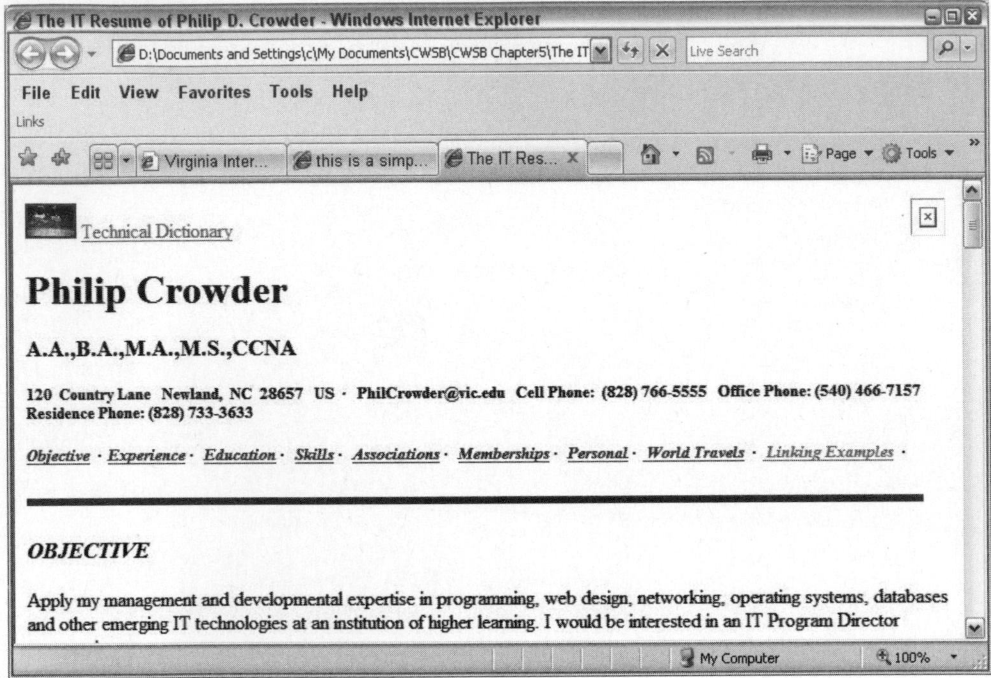

Notice in the preceding code example that, within the <img> tag, we have also put alt = ''waiting for a picture of the three bears to load''. The alt is a three-letter acronym that stands for *alternate*, and it provides a text description of the picture for slow-loading browsers, or for those users who are using text-only browsers or for helping blind people understand what images are on the page. The inclusion of alt is actually the first illustration of using an attribute in a tag.

An *attribute* is like an added feature or characteristic. So, if you were to place the image on the page and make it a certain size, you would describe the width as X and the height as Y. In coding, it would look like this:

```
<img src="goldilocksandthethreebears" alt="waiting for a picture of
the three bears to load" width="150" height="189" />
```

FIGURE 4-11

A good programming practice is to put all images together in a properly organized images folder. However, for the novice, it is easier to place all files for the Web page, including images, together into a single folder. This greatly simplifies referencing images.

Width and height are two characteristics of the `<img>` tag that help define the image for placement on the Web page. In other words, width and height are attributes. In this example, the `width` is defined as being 150 pixels and `height` as being 189 pixels. If the image isn't actually 150 × 189, then the browser will automatically shrink or expand it automatically to fit those dimensions.

Paragraphs

A paragraph `<p>` tag represents a block of content, typically text and typically, yes, a paragraph or at least a few lines of text. When a `<p>` tag is used, it causes a blank line to appear, separating the paragraph text in the <p> tag from the block element above. Paragraph tags can be used multiple times in the document code.

You may notice that the text you input in the <p> tags is not identical in the number of lines when the tags are rendered on the page. The reason is that the page dynamically allocates the length of the lines depending upon the browser window size. To maintain the appearance of the text to exactly mimic its appearance in the coding, it must be enclosed in <pre> tags — where "pre" means "preformatting." <pre> would more commonly be used for text-based tables, which is discussed in more detail in a later chapter.

Consider the following example:

```
<h2>The Story of Goldilocks and the Three Bears<h2>
<p>Once upon a time, there was a little girl named Goldilocks. She
went for a walk in the forest.  Pretty soon, she came upon a house.
She knocked and, when no one answered, she walked right in. </p>

<p>At the table in the kitchen, there were three bowls of porridge.
Goldilocks was hungry. She tasted the porridge from the first bowl.
</p>


<p>
"This porridge is too hot!" she exclaimed.
</p>
```

Remember that HTML ignores white space. Though we inserted a number of blank lines in the HTML coding between paragraphs, when rendered on the page, the appearance will be as follows:

The Story of Goldilocks and the Three Bears

Once upon a time, there was a little girl named Goldilocks. She went for a walk in the forest. Pretty soon, she came upon a house. She knocked and, when no one answered, she walked right in.

At the table in the kitchen, there were three bowls of porridge. Goldilocks was hungry. She tasted the porridge from the first bowl.

"This porridge is too hot!" she exclaimed.

Additional lines may be inserted between tag elements by using the break tag <br />. Thus, if you wanted to insert four blank lines, the coding would be as follows:

NOTE **The use of the break tag to insert a blank line is <br />. This is in conformance with XHTML.
 is an officially deprecated, but still functional, tag.**

```
<p>At the table in the kitchen, there were three bowls of porridge.
Goldilocks was hungry.  She tasted the porridge from the first bowl.
</p><br /><br /> <br /> <br />
<p>
"This porridge is too hot!" she exclaimed.
</p>
```

And the page would appear like this:

At the table in the kitchen, there were three bowls of porridge. Goldilocks was hungry. She tasted the porridge from the first bowl.

"This porridge is too hot!" she exclaimed.

Last, let's say you were to do the same paragraph with preformatting tags, as in the following:

```
<pre>
      At the table
        in the kitchen,
          there were three bowls
             of porridge.
              Goldilocks was hungry.
                She tasted the porridge
                   from the first bowl.
</pre>
```

The output would be exactly the same:

```
At the table
  in the kitchen,
    there were three bowls
       of porridge.
        Goldilocks was hungry.
          She tasted the porridge
             from the first bowl.
```

Unordered lists

As you may infer from the name of the tags, an *unordered list* <ul> is one that consists of elements listed in no particular sequence, and each item in the list is preceded by a bullet of some style. An example of an unordered list might be a list of groceries jotted down as you take inventory of the refrigerator and pantry before heading out for your weekly food shopping.

The default bullet is round (like a middot). However, you can use the `type` attribute to specify other geometric shapes and even tiny icons or images (which will be discussed in more detail later in this book) to prefix each element of the list. For example, you can use a circle, a square, or a disc.

NOTE **You may reference a full list of bullet options used in HTML coding at the `w3.org` Web site.**

The formatting for an unordered list using a circle is:

```
<ul type="circle">
<li>Item 1</li>
<li>Item 2</li>
<li>Item 3</li>
</ul>
```

The result would look like this:

o Item 1
o Item 2
o Item 3

Ordered lists

An *ordered list tag* — `<ol>` — is one that is identical in format to the unordered list, except that it lists items in a seemingly particular sequence. Examples are a list of birthdays or a list of names as in an address book. The sequencing for an ordered list is numeric but could be easily changed using the `type` attribute to change the ordering to letters (large or small), Roman numerals, or numbers.

The attributes for these designations are:

- *Lowercase alpha* — `<ol type = ''a''>`
- *Uppercase alpha* — `<ol type = ''A''>`
- *Lowercase Roman numeral* — `<ol type = ''i''>`
- *Uppercase Roman numeral* — `<ol type = ''I''>`
- *Numeric* — `<ol type = ''1''>`

The formatting for an ordered list using lowercase Roman numerals would be would be as follows:

```
<ol type="i">
<li>Item 1</li>
<li>Item 2</li>
<li>Item 3</li>
</ol>
```

The result would look like this:

i. Item 1
ii. Item 2
iii. Item 3

Both ordered lists and unordered lists have the identical formatting. This example shows an unordered list:

```
<ul>
                    <li><h6>Goldilocks said this heading was too
small</h6></li>

                    <li><h1>and this heading was too large</h1></li>

                    <li><h3>but that this heading was just
right</h3></li>
               </ul>
```

The resulting display of this code would look like this:

- **Goldilocks said this heading was too small**
- **and this heading was too large**
- **but that this heading was just right**

This example shows an ordered list:

```
<ol>
                    <li><h6>Goldilocks said this heading was too
small</h6></li>

                    <li><h1>and this heading was too large</h1></li>

                    <li><h3>but that this heading was just
right</h3></li>
               </ol>
```

The resulting display of this code would look like this:

1. **Goldilocks said this heading was too small**
2. **and this heading was too large**
3. **but that this heading was just right**

Definition lists

The *definition list* <dl> is similar in style to a dictionary definition. The following shows how the definition list is formatted:

```
<dl>
<dt>This is where the data term goes</dt>
<dd>This where the definition of the term goes</dd>
</dl>
```

If you were to look up in the dictionary a term such as "purview," then you would see "per-view: noun" as representing the data term <dt>, and "the body or enacting part of a statue" as representing the data definition <dd>. Thus, the code would look like this:

```
<dl>
<dt>per-view: noun</dt>
<dd><i>the body or enacting part of a statue</i></dd>
</dl>
```

The appearance on the page would be like this:

per-view: noun
    the body or enacting part of a statue

Heading tags

Heading tags govern the size of the enclosed text, with <H6> being the smallest size and <H1> being the largest, and they are used as headings for sections on a page. They automatically appear on their own line, so keep in mind that any text after a heading will be *below* the heading.

Let's now turn to designing your first simple Web page using the elements described thus far.

HTML Tools

A variety of tools are available today to help developers work in the complex world of HTML. This section examines a few of the common tools.

Link checkers

There's not much that can frustrate visitors to your site more than running into broken links. The Web changes so quickly that anyone who's been surfing for more than a day or two will expect to click some link and find the dreaded "404 - Web Page Not Found" error now and then. Dead links can happen but should be eliminated in testing. Dead links can lead to lost sales and lost customers. If people have trouble with your site, if they search for something and they can't find it, they may badmouth your site because of the lack of information accessibility. One or two dead links here and there are acceptable to any but the most high-strung people. But no one likes clicking on a whole series of dead ends — it's an annoying waste of time for them. If you let your visitors suffer this way, they'll remember your site for all the wrong reasons, and they won't be coming back in a hurry or recommending it to their friends.

Link checkers are programs or online services that perform the tedious task of following every single link on every page in your entire site and reporting back to you on which ones worked and which ones didn't. They can check them all in a few minutes — even on a very large site — saving you a lot of time and aggravation. The alternative is to stare at Web pages and click and click until your vision gets blurry and your mouse finger feels like it's about to fall off.

If you have lots of links to other sites, you're particularly vulnerable because other Webmasters have no obligation to keep you informed of their actions. Even if your site has no links to the outside world, you should still check it periodically because many times, when you make changes to your site, you risk breaking a link. Simply changing an image file (remember, images are linked into pages just as much as if you said "click here to see the picture") can result in a broken link.

Code validators

Whether you use plain vanilla HTML or toss in CSS, XML, and all the other alphabetical wonders of the Web, there's bound to be something somewhere in any large site that isn't right. *Code validation programs* like the one at `http://validator.w3.org` read through your creations and check for compatibility with published standards. Most of the time, the differences that are found and reported are negligible — no major Web browser has ever perfectly followed any published standard — but code validators do find real problems as well.

Many browsers do their best to render pages properly. There are so many different coding styles, however, that it is the most popular browsers that have been the ones that keep pages looking good almost regardless of how they were coded.

Compatibility testers

If you happen to have a dozen different versions of every kind of Web browser on your system and you've got plenty of time on your hands, you might want to look at every page in your site with every one of them. Really dedicated Web designers do just exactly that.

NOTE **But not professionals. Pros only check against Required Tier 1, and possibly Tier 2, browsers for compatibility. Tier 3/obsolete browsers are a waste of time.**

If you're not in that situation, then it's nice to be able to run your pages through a program called a *compatibility tester* that's trained to look for the common trouble spots. You'll get advice and warnings whenever the program spots things such as obsolete tags or company-specific features. It'll also tell you which elements on your page are limited to only newer browsers. It's up to you whether you change those features, but you should at least know about their existence.

The version nightmare

Why should you care which version of a Web browser someone is using? After all, everyone keeps up to date with the latest browsers, right? Nope. In fact, no one anywhere, no matter what figures they toss at you, has any idea how many of which brand of Web browsers are in use on the Internet, nor which versions of those brands people have.

The fact is that, for the average Web surfer, it's a pain in the mouse to keep up with all the version changes in even the two major Web browsers. The natural inclination of most people is, if the browser works, keep using it, and if it doesn't work, there must be something wrong with the Web site. The only time when average Web surfers will pay attention to upgrading is when a browser gives them enough trouble at a lot of Web sites or a browser upgrade is a required part of some software update, such as the operating system.

It's different for us, and maybe for you. But we get paid to keep up to date with the latest happenings on the Web. And things like patches for newly discovered security holes matter to us. That's just not the case with most people. Mention "frame spoofing" to your typical Webnaut and you're not likely to get the reaction, "But wasn't that fixed in Netscape 4.51 back in early '99?" No, you'll get a blank look.

The people who claim to know exactly how many people are using Internet Explorer versus Netscape Navigator or Opera or Lynx are talking through their hats, plain and simple. Because anyone anywhere can use any Web browser without having to tell anyone about it, there's no way of tracking what's on all the computers out there. You can, indeed, check to see which browser brand and version the people who visit any particular site are using, but that's all. And the sites that claim to track browser usage for many other sites won't admit that, until they can track every single Web site on the entire Web, they can't give honest, hard figures. Yes, you can argue that a statistically significant number of sites are being tested, but you need to keep Mark Twain's famous line in mind: "There are three kinds of lies: lies, damned lies, and statistics."

Does this mean that you should program for the lowest common denominator? Does it mean that you need to put up a sign saying, "This site best viewed in Internet Explorer 6.0 or greater"? Does it mean that you have to create a whole series of nearly identical Web sites, each of which caters to a different Web browser or version of that browser? Different Webmasters have chosen all of these possible options. It's up to you whether you join the bandwagon or ignore the problem.

Server monitors

Unless you run your own Web server, you're at the mercy of other people to make your Web site available on the Internet. Your Web site may even be physically stored on a machine on

continued

continued
the other side of the planet. A *server monitor service* periodically checks to see if the Web server that holds your site is up and running. Simply sign up with the service, and they'll automatically keep track of your server and notify you if it goes down. If the site is down, the service will notify you right away. Usually, this is done by e-mail, but the more sophisticated monitor services can even automatically trigger your beeper to let you know it's time to call up your Web space provider and demand action. There are also applications you can install on your own computer for monitoring your site, such as Intermapper and What's Up Gold. Just remember — if your own Internet connection goes down, these applications may give you false alarms, an issue a professional third-party service likely will not suffer.

TIP **There are lots of legitimate reasons why a Web server might be down temporarily, so it's a good idea to ask your provider what's happening before launching into a tirade.**

Authoring tools

All craftspeople are only as good as the tools they use. It doesn't matter if they're carpenters or artists — or Web site designers. A carpenter with an inaccurate measuring tape, a blunted saw, and a plane with a blade that keeps falling off will always produce lousy work. An artist whose brush is shedding and who has to work with old paint on a badly made canvas will never be able to create any masterpieces. And Web designers whose authoring programs are not suited to their individual needs won't win any awards, either.

On the flip side of the coin, no tools, no matter how fine and wonderful, can make the person who uses them into a winner. It is only the skilled craftsperson using the best tools who has a chance to produce the best work. A poor musician will play a Stradivarius as badly as a dime-store violin. A poet without heart will write bad poetry on a computer or with a quill pen. And Web designers who don't bring skill and artistry to the process won't benefit from the most sophisticated of programs.

The various chapters of this book cover both the skill and artistry parts. But there's one other thing that's needed, and you have to bring it — the earnest desire to make the best Web pages you can. If you have that, we'll supply the rest, and you can add a few more glittering strands to this wonderful place called the World Wide Web.

There are four basic types of Web page authoring tools:

- Text editors
- HTML editors
- WYSIWYG editors
- Word processors

FIGURE 4-12

The GWD Text Editor is a programmers' tool that can also be used for simple Web page creation.

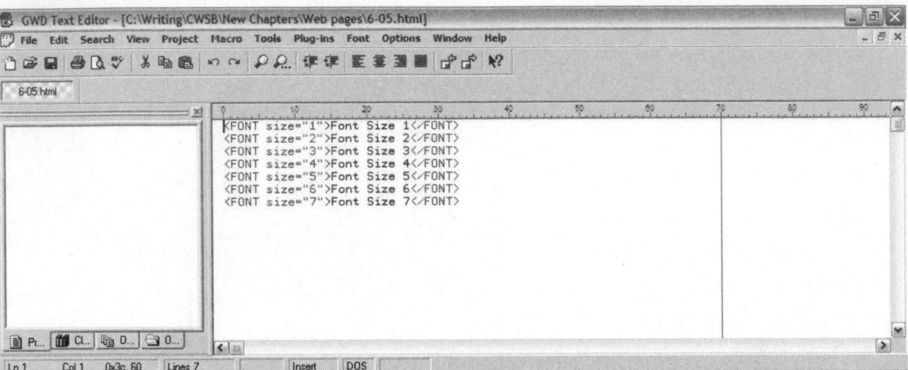

Text editors

Text editors are simple, no-frills programs that allow you to type from the standard keyboard and save a plain text file. These are the most difficult programs for beginners to work with because they offer no help. They require you to know everything there is to know about the languages you use and how their quirks can be applied to your situation. Many intermediate- to expert-level Web people, however, prefer to work this way. Different text editors offer various features, including spell checking and syntax highlighting (where different kinds of items in the code show up in different colors so that they can be easily identified at a glance). Figure 4-12 shows the GWD Text Editor, a tool designed for use by programmers. It can, however, be very useful to a Web page designer.

For Windows, the native Notepad is the best-known text editor. If you use the Linux operating system (or any other flavor of Unix), you doubtless have your own favorite — vi, Emacs, gedit, or whatever is the latest rage. And if you use a Mac, you're already familiar with SimpleText (OS 9) or TextEdit (OS X).

Tables 4-1 through 4-3 provide the World Wide Web addresses of several sites where you can find a variety of high-quality text editors.

HTML editors

These are specially enhanced text editors that are designed specifically for creating Web pages. The emphasis is still on typing code, but a wide variety of features are built in to make the process a lot easier. These are the best choice for many people, as they balance the power of hands-on code work with quite a bit of automated support.

Because many text editors today provide some degree of HTML support, it is sometimes hard to draw the line between a plain-text editor and an HTML editor. The programs in Tables 4-4 through 4-6 are, however, far superior to normal text editors and are specifically designed for writing the code for Web pages.

TABLE 4-1

Windows Text Editor Sources

Program	Web Address
Boxer 99	boxersoftware.com/pgb99.htm
Editeur	studioware.com
GWD Text Editor	gwdsoft.com
UltraEdit	ultraedit.com
WinEdit	winedit.com

TABLE 4-2

Linux Text Editor Sources

Program	Web Address
Cooledit	www.cooledit.sourceforge.net
JOE	http://trevormarshall.com/joe2.8.tar.Z
gedit	http://www.gnome.org/projects/gedit/
NEdit (Nirvana Editor)	www.nedit.org
TCL TextEdit	http://sourceforge.net/projects/tcltextedit/
Tk Notepad	http://home.earthlink.net/~joseph-ja
XEmacs	www.xemacs.org

TABLE 4-3

Macintosh Text Editor Sources

Program	Web Address
Alpha	www.kelehers.org/alpha
BBEdit	www.barebones.com/products/bbedit/index.shtml
Jedit	http://www.artman21.com/en
Style	www.merzwaren.com/style

TABLE 4-4

Windows HTML Editor Sources

Program	Web Address
Arachnophilia	www.arachnoid.com/arachnophilia
Coffee Cup HTML Editor	www.coffeecup.com/editor
HomeSite+	www.macromedia.com/software/homesite/trial
HotDog Pro	www.sausage.com/hotdog-professional.html
HTMLed Pro	www.ist.ca/htmledpro.html

TABLE 4-5

Linux HTML Editor Sources

Program	Web Address
August	lls.se/~johanb/august
Bluefish	www.bluefish.openoffice.nl
Quanta	http://kdewebdev.org/

TABLE 4-6

Macintosh HTML Editor Sources

Program	Web Address
BBEdit	www.barebones.com/products/bbedit.html
Taco Softwate	www.tacosw.com
PageSpinner	www.spinnerworld.com
Rage Software	http://www.ragesw.com/products/webdesign.html

WYSIWYG programs

WYSIWYG editors fully isolate their users from having to work with code. Typically, objects that are commonly used on Web pages are represented by icons that are grouped together in different *palettes* — floating windows that can be brought up or set aside as needed. Web pages are constructed by using your mouse to drag the objects from the palettes onto the working screen. Other floating windows enable you to customize the settings for the objects, choose and apply colors, and add special capabilities without having to learn programming. Macromedia Dreamweaver (see Figure 4-13) and Adobe GoLive are two popular WYSIWYG editors that both take this approach. Other approaches to WYSIWYG editing use menus and toolbars exclusively.

Despite the fact that they are simple enough so that just about anyone can use them, these kinds of programs also appeal to professional Web designers because the best WYSIWYG editors have more than one level to them. Yes, they can be used by a child who knows no programming to create a single page, but they can also be fully exploited by a skilled expert. Most of these programs, in addition to letting you work with a simple interface, also give you direct access to the code so that you can bypass the way the program works and manually override any decisions it makes. Even people who regularly use a text editor for their work will turn to a good WYSIWYG editor when a client wants a prototype Web site done "yesterday."

Tables 4-7 through 4-9 show the Web addresses for some of the best WYSIWYG software.

NOTE **Some of these programs come in both Windows and Macintosh versions, or both Windows and Linux versions, but the URL (Web address) is not always the same. NetObjects Fusion, which used to be available in both Windows and Macintosh versions, has discontinued Mac development, at least for the time being. As of this writing, the Windows version of Freeway was not yet available, but you should check the Web site for any updates on its status. WebSphere Home Page Builder, from IBM, was formerly known as TopPage.**

FIGURE 4-13

Dreamweaver uses an object-oriented approach.

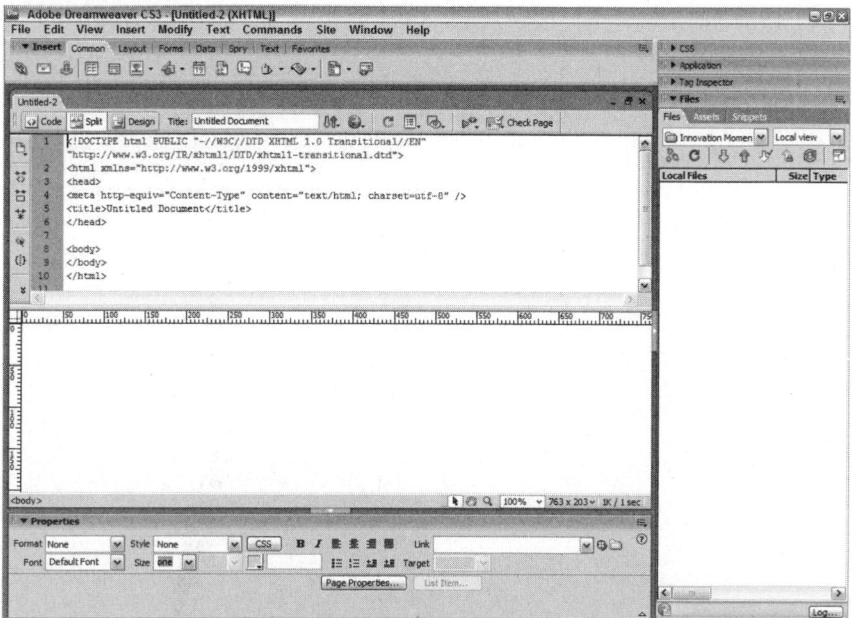

TABLE 4-7

Windows WYSIWYG Software Sources

Program	Web Address
Amaya	w3.org/Amaya
Dreamweaver	www.adobe.com/products/dreamweaver
Freeway	softpress.com
Expression Web	www.microsoft.com/expression
GoLive	www.adobe.com/products/golive/main.html
IBM WebSphere Home Page Builder	www-4.ibm.com/software/webservers/hpbuilder/win
NetObjects Fusion	www.netobjects.com/products/html/nf5.html

TABLE 4-8

Linux WYSIWYG Software Sources

Program	Web Address
Amaya	w3.org/Amaya
IBM WebSphere Home Page Builder	www-4.ibm.com/software/webservers/hpbuilder/linux
Siteseed	http://sourceforge.net/projects/siteseed
Wisewig	www.sourceforge.net/projects/wisewig

TABLE 4-9

Macintosh WYSIWYG Software Sources

Program	Web Address
Dreamweaver	www.adobe.com/products/dreamweaver
Freeway	www.softpress.com
GoLive	www.adobe.com/products/golive/main.html
NetObjects Fusion	www.netobjects.com/products/html/nf5.html

Word processors

If you can find a word processor that doesn't claim to be a Web authoring tool these days, we'd be shocked. All you have to do is type in your document, drag in a few graphics and save your document as an HTML file instead of as a normal document. It sounds good, but it doesn't usually work out well in practice. Word processors are designed for producing paper documents. They're wonderful for writing books and reports, but Web output format is something that was slapped on at the last minute as an afterthought. No word processor can possibly compete with programs that were designed from the ground up for the sole purpose of creating Web pages.

Word processors are also notorious for creating bad code. No professional Web designer we've ever heard of uses one in his or her work — other than for writing proposals and letters — but many of them do make a lot of money fixing up the problems created by clients who create Web pages in word processors.

Microsoft Word (see Figure 4-14) is the most popular of all word processing programs. If you work in a modern office, the odds are pretty good that you have it on your computer or, at least, someone in your office does. It's a very good word processor — we used it to write these words, and we have no complaints. It is, however, notorious for producing poorly written HTML code that produces some amazingly ugly results when viewed in anything but Microsoft Internet Explorer. (For more information, see the amusing article at `fourmilab.ch/webtools/demoroniser` or the more technical one at `www.cs.tut.fi/~jkorpela/unicode/greek.html`).

FIGURE 4-14

Microsoft Word is a fine word processor, but not a serious Web design tool.

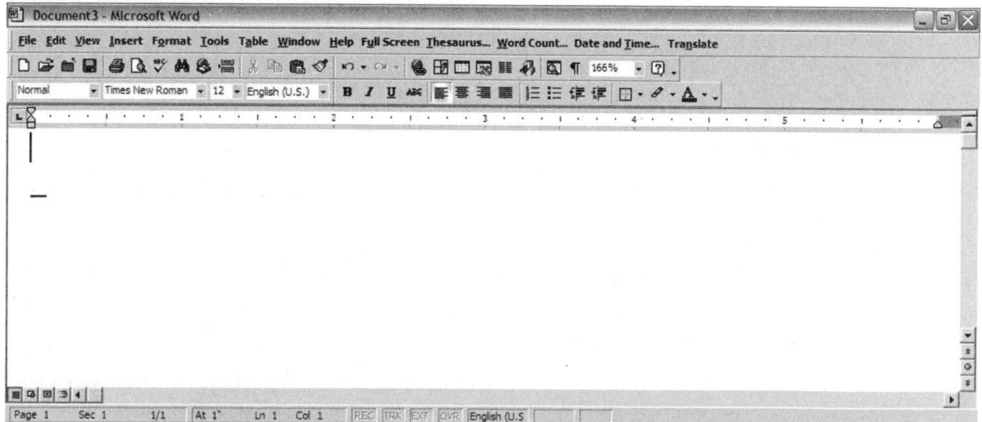

Word code gives HTML validator programs fits. However, most Web browsers perform a great deal of error checking and correction, so using Word to create Web pages is not a totally impossible option. If you want to work in a WYSIWYG environment on the Windows operating system and you have Word, you might as well give it a try before you buy a serious Web page creation program, but we'd advise against using it to do anything significant or important.

TIP **Be sure to always test any Web project you do with more than one company's Web browser. If possible, test with different versions of the same browser, too, and view the page on as many platforms as you can. If you're using Windows, for example, and don't have a Linux box or a Mac, ask a friend to surf to your pages and report on them. If you don't know anyone who has a different system, try asking for help on the `alt.www.webmaster` Usenet newsgroup.**

Exceptions to the rule

As with practically any "definitive" categorization, there are no doubt exceptions to this one, and it could easily be argued that there are some unusual Web authoring programs that fall between the cracks. What should you make of Caligari iSpace software, for example? Although technically a 3D Web graphics program that's usually employed in conjunction with a traditional Web authoring tool such as Dreamweaver, it can be used all by itself to create Web pages complete with text and an impressive number of bells and whistles.

Designing a Simple Web Page

The first thing to do is to click on Notepad, which will present you with a blank document. Then, type in the following:

```
<html>
<head>
<title> A first demonstration of tags</title>
<!--This web page was constructed by [your name] on [insert date].
Its purpose is to demonstrate the use of the following common tags:
<hx>, <p>, <ol>, <ul>, <li>, <address>  -->
</head>

<body>

<h2>How to make Kimchi<h2>

<p>Kimchi is a most flavorful and aromatic dish of Korea. It is very
nutritious for you providing lots of fiber, vitamins and minerals
needed daily for good health.</p>

<p>There are many kinds of kimchi, cabbage kimchi, radish kimchi,
cucumber kimchi, but cabbage kimchi is the most famous and served
in restaurants as a side dish breakfast, lunch, dinner and midnight
snack.</p>
```

```
<p align"center""> <h3>Making Kimchi using an ordered list<h3><p>

<ol>
<li>Take a head of cabbage and slice it into halves or
quarters.</li>
<li>Wash thoroughly.</li>
<li>Then lift and put salt between the leaves. (You should use sea
salt.) </li>
<li> After this preparation wait 4 or so hours.</li>
</ol>

<p>Preparing ingredients using an ordered list</p>
<ul>
<li>Dice a little ginger</li>
<li>Dice a lot of garlic </li>
<li>Chop up the green portion of leeks</li>
<li>Finely grind up radish</li>
<li>Prepare water flavored with dried minnows</li>

</ul>
<p>Note that several steps are involved which we have omitted
because the purpose of this is, after all, to demonstrate the use of
lists and not making food. But for the curious you add lots of red
pepper, sugar, other ingredients, stir them all together and let it
age. Several fine recipes for kimchi can be found at
www.fabulousfoods.com korean.allfoodrecipe.com, and many many other
fine sites too numerous to mention here. </p>


<p>If you would like to know further about kimchi you may contact at
the following fictional address used only for the purpose of
demonstrating the use of the address tag.</p>
<address>Kimchi World,
Kimchi Plaza,
NY, NY 21112</address>

</body>
</html>
```

Wordwrap

What might help you to read your coding as you write it and review it is to go to the Format menu of Notepad and click on Word Wrap to select that option. The default value of Notepad is to almost endlessly scroll to the right as you type on a single line. Wordwrap provides a soft carriage return at the right margin, so all that you type in remains visible on the screen.

FIGURE 4-15

After entering the HTML code, your new Web page contains a variety of formatting.

How to make Kimchi

Kimchi is a most flavorful and aromatic dish of Korea. It is very nutritious for you providing lots of fiber, vitamins and minerals needed daily for good health.

There are many kinds of kimchi, cabbage kimchi, radish kimchi, cucumber kimchi, but cabbage kimchi is the most famous and served in restaurants as a side dish breakfast, lunch, dinner and midnight snack.

Making Kimchi using an ordered list

1. Take a head of cabbage and slice it into halves or quarters
2. wash thoroughly
3. then lift and put salt between the leaves. (You should use sea salt.)
4. After this preparation wait 4 or so hours.

Preparing ingredients using an ordered list

- Dice a little ginger
- Dice a lot of garlic
- Chop up the green portion of leeks
- Finely grind up radish
- Prepare water flavored with dried minnows

Note that several steps are involved which we have omitted because the purpose of this is, after all, to demonstrate the use of lists and not making food. But for the curious you add lots of red pepper, sugar, other ingredients, stir them all together and let it age. Several fine recipes for kimchi can be found at www.fabulousfoods.com korean.allfoodrecipe.com and many many other fine sites too numerous to mention here.

If you would like to know further about kimchi you may contact at the following fictional address used only for the purpose of demonstrating the use of the
tag.
Kimchi World, Kimchi Plaza, NY, NY 21112

After you have finished coding in the Web page, your screen should look like Figure 4-15.

Notice the spacing between paragraphs that automatically happened when you used the `<p>` and the default formatting of the lists (both unordered and ordered). If you were to go back to your code (and you might want to do this just to see how white-space-insensitive HTML is), you could remove all white space between the lines of code, and it would not change the appearance of the Web page.

If your screen differs in appearance slightly, don't worry about it. But if your formatting does not show lists, everything shows up in the same font, or nothing shows at all, go back and recheck your code. Likely errors might include not using a closing tag `</>` for a two-sided tag, improperly opening or closing a comment tag or list tag, forgetting or transposing a line of code, or simply mistyping (transposition) or misspelling.

Now, you must give the file a name and save it as an `htm` file type. You do this by selecting the Save as... option from the drop-down File menu and then bringing up the Open File screen. Select the location of the folder where you want to save the HTML file. For the sake of simplicity, name the file `kimchi.htm` and save it in a folder called `CSWBChapter4`.

You will see *file type* immediately below *file name*. Click on the little triangle to the right and select the `htm` or `html` extension. If `html` is not one of the options listed, then select All Files and, in the filename, be sure to add `.htm` or `.html` file extension immediately after the filename. Use no spaces. Your screen should look like Figure 4-16.

FIGURE 4-16

As you save the file in Notepad with an .htm extension, notice the highlighted choice in File type is All Files.

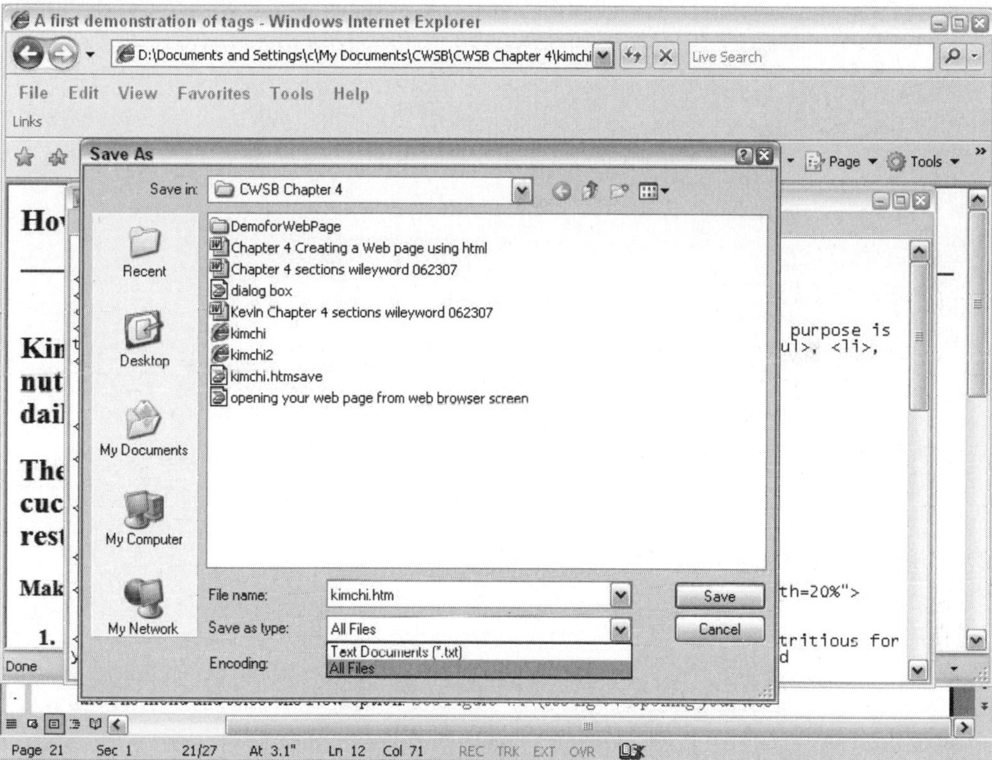

Your next step is to look at the coding as a Web page.

Click on your browser icon. Once your home page comes up, click on the File menu and select the New option as shown in Figure 4-17. A small dialog box will appear prompting you for input (if you know the path to the HTML file) or allowing you the option of clicking on the Browse button, as shown in Figure 4-18. The Browse button is the best button to use in most circumstances. Clicking on the Browse button will bring up the Open Screen window. From there, you navigate to the location of the file and select it by double-clicking. Your Web page should now appear.

Let's now develop the Web page a bit further by formatting the characters using both logical and virtual tags, adding a horizontal rule `<hr>`, and adjusting the alignment attribute of headers `<h1 align = "x">`.

FIGURE 4-17

You can open your Web page from your browser screen by using the drop-down File menu.

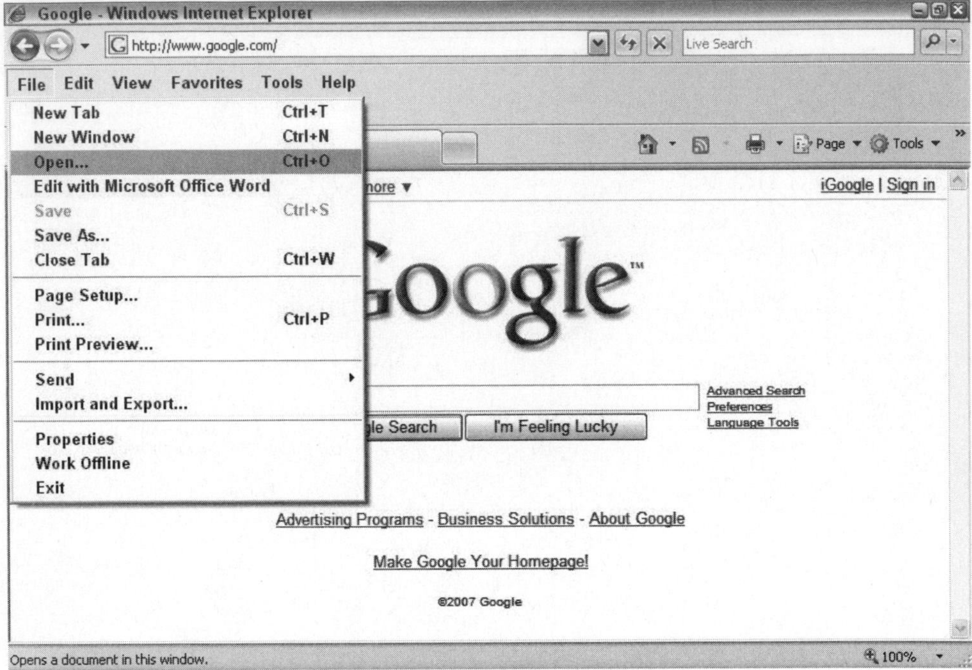

Logical and Physical Elements

Logical and physical elements are used to make formatting changes in characters or groups of words. For example, to make a word bold using the physical style, you would encompass the word in `<b>` tags. `<b>BOLD</b>` would be rendered BOLD in the browser. The logical (or virtual) equivalent of the <b> tag is `<strong>`. `<strong>BOLD</strong>` would also be rendered BOLD. Many of the tags have exact analogues in the virtual counterparts. `<strong>` and `<b>` both accomplish the same thing.

The physical tags give the programmer finer control over the appearance of the text in the document. Each physical tag will be rendered exactly as written.

FIGURE 4-18

A dialog box appears after you select Open in the Web browser. Click the Browse button to find the Web page you just created, and then press OK to bring it up.

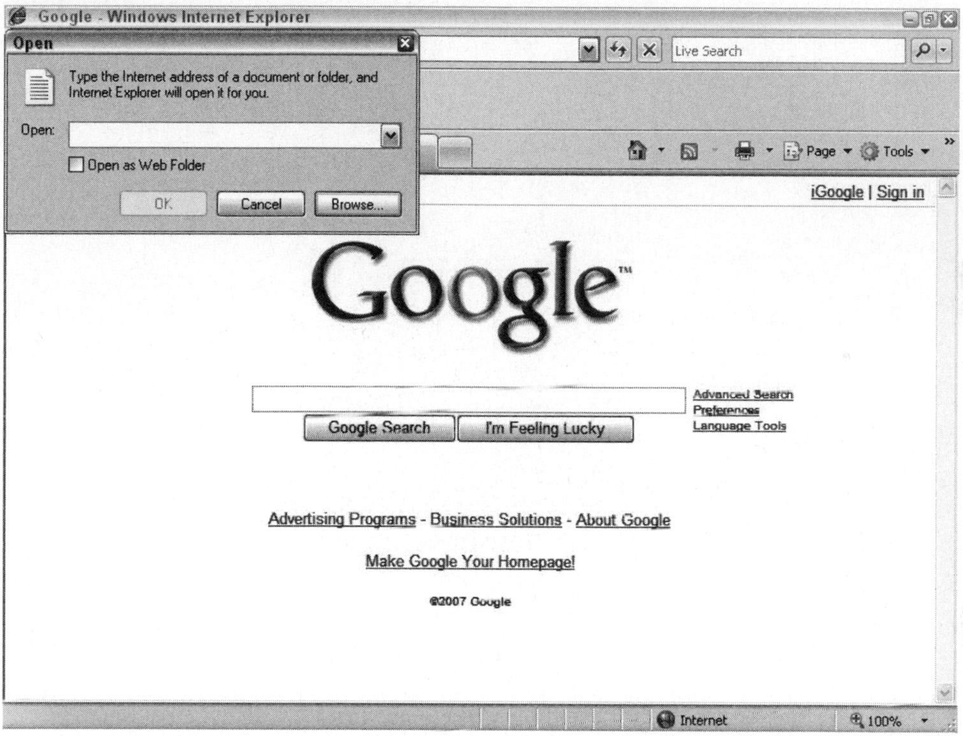

The logical tags are used because not all browsers or devices are capable of rendering all the physical tags. Additionally, emphasis may be presented differently for specific users, such as those with seeing difficulties, and so logical symbols are used. Using <em> for emphasis, for example, will simply indicate that the content between the <em> tags is to be emphasized in relation to the surrounding content, and will leave the specific style of emphasis to the rendering device. That could be bolding, highlighting, underlining, or italics. For example, consider the following:

```
<em> This is an example of logical or virtual rendering</em>
```

This would appear as follows:

This·is·an·example·of·logical·or·virtual·rendering¶

This·is·an·example·of·logical·or·virtual·rendering¶

This·is·an·example·of·logical·or·virtual·rendering¶

This·is·an·example·of·logical·or·virtual·rendering¶

Physical tags

The following code uses some common physical tags:

```
<b>bold</b>,
<big>Bigger text</big>,
<i>italicize</i>,
<small>Smaller text</small>,
<strike>Strikethrough text</strike>,
e=mc2 or why Albert Einstein <sup>should be looked up to</sup>,
That is <sub>beneath me. </sub>,
<u>Underline</u>
```

The result of executing this code looks like this:

bold

Bigger text

italicize

Smaller text

~~Strikethrough text~~

$e=mc^2$ or why Albert Einstein $^{\text{should be looked up to}}$

That is $_{\text{beneath me.}}$

Underline

These tags explicitly describe what the final appearance of the contained text should look like. If the rendering device does not have the capability to produce the specified physical tag, the formatting might be lost.

Logical tags

Here are some common logical tags:

```
<abbr>TCP/IP</abbr>

<acronym>SONET</acronym>

<cite>Don't quote me on this, but... </cite>

<code>if (form.query.value=="") {
                alert('Please make an entry in the product search
field.');
                return false;
            } else {
                return true;
            } </code>

     <dfn>terms and definitions</dfn>

<em>italic can be emphasis</em>

<strong>Strong and Bold</strong>
```

Logical tags do not include any final rendering guidelines. They describe instead how the content is to be represented in the context of the document. The benefit of logical tags is that the intent of the programmer can still be carried out.

Practice with tags of both styles and you will develop a subset of tags that fit your preferences as a developer to meet your programming needs.

Incorporating logical and physical tags

Now, let's work with some of those elements just described for your Web page. Let's use the following tags: `<b>`, `<i>`, `<u>`, `<center>`, `<hx>` (where *x* represents any number between 1 and 6), `<em>`, and `<strong>`. Enter the following code:

```
<html>
<head>
<title> A first demonstration of tags</title>

<!--This web page was constructed by [your name] on [insert date].
Its purpose is to demonstrate the use of the following tags: <b>,
<i>,  <u>, <center>, <hx> (where x represents any number between 1 and 6),
and <em>, <strong> -->

</head>

<body>
```

```
<center><h2><u>How to make <i>Kimchi</i></u><h2></center>

<p>Kimchi is a most flavorful and aromatic dish of Korea. It is very
nutritious for you providing lots of fiber, vitamins and minerals
needed daily for good health.</p>

<p>There are many kinds of <i>kimchi</i>, cabbage <i>kimchi</i>,
radish <i>kimchi</i>, cucumber <i>kimchi</i>, but
<strong>cabbage</strong> <i>kimchi</i> is the most famous and
served in restaurants as a side dish breakfast, lunch, dinner and
midnight snack.</p>

<p align="center">Making Kimchi using an ordered list<p>

<ol>
<li>Take a head of cabbage and slice it into <em>halves</em> or
<u>quarters</u></li>
<li>wash thoroughly</li>
<li>then lift and put salt between the leaves. (You should use sea
salt.) </li>
<li> After this preparation wait 4 or so hours.</li>
</ol>

<p>Preparing ingredients using an unordered list</p>
<ul>
<li><i>Dice</i> a little ginger</li>
<li><i>Dice</i> a lot of garlic </li>
<li><u>Chop up</u> the green portion of leeks</li>
<li><b>Finely grind up radish</b></li>
<li><em>Prepare</em> water flavored with dried minnows</li>
</ul>

<p>Note that several steps are involved which we have omitted
because the purpose of this is, after all, to demonstrate the use of
lists and not making food.  But for the curious you add lots of red
pepper, sugar, other ingredients, stir them all together and let it
age. </p>
<p>Several fine recipes for kimchi can be found at
www.fabulousfoods.com korean.allfoodrecipe.com and many many other
fine sites too numerous to mention here.</p>


<p>If you would like to know further about kimchi you may contact at
the following fictional address used only for the purpose of
demonstrating the use of the address tag.</p>
<address>Kimchi World,
```

```
Kimchi Plaza,
NY, NY 21112</address>
</body>
</html>
```

Your Web page now should resemble Figure 4-19.

Again, your screen may differ slightly in appearance. Compare the results in Figure 4-19 with the results shown in Figure 4-15. Notice in Figure 4-19 that the top heading is centered. Notice the formatting changes. Can you distinguish between logical and physical tags by looking at the page? How does your browser render an <em> tag? Try to center the address and put it in three separate lines.

Your new Web page may look kind of boring — and it is — but we'll spice it up a bit a bit later in the book. You should notice how a white background is nondistracting and focuses the viewer's attention just on the text of the page. Look at the effective use of white backgrounds in the top 10 Web sites (according to a March 2006 Nielsen ratings report): Yahoo!, Microsoft, MSN, Google, AOL, eBay, MapQuest, Amazon, Real, MySpace, and many others.

FIGURE 4-19

After entering the code, your Web page should have a new look.

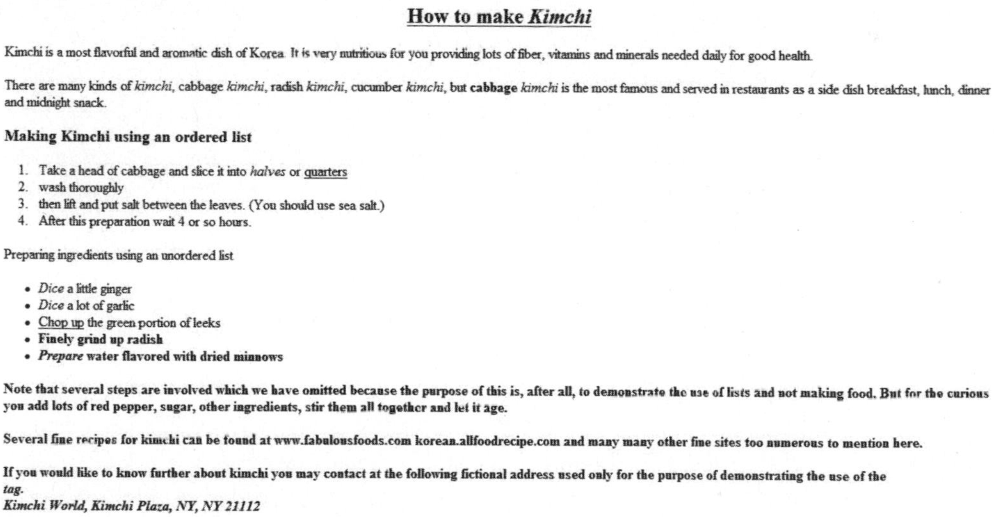

How to make *Kimchi*

Kimchi is a most flavorful and aromatic dish of Korea. It is very nutritious for you providing lots of fiber, vitamins and minerals needed daily for good health.

There are many kinds of *kimchi*, cabbage *kimchi*, radish *kimchi*, cucumber *kimchi*, but **cabbage** *kimchi* is the most famous and served in restaurants as a side dish breakfast, lunch, dinner and midnight snack.

Making Kimchi using an ordered list

1. Take a head of cabbage and slice it into *halves* or quarters
2. wash thoroughly
3. then lift and put salt between the leaves. (You should use sea salt.)
4. After this preparation wait 4 or so hours.

Preparing ingredients using an unordered list

- *Dice* a little ginger
- *Dice* a lot of garlic
- Chop up the green portion of leeks
- **Finely grind up radish**
- ***Prepare* water flavored with dried minnows**

Note that several steps are involved which we have omitted because the purpose of this is, after all, to demonstrate the use of lists and not making food. But for the curious you add lots of red pepper, sugar, other ingredients, stir them all together and let it age.

Several fine recipes for kimchi can be found at www.fabulousfoods.com korean.allfoodrecipe.com and many many other fine sites too numerous to mention here.

If you would like to know further about kimchi you may contact at the following fictional address used only for the purpose of demonstrating the use of the
tag.
Kimchi World, Kimchi Plaza, NY, NY 21112

Special Characters and Encoding Schemes: ASCII and Unicode

Look at your keyboard. Press A. Look at your screen. You see A. Press B. You see B, and so on. If you didn't know any better, you might even think that a big A was sent all the way from the keyboard to the computer, and the computer then forwarded it to the screen so you could see it. And you would be right, with qualifications.

All special character data, all numeric data, and all uppercase and lowercase letters appearing on the screen are a result of an encoding scheme called ASCII, which stands for American Standard Code for Information Interchange. It was created in the early 1960s as a joint project of both government and industry to permit machines from different manufacturers to exchange data. ASCII is a binary representation of the letters, numbers, and special characters you see on your keyboard (plus a few more relating to carriage return, line placements, and various beeps). Each of these letters and numbers can be encoded in a different pattern of 7 bits. And each bit goes down one of seven wires to make a unique pattern.

For example, the letter "A" is 65 in ASCII code, which would be the binary equivalent of 1000001. The digit "1", which is listed as element 49 in the ASCII code, would be represented in binary as 0110001. Each of these bits would go down a separate wire to form a group of 7 bits representing the "A" and then the "1."

NOTE **Bit, short for binary digit, simply represents the presence or absence of electrical current on a wire at a given moment.**

The ASCII codes 48 through 57 represent the digits 0 through 9, codes 65 through 90 represent the uppercase alphabet, and 97 to 122 represent the same in lowercase. A version called Extended ASCII has 255 representations available for a number of symbols not appearing on the keyboard.

You need to know about the existence of ASCII codes because sometimes in your coding there are symbols you want to insert, such as copyright symbol (`©`), a yen symbol (`¦`), a cent symbol (`¢`), or even a nonbreaking space between links (` `) — and not all of them are on your keyboard. You put them in by giving their proper numeric value in the ASCII code. You don't need to memorize all representations in the code. You can just look at any of a number of charts publicly available both online and in books dealing with Web design.

You will also notice that when you saved your HTML coding on Notepad, the default encoding type was ASCII. You also had a few other options for Unicode, but Notepad is what is called *plain* (or *simple*) *text*, and the only encoding scheme required for that is the first 127 numbers of the ASCII code.

NOTE **Unicode is an extension to ASCII that allows a number of special character representations from other alphabet systems. It can have up to 65,535 character representations, which is very useful for more complex languages or writing systems, such as Kanji or Mandarin. More information on Unicode is available at `Unicode.org`, or the Web site associated with this book.**

Element Quick Reference

The following provides a quick reference for key items discussed in this chapter:

- <html></html> — Tells the browser to render document content as a Web page.
- <head></head> — Contains code and block elements that do not appear in Web page as viewable content.
- <!-- --> — Used to insert a comment regarding purpose of code segment, and to give information about a program and programmer.
- <title></title> — Gives the title as it appears in title bar at top of the browser screen.
- <body></body> — Contains the content appearing on the Web page.
- <hx> *(where* x *represents numeric values 1 through 6)* — Gives the size of the content headings.
- <center></center> — Centers content contained between the tags.
- <p></p> — Separates blocks of content by a blank line.
- <ul></ul> — Provides a bulleted list.
- <ol></ol> — Provides a numbered or alpha-sequenced list.
- *Block level elements* — Elements that represent separate sections of a Web page (such as head, body, paragraph, address, title, comments, and lists).
- *Inline elements* — Elements that are contained within a block. They could be physical (such as <b> </b>, <i></i>, <center>, <u>), or virtual: (such as <em>, <strong>).
- *Function* — Returns a value or changes a state. Appears in the <head> element.

Summary

In this chapter, you learned that a Web page is created using HTML code as the language to create Web pages. This language may be viewed in the page's source code, which is accessed through View/Source or right-click/select in the browser's context menu. Tags are the structures that contain the commands regarding the physical layout structure of the site and govern the appearance of the content of the site. Content is what is displayed by the browser on the user's display, and is the material enclosed within the formatting tags.

Code contained in the head of an HTML document does not appear in the rendering of the Web page. Types of tags that appear in the head are metatags, title tags, scripts, and comments. Metatags are used by Web crawlers to categorize the Web page and add it to its parent database for search and retrieval by users of the search engine The <title> is used to give a name to the document. This name will appear in the title bar above the actual page. Comment tags are used to describe the purpose of the page, or to describe the purpose of some coding feature and, generally, to provide information regarding the site useful to developers working on the site at some later time. Executable code appearing in the head is contained in functions which are located in script tags. The purpose of a function is to return a value or change a state of an element of the Web page.

This chapter has reviewed some of the more common block-level elements used in Web page design — paragraphs, ordered and unordered lists, horizontal line, inline images — and the specifications of each. We have looked at the structure of two-sided and single-sided tags and their usage. We have looked at the head and the body sections, and noted the tag elements typical to each and both.

In this chapter, you developed your first Web page using Notepad as a text editor. In the first iteration, we used mostly block-level elements. We discussed the <img> tag and addressing, and how to most efficiently place the image in the same Web page folder as the code and other elements appearing on the Web page. In the second iteration of the Web page, we added inline elements to format specific selections of text. We used multiple formatting tags on one word to demonstrate the parallelism required for correct code usage. We saved the coding file as an HTML file using the `.htm` extension. We viewed it as a Web page by bringing it up in our Web browser.

Finally, this chapter introduced and related the use of ASCII and Unicode encoding schemes to coding for Web pages using simple text editors.

Chapter 5 will guide you in the creation of linking tags for your Web site.

Chapter 5

Links, Hotspots, and Web Site Navigation

IN THIS CHAPTER

Example Web site

Internal links with anchor tags

Developing a sample Web site

Absolute and relative paths

Previous and next links

External links

Storyboarding

Links quick reference

There are two fundamental types of hyperlinks: internal and external. You use *internal links* to create links to different sections of a single Web page, or links to other documents and sections within a Web site. The following is a snippet of code linking one document to a section of another document (Spr) in the same folder:

```
<a href="Course20Schedule.htm#Spr">Course
Schedule</a>
```

You can also create *external links* to Internet Web sites other than your own, to e-mail servers, to FTP servers, or to various discussion forums using Usenet groups. To make an e-mail reference, the code would be as follows:

```
<a href="mailto:madamimadam@pop.edu">
Madamimadam</a>
```

When you add links, the links will show up on the Web page underlined in blue, and the cursor will change from an arrow to a hand to indicate that the link can be clicked. Later in this chapter, you will learn how to manipulate links a bit by changing the default colors. You will also see how to use images as links, as shown in Figure 5-1. These are created the same way as text links; they are merely pictures or icons that you click on.

CROSS-REF **In Chapter 13, you will learn about other interactive maneuvers**

First up in this chapter, however, you will learn how to create an internal link within a document to move between the top of a document and its various sections. You will also learn how to jump back to the top of your document from any location in your document. By creating this internal link, you will learn to use #, `href`, `name`, and `id` attributes within the anchor tag pair `<a></a>`.

FIGURE 5-1

In this example of a clickable image, notice the border around the image at the top of the figure.

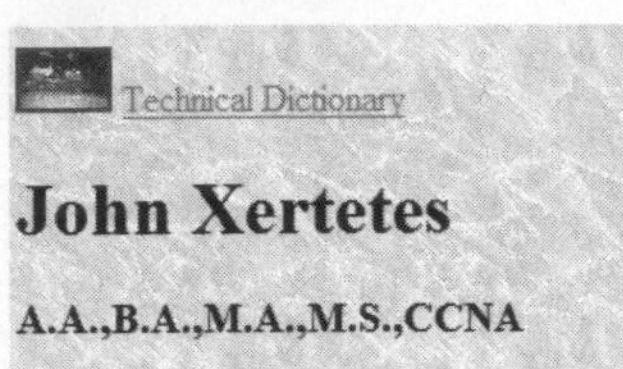

NOTE **The # is referred to as a *hash mark*. In the golden days of our youth, we referred to this as a number sign or pound sign.**

After you create and practice the internal Web page references, you will create additional links to other Web pages. You will learn how to jump to a specific section of another Web page, as well as going and returning from specific Web pages. You will explore navigating multiple pages using `previous` and `next` tags.

You will also learn how simple it is to create a tag to go to any Web site on the Web, as the following snippet will do:

```
<a href="www.yahoo.com" >A retrospective of the writing of Jonathan
Swift</a>
```

And, you will learn how to create a link to a Webmaster — the person who is generally in charge of running the site — using the `mailto:` URL type, and link to a Usenet. We will link via inline images, as shown here

```
<a href="http://www.space.com"><img src=="spaceship.jpg">
Atlantis</a>
```

You will learn how to link via hotspots using image maps, as well as how to use an image mapping utility.

Finally in this chapter, through the use of multiple links to multiple pages, you will develop a plan using storyboarding techniques to develop an efficient linking structure.

XHTML links

Another tag, the `link` tag, is used for linking resources to the page.

The following snippet of coding from the Wiley Web site shows a few examples of the `link` tag:

```
<!-- layout( Wiley Homepage ) -->
<html>
<head>
```

continued

continued

```
<link href="/WileyCDA/site/wiley2/include/style.css" type="text/css"
rel="stylesheet">
<title>
Wiley::Wiley

</title>
<script language="javascript" src="/WileyCDA/site/shared/form_validation.js"
type="text/javascript">
</script>
<!--[if lt IE 7]>
<link href="/WileyCDA/site/wiley2/include/style-ie.css" rel="stylesheet"
type="text/css">
<![endif]-->
</head>
```

The tag, as currently implemented, appears only in the `<head>` section of the document. As you can see in the line `<link href="/WileyCDA/site/wiley2/include/style.css" type="text/css" rel="stylesheet">`, the link refers to a stylesheet, `style.css`, located on the `WileyCDA` site. The second link refers to another stylesheet, `style-ie.css`, in the same location as the first `link` tag.

If you were to look at more `link` tags in the source code of this site, you would see that they all appear in the `<head>` section, and they all refer to stylesheets. What you may reasonably infer from this is that the `link` tag has limited applicability at present. The `link` tag may eventually have broader application, but it is presently mostly used only in the `<head>` section of a document to link to stylesheets.

And, as you now know, any element in the `<head>` does not appear in a Web browser's content pane.

Example Web Site

Listing 5-1 shows the source code of a site used in some of the examples for this chapter. The purpose of the source code shown here is to introduce the reader to several additional features of a Web page with links to other sites. This site incorporates links (internally and externally), images, and image maps. Each of the new features will be explained in context of the page, and then further illustrated in separate sections of the chapter.

LISTING 5-1

Example Source Code

```
<!DOCTYPE HTML PUBLIC "-//W3C//DTD HTML 4.0 Transitional//EN">
<HTML><HEAD><TITLE>Some Facts about John Xertetes</TITLE>
```

```
<META http-equiv=Content-Type content="text/html; charset=windows-1252">
<META content="MSHTML 6.00.2719.2200" name=GENERATOR></HEAD>
<BODY vLink=gray link=blue background="PDC Resume_files/granite.jpg">
<IMG src="PDC Resume_files/pdc1.jpg" align=right>
<A href="beach.gif"><IMG src="PDC Resume_files/beachthumb.jpg"><a
href="PDCResume.html"Home Page></a></A>
 <A href="http://webopedia.com/">Technical Dictionary</A>
<H1 align=left>John Xertetes</H1>
<H3>A.A.,B.A.,M.A.,M.S.,CCNA</H3>
<H5>314  Pie Circle Lane   Syracuse,  PI  12358  
US  ·   johnxertetes@pop.eye   Cell Phone: 
(828) 555-5555   Office Phone: (540) 555-5555   Residence
Phone: (828) 555-5555</H5>
<P>
<H5><I><A href="PDC Resume.html#OBJ">Objective</A> 
·  <A href="PDC Resume.html#EXP">Experience</A> ·
  <A href="PDC Resume.html#EDU">Education</A> ·
  <A href="PDC Resume.html#SKI">Skills</A> ·
  <A href="PDC Resume.html#ASS">Associations</A> ·
  <A href="PDC Resume.html#MEM">Memberships</A> ·
  <A href="PDC Resume.html#PER">Personal</A> ·
 <A href="Map.htm"> World
Travels</A> </A> ·  <A
href="LIN"> Linking Examples</A>
</A> ·   </A></I></H5>
<P></P>
<HR align=left width="97%" color=blue SIZE=6>
<H3><EM><A name=OBJ>OBJECTIVE</A></EM></H3>
<P>The objective of my current existence would seem to lie in the ceaseless pursuit
of truth in HTML, in other words, fact-checking, verifying, rechecking and then,
with fear and trembling in my heart, putting pen to paper, metaphorically of
course, to share my knowledge of web design and that to the utmost of my ability.
Then I happen to look up from my computer screen and see the Bradford pear trees
tossing their crowns in the hot winds of this summer afternoon and the dark storm
clouds gathering upon the rolling green hills beyond...and the sight fills my soul
with exultation.  I pause in wonderment and praise.</P><HR align=center width="55%"
color=black SIZE=4>
<P><H3><I><A name=EXP>EXPERIENCE</A></I></H3>
<HR align=left width="25%" color=blue SIZE=3>
<P><I><B>Director of IT, Nonsuche Ind, Ptl; ULtd.</P>
<P>Run the server farm for the webcast</P>
<P><I><B>Responsibilities</B></I></P>
<UL>  <LI>Monitoring and updating system
  <LI><p> Note: The following is an example of an infolder link</p> <A
href="file:///C:/My%20Documents/Resume%20folder/Course%20Catalog.htm#CIM
311">Developing  Server courses</A>
  <LI>Purchasing hardware and software.
  <LI>Scheduling staff training sessions.
```

```
  <LI>Hiring and training IT techs.
  <LI>In-house training. </LI></UL>
<HR align=left width="25%" color=blue SIZE=2>
<P><I><B>Director of IT</B> </I>(1999-2001,
Nongeek Ind,Pld )</P>
<P><I><B>Responsibilities</I></B></P><UL type=blue align="center"><I>
<LI>Management Information Systems
  <LI>Systems Analysis and Design  <LI>Database and Database Management
<LI>Network Design/Implementation (WANs and LANs)
  <LI>WIN NT 4.0 <LI>Visual Basic .net
  <LI>HTML,XML  <LI>MYSQL
  <LI>MicroSoft Office Suite all  <LI>Multimedia Communications
  <LI>Adobe Desktop Publishing 6.5 </I></LI></UL>
<HR align=left width="25%" color=blue SIZE=2>
<P><I><B>Technical Editor</I> </B>: <U>Guide to Upland Wireless
Communications</U>
Smokey Publishers, 2001; HAL.</P>
<HR align=center width="55%" color=black SIZE=4><P>
<H3><I><A name=EDU>EDUCATION</A></I></H3>
<HR align=left width="25%" color=blue SIZE=3><P><DL>
  <DT>Ball State University (July, 1969) Muncie, In.
  <DD><I><B>Master of Science in <A href="http://www.cics.bsu.edu/">Information
  and Communication Sciences</A></I></B>
  <P></P>  <DT>University of Southern California (1976) Far East
  <DD><I><B>Computer Systems Graduate Program</I></B>
  <P></P></DD></DL><HR align=center width="55%" color-black SIZE=4><P>
<H3><I><A name=SKI>SKILLS</A></I></H3><P></P>
<HR align=left width="25%" color=blue SIZE=3><P><DL>
  <DT><I><B>Networking </I></B> <DD><I>LAN <DD>WAN <DD>VLAN
<DD>Wireless</I><P></P><DT><I><B>Webpage</I></B> <DD><I>HTML
  <DD>Dreamweaver<DD>Java Script</I> <P></P>  <DT><I><B> Languages
</I></B> <DD><I>Java <DD>Visual Basic <DD>COBOL
  <DD>BASIC</I> <P></P><DT><I><B>Database</I></B>
  <DD><I>MYSQL</I> <P></P><DD><I>Technical</I><P></P>
  <DT><I><B>Technical editing/writing</I></B>
  <DD><I>College texts</I> <DD><I>Professional Journals</I>
  <P></P></DD></DL>
<HR align=center width="55%" color=black SIZE=4><P>
<H3><I><A name=ASS>PROFESSIONAL ASSOCIATIONS</A></I></H3>
<P></P><HR align=left width="25%" color=blue SIZE=3>
<UL> <P>  <LI><I>ACM <LI>IEEE<LI>IETF LI>ISOC <LI>Sig Comm</LI> </UL>
<P></P><HR align=center width="55%" color=black SIZE=4>
<P><H3><I><A name=MEM>MEMBERSHIPS</A></I></H3>
<P></P><HR align=left width="25%" color=blue SIZE=3>
<UL> <P>  <LI><I>Phi Theta Kappa <LI>Sigma Beta Delta <LI>Who's Who in Peace
Corps <LI>Royal Asiatic Society<LI>Association of US Army  <LI>Seoul Chamber of
Commerce <LI> Seoul School Board
  <LI>Watauga Gun Club</LI></UL>
```

```
<P></P><P><HR align=center width="55%" color=black SIZE=4>
<H3><I><A name=PER>PERSONAL</A></I></H3>
<H3><I><A name=LIN>Linking Examples</A> <IMG src="PDC Resume_files/case.bmp">
<P></P><HR align=left width="25%" color=blue SIZE=3>
<UL>  <P>  <LI><I>Hobbies  <LI>Interests  <LI>Newspaper articles <LI><A
href="file:///C:/My%20Documents/Resume%20folder/Alissa%20American.doc">Family</A>
<LI>Miscellaneous</I></LI></UL>
<P></P><HR align=center width="55%" color=black SIZE=4>
<H4 align=center><I>LINKS TO OTHER IN-FOLDER FILES</I></H4>
<H5 align=center><I><A href="Course%20Catalog.htm">Course
Catalog</A>   <A href="file:///A:/Course%20Schedule.htm#Spr">Course
Schedule</A></I></H5>
<HR align=center width="55%" color=blue SIZE=4>
<H3 align=center><I>Contact John Xertetes at:  <A
href="mailto: johnxertetes@pop.eye ">johnxertetes@pop.eye</A>
<HR align=left width="97%" color=blue SIZE=6>
</I></I></H3></H3></I></I></BODY></HTML>
```

Figure 5-2 shows the associated Web page that will demonstrate the various kinds of links as this chapter moves forward. Some of the examples in this chapter will use the JX Web page for image links, as well as for image maps.

TIP **You may cut and paste HTML code when creating your own Web page using links, image maps, and so forth, but you must also be aware that some images may be copyrighted and some JavaScript code may be as well.**

One of the things you should realize by now is that a lot of Web sites are created by borrowing from the source code of other sites. If you look at the third line in Listing 5-1, you will see the `Meta` tag defines the coding as 4.0 Transitional. There is a title and then the heading ends. A little terse, isn't it? If you were reprogramming this site, you might add to the `<head>` section so that the next programmer (such as you) could come along and immediately understand when this Web site was created, by whom, and what it is about.

Internal Links with Anchor Tags

The following code shows an internal *source* link with anchor tags:

```
<h3><I><A href="JXResume.html#OBJ">Objective</A><h3>
```

Let's break down this line of code:

- `<h3></h3>` — Note that the code for this link is enclosed in `<h3>` tags. These, of course, define the style of font that will be used to display the word "Objective." These heading tags are meant to section off the page by text importance and structure. Note that you cannot enclose block-level elements (such as heading tags) within the anchor; the link will not be rendered correctly.

- `<A></A>` — These inline anchor tags are contained within the block element. Within the `<a>` tag we have a *fragment identifier*:
  - `href` — This is the attribute that specifies the location of a resource.
  - `jxresume.html` — This is the URL to a page on your Web site.
  - `#OBJ` — This is the *fragment identifier*. The portion of the address signaled by the hash mark, #, is used to go to a specified section of that document. The hash mark can also be quite useful when trying to reference a particular section in another document.
- `Objective` — This is the text of the link representing the link destination.

NOTE **You can call the fragment identifier anything you wish. You must, however, use the same fragment identifier for the ID in the destination anchor. That is how source and destination uniquely identify each other.**

FIGURE 5-2

This sample Web page shows internal, in-folder, e-mail, and external links.

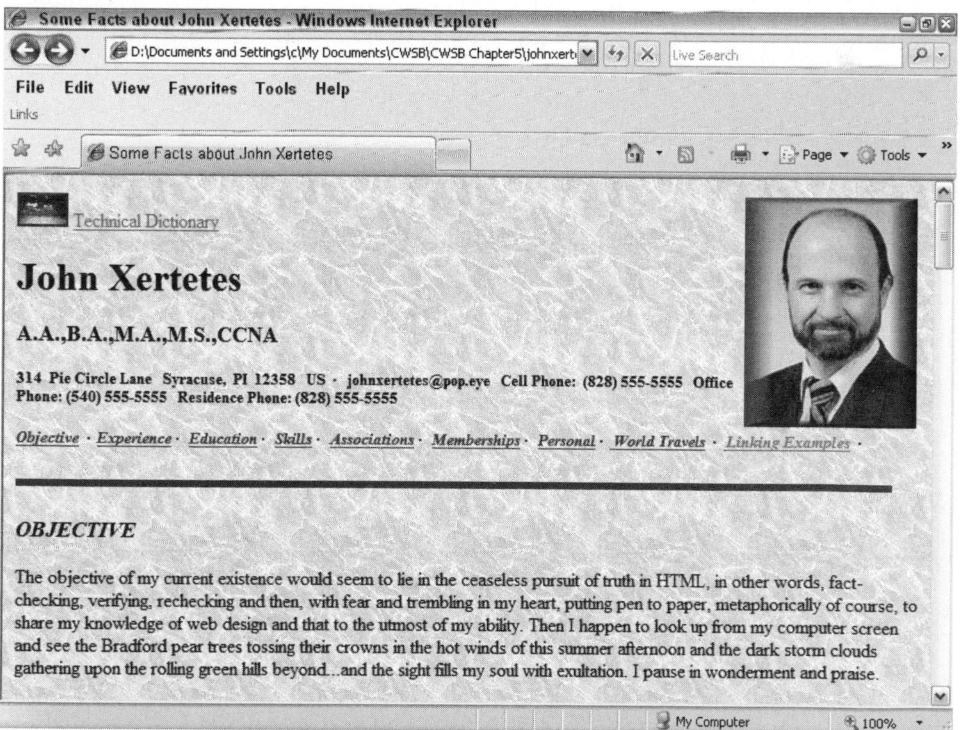

FIGURE 5-3

The Web page shows both source and destination anchors. Notice that source anchor is underlined as a link, while the destination anchor is not visually changed.

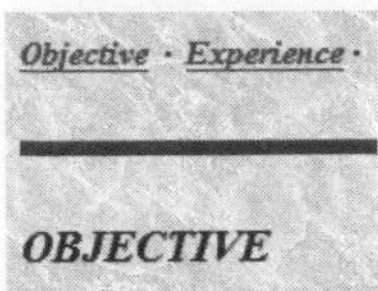

In this instance, the browser would go to section named "OBJ" on the destination page. On the Web page the *source anchor* would be rendered boldfaced and italicized. Had the fragment identifier been marked #EDU, the browser would have leaped to the part of the document with the "Education" subheading.

The following code defines a *destination anchor*:

```
<H3><EM><A name="OBJ">OBJECTIVE</A></EM></H3>
```

Let's break down this line of code:

- <H3></H3> — The destination anchor tag is also enclosed within block level element, <h3>.
- <EM></EM> — You remember that this tag emphasizes the content in some way without specifying to the browser exactly how. It could be by bolding, italicizing, underlining, blinking, or whatever that particular browser does to emphasize the content.
- name — The name attribute holds the value you give to the link. It can be any name you choose. In this example, the attribute is assigned the name OBJ as the name for the destination anchor. That is why we put #OBJ in the hypertext link to the source anchor (so the source would know what destination to link to). It should be apparent that each name within a document must be unique. If you had more than one OBJ, the source anchor would not know which one to link to.

NOTE **The destination anchor is not highlighted as a link.**

On the Web page, the destination anchor would be rendered with the word "Objective" simply boldfaced. Note that when you view the anchor on the Web browser, as shown in Figure 5-3, you will see that the subheading "Objective" is not interactive in any way. It does not need to be. It is the destination of the link. It is not clickable.

Now, there is more than one way to reference destination links. You may also use the <id> attribute in place of the name attribute. Think of <id> as an abbreviation for "identifier." Look carefully at the following two examples. First, look at this code using the name attribute in a destination anchor:

```
<H2><A name="OBJ">Objective</A></H2>
...break 25 birds...
```

```
<H2><A name="EDU">Education</A></H2>
...enough to be considered smart but...
<H3><A name="ASS">Associations</A></H3>
...only those my wife approves of...

Using an id attribute in a destination anchor.
<H2 id="OBJ">Objective</H2>
...my objective is to grow a crop of chamei...
<H2 id="EDU">Education</H2>  .
...not so much as to be considered useless...
<H3 id="ASS">Associations</H3>
...mostly harmless sort...
```

The name attribute must be used within anchor tags to give the element a unique value, as shown here:

```
<H2><A name="OBJ">Objective</A></H2>
```

However, the id attribute can be used within any other element to give it a unique value. Note that the anchor tags, <a></a>, are not used for the destination.

```
<H2 id="OBJ">Objective</H2>
```

The id attribute is also case-insensitive — EDU and edu would be seen as the same thing.

Technically, name has been deprecated by the newer id attribute.

Developing a Sample Web Site

Now, let's start to develop a new site devoted to you. It will have all the usual tags, the logical and physical formatting tags, and the attributes you worked with in Chapter 4. Additionally, this site will include internal links using the anchor tag, as well as both the id and the name attributes. Also, you must remember to use the hash marks, since you will be referencing links internally. Let's call the site "All About Me."

Follow these steps:

1. Open up Notepad and type in the following code:

```
<html>
<head>
<title> All About Me </title>
</head>
<body>
</body>
</html>
```

2. Now, go to the File menu and select Save As. Save the file with the name `AllAboutMe.htm` (do *not* forget the `htm` extension!). Ensure that the File Type is All Files. Save this file in a folder called `Chapter 5`, for example, and save it either in your `My Doucuments` folder or on your Desktop so that it'll be easy to find.

NOTE **Remember to save this file, and the other files you will be creating, in the same folder**

3. Next, go to your Web browser, and open the site using the Browse button on the dialog box.
4. Verify that the title bar shows "All About Me" in the title. There should be nothing on the screen, of course. You haven't input any content in the body, yet.
5. Close the page and open Notepad again, and add the following comments in the `<head>` section.

```
<!-- This web page was constructed by [your name] on [insert
date]. Its purpose is to demonstrate the use of source and
destination anchors using, hash mark, and both id and Name
attributes. These will be demonstrated by the development of an
autobiographical web Page -->
```

6. Within the `<body>` section, center an `h2` size of heading that will appear at the top of your Web page. Emphasize it in some way.
7. Now, make three links three lines below the heading. Enter the following code exactly:

```
<p><center><a href="#Fam">Family</a>  
<a href="#Spo">Sports</a>  <a
href="#Sch">Schools</a></center></p>
```

8. Go down a line. Put in a blue horizontal line all the way across the page. Go down two lines using the `<br>` tag.
9. Enter the following code, exactly as shown:

```
<h2><a href Name=Fam>Family</a> </h2></p>
<p>Paragraph on family.</p>

<p id="Spo">Sports</p>
<p>Paragraph on sports</p>

<p id="Sch">School</p>
<p> Paragraph on school</p>
```

10. Save the file and bring it up in your browser. It should look something like Figure 5-4. Test your links: They should work.

If your Web page doesn't have working links, or if it looks substantially different from Figure 5-4, go back and recheck your coding. You probably made an error in spelling or forgot to close a tag. If you can't find any errors, start over again.

FIGURE 5-4

The All About Me Web site shows source anchors and destination anchors.

It's about me!

Family Sports Schools

Family
Paragraph on family.

Sports
Paragraph on hobbies.

School
Paragraph on school.

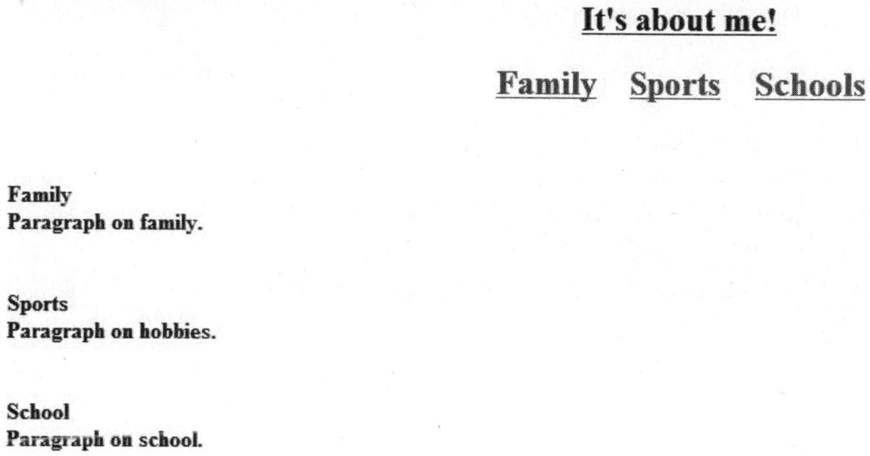

Congratulations! You have now finished creating your first sets of source and destination anchors within a document.

Navigating within your Web site

As you click on the links at the top of your Web page, the browser immediately jumps down to the section you selected. Let's make this Web page a little easier to navigate.

When you click on a link, the logic of the program brings you to the page section referenced in the link. If you want to get back to the top of the page, you must either use your scroll bar, or use the Back button in the navigation toolbar.

It would be better if you could actually navigate back to the top of the document while within the page. You already know how to do this. You place a link that you call `back to top` at the end of every section you have linked to. The `back to top` source anchor references an anchor at the top of the document.

The destination anchor could be an element, text, or image. So, let's create the `back to top` reference to be placed in the code, just after the `<body>` tag. For the source anchor, use the following code:

```
<p><a href="#sam">back to top</a></p>
```

For the destination anchor, use the following code:

```
<h1 id="sam"></h1>
```

The `id` selected, `sam`, is totally random. You can call the link anything you please. Just be certain to include the hash mark, #, before it in the source anchor.

Your Web page should now resemble Figure 5-5. All the links should work.

TIP **While you're free to create as many section names and links as you'd like on a page, keep in mind that some users may become confused if their clicks take them to a lower section on the page, where the main navigation and page title are no longer visible. So, if you do break your page up into multiple sections, consider duplicating the navigation and page title at each section, or providing links back to the page's navigation and title.**

If you find your internal links to sections aren't working, first confirm that the section name matches the link name perfectly. Because section names are case-sensitive, "top" and "Top" mean different things. In addition, it's best not to include any spaces or punctuation in your section names because they can easily be confused in the browser.

NOTE **The default color for an unvisited link is blue, and for a visited links it is gray. You may change these colors by assigning them different values in the `<body>` tag. For example, to use green for unvisited and red for visited links, the code would look like this:**

```
<body link="green" vlink="red">
```

We will show you other ways to do this in later sections of the book.

FIGURE 5-5

The sample Web page now shows internal links and links back to top of document.

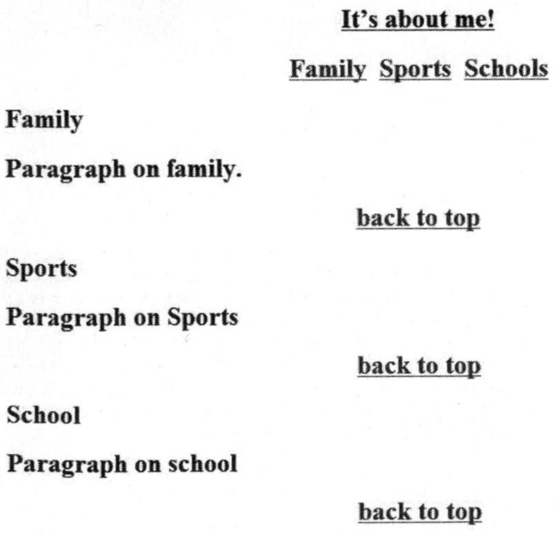

It's about me!

Family Sports Schools

Family

Paragraph on family.

back to top

Sports

Paragraph on Sports

back to top

School

Paragraph on school

back to top

Links between pages of a site

Let's now continue to expand the use of links by linking between documents (that is, Web pages) related to one another by being on the same site. As in the previous example, let's use the coding and illustrations from the All About Me document and its associated links.

Coding between documents is almost a duplicate of coding within a document. You use anchor tags to create both source and destination links, and you use the hash mark if you want to access a specific section of the linked document. To link from the All About Me home page to a related page called Family (in the same folder), use the following code:

```
<a href="Family.htm"> All about Family</a>.
```

To reference another in-folder link, Favorite Sports, you would use the following code:

```
<a href="Sports.htm#Bow">Bowling</a>
```

Note that, in this example, the link is first made to the document, and then to the fragment identifier `#Bow`.

If you click on the Family link, you will see the information shown in Figure 5-6. If you click on the Sports link, you will be taken to the Bowling subsection, as shown in Figure 5-7.

So, now that we see where we're headed, let's now add some content and get these links working properly.

FIGURE 5-6

Clicking on the Family link takes you to that page. Because the two documents were in the same folder, you could reference it by simply clicking on the Family link.

Family

Dad Mom Gretchen Maggie Ferdinand Swen

return to home page
Sports

Dad

Dad is 63 and owns a trucking business. He is very, very, very rich. He met Mom, see picture, when she was 16 and working as a clerk at the local PX. He was a driver in the transport unit. After he married Mom and got an honorable discharge, he returned to Bristol but still remained in the driving business, first as a trucker, then as truck owner, and then as a fleet owner. About that same time I came along and then Gretchen. The 4 of us always go to the Speedway to see the races. He also especially likes drag races and sponsors a few cars for the Thunder Valley Show in July every year. You know one of them: the big flying purple dragon with a yellow belly swooping down with flames shooting out of its mouth. Dad loves shooting flames. Every 4th of July he puts on a fireworks display at our home that's bigger than anything ever seen in New York, Los Angeles, Houston, and the first day of the battle of the Somme combined!

That's all about Dad.

back to top

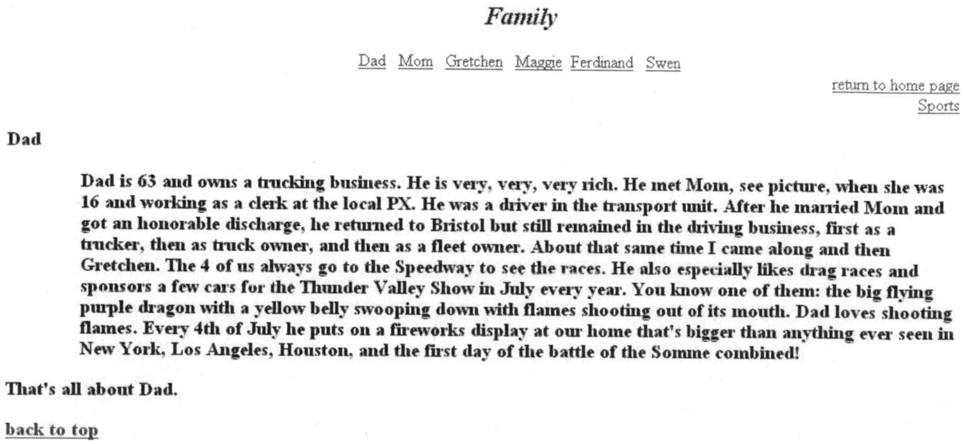

FIGURE 5-7

Notice the link went directly to the Bowling subsection of the Sports Web page, as specified in the fragment identifier.

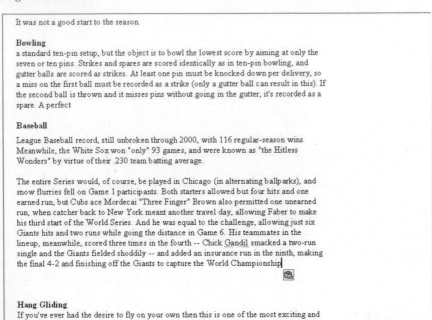

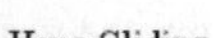

It was not a good start to the season.
Bowling
a standard ten-pin setup, but the object is to bowl the lowest score by aiming at only the seven or ten pins. Strikes and spares are scored identically as in ten-pin bowling, and gutter balls are scored as strikes. At least one pin must be knocked down per delivery, so a miss on the first ball must be recorded as a strike (only a gutter ball can result in this). If the second ball is thrown and it misses pins without going in the gutter, it's recorded as a spare. A perfect
Baseball
League Baseball record, still unbroken through 2000, with 116 regular-season wins. Meanwhile, the White Sox won "only" 93 games, and were known as "the Hitless Wonders" by virtue of their .230 team batting average.
The entire Series would, of course, be played in Chicago (in alternating ballparks), and snow flurries fell on Game 1 participants. Both starters allowed but four hits and one earned run, but Cubs ace Mordecai "Three Finger" Brown also permitted one unearned run, when catcher back to New York meant another travel day, allowing Faber to make his third start of the World Series. And he was equal to the challenge, allowing just six Giants hits and two runs while going the distance in Game 6. His teammates in the lineup, meanwhile, scored three times in the fourth -- Chick Gandil smacked a two-run single and the Giants fielded shoddily -- and added an insurance run in the ninth, making the final 4-2 and finishing off the Giants to capture the World Championship
Hang Gliding
If you've ever had the desire to fly on your own then this is one of the most exciting and
Close Full Screen

Creating Web Pages for Family and Sports

Let's now create anchors to other documents in your Web site. You have already created the basic outline of the first page of the site, All About Me. First, let's develop subsections on that page (Family, Sports, and School) by adding more data. Within each section, let's then create more links to them.

Let's begin with the Family Section. Insert the following code directly below the internal links of Family, Sports, and Schools:

```
<p>Paragraph on family. For link to Family page click
<a href="Family.htm">Family</a></p>

<p>Paragraph on school. For link to School page click
<a href="Schools.htm">Schools</a></p>

<p>Paragraph on sports. For link to Sports page click
<a href="Sports.htm">Sports</a></p>
```

Save the document. Note that none of the links will work because you haven't created anything to link them to, yet.

Now enter the following code:

```
<h2><a Name=Fam>Family</a></h2><p>

<ol>
<li>Wife, Reykya from <em>Sweden.</em> For additional info
on Reykya click
<a href="Family.htm#Mom">Mom</a></li>
<li>Swen, age 14.  For additional info on Swen click
<a href="Family.htm#Swe">Swen</a></li>
<li>Gretchen, age 12. For additional info on Gretchen click
<a href="Family.htm#Gre">Gretchen</a></li>
<li> Ferdinand, age 6.For additional info on Ferdinand click
<a href="Family.htm#Fer">Ferdinand</a></li>
</ol>
```

If you have coded correctly, your All About Me homepage should appear as shown in Figure 5-8.

Here, you are still linking to the Family document, but you are linking to a section of the document, depending upon which section you click. For example, if you go to Gretchen, you will see Gretchen's autobiography and so forth. Of course, the links still don't work, even though they should show up underlined in blue boldfaced fonts. But let's remedy that right now.

FIGURE 5-8

The All About Me home page now contains both internal links on the same Web page, and links to other Web pages in the same folder.

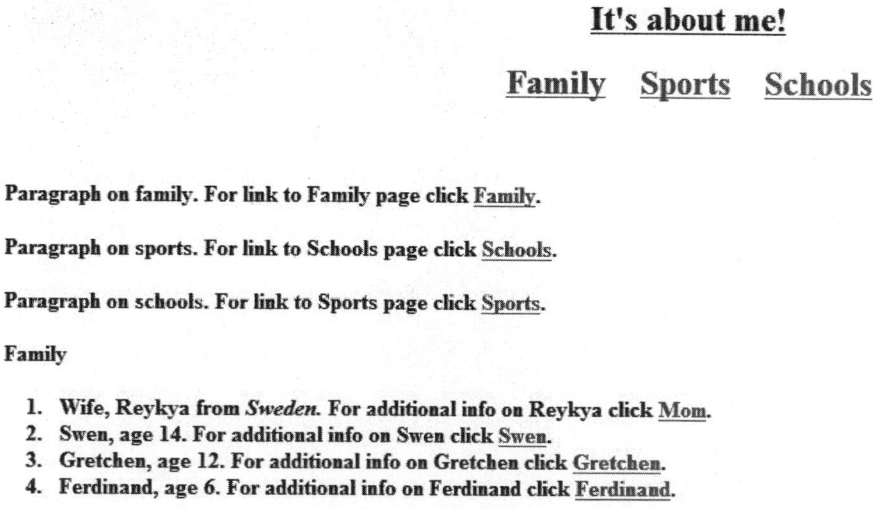

It's about me!

Family **Sports** **Schools**

Paragraph on family. For link to Family page click Family.

Paragraph on sports. For link to Schools page click Schools.

Paragraph on schools. For link to Sports page click Sports.

Family

1. **Wife, Reykya from *Sweden.* For additional info on Reykya click Mom.**
2. **Swen, age 14. For additional info on Swen click Swen.**
3. **Gretchen, age 12. For additional info on Gretchen click Gretchen.**
4. **Ferdinand, age 6. For additional info on Ferdinand click Ferdinand.**

Creating the Family page

At this point, you should be in Notepad. Enter the following generic code, which you will be filling out:

```
<html>
<head>
<title>All About My Family </title>
</head>
<body>
</body>
</html>
```

Don't forget to type in the head section the standard <!-- comments regarding purpose of the page and the creator, you. -->

Save the document as Family.htm. (Don't forget File type should be All Files). Then, bring it up in your browser and take a look at the title bar just to make sure you see the title in there.

You are now finished with the <head>. Let's go to the <body>. Enter the heading for Family, as shown here:

```
<h1 id="sam"></h1>
<p><h2><center><em>Family</em></center></h2></p>
```

Instead of using the deprecated <center></center> tags, you could also use a newer form:

```
<p><h2 align="center"><strong>Family</strong></h2>
```

Note that the first line is the link to the top of the page.

Now, insert the following internal links:

```
<center><a href="#Dad">Dad</a>   <a href="#Mom">Mom</a>
  <a href="#Gre">Gretchen</a>   <a href="#Mag">
Maggie</a>  <a href="#Fer">Ferdinand</a>   
<a href="#Swe">Swen</a></center>
```

Insert two links. One will to return to the home page. It is, surprise, named return to the home page. The other, named Sports, is used to go to the Sports page.

```
<p align="right"><a href="Allaboutme.htm">return to home page</a>
</p><p align="right"><a href="Sports.htm">Sports</a></p>
```

The Sports page, naturally, has two links: one to the Family page and the other is for return to home.

TIP **Make the links plain and simple to understand — both for your users and for you. It is amazingly easy to confuse links when you are coding them based on your memory.**

This next coding is fairly cut and dried. You create the sections that you will link to internally. The most difficult challenge is just remembering the abbreviations you have used and keeping them in order. Enter the following code:

```
<h3 id="Dad">Dad</h3>
<h3 id="Mom">Mom</h3>
<h3 id="Gretchen">Gretchen</h3>
<h3 id="Maggie">Maggie</h3>
<h3 id="Ferdinand">Ferdinand</h3>
<h3 id="Swen">Swen<h3>
```

Now, save your work and take a look at your Family document in your browser. It should look like Figure 5-9.

You can add whatever content you like for the blurbs about the family members. The equivalent coding would similar to that shown in Figure 5-10.

FIGURE 5-9

Your Web page should now include the infrastructure of links for the Family page.

Family

Dad Mom Gretchen Maggie Ferdinand Swen

FIGURE 5-10

In this coding for the infrastructure, notice the use of the definition list (`dl`) to format the appearance of the page.

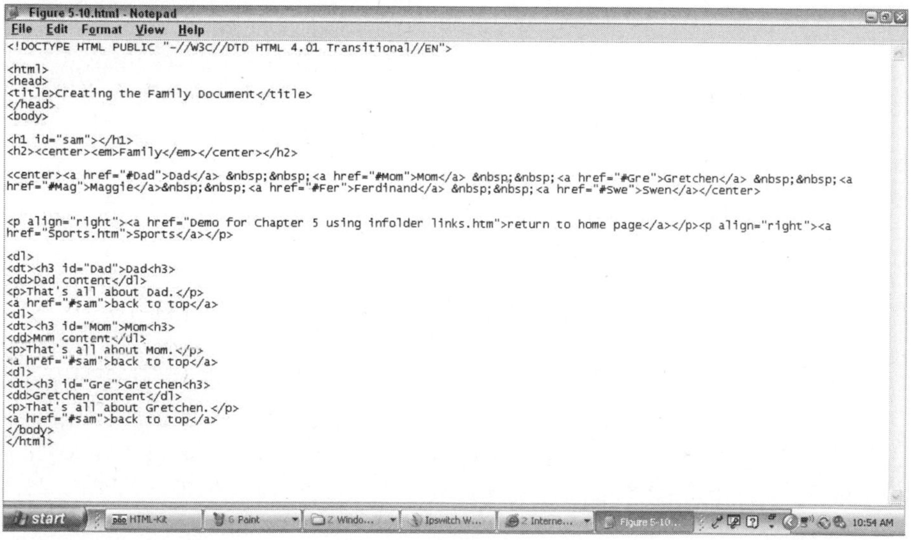

Figure 5-10.html - Notepad

File Edit Format View Help

```
<!DOCTYPE HTML PUBLIC "-//W3C//DTD HTML 4.01 Transitional//EN">

<html>
<head>
<title>Creating the Family Document</title>
</head>
<body>

<h1 id="sam"></h1>
<h2><center><em>Family</em></center></h2>

<center><a href="#Dad">Dad</a>   <a href="#Mom">Mom</a>   <a href="#Gre">Gretchen</a>   <a
href="#Mag">Maggie</a>  <a href="#Fer">Ferdinand</a>   <a href="#Swe">Swen</a></center>


<p align="right"><a href="Demo for Chapter 5 using infolder links.htm">return to home page</a></p><p align="right"><a
href="Sports.htm">Sports</a></p>

<dl>
<dt><h3 id="Dad">Dad<h3>
<dd>Dad content</dl>
<p>That's all about Dad.</p>
<a href="#sam">back to top</a>
<dl>
<dt><h3 id="Mom">Mom<h3>
<dd>Mom content</dl>
<p>That's all about Mom.</p>
<a href="#sam">back to top</a>
<dl>
<dt><h3 id="Gre">Gretchen<h3>
<dd>Gretchen content</dl>
<p>That's all about Gretchen.</p>
<a href="#sam">back to top</a>
</body>
</html>
```

start | HTML-Kit | 6 Paint | 2 Windo... | Ipswitch W... | 2 Interne... | Figure 5-10... | 10:54 AM

As an example of the type of content you might add (as referenced by `Dad content`, `Mom content`, and so on in Figure 5-10), Listing 5-2 shows some sample code for the Family page as it might appear in Figure 5-6.

LISTING 5-2

Example Content for Family Page

```
<dl>
<dt><h3 id="Dad">Dad</h3>
<dd>Dad is 63 and owns a trucking business.  He is very, very, very rich.  He met
Mom, see picture, when she was 16 and working as a clerk at the local PX. He was
a driver in the transport unit.  After he married Mom and got an honorable discharge,
he returned to Bristol but still remained in the driving business, first as a trucker,
then as truck owner, and then as a fleet owner.  About that same time I came along
and then Gretchen.
The 4 of us always go to the Speedway to see the races.  He also especially likes drag
races and sponsors a few cars for the Thunder Valley Show in July every year. You know
one of them: the big flying purple dragon with a yellow belly swooping down with
flames shooting out of its mouth.
Dad loves shooting flames.  Every 4th of July he puts on a fireworks display at our
home that's bigger than anything ever seen in New York, Los Angeles, Houston, and the
first day of the battle of the Somme combined!</dl>
<p>That's all about Dad</p>
<a href="#sam">back to top</a>
<dl>
<dt><h3 id="Mom">Mom</h3>
<dd>Mom must have been a real looker when she was young and walking along the
rocky crags of Smalands' hiking trails in the brief summers. But marriage, having a
few kids and a few decades of working hard side by side with her husband to develop
their truck business have matured her and her spryness is a wistful memory of the
past.  Though she still loves to walk and golf and garden, her joints cause her such
grief that she does not walk much anymore and Dad now affectionately calls her "Hippo
as they get into their golf cart to make the rounds of their private golf course for
their daily exercise.
Her favorite hobbies include doing macrame, organic gardening, cooking and creating
new varieties of linnea borealis.  Her dream one day is to create the first national
flower of Sweden which, sadly, is lacking one.
Every year she makes a trip back to Sweden to visit the graves of her parents and
visit relatives.</dl>
<p>That's all about Mom.</p>
<a href="#sam">back to top</a>
<dl>
<dt><h3 id="Mom">Gretchen</h3>
<dd>Gretchen is a lot like Mom when Mom was her age.  That, at least, is according
to Mom.  Gretchen strongly rejects that, of course.  She hardly has time for us
anymore but spends hours and hours and hours shut in her room on the cell phone. She
```

```
is obsessed with her hair, acne medicines, nail polish, lip gloss, and boys. She is
worried she is too fat and knows the intricacies of every diet ever advertised on the
Food channel.  She is very, very stuck up, and Dad says she has no sense of the
important things in life and shudders to think of the day she will encounter reality.
All of that is true, but she's a good little sis, even though she's a pain in the
rear at times, and I know she'll be turning out just fine (the way Mom did).</dl>
<p>That's all about Gretchen</p>
<a href="#sam">back to top</a>
<dl>
<dt><h3 id="Maggie">Maggie</h3>
<dd>Maggie is our dog.  She is a golden lab and very fat and lazy.  She looks
like one of those blimps for the Macy's Day parade.  She constantly begs for food
and wants to have her belly scratched all the time.  She does not go in water and
hates baths.  Playing fetch can be a solitary activity with her. She does not retrieve
balls or catch Frisbees in fantastic leaps into the air.  She just sits and pants and
smiles affectionately while I retrieve them.  When I walk she will follow.  When I run
she will watch.
She is, however, a good watchdog, and nothing will get past her whatever the size
or shape.</dl>
<p>That's all about Maggie</p>
<a href="#sam">back to top</a>
<dl>
<dt><h3 id="Me">Me</h3>
<dd>I like working on the Internet, and my plan is to be the first American to set
foot upon Mars and claim it for the USA.  My Dad applauds it. He says that's how
the West was won and America became great.  Anyway, I am good at math, but every-
body should be.  It's not easy, but the world is not easy. I am good at math because I
study hard at it and don't complain about the lousy teachers.  They'll always be with
us.  It's part of nature.  Dad says those who can, do; those who can't find an excuse.
He's right.  He's where he is because he never found an excuse.
In addition to being a math tutor and member of the Beta Club I also do track at the
school.  I run in the 400 meter relay.  I'm not the fastest on the squad, but I'm
always there for the practices and I always show up for the meets.  The coach appreci-
ates that. And we win a fair portion.
I'm doing this little family site just to help you design yours and show the use of
links between documents. Don't forget to put your own content in these tags, and your
page should turn out fine.</dl>
<p>Bye.</p>
<a href="#sam">back to top</a>
```

Your internal links should work, as should your link back to your home page.

TIP **Although suggested content can be found on the associated Web site to this book, you can fill your own page up with what you wish between the content tags.**

Creating the Sports and Schools sections

Now, let's add some content to the Sports and Schools sections. The following code is for the Sports and Schools sections:

```
<p id="Spo">Sports</p>
<ul>
<li>Soccer</li>
<li>Bowling </li>
<li>Baseball</li>
<li>Hang Gliding</li>
</ul>

<p id="Sch">School</p>
<ol>
<li>Elementary</li>
<li>Middle</li>
<li>Senior</li>
<li>West Point</li>
<li>London School of Economics</li>
</ol>
```

The links are left for you to complete.

You should now understand the basics of linking to other documents within a site and even to sections within documents. Now comes the real easy stuff: linking on the Web. The format for linking on the Web is real simple:

```
<a href="url">name of url</a>
```

For the All About Me Web site, let's add a section and call it, "Links to Internet sites about us, the Swedes of Sullivan County." You might want to have links to Sullivan County, Sweden, NASCAR, National Flowers, the History of Immigration, the Smithsonian, and the Yahoo! or Google search engines for further information. The section should look as follows

```
<h2>Links to Internet Sites about us, the Swedes of Sullivan
County</h2>
<ul>
<li><a href="http://www.sullivancounty.org">Sullivan County
</a></li>
<li><a href="http://www.sweden.se">Sweden</a></li>
<li><a href="http://www.nascar.com">NASCAR</a></li>
<li><a href="http://www.theflowerexpert.com">National Flowers
</a></li>
<li><a href="http://www.usdoj.gov/ins/">Immigration</a></li>
<li><a href="http://www.si.edu">Smithsonian</a></li>
<li><a href="http://www.yahoo.com">Yahoo Search Engine</a></li>
</ul>
```

Center it, bold it, list it, all as you wish. It's your site!

Absolute and Relative Paths

You may have noticed the emphasis we have put upon saving all documents in the same folder. There are a few reasons for this:

- It makes addressing the links easier.
- It makes portability easier.

However, as the sight grows, having all files in one folder can become unwieldy. So, as the site grows, it may make more sense to have multiple folders within the one big Web site folder.

In the world of links, there are (broadly speaking) two classes of links:

- *Absolute* — Absolute links provide the exact address of the location, the URL, which would include the domain and the root directory as part of its path.
- *Relative* — Relative links provide the location of a file in relation to its position with another (reference) file.

These days, my family and I travel often, and have the sour joke that our home is our suitcase. We normally stay at a hotel on Technology Parkway in Norcross, Georgia. We have stayed there so often that we know that hotel as if it were our own home. And the clerk will give us a room key with the room number, say, 101. And the location of that room is straight down the hall, almost to the exit, last room on the left.

Now, that is good knowledge. That is exact knowledge, and boy we don't waste a moment in finding the room. But that exact knowledge is of limited utility. We cannot transfer that mind map to any other hotel with assurance it will be accurate. In other words, it is not portable.

The first time we went to that hotel, we only knew the rooms relatively — relative to the lobby, relative to the swimming pool, or relative to the elevators.

And we find that this relative knowledge is more important to us than the absolute knowledge. With that relative structure, we can find our way to any room in another hotel relative to the elevator, or pool, or lobby.

If we were to take the hotel as a relative tree structure, and we were standing in the first floor lobby as our working directory, it might be coded something like this:

```
<A href="/FrontDesk/Room 115"> The room is on the same floor as the
lobby</a>

<a href="./FrontDesk/Room 214"> The room is up one floor relative to
the lobby but still in the same wing</a>
```

FIGURE 5-11

An absolute path to "a's Pictures" in the directory tree would be: D:\Documents and Settings/a/a's Pictures/. The relative version from a would be ../a/a's Pictures/.

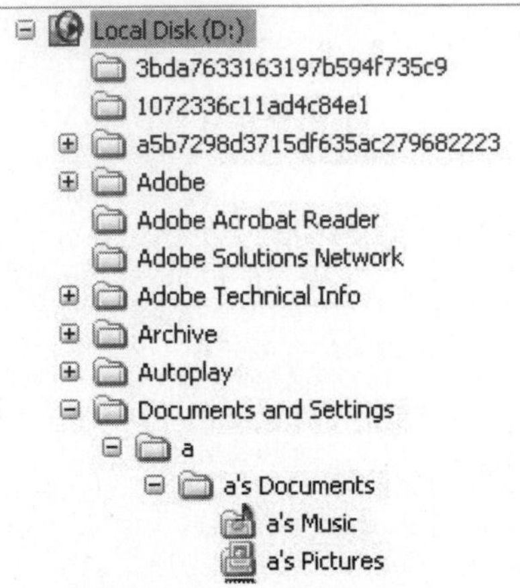

Both locations are encapsulated within the hotel, which, if we were to continue the analogy further, could be considered the root directory of the previous structure.

```
<a href="../Room 214W">The room is in the other wing relative to the
lobby but still in the same hotel</a>
```

A path is relative to its working directory (that is, the present location of where you are in a file system), while an absolute path does not change irrespective of which directory you are in. It normally points to the root directory. If you move the files, the root directory changes and the URLs are, absolutely speaking, no longer valid. However, if a file is two levels up relative to one file, or one level up relative to another, that will always be true (unless the whole directory structure is changed), even when you move to a different computer.

Paths are used extensively in computer science to represent the directory/file relationships common in modern operating systems, and are essential in the construction of URLs.

Look at Figure 5-11 for examples of relative and absolute directory structures.

Locking relative URLs with the BASE element

You can use the `BASE` element to force all links on a page to use the same domain name. For example, say that you wanted to create a page with links to your favorite books on the John Wiley & Sons Web site. Because all of the links on this page would be coded with the same starting part of the URL (`www.wiley.com`), putting that part of the URL in the `BASE` element could potentially save a lot of time when coding the page, as shown in the following code:

```
<HTML>
<HEAD>
<TITLE>My Web Page</TITLE>
<BASE href="http://www.yohansoldebookshoppe.com">
</HEAD>
<BODY>
<P>Yohan's Olde Bookshoppe has many great books. Here's some links to
my favorites:</P>
<P><A href="/burpee/burpee_index.html">Burpee</A> is the how-to
resource, from seeds to salads<BR>
<A href="/look&learn/index.html">Deke McClelland's Look and Learn
</A> series cuts to the chase to get you up and running quickly on a
new design application.<BR>
<A href="/bc/bc_index.html">Betty Crocker</A> is America's most
trusted name in the kitchen. This series includes cookbooks from
family classics to fine dining.</P>
<P><A href="http://www.mywebsite.com/index.html">Return to my
home page</A></P>
</BODY>
</HTML>
```

Notice that instead of typing `http://www.yohansoldebookshoppe.com` at the beginning of each link, only the folder and file names have been coded, as if these were relative links to pages within a specific Web site. Then, to override the `BASE` element, the entire URL (`http://www.mywebsite.com`) is included when linking to the home page because the domain was different than that listed in the `BASE` element.

Previous and Next Links

You may notice that there are a couple of ways to navigate a Web site. One is sequential, and one is through targeted searches such as what is used for drilling down to get the nuggets of data you are looking for. Sometimes the latter can seem rather random. To navigate sequentially through a Web site, you can use the *previous* and *next* arrows in the navigation bar of your browser. It's a fairly failsafe technique to get back, eventually, to the page you didn't realize you needed until a couple of clicks later.

You can also set up a *Previous/Next* link on your Web site for going from the beginning to the end in sequence, or somewhere in between, and it's really fairly simple to do.

Let's look at the Torah, more commonly known as Genesis, Exodus, Leviticus, Numbers, and Deuteronomy. The code to create a previous next link between Exodus and Genesis on the one side, and Exodus and Leviticus on the other, would be:

```
<p style= "text-align:center">
<a href= "Genesis.htm"> <img src= "prev.jpg" alt= "Previous Book" />
```

```
</a>
<img src ="Exodus.jpg" alt= "Exodus.jpg" />
<a href = "Leviticus.htm"> <img src = "next.jpg" alt = "Next
Book" /> </a>
</p>
```

The result is as shown in the `prevnext.tif` file in the `Chapter 5` folder.

This code can be replicated for each of the books of the Bible by simply substituting the names of the Scriptural works as you go back and forth.

External Links

As you have seen, links to other sections of the page, to other local documents, and even to other Web sites are added with the `<A></A>` (anchor) elements, as in the following example:

```
<A href="http://www.yahoo.com">Visit Yahoo!</A>
```

As with other container tags, you surround the content you wish use as a link with opening and closing `<A>` tags. As you have seen, the `href` attribute gives the specific location of whatever you are linking to. So, in the preceding example, the value of the `href` attribute tells the browser to link the words *Visit Yahoo!* to the Web site `http://www.yahoo.com`. As discussed earlier in this chapter, this is accomplished using an absolute URL.

A relative link back to Yahoo!'s home page from within the Yahoo! site might look like this:

```
<A href="index.html">Visit the Yahoo! home page</A>
```

By default, the user's cursor changes to a hand when it is moved over a link. This helps the user identify content that is clickable. For this reason, it is important to carefully select what is actually displayed as a link. Avoid using "Click Here" to label links (often referred to as the "Click Here syndrome," which is a common problem on Web sites). In addition, all the links should be pulled out into a brief list, except for ones in the text of the site.

To avoid confusing link errors, give yourself a few seconds to quickly scan your Web page. If you can't pick out the links and identify what they link to within a few seconds, you may need to rethink those link labels. A few simple changes can go a long way toward making the page, and the site as a whole much easier to navigate.

Getting hypertext references right

One of the biggest challenges in coding links lies in getting the hypertext references right. This means you must specify the appropriate path within the directory structure to properly link to a file.

FIGURE 5-12

This sample directory structure helps explain how to properly code hypertext references.

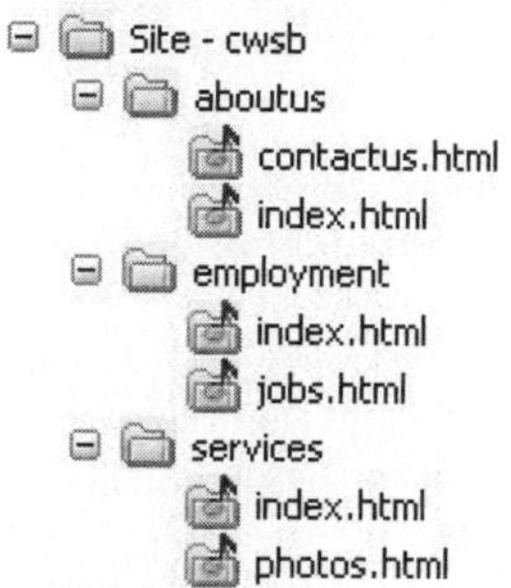

The directory structure shown in Figure 5-12 includes three folders, each containing two files. If you were coding a link on the page entitled `jobs.html` (located in the `employment` folder) that was supposed to take users to the Contact Us page, can you imagine what the hypertext reference would look like? Here's an example:

```
<A href ="../aboutus/contactus.html">Contact Us</A>
```

When moving around a Web site, you must tell the browser when to move up and down in the directory structure. Prefacing a folder or filename with `../` tells the browser to move back (or up) one level within the directory structure. If you leave off the `../` in the previous code example, and simply code the hypertext reference as `href="aboutus/contactus.html"`, the browser would have looked for a folder called `aboutus` within the `employment` folder. So, when a user clicks the reference, the link appears to be broken.

TIP **Many servers are also set up to recognize a single slash (/) as a shortcut back to the root level, or top directory. This can make coding the same thing on multiple pages of your site (such as a navigation bar) much easier because all the hypertext references can be the same, regardless of where the page lies within the directory structure. If you are unsure as to whether your server is set up to do this, contact your server's administrator or your hosting provider.**

Creating internal links with local anchors

So far in this chapter, you've only created internal links within a single page. What happens when you want to link to a specific section of a different page? As with links on the same page shown earlier in this chapter, you must first know the exact name of that section. Then, you add a hash mark and that section name after the page name in the `href` attribute of your <A> tag, as shown here:

```
<A href="shoes.html#size9">View our size 9 shoes</A>
```

This tells the browser to first look for the page called `shoes.html`, and then navigate to a section named "`size9`" on that page.

Sending e-mail with mailto links

While the majority of links you create will take users to other Web pages, you might also want to allow visitors to quickly access your e-mail address. To do so, preface your e-mail address with `mailto:`, as shown in the following example:

```
<A href="mailto:name@emailaddress.com">Email Me!</A>
```

When a visitor clicks a `mailto` link, a new e-mail message will be created with the specified e-mail address, in this case "`name@emailaddress.com`", in the `To:` field. Note that in order for your `mailto:` link to work, your visitors must have an e-mail program available on their systems.

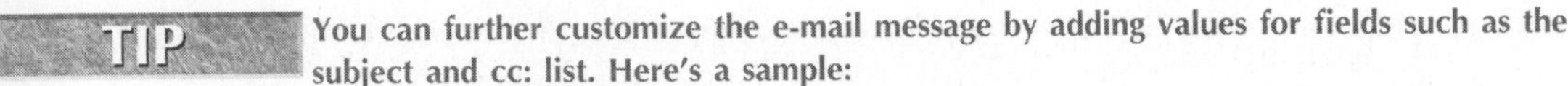

You can further customize the e-mail message by adding values for fields such as the subject and cc: list. Here's a sample:

<A href="mailto:name@emailaddress.com? Subject=Hello!&cc=anothername@emailaddress.com">Email Me!</A>.

Note that an ampersand (&) separates parameters of the `mailto:` link if you're defining more than one.

Other types of links

In some cases, it might be necessary to link to other types of information, such as downloadable files or newsgroup articles. When doing so, you continue to use the <A> tag and `href` attribute, but you change the value of the attribute accordingly, as shown in Table 5-1.

In order for links to newsgroups or news articles to work, users must have a browser and Internet connection capable of accessing newsgroups.

TABLE 5-1

Other Types of Links

Link Type	href Value	Sample Code
Downloadable file on an FTP site	`ftp://sitename.com/filename.pdf`	`<A href="ftp://sitename.com/filename.pdf"> Download from FTP site</A>`
Newsgroup	`news://group.name`	`<A href="news://alt.html">Visit the HTML newsgroup</A>`
Specific newsgroup article	`news://12345.67890@news.com`	`<A href="news://12345.67890@news.com">View this news article</A>`

Linking via images

Linking via images is the same as linking via Web address. The difference is that you click on an image. You make an image a link by embedding the reference to it inside the anchor tags.

The format for a source anchor is as follows:

```
<a href="destination id">name of link<</a> as in <A href="PDC
Resume.html#OBJ">Objective</A>
```

The format for making an image the link is as follows:

```
<a href="destination id"><img src="location of image"></a>
```

The following code would change "Objective" from the text link shown in the top of Figure 5-13 to the picture link shown in the bottom of the figure.

```
<A href="PDC_Resume.html#OBJ"><IMG src="PDC_Resume_files/
beachthumb.jpg"></A>
```

You can also add a little comment to the image so that its function will be clear to users when they slide their cursors over the link. This is done as follows:

```
<A href="PDC_Resume.html#OBJ" title="Click on this to get to the
Objective on the Web page><IMG src="PDC_Resume_files/beachthumb.
jpg"></A>
```

This produces the effect shown in Figure 5-14.

FIGURE 5-13

Objective is changed to an image link.

Objective · Experience · Education · Skills · Associations · Memberships · Personal · World Travels

· Experience · Education · Skills · Associations · Memberships · Personal · World Travels ·

FIGURE 5-14

You can add a popup comment to an image link.

John Xertetes

A.A.,B.A.,M.A.,M.S.,CCNA

314 Pie Circle Lane Syracuse, PI 12358 US · johnxertetes@pop.eye Cell Phone: (828) 555-5555
Office Phone: (540) 555-5555 Residence Phone: (828) 555-5555

Linking via Image Maps

Hotspots are transparent to the user. This means that they are so simple and convenient to use that the user does not spend a moment regarding the amazing complexity of that click.

A hotspot is a link. It has a URL. You cannot see the link until you pass the cursor over it. At that point, the shape of the cursor switches from an arrow icon to a hand icon.

Hotspots are a convenient way to link to several different sites from a single image. An example would be a map of the United States where a person could click on a state and be linked to that state, or a picture of the solar system and person could click on a planet, such as Saturn, and be whisked to Saturn. But how can a picture of the solar system *know* which planet to send you to?

It doesn't. The image overlays a grid, just like a spreadsheet made of pixels, and each of these pixels has a specific *x,y* location on the grid. You select certain locations on the grid and associate them with a URL you wish to link to and, voila, you are sent there.

Here is the coding to get to the planet Saturn from the image of the Solar System:

```
<!-- Beginning of Client Side Image Map -->
<img src="My Pictures/CWSB graphics/Chapter5/155035main_solar-system-
montage-browse.jpg" USEMAP="#Solar System" BORDER=0>
<map name="Solar System">
  <area shape="rect" coords="256,99,493,149" href=http://images.
google.com/imgres?imgurl=http://solarsystem.nasa.gov/planets/images"
alt="Satrun">
</map>
<!-- End of Client Side Image Map -->
</body>
</html>
```

The #is used to specify the location of the map within the Web page. Otherwise, if the map were located in a different Web page, you would use the format of `usemap="file"` to link to the map being used.

It might look a tad intimidating, but it's mostly because the addresses are long. The coding consists of the following tags and attributes.

First are the comments:

```
<!-- Beginning of Client Side Image Map -->
```

These explain what this section of the HTML is doing. In this instance, you could perhaps add what the map is about and what links you might be setting up in the map.

The second line consists of an inline element, IMG, with three attributes, src, usemap, and border:

```
<img src=" " USEMAP=" " BORDER>
```

Earlier in this chapter, you used the <img> tag to make an inline image into an image link. This time, the code manipulates the characteristics of an image of the solar system. The code gives it a BORDER value of 0 (zero). In other words, the image does not have a border (but you can add one if you wish by putting in a numerical value, such as BORDER ="5"). More importantly, you are associating the solar system image to a map. In this case, the map is called Solar System, and you are telling the program to apply (or use) the map (hence USEMAP) Solar System with the image at the following location:

```
My Pictures/CWSB graphics/Chapter5/155035main_solar-system-
montage-browse.jpg
```

Thus, the completed second line of code appears as follows:

```
<img src="My Pictures/CWSB graphics/Chapter5/155035main_solar-system-
montage-browse.jpg" USEMAP="#Solar System" BORDER=0>
```

Now, immediately below the img src tag is the set of <map></map> tags. This is where you define the links you will be using for different areas in the map, Solar System.htm. Notice that three separate areas are defined for the map, and each of these areas has a different shape attribute. The hotspot for Saturn is rectangular (rect), the hotspot for Jupiter is circular (circle), and the hotspot for the Martian North Pole is an irregular polygon (poly). You will further see that within each area is the hypertext reference to the destination link of the hotspot. For Saturn, this would be http://solarsystem.nasa.gov/planets/images/Saturn. So, the <map></map>tags surround the following lines of code:

```
<map name="Solar System.htm ">
  <area shape="rect" coords="256,99,493,149" href="http:
//solarsystem.nasa.gov/planets/images/Saturn"    alt=Saturn>
<area shape="circle" coords="311,263,29" href="http://Jupiter.com"
alt="Jupiter">
  <area shape="poly" coords="185,275,198,298,212,291,190,274"
href="http://www.mars.com" alt="Martian North Pole">
</map>
```

As you can see, creating an image map involves the following steps:

1. Select an image and reference it using the <img src> tag.
2. Create the map you will use for the image.
3. Associate the two by putting the name of the map in the usemap attribute of the <img> tag.

There are a couple of other points you might want to keep in mind:

- Don't try to figure out the positions of the coordinates yourself. It will drive you batty.
- Use any of several freeware and/or shareware products available. For the illustration provided here, we used CoffeeCup Image Mapper and found it more than satisfactory — it is quite easy to use and provides quick results.

Remember that you can also use the `title` attribute in an image map, with which you can advise the user of the destination of the hotspot.

You may also use the `target` attribute, which gives you the option of having a link appear in a secondary window, rather than replacing the image you clicked on. To use this attribute, simply include `target` in the list of attributes in the anchor tags. Figure 5-15 shows the result of using the `target` attribute in the following code:

```
<p>Paragraph on family. For link to Family page click
<a href="FamilyLinkDemo.htm"
target="_blank" title="This is an illustration of a popup">Family
</a></p>
```

FIGURE 5-15

This is an illustration of using the `target` attribute to bring up a link in a second window.

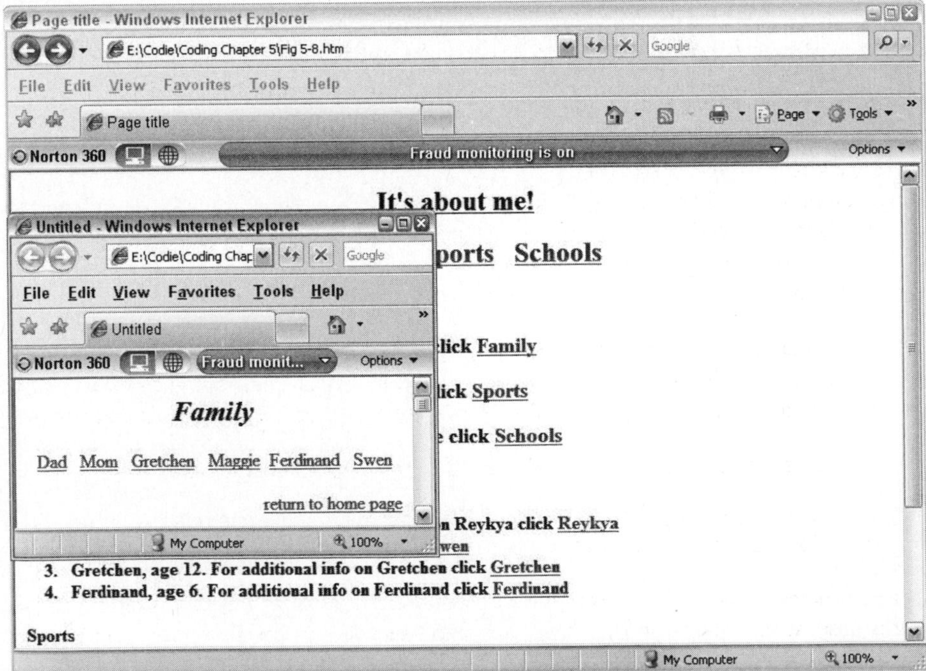

Storyboarding

Unfortunately, there are no hard-and-fast rules regarding development of the structure of the site. You might be tempted to develop links on the fly as you add and/or delete pages from the site — and succeed. But most likely, you won't, and you will spend long, exasperating hours tweaking it until the site somehow falls into place. (But you don't quite know how, and are too flummoxed to quite figure it out.) Then, when the time comes for the next modification, you are just a little reluctant to start making those changes — and only you know why.

There are always tradeoffs, but the general guidelines for links would be that you want to access a Web page within a site using as few *hops* as possible. (Remember, as mentioned previously, a hop is the distance traveled between any two points. If you were crossing a stream and you had to jump from one rock to another and then to another before reaching the bank on the far side, then that took you three hops.)

The smaller the number of pages, the fewer the links required to reach any one. The simplest type of linking is *linear*, where, for example, you might have three documents: A, B, and C. Document A would contain a link to Document B, Document B would contain a link to Document A and Document C, and Document C would contain a link to Document B. With three documents, the maximum hop to any single document is two, the maximum links in any single document is two, and total number of links on the site is four.

You cannot access Document C directly from Document A, and vice versa. It is, of course, possible to do so by adding another link to both Documents A and C, which would result in the number of links becoming six. It doesn't sound like much, but the tradeoff to increase efficiency to make all links a single hop has been a 50 percent increase in links.

Go back to the Web site you created earlier in this chapter. You have links from the home page to the child page Family, as well as to the child page Sports. Family has a link to the sibling page Sport, and to the parent page All About Me. Sport has a link to sibling page Family, and to the home page, All About me. Therefore, they are all linked to one another, and no page is more than one hop away from any other page.

Now, if you add the third page, School, to the existing links, and you require that it, too, be only a click away from any of its sibling sites and its parent site, how many links must each page have? Where would you put the links? Would it be top, bottom, or in a side column?

Here is an example of the coding for just one page for just three links:

```
<p align="right"><a href="Allaboutme.htm">return to home page</a>
</p><p align="right"><a href="Sports.htm">Sports</a></p>
```

If you increase that to five links, you can see where it is on its way to becoming clunky. And, by this time, with 5 pages and 20 links, you will waste lots of precious time tracking down where your links don't work as expected.

Now, let's bump up the number of linked linear pages up to 10. In the straight linear structure, the beginning and ending documents (Documents A and J, respectively) would have a single link, and every intervening document would have two links pointing to the previous and next Web page for a total number of links on the site of 18. The number of hops required to go from Document A to Document J is 9, though it is still only a single hop between any two adjacent Web pages. This is an obviously inefficient structure, time-consuming, and a great turnoff to any visitors to the site.

If you were to set up direct links to all pages as in the first example, each page would be required to have nine links and there would be almost a fivefold increase in the total number of links required! Not only would this situation be time-consuming to set up, even with the tools available today, it would not be particularly useful to the casual user, even though there is now a direct link to every page on the site.

Web sites with multiple pages typically do not use the linear structure just described — for the reasons just described:

- It is time-consuming to design.
- It is mind numbingly redundant.
- It is not actually all that user-friendly.

It is like having a single meal of all offerings on a menu. It would be overkill.

Sitting down and sketching out your site links (sometimes referred to as *storyboarding*) is a critical skill of practiced and successful Web designers.

Storyboarding allows you to determine the most efficient structure for your Web site links. You could take a baker's dozen and arrange them in a hierarchical structure so that no page would be more than two clicks away from the home page, and any page no more than two clicks away from any sibling page, as shown in Figures 5-16 and 5-17.

Let's go back to the John Xertetes site and look at the list of links spread across the top of the page. If we were to use the links as a linear structure from Objective through to World Travels, we would need to traverse seven links to reach the final page, World Travels. The coding would be the same as that used for the example of linking Genesis through Deuteronomy. What would change would simply be the link name of the present, previous, and next links. Similar to that example, you could only click through the previous/next links one Web page at a time to get to the beginning and ending pages.

FIGURE 5-16

In this example of links in linear structure, you must traverse 12 links to get from first to last page.

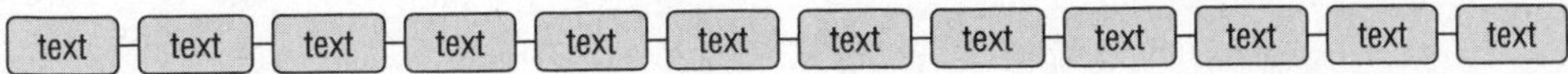

FIGURE 5-17

In this example of hierarchical links, notice you are no more than two links away from any page on the site.

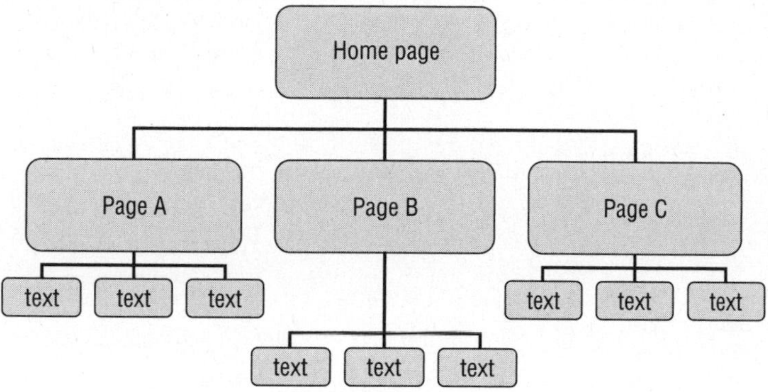


```
<p style="text-align: center">
   <a href="Objective.htm"><img src="prev.jpg" alt="Objective link"
style="border-width: 0" /></a>
   <img src="Experience.htm" alt="Experience" />
   <a href="Education.htm"><img src="next.jpg" alt="Experience link"
style="border-width: 0" /></a>
   <a href="Experience.htm"><img src="prev.jpg" alt="Experience
link" style="border-width: 0" /></a>
   <img src="Education.htm" alt="Education" />
   <a href="Skills.htm"><img src="next.jpg" alt="Skills" style=
"border-width: 0" /></a>
   <a href="Education.htm"><img src="prev.jpg" alt="Education link"
style="border-width: 0" /></a>
   <img src="Skills.htm" alt="Skills" />
   <a href="Associations.htm"><img src="next.jpg" alt="Associations
link" style="border-width: 0" /></a>
   <a href="Skills.htm"><img src="prev.jpg" alt="Skills link" style
="border-width: 0" /></a>
   <img src="Associatons.htm" alt="Associations" />
   <a href="Memberships.htm"><img src="next.jpg" alt="Memberships
links" style="border-width: 0" /></a>
   <a href="Associations.htm"><img src="prev.jpg" alt="Associations
link" style="border-width: 0" /></a>
   <img src="Memberships.htm" alt="Memberships" />
   <a href="Personal.htm"><img src="next.jpg" alt="Personal link"
style="border-width: 0" /></a>
   <a href="Memberships.htm"><img src="prev.jpg" alt="Memberships
link" style="border-width: 0" /></a>
   <img src="Personal.htm" alt="Personal" />
```

```
    <a href="World Travel.htm"><img src="next.jpg" alt="World Travel
link" style="border-width: 0" /></a>
<p style="text-align: center">
    <a href="Personal.htm"><img src="prev.jpg" alt="Personal link"
style="border-width: 0" /></a>
    <img src="World_Travel.htm" alt="World Travel" />
</p>
```

Links Quick Reference

The following provides a quick reference for key items discussed in this chapter:

- `<a> </a>` — These tags are used to create links.
- `<href>` — This attribute is used to point to location of hypertext document, or a link to a section in a page.
- # — The hash mark points to a segment of a page (also known as fragment identifier).
- `id` — Used to add a unique identification to an element. This attribute is used to point to the destination link.
- / — The forward slash delineates paths in a linking address.
- `<BASE>` — This allows you to access links even though directory structure has been moved.
- `<img src>` — This is an empty tag that is used to reference the location of images.
- `target` — This attribute references a window.
- `<map> </map>` — This defines an image map.
- `area` — This attribute is used to define the area of each hotlink on a map grid.
- `shape` — This attribute is used to define the structure of the hotspot as a rectangle, circle, or polygon.

Summary

In this chapter, you learned that to link a source with a destination is a two-step process. The first step is to create the destination of the link, called a destination anchor. The second step is to create a source anchor, the link to the destination, which, when clicked, will bring you to the destination. You also learned that it is not a good idea to try to use block elements within anchor tags. The discussion showed you how to navigate to the top of a long document, and showed you how to change default colors on links.

You learned that you may link to another document in your Web site by just using the URL reference, or that you could link to a specific section of an associated document. You developed your own Web site and created within it internal links, in-folder links, and then, within those, even more in-folder links.

This chapter showed how to use external links to reach the Internet, to set up an e-mail link and to contact usenet groups. You also learned how to link via images and how to create an image with hotspots. Hotspots are links under gridding-specific locations on a map. You learned how to use the MAP element and various attributes to define the hotspots.

And finally, you learned that storyboarding is the process of designing your links before you begin physically coding. Storyboarding allows you to consider several ways of linking your site to allow you to develop the most efficient linking structure based upon the purpose of your Web site. The goal of storyboarding is to provide a design that is both thorough and efficient.

Chapter 6 takes a look at using colors and backgrounds to enhance your Web pages.

Chapter 6

The Elements of Color and Images in Web Pages

Color is your most powerful tool when you create your Web site. How you use color in your Web site determines one of two outcomes:

- Visitors will come back to your Web site and perhaps comment on what a nice Web site you have.
- Your Web site will become the object of education in what not to do.

This chapter discusses not only how to set color attributes in HTML and CSS but, also the proper use of color so that you can avoid the second outcome. This discussion not only includes information about how to select background, text, and graphic colors to give your site's pages the greatest impact for visitors, but also how to select colors. While we cannot guarantee exact color matches across screen types, we can try to get as close as possible.

Setting Color Attributes

When you start your Web browser for the first time, the browser has default settings for how certain elements on a page (such as links, text, headers, and so on) will appear on the screen. However, you can customize the colors on the screen in Internet Explorer (IE), FireFox, and practically any other browser, no matter what computer or operating system you run.

Major browsers in computing today are Microsoft Internet Explorer, Firefox, Gecko, Safari, and Konqueror. Other top browsers would include Opera and America Online. No matter what computer and operating system you use, chances are that you will be using one or more of these two major types of browsers. So, this chapter discusses color issues that apply to these two classes of browsers. If you use another browser, check your browser's documentation for specific color support information.

Changing color settings

In IE, you can access color settings by following these steps:

1. Click the Tools option in the Internet Explorer menu bar. In Internet Explorer 7, press the Alt key to make the menu bar appear.
2. Click Internet Options in the Tools drop-down menu.
3. On the General tab of the Internet Options window, click the Colors button in the lower-left-hand portion of the window.
4. The Colors dialog box appears, as shown in Figure 6-1.

When the Colors dialog box appears, you will notice that there are two separate control areas: Colors and Links. The Colors area enables you to change the text (or foreground) color and the background color. The Links area lets you change the color of links. When you click OK in the Colors dialog box, IE reflects the changes on the page you're viewing, provided that the page does not have defined colors. If the reflected changes aren't what you're looking for, you can click the Colors button in the Internet Option's window's General tab again.

FIGURE 6-1

This is the Colors dialog box, where you customize colors in IE.

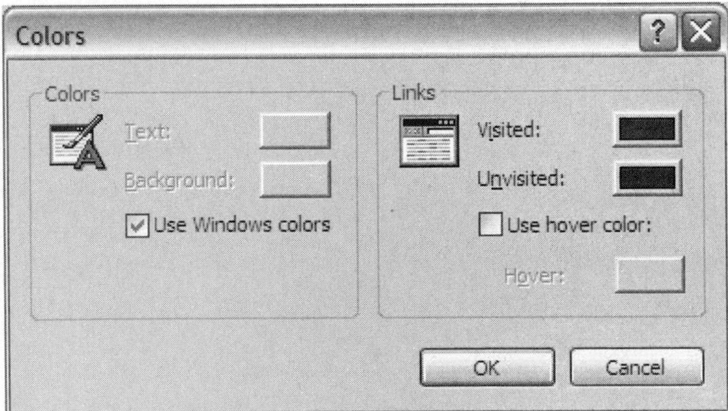

Setting background colors

The *background color* is the color that appears in the viewing area of your browser window. The background color does not apply if the Web page you are viewing has a specific background color that it displays, but if there is no specified background color on a Web page, then the background color you see will be the one you select in the Colors dialog box.

The default text and background color settings are the same as those in Windows. If you want to have a different background setting for IE, click the "Use Windows colors" check box to deselect it, and then click the color button to the right of the Background label. As Figure 6-2 shows, the Color dialog box appears, and selecting colors from this dialog box is the same as selecting a color in Windows. Select a color from the Basic Colors sample color display (called a *swatch*), or create your own custom color by clicking the Define Custom Colors button.

NOTE **You should probably not change any of the default settings for color. Many sites will override the settings. Therefore, your settings may not always "work," since site designers may override their settings when visiting a particular site. Finally, as a site developer, your browser settings won't affect anyone other than yourself.**

FIGURE 6-2

Select a basic background color in the Color dialog boxes.

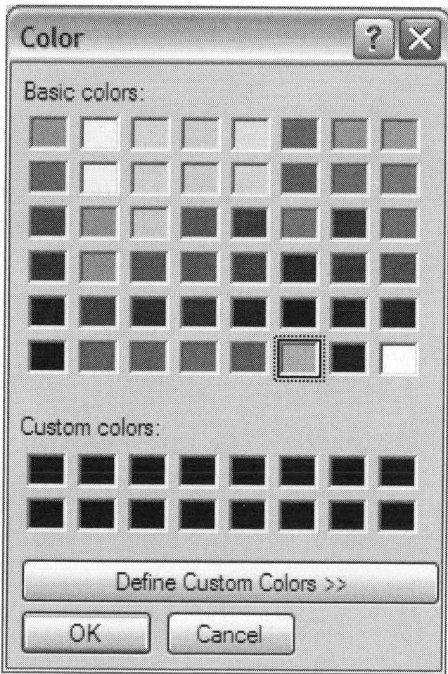

Specifying foreground colors

Specifying a *foreground* (or *text*) color in Internet Explorer is as easy as selecting the background color. You can choose a foreground color by clicking the color to the right of the Text label. The Color dialog box will appear, as shown in Figure 6-2, and you can select a color from the Basic Colors swatch, or create your own custom color.

Changing link colors for your browser

Internet Explorer can change the color of three types of text links that appear on the page: visited, unvisited, and active.

Links you have already visited reflect the Visited color that appears after the Visited label in the Links area. You can change the color, just as you can with the background and foreground colors.

Links you have not visited before reflect the Unvisited color that appears after the Unvisited: label in the Links area shown in Figure 6-1. You can change the color, just as you can with the background and foreground colors.

A link reflects the hover color when you move the mouse pointer over a link before you click it. The default setting in Internet Explorer is no hover color at all. If you want a hover color, click the "Use hover color" check box, and then click the color to the right of the Hover label, as shown in Figure 6-3. You can change the hover color, just as you can with the background and foreground colors.

FIGURE 6-3

The Hover color becomes available when you click the "Use hover color" check box.

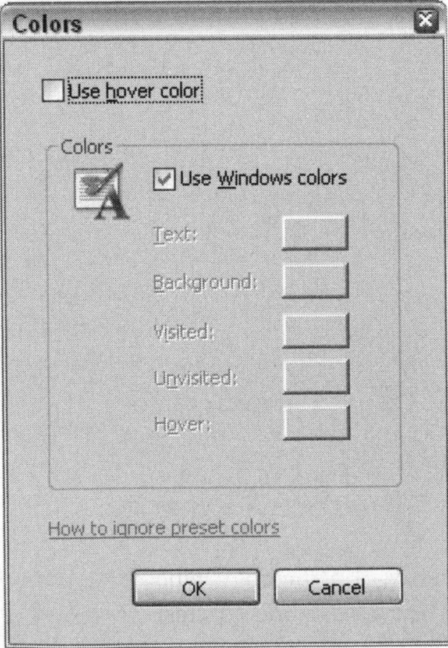

Using the Three C's: Complement, Contrast, and Coordination

How do you use color effectively? Effective color usage begins with the three C's of color management:

- *Complementary* colors are pleasing to look at.
- *Contrasting* colors make your elements stand out, not wash out.
- *Coordinating* colors throughout all the parts of your pages and site make your work look like a whole unit, not several different elements or pages jumbled together.

Planning for color should be one of the first things you do when planning your Web site. By keeping the three C's in mind, you will be able to create a site that's inviting, consistent, and memorable.

Choosing complementary colors

The World Wide Web is a semi-static medium. The Web is semi-static because you can add motion and other dynamic elements to your Web pages. However, most elements on a Web page are stationary, much like a page you read in a magazine or an image you view on a billboard.

CROSS-REF See Chapter 13 for more information about adding dynamic page elements.

If you've read any magazines or seen any billboards on the highway recently, the ads that probably caught your eye (though hopefully not for too long in the billboard case) were the ones that had good complementary color. That is, the colors look like they go well together, so the ad is pleasing to look at.

The same concept of complementary colors also applies to Web pages. If you have colors for your background, graphics, and text that go well together, your page will be not only be more readable, but also more pleasing to look at. The more pleasing your Web page is to look at, the more visitors (and more returning visitors) your page will receive.

But what are complementary colors, exactly? To illustrate the principle, take a look at Figure 6-4. Even though this book is in black and white, you can view the figure in full color on the accompanying Web site (`http://wiley.com/go/creatingwebsites`).

In the strictest sense, *complementary colors* are two colors that are opposite each other on the color wheel (a tool long used by traditional artists), as shown in Figure 6-4.

Analogous colors are ones that are right beside one another on the color wheel. Blue and blue-green, for example, are analogous to one another. In addition to the strictest definition of complementary colors, you can also consider any colors that are analogous to a complementary color as complementary. Complementary colors are those directly opposite each other on the color wheel. For example, orange is complementary to blue. The analogous colors for blue are blue-green and blue-violet, so both of those colors would also work well as complements to orange.

FIGURE 6-4

The color wheel is a basic artist's tool.

This color model provides basic information about how to use color on your pages, but it does not guarantee that different colors (or the colors in your background and text) will appear correctly. For that to happen, you must have the right color contrast.

Ensuring contrast and visibility

Complementary colors are also called *contrast colors* because they let the lighter colors stand out more against the darker colors. The most familiar contrasting colors are black and white. Books are printed with black ink on white (or light-colored) pages because that's easy to read. The same is true for the Web; it's much easier to see black text on a white background or, for example, on light gray wallpaper that you use as a background graphic.

If you try to read white text on a black background, you can't read the text as well. Black tends to mask the outer boundaries of the white text, and if you see any sites with black backgrounds, the text is usually in boldface to make the text easier to read. Some sites, such as the TrekWeb site (`www.trekweb.com`), use blue fields as the background to make the white text stand out even better.

If you have a *triad* or *split* complementary color scheme, the same contrast rules apply. For example, a triad color combination that has a background of red and green with blue text makes the text difficult to read. If you change the red to yellow, then the blue text stands out from the green-and-yellow background, so you can read the text more easily.

Coordinating color schemes

Coordination of your Web site's color schemes goes hand in hand with planning your Web site. (Refer to Chapters 1 and 4 if you need to brush up on planning your Web site.) Now that you have a firm grounding of how to complement and contrast colors on your site, it's time to coordinate how those colors will appear on your screen.

The audience for whom you are developing the Web site must determine your color schemes. For example, if your site is designed for seniors, then it may be a good idea to have a high-contrast color scheme (such as black text on a white background). If your site is designed for children, then having less contrast and more colors may be the best approach.

Understanding color warmth

If you want your site to be memorable, you must use color to create an emotional impact for your audience. Your visitors will come back to your site and encourage others to visit your site as well. You can manipulate colors by changing their values, thus producing strong, flamboyant colors or softer colors.

The color wheel shown in Figure 6-4 contains so-called warm and cool colors. *Warm colors* consist of red hues, from yellow to purple. Warm colors exude energy, so they stand out from the cool colors. These warm colors are best used as foreground colors.

Cool colors, on the other hand, consist of blue hues, from green to dark blue. Cool colors exude strength and calm. These colors are best used for the background so that the warm colors can stand out and do their work.

Although contrasting warm colors with cool colors is a good general rule, some colors contrast better than others. For example, if you use light blue and orange together, they won't contrast well because both colors are light. If you change the blue to a dark blue, or if you change the orange to black or brown, the colors will contrast much better, and visitors will have a much easier time viewing your page.

If you want more information about color theory, check out some of the Web sites in Table 6-1.

TABLE 6-1

Color Information

Web Site	URL
The 16,777,216 Colors of the Web	`the-light.com/16m/16m.html`
Web Color Reference	`webreference.com/html/reference/color`

Using Color Names and Hex Numbers

When a monitor displays colors on the screen, it uses the three primary colors of light: red, green, and blue (RGB). The monitor takes different amounts of each color, combines them, and projects them onto an area of the screen called a *pixel, which stands for "picture element."* If a pixel must be white, then the monitor displays 100 percent of the red, green, and blue light in that pixel. If a pixel must be black, then the monitor displays zero percent of the red, green, and blue light in that pixel.

HTML manages these RGB color combinations by using *hexadecimal notation* (or base-16).

Hex notation has a number set from 0 to 15, unlike the 0 to 9 numbers in the *decimal notation* (base-10) we use every day. Because we can use only one digit in each number place, hex notation uses A through F to denote the numbers 10 through 15. For example, when you translate the number 60 into a hex number, the hex equivalent is 3C. Writing down 3C is much easier than writing 111100 in binary notation.

When you pronounce a hex number that looks like a decimal number, such as 43, you don't say "forty-three" but "four three." This precise pronunciation avoids confusion; it's even better if you say "four three hex." (However, saying this may require you to reassure the person you're talking to that you're not casting a spell on him or her.)

Let's look at an example and play with it a little bit. Remember that a byte is 8 bits and a nibble is 4 bits. Well, when you take a number in binary and covert it into hex you do it a nibble at a time. That makes it easy.

The number 60 in binary is 00111100 — 32 + 16 + 8 + 4 = 60.

Each byte has 8 positions from the rightmost ones position to the leftmost 128th position. The "0" entries have no value associated with them. Therefore, you do include the equivalent positional value in the summing. It is just like taking the decimal number 109 and adding it up as one in the hundredths position, plus 0 in the 10s position, plus 9 in 1s position, and having it sum up to 109.

As you can see, these position values are based on the value of 2 raised to a power: 2^0 being 1, 2^1 being 2, 2^2 being 4, 2^3 being 8, 2^4 being 16, 2^5 being 32, 2^6 being 64, and 2^7 being 128. If you add them all together (1 + 2 + 4 + 8 + 16 + 32 + 64 + 128), you get 255, which in binary is 11111111.

To convert to hex, you take the four rightmost digits and add their corresponding values: 1, 2, 4, and 8, which will equal 15. According to the earlier description of hex notation, you know that 15 in hex is F. You then take the remaining four leftmost digits and add up their positional values: 16 + 32 + 64 + 128, which adds up to 240. Add 240 to 15, and you get 255. Thus, 255 in hex is FF.

Now, the more astute among you will have wondered why 1111 is 15 for the first set of digits on the right, but 1111 is added up to 240 on the left. And, if it is actually 240, how can it be F?

Good question, and this is one of the reasons so many of us gave up on math. It makes perfect sense, but it's difficult to explain.

You can really look it at two ways: as two nibbles of 15 each or as 1 byte of 255. We actually look at it as both. We think of the rightmost 4 digits holding their position values of 1, 2, 4, and 8 to have a total value of 15 (F). We think of this right nibble as the remainder of a number. Then we look at the left nibble and we think of its leftmost four digits as holding the positional values of 16, 32, 64, and 128 for a total value of 240. Now, if you divide 240 by 16, you get 15 (1111), which also equals F. Thus, you derive the left nibble as also being F. Thus you get 240 + 15 for 255 (FF). And getting FF when a byte is all ones is a perfect 255.

TIP **Remember that a bit is defined as a quantity of information that can be defined as either a yes-no or true-false value. (In other words, a bit is set if its value is 1 to indicate yes or true, and reset if its value is 0 to indicate no or false.) A nibble is 4 bits, and a byte consists of 8 bits. For the second nibble (left F), square the value 15. You'll get 225. Add 15 to that. You'll get 240. Then, add the right nibble value (15): 240 + 15 = 255.**

Decoding RGB triplets

HTML specifies colors by using a six-digit hex number, called a *color code*. The color code begins with a pound sign (#) and then the hex number follows. The six-digit hex number actually is a combination of three two-digit hex numbers that denote the RGB values. These RGB "triplets" enable you to set the red, green, and blue values of a color, and the color code combines these values and produces the color.

For example, the color code #FF00FF denotes the strongest red (FF), no green (00), and the strongest blue (FF). This color code produces a magenta color on your screen. Here are some additional simple color code examples:

- *#FFFFFF* — White (red, blue, and green)
- *#000000* — Black (no red, no blue, no green)
- *#FF0000* — Red
- *#00FF00* — Green (although the official HTML color name is "Lime")
- *#0000FF* — Blue

If you want a less intense color, you can lower the red, green, or blue color value in the color code. For example, if you want to display a lighter blue, you can use the color code #0000AA.

Facing limitations of named colors

Learning what color code value combinations produce the desired color can be a process of trial and error. Once you do find the color, the number of sticky notes to remind you of the correct color code can cover the entire perimeter of your screen. Fortunately, HTML does have common colors named, so you can enter the name of the color instead of the color code. Table 6-2 summarizes the named colors in HTML and their corresponding color codes.

So, for example, if you want to have the color blue as the color for the ubiquitous computing phrase "Hello, world!" you would enter the following HTML code:

```
<font color="blue">Hello, world!</font>
```

As you can see, the number of HTML color names is limited. If you don't want to go down the sticky-note path, you have other alternatives. One such alternative is the stylesheet. Stylesheets enable you to associate names with color codes so you only have to enter the color code once.

TABLE 6-2

English Color Names in HTML

Color Name	Hex Value
Aqua	#00FFFF
Black	#000000
Blue	#0000FF
Fuchsia	#FF00FF
Gray	#808080
Green	#008000
Lime	#00FF00
Maroon	#800000
Navy	#000080
Olive	#808000
Purple	#800080
Red	#FF0000
Silver	#C0C0C0
Teal	#008080
White	#FFFFFF
Yellow	#FFFF00

CROSS-REF You can learn more about stylesheets in Chapter 12.

Using color pickers

There are 216 *Web-safe colors*, which are colors that display solid colors on any computer, monitor, and Web browser. Colors other than these 216 exhibit *dithering* — geometric patterns appearing in the color that try to give the appearance of more colors.

What happens instead is that the dithered colors give the appearance of a freakish-looking quilt or tartan. What's more, a dithered color will look different on a different browser or on a different computer than the one you are using. So, using Web-safe colors is the only way to ensure that your Web site has a uniform look, no matter who accesses it.

One of the other alternatives to the sticky-note path (and an effective way to ensure that your site has Web-safe colors) is to choose your colors from a color picker. If you use a Web authoring program such as Dreamweaver, you can select from Web-safe colors directly in the program. If you choose to program directly in HTML, there are several sources on the Web for you to explore.

The Microsoft Developer Network Web site has a safety palette page at `http://msdn2.microsoft.com/en-us/library/bb250466.aspx`. This page, shown in Figure 6-5, contains all the Web-safe colors displayed in two ways: from beginning to end, and grouped by related colors. When you move your mouse pointer over the color you're looking for, the color code appears in a box next to the color.

FIGURE 6-5

The Microsoft Developer Network Web site has a safety palette with all the colors displayed.

The Colors dialog box in the 2007 version of Office provides a standard palette of Web-safe colors, as shown in Figure 6-6. This program displays the Web-safe colors for Internet Explorer. You can then copy the color codes from the program and paste them directly into your HTML code. If you have Windows, you can download the VQPalette program for free, or you can use the program directly within Internet Explorer.

The VisiBone Webmaster's Color Lab (`www.visibone.com/colorlab`), shown in Figure 6-7, displays its 216-color Webmaster's palette graphics on its site. If you click a color in the graphic, the site lists the color's name, the HTML color code, the RGB value information, and the CMYK (cyan-magenta-yellow-black) print color value information. This site has several unique features, including the following:

- Web-safe swatch collections that you can download for free and use with different Web-related graphics programs such as Adobe Photoshop and Macromedia Fireworks
- The capability to access the site in one of 16 languages
- The Webmaster's Palette, available for purchase as a poster for easy reference (or as wall art if you prefer), not to mention some pretty nice mouse pads

Table 6-3 provides the URLs of some other Web sites where you can also find color pickers.

FIGURE 6-6

The 2007 version of Microsoft Office provides a palette of Web-safe colors in its application suite.

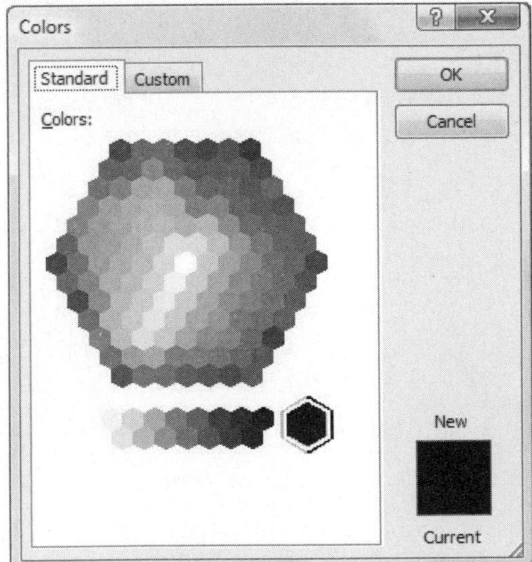

FIGURE 6-7

The VisiBone Webmaster's Color Lab displays a 216-color palette.

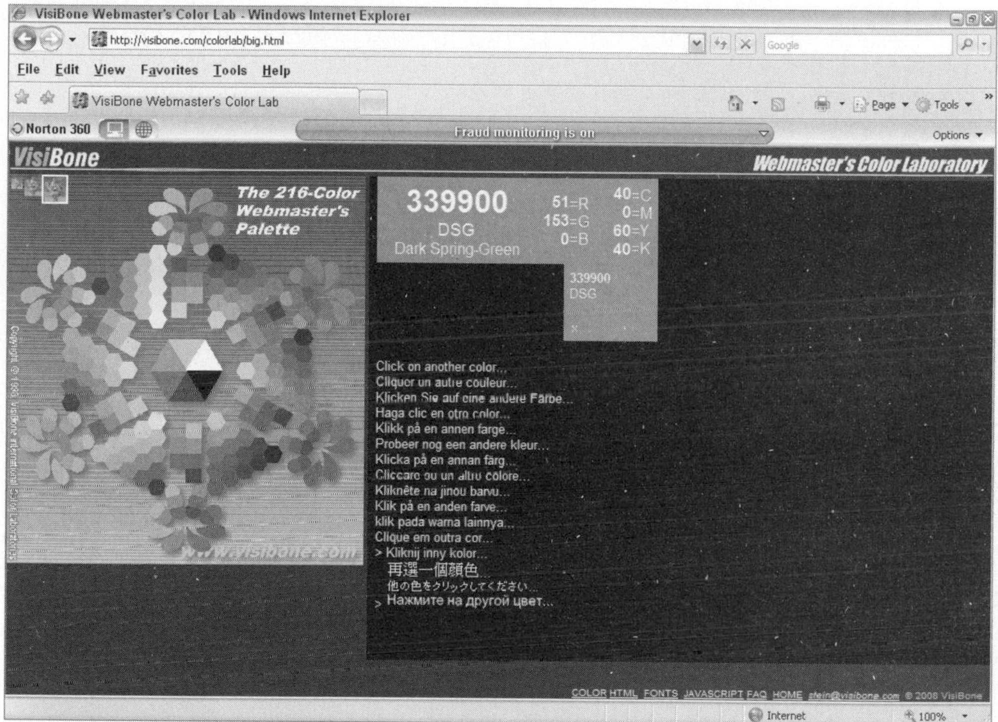

TABLE 6-3

Color Pickers

Web Site	URL
ColorMaker	`www.bagism.com/colormaker`
TomaWeb Hex Color Picker	`colors.tomaweb.com`
HTML Color Chooser	`geocities.com/colorchooser`
HTMLcolor	`bluefive.pair.com/htmlcolor.htm`
Kira's Web Toolbox	`lightsphere.com/colors`

Do "Web-safe colors" matter anymore?

The whole issue of Web-safe colors is based on the 256-color video display. Such video cards are more than a little bit outdated today, and computers from at least the past seven years are typically capable of displaying millions of colors instead. The only computers still displaying such a limited set of colors are rubbing elbows with the dinosaurs.

However, even though such systems are no longer sold (at least on the mass market), a lot of them are still in operation. Not everyone upgrades to the latest technology all the time, and companies, in particular, are still using older systems that are incapable of competing with the new computers.

It's the bugaboo of all Web designers — what audience are you creating your site for? If you want to cover all the bases, you have to use Web-safe colors so that everyone can visit your site. If you don't, you run the risk of losing visitors and, if you're promoting a business, potential customers.

Popular Graphics Formats

The following are three of the most popular types of graphics file formats on the Web:

- Graphics Interchange Format (GIF)
- Joint Photographic Experts Group (JPEG or JPG)
- Portable Network Graphics (PNG)

Let's take a look at these in a bit more detail.

Graphics Interchange Format (GIF)

The GIF graphics format is usually used to save icons, cartoons, logos, and the like. It supports 256 colors, and until it was revealed that its data compression algorithm, LZW, (named after the initials of its three co-inventors, Lempel-Ziv-Welch, in 1984) had been patented by Unisys (and that the copyright was being enforced for its use), it was probably the most common image-saving format utilized. It is still compatible with almost all browsers on the market today.

There are two versions of GIF files:

- *GIF 87* — This is the basic, original version of GIF files originally developed by a group of engineers from various software companies and sponsored by CompuServe.
- *GIF 89a* — This version supports transparent GIFs, animated GIFs, and a process of rendering images called *interlacing*.

Interlacing is a technique which loads an image through a series of alternating lines. It is a technique that improves image quality through several refreshes until the full resolution rendition comes up clear and crisp.

Non-interlaced GIF images are produced at full resolution, one line at a time from the top of the screen until the entire image is rendered. Each line of data is clear and crisp, but it takes time download the entire image.

Both ways of loading a graphic can be time-consuming depending on the visitor's Internet connection, although the advantage of interlaced GIFs is that you are able to get a preview of the whole picture. That preview may allow you to determine if you want to wait for the final download or just pass on it.

Another way to speed up the decision-making process is to use low-resolution (low-res) images to speed page download time. If you're using a very large image that you know is going to take forever to download, you may want to consider adding a low-res image to the mix as well. Low-res images are poor-quality copies of an image. They may, for example, be black-and-white or grayscale versions of a full-color image. Because of the smaller file size of low-res images, they don't take anywhere near as much time to download.

In HTML, you can specify that a low-res image be displayed on the Web page while the full version of the image is downloading, giving your visitors some idea of what they're waiting for. The low-res image is specified via the `lowsrc` attribute, as shown here:

```
<IMG src="huge_file.gif" width="1200" height="800"
lowsrc="small_version.gif">
```

CAUTION **The low-res version must have the same physical dimensions as the full version. If it doesn't take up the same space on the Web page, the display of the full version will be messed up.**

One way to speed up the downloading of the document is to simplify the color scheme. You do this by reducing the number of colors picked on the color palette.

Transparent GIFs

Transparencies are a way to blend GIF images into the Web page background. A transparent GIF is an image of an object where a selected color does not show when it is placed on the page, thus allowing the Web page background to show through the selected color instead.

A transparent GIF is an image, saved in GIF format, that has a color that you may elect not to display (in other words, you deselect it by using a tool such as Dreamweaver's Magic Wand utility). The color effectively becomes transparent. Thus, if you were to select an image of, say, a hibiscus in a white background, you could select the white background of the GIF to become transparent. Then, when you transferred the image to your Web page, only the hibiscus would appear against your existing background.

Animated GIFs

These are typically small drawings that are used in sequence to create the illusion of movement. Some can be comforting (as in the picture of an American flag flying in the breeze), but most are annoying (such as a dancing baby) and the novelty of movement soon wears out. Therefore, if you use them, they may actually have the effect of driving people away from your Web site because they are quite tired of seeing, say, a monkey bouncing from a tree, or the sudden appearance of a hideously colored smiley face appearing from the sun. You should be quite content that the physical constraints of this media (the book you are holding in your hands) prevents us from presenting actual illustrations to you. However, there are numerous collections of animated GIFs available for your eager perusal at such sites as `www.animationfactory.com`, `http://harrythecat.com/dorret/`, and `www.gifanimations.com`.

A good rule of thumb to use in deciding on use of animated GIFs is to ask yourself if you would want the animation (for example, an ugly dancing baby in diapers) to reside forever in your memory. If the answer is "no," then do not inflict it on another. Used properly, however, animated GIFs can be effective, and much more bandwidth-friendly than Flash animation, which is discussed later in this book.

Joint Photographic Experts Group (JPEG, or JPG)

The Joint Photographic Experts Group produced the JPEG (or JPG) standard in 1992. This format is best suited for photos because it can reproduce up to 16.7 million colors (as opposed to the maximum of 256 colors in GIF images). The size of the image can be controlled by compression algorithms that control the degree of detail contained in a copy of the image transferred across the Internet. The higher the compression, the greater the loss of detail will be when the file is decompressed and rendered on the receiving side.

Compression is used to speed up the transfer of data. Both GIF and JPG use compression algorithms. Larger file sizes take longer to download, especially over a slow connection. With compression, you reduce the file size and reduce the image quality, but you also reduce the time it takes to load on a page. The reduction of image quality is referred to as *lossy*. An image that is not compressed when it is transferred is referred to as a *lossless* image.

GIFs are much better at compressing simple artwork and line art. JPEG's inverse discrete cosine transforms are excellent for photographs.

Like its GIF cousin, a JPEG file can be rendered on the receiving browser just as an interlaced GIF image is, and for exactly the same reason — to allow a progressively better view of the image as it downloads.

Portable Network Graphics (PNG)

The PNG graphic format was developed to incorporate many of the favorable features of JPG and of GIF (without that little licensing issue associated with the latter). This format was designed primarily as an image-transfer program to send images across the Internet. PNG has all the features of GIF (interlacing, transparency, and animation), plus it also supports as many colors as JPG (16.7 million). Unlike JPG, however, it uses a lossless data compression algorithm. This means that no data is discarded or "lost" in data transfer.

NOTE **PNG compression ratio is 10 to 30% smaller than GIF. It is a lossless compression format which works best with solid blocks of color. It is not widely supported by older browsers, though it is available through plug-ins.**

The PNG format is consistent with the open standards philosophy of the development of the Internet. When it first came out in 1996, it suffered from the "new kid on the block syndrome" because it was not backwardly compatible with earlier versions of popular browsers. However, as time passes, compatibility is becoming less of an issue, and its advanced features make it a very attractive image format.

Setting Background and Foreground Color

Now it's time to have some fun, but we should also be a little careful here. We are going to show you how to set a page's background color using HTML 4.0 (which works just fine, and we're perfectly comfortable with), but the coding is *deprecated* — meaning that one fine day many, many years from now, if you use this HTML tag, your browser may not understand it. But don't worry. We'll also show you the new and improved way by using Cascading Style Sheet (CSS) styles.

Coding for background

To set a color background using HTML 4.0, you use the following:

```
<body bgcolor="color">
```

Let's say that you wanted to specify a background color of red in HTML for your Web site, All About Me, that you created in Chapter 5. The command sequence would be:

```
<body bgcolor="red">
```

By now, it should almost be second nature for you to recognize `bgcolor` as being an attribute of `<body>`. Of course, `red` is one of the many possible values of the attribute. It could be green, or yellow, or any of the 16.7 million colors of the color palette available. As mentioned earlier in the chapter, you don't have to remember all 16.7 million names of the colors. You can use RGB values or hex values instead.

NOTE **If anyone wonders where the figure 16.7 million came from, it is equivalent to 2^{24}.**

Recall that the RGB triplet is just the 3-byte coding for the color scheme. The range would be as follows:

- *Red* — 0–255
- *Green* — 0–255
- *Blue* — 0–255

For example, green would be `rgb(0,255,0)` or `#00ff00` in hex. The hash mark, in this context, signifies that the numeric sequence is hex. Inserted into HTML code it would be `<body bgcolor="rgb(0,255,0)">` or `<body bgcolor="#00ff00">` for hex.

Try the various combos in your Web page. Experiment; have a little fun.

TIP **You can see these RGB 0-255 ranges in a typical color dialog box.**

You can also do this stuff in CSS coding style. The code for setting a red background is as follows:

```
<body style="background-color: red">
```

We will just note the use of `style` in the `<body>` element. Note the quote marks around the attribute value pair `"background-color: red"`. Technically, `style` is a format description that tells the browser how to render each element. Therefore, the `style` is telling the browser to render the background color of the body as red.

Coding for foreground (text)

To set a color for the *foreground* (which means, actually, *text*) using HTML 4.0 format, use the following:

```
<body text="color">
```

However, that tag is deprecated. In more current HTML format, the code would be:

```
<body style="color: #8a2be2">
```

You may even combine background and text colors:

```
<body style="color: #8a2be2; background-color: red ">
```

Finally, you may even use an image as a background.

Adding Background Images

Background images, as with background color, can add immeasurably to the aesthetic appeal of a Web page — or they can destroy its usefulness and effectiveness. Properly chosen, a background image supplements the meaning and value of a Web page. Used improperly, it cripples it.

Following is an example of the coding for calling a background image from the same folder as the Web page:

```
<body background="bytebackground.gif">
```

Figure 6-8 shows how to use an image to provide a background for your All About Me Web page from Chapter 5. Again, there are countless images freely downloadable from the Internet or freely available in the public domain. Choose your favorite search engine and search for backgrounds, screen savers, or the like. The background in Figure 6-8 was downloaded from `www.freebackgrounds.com`. However, always check for copyright.

FIGURE 6-8

Adding a background image to a Web page can make the page more visually appealing.

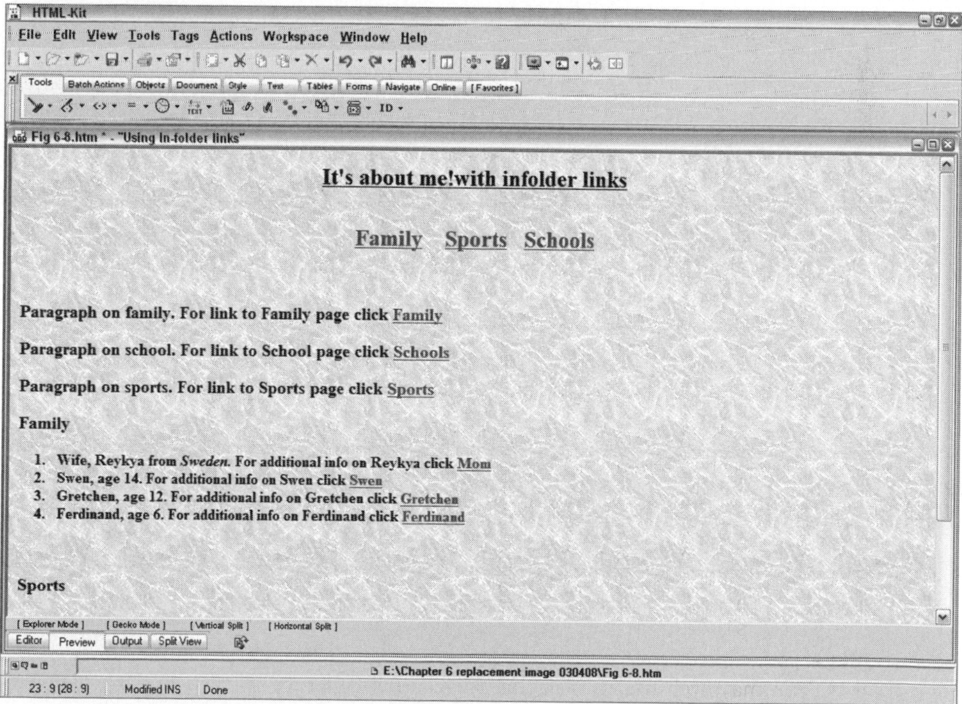

Calculating sizes for tiling

Since the background image repeats endlessly until it reaches the right margin, you should give some consideration to what happens to the last copy of the image on the line. Figure 6-9 shows a background image where the final copy is chopped off at the margin.

Because different visitors can have many different video settings, there is no way to avoid having someone, some time see a chopped-off background image. However, you can take steps to make it a rare occurrence.

The most common screen widths are 800 pixels and 1024 pixels (although there are still some old computers around with a width of only 640 pixels on their monitors). Some systems can show screens as wide as 1280 or even 1600 pixels, which is quickly becoming popular as more displays become widescreen instead of the old "full-frame" monitor style. All of these resolutions are evenly divisible by 32, so any background image that is 32 pixels wide will tile evenly in all settings.

FIGURE 6-9

This background image is chopped off on the bottom and the right side.

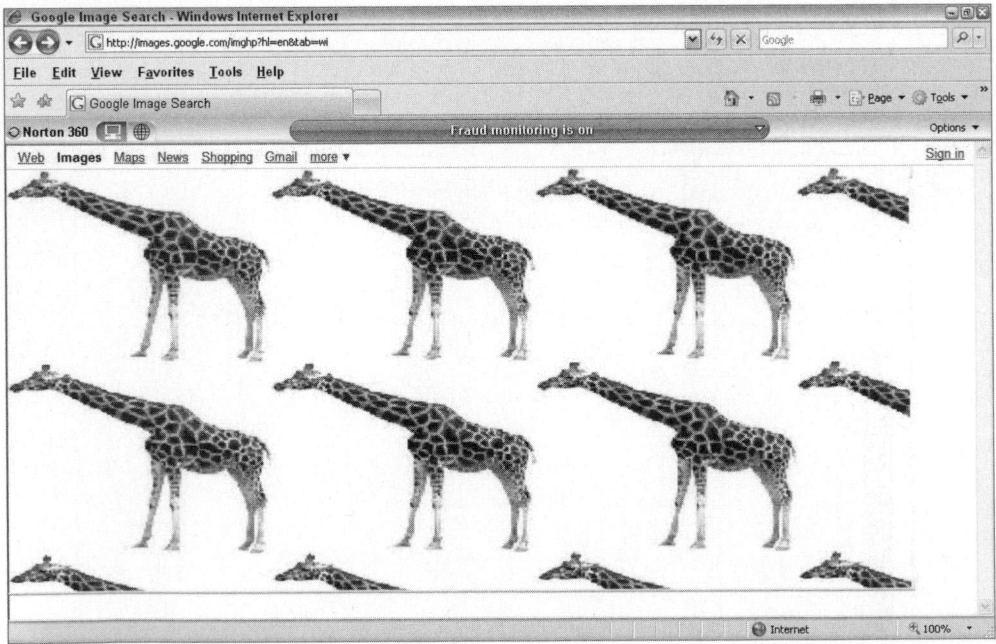

However, that's a pretty small size for many designs, so you might want to consider going up to 64 pixels instead. The problem with that is that it won't divide evenly into 800 — you'll get 12.5 copies tiling across the screen. Somewhere along the line, you have to throw up your hands and just accept that the situation will never be perfect.

Dealing with "sidebar" backgrounds

Sidebar background images require a slightly different approach because horizontal tiling isn't a concern. Instead, they're meant to take up the entire width of the page with a single image. Vertical tiling still takes place, however, so the single image is repeated from the top to the bottom of the Web page.

Figure 6-10 shows a typical sidebar background image on a Web page.

The actual image used for the background is shown in Figure 6-11. You can see in Figure 6-10 how the vertical tiling creates the illusion of a page of notebook paper.

Sidebar backgrounds violate one of the basic rules of background images, because they create an area where the overlying text is obscured. In order to prevent this situation from occurring, pages with sidebar backgrounds must position the text with a table or CSS "DIV" element so it doesn't overlap with the sidebar.

CROSS-REF See Chapter 8 for more information on how to use tables.

FIGURE 6-10

Sidebar images make a Web page appear as if it has a graphical design along the entire left side.

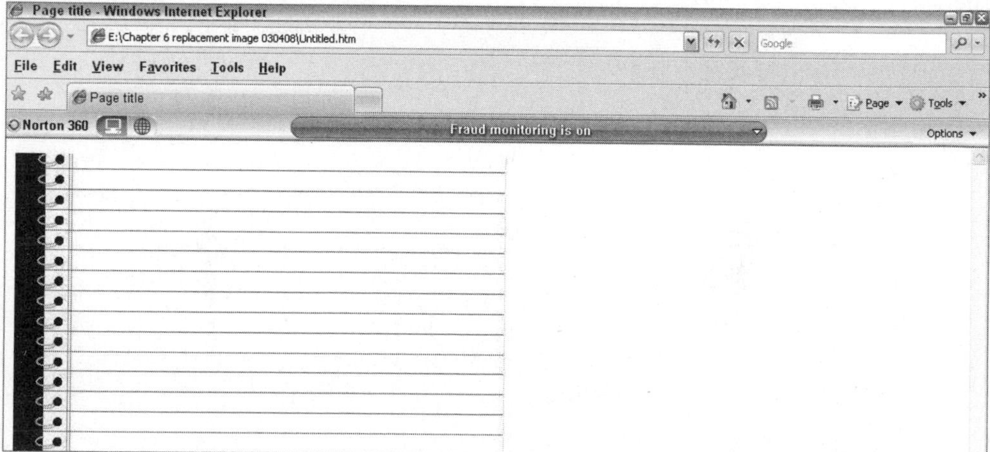

FIGURE 6-11

Sidebar images are composed of simple images that tile vertically.

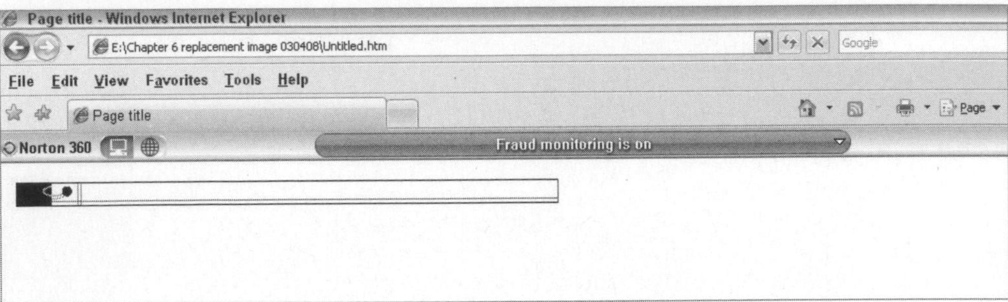

One of the most common annoyances on the Web is a bad sidebar image that makes the text of the page unreadable, as shown in Figure 6-12. This problem arises when a background image isn't wide enough, and it ends up tiling horizontally. However, this situation is totally avoidable.

FIGURE 6-12

Sidebar backgrounds that are too short will tile horizontally.

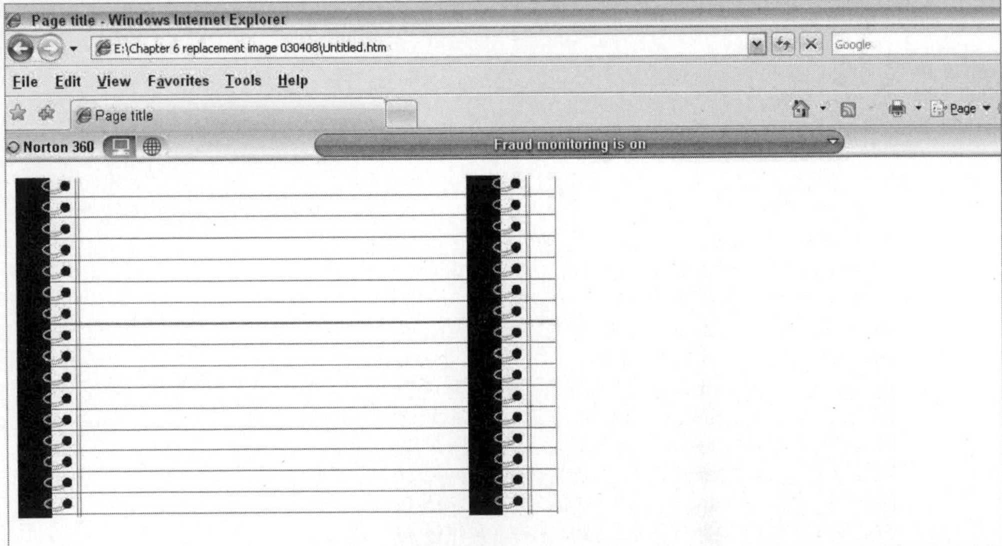

If you fail to appreciate the wide variety of screen resolutions used on the Web, you will experience horizontally tiling sidebar problems. What looks fine on an 800 × 600-pixel-wide resolution looks terrible when viewed on a 1024 × 768-pixel resolution. Solving this problem is incredibly simple — just make the sidebar image larger than you think you will ever need or set the image to only tile vertically using CSS. A Web browser, faced with a background image that's too large to fit on a single line, simply chops off the end of the image.

Make sure you test your work in multiple browsers and on multiple computers, of course, instead of assuming your site looks right!

When creating a sidebar image, make it as large as you think your most sophisticated visitor's screens will be. This means, in practice, that a typical sidebar must be at least 1280 pixels wide, and perhaps even 1600 pixels wide.

Checking seamlessness

The best kind of background image is one that tiles seamlessly — that is, an image that doesn't look like a bunch of repeated images, but a single image covering the entire Web page. Figure 6-13 shows a seamless background.

Figure 6-14 shows a seamed background image. Although the effect isn't a fatal defect, it can be distracting.

FIGURE 6-13

This figure shows a seamless background image.

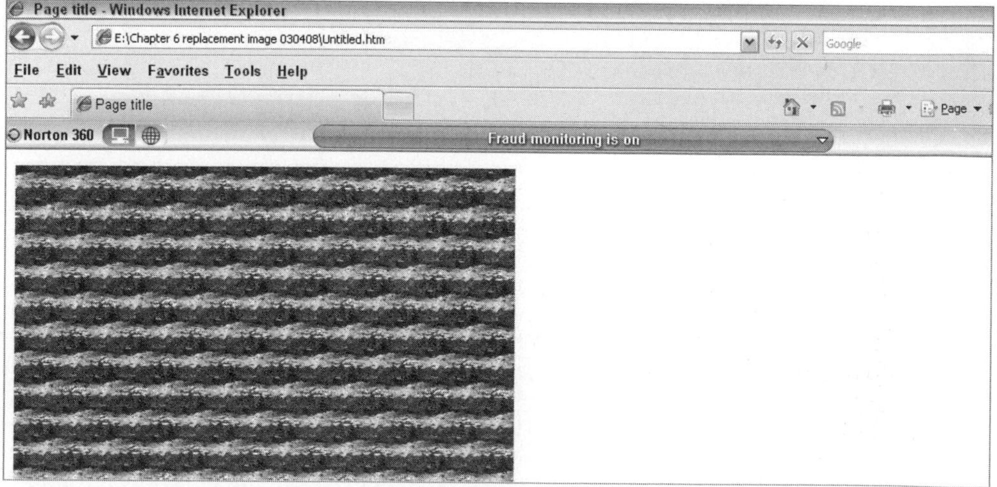

FIGURE 6-14

Seamed backgrounds can be distracting.

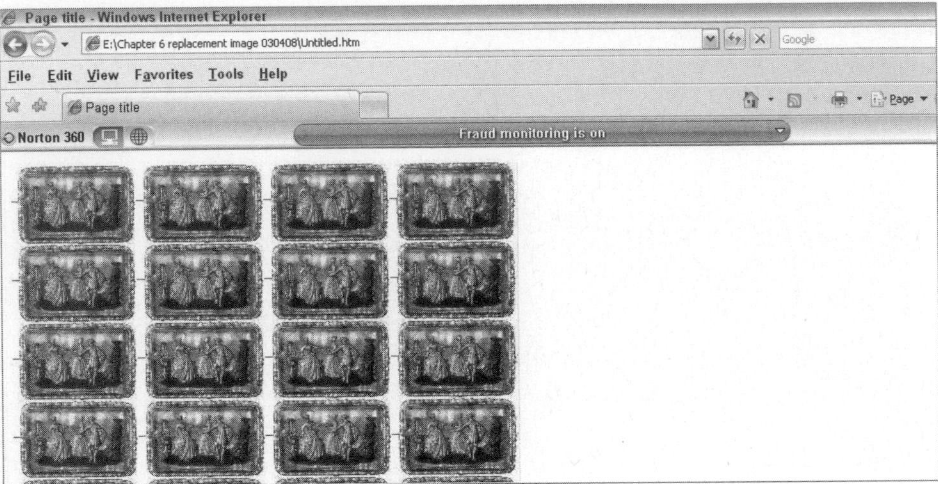

Avoiding busy backgrounds

Another common problem with background images is that some of them tend to be so complex and intricate that they distract a visitor's attention from the overlying text and images. Figure 6-15 shows such a busy background and how it detracts from the overlying elements.

Ensure that the background images you choose do not detract from the basic materials on your page.

Choosing color and contrast

A background image that is too close in color or value to the overlying text or images can be disastrous. It's amazing, though, how many times you find things like white text on a yellow background or purple on black. Pray that you never suffer a Web page with orange on red, such as the one shown in Figure 6-16.

Adding Images

Images are inserted into Web pages by using the `IMG` element. The name and location of the file are specified in the `src` attribute. Here's the basic code:

```
<IMG src="filename">
```

FIGURE 6-15

Some background images can interfere with the overlying elements.

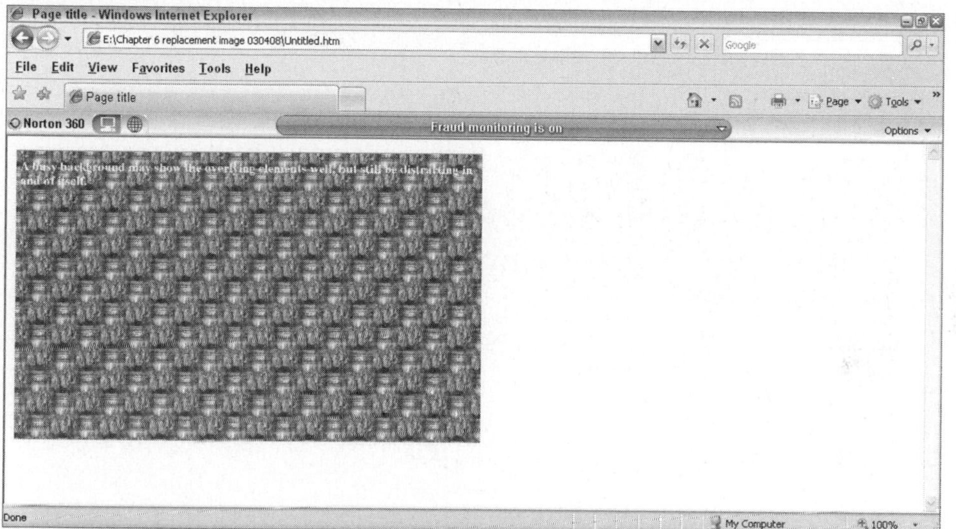

FIGURE 6-16

Backgrounds that are too close in color or value to the overlying elements can make Web pages hard to use. You can't see the color here, but you can see how bad it is!

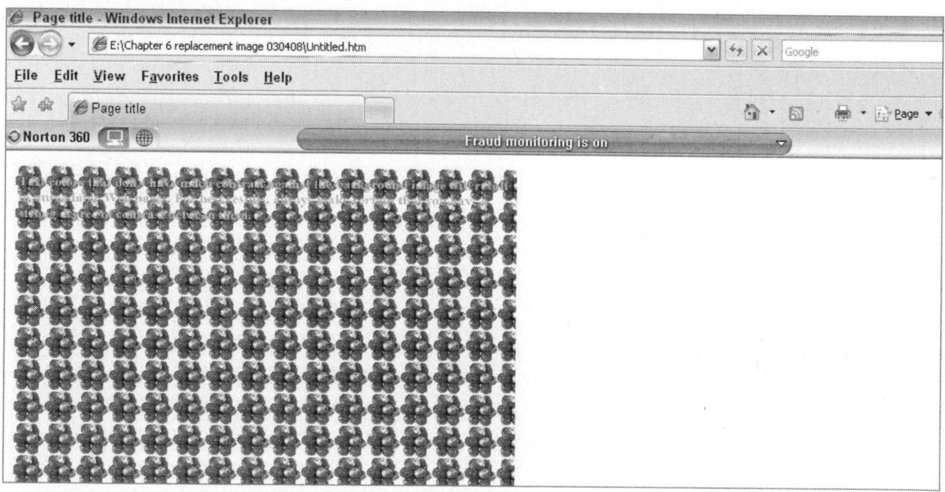

If the image file is in the same folder as the Web page it's displayed on, that's all you need. However, many Web designers keep their image files in a separate folder from their HTML files. In that case, you must specify the path to the file as well as its name. If, for example, you keep your image files in a subfolder called `images`, and you want to add a file called `toaster.jpg` to your Web page, you need to specify its location as follows:

```
<IMG src="images/toaster.jpg">
```

If the image file is on another Web server entirely, you need to use the full URL of the image file, like this:

```
<IMG src = "http://www.wheretheimageis.com/toaster.jpg">
```

CROSS-REF **See Chapter 5 for a discussion of URLs and file addresses.**

By the way, if you do link to an image located on someone else's server, be sure that you have their permission first. While it's as easy to do as typing the code in the preceding example, there are two problems with doing it:

- You inconvenience the other Webmasters by increasing the load on their servers — every time someone looks at your Web page, the other Webmaster's Web server has to serve up the linked image to your visitor's Web browser.
- You have absolutely no control over the contents of someone else's Web server. If they decide to rearrange files, remove the image file you're linked to, or if their server goes down or is out of business, your Web page won't work right any more. If you want to ensure that your site is always working, it's best to link only to images on your own system.

Coding for images using some CSS styles

Though it now has a background, your Web page, All About Me, does not yet have your image. Well, find a nice photo of yourself and get ready to put it up and align it.

The code for you to insert the image and align it on the right is:

```
<img src="myPhoto.jpg" align="right">
```

`myPhoto.jpg` should be changed to whatever you name your image file.

For purposes of demonstration, let's put up a picture of Swen's mom when she was young on the All About Me Web page, and make it left-aligned. The following code produces the result shown in Figure 6-17.

```
<IMG src="MaryPickford.jpg" align=left>
```

OK, it's really Mary Pickford, but they looked so much alike they could have been twins.

FIGURE 6-17

The image of Swen's mom on the All About Me Web page is currently left-aligned.

Aligning Images

As you saw in the previous example, HTML uses the attribute `align` within the image tag. `<img src align="position">`. A number of values are associated with alignment. Table 6-4 shows a deprecated list of tags for image alignment. For now, however, follow the Tao of your training and allow the photo to flow to the left or right margin on your page.

You will notice in Figure 6-17 that the text aligns at the right edge of the left-aligned image. You may move the text under the image by using the command `<br />` immediately below the `<img>` tag. The result will be as shown in Figure 6-18.

> **NOTE** **The `align` attribute for images doesn't actually align the image, but rather the surrounding text.**

If you want to have text next to the image, you can adjust its distance from the image by using either `hspace` or `vspace` attributes. `Hspace` creates a margin next to the image. In Figure 6-19,

TABLE 6-4

Image Alignment Settings

Align Value	Meaning
absbottom	Absolute Bottom — lines up the bottom of text descenders with the bottom of the image
absmiddle	Absolute Middle — lines up center of text with the center of the image
baseline	Puts the baseline of the text on the same level as the bottom of the image
Bottom	Same as baseline
Left	Drops the image out of its original location and moves it to the left margin
Middle	Lines up the baseline of the text with the center of the image
Right	Drops the image out of its original location and moves it to the right margin
Texttop	Puts the top of the image on the same level as the top of the text
Top	Same as texttop

FIGURE 6-18

Using the <br /> immediately below the <img> tag clears the image away from the text.

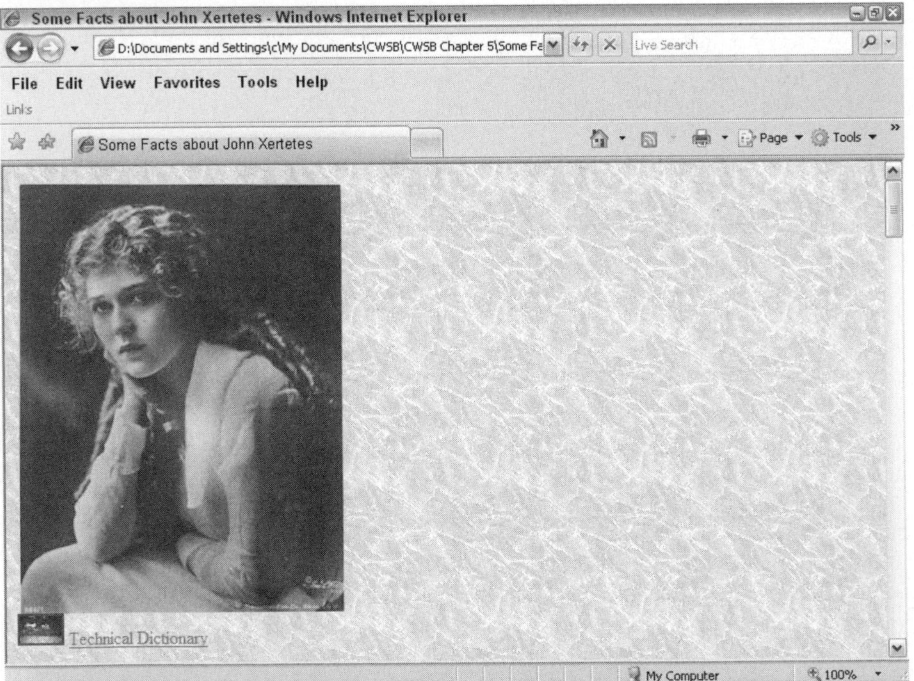

FIGURE 6-19

You can use the hspace and vspace attributes to add space between text and an image.

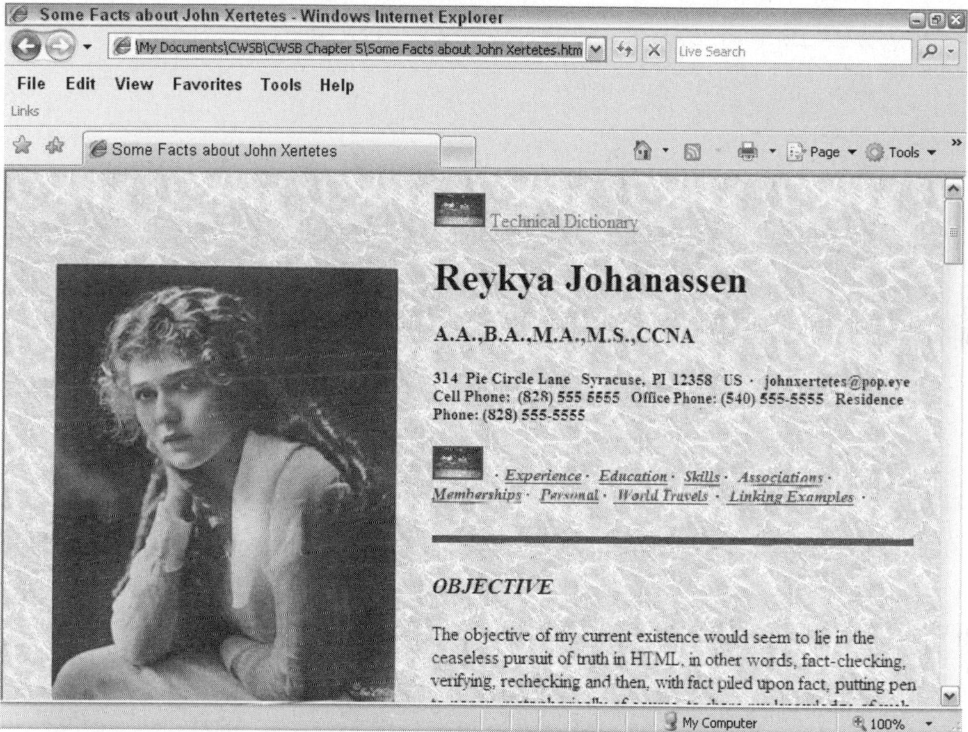

the `hspace` has been specified at 30 pixels, and the vertical space (`vspace`) has been specified at 60 pixels of space, to separate the top and bottom from the surrounding block. The equivalent to this with CSS is the padding, padding-left, padding-right, padding-top, and padding-bottom styles.

The `hspace` attribute sets both left and right spacing simultaneously, and the `vspace` attribute does the same for both top and bottom spacing. You cannot independently set the left margin to a different value from the right margin, or the top margin to a different value from the bottom one in traditional (or transitional) HTML.

Another alignment feature is called float. This occurs when text flows around an embedded image. Using float, you can place an image flush against the left or right margin of the page and have the content flow to wrap around the image. The following code produces the result shown in Figure 6-20:

```
<img src="imgxyz.jpg" style="float: right">
```

FIGURE 6-20

Notice how the text content flows around the right-aligned image.

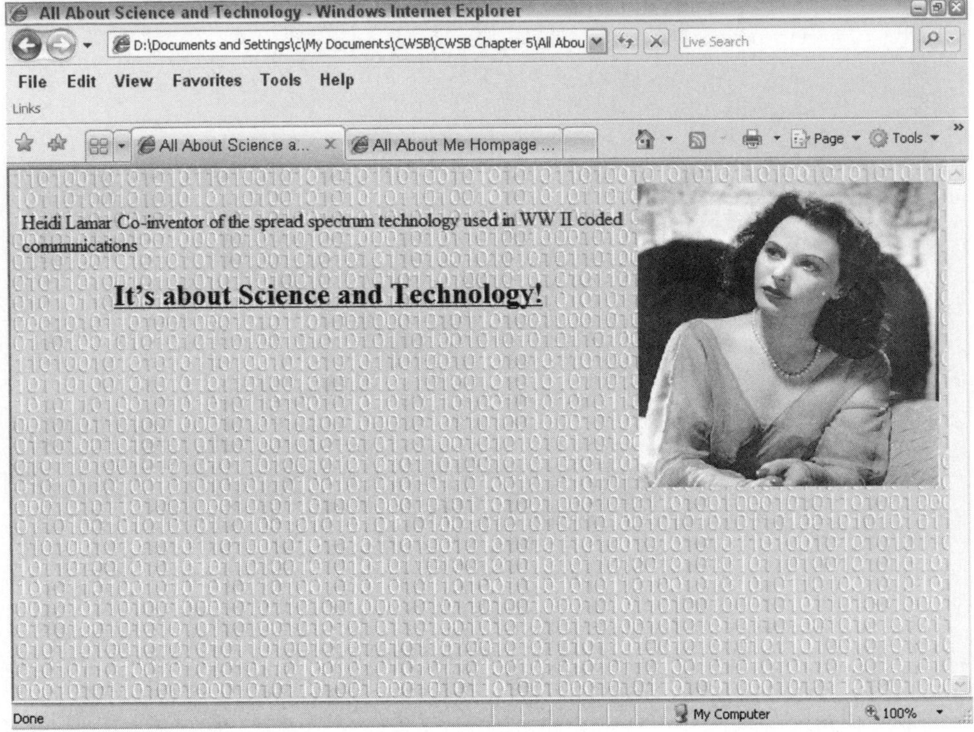

Notice the use of the style element in the previous example. Styles are format descriptions that tell the browser how to render each element of a page. You will use additional examples of styles when we cover the CSS language in Chapter 12.

You can use the `clear` attribute to prevent subsequent text from flowing around an image, as shown in Figure 6-21. The following code produces the desired result:

```
<HR align=left width="97%" color=blue SIZE=6 style="clear:left">
```

Although many Web designers use images as if they were block level elements, they are actually inline elements just like the ones used to make text bold or italic (the `B` and `I` elements). Thus, you can put an image right smack in the middle of a line of text and it sits there just as if it's another word in the sentence.

CROSS-REF **See Chapter 4 for more information on block and inline elements.**

FIGURE 6-21

Notice how the caption and header are repositioned to the first clear area below the image.

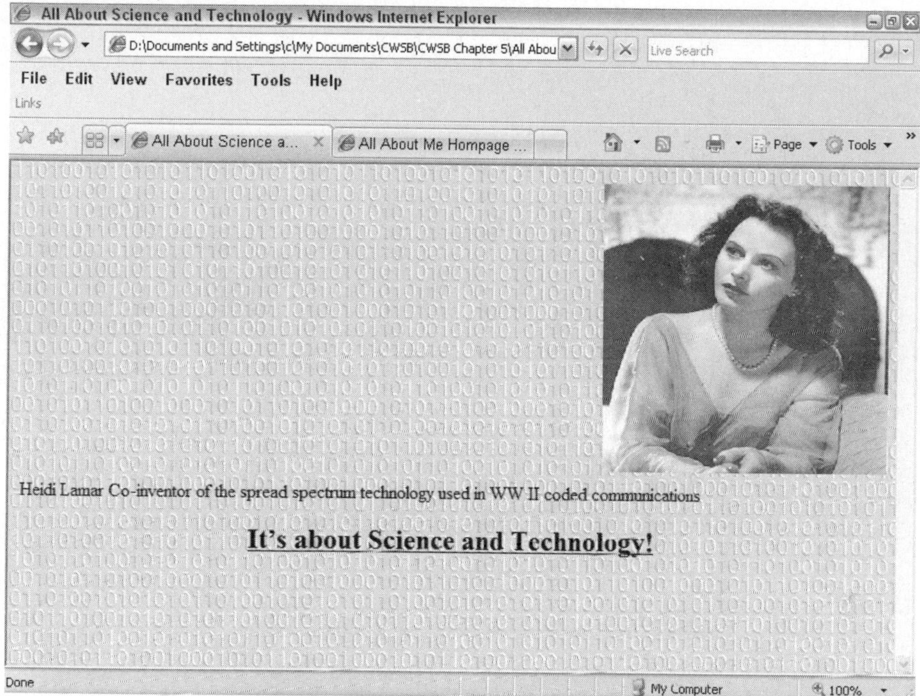

Of course, this creates a practical difficulty because the vast majority of images are considerably larger than most text. Figure 6-22 shows how a large image can disrupt the natural flow of a paragraph.

Small images called *icons*, however, are often used on the same line as text.

Aligning multiple images

When there is more than one image in a single line, the alignment becomes increasingly complex. All of the images' `align` values affect both the text preceding and following them. The following code sets up a situation where the first image is set to top alignment, and the second is set to bottom alignment:

```
<p>Try our veggies <IMG src="assorted_vegetables.jpg" width="200"
height="244" align="TextTop">and then our irresistible cake! <IMG
src="cake.jpg" width="150" height="142" align="bottom">You can't
beat either one.</p>
```

FIGURE 6-22

Large embedded images disrupt the flow of a paragraph.

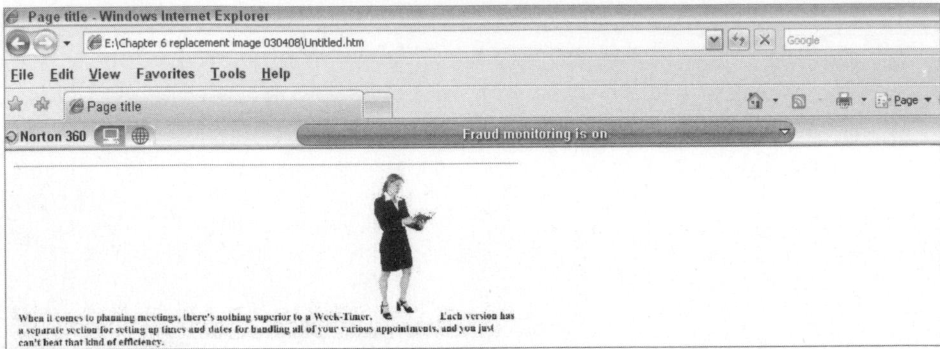

FIGURE 6-23

Multiple images can be difficult to align.

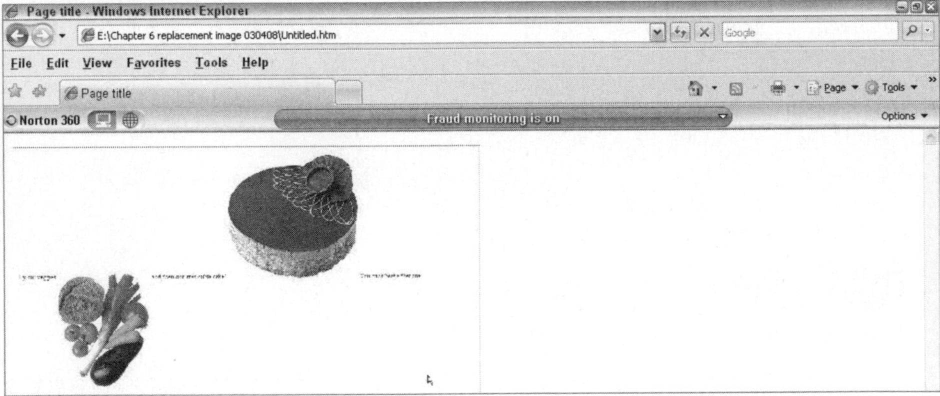

All the text is top-aligned with respect to the first image, and all the text is also bottom-aligned with respect to the second image. This means that the first image moves down to make room for the text to fit into the specified alignments. Figure 6-23 shows what happens in a case such as this.

Setting margins

Margins surrounding the image can be set with great flexibility using the four margin styles (`margin-top:`*`number of pixels`*, `margin-right:`*`number of pixels`*, `margin-bottom:` *`number of pixels`*, and `margin-left:`*`number of pixels`*) to set the distance from the image.

For example, the following will set a margin of 10 pixels equally around all four sides of the image:

```
<img src="imgxyz.jpg" style="float: right; margin:10">
```

In this example, you could insert `margin: 10, 20` to set the top and bottom at 10 pixels, and the right and left at 20 pixels.

If you use a three-sided figure, the same margin will be applied to top, right, and bottom margins, in a clockwise direction.

TIP **If you want to have images overlap with other elements to create overlay effects, you can use negative values in the margin styles.**

Setting borders

Images on Web pages can have a border — a frame for the picture, so to speak. But unlike physical artwork (such as cross-stitch or a painting), there is no canvas that requires a wood or metal frame. Digital images are similar to photographs — you may or may not want to frame one. Some images look better with a border at a certain size, while others don't. Borders are optional for images, and many designers prefer to leave most images borderless. It's one of those purely personal decisions that Web designers have to make, and you can be sure that you will never please everybody. When it comes to image links, however, there's a very good reason to make sure that the image has a border.

Figure 6-24 shows two images without borders. One of them is an image link, and the other is a plain image. Nothing indicates that there is any difference between them.

FIGURE 6-24

Borderless images — which is the image link?

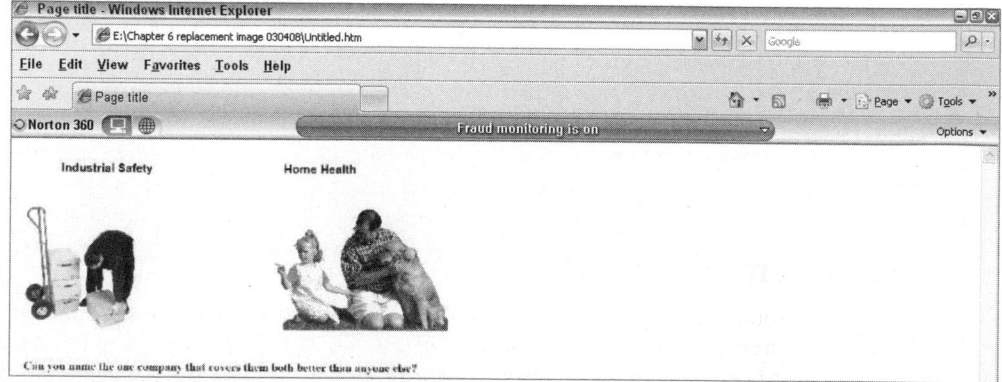

FIGURE 6-25

The border around an image link is a different color from a normal border (although it's difficult to discern in a black and white figure).

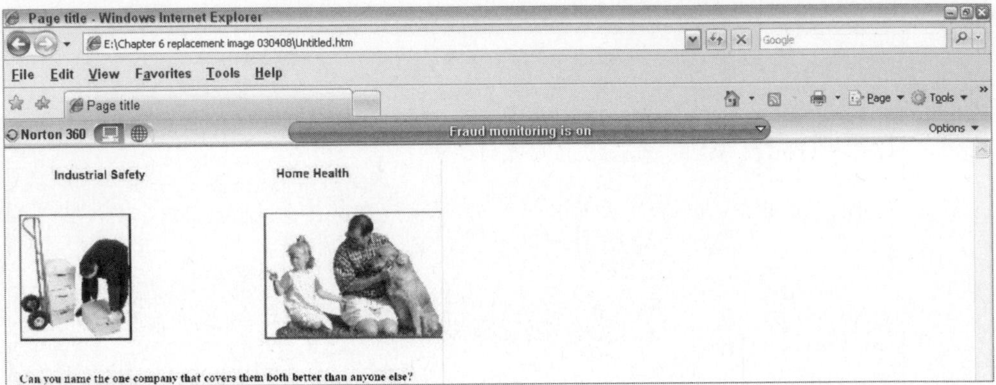

Figure 6-25 shows the same two images with borders. The plain one has a black border, but the image link has a blue border. This visual cue is standard on the Web as a clue for your visitors that the image link isn't just a plain old image, but has a special function. Of course, you don't have to put borders around plain images — you can just use borders on image links and leave your plain images borderless. If you don't like borders around image links, however, you can even eliminate them by setting the border width attribute to zero style as in `="border-width:0"` The important thing is to signify the importance and function of the image links on your page.

To insert a border around an image link, you would use code similar to the following:

```
<IMG src="imagelink.jpg" width="200" height="244" border="3"
alt="imagelink">
```

NOTE **The colors — blue for image links and black for plain image borders — are the same as for the same functions in the normal text colors. Plain text is black and link text is blue (see Chapter 5). Whatever color you set for the default text and link values also becomes the border colors for images. For example, if you set the default text color to red and the default link color to green, plain images will have red borders and image links will have green borders.**

Still, some Web designers don't use borders even for image links. There is no right or wrong decision. It's purely aesthetic. If there isn't a border — and, therefore, no special color marks the image as a link — how is anyone to know the link exists? Your site visitors do get two other clues. First, the mouse pointer changes shape if hovered over an image link. Instead of the usual arrow, the pointer becomes a hand. Second, the URL of the image link shows in the status bar of a Web browser when the mouse pointer is located over the image.

If your site visitors are seasoned veterans, they don't need borders to find image links — they know to move their mouse pointers over the images to see what happens. However, that means they still have to check out all the images one by one to see what each one is because there's no way to just look at them and tell. If your site's artistic motif can possibly accept the existence of bordered image links, you can make life a lot easier on your visitors by including them.

Setting Image Size

Setting image size is both simple and complex. It is simple to reduce the size of an image. Within an `<img src>` tag, you set the height and width attributes:

```
<IMG src="MaryPickford.jpg" align=left vspace= "0" hspace="10"
width="50" height="100" style="float: right; margin: 10;">
```

The image will be rendered according to the `height` and `width` size attributes, as shown in Figure 6-26. However, the file size remains unchanged. Therefore, in order to speed up the downloading time, you would need to actually reduce the size of the original image file. To change the actual size of an image, you must use an image-editing tool such as Xara, Corel, or Photoshop.

CROSS-REF **See Chapter 2 for more information on popular image-editing tools.**

Using the height and width attributes

When a browser loads a Web page, the text on the Web page appears right away, but the image file (being separate from the Web page itself) takes slightly longer to show up (the length of time depends on the size of the image file). If the Web browser doesn't know the width and height of the image, it can't tell how much space to set aside for it until the image file has been downloaded. In that case, the browser must rearrange the text after the image file (or files) have come in, which causes an automatic redraw of the screen — making all the existing elements jump around as the image comes in, and room is made for it. This unnecessary irritation can be avoided by specifying the `width` and `height` in the HTML code as in the following example:

```
<IMG src="toaster.jpg" width="200" height="234">
```

NOTE **If you use a Web authoring program such as Dreamweaver or HTML-Kit, the program automatically adds the width and height information when the image is inserted.**

The `width` and `height` attributes can be used to change how large the image is when viewed in a Web browser. It's simply a matter of changing the values. For example, if you want to display the toaster image at half its full size, alter the values as shown in this example:

```
<IMG src="toaster.jpg" width="100" height="117">
```

FIGURE 6-26

You can reduce an image size on the Web page, but you are not actually reducing the size of the file.

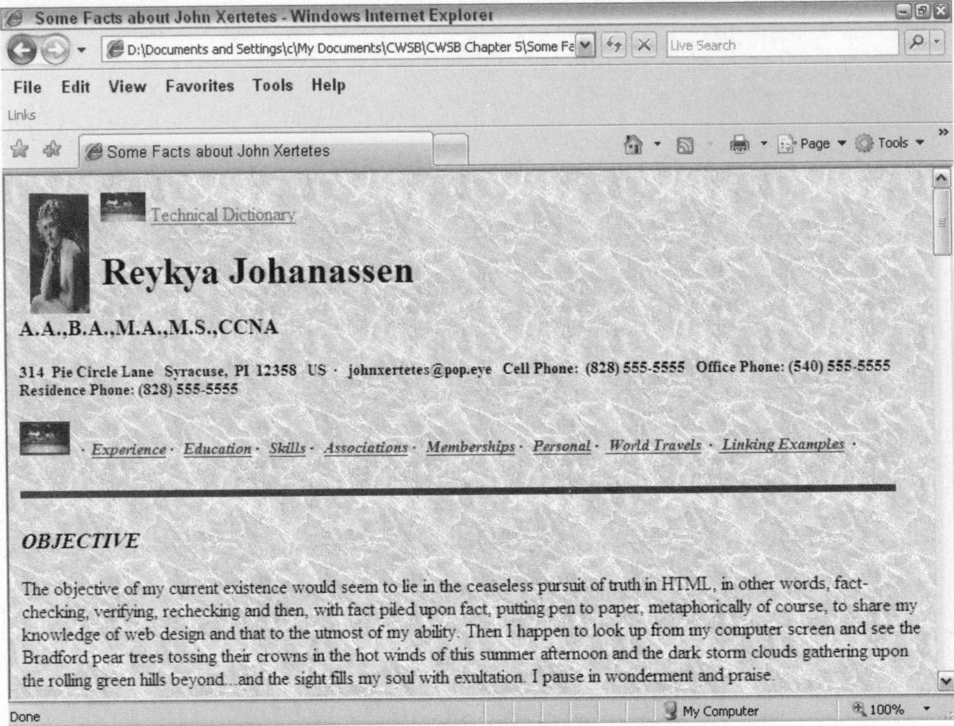

To make it show up at twice its normal size, double the values:

```
<IMG src="toaster.jpg" width="400" height="468">
```

You can also set `width="50%"` or `width="200%"` to halve/double the size of the image

Figure 6-27 shows the original toaster image, the half-size image, and the doubled version.

The doubled image is noticeably blocky. This is an unavoidable side effect of enlarging images with this method. It's important to realize that the image file itself is never affected by changing the width and height settings in the HTML code. The only change is in the way the image is displayed by the Web browser, and browsers aren't geared to fine-tune image variations. If you want to enlarge an image with less distortion, you have to do it in a professional graphics program such as Fireworks or Photoshop.

FIGURE 6-27

Image sizes can be manipulated with the width and height attributes.

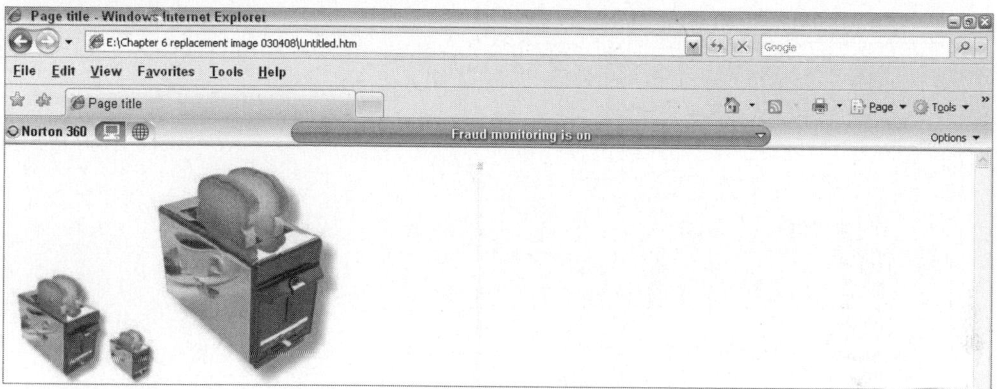

TIP **Although we carefully made sure that the proportions of the image were unchanged when we altered the width and height values, you can deliberately create some weird effects by using disproportionate values.**

Solving Image Problems

When working with images, there are some times when normal HTML methods just aren't very useful. Two of these are when there is an unavoidable delay caused by several large image files, and when there is a need to use fonts that just aren't supported by usual Web page methods.

Using thumbnail images to speed up page downloads

Thumbnails are small pictures that can be quickly loaded onto a page because their small size does not take up much bandwidth. They are links used to go to another associated Web page. You might be searching for cars and go to a site that has thumbnails of cars for sale. You can just click on the thumbnail of the one you like and be instantly connected to another page that has a larger image of the vehicle and additional information about it.

You can also make thumbnails of all your family members and use them for links to their respective autobiographical pages.

There are many programs for creating thumbnails. You may Google for them, and `www.download.com` and `www.tucows.com` are also good sources for popular freeware/shareware. Whatever sources you ultimately determine to use, only download from reputable sources.

In some cases, a Web page must deal with an awful lot of large image files. For example, how else can an art gallery be created online? But asking your site visitors to wait while a dozen — or a hundred — large image files download may be asking too much of their patience.

Thumbnails are simply image links composed of very small versions of the large images. Figure 6-28 shows a Web page that uses thumbnail images.

You will notice a blue border around a thumbnail to indicate it is a link.

The advantage to using thumbnails is that they provide enough of the full image for your visitors to decide whether or not they're interested in waiting for the full version. If so, they click the link and go make a sandwich. If not, they move down to the next thumbnail.

Embedding special fonts

The three fonts commonly used on the Web (Arial, Times, and Courier) do a pretty good job of handling the majority of text needs, but they don't do much in the way of satisfying artistic desires. Various attempts have been made over the years to come up with a workable method for using other fonts. One approach, for example, was to use any font you wanted, forcing your visitors to download fonts they didn't have. This, as you might imagine, resulted in an incredible lag time before the page could even be displayed. Web surfers hate long page download times more than anything else, and the idea of downloadable fonts is now gathering dust in a computer museum somewhere.

See Chapter 7 for information on how to set font families.

FIGURE 6-28

Thumbnail images can make pages with large numbers of images work better.

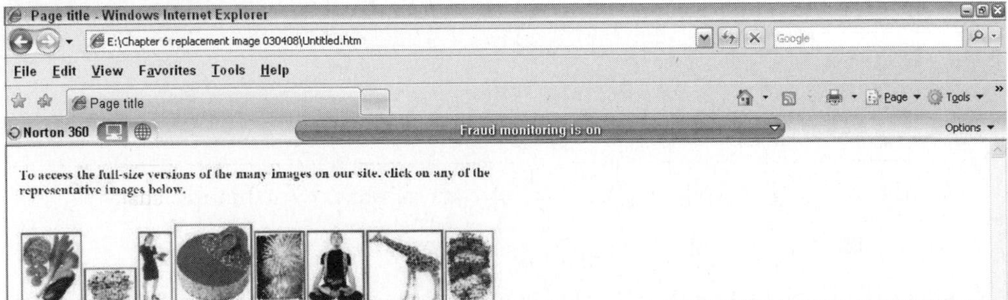

FIGURE 6-29

Text embedded in images can use any font. Note that this image is brought up by clicking on the thumbnail image in Figure 6-28

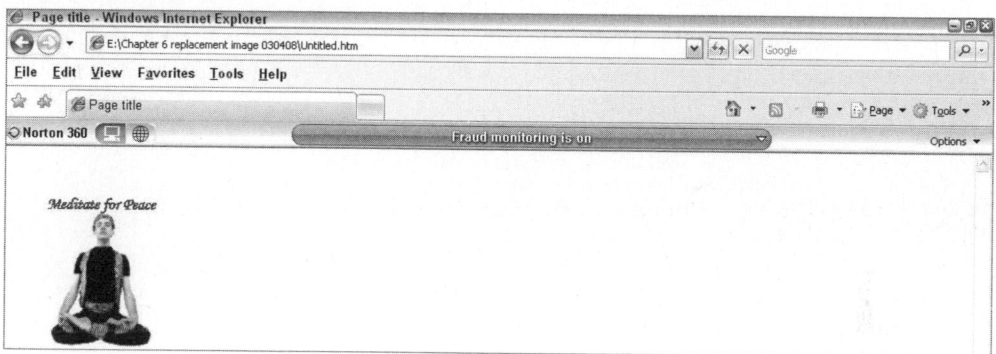

So, what do you do if you want to use a beautiful font that you have? You should embed it in an image in a graphics program and add that image to your Web page, like the example shown in Figure 6-29.

A similar approach, but without the potential handicap of having to tie the text in with a particular image, is to create the text as an image in its own right. Every good graphics program has some method for typing onto a blank canvas or an existing image, and different ones offer various methods for setting the font color and size. You may also have the ability to apply textures and special effects to the lettering.

NOTE **We do not, however, recommend this as the best approach. It would be better to use a stylesheet with preferred font and alternate fonts available if the first choice does not exist.**

CROSS-REF **See Chapter 11 for details on creating graphics.**

This approach is sometimes used to create *drop caps*, which are fancy capital letters used to begin paragraphs, a technique that is often seen in printed books. Figure 6-30 shows a drop cap in use on a Web page.

Quick Reference

The following are code snippets relating to the subjects covered in this chapter.

- Setting a color background using HTML 4.0:

```
<body bgcolor="color">
```

FIGURE 6-30

Drop caps are often used to spice up plain text.

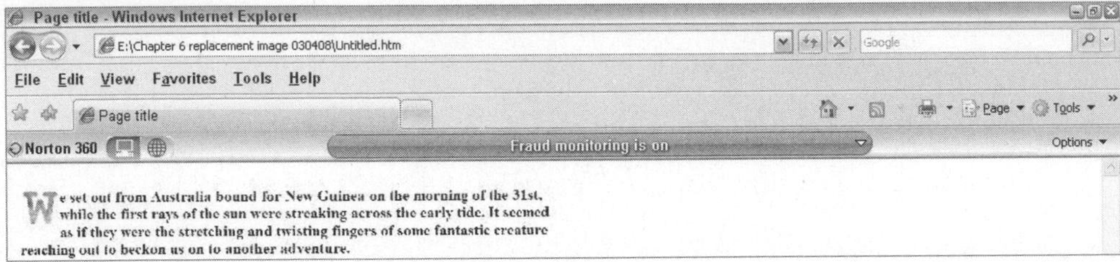

- Using CSS styles:
  ```
  <body style="background-color: red">
  ```
- Using RGB color settings:
  ```
  <body bgcolor="rgb(0,255,0)"> or
  ```
- Using hexadecimal notation:
  ```
  <body bgcolor="#00ff00">
  ```
- Combing foreground and background using styles:
  ```
  <body style="color: #8a2be2; background-color: red">
  ```
- Using a local image for a background:
  ```
  <body background="bytebackground.gif">
  ```
- Aligning to a margin in HTML:
  ```
  <img src="myPhoto.jpg" align="right">
  ```
- Setting margin around an image:
  ```
  <style="margin-bottom: 10">
  ```
- Sizing an image:
  ```
  <img src="myPhoto.jpg" height="250" width="250">
  ```
- Clearing an image using HTML:
  ```
  <br />
  ```
- Calling image, aligning image, sizing image using styles:
  ```
  <img src="MaryPickford.jpg" align=left vspace="0" hspace="10"
  width="50" height="100" style="float: right; margin: 10;">
  ```

Summary

Color is critical to your site's success. The proper use of color can make or break it. Images are also critical to the success of any serious Web site. The choice and proper use of images influences both the appearance and functionality of your site.

This chapter began with a discussion of how to set browser background colors, foreground colors, and links. You learned about the features of color: complement, contrast and coordination. You learned about a color chart and color warmth, and a number of color theory sites to visit.

This chapter explained hexadecimal code in relation to choosing colors. You learned about using RGB as a coding option, as well as the various color utilities available. We looked at a color chart, color picker, and safe palettes of colors.

This chapter reviewed the main features of each of the three most popular image formats. GIF is a 256-color format that has very wide browser support. It is compressed and supports transparency. It is not good for photos and has a patented compression algorithm. This chapter showed you some useful techniques to bring life to a static Web page through the use of transparencies and animated GIFs. JPG is great for photos and is also compressed (often yielding smaller file sizes than similar GIF images), but does not support transparency. PNG was designed to be the best of both worlds: 16.7 million color support like JPG, transparency like GIF, nonproprietary compression algorithms, and support from a growing number of browsers. However, PNG does experience an issue with backward compatibility for earlier browser versions.

You learned about the rendering of images on browsers and how each image type has its advantages. Non-interlaced graphics present a clear and crisp picture, eventually, one crisp line at a time. Interlaced image downloads progressively produce a clear image. You discovered how to use low-res images as an option for rendering graphics quickly and for using less bandwidth.

This chapter provided examples of the coding used to bring colors to Web sites. You learned about both the loose HTML way and the CSS way of setting style attributes. You learned about the coding used to download and attach images to Web sites.

You learned how to align images left and right using standard HTML and newer style formatting. The discussion demonstrated how to have text (content) wrap or not wrap around the image using either the `<br />` tag or the `clear` style. You learned how to work with margins and how to use borders with images.

This chapter examined how to align multiple images left and right using standard HTML, as well as newer style formatting. You learned how to use techniques in both standard HTML and CSS styles to resize images.

And, finally, you learned how to economize on space and bandwidth through the use of thumbnails, as well as about a technique for embedding fonts in images.

Next up, Chapter 7 examines the formatting of text.

Chapter 7

Text Formatting

Text is the heart of all Web pages. No matter how graphically oriented the site is, most information is transmitted by words. This chapter deals with how to use textual characters to make the most of your Web pages. At times, this chapter's information flies in the face of conventional wisdom and recommends flouting the advice of established standards bodies, but the focus is always on one thing — how to make your job as a Web page designer as easy as it can be.

IN THIS CHAPTER

Fonts

Look at your formatting toolbar and click on the drop-down list of fonts. You'll see dozens of specific fonts to choose from in five generic types:

- Serif
- Sans-serif
- Monospace cursive
- Fantasy

For most normal text output, you would be using either serif or san-serif fonts. It has been determined that it is easier to read large blocks of text on screen (and even off) using serif fonts, while headings and subheadings are better with san-serif. The proof, as they say, is in the pudding. Take a look at the font formats used in the book you now hold in your hand. What is serif? What is san-serif?

The Times New Roman font has a series of small lines called *serifs* that, many font artists believe, help the human eye catch and identify a letter more effectively. Fonts that do not have serifs are known as *sans-serif* fonts (*sans* being Latin for "without"). Figure 7-1 shows fonts both with and without serifs.

You may choose to be different and use uncommon font designs to proclaim your originality, you are in America after all, but then others may choose not to follow the beat of your different drum, and you could find yourself with a weird, wild, wonderfully wacky Web site that only you visit because browsers may not be able to render nonstandard fonts on computers as you intended — which sort of defeats the purpose of creating a Web site in the first place.

All font designs fall into one of two classes of fonts (*specific* and *generic*) and, as you have seen in the illustrations in earlier chapters, there are two ways of calling them:

- The happy, simple, and deprecated commands of transitional HTML 3.2 or 4.01 (transitional) or even 2.01 Fig. 1
- The newer Cascading Style Sheet (CSS) *styles*

The deprecated commands are easier to use, more intuitive, and terse (to the point), but they also lack in flexibility. (Deprecation is discussed in more detail later in this chapter in the section "Dealing with deprecation.")

You will remember that the general format of a normal HTML element tag is as follows:

```
<element attribute="value">
```

The general format of a style is as follows:

```
<element style="attribute:value; attribute:value; attribute:
value">
```

Notice also that a semicolon is used to separate each `attribute:value` pair.

When you use separate font types, however, you use a comma-separated list, such as in the following:

```
<font face="Times New Roman, Bodoni MT, Baskerville Old Face,
serif">Fickle finger of font</font>)
```

FIGURE 7-1

Sans-serif fonts do not have small lines at the ends of the letters.

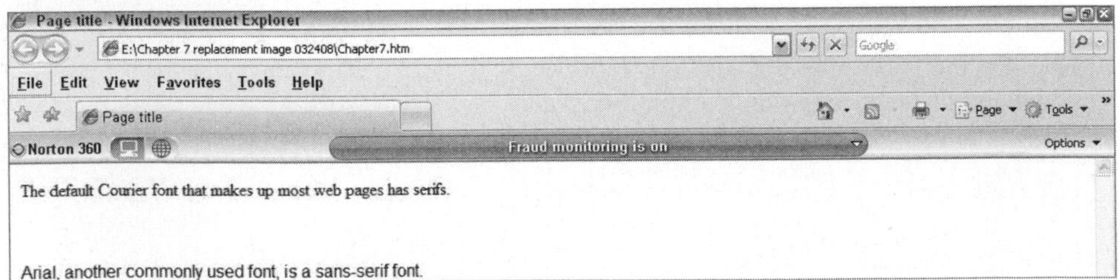

Be cognizant of the distinction, and your Web page will display a variety of fonts in a variety of formats quite nicely.

NOTE **In the font list example shown in the preceding paragraph, the last item in the list of fonts is the generic font type. This is good coding practice. It will ensure that the correct base font type is used even if the specific font design choices are unavailable.**

The same command sequence using styles would be:

```
<h1 style="font-family: Times New Roman, Bodoni MT, Baskerville
Old Face, serif">I attribute my style</h1>
```

Both deprecated HTML attributes and the newer CSS styles appear in the examples throughout this chapter.

Customizing Text with Character Styles

Character styles are HTML elements that modify the appearance of the text that they enclose. Character styles are most commonly used to add bold or italic styles to words. Character style elements are inline elements, which means that they do not create a new line because they are intended to be included in the middle of sentences.

CROSS-REF **See Chapter 4 for a description of inline elements versus block elements, as well as a general introduction to adding text to Web pages.**

Although the World Wide Web Consortium (W3C), the official standards body for the Web, has tried to phase out character styling elements in favor of Cascading Style Sheets (CSS), character styling elements are still in wide use. The reason for this is simple — they are easier to learn and more intuitive to use than CSS. CSS, on the other hand, rewards a little bit of study by giving you much richer style control capabilities.

CROSS-REF **Chapter 12 provides more details on using CSS.**

Italicizing text

Italics are used to place emphasis on particular words for various purposes. In this book, for example, whenever a technical term is used for the first time, it is italicized. Words from a foreign language that have not been assimilated into our native language are also usually italicized. Thus, an English speaker would italicize *nom de plume* (which is French for "pen name"), but would not italicize champagne or debris, because these words have become assimilated into English through common usage, even though they are also French in origin.

To add italics to text in HTML, you enclose the text in <I> and</I> tags, as in this example:

```
<P>The word <I>smaller</I> is italicized.</P>
```

Figure 7-2 shows the results.

FIGURE 7-2

Italicization is a common way of emphasizing words.

Bolding text

As with italics, bold is used for emphasis. Other than to make a word or phrase in a sentence stand out from the surrounding ones, the main use for bold print is to create headings. In HTML, however, heading elements are automatically bolded, unless overridden in stylesheets.

To make text bold, enclose it between `<B>` and`</B>` tags as in this example:

```
<P>The word <B>bold</B> is in bold print.</P>
```

Figure 7-3 shows the results.

Preformatting text

The basic text on a Web page is in a *proportionally spaced* font — that is, the amount of space taken up by a given number of characters depends on the particular letters used. The word "ion" doesn't take up the same space as the word "won," because a "w" is wider than an "i." With preformatted text, however, each character takes up the same amount of space, regardless of its size. This is because it uses a *monospace* font — one space for each character.

Other important differences occur when using *preformatted text*. For starters, preformatted text maintains all white space as it exists, without trying to condense it. For example, if the text contains ten space characters in a row in normal HTML, all but one of them is eliminated by the Web browser. In preformatted text, however, all space characters are left intact.

To set text as preformatted, place it between `<PRE>` and `</PRE>` tags as in this example:

```
<PRE>Preformatted text goes here.</PRE>
```

Figure 7-4 shows preformatted text with its effect on white space on a Web page.

CAUTION **If you use preformatted text, it is best to keep it as simple as it can be. If you add complex text such as superscripts and subscripts (see the next section), or modify the** PRE **element using CSS (see Chapter 12), Web browsers won't know how to handle the situation, and all bets are off.**

FIGURE 7-3

Bold print also emphasizes text.

FIGURE 7-4

Preformatted text is in a monospace font and maintains all white space.

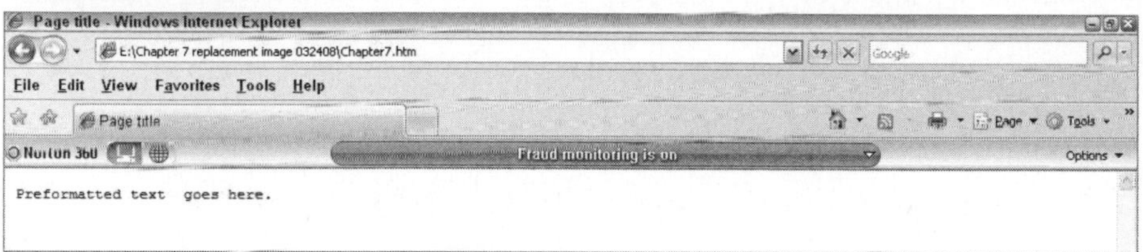

Adding superscripts and subscripts using HTML and CSS

Generally, all characters occupy the same level on a line. However, if you must add something such as the mathematical formula $E = mc^2$ or designate water as H_2O, you'll need to format the "2" as a superscript to raise it above the line, or as a subscript to drop it down a notch.

You can use a few special characters for terms such as squared or cubed (see the section "Using Special Characters and Entities" later in this chapter), but it's better in most cases to go with a generic solution that is applicable to all your needs for raising or lowering characters.

A once common problem on the Web was that the trademark symbol was not well-supported — if you added the symbol to your page, there was no guarantee that it would actually show up in a Web browser for a variety of reasons. While this problem seems tangential to the current topic, its simple and straightforward solution isn't — just superscript the letters TM. You superscript characters by putting them between the `<sup>` and `</sup>` tags as in the following code:

```
<P>We guarantee that CatMover<SUP>TM</SUP> will keep your
doorways unblocked.</P>
```

Similarly, subscripts are done with _{and} tags, as shown here::

```
<P>It was nice to get some good old H<SUB>2</SUB>0 after so
 long in the desert.</P>
```

Figure 7-5 shows superscripts and subscripts in action.

Another way (you knew this was coming) to do superscripts and subscripts is by changing the size value relative to the surrounding text using `style`.

For example, in addition to the superscript/subscript syntax, you may use the styles-based `vertical-align` attribute to precisely define how high (or low) you would wish the selected text to be in relation to the baseline.

The following command would set the selected text 50 percent higher than the surrounding text, or -50 percent to subscript it (that is, 50 percent lower than the surrounding text):

```
<p>Par<span style="vertical-align:-50%">agra</span>ph on
family.</p>
```

Unlike the subscript/superscript attribute of traditional HTML shown previously, by using this CSS method, you have a very fine degree of control in placement of the text. You can go up or down any amount. You can even use decimal increments (though good luck in trying to spot even a .999999999 percent degree of change on your monitor), thus providing a theoretically unlimited range of values you may use for text adjustment.

The following coding produces the result shown in Figure 7-6:

```
<p><center>I have gone<span style="vertical-align:50%">
up</span> by
50%.</center></p>
<p><center>I have gone<span
style="vertical-align:-50%">down</span>50%.</center></p>
<p><center>I have gone<span>
style=''vertical-align:-500%''>down</span>500%.</center></p>
```

FIGURE 7-5

Superscripts raise characters, whereas subscripts lower them.

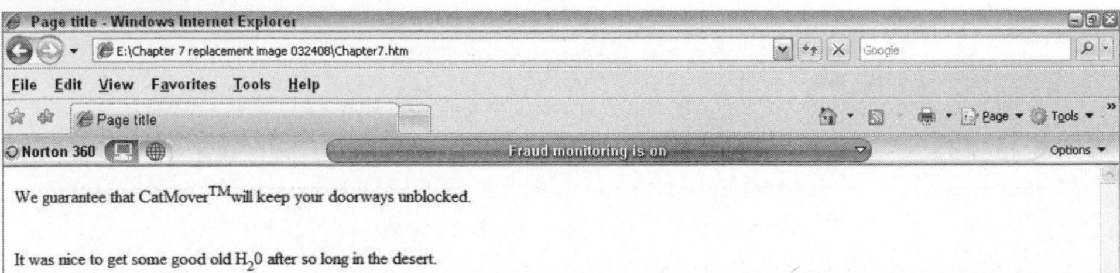

FIGURE 7-6

This example of subscripting and superscripting shows the vertical-align attribute within <span> tags of the inline style element.

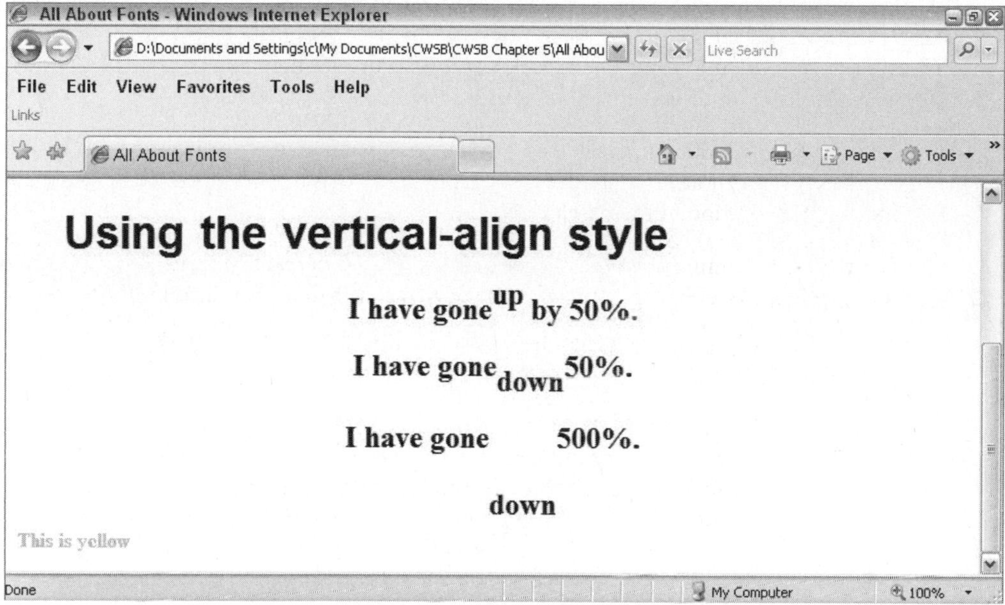

<span> and <div>

Notice the `<span>` tag in the code for Figure 7-6. The `<span>` tag is used to define a portion of text within an inline element. When you use the `<span>` tag, it selects a section of text for special treatment. This example metes out superscripting and subscripting by using the `vertical-align` attribute, and shows scalability of your Web page by using the `text-size` style to increase the heading size.

If you wanted want to select an entire block of text, you would use the `<div>` tag. Because you use `<div>` tags in conjunction with external stylesheets (and not inline elements), we will not demo it here. Chapter 12 provides more detail on using CSS (external stylesheets).

Using the FONT and BASEFONT Elements

The `FONT` element can be used to specify size, font face, and color for the text it encloses. The `BASEFONT` element (which is enclosed in the `HEAD` element of the Web page) serves an identical function, but for all the text on an entire Web page.

Specifying a size

For either the FONT or BASEFONT element, size is specified by the size attribute. Font sizes in HTML run from 1 (the smallest) through 7 (the largest). The default font size (that is, if no size is specified) is size 3, which generally is taken to mean a 12-point font. A *point* is $\frac{1}{72}$ of an inch, so a 12-point font is $\frac{1}{6}$ of an inch high. However, the actual size of a font on a visitor's screen is dependent on the browser Preference settings, so all you can do is create a hoped-for size. Figure 7-7 shows the relative sizes of the fonts on a normal Web page.

You can set an exact size for a font by using CSS, as detailed in Chapter 12.

To specify a font size of 6, write code as in this example:

```
<FONT size="6">Text goes here.</FONT>
```

The BASEFONT element works exactly the same way, except that it has no end tag — there is no such thing as </BASEFONT>. To set the global font size for the Web page to size 6, you would use the following code:

```
<HEAD>
<BASEFONT size="6">
</HEAD>
```

Font size options and inline styles

Let's take a look at the ins and outs of setting font sizing using inline styles. These might seem redundant, but each of these styles provides enhanced flexibility and very fine control compared to what you could previously exert using the limited attributes available in HTML. Styles extend the reach and degree of control over the design available to the programmer.

Using inline styles, the format of font sizing is:

```
<h1 style="font-size:length">
```

FIGURE 7-7

Font sizes vary from 1 to 7.

The `length` can be expressed in *absolute* units or *relative* units. Absolute measurements would be `mm` (millimeter), `cm` (centimeter), `in` (inches), `pt` (points), and `pc` (picas). Relative measurement would be via `em` or `ex` (which are discussed later in this chapter in the section, "Scalability and absolute measurement").

NOTE **The pica was one of two sizings popular during the decades of the typewriter. A pica is defined as 12 points. Since there are 72 points to an inch, there are 6 picas to an inch.**

Another measurement, points, provides a higher degree of granularity. In other words, you have a higher degree of control over the object.

There are four ways to change font sizes using the `length` style:

- Size can be expressed as a percentage, as you saw in previous examples.
- Size can be expressed as a unit of measurement. For example, the following code snippet produces the result shown in Figure 7-8:

  ```
  <p style="font-size:1.75cm">This text is 75% larger than text
  surrounding it.</p>
  ```

FIGURE 7-8

You can express size as a unit of measurement, in this case using em.

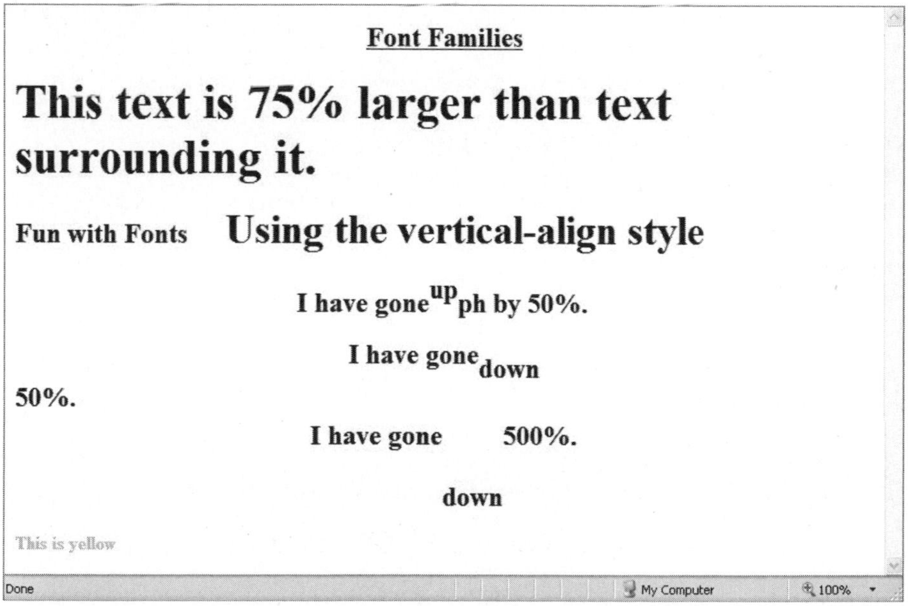

- Size may be indicated by using keywords such as `xx-small`, `x-small`, `small`, `medium`, `large`, `x-large`, or `xx-large`.
- Size may be indicated by keywords relative to the size(s) of the containing element. For example, you could use the keyword `larger` or `smaller`.

Notice that when you express size as a unit of measurement, you do not insert a space before the unit of measurement (in the previous example, this would be `em`). This is true of all length declarations — pica, point, pixel, or whatever. However, because pixel is the default, if you fail to specify a length type, the value will be calculated in pixels.

The following code produces the result shown in Figure 7-9:

```
<html>
<head>
</head>
<body>
<p style=''font-size:1.75em''>Using the font-size 1.75 em we have
made this text
75% larger than text surrounding it.</p -->
<p style=''font-size:larger''>Using the keyword ''larger'' we have
made this text
75%
larger than the text surrounding it.</p-->
<p style=''font-size:xx-small''>Using the keyword xx-small we have
made this text much much smaller than text surrounding it.</p>
</body>
</html>
```

FIGURE 7-9

The scale runs from xx-small, as in this instance, to xx-large. In HTML, the code used to resize segments of text (<font size = "value">text</font>) is deprecated.

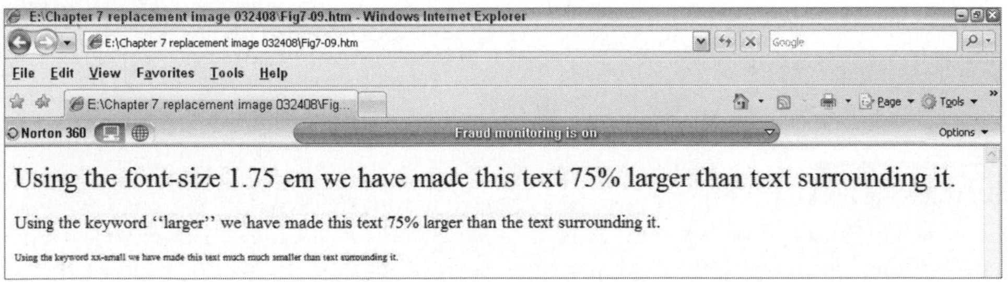

Figure 7-10 shows the result of using HTML coding.

FIGURE 7-10

This example shows both CSS and deprecated HTML to reduce relative size of text. Can you tell which is deprecated?

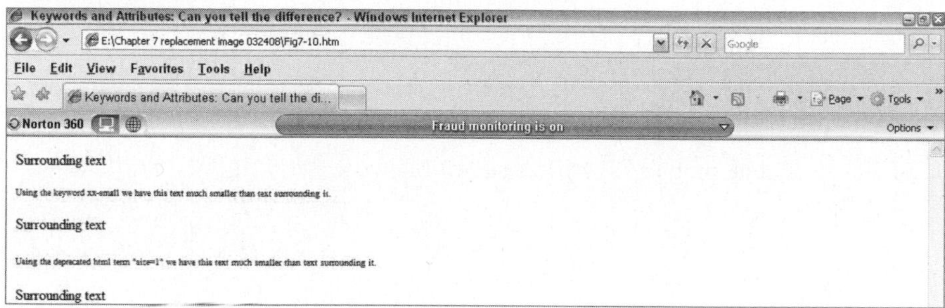

Scalability and absolute measurement

Scalability means the browsers renders the Web content in the same format irrespective of screen resolution — in other words, your Web page will appear readable in a variety of screen resolutions. You can produce scalability by keeping in mind the following:

- The `ex` keyword refers to the height of the letter "x" in lowercase.
- The keyword `em` refers to the width of the uppercase letter "M".

For example, if you would want a heading to appear 20 percent larger than the surrounding text, you would set the `size` value as follows:

```
font-size:1.2em.
```

An *absolute measurement* is one that does not scale to the size of the screen on which the font is being rendered. For example, if you were to insert text 6 inches high, it would be visible on most screens used today. But someone with Web access via a mobile phone with a 3-inch screen would not be able to read the text clearly.

NOTE **Of course, font-size may also be set by using pixels (which would be coded `px`). Indeed, this is the most common measurement used. It is so common that it is the default value and you do not even need to use `px` when giving a size. However, it is not an absolute measurement, because the size of a pixel varies on different browser types and screen resolutions.**

Inline style

An *inline style* simply means that the attribute style is used inside a tag. The following example selects a sans-serif font type to render the encapsulated phrase, "I attribute my style":

```
<h1 style="font-family: Arial, Tahoma, Verdana, sans-serif ">
I attribute my style</h1>
```

The following example subscripts the selected text "down" 50 percent:

```
<p><center>I have gone<span style="vertical-align:-50%">down
</center></span>50%.</p>
```

The following example turns the font color of the encapsulated text yellow:

```
<p><font><span style ="color:yellow ">This is yellow</span>
</font></p>
```

Using relative size in standard HTML coding

Font size can also be set relative to the default font size (or to the BASEFONT size, if one exists). To make the affected characters one size larger than the default, use this code:

```
<FONT size="+1">Text goes here.</FONT>
```

To make the characters two sizes smaller than the default, use a minus sign instead:

```
<FONT size="-2">Text goes here.</FONT>
```

Remember that there are only seven font sizes possible in HTML. You can't make anything smaller than size 1 or larger than size 7. So, if you had a default font size of 3 and used the following code, you'd still have only a size 7 font as a result:

```
<FONT size="+6">Text goes here.</FONT>
```

There is no way to get to a size 9 font, because it doesn't exist.

Comparing font size with heading size

Whoever first came up with heading sizes 1 through 6 and font sizes 1 through 7 had a keen sense of proportionality. If only there were an H0, then headings would fall into a perfect inverse ratio. The way it works is that an H1 heading is font size 6, an H2 heading is font size 5, and so forth, all the way down to where an H6 heading is font size 1. The only difference is that the heading text is automatically bold. Figure 7-11 shows this relationship graphically.

FIGURE 7-11

Heading sizes and font sizes are inversely proportional.

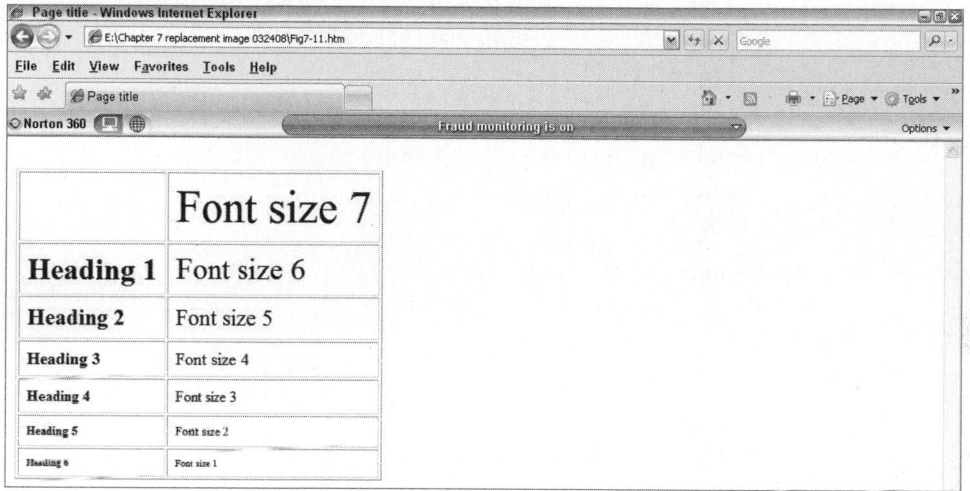

Overriding default font faces

By using the `face` attribute, you can override the default fonts used on Web pages. For example, the normal font used when you display a Web page on Windows systems is Times New Roman. However, it is customary for headings to be in a sans-serif font such as Arial instead. But on Web pages, headings and text are both in the same font.

The way to change this is to set a particular element on the Web page to a different *font face*. A font face is the way the lettering looks. For example, as you learned at the beginning of this chapter, the serif font Times New Roman has a series of small lines, while a sans-serif font such as Arial does not.

NOTE **"Serif" means "with feet" and "sans-serif" means "without feet."**

To change a particular element so that it has a different font face, use the following code:

```
<H1><FONT face="Arial">Changed text goes here.</FONT></H1>
```

NOTE **This is one of the places where CSS shines. Check out Chapter 12 for information on how to change all instances of headers to a different font.**

It is customary to specify more than one font face because not everyone using the World Wide Web is using the same computer system. While the most popular sans-serif font is called Arial on Windows computers, it is called Helvetica on Macintosh systems. To take things one step further, both Arial and Helvetica are in the sans-serif family. Thus, to cover all the bases, you would need to specify the font face as follows:

```
<H1><FONT face="Arial, Helvetica, sans-serif">Changed text goes
here.</FONT></H1>
```

By doing this, you enable the system used by your site visitors the greatest latitude in choosing a display font. If Arial is not available, the system tries for Helvetica. If neither is available, a different font from the sans-serif family is used instead. This approach ensures the likelihood that a visitor sees things the way you intended them to be seen.

This can be set globally for the entire Web page by using the BASEFONT element as follows:

```
<BASEFONT face="Arial, Helvetica, sans-serif">
```

Coloring text

The color of particular characters can be set with the color attribute of the FONT or BASEFONT element. To set it for a particular group of text (down to even a single character), use the following code:

```
<FONT color="red">Colored text goes here.</FONT>
```

To set all the text on the Web page to the same color, you can use the BASEFONT element as in this example:

```
<BASEFONT color="red">
```

CROSS-REF **The best way to set the text color for the whole page is to use the text attribute of the BODY element, as discussed in Chapter 6.**

Using fonts with style

All of the following illustrations are ways to make portions of Web page fonts stand out in some way to draw the attention of the viewer. Each of the examples here uses CSS techniques to create special font effects. You might use these techniques in advertising where you want to direct someone to a sponsor's link. You could use these techniques to draw attention to something significant in your own life (such as in the example All About Me Web page), or highlight an action of a member of your family (such as a new birth, marriage, graduation, or the like).

The basic format is to use `style=''attribute:value''` (as in `style= ''font-weight'': 800`). However, you can also manipulate text in variety of different ways.

You can use `text-decoration` to cause selected text have the following effects:

- `blink` — This causes selected text to blink.
- `overline` — This produces text with an overline.

- `underline` — This produces text with an underline.
- `line-through` — This produces text with a strikethrough effect.

You can also use `font-variant` in the same fashion to create special text effects such as small caps.

You can use more than one feature at a time. For example, the following code produces the words "LOOK AT THE BLINKING TEXT" in small caps with an overline and strikethrough effects, all while blinking on the screen:

```
<h1>Style="text-decoration:overline line-through blink; font-variant:
small-caps">Look at the blinking text</h1>
```

You use `font-weight` pretty much the same as you use <b> in HTML, though this CSS variant does offer finer control. You specify `font-weight` on a scale of 100 to 900, with 700 representing the equivalent to <b>. However, on good (but not exceptional) viewing devices, you probably won't really be able to tell if some thing is displayed with `font-weight` set at 700, 800, or 900. You can also use `font-weight` in relative terms by using of keywords `bolder` or `lighter`.

You can use `font-style` to change text to `italic` (or `oblique`, which is, pretty much, italic). Following is the CSS command sequence:

```
<h1 style="font-style:oblique">Italic</h1>
```

However, if you look at the following corresponding HTMLcode, you realize that, while there are instances where styles certainly provide advantages in terms of more thorough control over some elements, this doesn't appear to be one of those instances:

```
<h1><i>Italic</i><h1>
```

You can use `text-transform` to convert text to uppercase, lowercase, or initial caps (which means the first letter of each word is capitalized).

Kerning is the adjustment of the space between letters. You can effect kerning by using `letter-spacing` similar to the following example:

```
<h1 style="letter-spacing:25">Spaced out</h1>
```

The result of this code is as follows:

```
S    p    a    c    e    d    o    u    t
```

Tracking, on the other hand, is the adjustment of the space between words. You can effect tracking by using `word-spacing` similar to the following example:

```
<h1>style="word-spacing:25">Spaced out<</h1>
```

This code would produce the following result:

```
Spaced     out.
```

You can also work with indents using the `text-indent` style, where the value can be positive (to create a regular indent) or negative (to create a hanging indent). The style is used inside a list element. For example, to create a hanging indent in All About Fonts, you would use the following code:

```
<dd style="text-indent:-38">.
```

Figure 7-12 shows an example of the `text-indent` style using a negative number.

You can also create interesting effects in the header by manipulating line spacing using the `line-height` attribute to bring two lines of data closer together to enhance the visual impact. For example, the following command creates a line height of three times the normal amount:

```
style="line-height: 3em"
```

FIGURE 7-12

Using a negative value for the text-indent produces an interesting result.

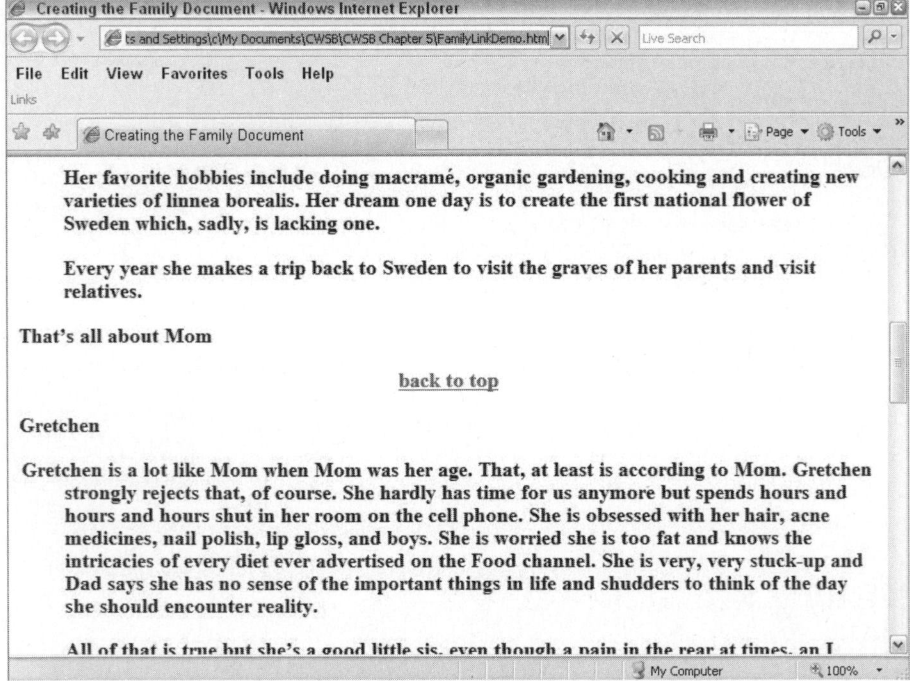

You can similarly use negative values to bring lines closer together.

Aligning and Indenting Text

The `P` (paragraph) element has four possible alignments — left, center, right, and justify. The same is true of the six heading elements (`H1` through `H6` — sometimes described collectively as the `Hx` elements, where *x* stands for the number). If you want to make a paragraph right-aligned, you can do it as in this example:

```
<P align="right">Paragraph text goes here.</P>
```

An `H1` element can be centered with this code:

```
<H1 align="center">Heading text goes here.</H1>
```

For justified text, simply use the word `justify` instead of `right` or `center`. Because left alignment is the default alignment, you don't have to specify it. Figure 7-13 shows some paragraphs and headings with various alignments.

FIGURE 7-13

Different alignment values create different results.

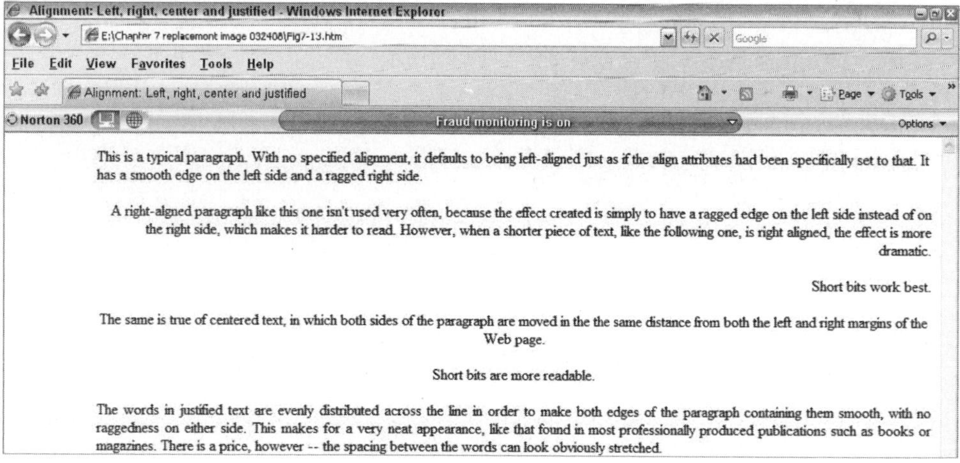

Dealing with deprecation

The deprecated `CENTER` element is a simple and easy way of aligning text, but it's frowned upon by W3C, which suggests doing it in a more complicated and potentially confusing manner.

According to the HTML standard, "A deprecated element or attribute is one that has been outdated by newer constructs." This would be no problem if the definition worked effectively, but in many cases, it has been applied to elements and attributes for which there is no better alternative available.

The W3C's reasoning relies on some old arguments about whether or not HTML should include elements and attributes that define how things look, or whether or not elements and attributes should describe the informational content of Web pages. It's very much a case of shutting the barn door after the horse is far over the horizon. Of course, these elements and attributes already exist and are already in worldwide use. It's as if you're trying to decide whether the English language should or shouldn't have adverbs in it.

No one's going to tear down the Web and rebuild all the old pages to suit the W3 C, and no sane browser maker is going to phase out backward compatibility, either. In fact, the HTML standard itself states that browsers should continue to support deprecated elements and attributes. All of this means that these deprecated methods are still fully functional, a lot easier than any alternative yet presented, and will be around for a long, long time to come.

Let's run a few examples past you to show just what we mean. Let's say that you want to center some text. We've already discussed how to do it for `P` and `Hx` elements. Here's another way to go about it:

```
<CENTER>Text to be centered goes here.</CENTER>
```

Simple, elegant, and as easy as it gets. And you can put just about anything between the `<CENTER>` and `</CENTER>` tags, including images (see Chapter 8). It has the same effect as writing this code:

```
<P align="center">Text to be centered goes here.</P>
```

But you're not supposed to use the `CENTER` element any more, or the `align` attribute, according to the W3 C. So, how do you do it?

You do what works for you.

NOTE **Don't get the idea that we're against using CSS. It does have its uses, and it can be a very powerful way to control your Web sites. We do, however, believe in using the best tool for any particular job, and using something as complex as CSS to replace simple existing elements is like using an atom bomb to crack open an egg.**

Indenting with BLOCKQUOTE

As you have seen, the `BLOCKQUOTE` element has a certain, specific purpose — to mark off long sections of material quoted from another source. However, it also has an interesting side effect.

It causes all the text contained within it to be indented equally from both sides of the screen. Figure 7-14 shows some normal text and some text indented using `BLOCKQUOTE`.

The process, once again, is simple:

```
<BLOCKQUOTE>Text to be indented goes here.</BLOCKQUOTE>
```

As you might expect, this is too easy, so the W3C has deprecated this use. To the best of our knowledge, it's the only use of an element that has ever been deprecated, even though it isn't possible under the HTML standard's definition of the word. The element itself hasn't been deprecated, but using it to indent text is officially frowned upon. The suggested alternative (as you might have guessed) is to use complex CSS instead. Take your pick of which way you want to do it; both of them work.

Choosing Character Sets

A character set is, basically, the manner in which a group of letters or symbols are *mapped* — that is, A is followed by B, and so forth. As a Web page creator, you do not need to concern yourself with the actual mapping, but you still need to pay attention to the character set you're using because different character sets represent the characters used in different languages. HTML recognizes one very important character set, called ISO 10646, also known as Unicode, the Universal Character Set, or UCS (see `www.unicode.org` for more information).

FIGURE 7-14

The BLOCKQUOTE element enables you to quickly indent text.

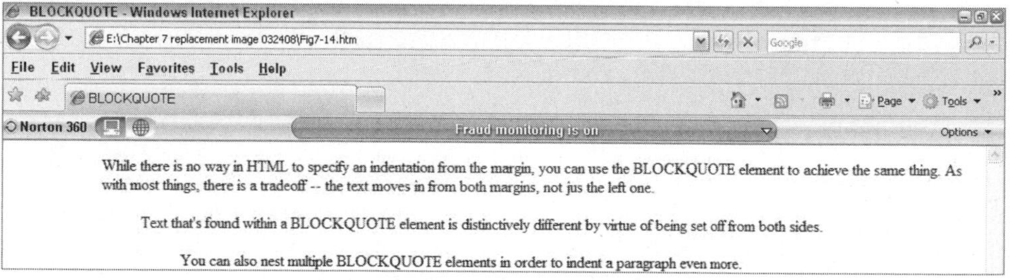

NOTE **The International Organization for Standardization (ISO) is the group responsible for promulgating character standards (and many other types of standards as well — the next time you buy film, notice that the film speed is also rated according to an ISO standard). The number is simply the ISO's reference for the particular character set.**

ISO 10646, however, is vast and far too unwieldy for normal use, so there are subsets of it that are normally used instead of the whole thing — the most common of which is known as ISO 8859-1 (also called Western or Latin 1). Until recently, this was the only character set used in HTML.

Character sets are specified in a META element with the charset attribute, as in the following example code:

```
<HTML>
 <HEAD>
 <META http-equiv="Content-Type" content="text/html;
charset=iso-8859-1">
 </HEAD>
 <BODY>
...
 </BODY>
 </HTML>
```

NOTE **The ellipsis (...) in the preceding code represents the portion of the Web page visible in a browser. It is not a part of the example's HTML code.**

If you're not interested in the details of what this code means, you can safely skip the next paragraph and just copy the META element exactly, substituting for ISO-8859-1 whatever character set you're using.

CROSS-REF **Metatags are also discussed in Chapter 4.**

For those who want to know the why as well as the how, the META element (which must be contained within the HEAD element) is a generic method for adding information to a Web page that is not a normal part of HTML. In this case, it is being used to supply information to a Web server about the character encoding method being used on the Web page. The information in the http-equiv attribute is read by the Web server handling the page containing the code, and is interpreted by the server as if it were an *HTTP header*. HTTP, as you recall, is the Hyptertext Transfer Protocol, the Web's native method of transferring information. Generally, the Web server itself generates the HTTP header information, but specifying an http-equiv value in the Web page overrides this behavior, causing the Web server to send the specified value to the Web browser when it sends the Web page to it to be displayed.

NOTE **The charset attribute is poorly named because it does not actually define a character set, but the method of encoding those characters. This and the exact definitions of many other terms relating to character sets and character encoding are the source of furious debate among technical folks. However, for all practical purposes, all a Web page author really needs to know is to use a charset value that includes the language grouping he or she is writing in.**

While ISO 8859-1 covers most of the characters the average American or Western European Web designer is ever likely to use, the fact that the World Wide Web is, well, worldwide, means that every language on Earth needs to be taken into account. The different characters used in countries such as Tibet, Greenland, Israel, and Russia are not included in ISO 8859-1.

Table 1 shows some of the other 8859-family character sets that are available and their common names. The ISO Reference column lists the character set numbers exactly as they should appear in your HTML code's `charset` attribute.

NOTE **An alternative Cyrillic character set, KOI8-R, is more popular in Russia than ISO-8859-5.**

TABLE 7-1

The ISO 8859 Family of Character Sets

ISO Reference	Common Name	Language Group
`iso-8859-1`	Western or Latin 1	West European — Danish, Dutch, English, Faeroese, Finnish, French, German, Icelandic, Irish, Italian, Norwegian, Portuguese, Spanish, and Swedish.
`iso-8859-2`	Latin 2	Central and East European — Albanian, Czech, English, German, Hungarian, Polish, Rumanian, Serbo-Croatian, Slovak, Slovene, and Swedish
`iso-8859-3`	Latin3	South European, Maltese, Esperanto
`iso-8859-4`	Latin4	North European — Afrikaans, Catalan, English, Esperanto, French, Galician, German, Italian, Maltese, and Turkish
`iso-8859-5`	Cyrillic	Bulgarian, Byelorussian, English, Latin, (Slavic) Macedonian, Russian, Serbian, and Ukrainian
`iso-8859-6`	Arabic	Arabic
`iso-8859-7`	Greek	Greek
`iso-8859-8`	Hebrew	Hebrew
`iso-8859-9`	Latin 5	Albanian, Basque, Breton, Catalan, Danish, Dutch, English, Faroese, Finnish, French (with restrictions), Frisian, Galician, German, Greenlandic, Irish Gaelic (new orthography), Italian, Latin, Luxemburgish, Norwegian, Portuguese, Rhaeto-Romanic, Scottish Gaelic, Spanish, Swedish, and Turkish
`iso-8859-10`	Latin 6	Danish, English, Estonian, Faroese, Finnish, German, Greenlandic, Icelandic, Sami (Lappish), Latvian, Lithuanian, Norwegian, and Swedish

Further extensions to the 8859 family are in the works:

- ISO 8859-11 (Thai)
- ISO 8859-13 (Celtic or Latin 7)
- ISO 8859-14 (Baltic Rim or Latin 8)
- ISO 8859-15 (Sami or Latin 9)

Oddly enough, the number 12 was skipped — perhaps someone, someday, will propose an ISO standard numbered 8859-12, but it apparently hasn't happened yet.

One other oddity — the 8859 series of standards (at least through ISO 8859-10) was not developed by the ISO, but by the European Computer Manufacturers Association (ECMA). In a further bizarre development, the ISO refuses to put the actual standards on the Web for free access, but sells them, while ECMA makes them available for free at `www.ecma-international.org/publications/standards/Standard.htm`. However, you have to dig through all of ECMA's documentation by topic, because the original versions, of course, don't have the ISO number. To save you the trouble, we've done it for you, and the results are shown in Table 7-2.

These are PDF files, which means that you must have Adobe Acrobat Reader installed to read them.

TABLE 7-2

The Original ECMA Versions of the ISO 8859 Standards

ISO Reference	ECMA Designation	URL
ISO 8859-1 through ISO 8859-4	Latin 1 through Latin 4	`www.ecma-international.org/publications/files/ECMA-ST/Ecma-094.pdf`
ISO 8859-5	Cyrillic	`www.ecma-international.org/publications/files/ECMA-ST/Ecma-113.pdf`
ISO 8859-6	Latin/Arabic	`www.ecma-international.org/publications/files/ECMA-ST/Ecma-114.pdf`
ISO 8859-7	Latin/Greek	`www.ecma-international.org/publications/files/ECMA-ST/Ecma-118.pdf`
ISO 8859-8	Latin/Hebrew	`www.ecma-international.org/publications/files/ECMA-ST/Ecma-121.pdf`
ISO 8859-9	Latin 5	`www.ecma-international.org/publications/files/ECMA-ST/Ecma-128.pdf`
ISO 8859-10	Latin 6	`http://www.ecma-international.org/publications/files/ECMA-ST/Ecma-144.pdf`

In addition to the ISO 8859 series of character sets, several others can be used for the same language groups, but if you stray from the ISO standards, you risk creating a Web page that will not display properly on all systems. The Windows-specific character sets created by Microsoft are particularly prone to wrecking a well-designed Web page because they violate the standard encoding methods in order to include some extra characters. This can cause serious problems on non-Windows browsers. Table 7-3 shows the Windows-specific character sets and the ISO character sets that are roughly equivalent to them.

Of course, if you're going to be doing a Vietnamese Web page, you have no option but to use `windows-1258`. In fact, all of the ISO 8859 family is limited to Western hemisphere language groups, although the Unicode project has gone further with its new work (see `www.unicode.org` for more information). However, there are several other Oriental language character sets, the most common of which are listed in Table 7-4.

TIP **For a more extensive list of character sets supported by major Web browsers, visit the World Wide Web Consortium's listing at** `www.w3.org/International/O-charset-list.html`.

Using Special Characters and Entities

You may need to use certain characters from time to time that are not found on your keyboard. How, for example, would you type a nonbreaking space? How would a Web designer in New York type a pound or yen sign? Two methods are available for adding these types of characters — by character code number and by character entity.

TABLE 7-3

Windows-Specific Character Sets

Microsoft Reference	ISO Equivalent
`windows-1250`	`iso-8859-2`
`windows-1251`	`iso-8859-5`
`windows-1252`	`iso-8859-1`
`windows-1253`	`iso-8859-7`
`windows-1254`	`iso-8859-9`
`windows-1255`	`iso-8859-8`
`windows-1256`	`iso-8859-6`
`windows-1257`	`iso-8859-4`
`windows-1258`	None (Vietnamese language)

TABLE 7-4

Eastern Hemisphere Character Sets

Language	Character Set
Chinese (Simplified)	gb2312
Chinese (Traditional)	big5
Japanese	Shift_JIS
Japanese (JIS)	iso-2022-jp
Japanese (EUC)	EUC-JP
Korean	euc-kr

When special character standards were first created, they were simply numbered by their order in the list. Thus, character number 160 was followed by character number 161, by character number 162, and so forth. Each special character was added to a Web page by typing a numeric value into the HTML code — for example, ` ` for character number 160 (all special character codes begin with an ampersand and end with a semicolon). The problem with this approach is that it's a bit difficult for everyone to remember that character number 160 is a nonbreaking space, while character number 8226 is a solid bullet.

That's where *character entities* come into the picture. The vast majority of character entities are simply shortened forms of the character you want to use. It's much easier to remember that you need to type ` ` for a nonbreaking space or `•` for a bullet than it is to memorize the numerical position of every character in the listings. Figure 7-15 shows how some special characters look on a Web page.

Tables 5 and 6 list the character codes and character entities from the HTML standard, but are rearranged into alphabetical order instead of numerical order for easier reference.

So, if you're writing a Web page in English and want to include the Spanish word *mañana*, you're in a jam because the standard English keyboard doesn't include the *ñ* character — an "n" with a tilde. To solve the problem, simply scan down the list of character entities until you find `ñ` — at that point, you can either enter the character entity itself or the numerical code (`ñ`), whichever you prefer to use. To use the character entity to write the word *mañana*, use the following code:

```
ma&ntilde;ana
```

Or you can do the same thing with the numerical code:

```
ma&#241;ana
```

FIGURE 7-15

Some special characters and their respective codes.

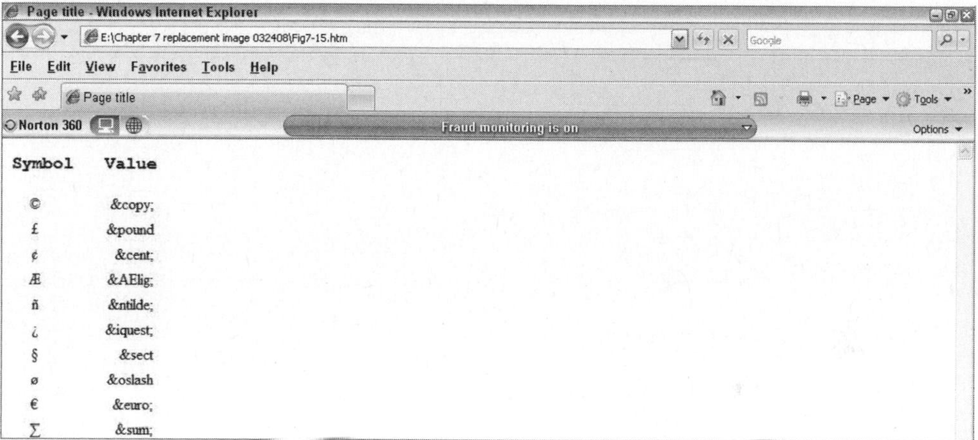

TABLE 7-5

Common HTML Character Entities and Codes

Character Entity	Character Code	Character Description and Appearance
Á	Á	Latin capital letter A with acute (′) accent
á	á	Latin small letter a with acute (′) accent
Â	Â	Latin capital letter A with circumflex (ˆ)
â	â	Latin small letter a with circumflex (ˆ)
´	´	Acute accent (ˆ)
Æ	Æ	Latin capital ligature AE (Æ)
æ	æ	Latin small ligature ae (æ)
À	À	Latin capital letter A with grave (‘) accent
à	à	Latin small letter a with grave (‘) accent
Å	Å	Latin capital letter A with ring above (Å)
å	å	Latin small letter a with ring above (å)

continued

TABLE 7-5 *(continued)*

Character Entity	Character Code	Character Description and Appearance
Ã	Ã	Latin capital letter A with tilde (Ā)
ã	ã	Latin small letter a with tilde (ā)
Ä	Ä	Latin capital letter A with diaeresis (Ä)
ä	ä	Latin small letter a with diaeresis (ä)
¦	¦	Broken vertical bar (¦)
•	•	Bullet (•)
Ç	Ç	Latin capital letter C with cedilla (Ç)
ç	ç	Latin small letter c with cedilla (ç)
¸	¸	Cedilla ¸
¢	¢	Cent sign (¢)
♣	♣	Black club suit (♣)
©	©	Copyright sign (©)
¤	¤	Currency sign ($)
°	°	Degree sign (°)
♦	♦	Black diamond suit (♦)
÷	÷	Division sign (÷)
É	É	Latin capital letter E with acute accent (É)
é	é	Latin small letter e with acute accent (é)
Ê	Ê	Latin capital letter E with circumflex (Ê)
ê	ê	Latin small letter e with circumflex (ê)
È	È	Latin capital letter E with accent grave (È)
è	è	Latin small letter e with accent grave (è)
Ð	Ð	Latin capital letter ETH
ð	ð	Latin small letter eth
Ë	Ë	Latin capital letter E with diaeresis (Ë)
ë	ë	Latin small letter e with diaeresis (ë)
½	½	Fraction one-half ($\frac{1}{2}$)
¼	¼	Fraction one-quarter ($\frac{1}{4}$)
¾	¾	Fraction three-quarters ($\frac{3}{4}$)

TABLE 7-5 *(continued)*

Character Entity	Character Code	Character Description and Appearance
`⁄`	`⁄`	Fraction slash (⁄)
`♥`	`♥`	Black heart suit (♥)
`Í`	`Í`	Latin capital letter I with acute (Í) accent
`í`	`í`	Latin small letter i with acute (í) accent
`Î`	`Î`	Latin capital letter I with circumflex (Î)
`î`	`î`	Latin small letter i with circumflex (î)
`¡`	`¡`	Inverted exclamation mark (¡)
`Ì`	`Ì`	Latin capital letter I with grave (Ì) accent
`ì`	`ì`	Latin small letter i with grave (ì) accent
`¿`	`¿`	Inverted question mark (¿)
`Ï`	`Ï`	Latin capital letter I with diaeresis (Ï)
`Ñ`	`Ñ`	Latin capital letter N with tilde (Ñ)
`ñ`	`ñ`	Latin small letter n with tilde (ñ)
`Ó`	`Ó`	Latin capital letter O with acute (Ó) accent
`ó`	`ó`	Latin small letter o with acute (ó) accent
`Ô`	`Ô`	Latin capital letter O with circumflex (Ô)
`ô`	`ô`	Latin small letter o with circumflex (ô)
`Ò`	`Ò`	Latin capital letter O with grave (Ò) accent
`ò`	`ò`	Latin small letter o with grave (ò) accent
`Ø`	`Ø`	Latin capital letter O with stroke (Ø)
`ø`	`ø`	Latin small letter o with stroke (ø)
`Õ`	`Õ`	Latin capital letter O with tilde (Õ)
`õ`	`õ`	Latin small letter o with tilde (õ)
`Ö`	`Ö`	Latin capital letter O with diaeresis (Ö)
`ö`	`ö`	Latin small letter o with diaeresis (ö)
`¶`	`¶`	Pilcrow sign, or paragraph sign (¶)
`£`	`£`	Pound sign (#)
`®`	`®`	Registered trademark sign (®)
`§`	`§`	Section sign (§)

continued

TABLE 7-5 *(continued)*

Character Entity	Character Code	Character Description and Appearance
`&spades:`	`♠`	Black spade suit (♠)
`¹`	`¹`	Superscript digit one (^{1})
`²`	`²`	Superscript digit two (^{2})
`³`	`³`	Superscript digit three (^{3})
`™`	`™`	Trademark sign (™)
`Ú`	`Ú`	Latin capital letter U with acute (Ú) accent
`ú`	`ú`	Latin small letter u with acute (ú) accent
`Û`	`Û`	Latin capital letter U with circumflex (Û)
`û`	`û`	Latin small letter u with circumflex (û)
`Ù`	`Ù`	Latin capital letter U with grave (Ù)
`ù`	`ù`	Latin small letter u with grave (ù) accent
`¨`	`¨`	Diaeresis (· ·)
`Ü`	`Ü`	Latin capital letter U with diaeresis (Ü)
`ü`	`ü`	Latin small letter u with diaeresis (ü)
`Ý`	`Ý`	Latin capital letter Y with acute (Ý) accent
`ý`	`ý`	Latin small letter y with acute (ý) accent
`ÿ`	`ÿ`	Latin small letter y with diaeresis (ÿ)

TABLE 7-6

HTML Technical and Math Character Entities and Codes

Character Entity	Character Code	Character Description and Appearance
`ℵ`	`ℵ`	Alef symbol
`Α`	`Α`	Greek capital letter alpha
`α`	`α`	Greek small letter alpha
`∧`	`∧`	Logical and
`∠`	`∠`	Angle
`≈`	`≈`	Asymptotic to
`Β`	`Β`	Greek capital letter beta
`β`	`β`	Greek small letter beta

TABLE 7-6 *(continued)*

Character Entity	Character Code	Character Description and Appearance
∩	∩	Intersection
Χ	Χ	Greek capital letter chi
χ	χ	Greek small letter chi
≅	≅	Approximately equal to
↵	↵	Downwards arrow with corner leftward
∪	∪	Union
↓	↓	Downward arrow
⇓	⇓	Downward double arrow
Δ	Δ	Greek capital letter delta
δ	δ	Greek small letter delta
∅	∅	Empty set
Ε	Ε	Greek capital letter epsilon
ε	ε	Greek small letter epsilon
≡	≡	Identical to
Η	Η	Greek capital letter eta
η	η	Greek small letter eta
∃	∃	There exists
∀	∀	For all
Γ	Γ	Greek capital letter gamma
γ	γ	Greek small letter gamma
≥	≥	Greater than or equal to
↔	↔	Left right arrow
⇔	⇔	Left right double arrow
ℑ	ℑ	Imaginary part
∞	∞	Infinity
∫	∫	Integral
Ι	Ι	Greek capital letter iota
ι	ι	Greek small letter iota

continued

TABLE 7-6 *(continued)*

Character Entity	Character Code	Character Description and Appearance
∈	∈	Element of
Κ	Κ	Greek capital letter kappa
κ	κ	Greek small letter kappa
Λ	Λ	Greek capital letter lambda
λ	λ	Greek small letter lambda
⟨	〈	Left-pointing angle bracket
←	←	Leftward arrow
⇐	⇐	Leftward double arrow
⌈	⌈	Left ceiling
≤	≤	Less than or equal to
⌊	⌊	Left floor
∗	∗	Asterisk operator
−	−	Minus sign
Μ	Μ	Greek capital letter mu
μ	μ	Greek small letter mu
∇	∇	Nabla
≠	≠	Not equal to
∋	∋	Contains as member
∉	∉	Not an element of
⊄	⊄	Not a subset of
Ν	Ν	Greek capital letter nu
ν	ν	Greek small letter nu
Ω	Ω	Greek capital letter omega
ω	ω	Greek small letter omega
Ο	Ο	Greek capital letter omicron
ο	ο	Greek small letter omicron
⊕	⊕	Circled plus
∨	∨	Logical or

TABLE 7-6 *(continued)*

Character Entity	Character Code	Character Description and Appearance
⊗	⊗	Circled times
∂	∂	Partial differential
⊥	⊥	Perpendicular
Φ	Φ	Greek capital letter phi
φ	φ	Greek small letter phi
Π	Π	Greek capital letter pi
π	π	Greek small letter pi
ϖ	ϖ	Greek pi symbol
∏	∏	N-ary product
∝	∝	Proportional to
Ψ	Ψ	Greek capital letter psi
ψ	ψ	Greek small letter psi
√	√	Radical sign
⟩	〉	Right-pointing angle bracket
→	→	Rightward arrow
⇒	⇒	Rightward double arrow
⌉	⌉	Right ceiling
ℜ	ℜ	Real part symbol
⌋	⌋	Right floor
Ρ	Ρ	Greek capital letter rho
ρ	ρ	Greek small letter rho
⋅	⋅	Dot operator
Σ	Σ	Greek capital letter sigma
σ	σ	Greek small letter sigma
ς	ς	Greek small letter final sigma
∼	∼	Similar to
⊂	⊂	Subset of
⊆	⊆	Subset of or equal to

continued

TABLE 7-6 *(continued)*

Character Entity	Character Code	Character Description and Appearance
∑	∑	N-ary sumation
⊃	⊃	Superset of
⊇	⊇	Superset of or equal to
Τ	Τ	Greek capital letter tau
τ	τ	Greek small letter tau
∴	∴	Therefore
Θ	Θ	Greek capital letter theta
θ	θ	Greek small letter theta
ϑ	ϑ	Greek small letter theta symbol
↑	↑	Upward arrow
⇑	⇑	Upward double arrow
ϒ	ϒ	Greek upsilon with hook symbol
Υ	Υ	Greek capital letter upsilon
υ	υ	Greek small letter upsilon
℘	℘	Weierstrass p
Ξ	Ξ	Greek capital letter xi
ξ	ξ	Greek small letter xi
Ζ	Ζ	Greek capital letter zeta
ζ	ζ	Greek small letter zeta

In either case, ensure that you always include the beginning ampersand (&) and the ending semicolon (;) — if you leave them out, you won't get the special character.

Most special characters in Table5 are designed to work only with the Latin 1 (ISO 8859-1) character set.

Summary

This chapter reviewed the format syles using both HTML 4.0x and new CSS styles, including the major font types (serif and san-serif).

This chapter examined the use of HTML-based text styles to italicize, boldface, or underline text. We also showed the preformatting tag and discussed appropriate uses of proportional and nonproportional fonts. We looked at the use of subscripts and superscripts both as HTML and CSS coding, and provided examples of each. The discussion noted the greater flexibility provided through styles. The examination looked at the use of the `span` tag and touched upon the use of the `div` tag in reference to its application in stylesheets.

This chapter also looked at several of the elements applicable to fonts. We have reviewed the ease of the `<BASEFONT>` tag to set all features through this one element. We have gone into the details of font specifications, discussing the numerous ways of sizing fonts, spacing both words and letters, transforming the appearance by using styles attributes (such as uppercase, lowercase, and small-capped), font faces, and font colors.

In this chapter, you have learned about the background of some decisions related to programming using tried-and-true formulas of character manipulation in HTML and the newer (and sometimes not user-friendly) methods of CSS. You also saw examples of block manipulation using `BLOCKQUOTE` tags.

The chapter concluded with a comprehensive overview of several of the character sets used in Web page encoding for multiple countries. The discussion included tables containing many of the more common codings for formatting and creation of symbols in HTML.

Chapter 8 discusses how to make tables and how to manipulate cells and cell contents.

Part III

Advanced Design Features

IN THIS PART

Chapter 8

Harnessing the Power of Tables

IN THIS CHAPTER

Adding tables and setting table size

Managing borders

Using padding and spacing

Aligning tables and cell contents

Spanning rows and columns

Working with images and color

Tables quick reference

Although tables on Web pages can be incredibly dull, they also can be the single greatest tool at your disposal. It all depends on how you use them. If a table does nothing but list row after row of numbers or words, then it's pretty hard to make it an exciting addition to your site. Of course, setting up neat and well-structured tabular data is a useful and often necessary way of presenting information. We're not exactly against it — you notice that we use tables of tabular data in the examples in this book from time to time when that's the best way to get something across.

But that's the pedestrian side of tables, and, even though it's all you can do with tables on paper, Web pages enable you to use tables in astonishing ways. Let's start with the basics: tables are groups of cells that contain information. The only difference between dull, plebian tables and powerful, delightful ones is what you choose to put in the cells of the table. Each cell in a table can hold nearly anything that can be put on a Web page — frames are just about the only exception, and that's because table cells can only contain things that also go into the `BODY` element. There's practically no limit to what you can do with a little imagination.

CROSS-REF **See Chapter 3 for a discussion of the `BODY` element and Chapter 9 for information on frames.**

Adding Tables and Setting Table Size

Savvy Web designers have used tables to structure their pages for years. Some of the most exciting and unusual designs — the ones that make you wonder, "How did they do that?" — are simply tables with the cells filled

FIGURE 8-1

Tables can also be used to structure Web pages and hold nontextual content.

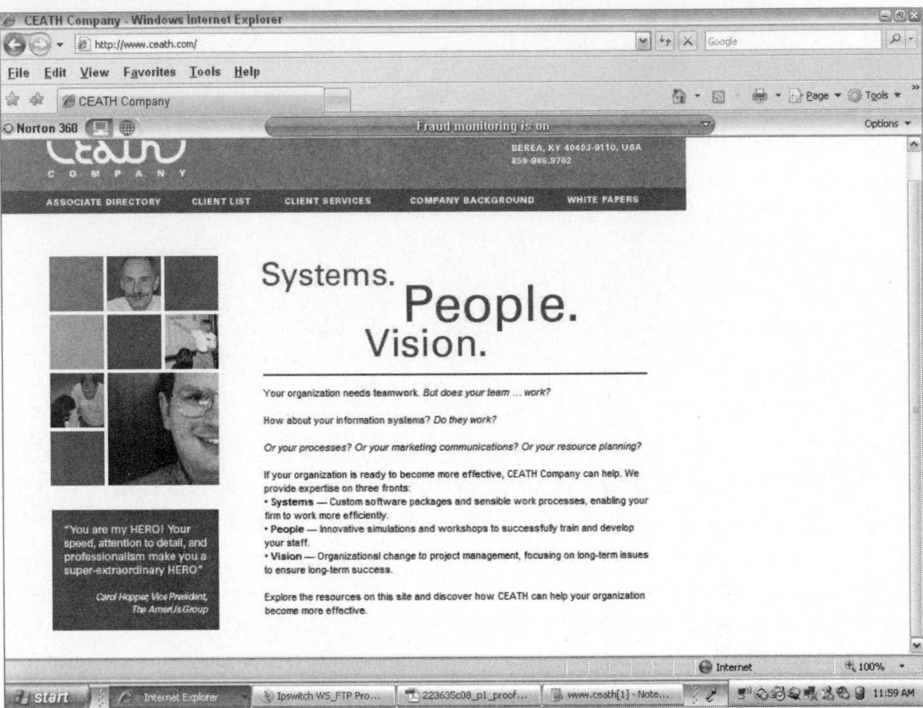

with different elements such as images or links. The Web page in Figure 8-1, for example, is nothing but a table filled with various elements.

Tables, predictably enough, are added using the TABLE element. The TABLE element contains one or more TR (table row) elements. The TR elements, in turn, contain one or more TD (table data) elements, which are usually referred to as *cells*. The HTML code for a typical table might look as follows:

```
<TABLE border="1">
<TR>
<TD>First Cell</TD>
<TD>Second Cell</TD>
</TR>
<TR>
<TD>Third Cell</TD>
<TD>Fourth Cell</TD>
</TR>
<TR>
```

```
<TD>Fifth Cell</TD>
<TD>Sixth Cell</TD>
</TR>
</TABLE>
```

This table contains three rows, with each row having two cells. The results are shown in Figure 8-2.

The width and height of a table, if they are not specifically stated in your HTML code, are determined by the size of the table's contents. The table automatically expands to accommodate whatever is put into its cells — even if the result means that the table is larger than the overall table size you specify in your HTML code.

To specify a particular size for a table, you use the `width` and `height` attributes. For example, to make the table take up the entire width and height of the screen as shown in Figure 8-3, you would use the following code:

```
<TABLE width="100%" height="100%" border="1">
```

NOTE **Of the two, `width` is far more often specified than `height` because Web pages effectively have infinite height, and people are used to scrolling to view whatever is below the current screen.**

Specifying size as a percentage works no matter what screen resolution a visitor is using. One hundred percent of the screen is the whole thing, period. Fifty percent of the screen is half of it, and so forth. You can also size the table with a set number of pixels. To create a table that is 400 pixels across and 250 pixels high, for example, you would state this:

```
<TABLE width="400" height="250">
```

The drawback to specifying a particular width is that you may force some of your site visitors to scroll horizontally to see the entire table. For example, if you fix your table at a width of 800 pixels and someone is using a screen resolution of 640 x 480 to view it, the right side of the table would be offscreen. It's usually better to use the percentage approach and leave the details of the display to the Web browser.

FIGURE 8-2

This is a basic table.

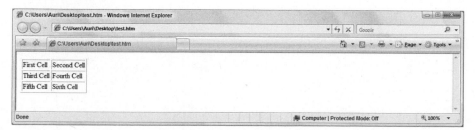

FIGURE 8-3

A table can take up the entire screen.

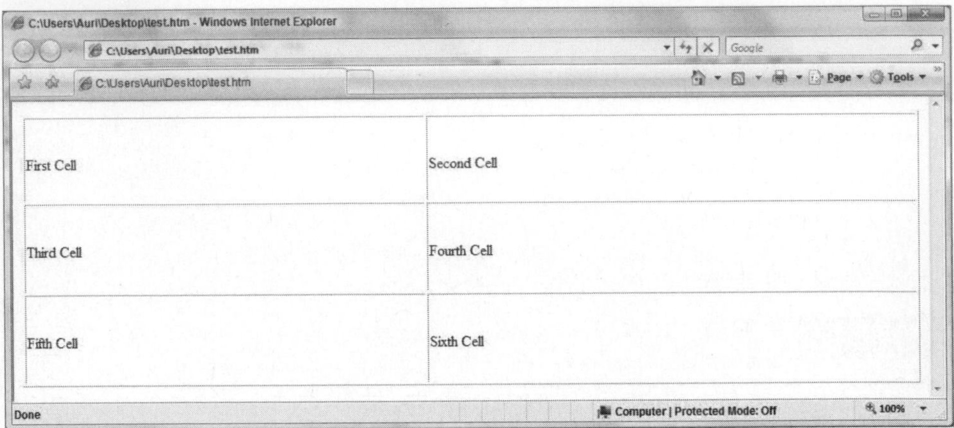

Both techniques can be combined, as well. To do so, simply use a percentage value with one attribute and a pixel value with the other. The following code, for example, fixes the width at 400 pixels, but still takes up three-quarters of the screen height, regardless of the screen resolution:

```
<TABLE width="400" height="75%">
```

You can also set the `width` and `height` of individual cells, although you must be careful of the impact of this on the rest of the table. Setting the height of one cell also makes every other cell in the same row change to that same height.

TIP **If you specify two sizes that conflict with one another, the larger one wins out. For example, if you set a cell to be 50 pixels high and set another cell in the same row to be 80 pixels high, all cells in that row will be 80 pixels high. If a third cell's contents are 100 pixels high, then all cells in the row become 100 pixels high.**

The `width` and `height` attributes work the same way for cells as they do for tables, with one important difference. When you set a percentage value for a cell, that's the percentage of the *table*, not the screen. Say, for example, that you have a table that's set to be 50 percent of the screen width, and you set a cell to take up 50 percent of the table width — that cell is only 25 percent of the overall screen width.

The following HTML code shows how to set the table from the preceding example so that its first column takes up one-third of the table, while its second row is fixed at 100 pixels in height:

```
<TABLE border="1">
<TR>
```

```
<TD width="33%">First Cell</TD>
<TD>Second Cell</TD>
</TR>
<TR>
<TD height="100">Third Cell</TD>
<TD>Fourth Cell</TD>
</TR>
<TR>
<TD>Fifth Cell</TD>
<TD>Sixth Cell</TD>
</TR>
</TABLE>
```

The results are shown in Figure 8-4.

NOTE **If you don't add any content to your table, the table won't show up in a Web browser. (Unless, of course, you add a border to the table.)**

If you start specifying sizes for different parts of tables, some bizarre situations may result. Setting a specific pixel size for individual cells tends to work best if you don't also set the table size that way. The following code, for example, doesn't work out because things don't add up properly:

```
<TABLE width="600" border="1">
<TR>
<TD width="200">First Cell</TD>
<TD width="100">Second Cell</TD>
</TR>
<TR>
<TD>Third Cell</TD>
<TD>Fourth Cell</TD>
</TR>
<TR>
```

FIGURE 8-4

You can set rows and columns to different values.

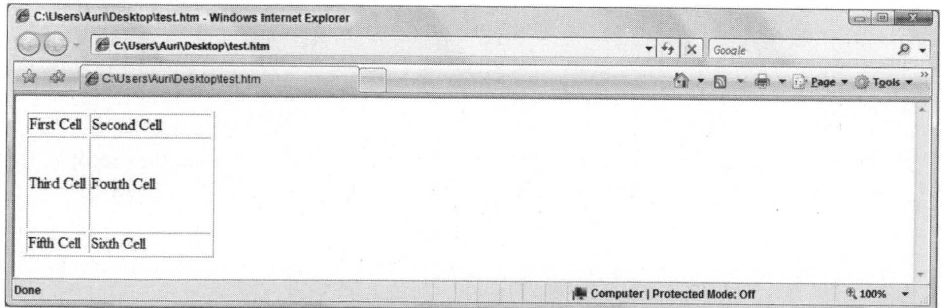

```
<TD>Fifth Cell</TD>
<TD>Sixth Cell</TD>
</TR>
</TABLE>
```

Fortunately, if you do end up with a situation such as this, Web browsers are usually smart enough to fix it so that the results are still viewable. The outcome of the preceding code sample, for example, is that the first column ends up being 400 pixels wide and the second one ends up at 200 pixels. The browser takes a look at the situation, realizes that things just won't add up, and decides to go with the table width of 600 pixels, maintaining the proportions (2 to 1, in this case) that you wanted for the cells.

Because the results are not what you intended, it's important to ensure that you don't create a size conflict problem.

It's easy enough to come up with percentage values that don't add up to 100 percent, too. Web browsers deal with that problem in the same way as they do with absolute values — by assigning the remaining percentage proportionally among the cells. In the case of values that exceed 100 percent, the excess is usually subtracted proportionally from each cell.

CAUTION **You should never assume the Web browser will take care of your errors. Always test and debug your Web site before deploying it.**

This behavior can actually be used deliberately to your benefit. Many Web designers, faced with the problem of setting up three cells of identical size in the same row, assign percentage values of 33 percent, 34 percent, and 33 percent, sacrificing a tiny bit of precision in order to make all the percentages add up to 100 percent. However, if you make them all 33 percent, most Web browsers automatically mix in the missing 1 percent to make them all perfectly even.

When dealing with the elasticity of cell heights and widths, you may also use the asterisk (*) symbol to complete a proportional table. If you wanted half a dozen cells per row, you could simply set the width of each cell to `width="*"` and the cells would be proportionally figured. This is great to use when you need to go back to a table and add or delete a cell while maintaining balance in the table.

As an example, the following code creates a table with four proportionally spaced cells using the asterisk symbol:

```
<html>
<head>
<title>Spacing by Asterisk</title>
</head>
<body>
<table width= "100%" border="3"  summary="This is a demo
 table using asterisk">
<tr>
<td width="*">1</td>
<td width="*">2</td>
```

```
<td width="*">3</td>
<td width="*">4</td>
</tr>
<tr>
<td width="*">1</td>
<td width="*">2</td>
<td width="*">3</td>
<td width="*">4</td>
</tr>
<tr>
<td width="*">1</td>
<td width="*">2</td>
<td width="*">3</td>
<td width="*">4</td>
</tr>
</body>
</html>
```

The top portion of Figure 8-5 shows the results of this code. Note in the bottom portion of Figure 8-5 that this dynamism holds even when the width of the table changes.

FIGURE 8-5

The table cells are automatically adjusted for width using the * symbol in the width attribute (top). The dynamism holds true even when the width of the table changes (bottom).

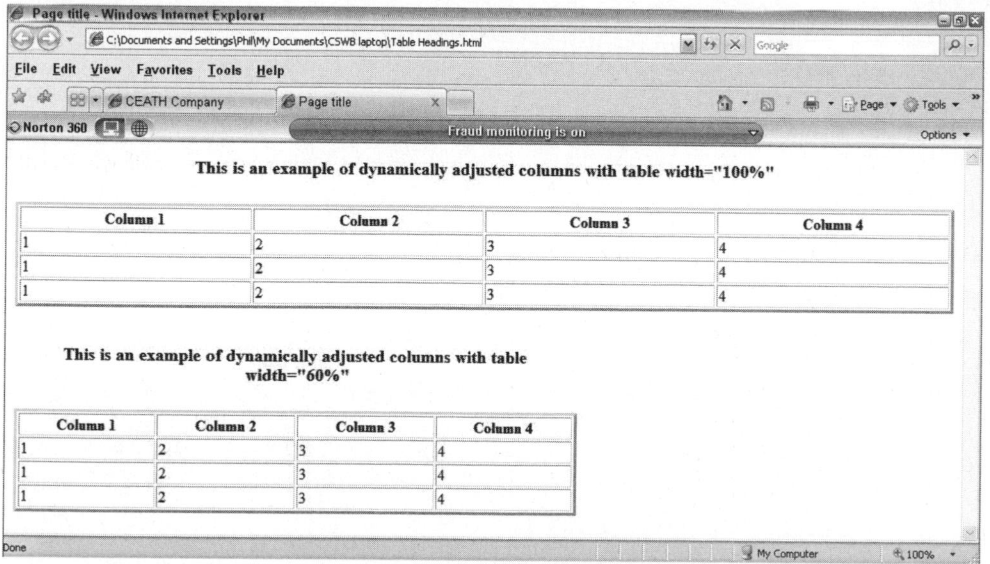

Managing Borders

Depending on how you're using tables, you may or may not want them to have a border. When tables are used to provide the underlying structure for a Web page, most designers prefer to leave borders out of the picture. But when you do need a border, it's easy to provide one.

To specify the thickness of a border, you set a value in pixels for the `border` attribute. The following example would create a thin border, 1 pixel wide:

```
<TABLE border="1">
```

Generally speaking, most people don't use very thick borders, preferring to stay in the range of from 1 to a maximum of 5 pixels. Figure 8-6 shows tables with various border sizes. You can also define borders with style elements when you want fine-tuned control.

Note that the border size has no effect on the internal borders around each cell. There is only one exception to this. If you make a table with no border by setting the value of the `border` attribute to `0`, this also removes the internal borders. The effect is to leave all of the table's structure intact, keeping the table itself from intruding.

FIGURE 8-6

Border sizes of more than 5 pixels are usually considered too large.

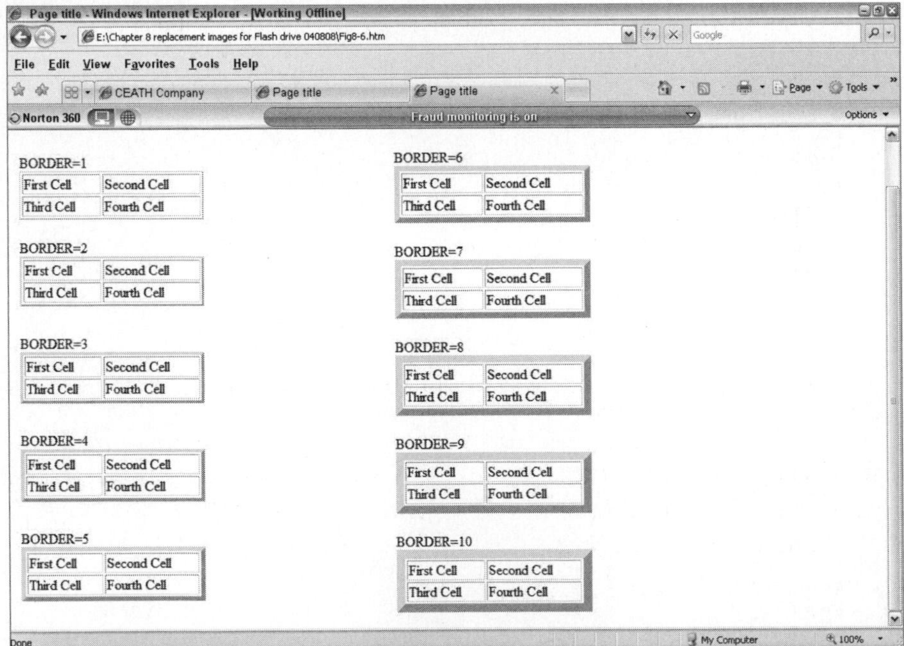

FIGURE 8-7

The top table shows a solid border.

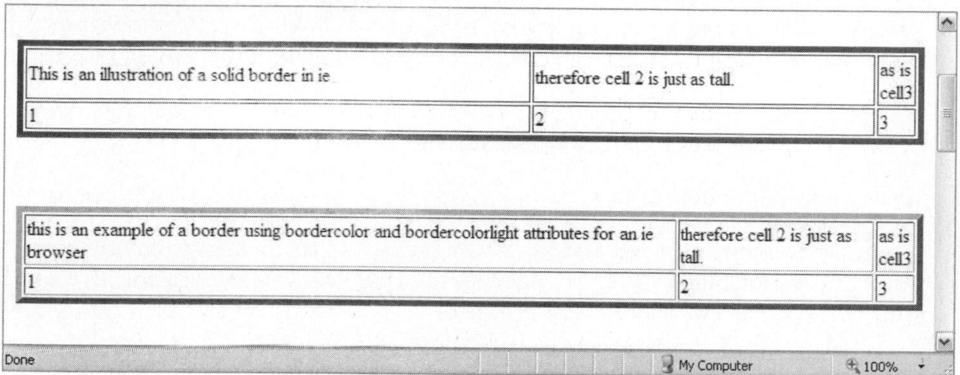

The shading of the border varies according to the browser. Of the more popular browsers, Internet Explorer (IE) provides a solid monochrome for all four sides.

The following code for IE uses two attributes in tandem — `bordercolor` and `bordercolorlight`:

```
<table border="5" bordercolor="blue" summary="">
<tr>
<td width="*">This is an illustration of a solid border in IE</td>
<td width ="*">Therefore cell 2 is just as tall.</td>
<td width="1%">as is cell 3</td>
</tr>
<tr>
<td>1</td>
<td>2</td>
<td>3</td>
</tr>
</table>
```

So, as shown in the results of this code displayed in Figure 8-7, you would see in the top table a solid border.

In the bottom portion of Figure 8-7, you see see a table with highlighted borders, which was produced with the following code:

```
<table border="5" bordercolor="blue"
bordercolorlight="rgb(102,204,204)">
<tr>
<td width="*">this is an example of a border using bordercolor and
```

```
bordercolorlight attributes for IE. You can see the left border is
light blue</td>
<td width ="*">and it is light blue across the top</td>
<td width="*">but the border is dark blue on the right and
bottom</td>
</tr>
</table>
```

Note that, in the bottom table shown in Figure 8-7, `rgb()` was used to define the color. Although the colors were selected from the safety palette, we could also have used the names of the colors or their associated hexadecimal values (such as `#c0c0c0` for `silver`).

Frames and rules

You can also create tables with borders, and then manipulate the appearance of the borders (and/or the rows and columns) within the table. The `frame` attribute allows you to manipulate the left, top, right, and bottom borders of the table. You may elect to have only left and right borders `frame="vsides"` or horizontally `frame="hsides"`.

The attribute values are easy to recall once you understand the shorthand used:

- `lhs` is left-hand side.
- `rhs` is the right-hand side.
- `above` gives a top border.
- `below` a bottom border.
- `void` creates an absence of borders.
- `box` and `border` both create borders on all four sides.

Figure 8-8 shows examples of some of these `frame` attribute values.

Similarly, the `rules` attribute allows you to control how gridlines are displayed within the table. You may use the following values:

- `cols` will show vertical lines.
- `rows` will show horizontal lines.
- `groups` will separate groups of data in a table. The tables defining `group` types are themselves in a table.
- `none` will have no grid lines showing in the table.
- `all` value shows all gridlines in the table.

The code in Listing 8-1 produces the results shown in Figure 8-9.

FIGURE 8-8

These are the values used with table frames. Note that either box or border value results in a table with borders on all sides.

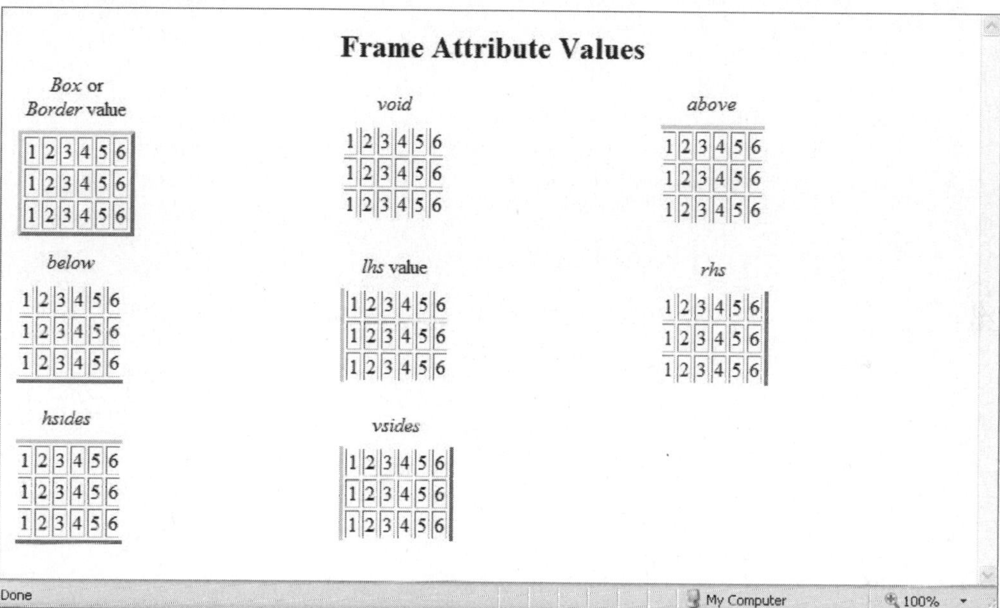

LISTING 8-1

Rules in a Table

```
<html>
<head>
<title>Rules illustrations</title>
</head>
<body>

<table width="100%">
<caption><h2>Table Rules Attributes and Values</h2></caption>
<tr>
<td width=*">
<table rules="all" width= "10%" border="3" summary="This is a demo
table using asterisk">
<caption> Table rules attribute  with <em>all</em> </caption>
<tr>
<td width="*">1</td>
```

```
<td width="*">2</td>
<td width="*">3</td>
<td width="*">4</td>
<td width="*">5</td>
<td width="*">6</td>
</tr>
<tr>
<td width="*">1</td>
<td width="*">2</td>
<td width="*">3</td>
<td width="*">4</td>
<td width="*">5</td>
<td width="*">6</td>
</tr>
<tr>
<td width="*">1</td>
<td width="*">2</td>
<td width="*">3</td>
<td width="*">4</td>
<td width="*">5</td>
<td width="*">6</td>
</tr>
</table><br><br>
</td>

<td width=*">
<table rules="none" width= "10%" border="3" summary="This is a demo
table using asterisk">
<caption>Table rules attribute  with <i>none</i>
value</caption>
<tr>
<td width="*">1</td>
<td width="*">2</td>
<td width="*">3</td>
<td width="*">4</td>
<td width="*">5</td>
<td width="*">6</td>
</tr>
<tr>
<td width="*">1</td>
<td width="*">2</td>
<td width="*">3</td>
<td width="*">4</td>
<td width="*">5</td>
<td width="*">6</td>
</tr>
<tr>
```

```
<td width="*">1</td>
<td width="*">2</td>
<td width="*">3</td>
<td width="*">4</td>
<td width="*">5</td>
<td width="*">6</td>
</tr>
</table><br><br>
</td>

<td>
<table rules="rows" width= "10%" border="3" summary="This is a demo
 table using asterisk">
<caption> Table rules attribute  with <em>rows</em> value</caption>
<tr>
<td width="*">1</td>
<td width="*">2</td>
<td width="*">3</td>
<td width="*">4</td>
<td width="*">5</td>
<td width="*">6</td>
</tr>
<tr>
<td width="*">1</td>
<td width="*">2</td>
<td width="*">3</td>
<td width="*">4</td>
<td width="*">5</td>
<td width="*">6</td>
</tr>
<tr>
<td width="*">1</td>
<td width="*">2</td>
<td width="*">3</td>
<td width="*">4</td>
<td width="*">5</td>
<td width="*">6</td>
</tr>
</table><br><br>
</td>
</tr>
<tr>
<td width=*">
<table rules="cols" width= "10%" border="3" summary="This is a demo
table using asterisk">
<caption>Table rules attribute  with <i>columns</i>
value</caption>
```

```
<tr>
<td width="*">1</td>
<td width="*">2</td>
<td width="*">3</td>
<td width="*">4</td>
<td width="*">5</td>
<td width="*">6</td>
</tr>
<tr>
<td width="*">1</td>
<td width="*">2</td>
<td width="*">3</td>
<td width="*">4</td>
<td width="*">5</td>
<td width="*">6</td>
</tr>
<tr>
<td width="*">1</td>
<td width="*">2</td>
<td width="*">3</td>
<td width="*">4</td>
<td width="*">5</td>
<td width="*">6</td>
</tr>
</table><br><br>
</td>
<td width=*">
<table rules="groups" width= "10%" border="3" summary="This is a demo
table using asterisk">
<caption>Table frame attribute with <i>groups</i>
value</caption>

<thead>
<tr>
<td width="*">1</td>
<td width="*">2</td>
<td width="*">3</td>
<td width="*">4</td>
<td width="*">5</td>
<td width="*">6</td>
</tr>
</thead>

<tr>
<td width="*">1</td>
<td width="*">2</td>
<td width="*">3</td>
```

```
<td width="*">4</td>
<td width="*">5</td>
<td width="*">6</td>
</tr>
<tr>
<td width="*">1</td>
<td width="*">2</td>
<td width="*">3</td>
<td width="*">4</td>
<td width="*">5</td>
<td width="*">6</td>
</tr>
</table><br><br>
</td>
</table>
</body>
</html>
```

FIGURE 8-9

Rules allow you to control the appearance of the grid within the table.

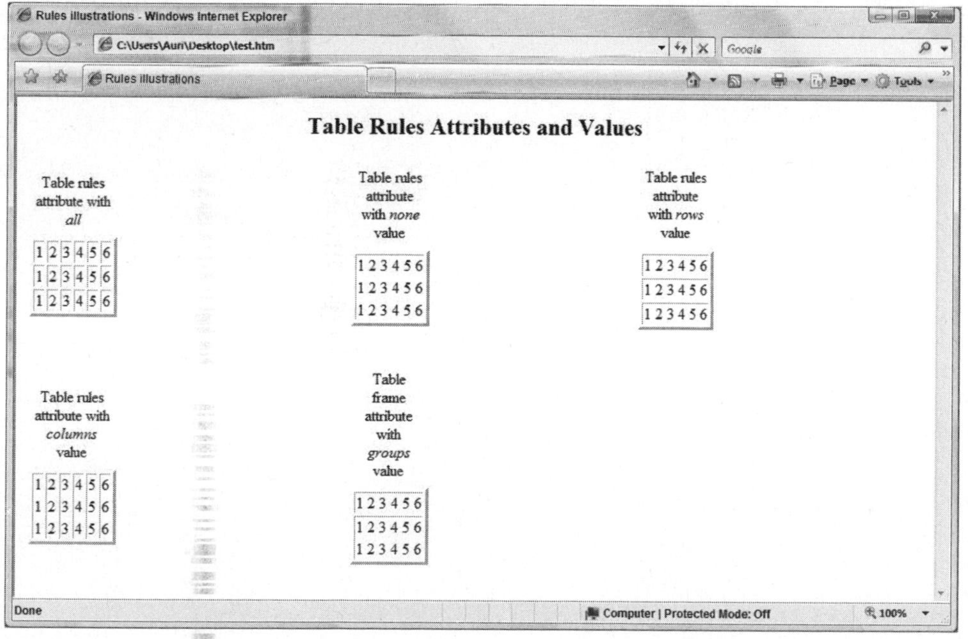

Tables within tables are called *nested* tables, which are used in several layout formats. The all-encompassing table is referred to as the *outer table*. The code in Listing 8-2 sets up nested tables.

LISTING 8-2

Nested Tables

```
<html>
<head>
<title>Frames and Rules illustrations></title>
</head>
<body>

<table width="100%"> <caption><h2>Frame Attribute Values<h2>
</caption>
<tr>

<td width=*">
<table frame="box" width= "10%" border="3" summary="This is a demo
table using asterisk"><caption><em>Box</em> or <em>Border</em>value</caption>
<tr>
<td width="*">1</td>
<td width="*">2</td>
<td width="*">3</td>
<td width="*">4</td>
<td width="*">5</td>
<td width="*">6</td>
</tr>
<tr>
<td width="*">1</td>
<td width="*">2</td>
<td width="*">3</td>
<td width="*">4</td>
<td width="*">5</td>
<td width="*">6</td>
</tr>

<tr>
<td width="*">1</td>
<td width="*">2</td>
<td width="*">3</td>
<td width="*">4</td>
<td width="*">5</td>
<td width="*">6</td>
</tr>

</table><br>
```

```
</td>
<td width=*">
<table frame="void" width= "10%" border="3" summary="This is a demo
table using asterisk">
<caption><i>void</i></caption>
<tr>
<td width="*">1</td>
<td width="*">2</td>
<td width="*">3</td>
<td width="*">4</td>
<td width="*">5</td>
<td width="*">6</td>
</tr>
<tr>
<td width="*">1</td>
<td width="*">2</td>
<td width="*">3</td>
<td width="*">4</td>
<td width="*">5</td>
<td width="*">6</td>
</tr>
<tr>
<td width="*">1</td>
<td width="*">2</td>
<td width="*">3</td>
<td width="*">4</td>
<td width="*">5</td>
<td width="*">6</td>
</tr>

</table><br>
</td>
<td>
<table frame="above" width= "10%" border="3" summary="This is a demo
table using asterisk">
<caption><em>above</em></caption>
<tr>
<td width="*">1</td>
<td width="*">2</td>
<td width="*">3</td>
<td width="*">4</td>
<td width="*">5</td>
<td width="*">6</td>
</tr>

<tr>
<td width="*">1</td>
```

```
<td width="*">2</td>
<td width="*">3</td>
<td width="*">4</td>
<td width="*">5</td>
<td width="*">6</td>
</tr>

<tr>
<td width="*">1</td>
<td width="*">2</td>
<td width="*">3</td>
<td width="*">4</td>
<td width="*">5</td>
<td width="*">6</td>
</tr>

</table><br>
</td>
</tr>
<tr >
<td width=*">
<table frame="below" width= "10%" border="3" summary="This is a demo
 table using asterisk">
<caption><i>below</i></caption>
<tr>
<td width="*">1</td>
<td width="*">2</td>
<td width="*">3</td>
<td width="*">4</td>
<td width="*">5</td>
<td width="*">6</td>
</tr>
<tr>
<td width="*">1</td>
<td width="*">2</td>
<td width="*">3</td>
<td width="*">4</td>
<td width="*">5</td>
<td width="*">6</td>
</tr>
<tr>
<td width="*">1</td>
<td width="*">2</td>
<td width="*">3</td>
<td width="*">4</td>
<td width="*">5</td>
<td width="*">6</td>
```

```
</tr>

</table><br>
</td>
<td width=*">
<table frame="lhs" width= "10%" border="3" summary="This is a demo
 table using asterisk">
<caption><i>lhs</i>value</caption>
<tr>
<td width="*">1</td>
<td width="*">2</td>
<td width="*">3</td>
<td width="*">4</td>
<td width="*">5</td>
<td width="*">6</td>
</tr>
<tr>
<td width="*">1</td>
<td width="*">2</td>
<td width="*">3</td>
<td width="*">4</td>
<td width="*">5</td>
<td width="*">6</td>
</tr>
<tr>
<td width="*">1</td>
<td width="*">2</td>
<td width="*">3</td>
<td width="*">4</td>
<td width="*">5</td>
<td width="*">6</td>
</tr>

</table><br>
</td>
<td width=*">
<table frame="rhs" width= "10%" border="3" summary="This is a demo
table using asterisk">
<caption><i>rhs</i></caption>
<tr>
<td width="*">1</td>
<td width="*">2</td>
<td width="*">3</td>
<td width="*">4</td>
<td width="*">5</td>
<td width="*">6</td>
</tr>
<tr>
```

```
<td width="*">1</td>
<td width="*">2</td>
<td width="*">3</td>
<td width="*">4</td>
<td width="*">5</td>
<td width="*">6</td>
</tr>

<tr>
<td width="*">1</td>
<td width="*">2</td>
<td width="*">3</td>
<td width="*">4</td>
<td width="*">5</td>
<td width="*">6</td>
</tr>

</table><br>
</td>
</tr>
<tr >
<td width=*">
<table frame="hsides" width= "10%" border="3" summary="This is a demo
 table using asterisk">
<caption><i>hsides</i></caption>

<tr>
<td width="*">1</td>
<td width="*">2</td>
<td width="*">3</td>
<td width="*">4</td>
<td width="*">5</td>
<td width="*">6</td>
</tr>
<tr>
<td width="*">1</td>
<td width="*">2</td>
<td width="*">3</td>
<td width="*">4</td>
<td width="*">5</td>
<td width="*">6</td>
</tr>
<tr>
<td width="*">1</td>
<td width="*">2</td>
<td width="*">3</td>
<td width="*">4</td>
<td width="*">5</td>
```

```
<td width="*">6</td>
</tr>
</table><br>
</td>
<td width=*">
<table frame="vsides" width= "10%" border="3" summary="This is a demo
 table using asterisk">
<caption><i>vsides</i></caption>
<tr>
<td width="*">1</td>
<td width="*">2</td>
<td width="*">3</td>
<td width="*">4</td>
<td width="*">5</td>
<td width="*">6</td>
</tr>
<tr>
<td width="*">1</td>
<td width="*">2</td>
<td width="*">3</td>
<td width="*">4</td>
<td width="*">5</td>
<td width="*">6</td>
</tr>
<tr>
<td width="*">1</td>
<td width="*">2</td>
<td width="*">3</td>
<td width="*">4</td>
<td width="*">5</td>
<td width="*">6</td>
</tr>
</table><br>
</td>
<td>
</td>
</tr>
</table>
</body>
</html>
```

`valign` is vertical alignment of the contents of the table cell.

You can use all of these formats to develop your own tables of, perhaps schedules of Little League teams, classes you might be taking (and their classroom numbers and times), a list of foods per meal for a diet, or even a static calendar of events.

FIGURE 8-10

You can use this generic table with headers and captions as a template to develop your own tables.

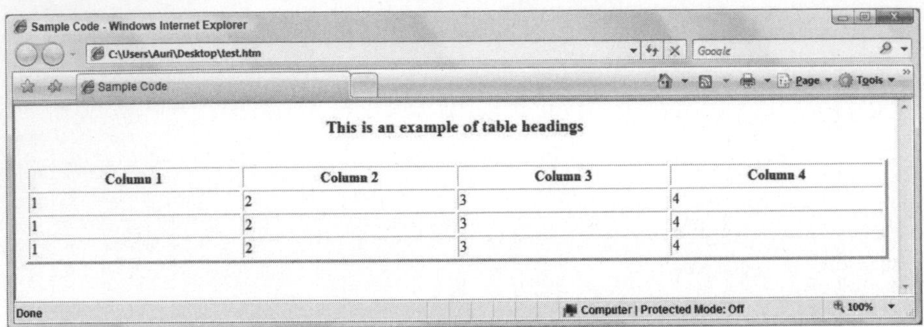

In the example code provided, notice that when you put the standard table elements together, you end up with something that looks like Figure 8-10. Note in particular the centered heading. This is actually a `<caption>` tag that appears bolded above the table. While the default style is `<center>`, the content is bolded by embedding `<h3>` tags within the `<caption>` tag pair.

By default, the column heading tags are centered and appear in bold text. If you want to align the column headings to the right or left, you specify this by using the `align` attribute. Also, in tables, text data in cells should be left-aligned; numeric data should be right-aligned. You do this by using `<align="left"` or `"right">`.

In the previous code examples, you may have noticed the `summary` attribute in the `table` tag. You could liken `summary` to the `<alt>` tag in that it provides a written description of the content. The description, however, is read through synthesized voice for users who are visually handicapped, and is rendered on computers so equipped and configured.

Look carefully at the following for a generic table. You can use this code and simply put in your own data, or to put other tables in cells. Try out the coding used for tables. Try bolding and aligning data. Change the captions and headings. Add rows. Add columns. Try putting lots of text in a cell and see what happens.

```
<table  width= "100%" border="3" summary="This is a demo table using
the columnheading tag, &lt;th&gt; The column heading tags by default
center and bold text.  If you wish to align to right or left you must
so specify use the align attribute. In addition, in tables text data
in cells should be left aligned and numeric data is right aligned.
You do this by using align="left" or "right">
<caption><h3>This is an example of table headings<h3></caption>
  <tr>
     <th width="*">Column 1</th>
     <th width="*">Column 2</th>
     <th width="*">Column 3</th>
     <th width="*">Column 4</th>
```

```
  </tr>
  <tr>
    <td width="*">1</td>
    <td width="*">2</td>
    <td width="*">3</td>
    <td width="*">4</td>
  </tr>
  <tr>
    <td width="*">1</td>
    <td width="*">2</td>
    <td width="*">3</td>
    <td width="*">4</td>
  </tr>
  <tr>
    <td width="*">1</td>
    <td width="*">2</td>
    <td width="*">3</td>
    <td width="*">4</td></tr>
</table>
```

We'll be merging cells and adding colors, headings, and backgrounds a bit later in this chapter.

TIP **Even when you plan to use a borderless table, it's best to keep the borders intact during the design phase. This helps you to visualize the exact location of each cell, and the relationships of the cells to one another. Setting the border to zero is one of the last steps before uploading the Web page to your site.**

Using Padding and Spacing

Depending on the contents of a particular cell, you may need to create some space between the border and the content, or avoid having any space at all. The space between the border and the content is called *cell padding*. Figure 8-11 shows two cells that have no padding at all. The first one contains an image, which fits perfectly within the cell. The second one contains text, which is rendered less readable by being crammed up against the cell's border.

Figure 8-12 shows the opposite situation, in which the cells have 2 pixels of padding that separate their contents from the border. The image now has an undesirable space around it, but the text has become more readable by virtue of the same padding.

CROSS-REF **See the section "Working with Images and Color" later in this chapter for details on adding images to tables.**

Cell padding is set via the `cellpadding` attribute of the `TABLE` element. You can only set padding for the table as a whole, not for individual cells. To get the 2-pixel cell padding shown in Figure 8-12, you would use the following code:

```
<TABLE cellpadding="2">
```

FIGURE 8-11

Images look best with no cell padding.

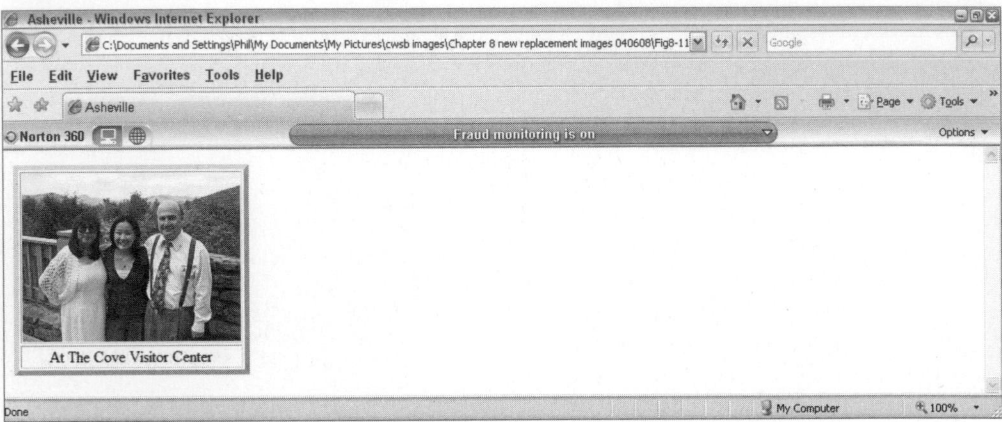

FIGURE 8-12

Text is more readable with some space between it and the cell walls.

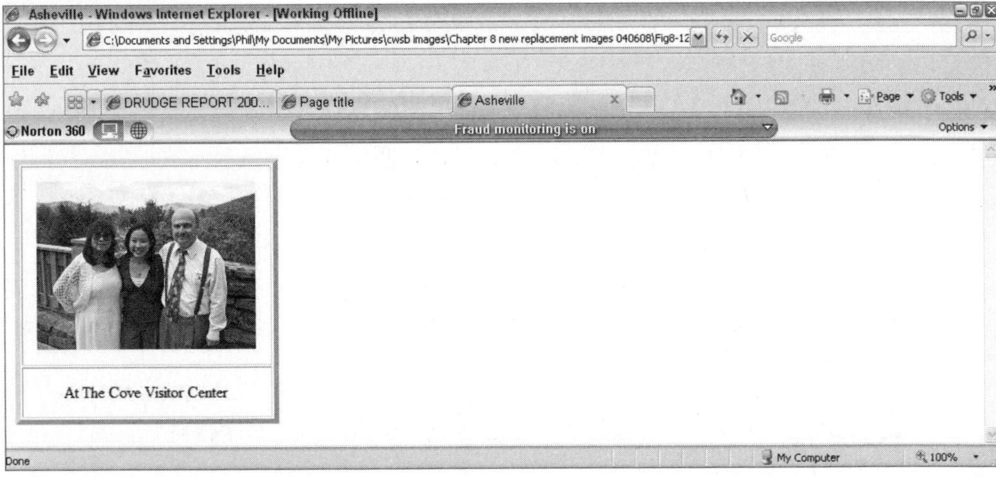

Cell spacing is different. Instead of setting the amount of space inside the cell's border, it sets the amount of space between the cells themselves. Figure 8-13 shows several tables with various cell spacing values.

FIGURE 8-13

Cell spacing determines how far apart each cell is from its neighbors.

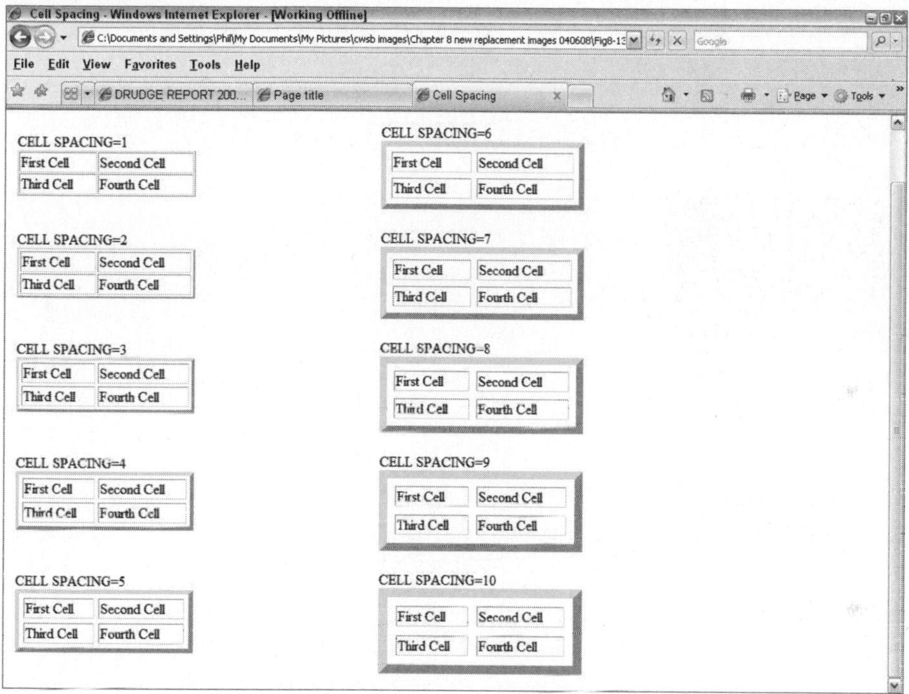

Cell spacing is set, as you might have guessed, with the `cellspacing` attribute of the `TABLE` element. The following code places each cell 5 pixels away from its neighboring cells:

```
<TABLE cellspacing="5">
```

The question of exactly how much, if any, cell padding or cell spacing to use is an aesthetic choice. A table with neither value set still works perfectly from a technical point of view.

Aligning Tables and Cell Contents

The alignment of a table is totally different from the alignment of rows and cells. *Table alignment* refers to where the table falls on the Web page. The possible values for the `TABLE` element's `align` attribute are `left`, `center`, and `right`. Left and right alignment put the edge of the table on the appropriate margin of the Web page, whereas center alignment puts it smack in the middle of the screen, with both edges of the table the same distance away from the margins. Figure 8-14 shows a right-aligned table.

FIGURE 8-14

A right-aligned table puts the edge of the table on the right margin.

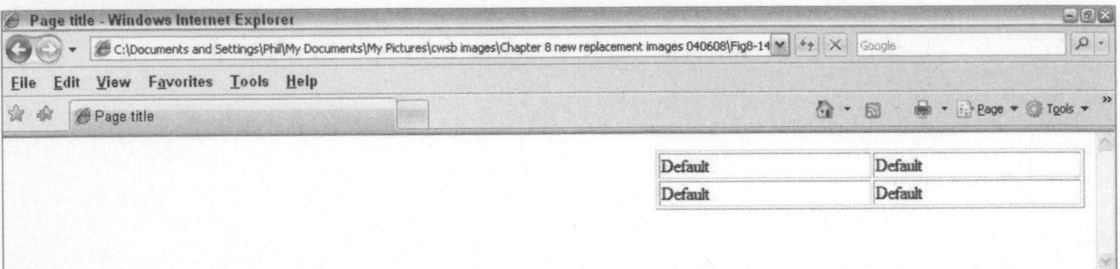

Setting horizontal alignment

The `align` attribute of the `TR` and `TD` elements, on the other hand, aligns the *contents* of the affected cells, not the cells themselves. Despite the fact that the exact same terminology is used for the attribute, and the same three values are possible — `left`, `center`, and `right` — there is no connection whatsoever between the way a table is aligned and the way rows or cells are aligned. Rows and cells, however, work exactly the same. It's only a question of how many cells are affected by the setting.

This is another one of those cases where the HTML container relationships come into obvious play. By default, the settings for the row become the settings for all the cells that the row contains. Thus, if a `TR` (table row) element is set to center alignment, then all the `TD` (table data, or cell) elements in that row automatically have that same alignment. To change the alignment of a specific cell, you must override the inherited attribute values.

The following HTML example shows a table that is center-aligned. It contains two rows, the first of which has no specified alignment. This means that all the cells in that row automatically have the default alignment, which is that their content is left-aligned. The second row is set to have center alignment, but one of the cells in it is set to have right alignment. Figure 8-15 shows the results.

FIGURE 8-15

Cell alignment overrides row alignment.

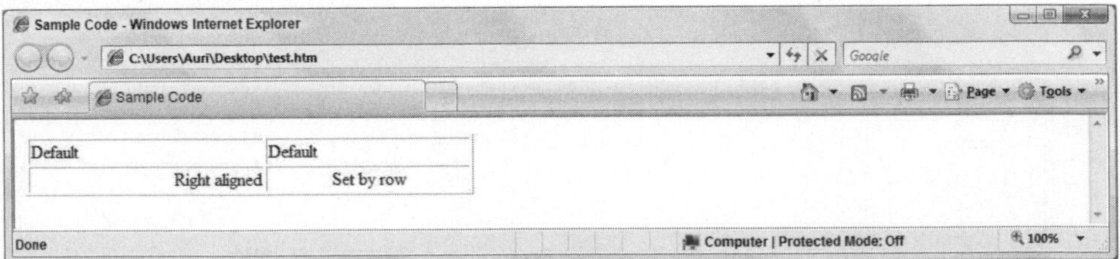

```
<TABLE width="400" border="1">
<TR>
<TD>Default</TD>
<TD>Default</TD>
</TR>
<TR align="center">
<TD align="right">Right aligned</TD>
<TD>Set by row</TD>
</TR>
</TABLE>
```

Using tables with forms

Good Web designers know that forms (which have a deplorable visual appearance in plain HTML) can be meshed with tables to create a carefully arranged appearance. This not only gives the form more visual appeal, but it also increases the ease of understanding for anyone faced with filling out the form. Figure 8-16 shows a form done in plain HTML, which was created using the following HTML code:

```
<FORM action="cgi-bin/checkident.pl" method="post">
<P>User Name: <INPUT type="text" name="username">
<BR>
Password: <INPUT type="password" name="pw">
</P>
<INPUT type="submit">
</FORM>
```

CROSS-REF **See Chapter 10 for a discussion on forms. The data on forms here is very narrowly focused on the application of a form within a table cell to add structure to a cell. Forms do a bit more than that, and adding structure to a table is fairly tangential to form function.**

Figure 8-17, on the other hand, shows how much better the same form looks when a table is added to the mix, and the form controls are carefully aligned.

FIGURE 8-16

Forms in HTML are naturally sloppy only if the designer is naturally sloppy.

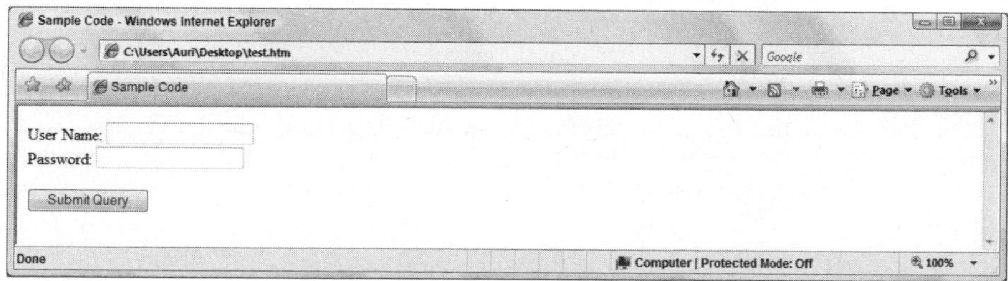

FIGURE 8-17

Tables can be used to make forms presentable.

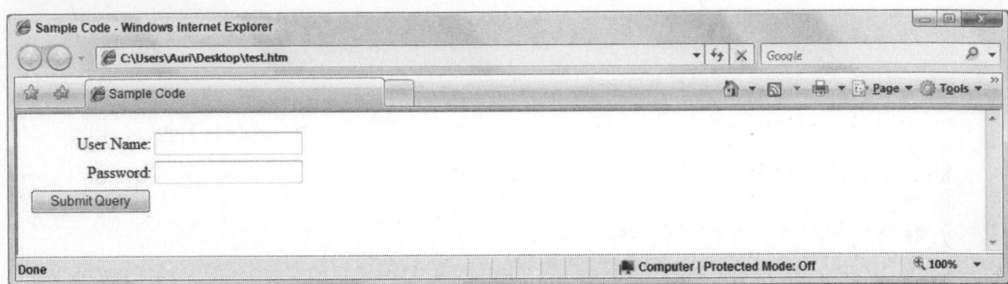

The following example shows how a table was added to the form so that the form controls would be meshed into the table for restructuring:

```
<FORM action="cgi-bin/checkident.pl" method="post">
<TABLE>
<TR>
<TD align="right">User Name:
</TD>
<TD align="left">
<INPUT type="text" name="username">
</TD>
</TR>
<TR>
<TD align="right">Password:
</TD>
<TD align="left">
<INPUT type="password" name="pw">
</TD>
</TR>
<TR>
<TD align="left">
<INPUT type="submit">
</TD>
</TR>
</TABLE>
</FORM>
```

To create this situation, the TABLE element is actually placed within the FORM element, rather than the other way around, because the only place you can put anything in a table is within an individual cell. Obviously, the entire form could not be put into such a small space, so the table necessarily goes into the form, not the other way around. This way, the structural capacities of the table are gained and the functional capabilities of the form are maintained.

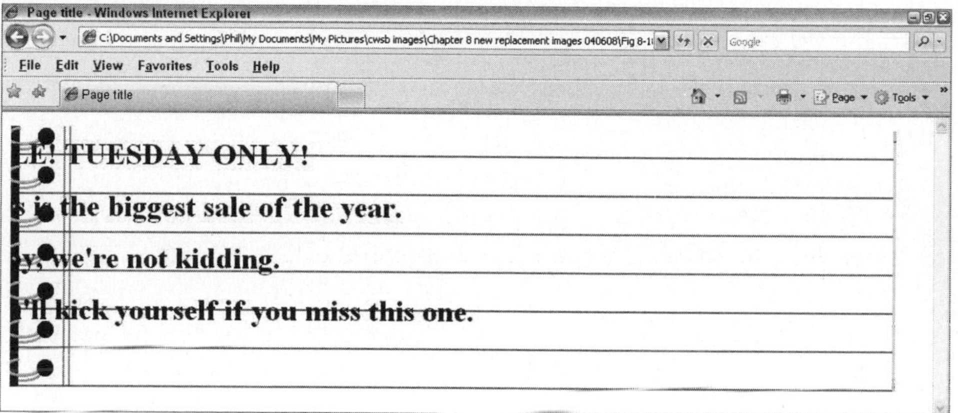

FIGURE 8-18

Sidebar background images interfere with page content.

By setting things up so that the table has two columns with the first column (which contains the descriptive text) right-aligned, and the second column (which contains the form controls) left-aligned, the form suddenly gains a nice, neat structure that is easy for the user to follow.

Using tables with sidebar images

Tables are absolutely essential when you use sidebar images on your Web pages. These backgrounds fill up the left edge of the screen with artistic or cute material that interferes with the display of text and other elements but leaves the rest of the screen in a proper condition. Figure 8-18 shows a typical sidebar background and its impact on a normal Web page's contents.

It's easy to use sidebar images, thus gaining the artistic look they provide, without having them mess up the rest of the page. As usual in HTML, there's more than one way to do this, but tables provide the quickest, simplest solution. At the lowest level of table usage, all you need is one cell to solve the problem. The following HTML code provides you with a basic Web page that enables you to use a sidebar background without interference:

```
<HTML>
<HEAD>
<TITLE>Sidebar Image Table Framework</TITLE>
</HEAD>
<BODY background="imagefile">
<TABLE width="80%" align="right" border="1">
<TR>
<TD>
Contents
```

```
</TD>
</TR>
</TABLE>
</BODY>
</HTML>
```

Figure 8-19 shows how the single-cell table this code creates is set away from the left side that is taken up by the sidebar image. The trick is in the combination of the table's alignment and width. Setting the right alignment puts it on the opposite side of the screen from the sidebar. Setting the width, so that the table takes up less than the full screen, keeps the sidebar from interfering with the table — and its contents.

To use this for your own Web pages, replace the placeholder *imagefile* with the name of your own sidebar background image file. Next, adjust the width of the table to fit the amount of space that the background image leaves open on your page. For example, you might be able to widen the table to 95 percent with some sidebar images — we're just playing it conservatively by setting the width to 80 percent in the example. When you have the table sized accurately, you'll probably want to eliminate the border so that the presence of the table won't be obvious to your visitors. To do so, change `border="1"` to `border="0"`.

From here on in, you can forget all about tables and background images. Simply replace the placeholder word *Contents* found between the `<TD>` and `</TD>` tags with the contents of your Web page. Everything on the entire page will fit into the one cell, which expands downward to accommodate anything you put within it. Figure 8-20 shows the same Web page that started off this section, but with all its content encapsulated within the single-cell table.

There are other ways to move the elements on the page out from the edge. You could, for example, encapsulate all your text in `BLOCKQUOTE` elements. Doing that, however, would have

FIGURE 8-19

A properly sized right-aligned table does not rest over the sidebar.

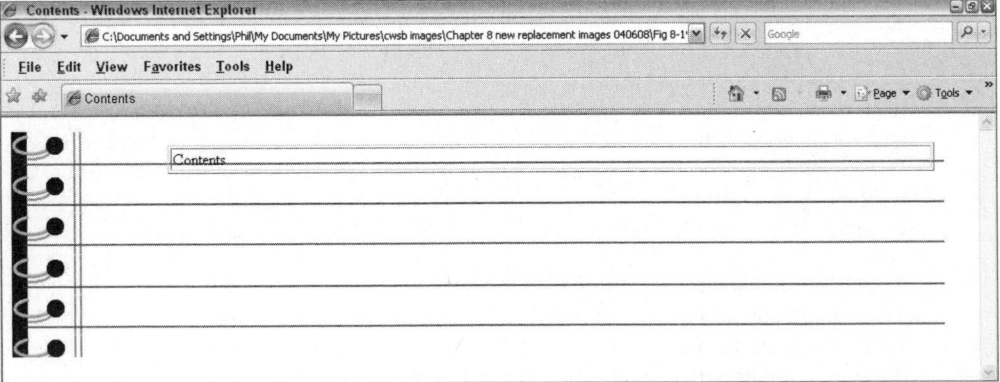

FIGURE 8-20

The addition of a table to the page makes the sidebar image work with the other elements.

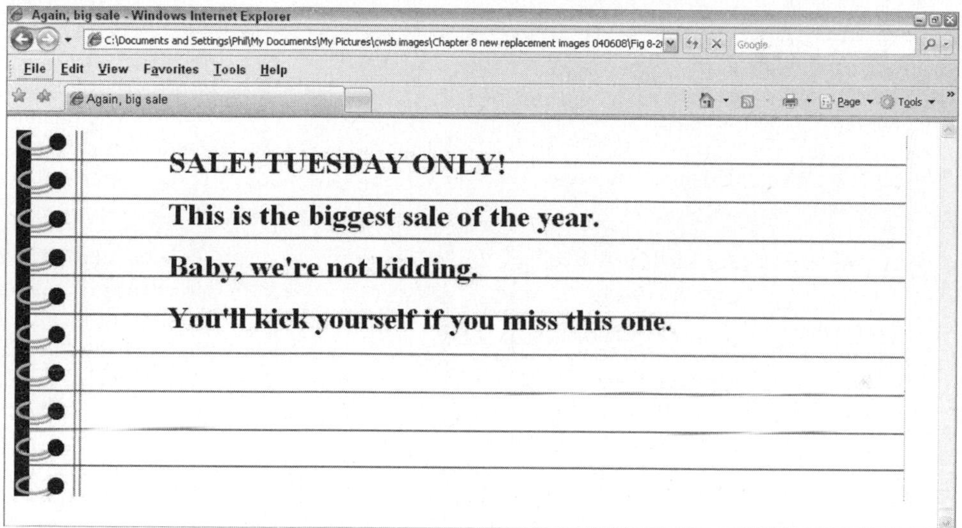

the undesirable result of moving the text in from both margins, when you're only trying to move it away from the left side. And this solution doesn't even begin to address what to do with non-textual elements.

You could also use CSS properties to set up a margin space on the left side of the page.

CROSS-REF **See Chapter 13 for a discussion of CSS. Note, however, that CSS is supported from HTML version 4.01 forward.**

Setting vertical alignment

In addition to horizontal alignment of row and cell contents with the `align` attribute, you can specify a vertical alignment by using the `valign` attribute. The four possible values for the vertical alignment are `top`, `middle`, `bottom`, and `baseline`. The first three are pretty much self-explanatory. The `baseline` value, however, is one of those attributes that has just never worked. Various browsers treat it differently, and there's no telling what will happen to the appearance of your tables if you use it. Just say "no" to its use. Stick with the basic three.

The following example of HTML code sets up a table with four rows. The first row has no explicit `valign` setting, so it defaults to center alignment. The second row is set to top alignment. The third row is set to bottom alignment. The fourth row is set to center alignment, but two of its cells override the setting with their own `valign` settings.

```
<TABLE height="400" border="1">
<TR>
<TD>Default</TD>
<TD>Default</TD>
<TD>Default</TD>
<TD>Default</TD>
</TR>
<TR valign="top">
<TD>Top aligned</TD>
<TD>Top aligned</TD>
<TD>Top aligned</TD>
<TD>Top aligned</TD>
</TR>
<TR valign="bottom">
<TD>Bottom aligned</TD>
<TD>Bottom aligned</TD>
<TD>Bottom aligned</TD>
<TD>Bottom aligned</TD>
</TR>
<TR valign="center">
<TD valign="top">Top aligned</TD>
<TD>Set by row</TD>
<TD>Set by row</TD>
<TD valign="bottom">Bottom aligned</TD>
</TR>
</TABLE>
```

The results are shown in Figure 8-21.

Preventing word wrap

Generally, when text in a table cell reaches the border of the cell, it wraps around and continues on the next line. If necessary, the height of the cell increases to accommodate the additional text. This is the way most Web designers leave things. However, if you have some need to keep all the text in a cell on a single line, you can simply add the `nowrap` attribute to it, as follows:

```
<TD nowrap>
```

This causes a reversal of the normal process. When the text in the cell reaches the border, the cell expands horizontally to accommodate the additional text to keep it all on one line. Figure 8-22 shows a table where one cell has been set to `nowrap`.

Using word wrap can affect table widths.

FIGURE 8-21

Vertical alignment in cells overrides vertical alignment in rows.

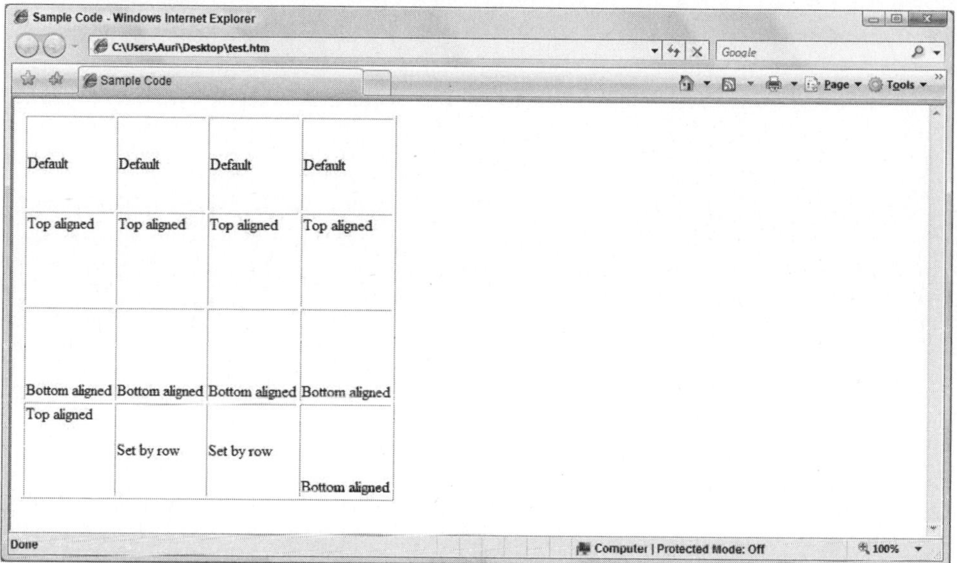

FIGURE 8-22

The nowrap attribute makes all text stay on one line.

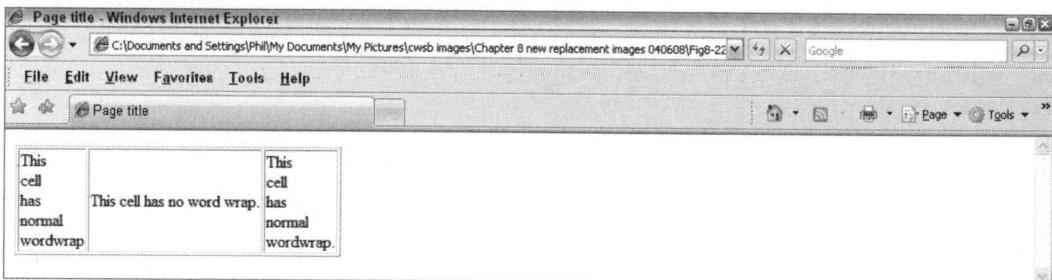

Spanning Rows and Columns

The basic layout of a table is purely symmetrical — each row has the same number of cells, every cell in a column is the same size, as is every cell in a row. But this doesn't have to be the case. The `colspan` and `rowspan` attributes of the `TD` (table data, or cell) element enable you to specify that one cell should extend across the space normally taken up by several cells. This is extremely useful in typical data presentation scenarios, where you may need to set up a title cell that applies to more than one row or column.

The following HTML code generates cell spanning as shown in Figure 8-23:

```
<TABLE border="1">
<TR>
<TD rowspan="2"></TD>
<TD colspan="2">Cats</TD>
<TD colspan="2">Dogs</TD>
</TR>
<TR> <TD>Male</TD>
<TD>Female</TD>
<TD>Male</TD>
<TD>Female</TD>
</TR>
<TR>
<TD rowspan="2"><P>Measured<BR>
Weight</P>
</TD>
<TD>17</TD>
<TD>12</TD>
<TD>40</TD>
<TD>35</TD>
</TR>
<TR>
<TD>15</TD>
<TD>16</TD>
<TD>34</TD>
<TD>27</TD>
</TR>
</TABLE>
```

FIGURE 8-23

One cell can span more than one row or column.

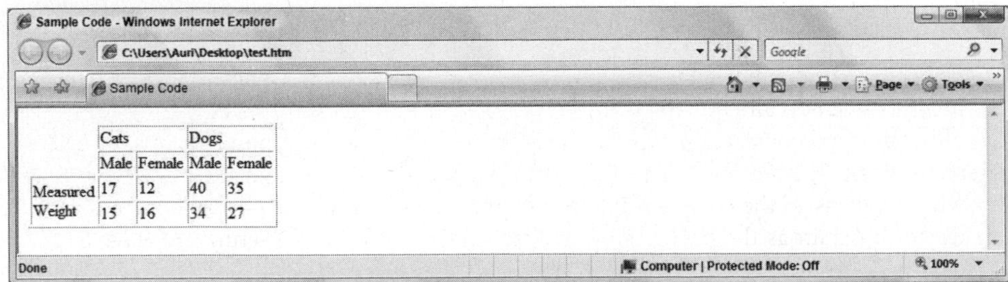

Despite the various bits of cell spanning, this is still a table that is basically measured as five columns by four rows. However, the change in the number of rows or columns that a single cell can fit into makes the HTML code harder to follow than a purely symmetrical table.

The first row works like this. The first (blank) cell occupies two rows, but only one column. The next two cells each occupy only this row, but take up two columns each. Thus, there are five columns accounted for.

The second row is a bit more complicated. Only four cells are apparently in it. However, the first cell in the row is actually the blank cell from the first row, which spans both the first and second rows. Thus, the four `TD` elements, added to it, make up the five columns.

The third row begins with a cell that spans the third and fourth rows, but only one column. The remaining four `TD` elements complete the five columns.

The final row, as with the second row, gives up its first space to the first cell from the preceding row, and adds four `TD` elements to finish up the table.

Working with Images and Color

Images are added to cells the same way they are added to a Web page — with the `IMG` element. The sole difference is that, this time, the `IMG` element goes in between a pair of `<TD>` and `</TD>` tags. The following HTML code shows how it's done:

```
<TD><IMG src="imagefile"></TD>
```

Figure 8-24 shows a table that includes an image. The table itself is not visible, however, because its purpose is to structure the Web page, with the image's placement controlled by the layout of the table. Therefore, the table's `border` value has been set to zero.

CROSS-REF See Chapter 6 for more information on adding images to Web pages.

Specifying background images

Entire tables can have background images, as can rows and individual cells. Candidly, there's not much real use for this ability. In fact, you can end up with some pretty ugly results. If you're using some of the more sophisticated table tricks, you run flat up against the fact that background images can undo all your work. For example, Figure 8-25 shows a table that uses a combination of background color, along with both visible and invisible foreground images, to create a seamless angular frame. It's a nice effect, and it takes a bit of work to get it just right. Figure 8-26 shows what happens to the table when a background image is added — it sends all that work right down the drain as the background image takes over the whole setup and wrecks the carefully designed layout.

FIGURE 8-24

Images can be included in tables just as with other elements.

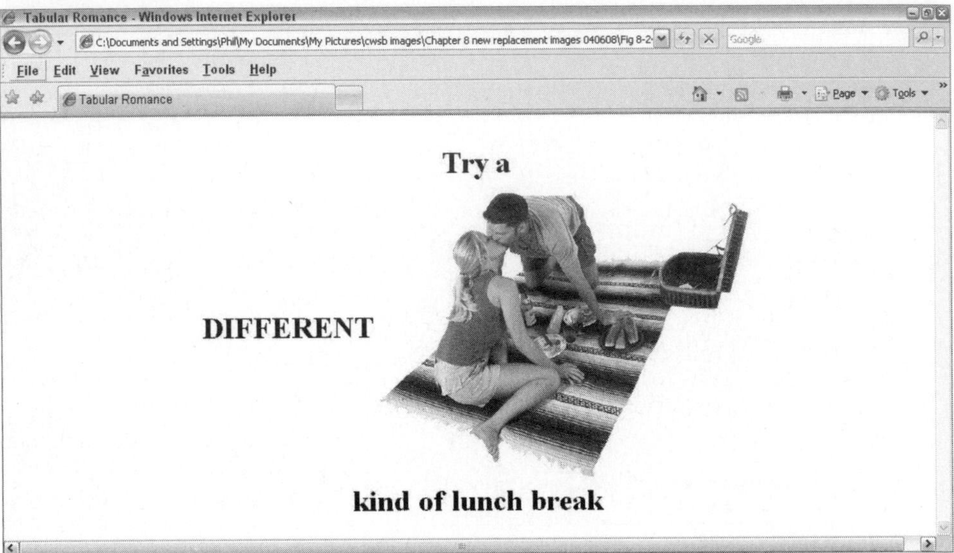

FIGURE 8-25

This figure shows a carefully crafted table with no background image.

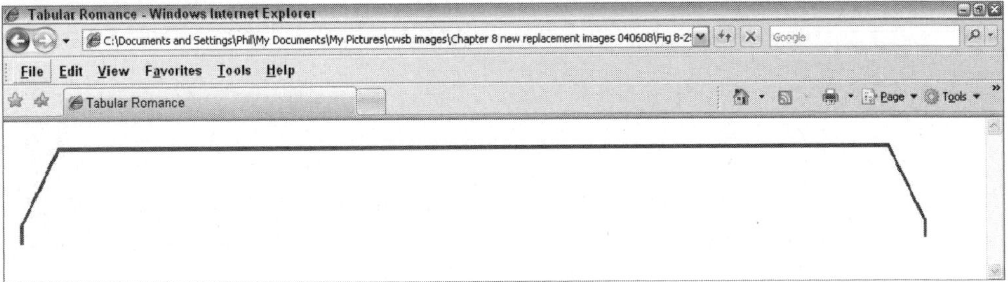

TIP **You may use images and HTML transitional as background in table elements, including `<table>`, `<th>`, `<td>`, and spanned cells.**

If you want (or need) to work with background images in tables, it's simple to do. You add the `background` attribute to the appropriate element and specify the location of the image file as the

FIGURE 8-26

Here is the same table, trashed by the addition of a background image.

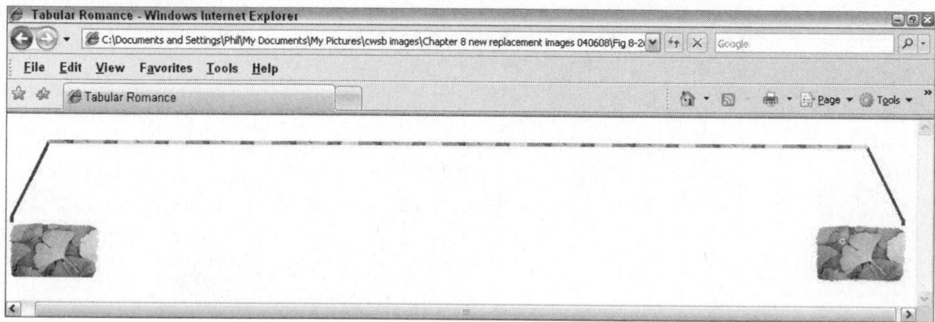

value. For example, if you wanted to add an image called `Lascaux-nef.jpg` to the table, and `Lascaux-nef.jpg` was in the same folder as the HTML file, you would use this code:

```
<TABLE background="Lascaux-nef.jpg">
```

As you can see in Figure 8-27, the image takes up the entire background of the table and expands beyond its limits. In a way, this does not matter because it does not affect the table content. However, you may want to resize it because of bandwidth (that is, download) considerations. It takes longer to download, and people may not wait around to see it.

FIGURE 8-27

This example shows a non-repeating image background.

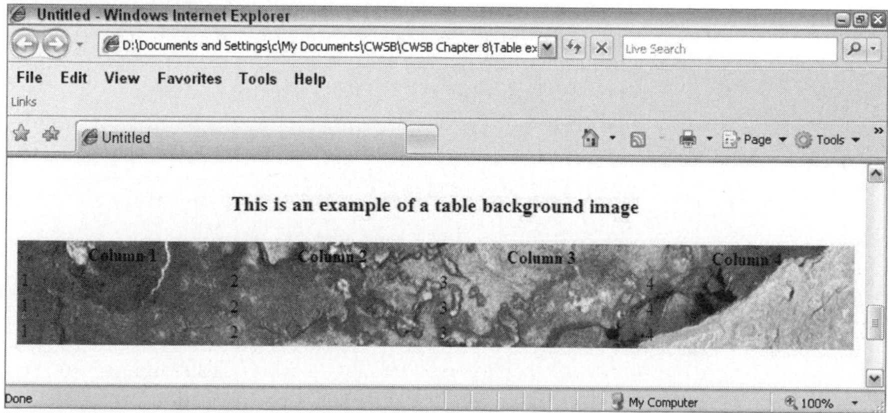

FIGURE 8-28

A tiled background can be used to fill the browser screen.

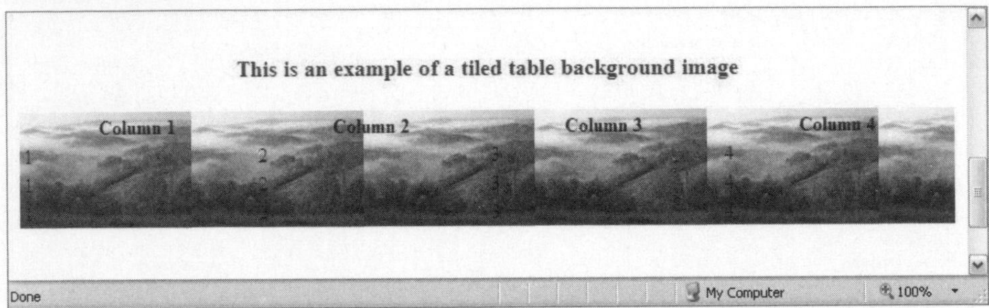

FIGURE 8-29

You can use a local element to override a global element. Local always takes precedence.

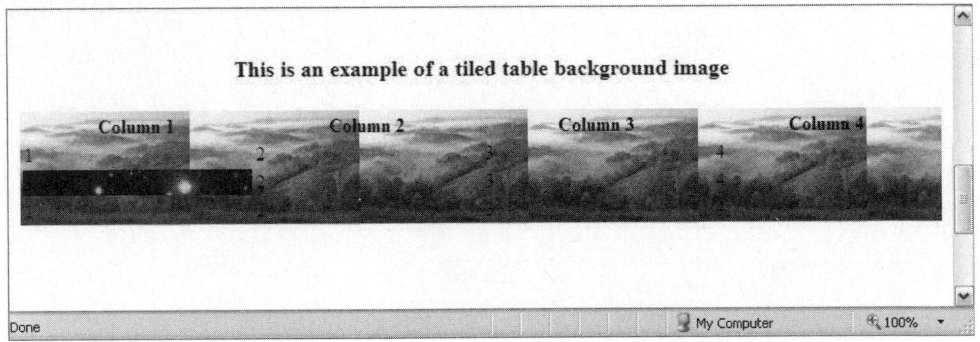

In Figure 8-28, the image is smaller and the default setting for the browser is to tile the image to fill the screen. In Figure 8-29, the local image in a cell `<TD background="HappyStars.jpg">` overrides the table background image.

Specifying background colors

Unlike background images, background colors are extremely useful in tables. For plain tabular data display, they can be used to delineate different rows to increase readability, just as with the alternating lines of color on spreadsheet printouts. Background colors can also make headings stand out from the data, emphasize the bottom line, or fulfill just about any other kind of attention-grabbing need. Figure 8-30 shows a simple table containing only data, with the various parts emphasized by background colors.

FIGURE 8-30

Background colors can emphasize cells.

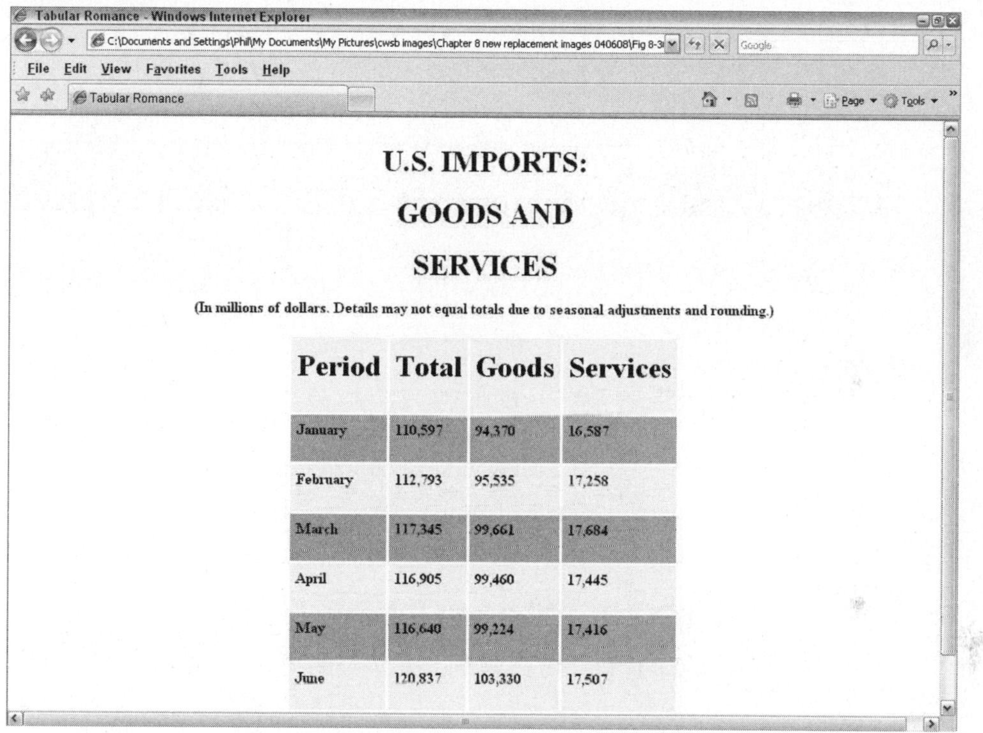

U.S. IMPORTS:
GOODS AND
SERVICES

(In millions of dollars. Details may not equal totals due to seasonal adjustments and rounding.)

Period	Total	Goods	Services
January	110,597	94,370	16,587
February	112,793	95,535	17,258
March	117,345	99,661	17,684
April	116,905	99,460	17,445
May	116,640	99,224	17,416
June	120,837	103,330	17,507

In Web design, table background colors really shine simply because you can make any cell be any size and color you want. This enables you to create color bars that are an integral part of the table. Especially in situations where you're going borderless, this opens up all sorts of possibilities.

A cell's background color won't show up in a Web browser unless there's some content in the cell. So, how do you get the color bar without spoiling it by covering the background color over with something else? The solution adopted by savvy Web designers has been devilishly simple.

What you do is to create a special image that's composed of nothing but a single, transparent pixel, and set that pixel so that it's transparent. This is called a *spacer image*. The end result is that an image that you can load into any cell without having to shrink it to make it fit into the cell, and which is invisible. The real beauty of this solution becomes apparent when you consider that you can deliberately alter the `height` and `width` values of any image, and that those values determine the size of the cell containing the image.

FIGURE 8-31

Color bars can be combined with images to produce dramatic effects.

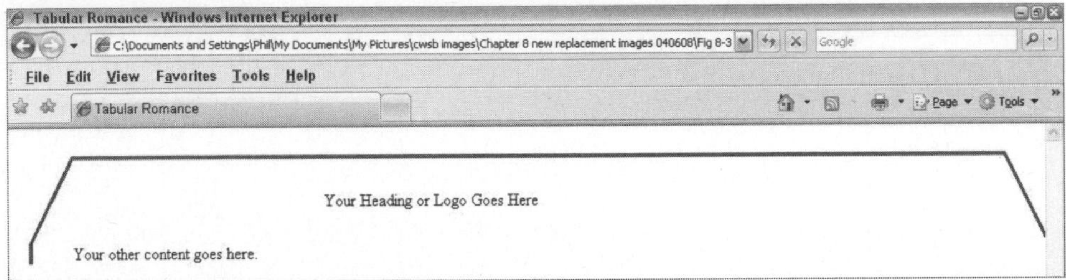

Here's a practical application of this technique that you can use on your own pages. Figure 8-31 shows a table composed of a series of color bars and a pair of images. The images are diagonal lines, and they're placed in opposite corners of the first row of the table. The horizontal and vertical lines in the table are the kind of color bars we've been talking about, where `IttyBittyClear.gif` is doing its work.

Here's the HTML code used to create that page:

```
<HTML>
<HEAD>
<TITLE>Creating Color Bars</TITLE>
</HEAD>
<BODY bgcolor="#FFFFFF">
<TABLE border="0" cellspacing="0" cellpadding="0" align="left">
<TR>
 <TD rowspan="2" align="right" colspan="2" valign="top">
<img src="TopLeft4.png" width="43" height="84" border="0" alt="top
left corner image"></TD>
 <TD bgcolor="#3C5897" valign="top" align="center"
width="100%">
<IMG src="IttyBittyClear.gif" width="1" height="4"
border="0" alt="top color bar set to 100%">
 </TD>
 <TD rowspan="2" align="left" colspan="2" valign="top">
<IMG src="TopRight4.png" width="43" height="84" border="0" alt="top
right corner image">
 </TD>
</TR>
<TR>
 <TD align="center" valign="middle" height="78"
width="693">Your Heading or Logo Goes Here</TD>
</TR>
<TR>
 <TD align="left" bgcolor="#3C5897" height="100%" width="4"
```

```
VALIGN="top">
<IMG src="IttyBittyClear.gif" width="4" height="1" border="0" alt="">
</TD>
<TD width="39"> <IMG src="IttyBittyClear.gif" width="39"
height="8" border="0" alt="">
 </TD>
 <TD colspan="3">Your other content goes here.
<IMG src="IttyBittyClear.gif" width="39" height="1" border="0"
alt="">
 </TD>
</TR>
</TABLE>
</BODY>
</HTML>
```

By the way, the purpose of setting the top color bar's width to 100 percent is to ensure that the table automatically stretches or contracts to accommodate the resolution of any screen resolution it's viewed on. You may recall from the section on sizing tables that, whenever the total size of all the cells in a row adds up to more than 100 percent (as it does in this case because there are other cells in this row), the Web browser automatically compensates. This keeps the table from being sized inappropriately.

Simply add your own content to the HTML code in the places indicated, and you have a Web page that's outlined in color. To add more rows so that the table can be expanded downward, simply copy the final TR element and its contents, then paste it in as many times as you need

FIGURE 8-32

The basic outline fills out well.

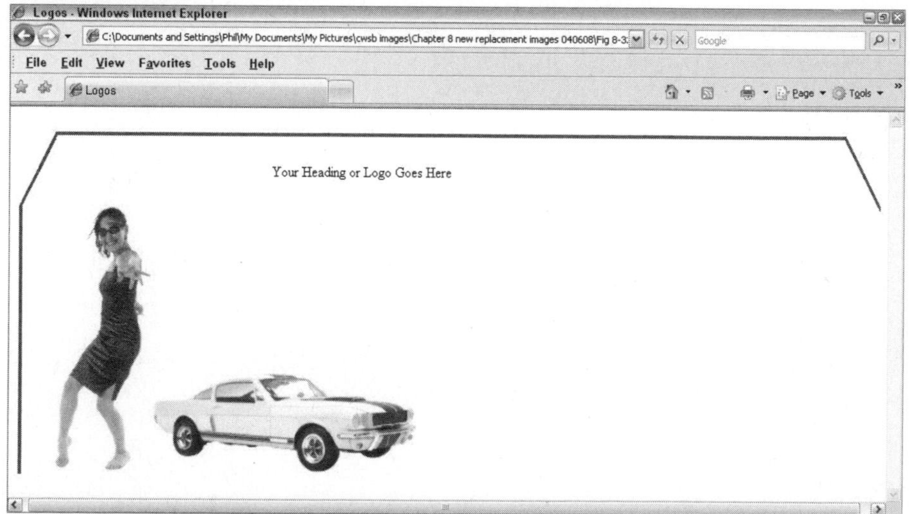

FIGURE 8-33

A basic e-zine layout using a color bar as a divider.

(we separated it with spaces above and below it in the example code so that you can pick it out easily). Figure 8-32 shows how this outline looks when it's filled with content.

Color bars don't have to sit on the fringes of the table, however. You can use them anywhere in a table. For example, Figure 8-33 shows a newspaper style design for an e-zine (online magazine) where a thin vertical line separates one article from another. As in the preceding example, you can use this right away on your own site — just fill in the blanks and you'll be ready to go.

Figure 8-33 shows the design where the first row, which holds the e-zine's logo, is composed of a single cell that spans all the columns. The next row is composed of three cells, with the center one holding the invisible image and having a black background color. The cells on the outside hold the articles. The bottom row, as with the top row, is a single cell that spans the other three columns. We recommend using it for links to other pages in the site, but that's up to you.

This is the HTML code that creates the framework:

```
<HTML>
<HEAD>
<TITLE>Creating a Newspaper Design</TITLE>
</HEAD>
<BODY>
<TABLE width="100%">
<TR ALIGN="center" valign="top">
  <TD COLSPAN="3">Logo Goes Here</TD>
</TR>
<TR valign="top">
  <TD width=50%>First article goes here.</TD>
  <TD bgcolor="Black" height="100%"><IMG src="IttyBittyClear.gif"
width="1" height="1" border="0" alt="one little dot"></TD>
  <TD width=50%>Second article goes here.</TD>
</TR>
<TR ALIGN="center" valign="middle">
  <TD COLSPAN="3">Links Go Here</TD>
```

```
</TR>
</TABLE>
</BODY>
</HTML>
```

NOTE **Because the color bar cell is set to 100 percent of the table's height, the line extends all the way down the entire article, no matter how large or small it is.**

Figure 8-34 shows the basic outline when content is added to the cells. We have also added a cell padding of 3, which increases the size of the central line in addition to moving the text out from the edges.

FIGURE 8-34

The newspaper style filled in.

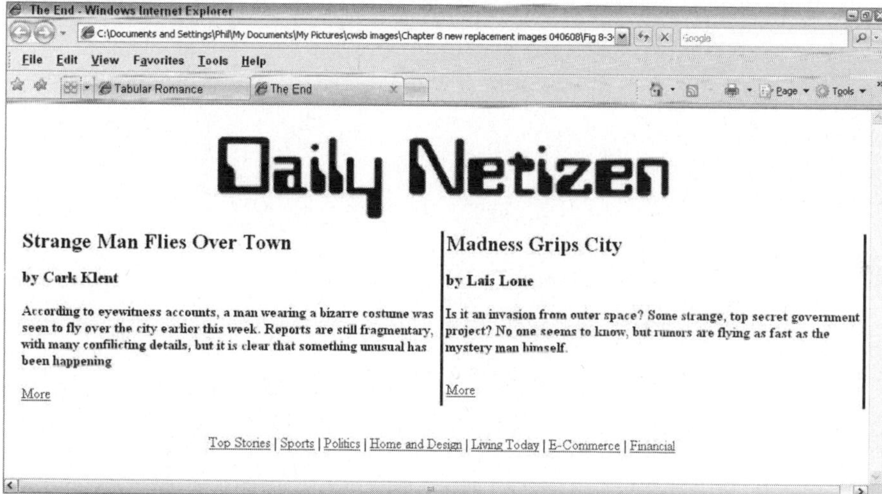

The same basic principles, of course, can be applied to more than just dividing two columns with a single line. Study the HTML code, let your imagination run free, and you'll find a lot of different ways to use color bars and tables.

Tables Quick Reference

The following provides a quick reference for key items discussed in this chapter:

- `<table></table>` — These tags are used to create tables.
- `<th></th>` — These tags are used to create table headings. The headings are centered and bolded by default.

- `<tr></tr>` — These tags are used to create a table row. Each row contains one or more cells. There can be many rows per table.
- `<td></td>` — These tags are used to create a table cell within a row. There can be several cells per row.
- `<caption></caption>` — These tags are used to present a brief description of the data. Other formatting elements may be encapsulated within the `caption` tags to modify the appearance of the caption.
- `summary` — This is an attribute used on specially equipped computers to render aurally the content of the table. It is positioned within the `table` tag.
- `align` — This is an attribute used within the `table` and `cell` tags. It specifies locations of the content with the values of `right`, `left`, and `center`.
- `height` — This is an attribute within cells that specifies the height of a cell.
- `width` — This is an attribute within cells and tables that specifies the width of cells.
- `*` — This is a value used within cells to proportionally allocate space in a table.
- Spanning cell — This is a cell that has merged with other cells. Cell spanning can be used for rows (`rowspan`) or for columns (`colspan`).
- `cellpadding` — This regulates the distance between the cell wall and the content.
- `cellspacing` — This regulates the distance between cells.

Summary

If there's a secret weapon in the Web designer's arsenal — it's tables. Tables can be used for a variety of purposes.

This chapter began with a review of the basic structure of a simple table and introduced the tags for developing a basic table. These tags are `<table></table>`, `<tr></tr>`, and `<td></td>`. They represent the coding to develop the table of rows and columns of cells. The discussion also examined the issue of proportionality in cell sizing, and provided ways to absolutely or relatively define table and cell size.

This chapter also looked at solid and highlighted colors using HTML attributes of `bordercolor` and `bordercolorlight`. We noted that this is a feature required in IE. We discussed when it was appropriate to use borders, and the range of acceptable border sizes, reaching the conclusion that though all sizes are permissible, not all sizes are expedient (a range of 1 to 5 pixels in thickness is best). We also looked at the manipulation of the border itself by using the attributes of `frames` (to manipulate the appearance of the table borders) and `rules` (to manipulate the appearance of the internal gridlines). We also introduced you to `captions` and `summary` attributes of common tables.

This chapter examined the features of cell spacing (the distance between two adjacent cells within a table) and cell padding (the space within a cell separating the content from the margin of the cell body).

We discussed the alignment of tables versus the alignment of content within cells. We discussed how to use tables to provide structure to forms that would make it easier for users to follow. We also looked at sidebars as an example of table layout. We pointed out that the contents of another (nested) table could be placed within one cell of an encompassing table. We looked at the range of options for `valign` and showed how to avoid word wrap within cells.

In this chapter, you learned how to create row and column spanning to control the appearance of your table, and to allow content within the table to be grouped for clarity. You learned how background images can add quite dramatic effects to your table, and provide visual clues to understanding the content. Images may be inserted into a table, may be resized, and may be tiled for effect. Tables in cells take precedence over images appearing at higher levels of the hierarchy. This can be summed up as "local overrides global." We discussed the difficulty of getting backgrounds to appear correctly if too many elements are in the mix, and we presented examples of well-formed table design such as in an e-zine.

Chapter 9 discusses frames.

Chapter 9

Organizing Your Site with Frames

Frames are used to put multiple Web pages on screen at the same time. Because each framed page resides within its own distinct and limited area of the screen, the effect is to create a seamless whole out of many parts.

All the frames together are contained within a different kind of Web page called a *frameset*. Framesets themselves are never seen by a site visitor. Only their contents — which consist of the borders of the frames and the framed pages — are visible.

The primary reason to use frames is to provide at least one area of the screen where the content remains stable while another area changes. The stable area keeps something important in front of your site visitors at all times. What this important item is varies from site to site. Most often, a special page showing a set of links to all the other pages in the site is kept in a small frame, while the pages themselves are displayed in the remaining screen area. The small frame with links is commonly called a *navigation frame*, because to navigate to any page in the site, visitors simply click one of the links in the frame, which loads the link in what could be called the "viewing" frame. By keeping the links content available at all times, visitors are able to move about the site more easily than if they had to constantly return to the home page to locate a links listing.

Although navigational content is the most common use for frames, frames are sometimes used for other types of static content, such as a legal notice or graphic that you want to always keep in your visitors' field of vision.

IN THIS CHAPTER

Designing Frame Layouts

The first step in designing your framed screen is to determine how many frames you need in order to display your content. While that varies from one situation to another, a good rule of thumb is to use the minimum possible number of frames. Part of that statement is pure aesthetic opinion, and you may well disagree with it. Still, it is a simple matter of practicality that every Web designer must face — there's only a certain amount of real estate available on a computer screen. If you want to cram 20 or 30 frames into a frameset, it can technically be done but the results won't be anything that anyone will be able to use easily. Figure 9-1 shows a Web page that has far too many frames — it's a horror that we created only so that it could serve as a bad example.

So, how many frames is right? Again, it depends on the needs of the particular Web site you're working on, but most Web designers would hesitate to have more than three to five frames on one screen. The smaller the content, the more frames you can get away with, but the key is to figure out what you really need to make the framed site work.

FIGURE 9-1

Too many frames can make a screen confusing or even unusable.

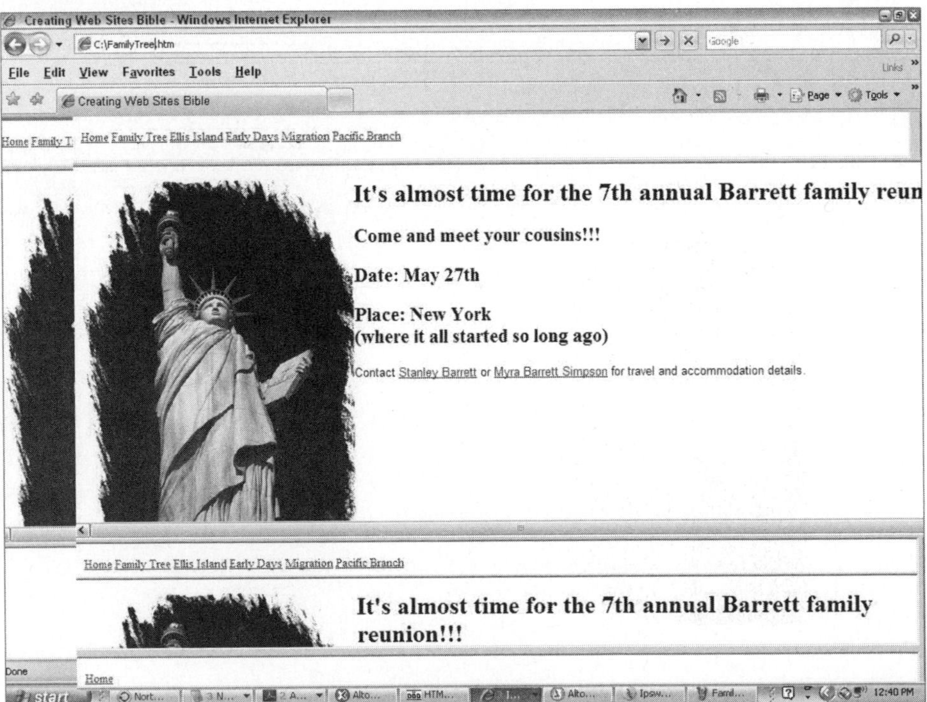

Analyzing functional needs

Do you have a corporate logo that you want to keep in front of visitors at all times? Frame it. Do you have a set of links that must always be accessible without users having to scroll up and down or retrace steps via the Web browser's Back button? Frame them.

Bearing in mind that the purpose of frames is to maintain some type of unchanging content for part of the screen layout, you must take a good look at which parts of your screen you want to lock into place, and which parts of it can be left free to scroll in the normal manner.

If you don't have anything that really needs to be locked into place, then you don't really need to be using frames at all.

Creating navigation layouts

The vast majority of framed pages on the Web exist for navigational purposes. With this approach, one frame holds a set of links that, when acted upon, change the contents of the other frame or frames. The most common arrangement is a two-frame setup in which the navigation frame is relatively small, and the content frame takes up most of the screen. Figure 9-2 shows a left-sided navigation frame.

FIGURE 9-2

The left-sided navigation frame is common on the Web.

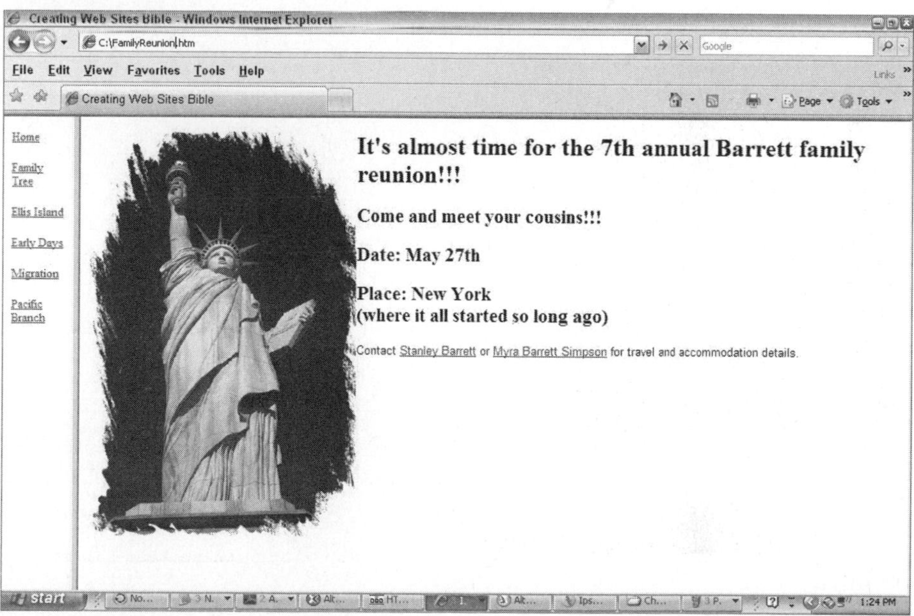

FIGURE 9-3

The top navigation frame is almost as popular.

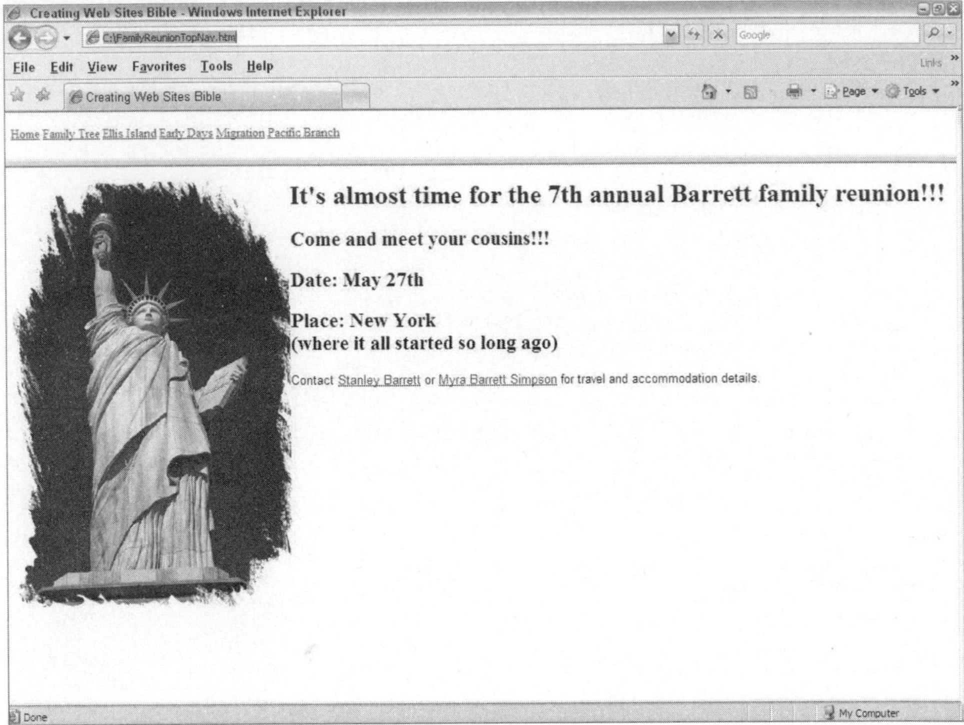

However, many designers use either the top or bottom of the screen to hold the navigation frame. Figure 9-3 shows the same Web site with a navigation frame on the top instead of on the left side. The right side is rarely used, but there is certainly no reason why it can't be, especially if your Web site is meant for an audience whose native language reads from right to left.

Some sites even have more than one navigation frame, depending on the needs of the material involved. It is even possible to load one frameset into a frame in another frameset. In that case, the second frameset may have its own navigation frame that works only within that smaller area (see the discussion on the `_parent` target in the section, "Using reserved frame names," later in this chapter).

Setting up action or result layouts

Frames are very useful when they are teamed up with JavaScript event handlers (see Chapter 13). Although HTML links can cause only one kind of change (a new file address is called upon), JavaScript programming is much more powerful than HTML alone.

FIGURE 9-4

JavaScript calculation pages often use frames to accept values and respond with results in separate screen areas.

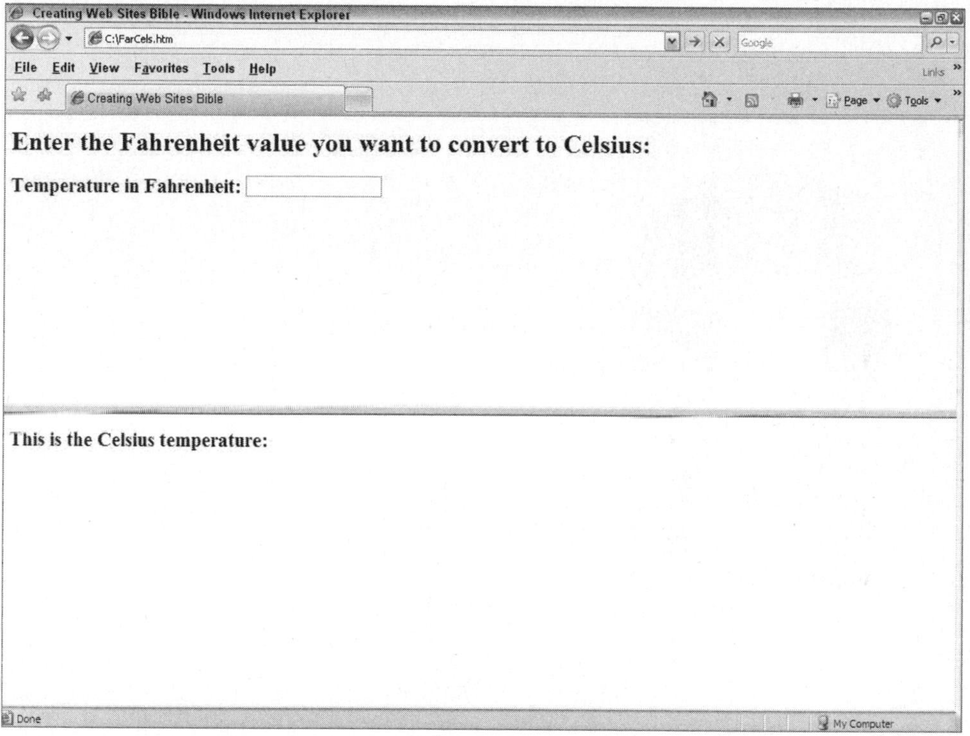

Figure 9-4 shows a Web site in which the top frame is used to enter values and the bottom frame is used to present the calculated results of those values.

Creating Framesets

Framesets are Web pages that define the areas of a Web browser's screen that will contain framed pages. In order to do this, framesets work a bit differently from the usual Web page. To save you from having to flip back to Chapter 4, here's the basic skeletal structure of a normal Web page:

```
<HTML>
<HEAD>
<TITLE>Web Page Title Goes Here</TITLE>
</HEAD>
```

```
<BODY>
Visible Web page content goes here.
</BODY>
</HTML>
```

The most important way in which frameset pages differ from regular HTML pages is that the BODY element is replaced by the FRAMESET element. The FRAMESET element contains two or more FRAME elements. You could, in theory, have only one frame, but there's no point to doing so — the result would be just one Web page on screen, and you don't need frames to do that. The following HTML code shows the outline structure of a frameset page:

```
<HTML>
<HEAD>
<TITLE>Frameset Title Goes Here</TITLE>
</HEAD>
<FRAMESET>
  <FRAME name="top" src="test.html">
  <FRAME name="bottom" src="test.html">
</FRAMESET>
</HTML>
```

Unlike all the other elements in this listing, the FRAME element does not have an end tag. The <FRAME> tags are indented to visually emphasize their containment within the <FRAMESET> and </FRAMESET> tags, but you do not have to indent them in your HTML code if you don't want to. Because HTML doesn't recognize leading white space, it's the same to a Web browser if you indent or not.

The FRAME element needs to have an src attribute that tells it what page to display in the frame. The name attribute is optional, but to use links in one frame to change content in another frame, the attribute is required (see the section, "Setting Targets for Your Links," later in this chapter).

NOTE **When a Web page is displayed in a browser, its title shows at the top of the browser. However, framesets contain multiple Web pages. Browsers solve this dilemma by showing the title of the frameset itself, instead of the title of one of the contained Web pages.**

The previous frameset has a problem in that only one frame is shown. That's because we need to specify the size of the columns and rows.

Setting columns and rows

As noted earlier, the first choice you must make is how many frames to have on screen. The second is whether to set up vertical or horizontal frames, or both at the same time. The following example uses the rows attribute to create a pair of horizontal frames, each of which takes up half of the screen:

```
<FRAMESET rows="50%,50%">
  <FRAME>
  <FRAME>
</FRAMESET>
```

FIGURE 9-5

The rows attribute sets up horizontal frames.

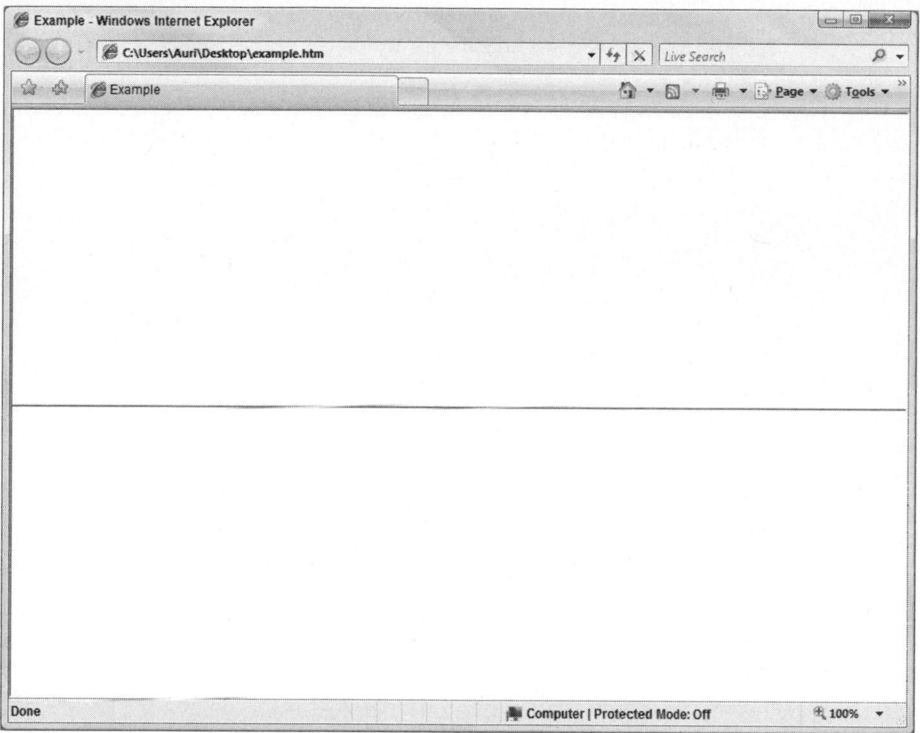

Figure 9-5 shows an evenly divided pair of horizontal frames.

To set a pair of vertical frames (columns) that each take up half the screen, you would use the same code, but substitute the cols attribute instead:

```
<FRAMESET cols="50%,50%">
  <FRAME>
  <FRAME>
</FRAMESET>
```

Figure 9-6 shows the results of this code.

If you want to have four columns, each one the same size, you could use the following code:

```
<FRAMESET cols="25%,25%,25%,25%">
  <FRAME>
  <FRAME>
  <FRAME>
```

```
    <FRAME>
  </FRAMESET>
```

NOTE **The number of size values in the `rows` or `cols` attribute specifies the number of frames to be created and sets how large each will be. Because we have given sizes for four frames, there must also be four `FRAME` elements.**

You do not have to set up symmetrical frames. Any frame can be any size you want. You could, for example, set up the preceding four columns like this:

```
<FRAMESET cols="10%,45%,15%,30%">
  <FRAME>
  <FRAME>
  <FRAME>
  <FRAME>
</FRAMESET>
```

FIGURE 9-6

The `cols` attribute sets up vertical frames.

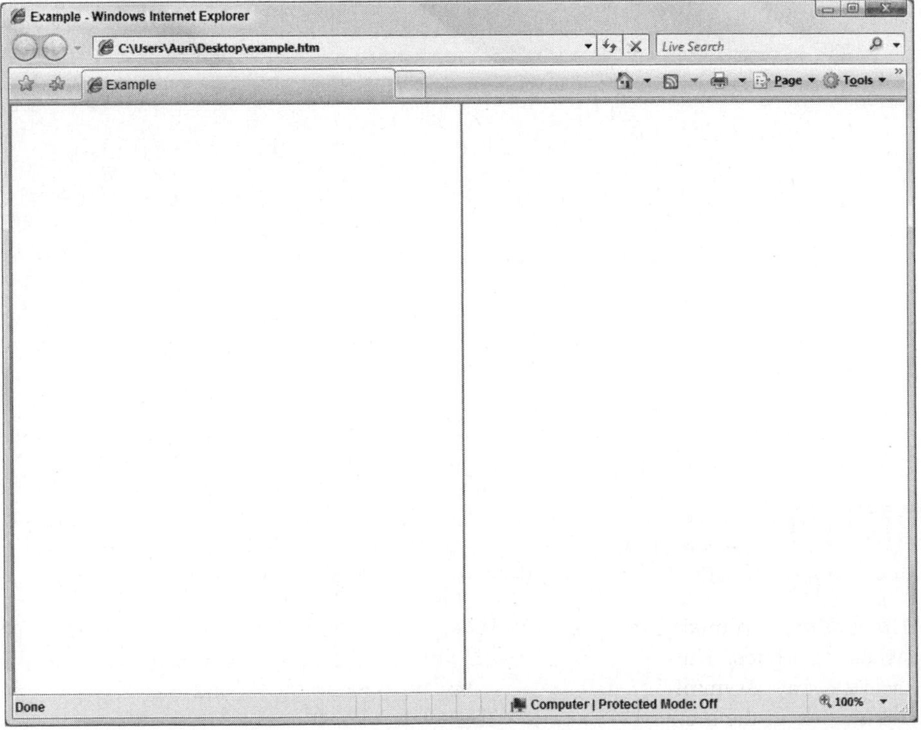

If you are setting up symmetrical frames, however, you can't use decimal points for your row and column sizes. The usual solution to this is to just drop any small amount of leftover pixels into one of the rows or columns. In the following code, it's impossible to create three equally sized rows and still have everything equal 100%, so the final row is 1 percent larger than the first two:

```
<FRAMESET rows="33%,33%,34%">
  <FRAME>
  <FRAME>
  <FRAME>
</FRAMESET>
```

This is a simple solution and the difference is virtually unnoticeable — very few people can tell the difference between two frames that are just a handful of pixels different in size.

It's common practice (and good programming procedure) to ensure that all the column or row percentages total 100 percent. However, if you fail to get the numbers exactly right, the Web browser used to view the frameset usually automatically compensates for your error. For example, if you specified each of the three rows in the preceding example as 33 percent in size, most Web browsers would simply make each frame equal to one third of the screen size (for more details on error correction by browsers, see the section, "Mixing pixel, percentage, and relative sizing," later in this chapter).

A frameset can contain both columns and rows at the same time by simply using both the `cols` and `rows` attributes. The following example, illustrated in Figure 9-7, makes eight frames by setting up two rows of four columns:

```
<FRAMESET cols="25%,25%,25%,25%" rows="50%,50%">
  <FRAME>
  <FRAME>
  <FRAME>
  <FRAME>
  <FRAME>
  <FRAME>
  <FRAME>
  <FRAME>
</FRAMESET>
```

The first four frames are placed in the top row, and the next four in the second row. The frames in each row are placed from left to right.

CAUTION **If you use both rows and columns in the same frameset, you must multiply the number of rows by the number of columns to determine how many frames are created. It's a common error to add the numbers of rows and columns instead of multiplying them.**

The drawback to mixing rows and columns in this manner is that you're limited to creating symmetrical grids. Thus, if you want to divide one column in half, you must divide all of them the same way. Asymmetrical frame layouts are possible, however, and they are discussed later in this chapter in the section "Nesting framesets."

FIGURE 9-7

The `rows` and `cols` attributes can be combined to create a grid.

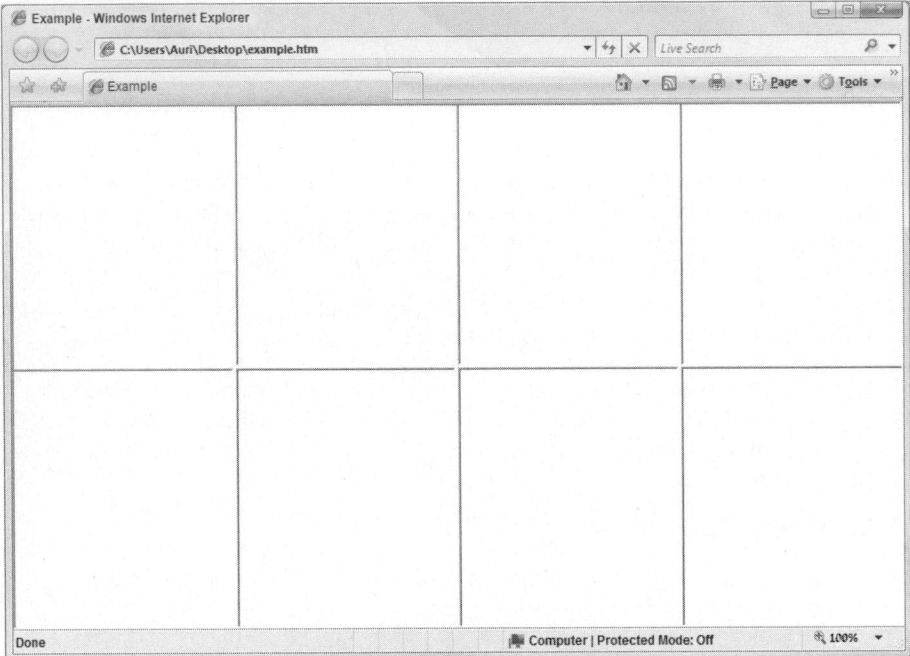

Mixing pixel, percentage, and relative sizing

So far, we have used only percentages of screen size when setting the sizes of frames. However, there are two other options. You can state a precise and absolute size in pixels for a frame, or use *relative sizing*. A frame that is relatively sized takes up all the space on the screen that isn't occupied by other frames. If there's half of the screen left for the relative frame to fill, then it takes up that half. If there's only 10 percent of the screen available, then that's how big the relative frame will be.

It's unusual to specify an exact size in pixels for all the frames in a frameset. It can be done, however, and Web browsers are smart enough to adjust for any difference between your intentions and the reality of the actual screen display. For example, the following code sets up two columns so that they add up to an exact width of 1,024 pixels:

```
<FRAMESET cols="200,824">
  <FRAME>
  <FRAME>
</FRAMESET>
```

If this frameset is viewed by someone using a screen resolution of 1,024 × 768, it works perfectly. However, if someone else views it using a screen resolution of 640 × 480, it will still work. The Web browser realizes the frameset can't fit on the screen and automatically resizes both frames so that everything fits into the available screen space. The resizing is done proportionally — each frame is shrunk by the same amount so that the layout remains intact. The same thing is true in reverse. If you specify a screen size that's too small, then both frames are proportionally enlarged to fit.

Although the HTML specification doesn't include percentages that are too large or too small (it only tells Web browsers how to handle errors in absolute values), both of the major browsers handle percentage errors just as they do absolute errors. If you make three frames take up only 70 percent of the screen among them, the remaining 30 percent of the space is used up by providing 10 percent more screen width to each of the three frames. If you make two frames take up 140 percent of the screen between them, the excess 40 percent is taken up by making each frame 20 percent of the screen size smaller.

Absolute values are commonly used in tandem with relative sizing. For example, you might specify that two columns are to be divided so that the first column is 200 pixels wide and the second one will be relatively sized, taking up all of the remaining space. To do so, you would write the following code:

```
<FRAMESET cols="200,*">
  <FRAME>
  <FRAME>
</FRAMESET>
```

The asterisk (*) is the relative size character. Exactly how much space is allotted to the second column depends on the screen resolution being used by a visitor to your site. If the display is 640 pixels wide, for example, then the second column will be 440 pixels wide (640 – 200). Figure 9-8 shows the results of this code on a 1024-pixel-wide screen where the size of the second column becomes 824 pixels wide (1024 – 200).

NOTE **It's not as easy to calculate exactly how relative sizes for rows will turn out, because every Web browser takes up some of the vertical screen space with its menus and icons — and the exact amount of vertical space depends on user Preference settings. Some browsers also use up some of the horizontal screen space. For example, when you click the History button in Internet Explorer (IE), the History window opens on the left side of the screen. When that happens, the available space for columns is also affected.**

You can set relative sizes for multiple frames as well. To set up three rows in which the first is 200 pixels high and the other two each take up half of the remaining space, you would use this code:

```
<FRAMESET rows="200,*,*">
  <FRAME>
  <FRAME>
  <FRAME>
</FRAMESET>
```

FIGURE 9-8

Relative sizing enables you to specify an exact size for one frame and let the remaining frame take up whatever space is left.

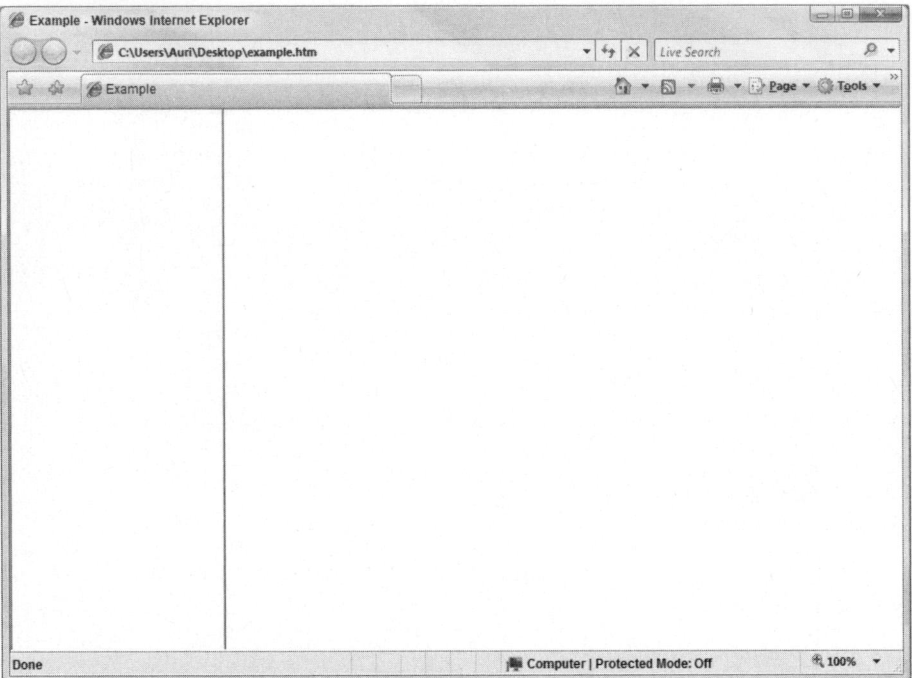

This means that, if the screen height is 768 pixels, the last two rows split the remaining 568 pixels, and each is thus 284 pixels high. For a screen height of 600 pixels, all three rows are 200 pixels high (400/2). If the screen height is 480 pixels, then the last two rows are each only 140 pixels high (280/2).

If you want the center row to be the one with the absolute size, the code is modified like this:

```
<FRAMESET rows="*,200,*">
  <FRAME>
  <FRAME>
  <FRAME>
</FRAMESET>
```

If none of the frames has a specific size, then all are proportionally distributed. The following code sample sets up four equally sized frames using relative sizing:

```
<FRAMESET rows="*,*,*,*">
  <FRAME>
```

```
    <FRAME>
    <FRAME>
    <FRAME>
  </FRAMESET>
```

The effect is the same as if each frame had been set using a value of 25 percent.

You can also specify relative sizes by stating the proportions to be allotted to each frame. Thus, 2* is twice as much space as *, and 3* is three times as much as *. To make a trio of columns in which the center column is four times as wide as the other two, write this code:

```
<FRAMESET cols="*,4*,*">
  <FRAME>
  <FRAME>
  <FRAME>
</FRAMESET>
```

Any combination of the three approaches can be used together. The following example shows how to make three rows in which the first row is 100 pixels high and the second is twice as high as the third:

```
<FRAMESET rows="100,2*,*">
  <FRAME>
  <FRAME>
  <FRAME>
</FRAMESET>
```

Likewise, you can specify percentages for some frames while others are left to relative sizing. In this example, the first row takes up 35 percent of the screen height, and the second row is one fifth of the height of the third row:

```
<FRAMESET rows="35%,*,5*">
  <FRAME>
  <FRAME>
  <FRAME>
</FRAMESET>
```

You can mix all three techniques together, as in the following code:

```
<FRAMESET rows="25%,*,80">
  <FRAME>
  <FRAME>
  <FRAME>
</FRAMESET>
```

This sets the first row to one quarter of the screen height, sets the final row to 80 pixels in height, and leaves the center row to take up all the remaining space.

Preventing resizing

The default behavior of Web browsers is to allow users to resize frames at will by dragging the frame border to a new location. Generally speaking, it's preferable to leave your site visitors with this option intact. However, if there is some reason why your framed design would suffer if anything were changed, you can ensure that the frames cannot be resized simply by adding the `noresize` attribute to the `FRAME` element:

```
<FRAME noresize>
```

Specifying frame names and contents

Each frame must have a name if you are ever going to change its original content. Although you can put a Web page into a frame just by specifying it in the initial frame declaration, the only way to tell which frame to load a new Web page into is by using the frame's name (see the section "Setting Targets for Your Links" later in this chapter).

NOTE **When we refer to the contents of a frame as a Web page, we are simply recognizing that most people use frames for displaying Web pages. However, there is nothing to stop you from putting any Web-displayable file into a frame. For example, you could specify a JPEG image file for the contents just as easily as you could a Web page. You can even use another frameset as the contents instead of a normal Web page, although that's pushing the capabilities of most Web browsers to the limit and begging for a crash.**

There are very few limits on creating frame names. There are some reserved names that you cannot use: `_blank`, `_parent`, `_self`, and `_top`. The first character of your frame name must be a letter (the reserved names are the only ones that don't follow this rule). Beyond that, the name may contain letters, numbers, hyphens, underscores, colons, or periods. Table 9-1 provides examples of legal and illegal frame names.

Although this means that you can create practically any names you want for your frames, it's good practice to use descriptive names. For example, `MainDisplay` is much easier to comprehend than something like `Frame3`.

TABLE 9-1

Frame Naming Conventions

Valid Name	Invalid Name
`secondframe`	`2ndframe`
`AboveTheOthers`	`_AboveTheOthers`
`left-Side`	`-leftSide`
`a9q:-._`	`a9q:-._,?/`

The name of the frame is an attribute of the FRAME element and is assigned by using the name attribute. So is the location of the Web page that will initially fill the frame; the location is shown by the src (source) attribute. The following line of code shows how the name and source are specified:

```
<FRAME name="LeftSide" src="firstpage.html">
```

NOTE **The location of the Web page in the src attribute follows the same rules about absolute and relative URLs that the href attribute does in anchors, as discussed in Chapter 5.**

Figure 9-9 shows a genealogy Web site with two frames. The small top frame holds a Web page in which the sole content is a graphics file that shows a fancy image of the family name. The larger bottom frame holds the event announcement page for the site.

FIGURE 9-9

This figure shows a framed genealogy Web site.

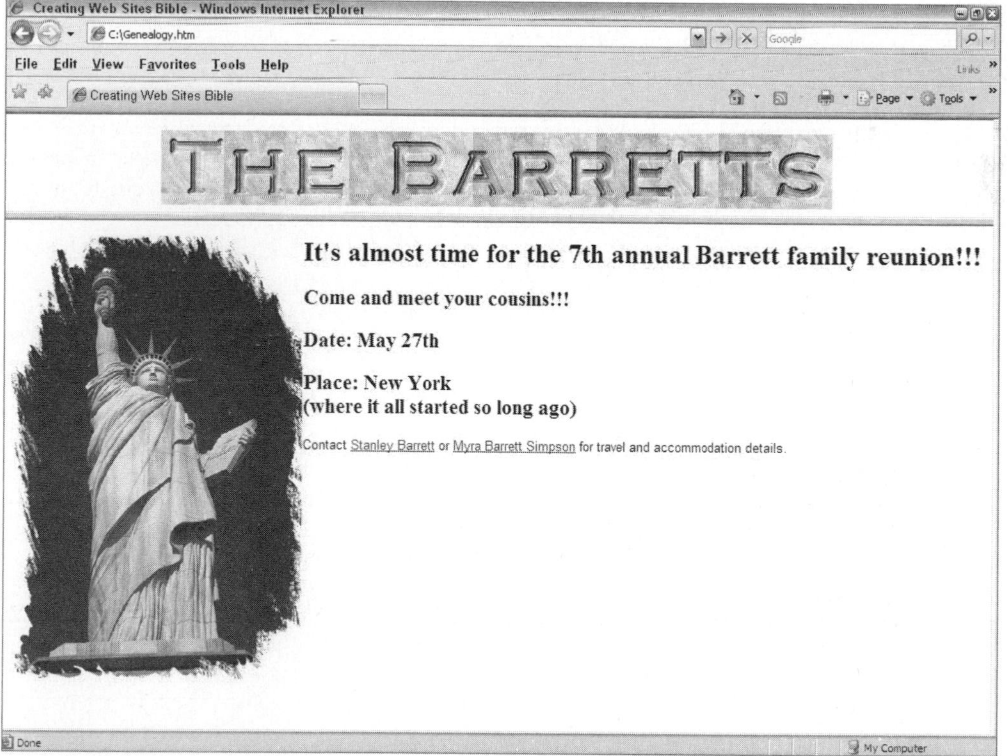

The frameset and contents were specified using the following code:

```
<HTML>
<HEAD>
<TITLE>The Barrett Family Genealogy Page</TITLE>
</HEAD>
<FRAMESET rows="105,*">
  <FRAME name="banner" src="barrettslogo.html">
  <FRAME name="mainpage" src="family.html">
</FRAMESET>
</HTML>
```

The top frame is set to a height of 105 pixels because that gives the graphic in the Web page contained in that frame a little bit of room around it. The bottom frame is set to relative sizing, taking up whatever remains of the available vertical space.

Don't forget that if you want the frameset to be the default page for your site, you need to save it as `index.html`.

Nesting framesets

In addition to containing frames, framesets can contain other framesets. This technique is called *nesting*. You would want to do this to overcome the basic limitation of frames — that they must be either horizontal or vertical. By nesting one frameset within another frameset, you can set one to vertical and the other to horizontal, resulting in a much more complex and useful screen layout.

The skeleton structure of a nested frameset page shows that the internal frameset is equivalent to a regular frame:

```
<HTML>
<HEAD>
<TITLE>Frameset Title Goes Here</TITLE>
</HEAD>
<FRAMESET>
  <FRAME>
  <FRAME>
  <FRAMESET>
    <FRAME>
    <FRAME>
  </FRAMESET>
</FRAMESET>
</HTML>
```

The genealogy page in the preceding example uses a simple pair of horizontal frames. That kind of setup maximizes the screen area that the main Web page has to sprawl out in, but it also means that frames aren't being used to their full advantage. All the links for the site will have to be contained within the Web page itself, which also puts constraints on the layout, content, and functionality of that page.

FIGURE 9-10

A second frameset enables you to include more content.

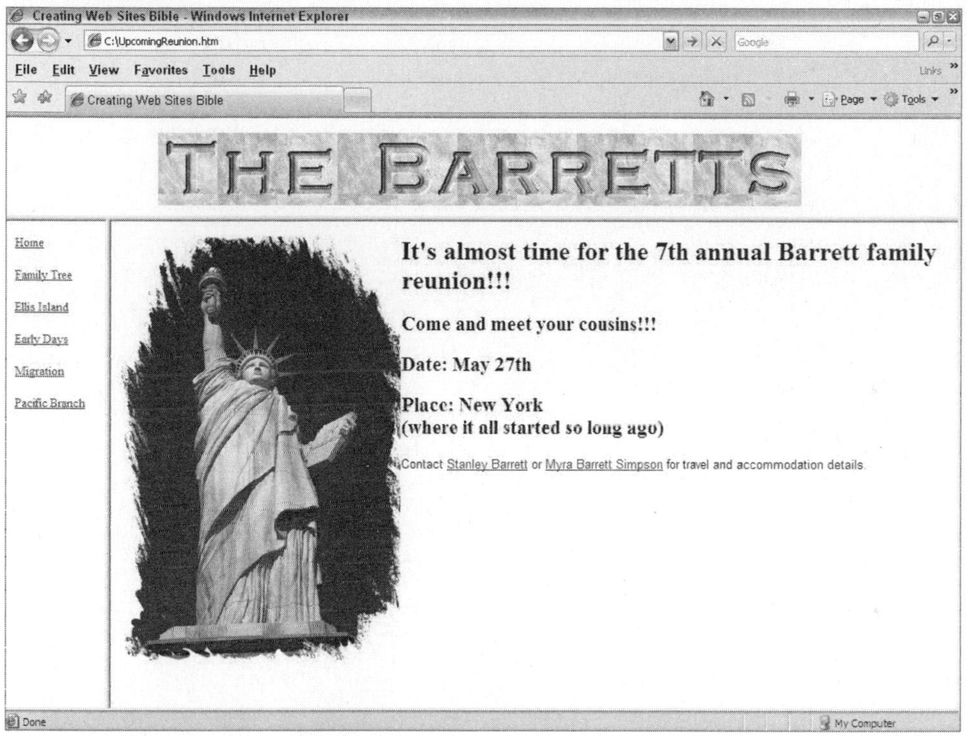

You could solve the problem by putting a set of links to other pages in the site into the top frame, but the tradeoff is that you must replace the logo graphic with the link set. If a second frameset is added, however, the top frame can remain as it is and site links can be placed to the side of the main page, as shown in Figure 9-10. This not only frees up the main page for any other type of content you want to add to it, but it keeps the link listing constantly available as other Web pages are loaded into the main frame.

This is the HTML code that achieves the modification:

```
<HTML>
<HEAD>
<TITLE>The Barrett Family Genealogy Page</TITLE>
</HEAD>
<FRAMESET rows="105,*">
  <FRAME name="banner" src="barrettslogo.html">
  <FRAMESET cols="110,*">
    <FRAME name="navpage" src="barrettlinks.html">
```

```
    <FRAME name="mainpage" src="family.html">
  </FRAMESET>
</FRAMESET>
</HTML>
```

The containing frameset is still the same as before — it divides the screen into two rows with the top row containing the graphic. The content of the bottom row, however, is no longer a frame, but rather another frameset. That frameset divides the bottom row into two columns. The left column is set to a width of 110 pixels, and the right column uses relative sizing. The left column contains a new Web page that has the links to the rest of the site. The right column contains the same page that used to take up the entire bottom row.

Adding NOFRAMES content

The NOFRAMES element has only one purpose — to provide some visible content for users of browsers or browsing tools that don't display framesets (the text-to-speech browsers used by blind people, for example). All modern computer-based browsers support frames, but devices such as mobile phones and PDAs often do not. In this respect, it is much like supplying alternative text for images (see Chapter 8). No one knows how many people are using browsers that can't handle frames, so you should always make some sort of provision for that possibility.

The NOFRAMES element is not, as you might expect, contained within the FRAMESET element. Because it's not a part of the frame scenario, but rather an alternative, it goes outside. The following HTML code shows where it fits:

```
<HTML>
<HEAD>
<TITLE>Frameset Title Goes Here</TITLE>
</HEAD>
<FRAMESET>
  <FRAME>
  <FRAME>
</FRAMESET>
<NOFRAMES>
Content for browsers without frame support goes here.
</NOFRAMES>
</HTML>
```

Within the NOFRAMES element, you enter everything you want to be displayed in case a browser that isn't capable of showing frames is used to view the frameset page. That content depends upon your own site's intentions, audience, and capacity.

Many framed sites use a blunt and simple approach, as you see in this example:

```
<NOFRAMES>
<P>This Web site uses frames. Your browser does not support them.</P>
</NOFRAMES>
```

However, it is better to provide a link to a version that doesn't use frames:

```
<noframes>
  <h2>Frame Alert</h2>
  <p>
  This document is designed to be viewed using the frames feature.
You are using a non-frame-capable browser.
  <br>
  See the <a href="noframe.html">Non-frame version</a>.
  </p>
</noframes>
```

The contents of the NOFRAMES element can be as complex as any Web page. We'll explore this in the following project.

Setting Targets for Your Links

It is possible that you could set up a framed site in which none of the contents of any of the frames ever changes, resulting in a simple, static layout that's no different from a normal Web page except for the fact that it's composed of multiple HTML files. However, people generally use frames so that their content can be more organized.

Targeting custom-named frames

Generally, when someone clicks a link on a Web page, the new Web page simply replaces the old one on his or her screen. Frames are different, however. Different frames can be specified as the *target* for the link — the frame in which the link will open. Links between frames have a variety of different behaviors, depending on what target is set for the link (see Chapter 5 for more information on creating links). The syntax for setting a link's target is as follows:

```
<A href="url" target=-"framename">
```

When you click a link that's on a framed Web page and no target is specified, the linked Web page opens in the same frame that the link was in, replacing the linking page. If you specify another frame as the target, then the linked page opens in the specified target frame instead, replacing whatever is in that frame, but leaving the linking page unaffected.

For example, let's say you have two frames, one of which is named `frameone` and the other `frametwo`, and you have a links page in `frameone`. If you used the following code in a link in `frameone`, then the linked page would open in `frameone`:

```
<A href="somewhere.html">Over The Rainbow</A>
```

In this case, the Web page named `somewhere.html` would be loaded over the links page in `frameone`, and there would be no effect at all on `frametwo`.

However, if you gave an additional instruction by adding the `target` attribute to the code and specifying `frametwo` as the target, the results would be different:

```
<A href="somewhere.html" target="frametwo">Over The Rainbow</A>
```

This would cause the Web page named `somewhere.html` to open in `frametwo`, leaving the links page in `frameone` intact.

If you use a target name that doesn't exist, the linked page opens in a new browser window.

The following is the HTML code for the links page that was used in the navigation frame for the genealogy page in the preceding section:

```
<HTML>
<HEAD>
<TITLE>Barrett Site Links</TITLE>
</HEAD>
<BODY>
 <P><A href="family.html" target="mainpage">Home</A></P>
 <P><A href="familytree.html" target="mainpage">Family Tree</A></P>
 <P><A href="ellis.html" target="mainpage">Ellis Island</A></P>
 <P><A href="earlydays.html" target="mainpage">Early Days</A></P>
 <P><A href="migration.html" target="mainpage">Migration</A></P>
 <P><A href="pacific.html" target="mainpage">Pacific Branch</A></P>
</BODY>
</HTML>
```

The main display area in that site's frameset was a frame named `mainpage`, and each of the links in the navigation page is set to have that frame as its target. Without that target specification, the linked pages would all open within the narrow navigation frame.

Base target element

However, you can simplify the coding and still make it accomplish the same thing through the use of `base target="mainpage"`. The `BASE` element is placed within the head because it does not display content.

```
<HTML>
<HEAD>
<BASE target="mainpage">
<TITLE>Barrett Site Links</TITLE>
</HEAD>
<BODY>
 <P><A href="family.html">Home</A></P>
 <P><A href="familytree.html">Family Tree</A></P>
 <P><A href="ellis.html">Ellis Island</A></P>
 <P><A href="earlydays.html">Early Days</A></P>
 <P><A href="migration.html">Migration</A></P>
```

```
 <P><A href="pacific.html">Pacific Branch</A></P>
</BODY>
</HTML>
```

Note that all individual references to mainpage have been replaced by the single reference to mainpage in the base target element. The Web page functions exactly as it did in Figure 9-10.

Expandable and collapsible list

Suppose that you want to set up your links frame so that the content may appear to expand and collapse. To achieve that effect, you need a couple of things. The first thing you would need would be to create a link in the existing coding to link to a menu that will appear in the same space as the link frame menu when it is clicked.

Here is the way to create a link to a list of expanded links within the Barrett site links code:

```
<HTML>
<HEAD>
<BASE target="mainpage">
<TITLE>Barrett Site Links</TITLE>
</HEAD>
<BODY>
 <P><A href="family.html">Home</A></P>
 <P><A href="familytree.html">Family Tree</A></P>
 <P><A href="expandedlist.htm" target="_self">Historical List
       of Links</A></P>
 <P><A href="ellis.html">Ellis Island</A></P>
 <P><A href="earlydays.html">Early Days</A></P>
 <P><A href="migration.html">Migration</A></P>
 <P><A href="pacific.html">Pacific Branch</A></P>
</BODY>
</HTML>
```

In this example, a link, expandedlist.htm, has been added to the current links within the Barrett Site Links page. When you click on "Historical List of Links," that Web site will be rendered in the same frame. This is because the "_self" value opens the clicked-on link in the same frame as the source. "_self" is one of four reserved names in HTML. All of them are discussed in the following section. All other links will be rendered in the frame, mainpage.

Following are the sites that will appear under the link once expandedlist.htm link is clicked:

- Home
- Family Tree
- Historical List of Links
  - Australopithecus
  - Homo Habilis

- Java Man
- Neander
- Wise Man

- Ellis Island
- Early Days
- Migration
- Pacific Branch

The coding to include these links is as shown here. Listing 9-1 contains `Barrettlist.htm` and Listing 9-2 contains `earlyMan.htm`.

LISTING 9-1

Code for Barrettlist.htm

```
<HTML>
<HEAD>
<BASE target="mainpage">
<TITLE>Barrett Site Links</TITLE>
</HEAD>
<BODY>
<P><A href="family.html">Home</A></P>
<P><A href="familytree.html">Family Tree</A></P>
<P><A href="earlyMan.htm">Historical List of Links</A></P>
<P><A href="ellis.html">Ellis Island</A></P>
<P><A href="earlydays.html">Early Days</A></P>
<P><A href="migration.html">Migration</A></P>
<P><A href="pacific.html">Pacific Branch</A></P>
</BODY>
</HTML>
```

LISTING 9-2

Code for earlyMan.htm

```
<HTML>
<HEAD>
<BASE target="mainpage">
<TITLE>Barrett Site Links</TITLE>
</HEAD>
<BODY>
<P><A href="family.html">Home</A></P>
<P><A href="familytree.html">Family Tree</A></P>
<P><A href="Barrettlist.htm" target="_self">Historical List of Links</A></P>
  <A href="australopithecus.htm">Australopithecus</A></P>
```

```
  <a href="homohabilis.htm">Homo Habilis</a></p>
  <a href="homoerectus.htm">Java Man</a></p>
  <a href="neanderthalman.htm">Neander</a> </p>
  <a href="homosapiens.htm">Wise Man</a></p>

<P><A href="ellis.html">Ellis Island</A></P>
<P><A href="earlydays.html">Early Days</A></P>
<P><A href="migration.html">Migration</A></P>
<P><A href="pacific.html">Pacific Branch</A></P>
</BODY>
</HTML>
```

NOTE **Each of the links under the expanded list has been indented slightly because of the nonbreaking space "` `" inserted before each of them.**

Note that clicking on "Historical List of Links" in the `Barrettlist.htm` causes the list to expand as follows:

```
Family Tree
Historical List of Links
   Australopithecus
   Homo Habilis
   Java Man
   Neander
   Wise Man
Ellis Island
Early Days
Migration
Pacific Branch
```

Clicking on it again causes the list to collapse to its original size, as shown here:

```
Home
Family Tree
Historical List of Links
Ellis Island
Early Days
Migration
Pacific Branch
```

This is because when you click on "Historical List of Links" the first time in `Barrettlist.htm` it calls another Web page (`earlyMan.htm`), which appears in the place of it. So, the list is not really expanding or collapsing at all. Each time the "Historical List of Links" is clicked, it calls the Web page, `earlyMan.htm`, and when you click on it again it calls `Barrettlist.htm`.

If you have been following the code, you will see that the clickable link, "Historical List of Links," actually has two separate addresses, `Barrettlist.htm` and `earlyMan.htm`, which switch back and forth, giving the illusion of an expanding and collapsing list.

TABLE 9-2

Reserved Frame Name Functions

Frame Name	Function
`_self`	Opens the linked Web page in the frame that holds the link. This is the same as the default linking behavior if no target is specified.
`_top`	Opens the linked Web page in the full browser window, obliterating all the frames.
`_blank`	Opens the linked Web page in a new instance of the Web browser.
`_parent`	Opens the linked Web page in the next highest frame or window.

Using reserved frame names

Each reserved frame name serves a special purpose. Table 9-2 explains what each of them does.

CAUTION **HTML is not case-sensitive, which means that `FRAMENAME` and `framename` are the same to it. However, that's not the case with the reserved frame names; they must be all lowercase all the time.**

Three of the reserved frame names — `_self`, `_top`, and `_blank` — are clear and unambiguous. The `_parent` name, however, is a source of confusion to most Web designers. Most of the time, it acts just like `_top`. Only when one frameset is contained within another one does the difference become apparent.

We're referring here not to the practice of creating nested frames in your HTML code but to using a second frameset page as the contents of one of your frames. It doesn't matter if it got there as the frame's original content because you put it there using the `FRAME` element's `src` attribute, or as a result of a link from the original content being loaded as the second frameset into the frame. If a link in any of the frames in the second frameset has its target set to `_parent`, then the linked page appears in the frame that holds the second frameset, overwriting the second frameset, but leaving all the frames in the first frameset intact.

Customizing Frame Borders and Margins

The borders that separate one frame from another are usually left alone. However, you do have several options you may want to pursue, such as changing the width or color of the border. The amount of space around the contents of frames is also open to manipulation.

FIGURE 9-11

You can display frames without borders.

Setting border width

The width of the borders between frames (in pixels) is set with the `border` attribute. Setting the value of `border` to 0 (zero) removes all frame borders, as shown in Figure 9-11. Any setting from 1 on up changes the width and is a matter of personal preference. This should be determined by the needs of a particular Web site's design.

CROSS-REF **You can create the same effect without using frames. To see how to use tables to create a layout of this sort, see Chapter 8.**

CAUTION **The `border` attribute is not supported in XHTML or XML and only has sporadic support across browsers.**

If we were to change the genealogy Web site so that it had borders that were 30 pixels wide, for example, it would pretty much ruin its appearance. The following change in the first `FRAMESET` element is all that's required to mess up the site, as shown in Figure 9-12:

```
<FRAMESET rows="105,*" border="30">
```

FIGURE 9-12

Changing the border size can have unfortunate effects on the display.

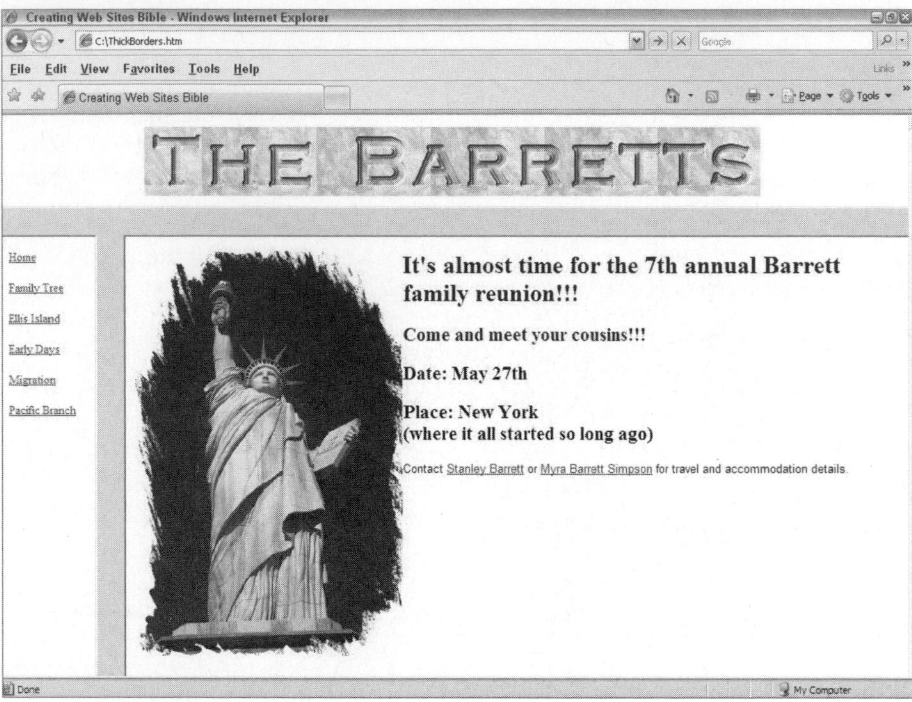

If you add the `border` attribute to the second `FRAMESET` element instead of the first one, you begin to get a sense for how frustrating it can be to monkey with borders — IE implements the change in border size for the specified frameset only. If you add different border sizes to both framesets, IE the second one.

In addition to setting the border value to zero, you can remove all borders between your frames with the `frameborder` attribute:

```
<FRAMESET frameborder="no">
```

The values for `frameborder` can be `yes` or `no`. Alternatively, you can use `1` for `yes` and `0` for `no`. There is no reason to use this attribute if the value is going to be `yes`, however, because that's the default setting, anyway.

The same attribute can be used with individual `FRAME` elements as well. Here, though, the going gets even rougher. Depending on the layout of frames in your site and which browser is used to view it, the appearance can be anything but what you intended. Any border can be viewed as belonging to both of the frames it divides, and various browsers take different approaches, so be sure to check the resulting screen in all browsers you intend to serve.

Handling border colors

The bordercolor attribute is the one that handles border colors:

```
<FRAMESET bordercolor="fuchsia">
```

The same attribute works with the FRAME element as well.

Border colors between frames can be tricky. Unless you want all your frame borders to be the same color (which we would generally recommend), you again run up against the fact that a single border touches on two frames. If you set the first frameset in the genealogy site to one color and the second one to another, IE will go along with your desires.

If you set the first frame in each frameset to yet another color, you'll finally find popular Web browsers in agreement — the frame colors generally override the frameset colors.

As with border sizes, it's worth a little bit of experimentation to get the hang of it.

The bordercolor attribute is not supported in XHTML or XML and only has sporadic support across browsers. It may be used with both <frame> and <frameset> elements.

Setting margin width

Margins (the amount of space between the content of a frame and the borders of that frame) are set with the marginheight and marginwidth attributes of the FRAME element. The first sets how much vertical space (in pixels) there is between the top and bottom of the frame and its content. The second does the same for the horizontal space between the left and right sides of the frame and its content.

Thus, if you want to specify a 20-pixel space horizontally and a 40-pixel space vertically, you would use this code:

```
<FRAME marginwidth="20" marginheight="40">
```

Setting Scroll Bar Options

The default behavior of scroll bars in frames is auto, which means that, if they're needed, they'll appear. Basically, that means that if the contents of the frame are larger than the space allotted for the frame itself, you get scroll bars. However, you can specify that they must appear regardless of need, or that they can't appear under any circumstances. In our opinion, the default setting should be left intact in any but the most unusual situations. Just in case you're facing one of those unusual situations, here's how to manage it.

To set scroll bars so that they cannot appear in a frame, use this code:

```
<FRAME scrolling="no">
```

Just change the "no" to "yes" and you have made it so that they must appear.

Alternatives to framesets and frames

There are alternatives to the use of frames to show fixed content on each page of a Web site: iframes (internal frame), server-side includes (SSIs), and XML with XSL transformations. Each option, including frames, has its advantages and disadvantages. The main disadvantage of frames is that you must specify the size of the frame, yet you don't know the size of the user's window, so your page may not be displayed as you wish. With SSIs and XML with XSL transformations, you can take advantage of the formatting properties of standard HTML and let the browser decide how to lay out the pages. When using iframes, the size doesn't need to be specified.

An obstacle to wider use of frames is they make it difficult for search engines to "read" and index the page. Most search engines frown on sites using frames.

Iframes

Using frames and framesets, you define a template and include Web pages inside the frames. However, sometimes you may have to do the opposite and put a frame inside a Web page. Using an iframe, you can embed a Web page in the current page in much the same way as you display an image in a Web page.

One advantage of using iframes is that you have control over how they are aligned within surrounding text. They can move around as a user resizes the page, and they can appear in any part of the page. So, they don't have to divide your harmoniously designed Web page into squares.

The way to do this is to use an `iframe` tag:

```
<IFRAME src="encrusted.html" width="300" height="300"
frameborder="0">
  Your browser does not support internal frames. See the
  <A href="encrusted.html">non-frame content</A>.
```

The width and height are in pixels or can be percentage values relative to the parent element. Writing `frameborder="0"` specifies not to draw a border. If you don't specify the attribute, the default is a border of 1 pixel.

Programs in JavaScript sometimes use iframes to mimic a slide show or reload information that changes (such as stock quotes).

Following are some similarities between iframes and frames:

- Both are scrollable
- Both show external HTML pages

Following are some differences between iframes and frames:

- You don't have to specify the size of an iframe.
- iframes are not resizeable by the user.

Instead of a `noframes` tag, the iframes content is displayed if the browser does not support iframes.

Iframes are also a way of displaying other Web sites' content seamlessly on your own page.

Server-side includes

You may have noticed that some pages on the Web have the extension `.shtml`. That is because these pages have content that is generated or included by the Web server.

Most people use frames because they want a standard header, footer, or navigation bar on each page. You can accomplish the same thing with SSIs.

For example, consider the following file, `ssi-example.shtml`:

```
TABLE>
<TR>
  <TD><!--#include virtual="header.html" --></TD>
</TR>
<TR>
  <TD><!-#include virtual="navigationbar.html" --></TD>
  <TD>Content goes here</TD>
</TR>
<TR>
  <TD><!--#include virtual="footer.html" --></TD>
</TR>
</TABLE>
```

The contents of the files are included just as if you had done a copy-and-paste operation and so shouldn't contain the `<html>`, `<header>`, or `<body>` tags — just the content that you want, as shown in the following example:

```
If you want to get really flashy, you can automatically include the
modification date of the file.
```

CAUTION **As just as a word of warning, you should be aware that the SSI support depends on your Web server and its configuration. You should check before designing your whole Web site using SSIs. The Apache Web server does support them but must be configured to do so. Microsoft's IIS 5 Web server supports them by default, yet IIS 6 and above must be configured to support them.**

XML and XSL

Another alternative is to write the page content in XHTML and use XSL to form the template for the pages. This will be covered in greater detail in Chapter 15.

Avoiding Frame Problems

Even if you do everything perfectly and avoid all typographical errors and syntax blowups, there are still a few "gotchas" you need to be on the alert for.

Making sure that you have enough frames

If you've been banging your head over your HTML code and just can't figure out why your frames won't display as intended, take the time to count the number of frames you've specified. Remember that the number of sizes stated in your FRAMESET elements must match up with the number of FRAME elements that it contains. If you have code like this, you'll have problems because you have an extra frame that won't display:

```
<FRAMESET rows="200,100">
 <FRAME>
 <FRAME>
 <FRAME>
</FRAMESET>
```

And, if you have code like this, you'll have problems because you'll end up with an empty third frame:

```
<FRAMESET rows="200,100,*">
 <FRAME>
 <FRAME>
</FRAMESET>
```

Adding foreign elements

If you put any element that might be found in a normal Web page's BODY element (or the <BODY> tag itself) before the FRAMESET element, the frameset will not work. This should not be an issue if you create every page from scratch, but many Web designers use template pages for all their work. If the template page you're using to create your framesets contains anything at all that shouldn't be in a frameset, you're risking making the whole thing not work. If your frames aren't showing up, check the frameset page's HTML code carefully before you do anything else.

The same problem can also be caused by failing to include the </FRAMESET> end tag.

What size is the user's screen?

One serious problem when using frames is that you have no idea what the dimensions are on the users' screens — 640 × 480, 800 × 600, 1024 × 768, 1152 × 864, 1280 × 1024, or 1600 × 1200 or even something else, such as in the case of widescreen displays.

But how can you design your site so that it looks good at any screen resolution? What if you've put in a frame that isn't resizable and only displays half of the menu?

Some sites try to standardize things by giving users instructions to change their resolutions to 800 × 600. But it's unrealistic to expect users with high-end graphics workstations to halve their screen resolution just to see your site. Most users as of this writing have 1024 × 768 displays, but that will most definitely become higher as technology advances.

Most HTML is designed to resize the layout of the page depending on the size of the content and the size of the screen. Frames are an exception; you have to specify a fixed size or a size relative to the size of the browser window. However, since you don't know the size of the content of your page nor the size of the window, it's impossible to get it right every time.

Many experts on Web page design discourage the use of frames for this reason. They advocate the use of non-frame HTML. The choice is yours.

Using too many frames

It's easy to get carried away with frames, especially for those people who like to put everything into neat little boxes. And that's what frames are, right? Well, not exactly. Only a limited number of frames make a workable Web site — generally, we'd recommend no more than three to five frames on one screen.

It's important to remember that even though a framed Web site looks like a single Web page, in reality, every frame is holding a different Web page. That means that, with only three frames, you're making a visitor to your site download three Web pages at once. And if each of those pages has its own graphics as well.... You begin to see the problem? It's an issue of downloading time. Not everyone has a broadband connection to the Internet, and tripling, quadrupling, or quintupling, the download time is enough of a burden without unnecessarily adding even more Web pages to the display.

Providing backup navigation

You've designed your Web site to use frames and, specifically, a navigation page tucked over on the side, top, or bottom of your main entry point. However, people may come into your site from other sites that have linked to an individual page instead of your entry point. This generally happens when visitors come to your site using the results from a search engine.

In that case, such visitors are never going to see your nice navigational setup, and, unless you provide at least a minimal alternative, the single page is all they'll ever see of your site. At rock-bottom minimum, ensure that every page on your site has a link to your home page (the framed entry point), or you'll lose some visitors for sure.

Legal challenges to framing

Framing your own pages does not create any kind of legal problem, but when you frame someone else's pages on your own site, a bit of a risk is involved. Some commercial Web sites have objected

continued

continued
to becoming part of another site through the use of frames, claiming that they are losing advertising revenue by being "hijacked."

So far, the difficulty seems to be limited to situations in which one site that makes its money from advertising incorporates pages from another site that also has paid advertisements. The *framee* claims that the *framer* is capitalizing on the *framee's* work, displaying it within a frame that contains ads from the *framer's* sponsors. The result is that the framer is making money off someone else's copyrighted publication.

What's funny to anyone who knows even a little bit about the Web is that any page can be set so that no one can put it into a frame. Certainly, if anyone cares about preventing others from displaying their pages in unauthorized frames, it's a lot cheaper to pay a JavaScript programmer for a few minutes of work than to hire a battery of lawyers and go to court.

Whatever the merits to the claims of the parties, the legalities are following the usual run of absurdities — in Web-related law, it is often lawyers who don't understand the Web who argue their cases in front of judges who don't understand the Web. While this may all seem amusing to technical people, the stark reality of the situation is that lawyers and judges create the legal framework that affects us all, and the decisions handed down by judges can be used against you.

Because many of the framed sites on the Web do display material from other Web sites, such court cases can have far-reaching impact. If you want to ensure that you're covered, consider asking permission from the Webmasters whose sites you want to frame. In most cases, they'll be more than happy to cooperate. If not, then you'd better leave them out of your plans.

Frames Quick Reference

The following provides a quick reference for key items discussed in this chapter:

- `<FRAMESET></FRAMESET>` — These provide structure within which frames are developed.
- `<FRAME>` — This is the element that defines the content. They are empty tags.
- `"rows"` — This is an attribute of `<FRAME>` that defines rows within a Web page frame structure.
- `"cols"` — This is an attribute of `<FRAME>` that defines columns within a Web page frame structure.
- `FRAME frameborder="value"` — When `value` is equal to 1 or 0, this sets (1) or removes (0) borders of the frame.
- `FRAMESET border="value"` — This is set as a specific size in pixels for the frameset.
- `bordercolor="color"` — This is expressed in hex values or color name.

- "noresize" — This is an attribute of <FRAME> that fixes the frame size.
- "name" — This is an attribute of <FRAME> that is used to uniquely identify that frame.
- *Reserved names* — These are precoded and are used to determine the location (or target) of linked documents.

Summary

Frames present an alternative method for displaying Web pages. They allow you to put multiple Web pages on screen at the same time.

This chapter discussed the uses of frames for displaying static and dynamic content simultaneously through the development of a frame for a logo and dynamic navigation frame. Frames are a way of offering multiple content on a single page. Content may be links, menus, images, or even another Web page.

Frames allow you to see content from different Web pages within your own site. Within the `frameset` tag itself are attributes of `row` and `column`. The dimensions of each may be defined by percent of screen, size in pixels, and by an asterisk (which will fill out the remainder of the browser window with the row or column).

Rows and columns may be symmetrical or asymmetrical. You control resizing by using the `noresize` attribute. You may name frames so that they may be referenced by the `target` attribute. The code for rendering frame content on browsers incapable of supporting frames is to include a non-frames Web page within a <NOFRAMES></NOFRAMES> element pair.

This chapter also discussed the attributes of frames and framesets, such as `src` and `name`. We also presented reserve target names and their functions. We gave examples of coding for expanding and collapsing lists.

In this chapter, you learned about border widths, border colors, and margin widths and heights. We reviewed coding for scroll bars, and discussed the use of iframes and SSIs.

In Chapter 10, we introduce forms and, associated with that, the concepts of events and event handlers.

Chapter 10

Getting Input with Forms

Forms provide a way for your site's visitors to give you information. Using a variety of different input techniques, forms enable you to gather all sorts of data, ranging from simple "yes" or "no" answers to complex written responses.

Forms are used for several different purposes. Most often, they are used to gather contact and delivery information for situations ranging from e-mail newsletters to the shipment of physical products. As HTML's native method for acquiring user input, forms are a powerful part of your Web design repertoire, enabling limitless opportunities for gathering information.

When it comes to visual presentation, however, forms leave a little bit to be desired. In fact, if you stick with the plain method of adding form controls and their accompanying text to your pages, you end up with a pretty sorry-looking design. To avoid this, embed your forms within tables, as the majority of Web designers do to keep their forms neat and attractive. This chapter is dedicated only to the use of forms. The technique for meshing them with tables is covered in detail in Chapter 6.

IN THIS CHAPTER

Adding Forms

As shown in Figure 10-1, forms in HTML are made up of elements such as text boxes, check boxes, and option buttons. Collectively, these elements in a form are known as *controls*. A form begins with the `<form>` tag and ends with the `</form>` tag. All of the form's controls are placed between them.

FIGURE 10-1

This figure shows various form controls.

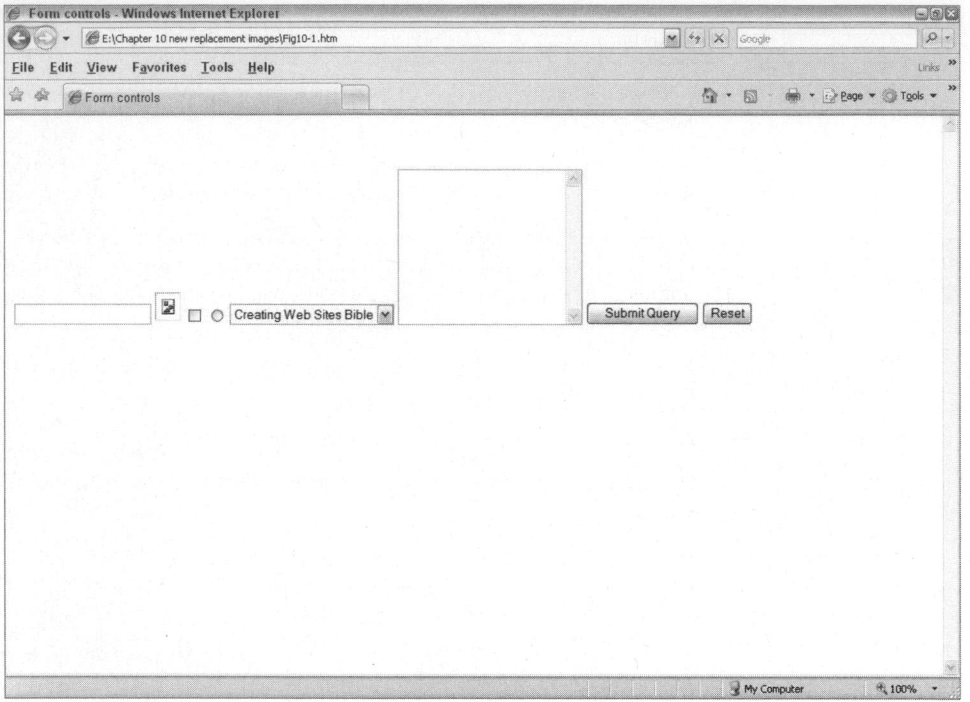

NOTE **Option buttons are also sometimes referred to as *radio buttons.***

NOTE **Form controls can actually be used outside a `FORM` element, but to keep things working properly, put them inside a `FORM` element.**

The INPUT element

The majority of form controls are variations on a single element called `INPUT`. This is a unique situation in HTML in which items that have a totally different appearance and method of operation are represented by distinct elements. The `TABLE` element can't be used for anything but to create a table, the `IMG` element can only be used to add an image, and so forth. Yet, the `INPUT` element has 10 different types, some of which are very similar to one another, whereas others are totally different. Table 10-1 summarizes the many faces of the `INPUT` element.

TABLE 10-1

INPUT Types

Type	Description
Button	A custom button without a defined function in HTML. May be used to trigger JavaScript actions.
Checkbox	A small square that, when checked (filled), means "yes" and when empty, means "no." Any number of check boxes can be selected simultaneously.
File	A specialized text box (see the entry for "Text") into which a filename is entered. The file may also be selected by clicking a Browse button that automatically accompanies the file text box. The specified file is uploaded, along with other form information.
Hidden	Information that is not displayed to the user, but is still transmitted along with the other form information.
Image	An image that functions as a Submit button.
Password	Identical to `text` except for the fact that it disguises the input but does not encrypt it.
Radio	A small circle that, when checked (filled), means "yes" and when empty, means "no." These buttons are distinguished from check boxes by the fact that you cannot select more than one button in a group.
Reset	A button that resets all entries users have made in the form to their initial values.
Submit	A button that causes the form information to be transmitted.
Text	A text box that enables users to enter short information.

Each variation of the `INPUT` element is specified by its `type` attribute. For example, the following code creates a text box and a Submit button:

```
<FORM>
<INPUT type="text">
<INPUT type="submit">
</FORM>
```

Naming elements

Each element should also be given a distinctive name. That, as you might guess, falls in the province of the `name` attribute. The reason for this is that the name of the element is paired with the value of its entry when the form data is submitted. If the element has no name, there is no way to tell what the entry itself means.

To illustrate this, let's say you have a text box that asks visitors to state their age. You give it the name `"age"` so that it's clear what the entered number means when it shows up in a report based on the form submission. This is accomplished by the following code:

```
<INPUT type="text" name="age">
```

If a user enters the number 37 into that text box when the form is submitted, the data that is transmitted is `age=37`, which clearly tells you — or the data processing program that receives the form input — what is meant.

If you want to use JavaScript with your controls, then you should also give them an `id` attribute. To keep things simple, make the `id` attribute identical to the value of the `name` attribute. This is because the `name` attribute is sent to the server and the `id` attribute is used locally to refer to the control. Ideally, there should be only one definition of the `name` and `id` attributes. The HTML standard is moving toward just using the `id` attribute, but as you can see, there is still some way to go.

NOTE **The one exception to the rule of giving each element a separate name is with option buttons. Option buttons that are grouped together all share one name.**

Of course, each type has a more complex series of settings than what we've covered so far. The following sections explore the details of the `INPUT` element, as well as the other three elements that are used inside forms.

Getting Short Data with Text Boxes

Text boxes are used to collect short strings of information such as first and last name, street address, and so on. They are the single most often used type of form control. Some forms, in fact, consist of nothing but a single text box and a button to submit the text box's contents. This is the case with the most popular search engines (see Figure 10-2), although they may also have a second, more complex, form available.

Generally, if there is only one text box in a form and the user presses Enter, the form is automatically submitted, as you may have noticed in Google.

Password fields are similar to text boxes. However, when someone enters a password, the password field displays a string of asterisks instead of showing the actual password. This is a security precaution. Although the password itself is correctly passed through the form, it is impossible for anyone to identify the password by simply looking at the screen. Figure 10-3 shows a typical login screen that uses both a text box and a password field.

Remember that if you're using HTTP, the password is not encrypted when it's sent over the Internet; it is, however, in the case of HTTPS. To check that the connection is secure, look for a locked padlock or key icon at the bottom of the browser window, or ensure that the URL in the address bar starts with `https`.

FIGURE 10-2

Google, one of the most popular search engines, uses a simple form interface.

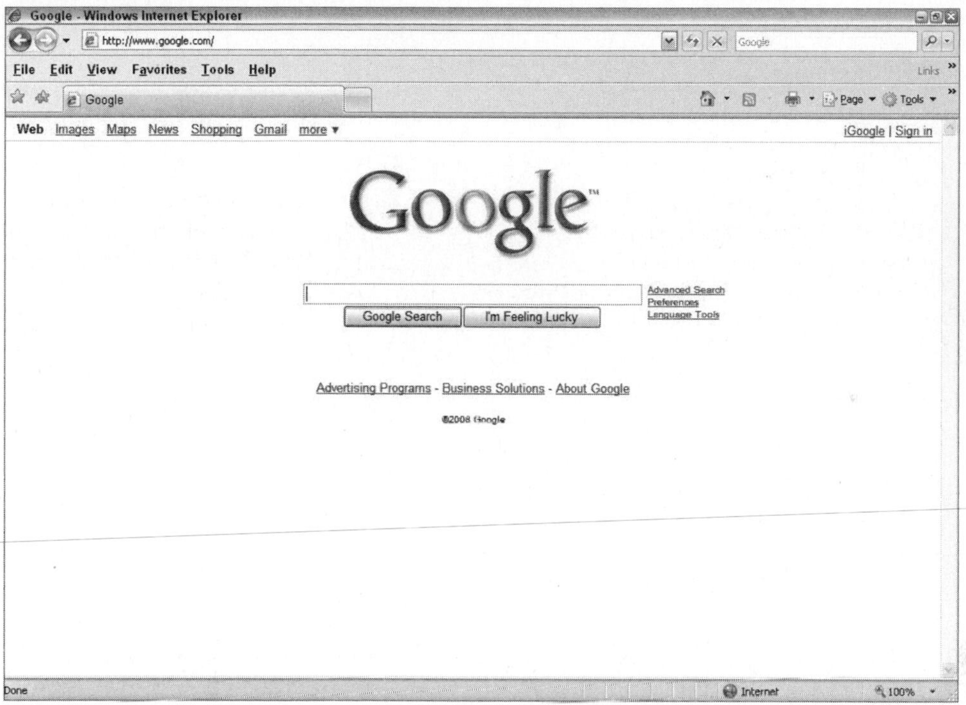

Setting box size

The physical width of a text box is set with the `size` attribute. Unlike `width` and `height` settings, this setting does not use pixels as the default unit for measurement. Instead, it uses characters. Thus, the following code creates a text box that is the same width as 20 letters:

```
<INPUT type="text" size="20">
```

NOTE **The exact number of how many characters fit in a box vary when using proportional width fonts, because each character takes up a different amount of space. You can fine-tune the font widths using styles. This would provide uniformity of size. It's also a good idea to test your Web pages on several browsers before you go into production.**

Figure 10-4 shows several text boxes, ranging in size from 10 to 50 characters wide.

FIGURE 10-3

The only difference between password fields and text boxes is the display of the user's entry.

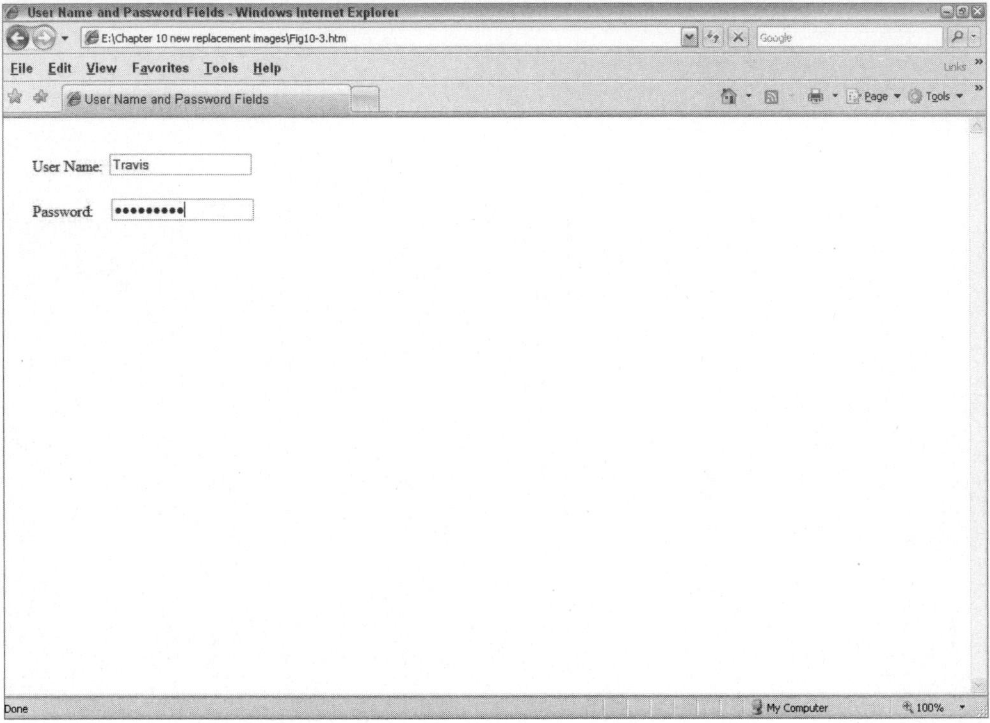

Defining the maximum length of input

The physical width has nothing to do with how much text can fit into a text box. If you have a text box that's 30 characters wide, and a visitor to your site enters 80 characters, the text box still takes the input. The text simply scrolls as it's entered, as shown in Figure 10-5. The amount of text that can be input is unlimited.

However, the processing program receiving the form's information may have an input size limitation. That's where the `maxlength` attribute comes into play.

Say, for example, that the data-processing program can only accept text input that's 30 characters or less, yet your design constraints mean that you still have to use a 20-character-wide text box. The following code solves both problems in one swoop:

```
<INPUT type="text" size="20" maxlength="30">
```

FIGURE 10-4

Text boxes can be set to any width in characters.

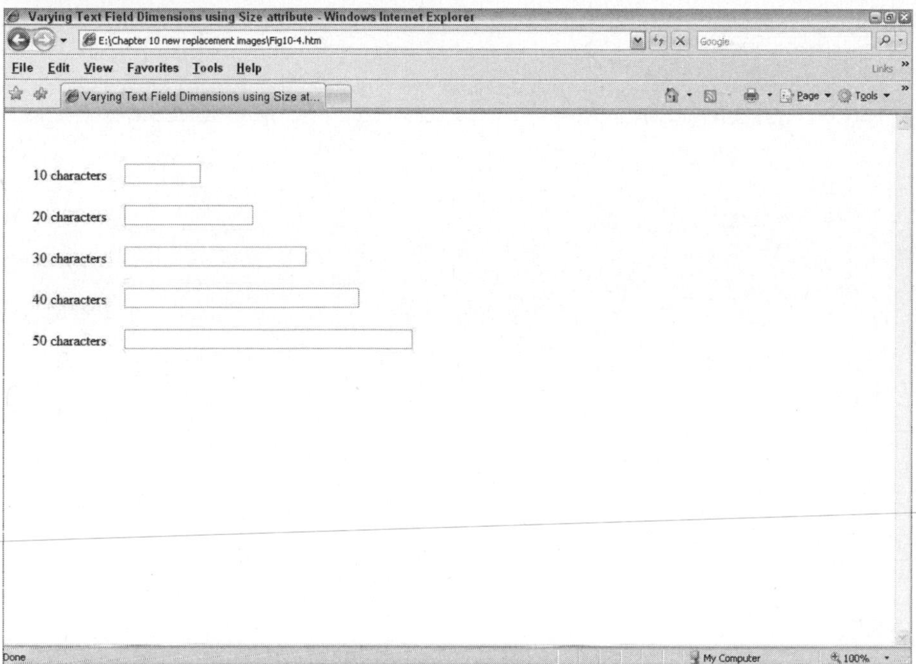

Of course, there is no requirement that the `maxlength` value be larger than the `size` value. They could be set to the same number, which would mean that there would be no scrolling at all, but the text box could still be filled completely. The following code accomplishes this:

```
<INPUT type="text" size="20" maxlength="20">
```

NOTE **You can actually set the `maxlength` value so that it is less than the `size` value. Even though this is possible, it could create a counterintuitive form that would only confuse users. It's better to keep `maxlength` at least equal to `size`.**

Prefilling a text box

There are times when you can presume to know what value a visitor will enter in a text box. For example, if you're selling a magazine subscription, the odds are pretty good that one person will order only one copy — very few, if any, people want multiple copies of the same magazine sent to them every month.

FIGURE 10-5

Text entries that are larger than the text box scroll across it.

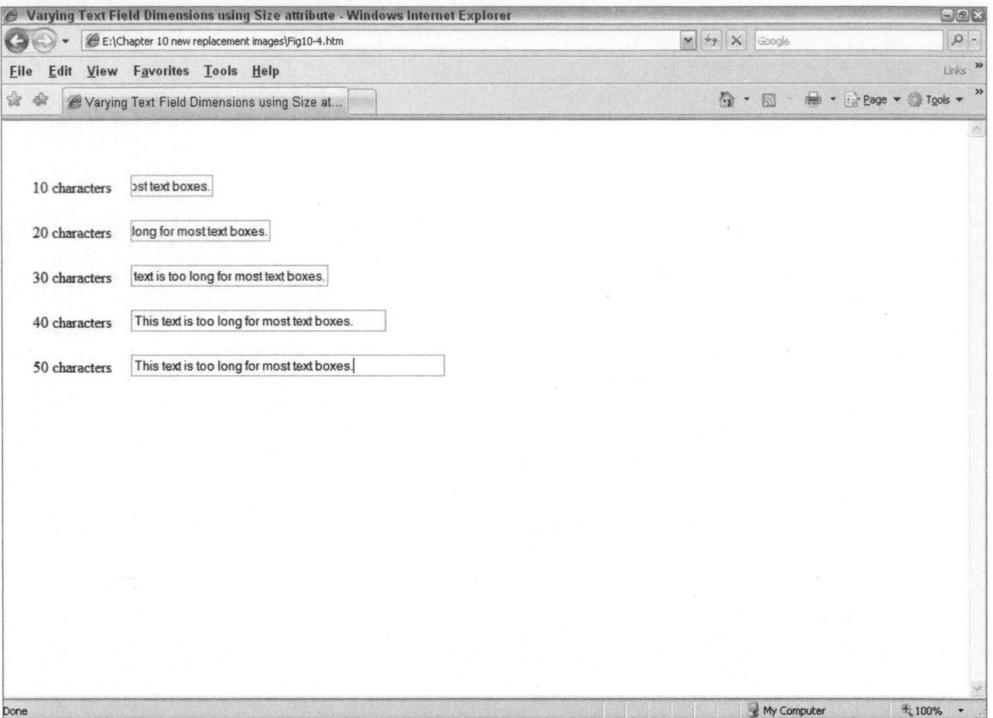

In that instance, it would be safe to specify "1" as the value for the number of subscriptions ordered. However, if someone does have a need for multiple copies, it's wise to not lock them in to ordering just one. To accomplish this, specify content for the text box that can be altered by anyone who fills out the form. Thus, the majority of subscribers are saved the trouble of filling in the number, whereas the minority can still do what they want.

This is accomplished with the `value` attribute, as in the following code:

```
<INPUT type="text" size="3" name="numberofsubs" value="1" maxlength
="2">
```

NOTE **There should be a `maxlength` of 2 to show that the designer must still think about limiting user input to what is expected.**

The results are shown in Figure 10-6.

NOTE **Setting the `maxlength` to 3 allows a potential subscriber to order up to 999 subscriptions.**

FIGURE 10-6

For this simple form we set a default value.

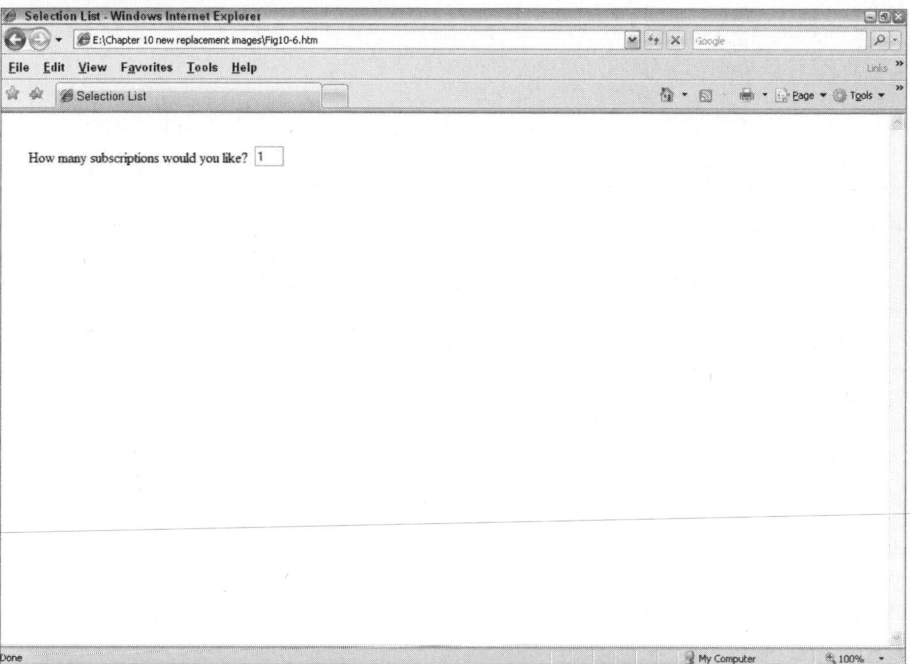

Locking content with readonly and disabled

If you're absolutely, totally certain that you want to lock into place a particular value for a text box's content, use the `readonly` attribute. It's simply a matter of specifying the content and adding that attribute to the code, as in the following example:

```
<INPUT type="text" size="1" name="numberofsubs" value="1" readonly>
```

However, there is a drawback to this approach — users filling out the form are shown a text box, an element into which they are used to entering information, but one that refuses to cooperate with them. The potential for user frustration — and, therefore, for refusal to complete the form — is high with this approach.

An alternative would be to disable the text box using the `disabled` attribute. This prevents the user from even placing the cursor in the text box. Disabled controls are normally displayed as grayed out. The following code accomplishes this:

```
<INPUT type="text" size="1" name="numberofsubs" value="1" disabled>
```

NOTE **The content of a control is sent to the server if it is marked `readonly`, but not if it is marked `disabled`.**

If you just want to send some data to the server, a far better technique is to use the `hidden` type, which is discussed in the section, "Adding Hidden Fields," later in this chapter.

Gathering Information with Text Areas

Text boxes are good for information that can be entered in one line, such as a first name, last name, or ZIP code. But what about situations in which you need a multiline response — such as directions to a farm or comments on the usefulness of a product? The `TEXTAREA` element enables you to accept multiline responses. Figure 10-7 shows how a text box compares to a text area.

Sizing text areas

The number of characters you want to be displayed sets the width of text areas, as is the case with text boxes. However, because text areas have more than one line, you can also set the height of the text area. The width is set by the `cols` attribute, and the height by the `rows` attribute. Each column equals the width of one character, and each row is the height of one line of text. The following example shows how to set a text area that is 50 characters wide and 10 lines high:

```
<TEXTAREA cols="50" rows="10">
</TEXTAREA>
```

FIGURE 10-7

Text areas are capable of holding multiple lines of text.

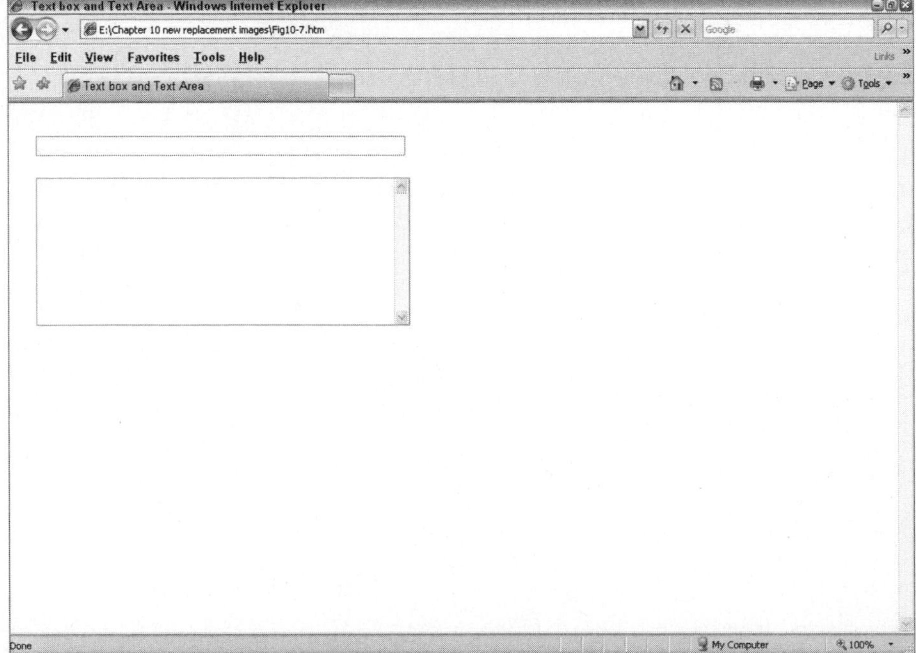

NOTE **While you may also be able to use styles to determine rows and columns (for example, `<textarea name="foofighter" style="width: 200px; height: 100px;">`), under new browser versions of Firefox or Internet Explorer, styles may not work for rows and columns in many other circumstances. The long and short of it is that you should use rows and columns, but if that doesn't work, then use styles.**

Figure 10-8 shows several text areas of various sizes.

Setting wordwrap

There are a few different ways in HTML for the input of text areas to be wrapped, but only two of them have any effect on how the text is actually displayed on the screen of a Web browser. Wordwrap is controlled by the `wrap` attribute, as in the following example code:

```
<TEXTAREA wrap="virtual">
</TEXTAREA>
```

Table 10-2 shows what each value of the `wrap` attribute means.

FIGURE 10-8

Text areas can be set to any character width or number of lines.

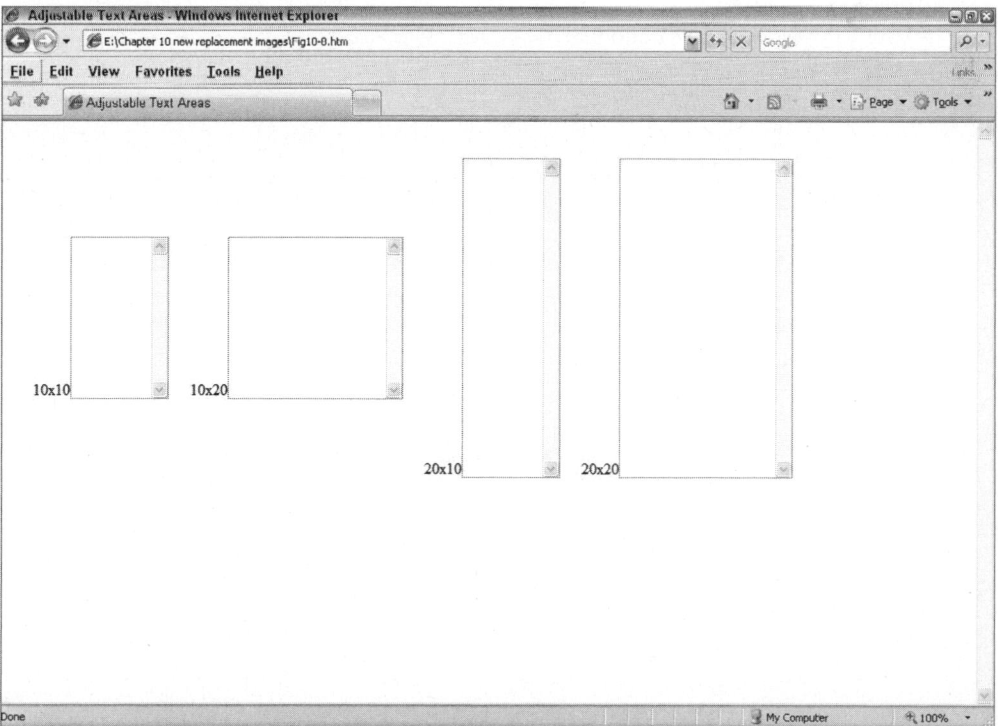

TABLE 10-2

Wordwrap Values

Value	Description
off	The text is displayed on one line until the user presses the Enter key, at which point a new line begins. If the line is longer than the text area is wide, the text scrolls.
virtual	The text wraps to the next line when it reaches the edge of the text area. However, it is sent as one long line when the form is submitted.
physical	The text wraps to the next line when it reaches the edge of the text area, and is sent as displayed when the form is submitted.

If no value is specified, the wordwrap relies on the default behavior of the particular Web browser that's used to view the form. In Internet Explorer and Firefox, it is the same as `virtual`.

Figure 10-9 shows both scrolling and nonscrolling text areas.

FIGURE 10-9

Text areas can be made to wrap or scroll.

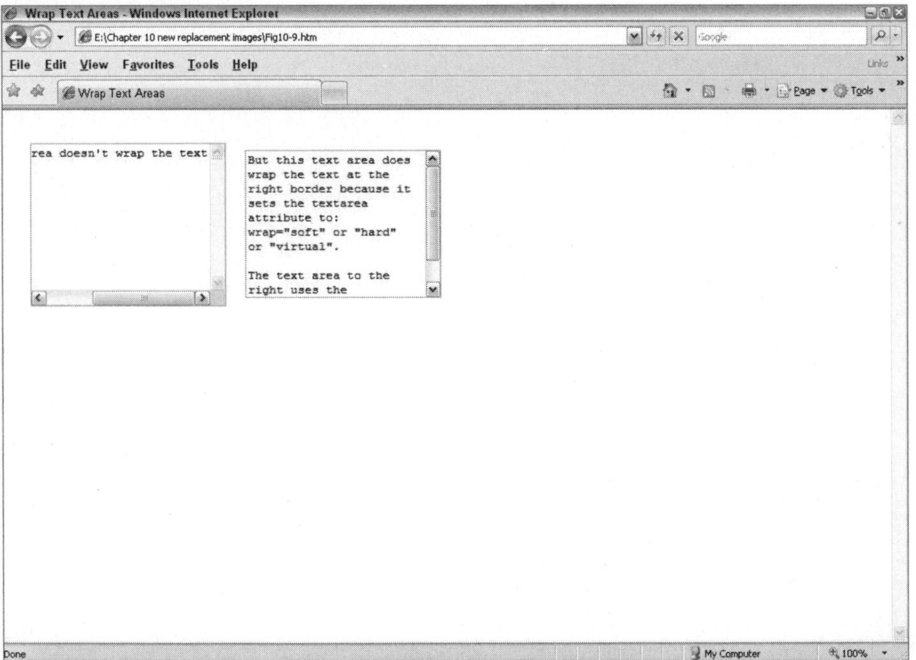

Setting default contents

As with text boxes, text areas can hold default content; however, there is no attribute to be set. Instead, any text that is placed between the <textarea> start tag and the </textarea> end tag shows up onscreen as the default content.

For example, the following code displays a helpful message in a text area:

```
<TEXTAREA name="comments" cols="50" rows="10">
Please tell us what you think.
</TEXTAREA>
```

The results of this code are shown in Figure 10-10.

FIGURE 10-10

Text areas can have default content.

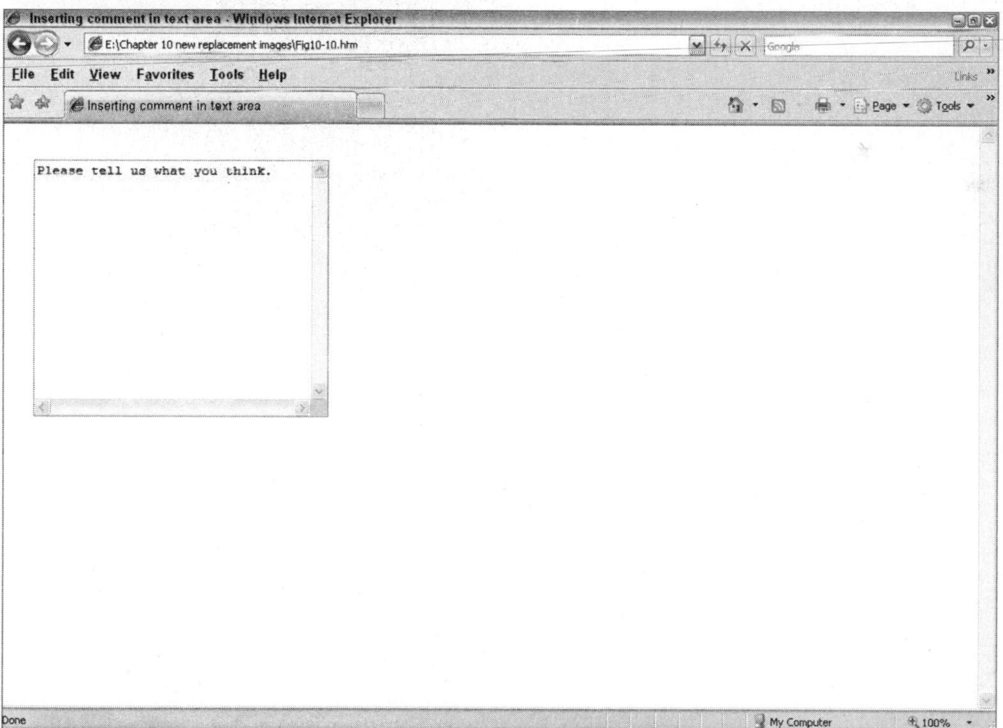

Making Choices with Check Boxes and Option Buttons

While text input is important in forms, it is often easiest — for both you and your visitors — if you present a set of choices instead. Check boxes and option buttons solve this problem handily. Both are types of the `INPUT` element, and are very similar in function and appearance. Check boxes are, as the name implies, square, whereas option buttons are round, as shown in Figure 10-11. Beyond that, however, they are pretty much the same thing — a user clicks them to select a choice from a list of items, such as "yes" or "no."

There is, however, one critical difference in the way they can be used, as discussed in the following sections.

FIGURE 10-11

Check boxes and option buttons are similar, but have important differences.

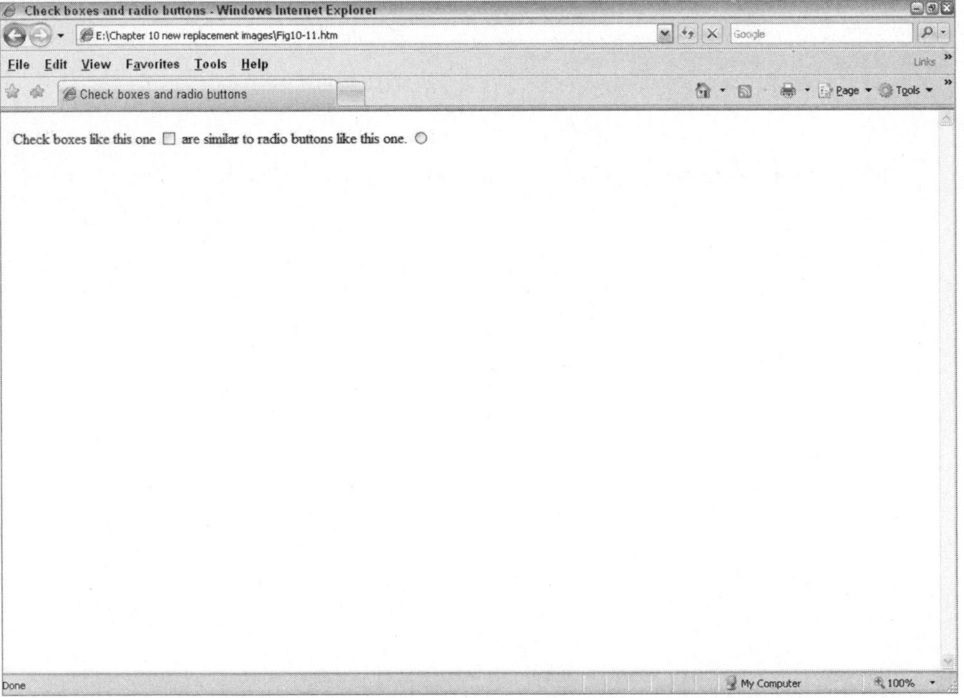

Adding check boxes

Check boxes are used when a choice to be made does not conflict with another possible choice. For example, you might use check boxes if you are offering information on several different products. You certainly wouldn't want to limit your visitors to asking for only one brochure! The form in Figure 10-12 shows a set of check boxes that offer such a set of choices.

Even a single check box, offering one simple "yes" or "no" possibility, makes sense. For example, at the bottom of a form asking for personal information, you often see a single check box that asks whether or not you want to receive mailings from third parties. Such a check box may be coded as follows:

```
<INPUT type="checkbox" name="askmailing" value="permissiongranted">
```

FIGURE 10-12

Check boxes offer noncompetitive choices.

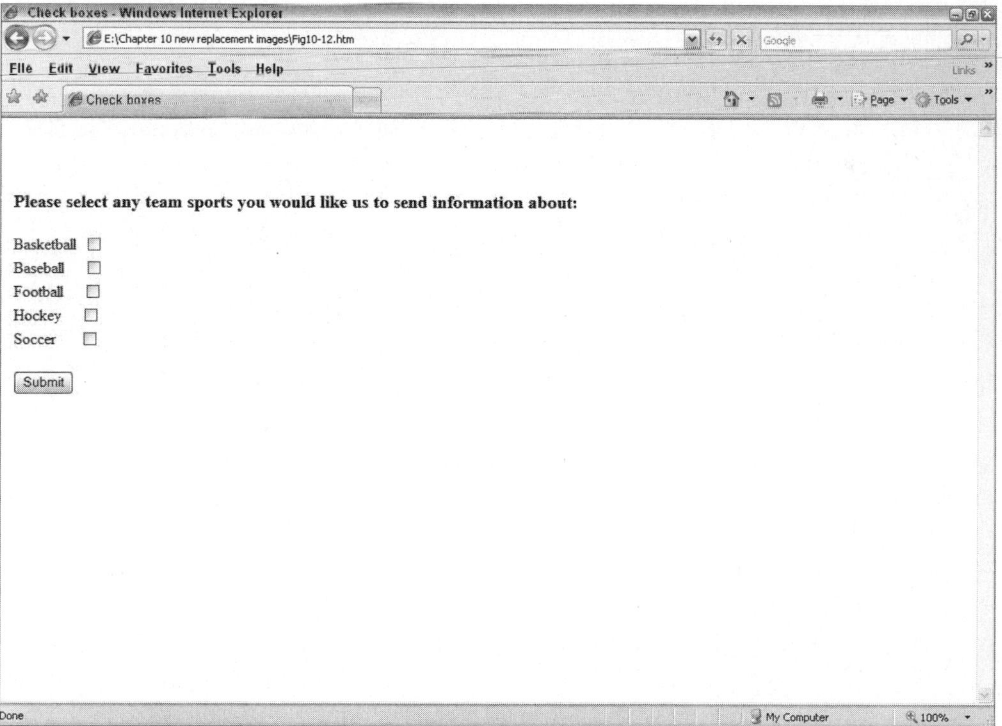

If a visitor does click the check box to select it, when the form is submitted, the name/value pair `askmailing=permissiongranted` is sent. If the check box remains unselected, it is ignored when the form is submitted, and no input from it exists.

Grouping option buttons

As noted earlier, option buttons are different from all the other elements that make up forms. Although you can use an individual option button in the exact same way as an individual check box, the true power of option buttons comes when they are used in groups. Because option button choices are mutually exclusive, when they are grouped together as a unit and you choose one option button in that group, you are prevented from making a conflicting choice.

For example, say that you are selling hats. A visitor can order a small, medium, or large hat, but one hat cannot be two or more sizes. If you were to use three check boxes, it would be possible for someone to place an order for a single hat that was small, medium, and large. When you received the form data, you would not be able to tell if the person filling out the form wanted three different hats, or was simply confused. The input would be totally useless.

Three option buttons, however, would be perfect for the job. If your customers used the form shown in Figure 10-13, and they chose the radio button for Small, but also clicked the Medium button, the Small button would be automatically deselected. If the user continued on to click the Large option, the Medium option button would, in turn, be deselected. As you can see, this process totally eliminates any possibility of confusion among a set of conflicting choices.

Although all other elements in a form must have separate names, option buttons are a different story entirely. An option button group is created by giving the same name to more than one option button. The `value` attribute of each option button is what distinguishes one from the other. The hat size option button group, for example, would be created by code such as this example:

```
<INPUT type="radio" name="hatsize" value="small">
<INPUT type="radio" name="hatsize" value="medium">
<INPUT type="radio" name="hatsize" value="large">
```

NOTE **Care should be taken to ensure that all option buttons in a group are actually placed in the same area of the form. There is nothing in HTML to prevent you from creating a group that is scattered about the form in different locations, but the effect of doing so may be confusing to the user.**

Setting a default choice

Both option buttons and check boxes can be set as the default choices in a form. Returning to the example of a visitor being asked permission to share private information with third parties, some Web sites force the issue by setting the check box so that it is selected from the start without any action on the part of the visitor. To do so, they simply add the `checked` attribute as in the following example:

FIGURE 10-13

Option buttons offer mutually exclusive choices.

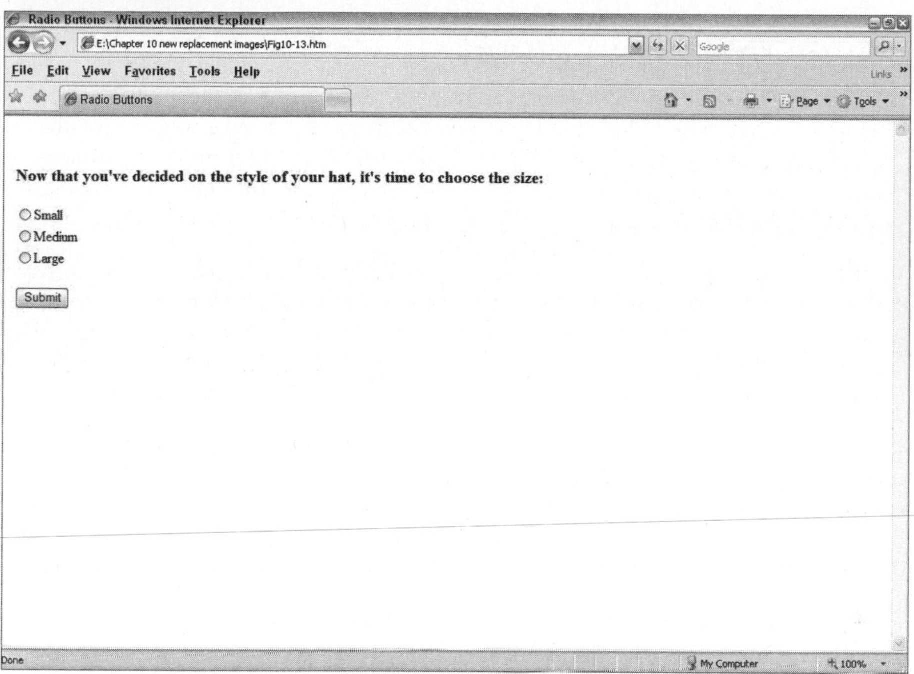


```
<INPUT type="checkbox" name="askmailing" value="permissiongranted"
checked>
```

Now, a visitor must click the check box to deselect it. If not, the permission has been given.

This technique (in addition to being commonly used to trap unwary people into giving permission for things they wouldn't want) has perfectly valid uses. Anytime you have an option that you believe most people would select, it makes sense to have it preselected to save your visitors the bother of filling out every detail — and to save yourself the frustration of an incomplete form being submitted. It's similar to adding default content to a text box or text area.

For option buttons, you should set only one in the group. For example, if you know that almost every order you get is for a medium-sized hat, the following code would create a form that assisted most of your customers:

```
<INPUT type="radio" name="hatsize" value="small">
<INPUT type="radio" name="hatsize" value="medium" checked>
<INPUT type="radio" name="hatsize" value="large">
```

CAUTION Although it is possible to add the `checked` attribute to more than one option button in a group, you need to ensure that this doesn't happen. The result in Internet Explorer is that only the last one with the `checked` attribute is shown as checked. Ensure that you test with the browsers you want to support (such as Safari, Firefox, and Opera) to make sure these inconsistencies are known and resolved.

Saving Space with the SELECT and OPTION Elements

If you only have to add a few options (such as Small, Medium, or Large) to your form, check boxes and option buttons are definitely the way to go. But what if you need to do something a lot more complex than that? What if you have to add choices for all 50 U.S. states, or every country in the continent of Europe? As Figure 10-14 shows, you end up with so many boxes or buttons that your form is an unusable mess.

FIGURE 10-14

Too many check boxes or option buttons make a form look cluttered.

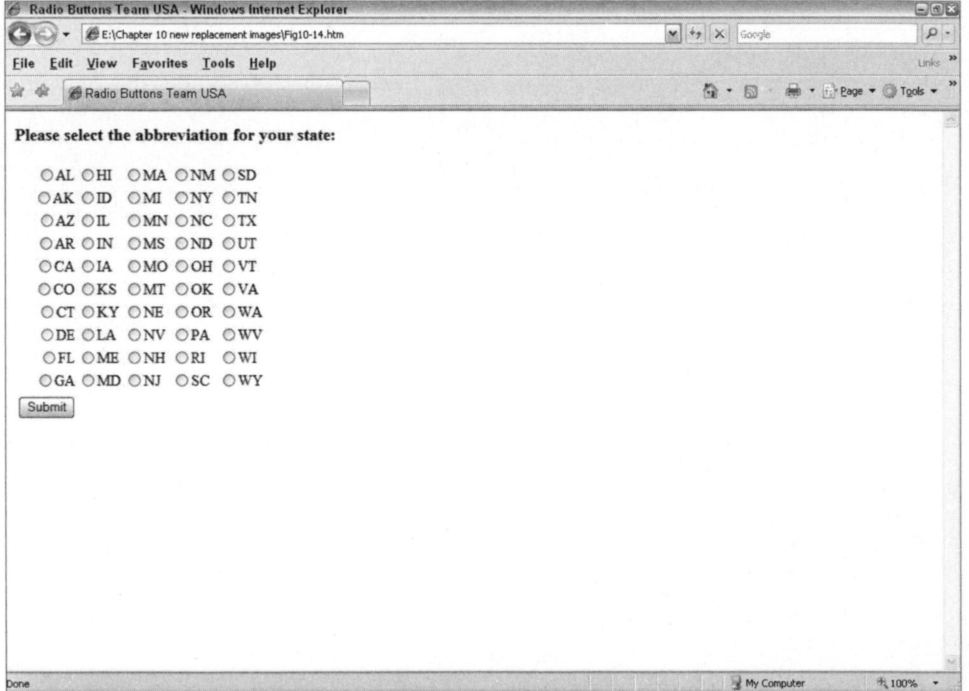

That's where drop-down lists and list boxes come into the picture. As you can see in Figure 10-15, the use of a drop-down list creates a much more pleasing form, and still enables all the necessary options to be included.

Both drop-down lists and list boxes are created using a combination of the SELECT and OPTION elements. The major difference between them is their appearance on screen. A drop-down list is a list of options showing multiple choices that are accessed by clicking an arrow that opens the list for selection. A *list box* is simply a list of options on screen.

The following code creates a drop-down list enabling users to select one of four geographical regions:

```
<SELECT name="region">
<OPTION>South</OPTION>
<OPTION>North</OPTION>
<OPTION>East</OPTION>
<OPTION>West</OPTION>
</SELECT>
```

FIGURE 10-15

Drop-down lists contain a lot of options in a small area.

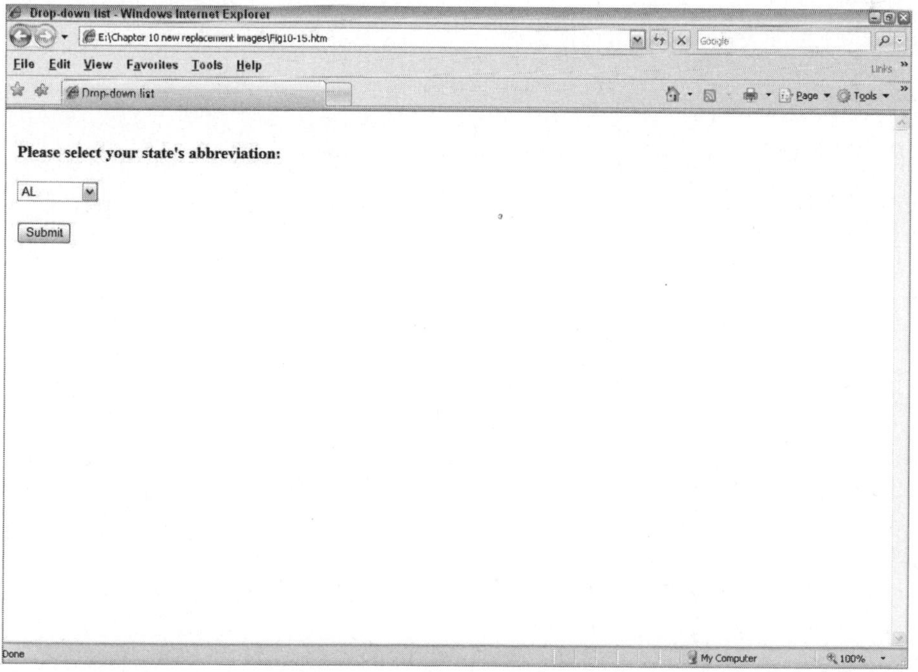

The SELECT element defines where the drop-down list begins and ends, whereas the OPTION elements specify the choices included in the list.

The OPTION element does not take a name.

You can also set size via styles as in the following:

```
<select name="region" style="width: 100px;">
```

A variation on the drop-down list is the selection list. The selection list shows all options when the visitor clicks an arrow, as can a drop-down list. The selection list, however, has the selection also appear in the text box at the top of the list. Figure 10-16 shows the selection list when a visitor clicks its arrow.

Specifying values

The name/value pair (which is sent when the form is submitted) would be region=South if the first option were chosen, region=North for the second option, and so forth. However, there are times when a value needs to be submitted that doesn't make a good, readable option for people

FIGURE 10-16

Selection lists display all the choices when activated.

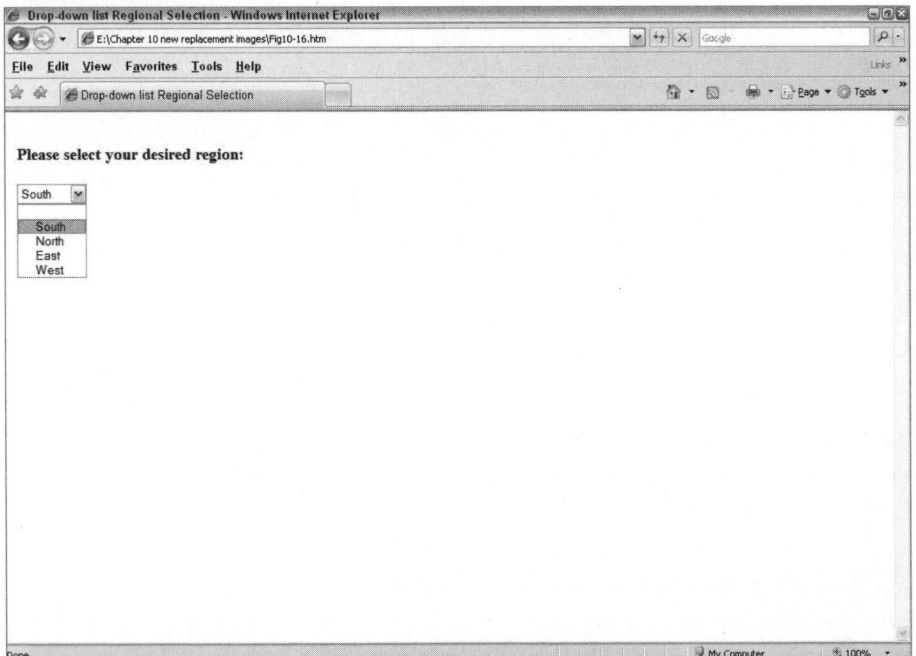

to choose. For example, what do you do if company regulations specify that the southern region is to be referred to by some internal code such as SoReg, but the form is to be used by customers who aren't familiar with such abbreviations?

The optional value attribute for the OPTION element can solve this problem easily. If it is specified, it overrides the content of the option. The preceding example can be modified as follows:

```
<SELECT name="region">
<OPTION value="SoReg">South</OPTION>
<OPTION value="NoReg">North</OPTION>
<OPTION value="EaReg">East</OPTION>
<OPTION value="WeReg">West</OPTION>
</SELECT>
```

Thus, the users of the form see easily comprehensible choices, but the internal code is submitted instead of the plain language.

Setting menu types

The same options could be presented as a list box simply by specifying how many of the options should be visible. This is done with the size attribute. If you wanted all four of the options to show at once, you would change the code as follows:

```
<SELECT name="region" size="4">
<OPTION value="SoReg">South</OPTION>
<OPTION value="NoReg">North</OPTION>
<OPTION value="EaReg">East</OPTION>
<OPTION value="WeReg">West</OPTION>
</SELECT>
```

To make three of the options show at once, the following code would do the trick:

```
<SELECT name="region" size="3">
<OPTION value="SoReg">South</OPTION>
<OPTION value="NoReg">North</OPTION>
<OPTION value="EaReg">East</OPTION>
<OPTION value="WeReg">West</OPTION>
</SELECT>
```

If the number of options showing is less than the total, scroll bars appear, enabling users to scroll up and down through the list. Figure 10-17 shows two samples of this list box, one set to show three of the options and the other set to show all of them.

Allowing multiple selections

Aside from the difference in appearance, one significant difference between popup menus and list boxes exists. There are times when you want someone to be able to make more than one choice

FIGURE 10-17

List boxes can be set to show different numbers of options.

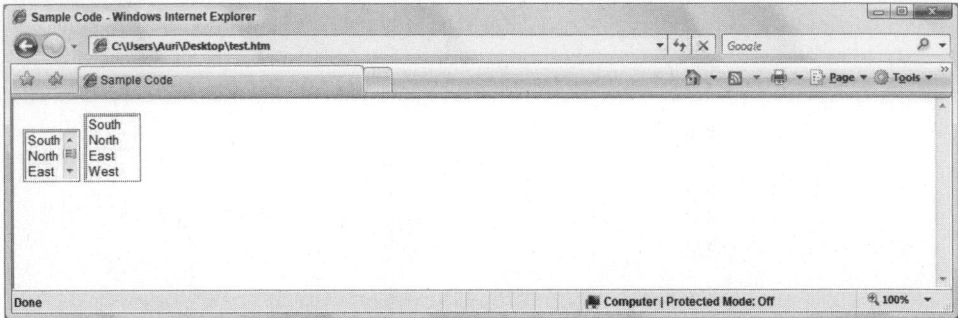

from among the options, and list boxes enable you to do so using the `multiple` attribute. The following code illustrates its use:

```
<SELECT name="region" size="4" multiple>
<OPTION value="SoReg">South</OPTION>
<OPTION value="NoReg">North</OPTION>
<OPTION value="EaReg">East</OPTION>
<OPTION value="WeReg">West</OPTION>
</SELECT>
```

NOTE **In fact, you do not even need to specify the size of a list box that has the `multiple` attribute, unless you want the list to show less than the full amount of options. The presence of that attribute automatically changes a popup menu into a list box, because popup menus don't have multiple choices as a possibility.**

Figure 10-18 shows a list box with multiple options selected.

FIGURE 10-18

List boxes can enable multiple choices.

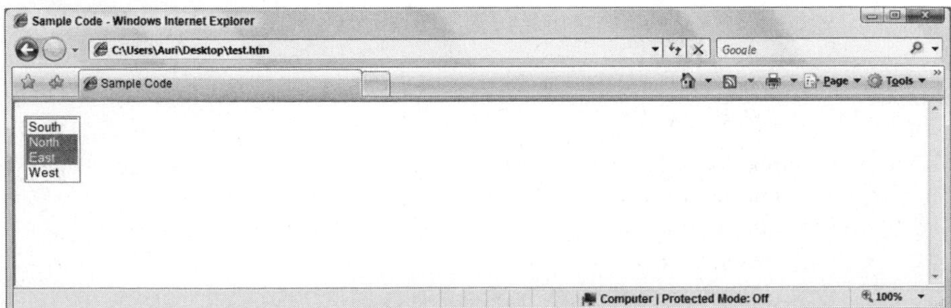

Setting a default choice

As with check boxes and option buttons, default choices can be set for popup menus and list boxes. However, the attribute is different — in this case, the `selected` attribute is used. If you want the first attribute to be selected, you don't have to do anything, because that's the default selection. However, if you wanted, for example, the third option to be the default choice, you would change the code as follows:

```
<SELECT name="region" size="4" multiple>
<OPTION value="SoReg">South</OPTION>
<OPTION value="NoReg">North</OPTION>
<OPTION value="EaReg" selected>East</OPTION>
<OPTION value="WeReg">West</OPTION>
</SELECT>
```

You can set more than one option to be selected, at least with list boxes. Popup menus do not enable multiple selections.

Using INPUT Buttons

All forms have buttons that trigger various actions. The most common are the two basic buttons, Submit and Reset. Beyond those two, you can also create custom buttons that do whatever you decide, or you can replace the plain Submit button with a graphical one of your own design. All four of these are various types of the `INPUT` element.

Adding the Submit button

The Submit button does just what it says — it causes the information in the form to be sent to the data processing program. It has no other function, and no form can do anything without this button unless its creator has worked a custom JavaScript program into the equation. The Submit button is required on most forms.

NOTE **The HTML standard specifies that you can have more than one Submit button in a form. This is for cases when the program that receives the form should do something different, depending on the button pressed. For example, the "Next" and "Previous" Submit buttons for a series of forms could be used to submit the data, regardless of which direction the user chooses, and then go to the next or previous form.**

The simplest code for inserting a Submit button is this:

```
<INPUT type="submit">
```

There are a number of possible options you can play with. If you don't specify the text to be used on the Submit button, it simply says "Submit Query," which is accurate, but dull. To change the caption on the button to something more interesting such as the one shown in Figure 10-19, you can use the following code:

```
<INPUT type="submit" value="Place My Order!">
```

FIGURE 10-19

A Submit button can say anything you want it to.

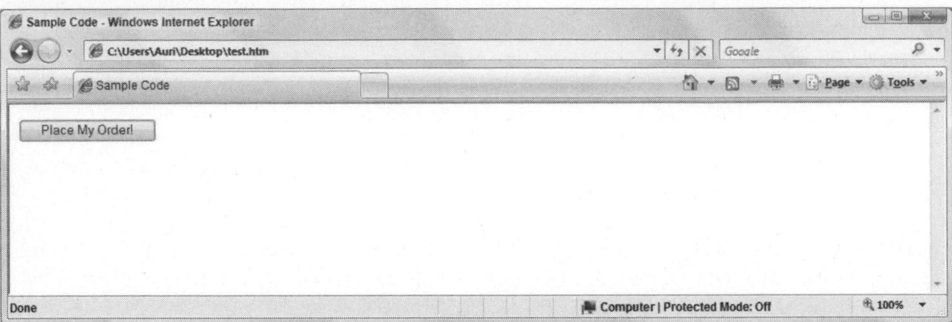

The button expands, if necessary, to be large enough to display the entire caption.

You can also change the size of the button by specifying values for its `width` and `height` attributes. The following code specifies a Submit button that is 100 pixels wide and 50 pixels high:

```
<INPUT type="submit" width="100" height="50">
```

This is perfectly valid, just as for any other type of the `INPUT` element. However, Internet Explorer does not recognize the values. It always displays a Submit button at the same size unless a custom caption forces it to expand.

NOTE **Size may also be given using styles as in the following:**

```
<INPUT type="submit" style="width: 100px; height: 50px;">
```

Adding a Reset button

The Reset button has only one function — to clear all information that a visitor has entered into the form. It returns all the form controls to their default settings and restores any initial values you may have specified, such as text area content or selected options in list boxes.

While the Reset button is present in nearly every form you see on the World Wide Web, its usefulness is open to question. After all, can you ever imagine a circumstance in which someone would want to start completely from scratch after filling out a form? Granted, a visitor may want to change a thing or two, but we're talking about *everything*. It's a bit unlikely that anyone would complain too much if there were no Reset button to be found.

However, if someone did want to reset all the items in the form, it would be a lot easier to add the Reset button than to code and maintain a "clear all fields" function.

TIP **You can alter the size and caption of the Reset button just as with a Submit button.**

Creating custom buttons

Custom buttons are not for the casual Web page designer, because they require the use of JavaScript in order to be effective. Custom buttons, called *push buttons* in the HTML standard, enable you to do just about anything you want, but require a lot more knowledge — and work — on your part than using regular buttons.

The code needed to create a custom push button is as follows:

```
<INPUT type="button" name="dosomethingspecial" value="showthistext"
onClick="runthisScript">
```

The value of the `value` attribute is displayed in a Web browser as the text on the custom push button. The `onClick` value launches a JavaScript program that you have designed to exploit the existence of the custom push button.

CROSS-REF **See Chapter 13 for information on using JavaScript.**

TIP **You can alter the size of a push button in the same way as a Submit button.**

Going pictorial with graphical buttons

When the basic Submit button that HTML supplies just won't do the job, it's time to create your own. A graphical Submit button won't do anything that the plain Submit button won't do, but it can look a great deal nicer. If you're into plain utilitarianism when it comes to forms, this won't interest you. But if you'd like to toss in a little bit of flair, this is pretty much the easiest way to do it.

CROSS-REF **See Chapter 18 for information on creating images.**

Figure 10-20 shows a graphical Submit button instead of the plain one.

TIP **Because this button is designed to replace the functionality of the typical Submit button, it should display some type of text that fits in with that function, such as "Click Me" or "Place My Order."**

As with so many other form controls, this is a variation of the `INPUT` element. HTML code, as found in the following example, is required in order to add a graphical Submit button:

```
<INPUT type="image" name="pictureSubmit" src="graphicbutton.jpg">
```

CROSS-REF **See Chapter 4 for a discussion of URLs and file addresses.**

The size of the button is the same as the size of the image. Graphical Submit buttons, because they are images by their very nature, also use the `align` attribute. This affects the display of any other element found in the same line — or, effectively, the same block-level element — with the graphical Submit button.

FIGURE 10-20

You can beautify your forms with graphical Submit buttons.

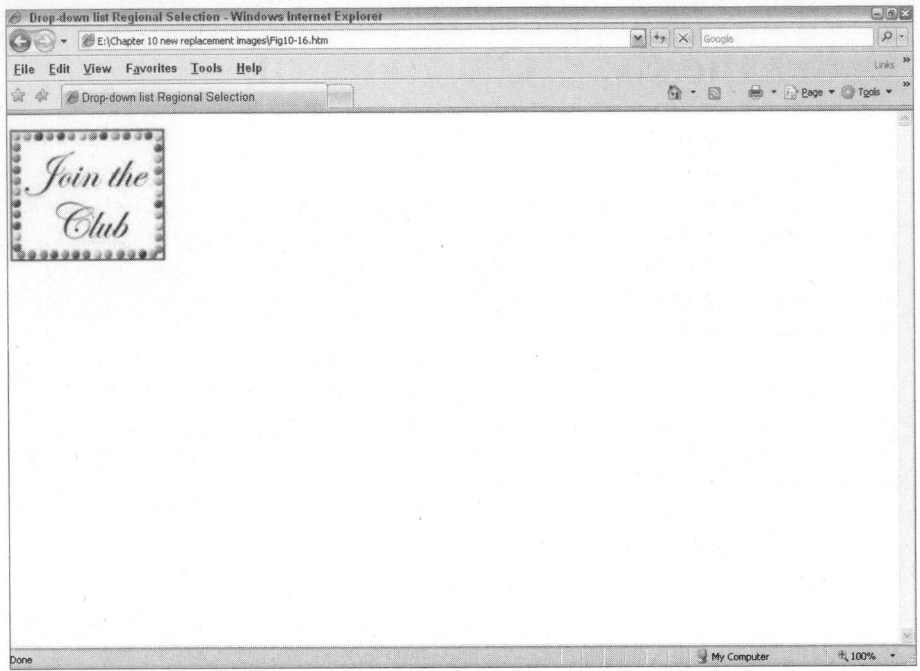

CROSS-REF See Chapter 6 for information on aligning images.

One of the most fascinating things about graphical buttons is that the HTML standard intended for them to be able to do much, much more than simply replace the usual Submit button with a prettier alternative. A graphical Submit button is, in fact, a miniature image map. When the form information is sent to the data-processing program, the location of the pointer when the graphical Submit button was clicked is included along with all the other information.

CROSS-REF See Chapter 5 for more information on image maps.

The location of the mouse pointer measuring from left to right (the X axis) and from top to bottom (the Y-axis) is sent at the time of submission. Each of these coordinates is appended to the name of the graphical Submit button by adding `.x` and `.y` to the button's name. Using the preceding code example as a base, the values of the mouse pointer coordinates would be sent as `pictureSubmit.x` and `pictureSubmit.y`.

This provides one way to create a server-side image map. An example of a good use of this is that, instead of presenting all the countries of the world in a drop-down list box on your Web page, you could show a map of the world and prompt users to click on an area that marks the location where they live. This would add a much more dynamic feel to your Web site.

Using the BUTTON Element

Often, there's more than one way to do the same thing in HTML, and each approach has its own ups and downs. A classic example is the BUTTON element in forms. We've just covered four different ways to create buttons in forms, all of which use the INPUT element and specify a particular kind of button via the type attribute. Well, you can do the same thing with the BUTTON element's type attribute, too. But there's a major difference here — the BUTTON element has both a start tag and an end tag, which means that it can hold content. And the content is displayed on the button.

There are three possible values for the type attribute for this element: button, submit, and reset. They create, in order, push buttons, Submit buttons, and Reset buttons. The following code, for example, creates a Reset button that is identical in both function and appearance to the standard one:

```
<BUTTON type="reset">
Reset
</BUTTON>
```

The possibilities, however, are many. Think of this kind of button as a tiny Web page. The content can include character styles such as bold and italic lettering. It can be an image or just about anything else. We once added a table to a form button in this way, as shown in Figure 10-21. Not that there's a practical use for doing that, but it does illustrate how much latitude you have.

The only thing that is explicitly forbidden to use in a BUTTON element is an image map. However, as with the table-in-a-button example, the fact that you can pull something off in HTML doesn't necessarily mean that it has real value. Because the INPUT element already has the capability to display an image on a button, and the three values of the type attribute for the BUTTON element are duplicates of the ones in the INPUT element, only one true, practical difference exists between INPUT-based buttons and BUTTON-based buttons.

The best use of this element is to include formatted text as the button caption. The following code creates a Submit button that uses various text styles to make the final word red in color and two sizes larger than the preceding text:

```
<BUTTON type="submit" name="colorsubmit" value="submit">
SEND IT RIGHT <I><FONT color="#FF0000" size="+2">NOW!</FONT></I>
</BUTTON>
```

Figure 10-22 shows the difference between this custom button and a normal Submit button.

FIGURE 10-21

You can do just about anything with the BUTTON element.

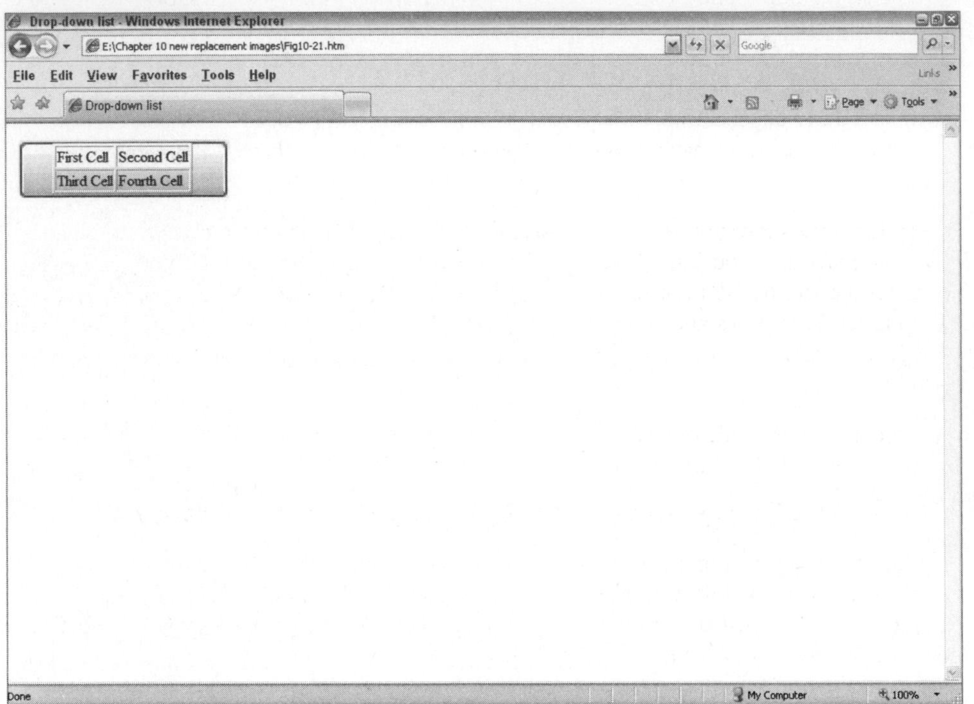

FIGURE 10-22

Character styles can be used to beautify buttons.

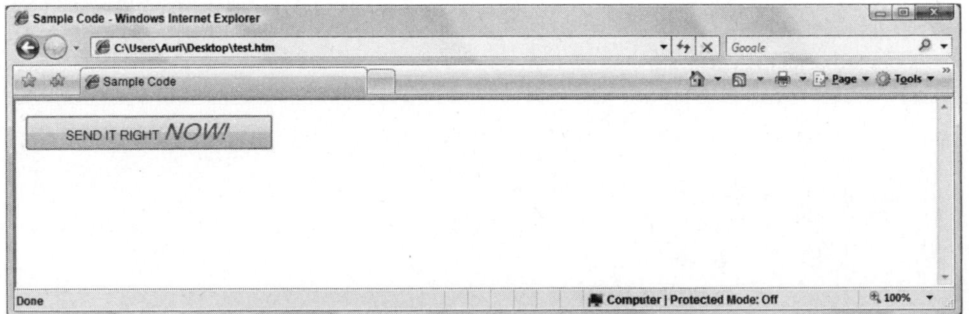

Adding Hidden Fields

For all the information that you want to have, but don't want your visitors to see or alter, *hidden fields* are the answer. We have already talked about the possibility of setting some form fields so that they could not be altered (see the section, "Locking content with readonly and disabled," earlier in this chapter), but that practically ensures that some of your visitors will become frustrated. After all, the whole purpose of a form is to get user input. If users can't provide that input — or at least make changes to your default entries — there's no point to the display existing at all.

Hidden fields give you the best of both worlds. They enable you to include information that may be important to you, but should not be altered by visitors, and at the same time, shield visitors from the fact of the information's existence. You may, for example, have an identical form on different Web pages and want to know which page the submission came from. This isn't the kind of information that needs to go onto a form to be shown to your visitors, but it's perfect for the `hidden` type.

You can achieve this by using the following code in your forms, changing `"thispage"` to show the name or URL of the page the form is on:

```
<INPUT type="hidden" name="whichpage" value="thispage">
```

You should bear in mind that it is possible for someone with technical skills to change your page so that it sends a different value. Don't put the price you will charge for some goods in a hidden field and then trust this value when it gets to the server. There is no way around this; you just have to take it into account when you design your Web application.

Adding Labels

There isn't, in our opinion, much real use for form labels, and browser support for them is spotty at best. However, they do exist, so we'll briefly talk about them. Almost every form control has some kind of text relating to it. A check box, for example, may have some text that says, "Click in the box if you want to get our monthly newsletter."

Generally, this is accomplished by the simple expedient of entering text into the form along with the form controls, such as this:

```
<FORM>
<P>
First Name:
 <INPUT type="text" name="firstname" size="20" maxlength="50">
</P>
<P>
Last Name:
 <INPUT type="text" name="lastname" size="20" maxlength="50">
</P>
```

```
<INPUT type="submit">
<INPUT type="reset">
</FORM>
```

This tends to satisfy the needs of 99.9 percent of form makers. However, there is one small factor to take into consideration when adding labels instead of normal text (and it's the only difference there is) — labels are directly associated with the form control they're attached to. This means that, if you click the label, it's the same as if you select the form control. This is hardly a great thing to get excited about, in our opinion, but if it happens to be what you need or want, here's how to go about it.

First, you need to define the text as a `LABEL` element. Then you need to use the `for` attribute to explain to the Web browser which form control the label text is attached to. The following variation on the preceding code shows the relationship:

```
<FORM>
<P>
<LABEL for="firstname">First Name: </LABEL>
<INPUT type="text" name="firstname" size="20" maxlength="50">
</P>
<P>
<LABEL for="lastname">Last Name:
</LABEL>
<INPUT type="text" name="lastname" size="20" maxlength="50">
</P>
<INPUT type="submit">
<INPUT type="reset">
</FORM>
```

You can also go for what is technically known as an *implied relationship* using the `LABEL` element, where the associated form control is contained within the `<label>` and `</label>` tags:

```
<FORM>
<P>
<LABEL>First Name:
 <INPUT type="text" name="firstname" size="20" maxlength="50">
</LABEL>
</P>
<P>
<LABEL>Last Name:
 <INPUT type="text" name="lastname" size="20" maxlength="50">
</LABEL>
</P>
<INPUT type="submit">
<INPUT type="reset">
</FORM>
```

Setting Tab Order

By default, the *tab order* — the order in which the controls in a form become active (or *receive focus*, if you want to use the technical phrase) as a user presses the Tab button on a keyboard — starts from the first FORM element and ends at the last FORM element. At that point, instead of wrapping around and beginning the whole process over again at the first FORM element, the tab order moves to the Address bar of the Web browser. One more press on the Tab button and you're back in the first FORM element.

Generally speaking, this is the way that most Web designers want their forms to work (with the possible exception of the detour through the Address bar). However, if you have some unusual situation where you want to change the tab order, it can be done. There is, unfortunately, no way to keep the tab order from including the Address bar — this technique is strictly for specifying which form controls are activated in which order.

The tabindex attribute works with all the FORM elements with one exception — the OPTION element, where it isn't needed or useful. OPTION elements are always contained within SELECT elements, and the tab order of the SELECT element would automatically encompass its contents.

The FORM element with the lowest tabindex value is the first one in the tab order, whereas the one with the highest tabindex value is the final one in the tab order. In the following example, the First Name text box is first, whereas the Last Name text box is second, while the Submit and Reset buttons are third and fourth, respectively:

```
<FORM>
<TEXTAREA>
First Name:
 <INPUT type="text" name="firstname" size="20" maxlength="50"
  tabindex="1">
</TEXTAREA>
<P>
<INPUT type="submit" name="lastname" tabindex="2">
</P>
<INPUT type="submit" tabindex="3">
<INPUT type="reset" tabindex="4">
</FORM>
```

Specifying Access Keys

Access keys (which have nothing to do with handicapped access) are common features in all programs. For example, nearly every program already defines Ctrl+S as the way to save a file and Alt+F as the way to open the File menu. So, you might confuse users if you try to use access keys with forms.

The access key you assign for your form overrides the same one in the Web browser. Internet Explorer already uses F, E, V, A, T, and H for its own menu access keys. Even if your needs can be taken care of by working around those letters, you must consider the possibility that future versions of Internet Explorer, or your browser of choice, may have different menu access keys.

With these caveats in mind, if you still want to assign access keys to your form, it's a simple enough matter. Just add the `accesskey` attribute and specify which key you want to use as the value:

```
<INPUT type="text" name="initial" accesskey="I">
```

It doesn't matter if you use a capital or lowercase letter for the value.

You can even use access keys to submit the form by specifying the `accesskey` attribute for the Submit button.

When an access key has been assigned, Windows and Linux users can access the control by using the access key in combination with the Alt key; Mac users use the Command key instead.

Because there is no indication to the user that the access key exists, you'll have to take care of that yourself. If you want to use the standard approach of showing the access key by underlining the appropriate letters, you could do it as follows:

```
<P><U>I</U>nitial: </P>
<INPUT type="text" name="initial" accesskey="I">
```

Figure 10-23 shows the results.

FIGURE 10-23

This is one example of how to use access keys in your form.

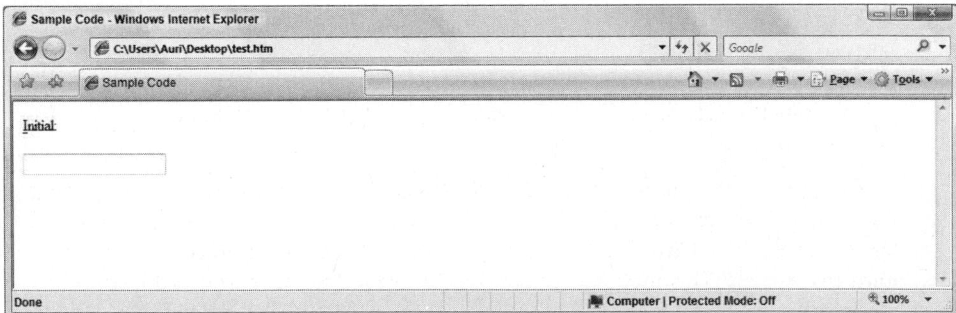

Submitting the Form

There are two attributes of the `FORM` element that must be specified for a form to be submitted properly when a user clicks the Submit button: `action` and `method`. The *action* is the URL of the program that handles the submitted data. The *method* specifies the manner in which the data is transmitted.

Two different possibilities exist for the value of the `method` attribute: `get` and `post`. Of the two, `post` is generally preferred, because it is the most flexible and efficient. The `get` method works by appending the name/value pairs from the form to the URL specified in the `action` attribute, which limits the amount and types of data that can be sent using that approach.

Since the information that the `get` method sends is visible in the navigation bar, it's not a good option to use if you want to keep your password secret. Also, since the browser remembers the URLs for the pages you visited, if you visit the page again by clicking on the back arrow, the browser may send the form information again (not too good of an idea if the form was to transfer money from your bank account).

However, the `get` method is great for search engines, particularly where you want people to be able to bookmark a search and it doesn't matter how many times it is executed. The `post` method, on the other hand, sends the form data separately from the URL, thus allowing it to send an unlimited amount of information. If you want to use a file input box, you must use the `post` method and specify the content encoding of the form using the attribute `enctype="multipart/form-data"`.

There are various ways to handle the form data. Some of the most common are Java servlets, Java Server Pages (JSPs), PHP programs, Active Server Pages (ASPs), and Common Gateway Interface (CGI) programs.

Java runs on any platform — including Windows, Mac, Linux, and Unix. Also, the software to create the pages and programs, as well as the application server to run them, is free of charge. If you have worked with JavaScript, you'll find the Java language is quite similar.

PHP (which started up as a scripting language to make personal Web sites, but is used now in large systems) is also free and works on any platform.

Microsoft's ASP.NET allows you to write Internet applications in many languages (such as BASIC, C#, C, and others), and runs on many Web servers running on the Windows platform, as well as, to a much more limited extent, Linux/Unix systems running Mono and Apache or other Web servers.

CGI programs are a means of getting information from Web pages into external programs for processing. Thousands of CGI programs are available either at no cost, or for a very reasonable fee. However, they have the disadvantage of starting a separate process on the server for every form that is sent. This may not seem like a problem, but when you suddenly find your site on the Internet news site Slashdot (`http://slashdot.org`), you might have performance issues.

There are several technologies designed to be more efficient. Most of these combine a programming language with HTML in a hybrid format.

To illustrate how form submission works, if you had a page that was designed to enable registered users to log in to a private section on your site, it would have to accept as its input the user's name and password. You could pass this data to a program called, let's say, `action.php`. The following form would handle all the necessary parts:

```
<FORM action="action.php" method="post">
<p>User name: <INPUT type="text" name="username" /></p>
<p>User password: <INPUT type="password" name="pw" /></p>
<p><INPUT type="submit" /></p>
</FORM>
```

In addition to programs that you house on your own Web server, a growing number of programs are hosted by other company's Web servers. You can, nonetheless, use a remotely hosted program as the action for your own form.

For example, a form mailer sends the request to a Java servlet. This, in turn, sends the form contents by e-mail to a specified address, and redirects the browser to the next page in your site. Note that you must specify the mail address and the next page to be shown as hidden fields in the form in this example, although some external mail applications may require different settings.

```
<FORM action="http://www.samplemailer.com/mailer" method="post">
<INPUT type="hidden" name="mailto" value="myemail@myhost.com">
<INPUT type="hidden" name="redirectto"
value="http://www.myhost.com/next.html">
<INPUT type="text" name="username">
<INPUT type="text" name="comment">
<INPUT type="submit">
</FORM>
```

Simple DOM

The Document Object Model (DOM) can be represented as a tree-like structure having a root, trunk, and many branches, as shown in Figure 10-24. An implementation of a DOM will have the Document as one of the branches with Form being one of the branches of Document. From the form itself, you have derivatives for text boxes; labels; option or radio buttons; Submit, Reset, and command buttons; lists; and other objects that make up the structure of the form.

The DOM is a programmable representation of a document. In other words, you might see the following list in a Web page

FIGURE 10-24

DOM can be represented as a tree-like structure.

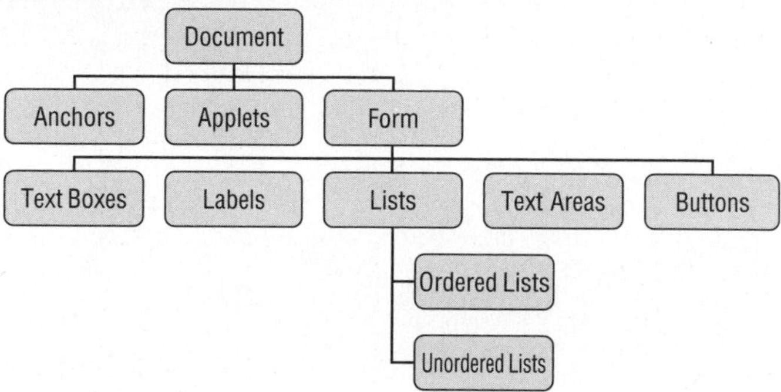

- The to do list
- Get school sticker for daughter's car
- Get school schedule for daughter
- Get immunization record for daughter
- Get school parking space for daughter

But the browser actually sees this:

```
<p>The to do list</p>
<ul>
<li>Get school sticker for daughter's car</li>
<li>Get school schedule for daughter</li>
<li>Get immunization record for daughter</li>
<li>Get school parking space for daughter</li>
</ul>
```

The partial DOM representation would be as shown in Figure 10-25.

This would be represented as part of a tree extending straight up to the Web page document itself. In the same way, you have a tree structure representing the Document and Form as the parent and its many children, each with content that can be manipulated, added to, or deleted from the structure.

Thus, while you see a page as a visual construct, the browser recognizes it as a tree structure of elements and their properties. The DOM is used to make the elements of the document accessible for manipulation.

FIGURE 10-25

This figure shows the DOM representation of the <UL> element.

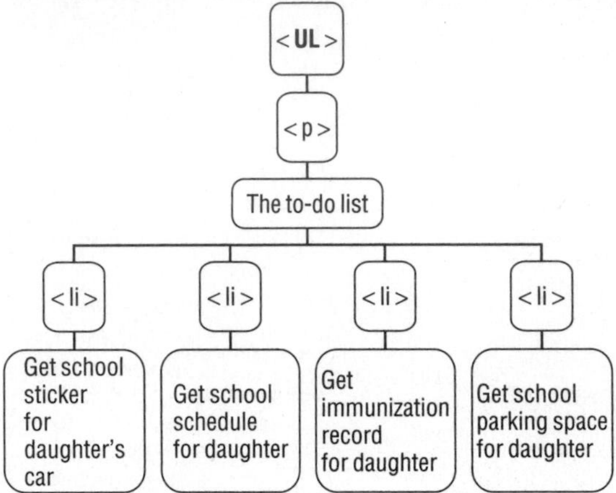

Its predecessor, Dynamic HTML (DHTML), was an admixture of CSS, JScript, and HTML 3.2 and after. This never really matured because a different DOM had to be written for each browser type. In the mid-1990s, browsers were coming and going at a dizzying pace. In addition, this mixture never had the official stamp of W3C. When a cross-platform DOM became available from W3C, DHTML went by the wayside.

Summary

Forms are the one major way for gathering user input on Web pages. Although you may devise other methods using sophisticated programming techniques, this is the way that most of your visitors are used to.

In this chapter, you learned that the `INPUT` element is the only one you have to use in order to create workable forms. Each element within the form should be given a distinctive name so that it will be clear what kind of information is presented when the form is submitted.

You learned that when writing JavaScript programs, each element should also have a unique `id` attribute so that it can be referenced.

You learned how text boxes (single line, rectangular areas) are useful for the gathering of information like names and addresses. Text areas (multiline, rectangular areas) are used for getting more complex information like shipping instructions. Check boxes are used for making choices among several nonexclusive alternatives. Option buttons are used for making choices between absolutes.

This chapter discussed how the `SELECT` element is used to present multiple options in a list.

And, finally, you learned that the DOM is a programmable tree-like structure of nodes which represents a hierarchy of objects within a document.

Chapter 11 introduces you to using audio and visual applications to increase the versatility of content offered on your Web site. It discusses implementations of the most recent formats in use, and presents step-by-step development of a movie using Adobe CS3 Flash.

Part IV

Making It Look Professional

IN THIS PART

Chapter 11

Adding Multimedia and Other Objects

This chapter reviews some of the ways to be creative and expand the functionality of your Web site through the use of plug-ins and extensions.

IN THIS CHAPTER

While a browser's inherent capabilities are for displaying styled text and limited image styling, its capabilities can be extended by the use of newer technologies that allow streaming audio and video, enhanced interactivity for forms, easier development environments for Web designers, downloading and integration of greater security features, and improved data storage and retrieval methods. These technologies are often freely available and are more commonly known as *plug-ins* or *extensions*.

A plug-in, like an extension, is a program that extends the capabilities of a browser. These may be used within software development environments, with e-mail clients, with graphics software and media players and, most relevant to this chapter, Web browsers. Some popular Firefox customizable extensions (plug-ins) would be Acrobat Reader, Flash, Java, QuickTime, RealPlayer, and MediaPlayer.

NOTE **We will be discussing in great detail the use of the Flash plug-in as it is currently used in CS3.**

Though the list is constantly shifting, some very useful extensions for Web development are FireFTP, WebDeveloper (also known as the "Swiss Army Knife for coding"), Firebug (for taking care of CSS, JavaScript, and HTML), Greasemonkey (create and or implement previously created JavaScript on your Web page), Internet Explorer Tab (for rendering sites on Internet Explorer), and Nuke Anything Enhanced (allows you to just get the desired content and not the extraneous advertising from a Web page).

Different plug-ins have varying attributes, so you really need to fully acquaint yourself with any new plug-in in order to use it to the fullest possible extent. If you would want to explore the outer limits of what you can do with Web pages, you must be willing to sail in the mystical waters of the siren sea and hear the haunting melodies of the Web (and beware the dragons, of course!).

Here is a short list of good references to plug ins to get you started

- `www.chami.com/htlm-kit/plugins`
- `desktop.google.com/plugins`
- `www.wmplugins.com`
- `http://adobe.com/products/plugins/photoshop/`
- `https://addons.mozilla.org/en-US/firefox/`
- `http://thepluginsite.com/`

NOTE **There is a technical distinction between a plug-in and an extension. A plug-in is a well-defined program that often runs on a host application's user interface. An extension may run on its own interface and is not as tightly defined. We tend to use both terms interchangeably.**

Adding Audio

Before we get into the details of how to embed an audio file in your Web page (in other words, to make the sound an automatic and integral part of the page), consider that there's a very easy way to add sound. And it's a way that avoids a common problem.

One of the most important rules of good Web design is this: *If you're going to use background sound on your site, ensure that you give your visitors some way to turn it off*. Not everyone appreciates a soundtrack accompanying his or her Web surfing. And, even if people do enjoy sound, they grow tired of the same thing repeating endlessly. If you make it impossible for visitors to opt out of the sound, you'll lose some of them. There are ways to do this with embedded sound, as shown later in this chapter, but there's also a simple way to keep everyone happy.

Simply by linking to the sound file instead of embedding it, you give your site visitors the option of whether to listen to the sound or not. All you do is create the same kind of link as you would to another Web page or a graphics file. For example, if you wanted to play an MP3 song, you could use this code:

```
<A href="overtheseatoskye.mp3">Click here to listen to the
reflection of your soul</A>
```

That's all there is to it. Anyone who wants to hear the music can click the link. Anyone who doesn't want to hear it doesn't have to.

Choosing a file type

Plug-ins enable you to play practically any kind of audio file in a Web browser. However, you need to consider just how important the music (or other sound) is compared to how much it can delay the download of your Web page. You have several different file types from which to choose:

- *WAV* — A sound file in the WAV format (Waveform audio file) is hideously large when compared to other options. This file type has proven to be enduringly popular for Windows users. It can use either 8- or 16-bit sampling rates, recorded in either mono or stereo, and has `.wav` as its extension. It was jointly developed by both Microsoft and IBM. Waveform, of course, refers to the analog nature of sound that is digitally sampled and transferred to other formats.
- *WMA* — An audio file format for encoding digital audio. It is similar to MP3, though capable of compressing digital audio files at a higher rate and matching a variety of bandwidths. Its extension is `.wma`.
- *MIDI* — When it comes to audio file formats on the Web, for the longest time, MIDI files (which end in either `.mid` or `.midi` extensions) were king. MIDI files, rather than being recordings in digital format, are sets of instructions on how to reproduce a sound by using common instruments. They are pretty restricted in use to music files, since they record data on note characteristics such as pitch and length, and music synthesizers. You would not use this format to record sounds that roll trippingly off the tongue. However, their file sizes can be very small, making them ideal for non-speech use on Web pages.
- *Au* — This derives from *au*dio. It records in 8-bit mono and is used with Unix systems.
- *RealAudio* — RealAudio is a proprietary format of Real Networks used for streaming audio data to a source over limited bandwidth systems. Its typical extensions are `.rm`, `.ra`, and `.ram`. Because file sizes tend to be smaller than some other file types, the sound quality may be lower.
- *SND and AIFF* — For the growing base of Mac aficionados, you have SND and AIFF file types. AIFF (Audio Interchange File Format) is rather like the WAV file type in terms of capabilities (such as variable sampling rates, as well as mono or stereo options). SND is currently not a very well-supported file format, but it may gain increased support as the Apple share of the digital music market expands.
- *Ogg* — This is an open source audio compression format for the playing and storage of digital music. It uses Vorbis. The extension of Ogg is `.ogg`. Another popular free open source audio compression format, flac, is available at: `flac.sourceforge.net/`.
- *MP3* — With its compression algorithm, the MP3 file format offers an almost unbelievable capacity for storing CD-quality sound in a relatively tiny file compared to earlier digital recording formats. The key word here is "relatively" — the longer the music (or other sound), the larger the file. It's not unusual for a 2-minute song to take up 3MB, and that adds a stiff penalty to your Web page's download time. Whatever format you

use, it's a really good idea to keep the sound duration as short as you can. Unless you're selling digital albums, think in terms of seconds, not minutes.

- *MP4* — Though designed to transmit video and images over a smaller bandwidth, MP4 also is used for audio transmit through ACC MPEG-4 Audio. iTunes uses it. The extensions are `.m4a` and `.m4p`.

This is an area of high fluidity, and changes/improvements are constantly being made.

Embedding audio

We recognize that background sound (sort of a soundtrack to a Web page) does appeal to some Web designers. We'll show you how to make your background sound jump through hoops if you want it to.

Many Web browsers can natively play music and do not need plug-ins do the job. In any event, except for one issue that we cover, you will not need to concern yourself with the particular brand of music plug-in your visitors are using. Many different ones exist, and few Web browsers lack the capacity to play MIDI, MP3, or several other audio files currently on (and off) the above list.

Audio files are embedded in Web pages with the `OBJECT` element or the `EMBED` element. The basics can be handled relatively easily, as the following example demonstrates:

```
<html>
<body>
<object title="A Cool Song" data="Mission_Impossible.mid">
Sorry I can't play your song!
</object>
</body>
</html>
```

If you use the `<embed>` tag, rather than the `<object>` element, to link to an audio file,

```
<EMBED src="url_of_file" width="number" height="number">
</EMBED>
```

This code has the absolute minimum amount of information necessary to add sound. All it does is to specify the location and name of the audio file. If you wanted to play a MIDI file called `softsong.mid`, you could fill in the blanks like this:

```
<EMBED src="softsong.mid" width="200" height="100">
</EMBED><object title="A Cool Song" data="Mission_Impossible.mid" >
```

The `width` and `height` attributes, which are required, seem a bit strange at first — after all, this is a `sound`, not an image or a movie. How can it have dimensions? Well, it's the controls that are used to start, stop, and play the sound, as well as to change its volume, that are at issue here. The problem is that you don't know what plug-in someone's using. That means you don't know what the controls are going to be, let alone how large they'll be. The ones in the example code pretty much cover all the bases, however.

You can actually set up things so that the controls don't show on the Web page. However, you still have to specify the `width` and `height` attributes. Of course, the numbers could be anything you wanted under those circumstances. To make the controls disappear, you use the `hidden` attribute:

```
<EMBED src="softsong.mid"" width="200" height="100" hidden="true">
</EMBED>
```

This attribute takes a value of either `true` or `false`, but there's not much point to using `false` — if you don't want the controls hidden, just don't use the `hidden` attribute.

CAUTION **If you hide the controls, you make them inaccessible to your visitors, which means that they cannot turn off the sound. This is a fast way to annoy people. It's usually preferable to leave the choice up to them.**

A less invasive attribute is `autostart`, which does just what its name implies — it plays the sound file automatically when the page loads into a visitor's Web browser. It also takes values of `true` or `false`, and once again, there's no reason to use `false`, because that just yields the same result as not using `autostart`.

```
<EMBED src="softsong.mid" width="200" height="100" autostart="true">
</EMBED>
```

If you want the sound to play more than once, you can set it to start over again when it finishes. This is done with the `loop` attribute. This attribute takes a value of `true`, `false`, or the number of times to play the sound. As you'd expect, there's no point to specifying `loop="false"` because `false` is the default value. To set a sound to play forever, you use the following code:

```
<EMBED src="softsong.mid" width="200" height="100" loop="true">
</EMBED>
```

To set it to play four times, specify that number as the value:

```
<EMBED src="softsong.mid" width="200" height="100" loop="4">
</EMBED>
```

CAUTION **This, as you might imagine, is another touchy area. While some people enjoy listening to a hot new song over and over again, even the best music can get old very quickly if it's repeated endlessly.**

Setting volume

The volume of a sound file is only sort of under your control. Although you *can* set how loud you want it to play back, this setting is relative to the volume at which a visitor's speakers are set. In other words, if you set your sound file to play at 100 percent volume, that's just the normal volume at the visitors' end of things. If their speakers are cranked up, your sound plays loudly; if they're turned way down, your sound is gentle. All you can do is to accept this, or lower the volume. Thankfully, Web designers have no way to turn up the volume on a visitor's computer speakers.

The value of the `volume` attribute sets what percentage of the current full volume your song plays at. A value of `0` means that no sound is heard, whereas a value of `100`, as in the following code, means that the song is played at full volume:

```
<EMBED src="softsong.mid" width="200" height="100" volume="100">
</EMBED>
```

Using NOEMBED

The `NOEMBED` element enables you to add some message for those people whose Web browsers cannot play the sound, much as with the `Alt` text used with images and other elements. It is placed within an `EMBED` element as follows:

```
<EMBED src="softsong.mid" width="200" height="100" volume="100">
<NOEMBED>
Sorry, your Web browser cannot play this song.
</NOEMBED>
</EMBED>
```

Finding digital audio sources

Copyright is always an issue on the World Wide Web, but perhaps nowhere more in recent times than with the music industry. The person who creates a song owns the copyright, which means just what it says — they own the right to make copies. This includes the right to perform the song, either live or on some kind of recording medium. So, if you write the music, you own the rights to it. Otherwise, someone else does. And that someone just might come after you with a battery of lawyers if you don't watch your step, because you infringe on their copyright.

You can, of course, get permission to play popular music by paying money to the big recording studios (some of the money, we understand, even trickles back to the singers, musicians, and songwriters, after the lawyers and executives are finished taking their slices). You can get also permission directly from the artists if you know them. But, even if you happen to be on a first-name basis with a famous recording artist, you're probably still out of luck. Very few of them write their own music and lyrics, which means you'd have to get the composer's and, if applicable, the lyricist's permission, too, along with permission from the singer. It all gets so complicated that not even the lawyers really know what's going on.

There are two basic approaches you can take to avoid all these problems, however. You can make your own music, or buy music custom-made for you by someone else. And the Web puts you on the fast track to getting the music you need, either way.

The state of laws (and interpretations thereof) is "fluid" regarding making recordings, so we won't go into detail about any applications or programs that may presently be on the market. However, your local teenager may be a very good source on the current state of the recording industry as far as the Web is concerned.

Making your own music

You can make your own kind of music. If you're an accomplished digital musician, the last thing you need is our advice on what kind of recording studio equipment to use. If you're not, though, and you still want music you can call your own, the answer to your prayers is a Web site in Japan that you should visit:

```
http://hp.vector.co.jp/authors/VA014815/music/English/autocomp.html
```

While you're there, download a copy of Tetsuji Katsuda's Automated Composing System (available in both Windows and Macintosh versions). This precious little lifesaver of a program, shown in Figure 11-1, enables you to create your own music by just making a few choices such as whether you want jazz or hard rock, or what kind of instrument(s) you want to simulate — a harmonica or a string quartet.

FIGURE 11-1

The Automated Composing System creates a wide variety of tunes.

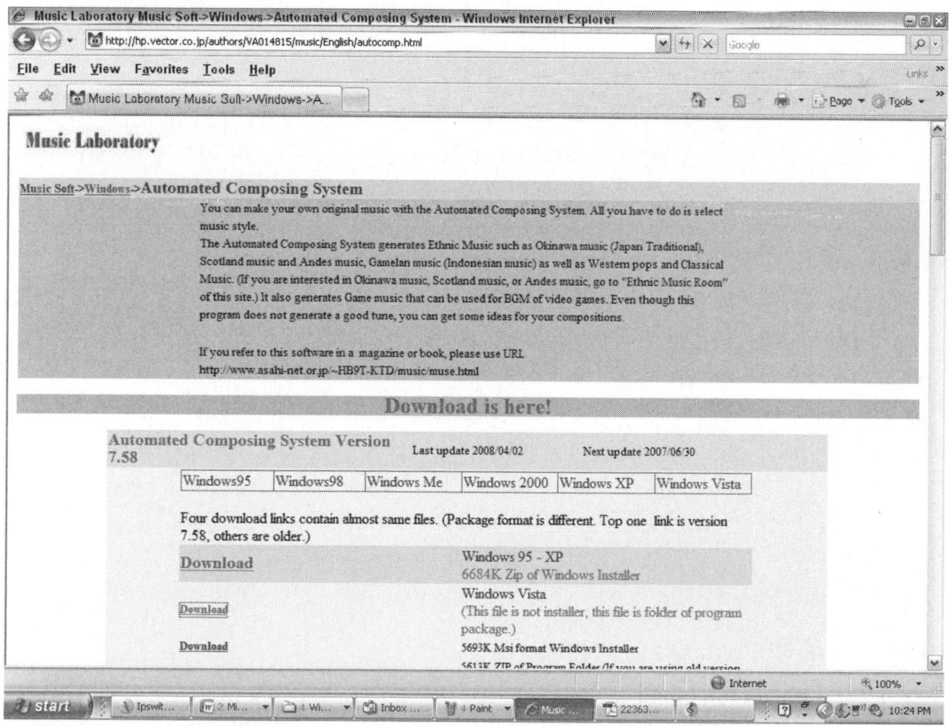

If you have even a passing knowledge of music (or, if you simply enjoy playing around with program settings to see what happens), you can come up with an astonishing variety of digital song files. Because you make them, you own the copyright — and they're unique, which means that no one else will have the same songs on their Web sites (unless they coincidentally make the same choices for their own settings). Granted, you won't get the same quality as you would get if you hired a professional digital composer, but the tunes are surprisingly good. And you cannot beat the price with a stick — the Automated Composing System is shareware.

The song files created with the Automated Composing System are in MIDI format, which are fully compatible with use on Web pages. However, you can easily convert them to other formats such as MP3 if you want. Our recommendation for this purpose is a program called Melody Assistant, which can be found at the `Download.com` Web site at `www.download.com/Melody-Assistant/3000-2133_4-10308195.html`. This is another great program that, in addition to simply converting digital music formats, is an impressive little music-composing system all on its own, including professional features such as real-time input from a MIDI keyboard. It requires at least some knowledge of music if you're going to use it for anything but file conversion, but it can be enjoyed by musicians of all levels. And all it costs is $15 — about the price of a bucket of fried chicken.

Table 11-1 shows where to find other digital music software.

TABLE 11-1

Other Sources of Digital Music Software.

Site	Address
Algorithmic Arts	`http://geneticmusic.com`
Wal-Mart	`http://musicdownloads.walmart.com/catalog/servlet/MainServlet`
Cakewalk	`www.cakewalk.com`
Digidesign	`www.digidesign.com`
Dream Station	`www.dreamstation.de`
Drumtrax	`www.drumtrax.com`
Magix	`www.magix.com/us`
Shareware Music Machine	`www.hitsquad.com/smm`
Sonic Foundry	`www.sonicfoundry.com/products`
Squeezer Virtual Band	`www.hmmsoftware.com/squeezer`

NOTE A kind of in-between approach is also available — using public domain music (songs that no one owns the copyright to). However, this involves meticulous legal research, where a mistake can land you in court. Plus, you have to enter the sheet music into a composing program, which is nearly as much work as creating your own.

Buying music

If you're looking for custom music, you need to find a composer who is comfortable with creating digital music. So, where do you look? The same place that has been in the news so much lately. `MP3.com` (see Figure 11-2) is a marvelous gathering of musicians from every genre. If you're looking for country and western, you'll find it there, along with progressive rock, trance, new age, classical, jazz, and some other kinds you've never heard of before. MP3.com is your composer supermarket. Go there, spend some time listening, and you may find the sound that you are looking for. Once you do, just click the link to contact the recording artist and tell them what you want. It's a lot faster than advertising for and auditioning composers.

FIGURE 11-2

MP3.com is a great place to find digital recording artists.

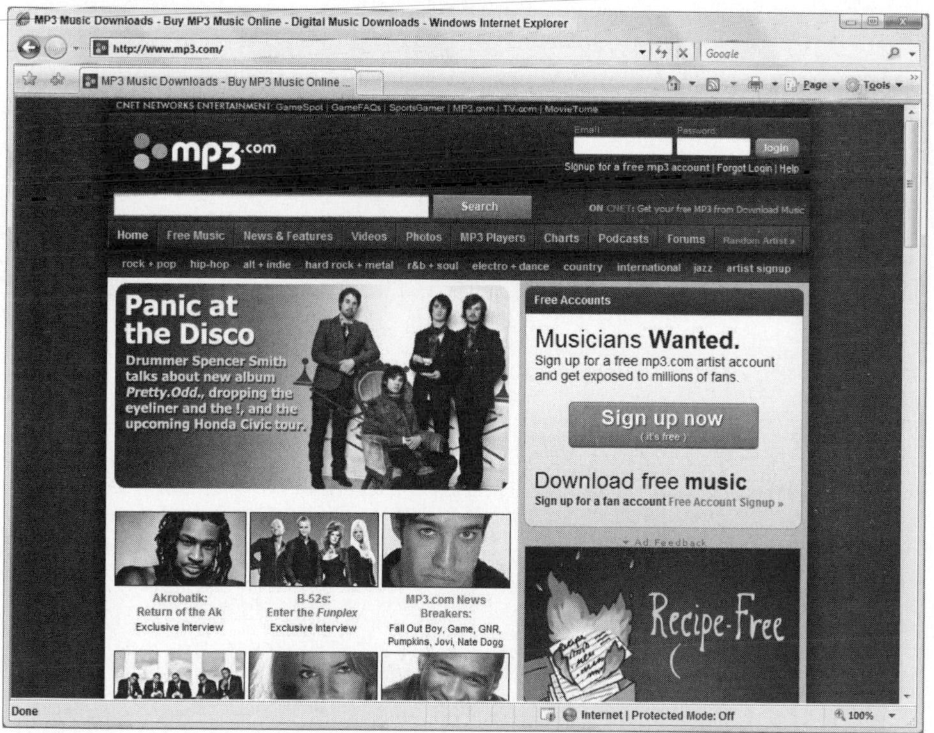

Of course, not everyone who's listed at MP3.com is a musician. You may not, for example, need a songwriter as much as you need a composer. But if you do, all aspects of music creation are represented. And not every composer is interested in whipping up a 5-second ditty or a bit of background music for a Web site. But you will find that most starving artists are perfectly willing to jump on the chance to put a little bread on the table by doing what they love most. You make the deal directly with an artist whose work you already respect. No mega-corporations or law firms get in the way, either, so you keep your costs down and the composers maximize their own profits.

You can also check out the Band and Composers Sites listing at `http://midimusic.about.com/musicperform/midimusic/msub15.htm`.

CAUTION **Ensure that you have at least some sort of minimal contract, stipulating exactly what rights you have to use the music. This helps prevent any possible misunderstandings down the road.**

If you're willing to settle for music that's not unique, and that your visitors may recognize from other Web sites they visit, you can always buy some prerecorded digital music. Table 11-2 lists the URLs of several sites on the World Wide Web where you can either purchase CDs or download (for a fee) some existing digital music files that can be used on your Web sites. Although you always must ensure that you double-check the legal details, you can generally use such music without paying any fee beyond the original CD price or download fee.

Finally, and quite importantly, a lot of the best music is actually public domain. And that, for those of us with good musical tastes and who are on a tight budget, is a very attractive option.

TABLE 11-2

Online Sources of Digital Audio

Site	Address
Classical Music Archives	`www.prs.net`
Dawn Audio Worldwide Music	`www.dawnmusic.com`
Ardour	`www.ardour.org`
Free Up Down Under	`www.royaltyfree.com.au`
musicandsfx.com	`www.musicandsfx.com`
Partners in Rhyme	`www.partnersinrhyme.com`
Web Sounds	`www.sonicimplants.com`

Embedding Video

Video is embedded with nearly the identical code you use to add audio files — both use the EMBED element, and both are played by the plug-in appropriate to the file type. Video clips, of course, differ from audio in that they are visible, and this means that they have a greater impact on the appearance of your site than just the presence or absence of audio controls.

For video, you'll need to know the width and height of the movie. The wrong settings make it look distorted, stretched, or compressed horizontally, vertically, or both. If you recorded the video yourself, there's no problem, because you doubtlessly know what settings you used. If you're using a commercially available video clip, the documentation should tell you all the parameters you need to set. If you don't have this information, you'll have to rely on either a Web authoring program such Adobe GoLive or another graphics program that recognizes that video format to get the information from the file for you.

If you do not know the sizes, and your Web authoring or graphics software does not automatically provide it, you can use a standalone media player that recognizes the file type. For example, if you are embedding a video in Apple's popular QuickTime format (`.mov`), you can find the size in QuickTime Player by following these steps:

1. Select File → Open Movie from the QuickTime Player menu.
2. Navigate to the movie file.
3. Select the filename and click the Open button.
4. Select Move → Get Info from the QuickTime Player menu.
5. In the dialog box that pops up to the side of the movie, choose Size from the right-hand drop-down list (see Figure 11-3).

Otherwise, the only solution is to discover the proper settings for the `width` and `height` attributes by trial and error.

FIGURE 11-3

You can get the size of a QuickTime movie with QuickTime Player from this dialog box.

Obtaining the size of the video file using Windows Media Player is simple. You just click on your videos in the main screen and then right-click on any video to get the size. You can do the same thing by clicking on the Size menu on the menu bar across the top. To get width and height, you just right-click on the video, select Properties from the context menu, and then select the Details tab.

You also should be aware of a couple of slight differences between QuickTime movies and sound files. The `autostart` attribute for sounds is replaced by `autoplay` for movies. And the `controls` attribute becomes the `controller` attribute. Other than the slight difference in name, they work the same way. This is a classic example of the need to check the documentation for any type of plug-in you plan to use.

Do not use the `hidden` attribute with a video clip. If you do, it hides the video.

Running a movie

There are a couple of differences in approach, if not in coding, when dealing with movies. Many video clips *must* be infinitely looped in order to have the greatest impact. The same code that produces an incredibly annoying perpetual background sound enables a looped video clip to be seamlessly consistent. By the same token, because the video is likely to be an integral part of the Web page, it is fair to hide the controls. Another reason for this is that the video, as with a still image, moves off screen if a visitor scrolls down the page. Background music, on the other hand, is present all the time, regardless of what part of the page you're looking at.

The following simple Web page illustrates how to add a video clip:

```
<HTML>
<HEAD>
<TITLE>Hot video clip</TITLE>
</HEAD>
<BODY bgcolor="#FFFFFF" text="#000000">
<EMBED autoplay="true" controller="false" loop="true"
src="RF103T.mov" width="200" height="200">
<NOEMBED>
<P>This is a video clip of flames. Your browser isn't set up to
support embedded videos.</P>
</NOEMBED>
</EMBED>
</BODY>
</HTML>
```

FIGURE 11-4

Digital video such as this clip from Artbeats.com can add a thrilling bit of dash to your Web pages.

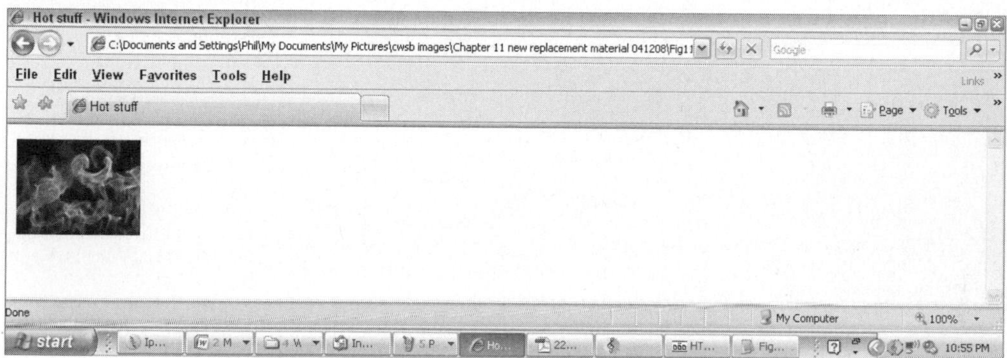

The results are shown in Figure 11-4.

Finding digital video sources

Table 11-3 gives the URLs of several sites on the World Wide Web where you can find digital video sources.

TABLE 11-3

Online Sources of Digital Video

Site	Address
Artbeats	`www.artbeats.com`
Digital Juice	`www.digitaljuice.com`
Hubble Source	`http://hubblesource.stsci.edu/sources/`
Wrightwood Laboratories	`www.wrightwood.com`

Animating with Adobe Flash

Adobe Flash, a component of Creative Suite 3 (CS3) discussed in Chapter 2, is a vector animation application that creates sequences of interactive action and sound, which are referred to as *Flash animations, Flash movie clips* or *Flash movies*. Flash movies can be played on Web sites or even as standalone applications. The application's strong points are that it greatly automates creating the movies and uses vector graphics that create relatively small files. If you have ever created an animated GIF frame by frame using a photo-editing program, you will definitely appreciate the work you can save by using Flash.

Flash organizes the space and time used by a video in a format that enables you to control the action as you work. The Stage is the space for your movie's action, and the Timeline enables you to set up the sequence for that action. Although bitmaps can be imported into Flash movies, they add to the file size and take longer to load into the user's browser than if you were to create all your animations in Flash.

Understanding the Flash Layout

Although you can create still graphics in Flash, you are most likely to use Flash to animate your Web pages. A Flash movie could consist of a menu with menu items presented so that they change in some way to create the effect of motion. For example, text can change color when the mouse is passed over it, or it is selected with a mouse click.

NOTE **Flash animations can't be crawled by Web spiders. This means that sites with only Flash content, and no HTML alternative, will be basically "invisible" to search engines, and you may have a lower placement in the search engines.**

Launching Flash for the first time reveals a screen with title bars showing Movie1, Scene1, and Layer1. The Flash layout consists of the following components, which are discussed in this section:

- Stage
- Scenes
- Layers
- Timeline
- Toolbox and Tool panels

The Stage

When you launch Flash and open a new file, you see a large, white space in the middle of your screen called the *Stage* (see Figure 11-5). This is where you place the objects and set the action for your movie.

FIGURE 11-5

The Stage is the main part of the Flash layout.

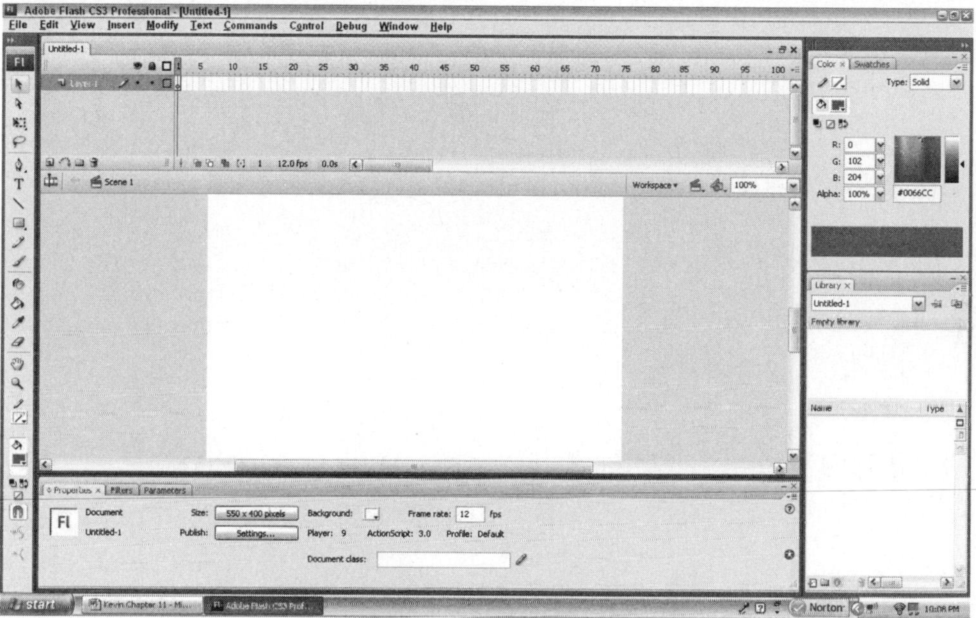

You can control the size, shape, and color of the Stage, depending on what type of movie you are making. For example, if your movie were a Web page banner, you might want to shape it as a wide rectangle to span the top of the Web page. To modify the size and color, select Document from the Modify menu. The Document Properties window that pops up (see Figure 11-6) enables you to change the Stage dimensions, the movie frame rate, background color, and the measurement units (pixels, inches, and so on). In addition, you can choose to have the Stage mimic a printer page (Printer) or the actual objects (Contents) already placed on the Stage.

Scenes

A movie can have multiple *scenes*. Each scene consists of its own Stage, Layers, and Timelines. You simply set the Stage for each scene, just as if you were setting the stage for a play with different scenes. When the movie is played, the scenes follow each other in the sequence they were created. You can select each scene (if there is more than one) by clicking the Edit Scene icon at the right side of the Scene title bar. If you need to rearrange the sequence, you can do so by clicking and dragging a scene up or down in the list.

NOTE **You can also use ActionScript and/or Java to jump to scenes.**

FIGURE 11-6

View the Document Properties window on the Modify menu.

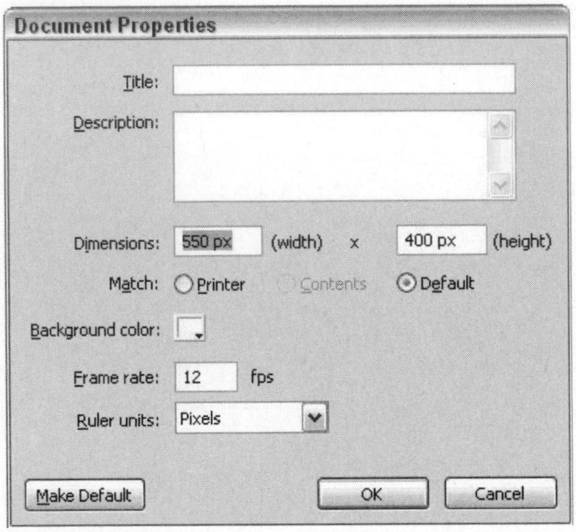

Layers

Above the Scene title bar is the Layer area. Layers are important because they separate graphics within the same scene. A scene can have many layers. You should name each layer differently to indicate what it does in the scene. For example, you could name a layer *Background* if it contains the movie backdrop. You create a new layer by clicking the plus sign in the lower-left corner of the Layer area. The new layer appears above the original layer (as shown in Figure 11-7), so that the oldest layer is on the bottom and the newest layer is on the top, near the Scene title bar. Double-click the layer name to rename it according to the new layer's theme.

NOTE **Usually, you work from the bottom up, but you can drag layers up and down to change locations. For example, you might want to change a layer's location if you created a foreground layer before the background layer.**

The Timeline

In the right pane of the Layer area, a ruler is displayed containing numbers incremented at regular intervals. This is the *Timeline*, which represents the time span of the movie. It enables you to direct the action. Using the Timeline, you can determine the sequence in which your objects move. A Timeline can be broken into a series of points that are called *frames*, in which some activity or change from previous activity takes place. Each layer you create has its own Timeline.

FIGURE 11-7

You can view two layers.

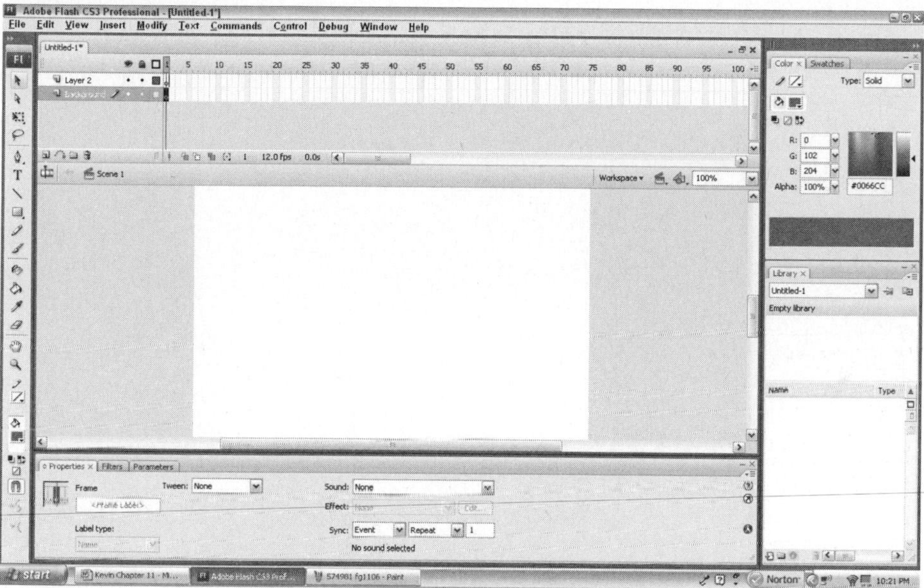

NOTE **To add a frame to a Timeline, you place the cursor on one of the Timeline points, which resemble rectangular boxes, and right-click to select the Insert Frame option from the Shortcut menu.**

The toolbox

The Flash Tools panel provides the set of tools that enables you to select and manipulate objects on the Stage. The Tools panel is usually positioned on the left side of the work area. Sometimes called the Drawing toolbar, the Tools panel items enable you to draw, paint, and write. Unlike the toolbox, most of the Toolbar tools are generic and work similarly to those in other programs. Adobe has actually worked hard to make most of its applications look similar, so if you learn one Adobe application, it's easier to pick up the rest.

NOTE **To float the Tools panel, click and drag it with the mouse. Grab it by the gray area above the icons. Move the Tools panel to a part of the screen you find more convenient. The Tools panel is now floating, as shown in Figure 11-8. You can replace (dock) the Tools panel by returning it to the area on the left side of the screen under the File menu.**

FIGURE 11-8

The Flash Tools panel can be floated into any position.

Most of the Tools panel items have selectable modifiers to enable you to vary the action. For example, you can select the Radius modifier for the Rectangle tool to add curved corners to the rectangles you draw. You can, of course, select line or fill color for all of the tools, with the exception of the Eraser, Lasso, Arrow, and Subselect tools. Table 11-4 shows the major functions for each tool in the Tools panel.

Tool panels

Panels are windows containing various tool options and can be accessed from the Window menu. Each of the tools in the Tools panel has a set of options, which are displayed immediately under the toolbox and are incorporated in the Tool panels. You also can select a layout from the Workspace item on the Window menu shown in Figure 11-9. Once you select a layout, you can reposition the panels to suit your preference and save the layout with a name. Then you can recall it to view your preferred panel layout.

NOTE **Although the top of the Tools panel remains the same, the options at the bottom of the Tools panel change, depending on the currently selected tool.**

TABLE 11-4

Tools and Functions in the Tools Panel

Tool	Function
Selection	Enables you to select objects.
Subselection	Creates handles, which enable you to modify the selected object.
Free Transform	Enables you to rotate, scale, distort, envelope, and snap to objects.
Lasso	Creates an irregular selection area of objects, based on the line drawn. Polygon and Magic Wand modifiers change the selection area.
Pen	Enables you to draw Bezier curves with nodes.
Text	Enables you to create text. You can modify the font size, color, style, line spacing, and margins, and set the paragraph alignment.
Line	Enables you to draw lines. You can select line color.
Oval/Rectangle	Enables you to draw oval and circular shapes. You can select line and fill colors. Also enables you to draw rectangular and square shapes. You can select line and fill colors and change the radius.
Pencil	Enables you to draw freeform lines. You can select tool modifiers to straighten and smooth lines. You can also select line color.
Brush	Enables you to paint using different brush sizes and shapes. You can also select fill color as well as modifiers for Normal, Fills, Paint Behind, Paint Selection, and Paint Inside modes.
Ink Bottle	Changes color, thickness, and style of lines based on the currently selected color.
Paint Bucket	Enables you to fill objects with color. Modifiers set the gap size to be closed by the Paint Bucket.
Eyedropper	Copies line, fill, and text styles from the drawing.
Eraser	Erases lines and fills. Modifiers set the mode to Erase Normal, Fills, Lines, Selected Fills, or Inside, and set the size and shape of the Eraser.
Hand	Moves the drawing's viewpoint.
Zoom	Enlarges or shrinks the drawing's view.
Stroke Color	Enables you to change the color of your stroke.
Fill Color	Enables you to transform gradient or bitmap fills and snap to objects.

FIGURE 11-9

The default layout can be customized.

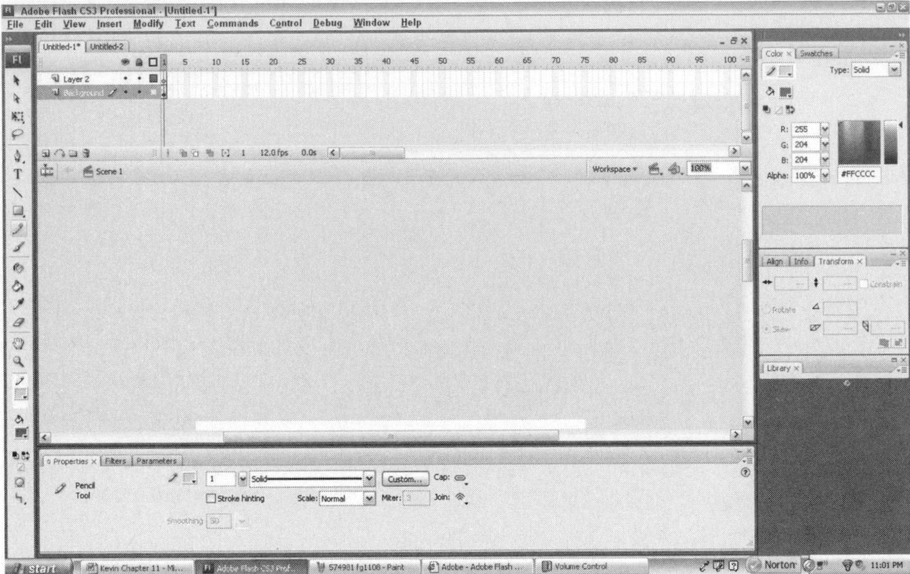

Flash classifies most of its panels into three categories: Design Panels, Development Panels, and Other Panels, which can be accessed through the Window menu. Tables 11-5 through 11-7 list the various panels by category.

TABLE 11-5

Design Panel

Panel	Function
Align	Enables you to change the alignment of elements with respect to one another and to the Stage.
Color Mixer	Enables you to mix the colors Red, Green, Blue, and Alpha transparency by percentage values. Also displays Line and Fill palettes, Black and White, No color, and Swap color options.
Color Swatches	Displays a palette of colors and gradients.
Info	Shows the coordinates X and Y, Width and Height dimensions, and Red, Green, Blue, and Alpha (transparency) values.
Transform	Enables you to resize, rotate, or skew objects.

TABLE 11-6

Development Panels

Panel	Function
Actions	Enables you to add scripted actions to your files.
Behaviors	Enables you to add scripted behaviors to your files.
Components	Provides a centralized source for dragging common components such as buttons onto the Stage.
Component inspector	Provides information on the selected component.
Debugger	Traces problems in your `.swf` files.
Output	Keeps track of variable values and such as your file runs.
Common Libraries	Enables you to add objects from either the default libraries or your own custom ones.

TABLE 11-7

Other Panels

Panel	Function
Accessibility	Sets name, description, shortcut, and tab index for objects.
History	Keeps track of all changes.
Scene	Enables you to duplicate, add, or delete scenes.
Strings	Provides an avenue for language translation.
Web Services	Lists Web service URLs.

Creating Objects

An *object* is anything you create or import into Flash. When you create an object on the Stage, you can direct how it appears and functions. You can change its color, size, and shape, as well as specify which frames it appears in and what it does.

FIGURE 11-10

You can draw lines with the Line tool.

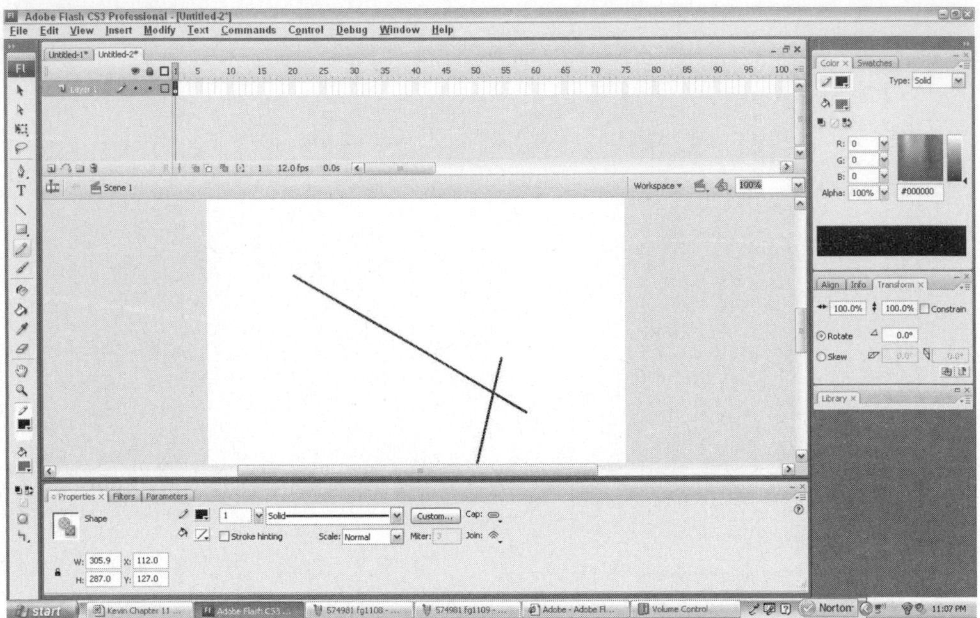

Drawing lines with the Line tool

Use the Line tool when you want to draw completely straight lines, as shown in Figure 11-10. The Pencil tool is for freehand drawing, although you can use the tool modifiers to smooth the lines it draws. Select the Line tool and draw a line on the Stage by clicking at one point and dragging the mouse to another point. Then release the button, and a line forms between the two points.

Smoothing a line is called *anti-aliasing*.

Setting stroke characteristics

Select the Line tool by clicking it with the Arrow selection tool. Click the line color palette in the Colors area in the Tools panel, and select the color red from the palette. Use the mouse to draw a line on the Stage. You can thicken the line using the Property inspector. Use the slider on the arrowed list box to increase the line thickness or enter the desired number in the box.

NOTE **The Property inspector can be accessed by selecting Window → Properties → Properties. The line-thickening feature can then be accessed by selecting options in the Stroke Style dialog box and clicking OK.**

FIGURE 11-11

You can draw an infinity symbol with the Pencil tool.

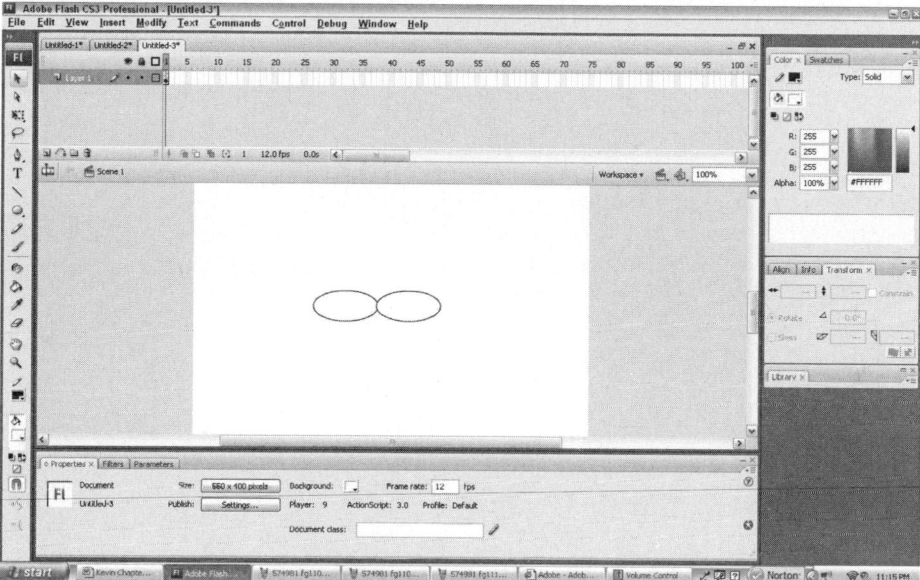

You can use the modifier tools to change the way the Pencil tool draws lines. Select the Pencil tool. Notice that a stair-step icon opens below the Options area at the bottom of the Tools panel and the Colors box. Select the icon, and then select the Smooth tool modifier. Now, draw an infinity symbol on the Stage, as shown in Figure 11-11. Do not worry about drawing a perfect infinity symbol. The Smooth modifier makes the curves smoother than you draw them. Release the button when you complete the infinity symbol. The shape probably looks much better than when it was drawn. You can experiment with the Straighten and Ink modifiers. They greatly affect the way shapes look when drawn with the Pencil tool.

You can use the Ink Bottle tool to change the characteristics of lines after they have been drawn. Select the Ink Bottle tool. Select the dotted line from the list box on the Stroke panel. Change the line width to 8 points. Now, use the Ink Bottle tool to click anywhere on the outline of the infinity symbol you just drew. Presto! The line changes style and thickness.

Selecting and deleting objects

By now, your drawing area is somewhat cluttered. You can remove unwanted artwork several different ways. You can select a line by double-clicking it and pressing the Delete key. When an object is selected, it appears crosshatched or grayed out. Alternatively, you can use the Selection tool to draw a selection box around the object you want to delete and then use the Delete key to erase it. You also can use the Eraser tool to erase unwanted objects from the Stage. Yet another way to remove objects is to use Edit → Select All, then select Edit → Clear to clear the entire Stage. Use your preferred method to remove the lines and infinity symbol.

Making shapes with tools

You can make different shapes just as easily as you can draw lines on the Stage. Select the Oval tool and draw a circle on the Stage, as shown in Figure 11-12. You will notice that the circle has the same line thickness, style, and color as the infinity symbol. Change the line style by selecting the wavy pattern from the Style list box in the Property inspector.

Select the Rectangle tool and draw a square or rectangular shape. This time, change the fill color rather than the line color. Select a fill color that contrasts with the line color. Select the Paint Bucket tool and click inside the rectangle. The color fills the inside perfectly. Now, use the Selection tool to select the fill by clicking only on the fill (don't double-click or click the line). Press the Delete key to remove the color.

Select the Brush tool and paint inside the rectangle. If you aren't careful, the fill color will "splash" outside the lines. You can control this by using the Paint modifier. With the Brush tool selected, click the Brush Mode icon in the top of the Options area. Now, select Paint Inside from the drop-down menu. Paint the rectangle. This time, the paint stays inside the lines. Of course, you must make several strokes to completely fill the rectangle. You can make this easier by selecting a larger brush from the Brush Size modifier in the Options area.

FIGURE 11-12

You can draw a circle on the Stage.

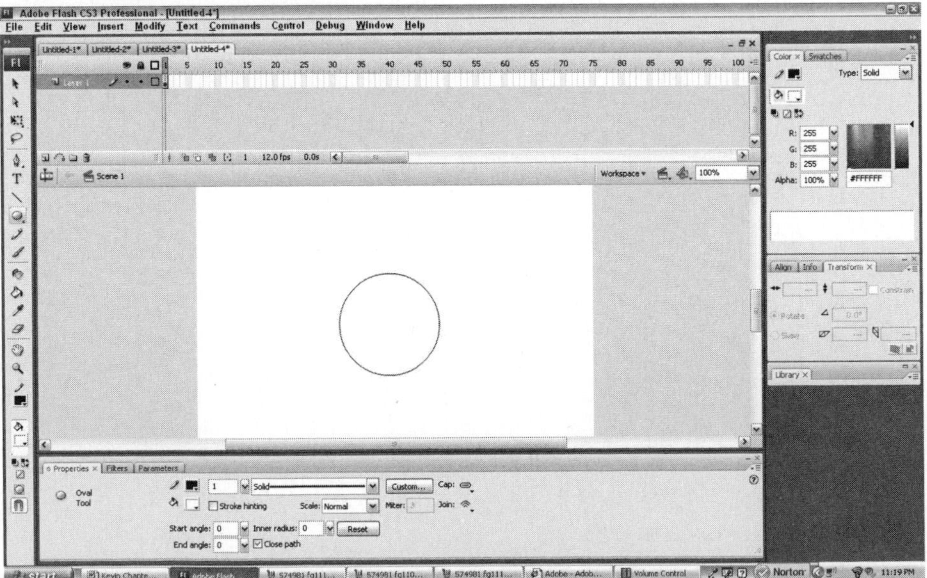

Saving your work

If you create any movie or part of a movie that you may want to build upon or reuse, you should save it. Remember all of the steps you went through to create even a simple shape with a gradient fill. To save your work, select File → Save. Your file is saved in the default location as Movie1, Movie2, or whatever the current movie name is. If you did not rename your movie, it is named Movie with a number appended.

If you want to give your movie a specific name, use File → Save As and type the name you want in the File name box. The Save box shows the current default folder where the file is located. You can click the icon showing a folder with an up arrow to move to a parent folder. Save your current file as `test`. Flash appends the `.fla` extension to the file name, signifying the Flash Movie file type.

Importing art

Importing art created in other applications is as easy as selecting File → Import. Most image types can be imported into Flash, including the following formats:

- TIFF (`.tif`)
- JPEG (`.jpg`)
- GIF (`.gif`)
- Windows Bitmap (`.bmp`)
- Adobe Illustrator (`.ai`)
- Enhanced Metafile (.emf)
- Windows Metafile (`.wmf`)
- PhotoShop (`.psd`)
- AutoCAD (`.dxf`)
- Macintosh PICT (`.pct`).
- Portable Network Graphics (`.png`).

In addition, Flash supports several animated file types, including the following:

- QuickTime Movie (`.mov`)
- Animated GIF (`.gif`)
- Flash Player (`.swf`)

Flash also imports sound formats such as the following:

- Windows Wave (`.wav`)
- MP3 Sound (`.mp3`)
- AIFF (`.aif`)

NOTE Windows Media Video files can be imported and played in Adobe Premiere Pro 2.0. From Adobe CS3 Flash 9.0 Professional, support has been provided for MPEG 4, H.264 (video codecs), and HE-AAC and Real Audio (audio codecs). In other words, Flash supports `.mwv` and `.mwa`, though there is some trouble running `.swf`. Note, however, that H.264 does not provide support for alpha channel and does not have the capability to embed video into a `.swf` file.

You can use imported bitmaps as a patterned fill for shapes you draw. Other uses for imported art include animating images by changing the size, shape, and orientation to simulate animation. You can use this technique with still photos to create the illusion of movement. Also, bitmaps and vector art often make good backgrounds for movies.

Imported files are amazingly large, particularly for some movie types and PostScript files. They can easily climb into the double-digit megabyte range. Bitmaps also increase the file size of the authoring file (`.fla`) and the compiled Flash Player version (`.swf`). The file size and the browser downloading time are important to keep in mind when creating Flash movies, because large files force your visitors to wait forever until they see the movie. Obviously, waiting for many minutes to see your movie is not going to create a favorable attitude toward your Web site.

NOTE PostScript is a standard language for defining images and print. In addition, PostScript files are vector graphics files that are scalable. They can be printed at various resolutions, according to the capabilities of the output device.

Using the Library panel

When you import images, they appear in the Library panel. You can access this panel by selecting Window → Library or Import to Library. The Library panel displays the names of all imported objects. Clicking a name in the list displays the object in the Library panel. Items listed in the Library panel can be reused in other scenes and even other movies.

Modifying Objects

You have seen how easily you can create objects on the Stage. You have also experimented a little with modifying them. But you are not limited to the oval and rectangular shapes in Flash. You can easily change the nature of the shape by using a click-and-drag routine.

Stretching and distorting objects

Clear the Stage and select the Oval tool to draw a new oval. Ensure that the object's line or fill is not selected. Choose the Selection tool and bring it very close to the edge of the oval shape. Be careful not to select it. When you see a tiny arc symbol form below the pointer, you can click and drag to pull the shape outward or inward (see Figure 11-13). Practice pushing and pulling the edge of the shape until it becomes distorted and the shape changes. If the oval object moves its position instead of changing shape, you have accidentally selected it. Just select Undo from the Edit menu to return it to its original position.

FIGURE 11-13

You can change the oval object's shape.

NOTE **When the Selection tool is touching a line, a right-angle symbol (it looks as if it's a corner) or an arc symbol appears below the cursor. The angle means that if you drag the line at that point, it pulls into a straight angle, and the arc signifies that any manipulating gives the line a curve.**

Flash has a feature that becomes a little tricky when dealing with multiple objects. This is especially true when it catches you by surprise.

With your distorted oval object on the Stage, select the Oval tool again and draw a small oval shape partly on top of the original object; be sure that the new object overlaps the existing one. Now, use the Selection tool to select the new oval object. Double-click to verify that the fill and outline are both selected. When selected, click and drag the shape away from the original object. A hole is now revealed in the first oval shape, as shown in Figure 11-14.

When objects come in contact with one another on the same Layer, they connect, causing the object on top to displace the covered portion of the bottom object. When you move the top object, the corresponding portion of the bottom object disappears as if it were displaced by the connection.

FIGURE 11-14

You can change the old shape by moving the new one.

Grouping objects

To learn about this feature, clear the Stage. Select the Oval tool and draw a new oval shape. Select Modify → Group to create a group. Now, select the Oval tool again and select a new, contrasting fill color from the Color area of the Tools panel. Draw another oval shape overlapping the first one. Now, select the overlapping oval object and move it away from the original one. This time, the object remains unchanged.

NOTE

When grouping objects, those most recently grouped appear to be on top of the other objects.

Scaling

You can scale objects using the Free Transform tool. Select the Oval tool and draw a new oval shape. Select the Paint Bucket tool and select any color you like from the Fill Colors box (appearing below the Paint Bucket). Click inside the circle to color it. Choose the Selection tool and double-click the oval object to select both the line and fill.

NOTE

When both line and fill are selected, the fill appears in a crosshatched pattern and the line becomes darker and thicker.

FIGURE 11-15

You can scale the oval.

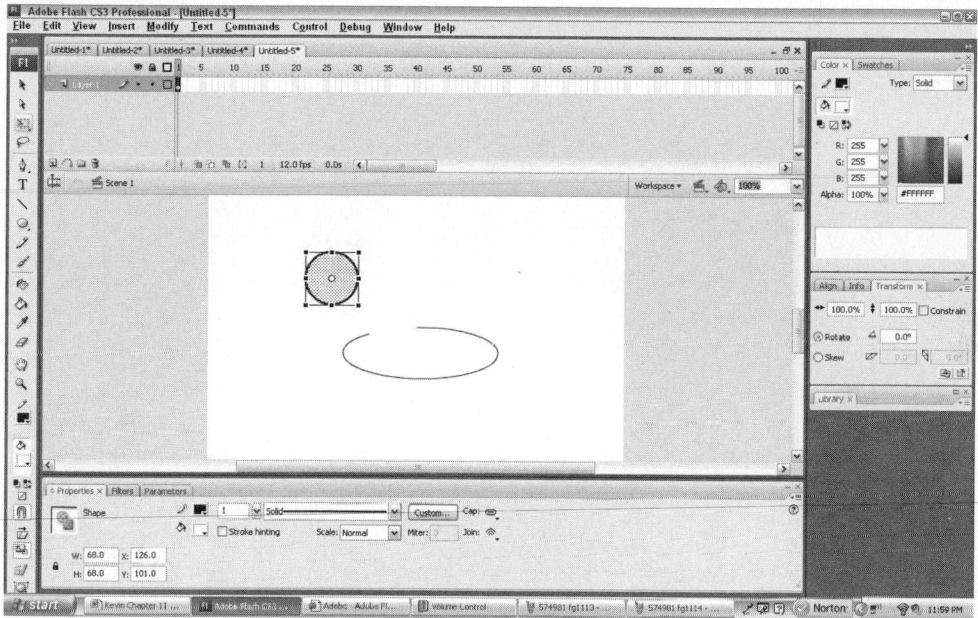

Select the Scale modifier by clicking Modify → Transform → Paste. Small square tabs form around the oval object, as shown in Figure 11-15. Grab one of the corner tabs and drag toward the center of the object to make it smaller.

NOTE **The differences between bitmaps and vector images are illustrated and discussed in Chapter 2.**

You also can distort the object into an egg or oval shape by grabbing one of the middle tabs and dragging it toward the center.

Rotating and skewing

Rotating an object is similar to scaling it. Select the Free Transform tool and select the Rotate and Skew modifier in the Options area. Grab one of the corner tabs and drag in either clockwise or counterclockwise direction. The oval should now be upended, as shown in Figure 11-16.

NOTE **When you select the Free Transform tool, a small rectangular box appears just to the right and contains two options: Q and F. This is the Options area. If you want the Free Transform tool, select the Q option. Otherwise, if you want the Gradient Transform tool, select the F option.**

FIGURE 11-16

You can rotate the oval.

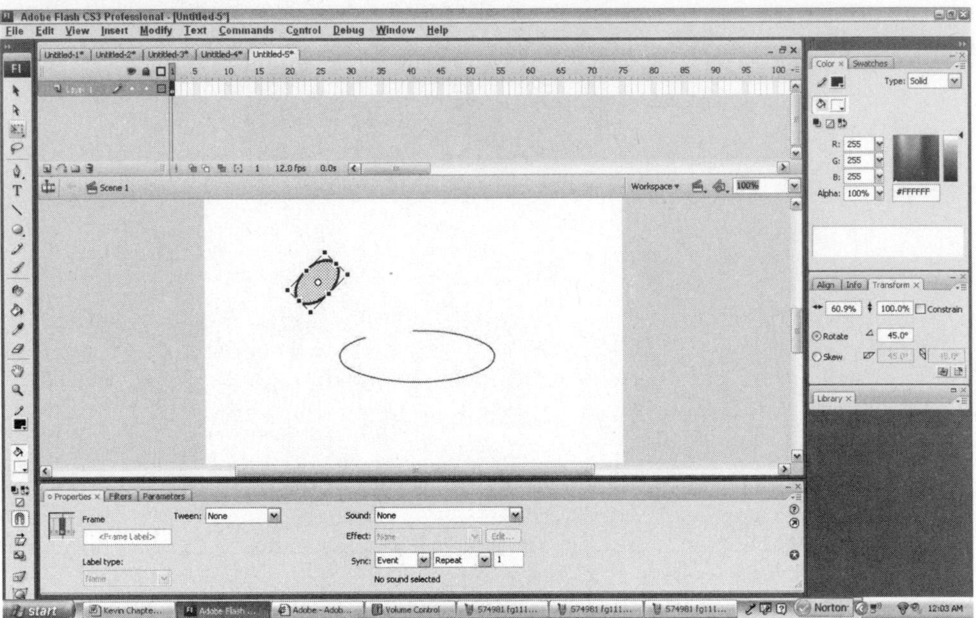

Straightening and smoothing

With the Selection tool, you can use the Straighten and Smooth modifiers in the Options area to modify shapes. Clear the Stage and select the Pencil tool. Draw a wavy line across the Stage. Choose the Selection tool and select the line you drew. Select the Straighten modifier in the Options area. Select the line and see if it changes. Now, select the Smooth modifier. Select the wavy line. How much difference you see in the shape of the line depends on the nature of the line drawn. Depending on how the line was drawn, the Smooth or Straighten modifier changes it more or less. As you can see, learning your way around Flash requires some experimentation. It is a good idea to experiment a lot before beginning serious projects.

Using gradient fills

So far, you have used solid colors for stroke and fill in the objects you created on the Stage, but there is a lot more you can do with color. You can select one of the premixed gradients by clicking the Fill color button (shown with the Paint Bucket icon) in the Color area. You also can select Window → Design Panels → Color Mixer to choose a fill type (solid, linear, or radial) and a fill color. At the bottom of the Fill color palette, you will see a selection of linear and radial gradient mixes.

A *linear gradient* shades in a straight line from the beginning to the end of the object being filled. A *radial gradient* shades in a circular pattern.

Just a reminder that the same Icon tool can be used to create an oval or a rectangle

Here's how to add a gradient:

1. Clear the Stage and select the Rectangle tool to draw a square or rectangle.
2. If the Color Mixer panel is not showing, select Window → Design Panels → Color Mixer.
3. Select Radial gradient from the drop-down list box in the Color Mixer.
4. Select the rightmost pointer under the mixer bar, representing the outside of the rectangle. Choose a color by clicking the Color area, setting the basis for the gradient. Now click the pointer on the far left. Select a different color from the palette. Move the pointers displayed below the slider bar to change the color mix until you are satisfied with the gradient sample shown in the Gradient Preview box (see Figure 11-17).

FIGURE 11-17

You can fill the rectangle with a gradient.

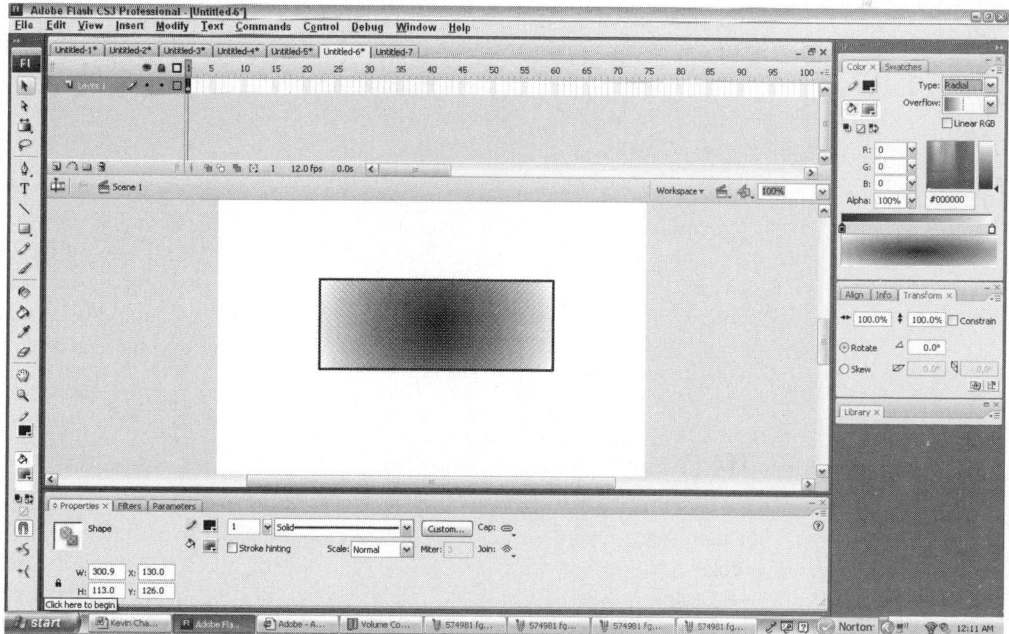

Working with bitmap fills

Not only can you fill objects with gradients and solid colors, you also can use bitmaps as fills. You can select a bitmap in the drop-down box on the Fill panel, where you just selected the Radial gradient. First, select the Rectangle tool and draw a rectangle on the Stage.

NOTE **Refer to Chapter 2 for additional information on bitmapped or raster graphics.**

Here's how to add a bitmap fill:

1. Clear the Stage and select the Rectangle tool to draw a square or rectangle.
2. If the Color panel is not visible, select Window → Color.
3. Select Bitmap gradient from the drop-down list box in the Color Mixer.
4. In the Import to Library dialog box, navigate to the bitmap file you want to use, select it, and then click on the Open button to display the imported bitmap.
5. Select the Paint Bucket tool, and click inside the rectangle. It will be tiled with the bitmap (see Figure 11-18).

FIGURE 11-18

You can fill an object with a bitmap pattern.

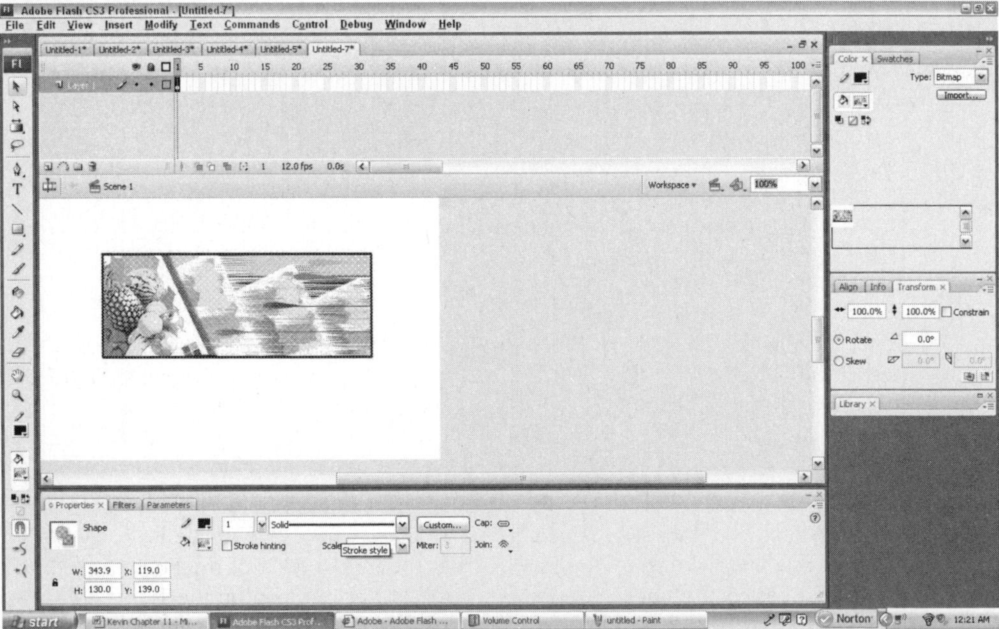

Working with Text

It is easy to add text to your movies. You will find that you can transform text as simply as you can alter lines and shapes. Text is a great way to create stunning effects without creating a movie with a large overhead.

Excellent examples of the uses of text in Flash movies can be found on the Internet. Some examples combine text and sound with no other graphics. Together, these create great effects.

Adding text

You add text using the Text tool on the Tools panel. Buttons and list boxes in the Property inspector enable you to select a font, a font size, tracking, kerning, and normal, superscript, and subscript, as well as the bold and italic styles and font color.

Choosing fonts

When you select a font and publish it with your movie, it will be exported with the Flash Player (`.swf`) file, so that font does not need to be installed on the user's system. Device fonts shown at the top of the fonts list (`sans serif`, `serif`, `typewriter`) are not embedded in the exported Flash movie. Using a device font causes the movie to use the font on the user's system that most closely resembles the selected device font. The purpose of using device fonts is to create a movie with a smaller file size because the font is not embedded in the `.swf` file.

NOTE **Any fonts that are purchased may not be allowed to be exported. A Web designer or developer should secure copyright and export permissions before deploying a font without distribution rights.**

You select a font from the list of fonts you have installed on your system. Sometimes the fonts are installed automatically when you install a new application, so you may not have used many of the fonts available to you. Windows and Mac users usually have many TrueType or PostScript fonts from which to choose.

Fonts are available from the slider in sizes from 8 points to 120 points. But size is relative to the size of the Stage in your movie. If you really need bigger fonts, you can type numbers ranging from 0 to 2500 into the Font Size list box instead of using the slider.

Setting font characteristics

There are many ways to select a font. Enter the point size as 48 in the Property Properties submenu of the Window menu; click the down arrow to the right of the Font Size list box and use the slider to select a 48-point size, or simply click the Text icon on the Tools toolbar or Standard toolbar. Select a bright color and begin typing on the Stage. As you can see in Figure 11-19, 48 points doesn't look very large when displayed on the default movie Stage.

FIGURE 11-19

You can insert type on the Stage.

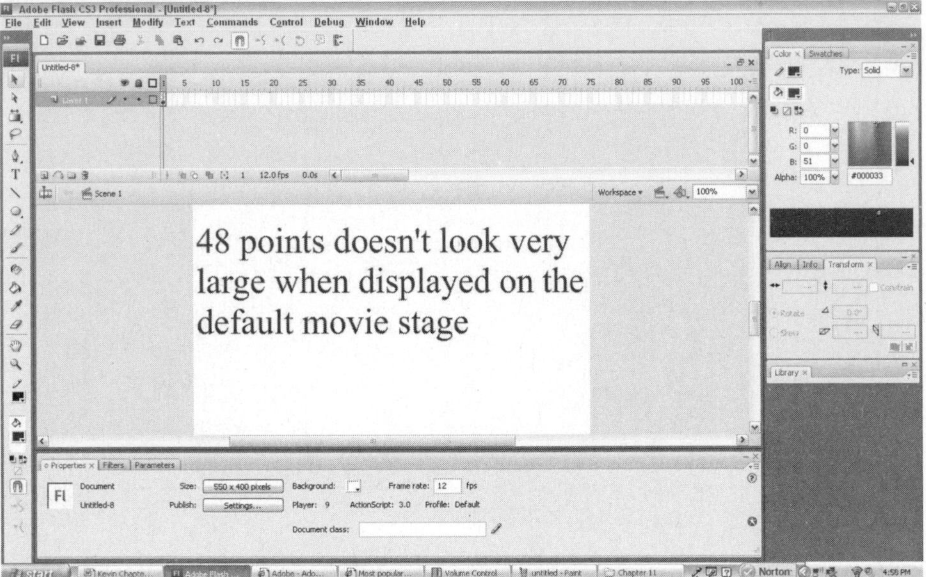

In addition to font size and color, you can change the character spacing, also called kerning. An increase in the character spacing increases the space between letters. Use the Selection tool to select the text block just created. Select the down arrow on the Character Spacing list box, and use the slider to increase and decrease the value. Figure 11-20 shows the space between the letters when the character spacing value is increased to 18.

Kerning controls the space between certain letters. In kerned text, differing amounts of space exist between letters, depending on the space the letter takes up. For example, in the preceding sentence, the space used by the letters *t* and *a* in the word *takes* is less than that used by the letters *k* and *e*. For the most part, kerning is not a major concern in Flash movies.

You also can use the Selection tool and the Scale modifier to stretch the text block. With the text block selected, use the Selection tool and the Scale modifier, and drag one of the tabs formed on corners of the text block to enlarge or decrease the size. Drag a middle tab to scrunch or elongate the text. Dragging the middle tabs distorts the text, whereas dragging a corner tab maintains the aspect ratio while adjusting the size.

FIGURE 11-20

Adjust tracking to increase the spacing between characters.

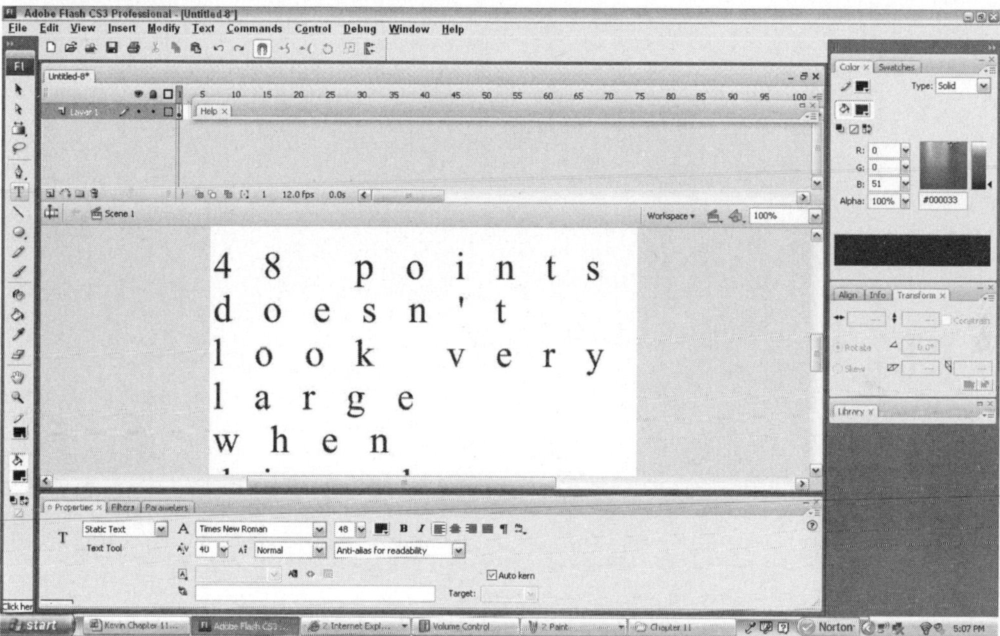

Creating text effects

You can create some great effects using the Flash tools, including making pictures out of text by following these instructions:

1. Delete your text to clear the Stage.
2. Select the Text tool, click on the Stage, and type **I LOVE** on one line.
3. Click the mouse button on the Stage immediately below that text block to begin a new text block, and then type **MY WIFE**.
4. Select the I LOVE text block and select Modify → Break Apart to break apart the text block, as shown in Figure 11-21. This is necessary so that you can manipulate individual letters. Now you can change the shapes of each letter using the various transformation tools.

FIGURE 11-21

Breaking apart the text block yields five text blocks instead of one.

Working with Animation Timelines

The Timeline is the basis for your Flash animation. The area above the Stage and immediately below the Scene title bar shows a ruler containing numbers incremented at regular intervals. The Timeline represents the time span of the movie. By using the Timeline, you can determine the sequence of your objects' movements. You can animate the objects on the Stage by selecting different frames on the Timeline and changing the placement of objects.

Using frames

Each box directly below the numbers on the Timeline is a frame. A *frame* is a unit of time on the Timeline. For animation to appear, each successive frame must differ from the preceding one. If you ever created your own animated GIF movie frame by frame, you understand the amount of work involved. This is termed *frame-by-frame animation*, and it requires that you create a series of still images, each slightly different from the others, so that when these are viewed in succession, they appear to move. In fact, a motion picture is really a lot of frames (still photos) displayed in rapid succession. Using the Timeline, you can automate this process so that you do not need to create a specific action for each individual frame.

Assigning keyframes

Keyframes are those frames you use to identify events. Each keyframe marks a change in objects on the Stage. You can simplify animation by placing keyframes at strategic points along the Timeline. To create a keyframe, right-click a frame somewhere on the Timeline, and select Insert → Keyframe from the shortcut menu. A black dot appears in that frame to signify it is a keyframe.

Adding Layers

Each layer has its own Timeline. Layers are important because they enable you to separate objects in the same scene. When the objects are on different layers, you do not have to worry about object interaction as you did in the shape exercise earlier in this chapter. That is, when objects are on different layers, they cannot affect one another. You add new layers by clicking Insert Layer button at the bottom left of the Timeline area, above the Scene title bar.

NOTE **You may also right-click a layer name and select Insert Layer from the context menu.**

Clear the Stage to begin a new movie. Double-click the layer name (Layer 1), and rename it to Background. Naming the layers according to their functions is helpful. Click the Insert Layer button in the lower-left corner of the layer area to add a new layer. Double-click the new layer and rename it Action. You now have two layers and two Timelines, as shown in Figure 11-22.

FIGURE 11-22

You can add and name a new layer.

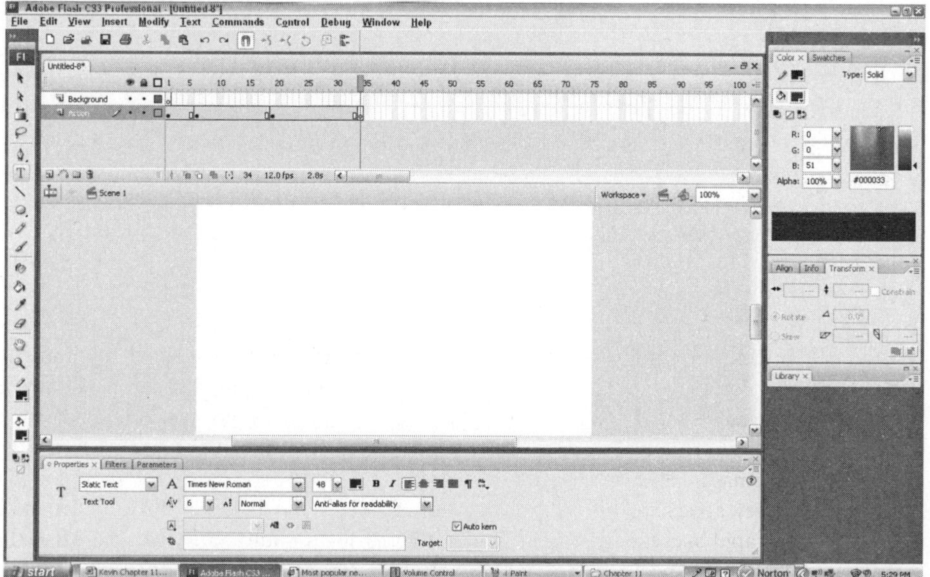

FIGURE 11-23

You can add an object to the layer.

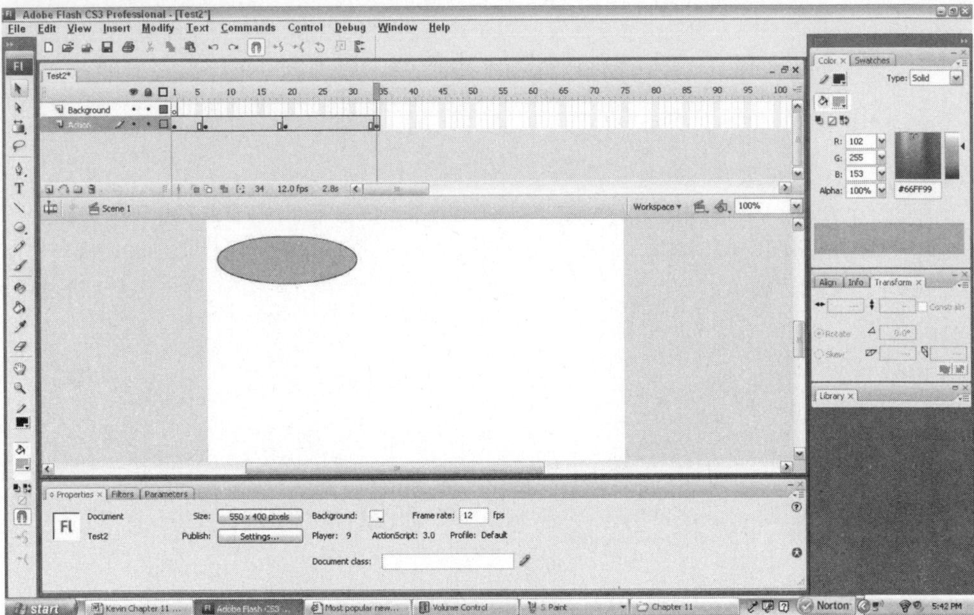

Adding objects to the Layers

To add content to your document, you need to add objects to the Stage. It is important to identify the layer on which you are adding the objects. The active layer is the one you currently have selected. Select the Action layer and draw an oval shape near the top of the Stage. Use the Paint Bucket tool to select a light green fill. Click inside the oval to color it green (shown as a gray shade in Figure 11-23).

This is a good time to save your movie. Select File → Save As and name the movie Test2. Type the name in the File name box, and check the Save box to ensure that you are saving it in the correct folder. If you want to change the folder, click the down arrow next to the Save in box to show all the folders on your system. You can move up one level by clicking the folder icon with the up arrow symbol.

Converting objects to symbols

Symbols can be reused in different scenes and also in different movies. When your project requires a number of similar objects, one symbol can be slightly changed several times to create different instances of the symbol. Each copy of a symbol is referred to as an *instance*.

In addition to saving time, converting an object to a symbol prevents accidental deletion or distortion. Once converted, symbols also appear in the Library panel and in the Library list. You can click and drag symbols from the Library panel onto the Stage as needed. Actions carried out on a symbol also affect all instances of a symbol.

Select the oval shape you just drew and select Insert → New Symbol. When the Create New Symbol window pops up, rename the symbol to GreenOval and click OK. Select Window → Library to verify that the symbol appears on the Library list.

Creating animation

Although you can change objects that have not been converted to symbols, you will find symbols in frames on a Timeline much easier to manage than simple objects. The first keyframe on a Timeline is always created for you when the layer is added. To make the green oval object appear to move and, at the same time, change color, follow these steps:

1. Right-click the 15th frame on the Action layer Timeline, and select Insert → Keyframe from the shortcut menu.

NOTE **Be sure that you have the correct layer selected before changing the action or attributes of objects or symbols. It is very easy to select the wrong layer, so check to see that the desired layer is highlighted.**

2. Drag the oval downward to the center of the Stage.
3. Select a bright pink color in the Property inspector.
4. Play the movie by selecting Control → Play. Be sure the first frame is selected, or you will need to select Control → Rewind then Control → Play. When the movie plays, the oval stays put until the 15th frame, in which it jumps to the new position and changes color (see Figure 11-24).

Now, this may not seem astonishing, but it is animation. If you want to change the action frame by frame, you could just move the oval in short increments by adding keyframes to every frame between 1 and 15. However, there is a much better and easier solution.

Tweening action

The solution to automating animation is called *tweening*. You can have your oval float gracefully down to center stage and change color gradually by tweening the action:

1. Select the first frame on the Action layer Timeline.
2. Choose Insert → Timeline → Create Motion Tween.

   An arrow forms on the Timeline between the first and the 15th keyframe. This signifies motion. In this case, the symbol is moving through space and changing color simultaneously. Both events involve motion tweening.

3. Play the movie by selecting Control → Play. The action should be significantly better than the abrupt change experienced before the action was tweened.
4. You needn't stop with one tweened action. You can extend the action by adding a keyframe to the 40th frame. Right-click the 40th frame of the Action layer and select Insert → Keyframe from the shortcut menu.
5. With the 40th frame selected, drag the oval to the far right of the Stage.
6. Choose a bright blue from the Property inspector.
7. With the 15th frame selected, choose Insert → Timeline → Create Motion Tween.
8. With the first frame selected, use Control → Play to view the movie. The movie should be decidedly better than the last change you made. Now the oval changes colors and moves in different directions, and for a longer time span (see Figure 11-25).

Creating more Layer effects

Now that you have something going on for the Action layer, you can turn your attention to the Background layer. The movement and color shift of the oval can be more interesting if you create an interesting background.

FIGURE 11-24

You can add a new keyframe to the Action layer Timeline.

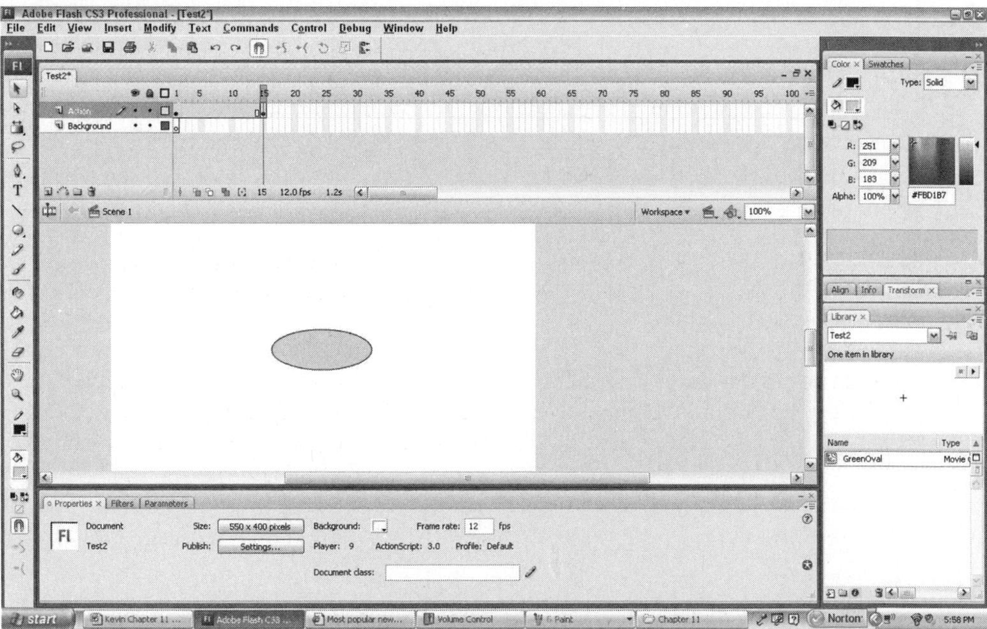

FIGURE 11-25

A new effect is introduced when you play the tweened movie.

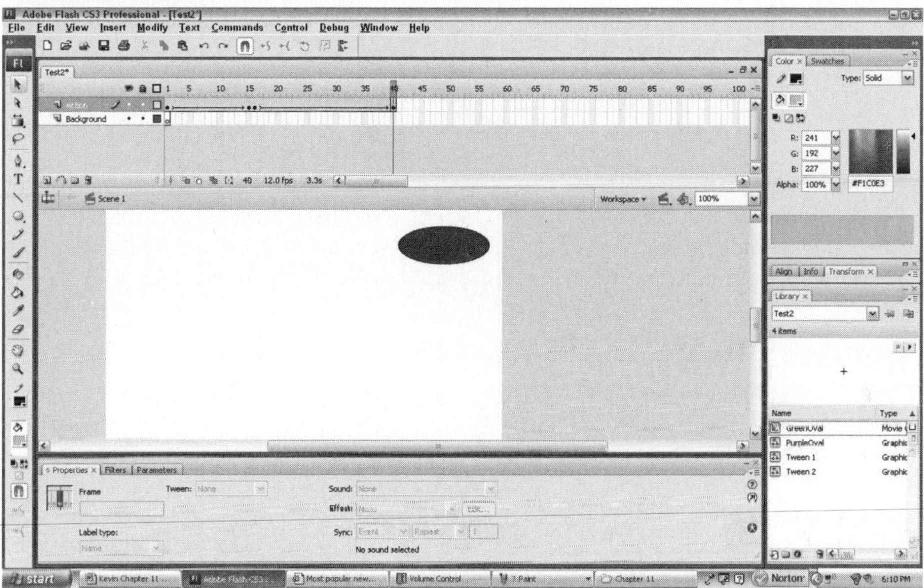

To make a simple background, select View → Zoom Out to view the entire Stage. Select the first frame on the Background layer. Then, select the Rectangle tool to draw a rectangle around the area of the Stage where the action takes place. You can then select a fill color and use the Paint Bucket to fill the rectangle with a color or gradient. Add a keyframe to the 40th frame directly below the keyframe for the Action layer. Play the movie, using Control → Play. The oval show now floats over a backdrop, as shown in Figure 11-26.

NOTE **To prevent making unwanted changes to layers, you can lock layers you are not working on. Click the dot in the column headed by a padlock symbol on the layer you want to lock.**

You can add more features to the background if you want. Click the dot in the column headed by the eye symbol on the Action layer. This removes the oval object from view, which is handy when you want to remove the distraction of objects that you are not currently working on.

1. Select View → Zoom In to zoom back into the Stage.
2. With the first frame in the Background layer selected, draw several shapes around the Stage.
3. Play the movie. Now, the oval action plays on a more interesting backdrop, as shown in Figure 11-27.

FIGURE 11-26

You can view the added background.

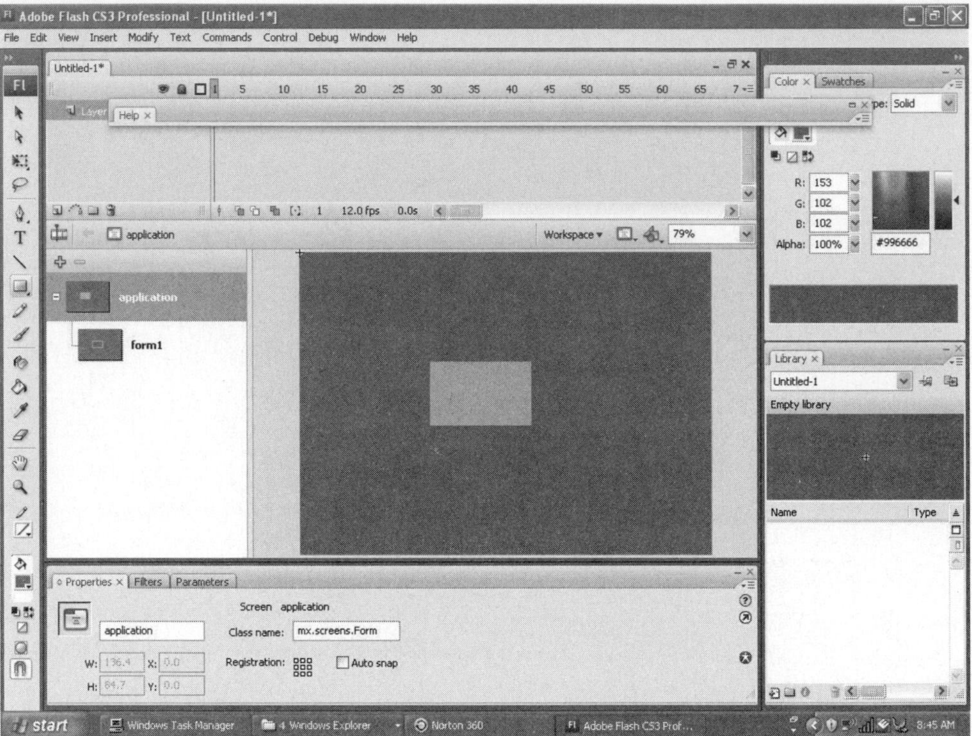

Using sound

As discussed earlier, you can import several types of sound files into Flash movies, including the Windows Wave (`.wav`) format, the Macintosh AIFF format, and QuickTime 7.5 format, as well as HE-AAC and Real Audio codecs. The MP3 format is supported by both platforms. Though AAC (MPEG-4 Audio) is smaller, as is WMA, and both have higher perceptive quality at lower bit rates, the MP3 format is still considered the standard compression format, and so is most often used in Flash movies.

Sound adds a great deal to Flash movies, as you experience from Web site introductions on the Web. Many Web sites use text and sound without graphics. Presumably, the combination of sound and text has a greater presence than text and graphics. The tradeoff in the form of a smaller file size caused by the absence of graphics probably influences the decision not to include them.

FIGURE 11-27

You can now play the completed movie with an interesting background.

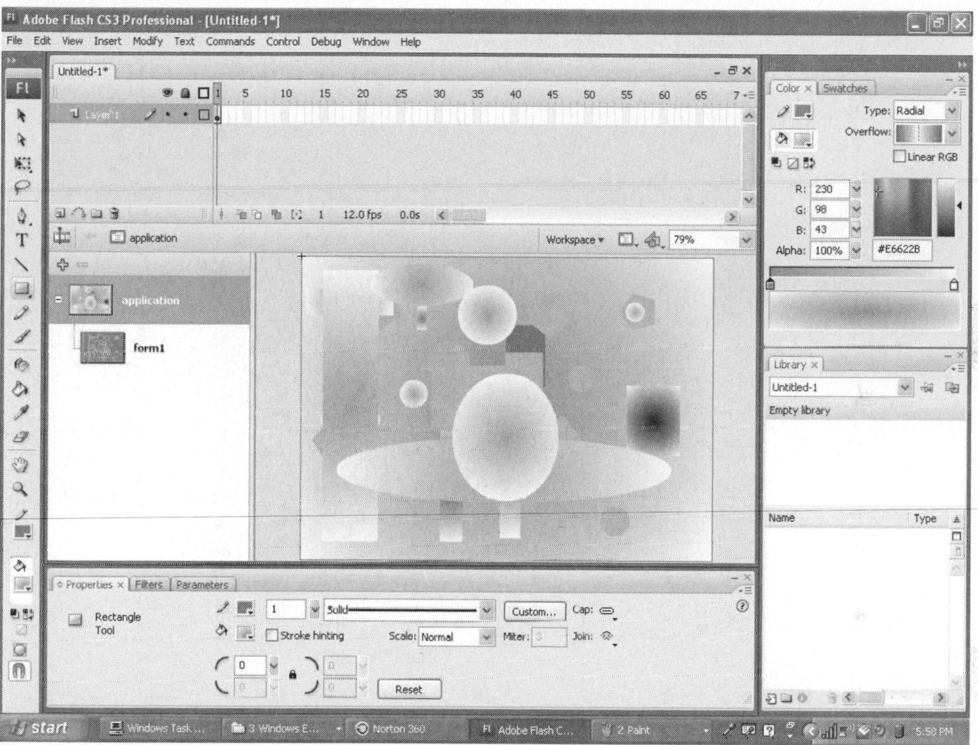

Importing sound files is as easy as selecting File → Import → Import to Library. Once imported, the sound files appear in the Library list. When selected, the wave forms of the sound files display in the Library window, as shown at the bottom of Figure 11-28.

To incorporate the sound in your movie, select the layer and keyframe with which you want the sound associated. Drag the sound file from the Library onto the Stage. The sound begins playing when the associated keyframe is displayed and continues playing until the sound is complete.

Adding MP3 sound

Because MP3 sound is a highly desirable format to use in Flash movies, you must have a way of converting other file formats to MP3. You will also be able to download sound files from the Web that are already in MP3 format. To find file downloads, you can simply perform a search for "sound files" to get a list of potential sites. When you are learning, the actual sound effect is not important because you are just practicing using it in Flash.

FIGURE 11-28

Wave forms are displayed in the Library window.

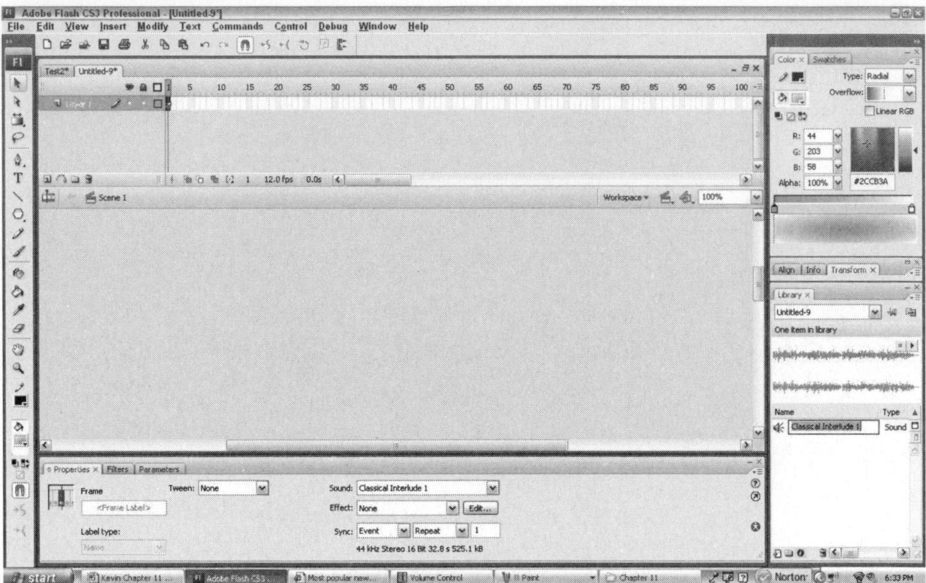

If you have a number of Windows `.wav` files, you can use a sound-conversion program to convert them to MP3. These programs are available in trial versions on the Web. They can also be purchased in any software store. There are many different sound editing and conversion programs. Most of them will do well, but be sure the product's documentation indicates that it converts your existing sound format into MP3.

Flash can compress MP3s.

Synchronizing sound and action

To synchronize sound with events, select Event from the Sync list box in the Property inspector. The list box also includes a Stream option that can save loading time on the Web. Instead of waiting for the entire sound file to download before playing the movie, you can *stream the sound*, meaning that the sound begins playing almost immediately while continuing to download the rest of the file. Streaming the sound causes Flash to synchronize the sound and animation. If you stream sound, you should not enter a value in the Sound Panel Loops list box, because this lengthens the movie beyond the frames you select.

FIGURE 11-29

You can recompress an MP3 file from the Sound Properties dialog box.

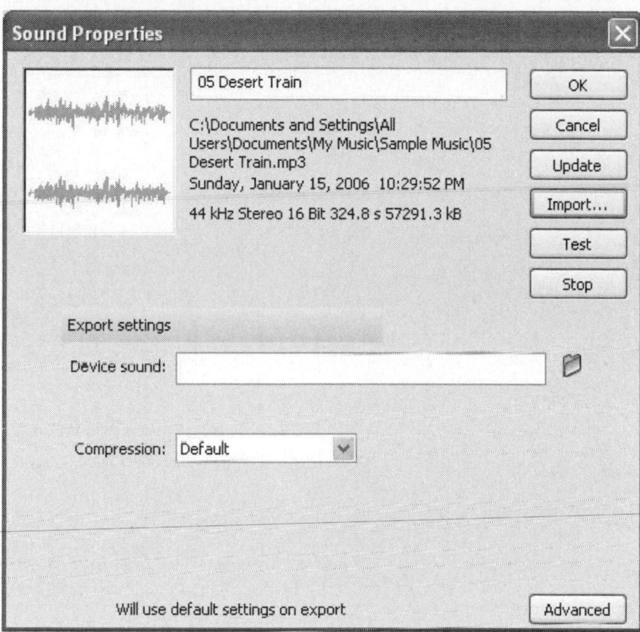

However, you must compress (or recompress) MP3 files before publishing your movie. One advantage of using a Wave file instead of an MP3 file is that the Wave file exports without recompression when the movie is published. To recompress the MP3 file, right-click the sound file in the Library panel and select Properties from the shortcut menu. In the Sound Properties Dialog box, select MP3 compression from the Compression list box, as shown in Figure 11-29, then click OK.

Using Advanced Techniques

Once you have tried and mastered the basic skills outlined in this chapter, you are ready to learn some more advanced techniques. It is not essential that you program in ActionScript (the built-in object-oriented programming language) in order to create great Flash movies. However, there are some projects that require these more advanced skills.

Programming with ActionScript

ActionScript is an object-oriented, scripting language similar to other object languages such as JavaScript and Visual Basic. You can build applications in Flash that interact with the user. Using ActionScript, you can create scripts that respond to a mouse click by displaying a Web site or playing a Flash movie. You can use this powerful tool in the Normal or Expert mode.

Adding actions

Using the Normal mode (Window → Development Panels → Actions) provides you with a selection of preset scripts. Clicking the right arrow in the upper right-hand corner of the Actions panel displays a list of options, including the Normal or Expert setting for your ActionScript task. You can choose from options on the Toolbox list, and Flash creates the ActionScript code for you. However, you can edit the code if you want. Using Expert mode, you are required to type code in the text box on the right side of the Action panel.

Basic actions provide a list of built-in actions, and when selected, generate the boilerplate code displayed in the text box. The basic actions for which Flash generates the code are shown in Table 11-8.

TABLE 11-8

Basic Actions in ActionScript Action Panel

Action	Description
Go To	Goes to a frame or scene.
Play	Plays a movie.
Stop	Stops a movie playing.
Toggle High Quality	Adjusts the quality of the movie.
Stop All Sounds	Stops all sounds playing.
Get URL	Displays a URL in a browser.
FSCommand	Controls Flash Player.
Load Movie	Loads and plays a movie from local drive or URL.
Unload Movie	Unloads a loaded movie.
Tell Target	Specify path and control movies.
If Frame Is Loaded	Specifies actions taken if a particular frame is loaded.
On Mouse Event	Identifies actions taken when specified mouse event occurs.

Once you have begun using ActionScript, you may find that you need to troubleshoot some errors in running the scripts. The script debugger can be launched from Window → Debugger. To debug a movie in Test Movie mode, you select Control → Debug Movie.

Exporting and Publishing Movies

Exporting is different from publishing. Exporting means that you convert your movie (or a frame from it) to a file format other than Flash. Exporting into some formats will not include the sound files in the exported movie. *Publishing* converts your Flash movie to the Flash Player format. In a sense, it is compiled. All files incorporated into your movie (such as bitmaps and sound) are combined into the Flash Player file.

Exporting movies

You can export your movies just as you imported images into them. Why would you want to export a movie? There are at least two reasons. First, you might want to export a still image from one of the movie's frames to use in an advertisement or a promotion. Second, you could export your movie to be played in a different player than Flash Player.

Flash exports both still image and animated formats. Images from your movies can be exported as bitmap and vector graphic files. Following are some of the specific formats Flash exports:

- *Bitmap graphic* — JPEG, GIF, PNG, BMP, PCD, PICT, PCX, or TIFF
- *Vector graphic* — AI, CDR, CMX, CGM, DXF, WMF, EPS, SVG, or SWF

When you export an image in your movie as an `.swf` file (which is the same format as the Flash movie file), the result is a still image of the first frame of the movie.

Mac users cannot use files exported from Windows in the Windows Metafile format. If you are a Mac user exporting to a Windows user, you can export in nearly any format because most image-editing programs (such as PhotoShop and PhotoPaint) can import the Mac PICT format.

Open the `Test2.fla` file that you saved previously. Select File → Export Image. In the Export Image dialog box, select JPEG Image (`*.jpg`) from the "Save as type" dialog box. Type **test** in the "File name" box and click the Save button. The `Test2.jpg` file will contain the frame displayed on the Stage at the time it was exported.

You can export movies in movie (animated) formats just as easily as you can export still images. There are some additional consequences you need to be aware of when you export movies. When you export a movie from Flash instead of publishing it as a Flash Player file, it is going to be because you expect your recipients to play it using software other than Flash.

Exporting in different formats yields different results. Export the file in two or three formats, and if you have more than one movie player, you can open it in each player and compare the results.

For example, most Windows users have Windows Media Player because it is distributed with Windows. Mac users are likely to have QuickTime because it is an Apple product.

NOTE **Many player programs for the Windows or Macintosh platform can be downloaded for free from the Internet. Windows Media Player is available at** `www.microsoft.com` **and is usually included with the operating system, QuickTime can be found at** `www.apple.com/quicktime`**, and RealPlayer has a free basic player at** `www.real.com`**.**

Among so many formats, how do you know which is best? The answer is that you select the best export format based on the player that will be used to play the movie. The Windows Media Player plays MPEG, MP3, MPEG-4, MPG, MP2, AVI, and WMV files. RealPlayer plays MPEG, MPG, MP2, MP3, and MPV formats. QuickTime plays MPEG, MP3, MPEG-4, MOV (QuickTime movies), and AVI formats, among others, including Flash!

To determine which file format to use in exporting a movie, it is best to experiment by exporting and playing the files to test them in the selected player on the platform you intend to use. The Flash Player format works well across the Windows and Macintosh platforms. If possible, it is best to publish (in the Flash Player format) rather than export the movie.

A further consideration in movie file exporting is the file size. Some files may be extremely large. For example, movies exported in the AVI format and also in Encapsulated PostScript (EPS) tend to be very large. A Flash movie that is less than 1MB when saved in the FLA format may be over 20MB when exported as an AVI file. Such a large file size will not work on the Web.

Select File → Export → Export Movie. In the Export Movie dialog box, select the Windows AVI under "Save as type." Name the file `Test2.avi`. Accept the defaults in the Export Windows AVI dialog box, and click OK to save.

Start QuickTime, Windows Media Player, or RealPlayer. Any of them should be able to play your exported movie. If you have old versions of these programs, you can download the current version of each player from the Internet at `www.microsoft.com`, `www.apple.com`, or `www.real.com`. Next, launch Windows Explorer or use the Macintosh Finder to locate the `Test2.avi` and the `Test2.fla` files to compare. The AVI file is probably over 2MB, while the Flash movie file can be well under 100KB. Clearly, you would want to be selective about the movies you export.

Publishing movies

When you publish your movie, all the images, sounds, and symbols that you added to the movie are compiled into the Flash Player file. A Flash Player movie (`.swf`) is the compiled version of the Flash authoring (`.fla`) file. There is no need to copy all of these files to your Web site. Flash

FIGURE 11-30

You can set the file formats in the Publish Settings window.

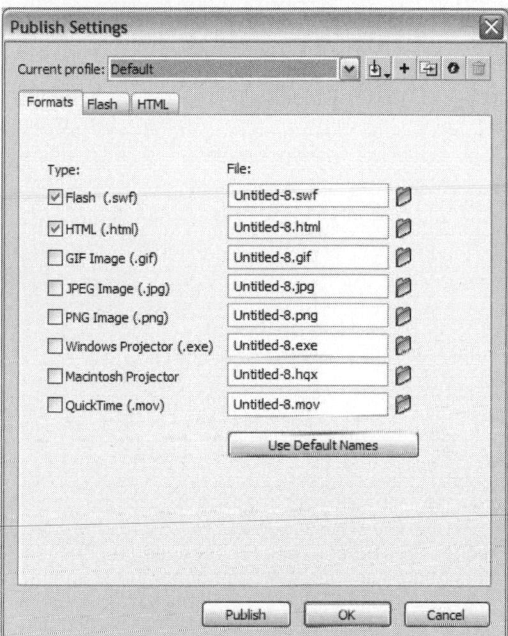

takes care of that when the movie is published. You can also select a number of different settings for your published movie.

Select File → Publish Settings to view the Publish Settings window. Select the Formats tab. The file types Flash (`.swf`) and HTML (`.html`), are selected by default, as shown in Figure 11-30. You also have the option to create other files during publishing. If you create a Windows Projector file, it can be executed by double-clicking the filename.

Select the Flash tab (see Figure 11-31). You can determine the load order (the order in which objects load from bottom up or from top down). You also can generate a size report to show the resources used by each element in the movie. You can protect your product from import online. You can choose to permit or not permit debugging. You can use the JPEG Quality slider bar to adjust the bitmap quality. If you are streaming audio, you can modify these settings. You also can publish in previous versions of Flash.

FIGURE 11-31

You can view the Flash tab in the Publish Settings window.

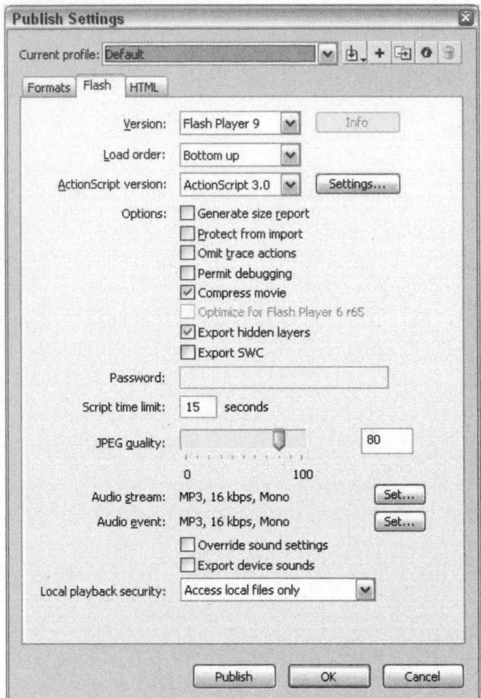

The HTML tab (see Figure 11-32) affects the HTML file (`Test2.html`) settings. You can determine the template to use, the movie dimensions, the Playback options, and whether Flash Player will display a menu. If you are playing the movie as part of a Web site, you probably won't want a menu showing at the top of the action. You can modify the settings and play back the movie in Flash Player to experiment with the different effects.

Click the Publish button, and then click OK. Locate your `Test2.swf` file on your system and double-click to play it in Flash Player. Does the movie play as it did when you selected Control → Play or Control → Test Movie?

If you use a Web Publishing application such as Adobe Dreamweaver, you can use it to publish your new Web page containing the Flash movie. Dreamweaver automatically creates the HTML

FIGURE 11-32

You can modify the HTML Publish Settings.

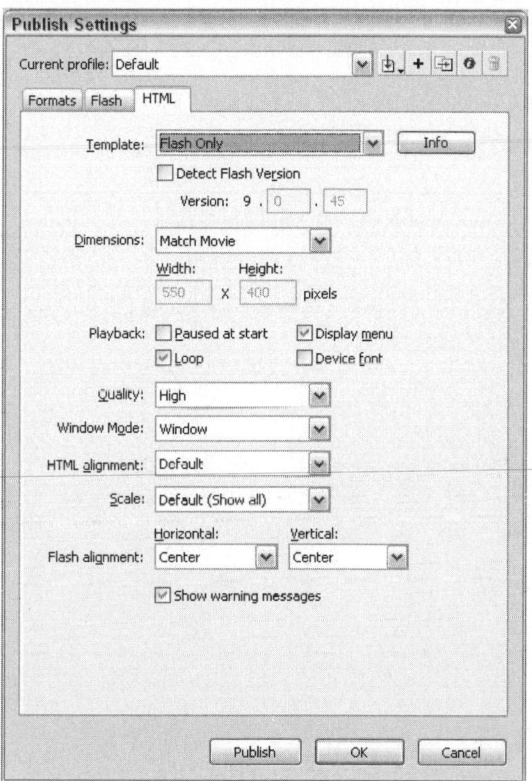

code for your Flash Player movie. You also can use any Word processor as an HTML editor, provided that it has an option to save the file in HTML format. The `Test2.html` file generated by Flash can be used just as it is by adding the page to an existing Web site.

NOTE **If you have FTP access, you can upload the `.swf` file directly to the Web site. Usually you have FTP access if you have your own domain name. FTP (File Transfer Protocol) provides access to file uploading and downloading.**

FIGURE 11-33

You can view the Test2.html file in Notepad.

```
Test2 - Notepad
File Edit Format View Help
                AC_FL_RunContent(
                        'codebase', 'http://download.macromedia.com/pub/shockwave/cabs/flash
                        'width', '550',
                        'height', '400',
                        'src', 'Test2',
                        'quality', 'high',
                        'pluginspage', 'http://www.macromedia.com/go/getflashplayer',
                        'align', 'middle',
                        'play', 'true',
                        'loop', 'true',
                        'scale', 'showall',
                        'wmode', 'window',
                        'devicefont', 'false',
                        'id', 'Test2',
                        'bgcolor', '#ff0000',
                        'name', 'Test2',
                        'menu', 'true',
                        'allowFullScreen', 'false',
                        'allowScriptAccess','sameDomain',
                        'movie', 'Test2',
                        'salign', ''
                        ); //end AC code
        }
</script>
<noscript>
        <object classid="clsid:d27cdb6e-ae6d-11cf-96b8-444553540000" codebase="http://downlo
        <param name="allowScriptAccess" value="sameDomain" />
        <param name="allowFullScreen" value="false" />
        <param name="movie" value="Test2.swf" /><param name="quality" value="high" /><param
        </object>
</noscript>
</body>
</html>
```

When you publish your movie, the `Test2.swf` file is created by default as an HTML file (`Test2.html`) that handles the HTML code on your Web page. The HTML code is generated for you to copy and paste into the Web page where you want the movie to play (see Figure 11-33). The HTML code can be tailored to specific needs according to the settings you select.

When you use Windows Notepad or any text editor to view the `Test2.html` file generated by Flash, you will see that an entire Web page has been generated for you. If you already have a Web page, edit it by selecting the lines that are placed between the HTML `BODY` tags. Select the lines between the HTML tags, `<BODY>` and `</BODY>`. Copy these tags and paste them into the HTML code on your Web page as shown. Be sure to paste the code within the `BODY` element.

Tips for optimizing your movies

There are several things to keep in mind when designing your movies in order to make them run better:

- Convert all reusable objects to symbols.
- Tween animations.
- Don't animate bitmaps.
- Don't embed large font files.
- Use small sound files, get looped music from sites such as `Flashkit.com`.
- Use small bitmaps.
- Use vector (WMF) instead of bitmap (GIF, JPG, and so forth) graphics.

Some of these options can be managed by the File → Publish options, and some by what you import into the movie. Using the previous suggestions, you can make any necessary modifications to reduce the download time and system requirements. Also, when you design and create new movies, you can keep the memory and connection speed factors in mind.

Summary

Multimedia — basically, the addition of audio and video to your Web pages — is the secret of lots of the glitz and splash of Web sites. Adobe Flash is the program of choice for most Web designers when it comes to creating Web animations.

In this chapter, you learned that sound can be added to your Web page as an optional feature — just a link like any other link. The `EMBED` element can be used to add sound to any Web page regardless of which Web browser is used to access it. The volume you set for a Web page is a percentage of the normal volume your visitors have set for their own speakers. Professional musicians are waiting to provide you with the small amounts of music you need at worthwhile prices. Alternatively, prewritten music may suit your needs.

You also learned that video can be added in almost the same manner as audio.

Flash movies are made up of scenes. Each scene contains a Stage, Layers, and Timelines. Objects can either be created within Flash or imported into it. Animation is created by assigning events to keyframes.

Chapter 12 introduces you to the features and functions of Cascading Style Sheets.

Chapter 12

Styling Web Pages with Cascading Style Sheets

Cascading style sheets (CSS) have the potential to provide Web page designers with a fabulous degree of control over the appearance and functionality of their sites. Using CSS, you can specify the styles used in HTML pages for a whole Web site, per page, or for each tag. This allows the designer to separate the content from the presentation — a good idea when it comes to making changes in a 1,000-page Web site.

NOTE **All of the formatting instructions in HTML have been deprecated in favor of their CSS equivalents.**

Using CSS, you can reduce the size of your HTML files, which in turn reduces the download time, improving user satisfaction because the page downloads faster. It also reduces the disk space used on both server and client machines, and lessens the load on the server and network. All of this means that your Web site can support more users.

What if you don't use CSS? Several well-known office applications create HTML files that don't use CSS. However, the same files with CSS can be reduced by half or more of their original size, and so will download two to three times faster (but the images won't). However, there are drawbacks.

First, the CSS specifications are large and complex. Second, the browser doesn't give any error messages if there are errors in the stylesheet. And third, while all modern browsers support CSS, there are sometimes minor formatting differences, which may, on occasion, cause unexpected results.

This chapter provides a general overview of how CSS works within a Web page and across a Web site. This chapter also discusses the uses of the `<div>` and `<span>` tags in relation to formatting Web page segments.

IN THIS CHAPTER

- Testing your browser
- Coping with browser support issues
- Cascading priorities
- Redefining HTML elements
- Assigning classes
- Using IDs
- Defining nested elements with contextual selectors
- Consulting the CSS reference
- Using stylesheet-creation programs
- Interesting CSS sites
- Adding layers
- Clipping layer content
- Handling large elements with overflow attributes

Subsequent chapters explore specific implementations of these principles and how you can exploit them to your best advantage.

Testing Your Browser

The World Wide Web Consortium (W3C) has an online test suite through which you can see how well the browser you're using handles selected CSS properties. The test suite is located at `www.w3.org/Style/CSS/Test`.

There are three different CSS specifications, CSS1, CSS2, and CSS2 revision 1, all of which are simultaneously in effect. CSS1 was issued way back in the dim mists of Web history (1996) and CSS2 came out in 1998. CSS1 was then revised in 1999. That's right — not CSS2, but CSS1, the year after CSS2 came out. And work is underway on CSS3. It's enough to make you wish you were back in the days when people used sticks to scratch messages on clay tablets. But this is the crazy world that Web designers have to cope with today. Following are the locations of the official Web sites for the three CSS specifications:

- CSS1: `www.w3.org/TR/REC-CSS1`
- CSS2: `www.w3.org/TR/REC-CSS2`
- CSS2: revision 1 `www.w3.org/TR/2004/CR-CSS21-20040225`

NOTE **CSS3 is the latest spec in the works. For more information on CSS, go to** `www.w3.org/Style/CSS/current-work`.

Coping with Browser Support Issues

New browser versions (both major and minor) come out at such odd and unpredictable intervals that it is impossible for any book to keep fully up to date with them. Although we will document the current state of browser support for the CSS properties covered in this chapter, you need to be aware that this could all change at any time. Tomorrow, Microsoft, Apple, and Opera, all could fully implement every feature of CSS1 or CSS2 (or the nascent CSS3), and the developers could implement a crash program to have the new browser finished in a month. It's just as possible that they might ignore CSS2 entirely and go straight into adding support for CSS3, as tentative as that proposal is right now. Or, perhaps some of them will ignore the CSS support problem entirely and even introduce bugs in their latest versions that invalidate earlier CSS functionality. Stranger things have been known to happen.

So, how do you, as a conscientious Web designer, know what's going on now? The answer, as you've probably guessed, is on the Web itself. There are several Web sites that keep track of browser version issues, including the state of their CSS support. Table 12-1 lists some sites where you can get the latest news.

TABLE 12-1

CSS Support Information Sites

Web Site	Address
QuirksMode	www.quirksmode.org/home.html
The Developer Archive	www.dev-archive.net
Index DOT Css	www.blooberry.com/indexdot/css
HTML Dog	www.htmldog.com/guides/cssadvanced
RichInStyle.com	www.richinstyle.com/bugs
Alsacreations	Tutorials.alsacreations.com

Cascading Priorities

Cascading Style Sheets are called that for a good, solid reason. There are four different levels at which styles can be applied. An element can have its own style using the `style` attribute, a Web page can have a global style that is controlled by an embedded stylesheet created with the `STYLE` element, the styles on the same page can also be controlled by an external stylesheet that is linked to that page, and the user can specify his or her own stylesheet in the browser. With four different ways of styling the same element, the possibilities for conflict are practically endless.

So, how could the designers of CSS manage to leave as much flexibility as possible for Web designers, yet still manage to handle the inevitable conflicts? The solution for this was to establish a set of priorities. The lowest-level style setting — an individual element's `style` attribute — has the highest priority, and it will override any conflicting setting in both the `STYLE` element in its containing Web page and any linked stylesheet. The `STYLE` element in a Web page similarly overrides any conflict created by an external stylesheet that it's linked to. The external stylesheet has the lowest priority of all, and any time it creates a conflict, it loses out. This prioritization system is seen as a sort of multilevel waterfall effect, and thus the term *cascading* came into use to describe it.

Going inline with the style attribute

The simplest way to set the style for an individual element is via its `style` attribute. For example, if you wanted to make a particular `H1` element turn magenta instead of its default black, you could use the following code:

```
<H1 style="color: magenta">Everything in this heading is
 magenta-colored.</H1>
```

NOTE **Look at the syntax involved in an inline style statement:** `style="property:value; property:value;"`**. Notice that property value pairs use colons to relate to each other, and that each** `property:value` **pair is separated by a semicolon. In HTML, the relationship is established by the equals sign (=), and quotation marks around the property value are frequently optional (depending on browser version, naturally). The semicolon is optional if only one** `Style` **element is used.**

This example sets the CSS `color` property to a value of `magenta`. If you want to set more than one CSS property, simply separate them with a semicolon (this is known as *grouping* the properties). The following example expands on the earlier one by also changing the `H1` element so that it also uses a Helvetica or Arial font:

```
<H1 style="font-family: Helivetica, Arial, sans-serif; color:
 magenta">Everything
 in this heading is magenta-colored and uses a Helvetica
 font.</H1>
```

Embedding with the <style> tag

Setting a CSS property for one element is child's play compared with the kind of power that CSS was meant to supply. After all, there are already native capabilities in plain old HTML that enable you to do many of the things that CSS can do — for each individual element, that is. Creating an *embedded* stylesheet (one that controls the whole Web page), however, gives you quite a bit more power.

The `<style>` tag enables you to establish a broader impact. For example, you could set the CSS properties for *every* `H1` element at once, instead of having to set each one, one at a time. You can save yourself an awful lot of work by just making one global setting like this:

```
<HEAD>
<STYLE>
H1 { color: magenta }
</STYLE>
</HEAD>
```

NOTE **The** `<STYLE>` **tag has to go within the** `HEAD` **section of the HTML document.**

The syntax is very similar to that used in the `style` attribute, but there is a slightly different approach, and you have to be careful to get it just right. Between the `<STYLE>` and `</STYLE>` tags, the name of the element to be styled comes first (`H1`, in this case). In CSS, it is called the *selector*. Next comes the opening curly bracket ({), then the name of the CSS property (`color`, in this case). The property name is separated from the value of the property (`magenta`, here) by a colon (`:`). Finally, you must close the style declaration with a closing curly bracket (}). Leave out any one of those items and the whole thing won't work.

CAUTION ***Never*** **treat the selector as a tag instead of an element. In other words, you cannot put angle brackets** `<>` **around a selector. If you used** `<H1>` **instead of plain** `H1` **as the selector, no Web browser in the world would forgive the mistake.**

You can set multiple global CSS properties simultaneously, just as you can with the `style` attribute for individual elements. With the `<STYLE>` tag, however, it's customary to put each property on a separate line. This is not a requirement, but it does make it a lot easier to read and understand the HTML code.

```
<HEAD>
<STYLE>
H1 {
font-family: helvetica;
color: magenta
}
</STYLE>
</HEAD>
```

Linking external stylesheets

External stylesheets follow the same syntax as an embedded stylesheet, with one exception. There is no `<STYLE>` tag involved because an external stylesheet simply isn't a Web page, so it doesn't use any HTML. Instead, it's a CSS file, and it ends in a `.css` extension. The function of a CSS file is to provide information on how the various elements on a Web page should be styled. A portion of an external stylesheet might look like this:

```
H1 {
font-size: 1in;
margin-left: .5in
}

H2 {
font-size: .75in;
margin-left: .5in
}

H3 {
font-size: .5in;
margin-left: .5in
}
```

This segment specifies the size of `H1` elements as 1 inch high, `H2` elements as ¾ of an inch high, and `H3` elements as ½ inch high; it also sets all of them ½ inch away from the left border of the Web page.

If the CSS file that held these declarations were called site `_xt_sheet.css`, it would be attached to a Web page by the following code:

```
<HEAD>
<LINK rel="stylesheet" href="site_x_sheet.css" type="text/css">
</HEAD>
```

Just like the `<style>` tag, the `<link>` tag has to go into the `<HEAD>` section of an HTML document (that is, the Web page).

The best and highest use of stylesheets comes when the look of an entire Web site is established and controlled by a single external stylesheet. We once had a site with hundreds of pages and got tired of the look after a while, so we began to experiment a bit. We finally settled on a new appearance that we liked better and, in those days before stylesheets, we had to recode each one of the affected elements on every single page by hand. If we had been able to use a single stylesheet linked to each Web page in the entire site, all we would have had to do would be to make a few changes in that one CSS file, and the look of hundreds of Web pages would have changed instantly.

You can also link more than one CSS file to a single Web page, just by stacking `<link>` tags like this:

```
<HEAD>
<LINK rel="stylesheet" href="site_a_sheet.css">
<LINK rel="stylesheet" href="site_b_sheet.css">
<LINK rel="stylesheet" href="site_c_sheet.css">
<LINK rel="stylesheet" href="site_d_sheet.css">
</HEAD>
```

This is simple to do, although it does have the potential to tremendously complicate things. It's not a problem for a Web browser because the rules for cascading in this case are about as easy as they can get — whichever stylesheet is linked first has priority over any that come after it. The problem is that, if you have many conflicting declarations in the multiple CSS files, you may not be able to figure out what the results will be until you see them on screen. And they may not at all be what you had in mind.

You can also import a stylesheet, as shown here:

```
@import url(style.css);
body { background-image: url(sky.png);}
```

In this case, the imported stylesheet has less priority than the stylesheet that includes it.

Redefining HTML Elements

The most potent way to use CSS is to redefine how an HTML element works — not an individual instance of that element, but all occurrences of it throughout an entire web site. You can, for example, make all `P` elements have purple text. We're not sure why you'd want to, but you can do it. Or, you could make every `H3` centered. Or, you could make all images invisible. CSS gives you the power, but, like all power, it's open to either constructive use or unfettered abuse.

Note, however, that the most common uses for CSS are setting the fonts and link colors on a page.

You may want to assign a Helvetica-style font to all your heading elements, for example. Most Web designers have done this for eons, but they had to deal with it on an individual basis, heading by heading. This is a clearly constructive use of the power of CSS. Deliberately setting all P elements a certain distance from the edges of the screen would be another good example of constructive use.

You could, however, just as easily make all the tables on your pages use dingbat fonts — deliberately or otherwise. Take care when using redefinition of elements to ensure that you are, indeed, getting the exact effect you want, because doing so causes a sweeping and possibly overpowering change all across every page that's affected by the style.

With these cautions in mind, here's an example of how element redefinition works in CSS:

```
<HTML>
<HEAD>
<STYLE>
P {color: purple}
</STYLE>
</HEAD>
<BODY>
<H1>This text is black.</H1>
<P>This text is purple.</P>
</BODY>
</HTML>
```

Assigning Classes

Classes are a wonderful balancing act between the unfettered power of element selectors and the old style of doing things in plain HTML. They avoid the sweeping changes dictated by redefining entire tags, and enable you to limit the impact of a CSS property declaration to specified elements on your Web page.

To assign a class and apply it to different elements on your Web pages, two things are necessary: the declaration of the class in the STYLE section in the HEAD of the Web page (or in an external stylesheet) and the addition of a class attribute to the elements you want to alter. The following example code shows how it's done:

```
<HTML>
   <HEAD>
   <STYLE>
   .helv16 {font-family: Arial, Helvetica, sans-serif; font-size:
    16px}
   .mustardcolor {color: #FFCC00}
   </STYLE>
   </HEAD>
```

```
<BODY>
<p class="helv16">This is an example of class 1.</p>
<p class="mustardcolor">This is an example of class 2.</p>
</BODY>
</HTML>
```

NOTE **The class declaration must be preceded by a period (.), but the period is not used in setting the `class` attribute.**

The first class declaration (`helv16`) sets the font to a Helvetica font, 16 pixels in height. The second class declaration (`mustardcolor`) sets the font to a mustard yellow color, but affects it in no other way.

Using IDs

While ID selectors aren't as useful or powerful, generally speaking, as redefining an HTML element or assigning a class, they do have a place. At first glance, this seems a pretty limited capability, however. Why? Because an ID selector is usable only with a particular, individual element — not all instances of an element, but an individual use of it. For example, the following code creates an ID selector and then applies it by assigning an `id` attribute to one item on the Web page:

```
<HTML>
<HEAD>
<STYLE>
#truegreen {color: #00FF00}
</STYLE>
</HEAD>
<BODY>
<p id="truegreen">This is an example of id assignment.</p>
</BODY>
</HTML>
```

NOTE **The ID declaration must be preceded by a hash mark (#), but the hash mark is not used in setting the `id` attribute.**

No other item on the entire page can have the same `id` value, which means that all the power of CSS is brought to bear upon one little spot on the Web page. There are times when it can be a handy tool. For example, if you have a header, footer, or menu and you want to specify how they should be formatted on every page, it's a good idea to give each an `id` and then use an external stylesheet to change their appearances.

Defining Nested Elements with Contextual Selectors

If one element is nested inside another, and the parent element has a CSS property set, then, in most cases, the child element automatically has the same setting, even if it is not specified in the child element. This phenomenon is known as *inheritance*. To illustrate how it works, consider the following example:

```
<HTML>
<HEAD>
<STYLE>
H1 {color="red" }
</STYLE>
</HEAD>
<BODY>
<H1>All Heading 1 elements <I>must</I> be red in color.</H1>
</BODY>
</HTML>
```

The I element, as well as the H1 element, will be red in color. However, there are many times when you may want to override inheritance and have, instead, a specific CSS property show up. In those cases, *contextual selectors* are the key. A contextual selector is one that specifies that one element, when contained within another, is to be shown in a certain manner. For example, you may want all italicized items within Heading 1 elements to be shown in a blue color. The following code would accomplish this handily, overriding the inheritance factor:

```
<HTML>
<HEAD>
<STYLE>
H1 {color="red" }
H1 I {color="blue" }
</STYLE>
</HEAD>
<BODY>
<H1>All Heading 1 elements <I>must</I> be red in color.</H1>
</BODY>
</HTML>
```

Cool effects with CSS

Many people use JavaScript to make menus, but few people realize that you can do the same thing with CSS. For example, the following code creates a menu that has images of stars instead of dots, and, as the user hovers over each link, it changes color and the text grows larger (Figure 12-1).

FIGURE 12-1

Menus can be built with CSS.

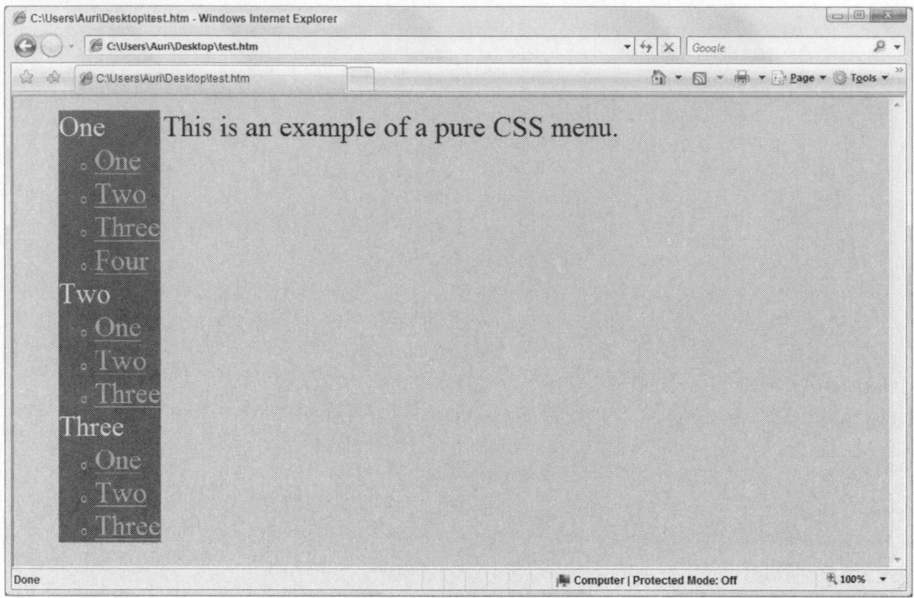


```
<html>
<head>
  <link rel="stylesheet" href="hoverMenu.css" type="text/css" />
</head>
<body>
<ul id="menu">
  <li>One
        <ul>
        <li><a href="">One</a></li>
        <li><a href="">Two</a></li>
        <li><a href="">Three</a></li>
        <li><a href="">Four</a></li>
        </ul>
  </li>
  <li>Two
        <ul>
        <li><a href="">One</a></li>
        <li><a href="">Two</a></li>
        <li><a href="">Three</a></li>
        </ul>
  </li>
```

```
    <li>Three
        <ul>
        <li><a href="">One</a></li>
        <li><a href="">Two</a></li>
        <li><a href="">Three</a></li>
        </ul>
    </li>
</ul>
This is an example of a pure CSS menu.
</body>
</html>
```

Following is the file hoverMenu.css:

```
body { background-color: lightblue;font-size: x-large; }
/* The background is lightblue with extra large fonts. */

#menu { background-color:blue;float:left; }
/* The menu has a blue background and is floated to the left
hand side. */

#menu li { list-style-image: url(ylwstar.gif); font-size: x-large;
color:yellow; }
/* The list items in the menu have a star as the image and are in a
large yellow font. */

#menu li a { color:lime; } /* the links are lime colored */

#menu li a:hover { color:red; background-color: white; font-size:
larger; }
/* When the user hovers over a link it changes to red, the
background to white, and the font grows larger. */
```

Just by changing the CSS stylesheet (as shown in the following code), we can hide each submenu initially and then have it appear as the user hovers over the menu items (see Figure 12-2).

FIGURE 12-2

Submenus are hidden with a slight change in the stylesheet.

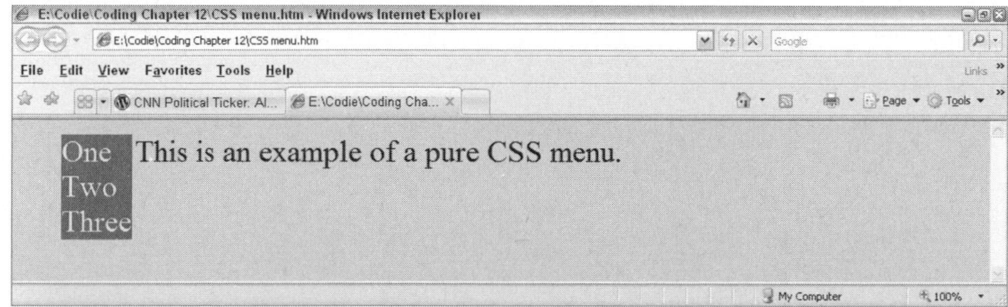

```
body { background-color: lightblue;font-size: x-large; }
/* The background is lightblue with extra large fonts. */
#menu { background-color:blue;float:left; }
/* The menu has a blue background and is floated to the
left-hand side. */
#menu li { font-size: x-large; color: yellow; }
/* The list items in the menu are in a large yellow font. */

#menu li:hover { color:red; }
/* List items change to red when the mouse passes over.*/

#menu li a { color:lime; }
/* The links are lime colored. */

#menu li a:hover { color:red; background-color: white; }
/* The links change to red with a white background when the mouse
passes over. */

#menu li ul {display:none;position:absolute;background-color:blue; }
/* Submenus are not displayed initially, absolutely positioned, and
have a blue background. */

#menu li:hover ul { display:block; }
/* When the mouse passes over a list item its submenu is
displayed. */
```

Consulting the CSS Reference

The CSS1 specification is the most widely supported one among the major Web browsers. However, many CSS2 properties (such as absolute positioning) are also important.

CSS1 properties

We have compiled the information in this section from contents in the W3C's CSS1 specification, originally dated December 17, 1996, and revised January 11, 1999. This specification carries the status of a W3C recommendation. The URL of the specification is `www.w3.org/TR/REC-CSS1`. Although the specification carries no specific copyright notice, we assume that the usual requirement of adding the following notice to information taken from W3C documents still applies:

The properties in the following listing are specified by name (in alphabetical order) followed by this information:

- *Value* — Shows all possible values that can be used with this property.
- *Initial value* — Shows the default value if none is specified.
- *Applies to* — Shows the elements the property can be applied to.
- *Inherited* — Shows if the property can be inherited.
- *Percentage values* — Shows how percentages are handled.

Following is a breakdown of CSS1 properties.

background

- *Value* — `<background-color> || <background-image> || <background-repeat> || <background-attachment> || <background-position>`
- *Initial value* — Not defined for shorthand properties
- *Applies to* — All elements
- *Inherited* — No
- *Percentage values* — Allowed on `<background-position>`

background-attachment

- *Value* — `scroll | fixed`
- *Initial value* — `scroll`
- *Applies to* — All elements
- *Inherited* — No
- *Percentage values* — N/A

background-color

- *Value* — `<color> | transparent`
- *Initial value* — `transparent`
- *Applies to* — All elements
- *Inherited* — No
- *Percentage values* — N/A

background-image

- *Value* — <url> | none
- *Initial value* — None
- *Applies to* — All elements
- *Inherited* — No
- *Percentage values* — N/A

background-position

- *Value* — [<percentage> | <length>]{1,2} | [top | center | bottom] || [left | center | right]
- *Initial value* — 0% 0%
- *Applies to* — Block-level and replaced elements
- *Inherited* — No
- *Percentage values* — Refer to the size of the element itself

background-repeat

- *Value* — repeat | repeat-x | repeat-y | no-repeat
- *Initial value* — repeat
- *Applies to* — All elements
- *Inherited* — No
- *Percentage values* — N/A

border

- *Value* — <border-width> || <border-style> || <color>
- *Initial value* — Not defined for shorthand properties
- *Applies to* — All elements
- *Inherited* — No
- *Percentage values* — N/A

border-color

- *Value* — <color>{1,4}
- *Initial value* — The value of the color property
- *Applies to* — All elements
- *Inherited* — No
- *Percentage values* — N/A

border-style

- *Value* — `None | dotted | dashed | solid | double | groove | ridge | inset | outset`
- *Initial value* — `None`
- *Applies to* — All elements
- *Inherited* — No
- *Percentage values* — N/A

border-top, border-right, border-bottom, border-left

- *Value* — `<border-top-width> || <border-style> || <color>`
- *Initial value* — Not defined for shorthand properties
- *Applies to* — All elements
- *Inherited* — No
- *Percentage values* — N/A

border-width

- *Value* — `[thin | medium | thick | <length>]{1,4}`
- *Initial value* — Not defined for shorthand properties
- *Applies to* — All elements
- *Inherited* — No
- *Percentage values* — N/A

border-top-width, border-right-width, border-bottom-width, border-left-width

- *Value* — `thin | medium | thick | <length>`
- *Initial value* — `medium`
- *Applies to* — All elements
- *Inherited* — No
- *Percentage values* — N/A

clear

- *Value* — `none | left | right | both`
- *Initial* — `None`
- *Applies to* — All elements

- *Inherited* — No
- *Percentage values* — N/A

color

- *Value* — `<color>`
- *Initial value* — UA specific
- *Applies to* — All elements
- *Inherited* — Yes
- *Percentage values* — N/A

display

- *Value* — `block | inline | list-item | none`
- *Initial value* — `block`
- *Applies to* — All elements
- *Inherited* — No
- *Percentage values* — N/A

float

- *Value* — `left | right | none`
- *Initial value* — `None`
- *Applies to* — All elements
- *Inherited* — No
- *Percentage values* — N/A

font

- *Value* — `[ <font-style> || <font-variant> || <font-weight> ]? <font-size> [ / <line-height> ]? <font-family>`
- *Initial value* — Not defined for shorthand properties
- *Applies to* — All elements
- *Inherited* — Yes
- *Percentage values* — Allowed on `<font-size>` and `<line-height>`

font-family

- *Value* — `[[ <family-name> | <generic-family> ],]* [ <family-name> | <generic-family> ]`
- *Initial value* — Depends on user agent

- *Applies to* — All elements
- *Inherited* — Yes
- *Percentage values* — N/A

font-size

- *Value* — `<absolute-size> | <relative-size> | <length> | <percentage>`
- *Initial value* — `medium`
- *Applies to* — All elements
- *Inherited* — Yes
- *Percentage values* — Relative to parent element's font size

font-style

- *Value* — `normal | italic | oblique`
- *Initial value* — `normal`
- *Applies to* — All elements
- *Inherited* — Yes
- *Percentage values* — N/A

font-variant

- *Value* — `normal | small-caps`
- *Initial value* — `normal`
- *Applies to* — All elements
- *Inherited* — Yes
- *Percentage values* — N/A

font-weight

- *Value* — `normal | bold | bolder | lighter | 100 | 200 | 300 | 400 | 500 | 600 | 700 | 800 | 900`
- *Initial value* — `normal`
- *Applies to* — All elements
- *Inherited* — Yes
- *Percentage values* — N/A

height

- *Value* — `<length> | auto`
- *Initial value* — `auto`

- *Applies to* — Block-level and replaced elements
- *Inherited* — No
- *Percentage values* — N/A

letter-spacing

- *Value* — `normal | <length>`
- *Initial value* — `normal`
- *Applies to* — All elements
- *Inherited* — Yes
- *Percentage values* — N/A

line-height

- *Value* — `normal | <number> | <length> | <percentage>`
- *Initial value* — `Normal`
- *Applies to* — All elements
- *Inherited* — Yes
- *Percentage values* — Relative to the font size of the element itself

list-style

- *Value* — `[disc | circle | square | decimal | lower-roman | upper-roman | lower-alpha | upper-alpha | none] || [inside | outside] || [<url> | none]`
- *Initial value* — Not defined for shorthand properties
- *Applies to* — Elements with `display` value `list-item`
- *Inherited* — Yes
- *Percentage values* — N/A

list-style-image

- *Value* — `<url> | none`
- *Initial value* — `none`
- *Applies to* — Elements with `display` value `list-item`
- *Inherited* — Yes
- *Percentage values* — N/A

list-style-position

- *Value* — `inside | outside`
- *Initial value* — `outside`
- *Applies to* — Elements with `display` value `list-item`
- *Inherited* — Yes
- *Percentage values* — N/A

list-style-type

- *Value* — `disc | circle | square | decimal | lower-roman | upper-roman | lower-alpha | upper-alpha | none`
- *Initial value* — `disc`
- *Applies to* — Elements with `display` value `list-item`
- *Inherited* — Yes
- *Percentage values* — N/A

margin

- *Value* — `[ <length> | <percentage> | auto ] {1,4}`
- *Initial value* — Not defined for shorthand properties
- *Applies to* — All elements
- *Inherited* — No
- *Percentage values* — Refer to width of closest block-level ancestor

margin-top, margin-right, margin-bottom, margin-left

- *Value* — `<length> | <percentage> | auto`
- *Initial value* — `0`
- *Applies to* — All elements
- *Inherited* — No
- *Percentage values* — Refer to width of the closest block-level ancestor

padding

- *Value* — `[ <length> | <percentage> ] {1,4}`
- *Initial value* — Not defined for shorthand properties

- *Applies to* — All elements
- *Inherited* — No
- *Percentage values* — Refer to width of closest block-level ancestor

padding-top, padding-right, padding-bottom, padding-left

- *Value* — `<length> | <percentage>`
- *Initial value* — `0`
- *Applies to* — All elements
- *Inherited* — No
- *Percentage values* — Refer to width of closest block-level ancestor

text-align

- *Value* — `left | right | center | justify`
- *Initial value* — UA specific
- *Applies to* — Block-level elements
- *Inherited value* — Yes
- *Percentage values* — N/A

text-decoration

- *Value* — `none | [ underline || overline || line-through || blink ]`
- *Initial value* — `none`
- *Applies to* — All elements
- *Inherited* — No, but elements should match their parent
- *Percentage values* — N/A

text-indent

- *Value* — `<length> | <percentage>`
- *Initial value* — `0`
- *Applies to* — Block-level elements
- *Inherited* — Yes
- *Percentage values* — Refer to parent element's width

text-transform

- *Value* — `capitalize | uppercase | lowercase | none`
- *Initial value* — `none`

- *Applies to* — All elements
- *Inherited* — Yes
- *Percentage values* — N/A

vertical-align

- *Value* — `baseline | sub | super | top | text-top | middle | bottom | text-bottom | <percentage>`
- *Initial value* — `baseline`
- *Applies to* — Inline elements
- *Inherited* — No
- *Percentage values* — Refer to the `line-height` of the element itself

white-space

- *Value* — `normal | pre | nowrap`
- *Initial value* — `normal`
- *Applies to* — Block-level elements
- *Inherited* — Yes
- *Percentage values* — N/A

width

- *Value* — `<length> | <percentage> | auto`
- *Initial value* — `auto`
- *Applies to* — Block-level and replaced elements
- *Inherited* — No
- *Percentage values* — Refer to parent element's width

word-spacing

- *Value* — `normal | <length>`
- *Initial value* — `normal`
- *Applies to* — All elements
- *Inherited* — Yes
- *Percentage values* — N/A

CSS2 properties

This section contains the official list of all CSS properties from the World Wide Web Consortium's CSS2 specification, which carries the status of a W3C Recommendation. The URL of the specification is www.w3.org/TR/REC-CSS2. Although the specification carries no specific copyright notice, we assume that the usual requirement of adding the following notice to information taken from W3C documents still applies:

The properties in the following listing are specified by name (in alphabetical order), and then the following information is presented:

- *Values* — Shows all possible values that can be used with this property.
- *Initial value* — Shows the default value if none is specified.
- *Applies to* — Shows the elements the property can be applied to.
- *Inherited* — Shows if the property can be inherited.
- *Percentages* — Shows how percentages are handled.
- *Media groups* — Shows which media group (visual, aural, print, and so on) the property is intended for.

Following is a breakdown of CSS2 properties.

azimuth

- *Values* — <angle> | [[left-side | far-left | left | center-left | center | center-right | right | far-right | right-side] || behind] | leftwards | rightwards | inherit
- *Initial value* — center
- *Applies to* — All
- *Inherited* — Yes
- *Percentages* — N/A
- *Media groups* — Aural

background

- *Values* – ['background-color' || 'background-image' || 'background-repeat' || 'background-attachment' || 'background-position'] | inherit
- *Initial value* — Not defined for shorthand properties
- *Applies to* — All
- *Inherited* — No
- *Percentages* — Allowed on background-position
- *Media groups* — Visual

background-attachment

- *Values* — `scroll | fixed | inherit`
- *Initial value* — `scroll`
- *Applies to* — All
- *Inherited* — No
- *Percentages* — N/A
- *Media groups* — Visual

background-color

- *Values* — `<color> | transparent | inherit`
- *Initial value* — `transparent`
- *Applies to* — All
- *Inherited* — No
- *Percentages* — N/A
- *Media groups* — Visual

background-image

- *Values* — `<uri> | none | inherit`
- *Initial value* — `none`
- *Applies to* — All
- *Inherited* — No
- *Percentages* — N/A
- *Media groups* — Visual

background-position

- *Values* — `[ [<percentage> | <length> ]{1,2} | [ [top | center | bottom] || [left | center | right] ] ] | inherit`
- *Initial value* — `0% 0%`
- *Applies to* — Block-level and replaced elements
- *Inherited* — No
- *Percentages* — Refer to the size of the box itself
- *Media groups* — Visual

background-repeat

- *Values* — `repeat | repeat-x | repeat-y | no-repeat | inherit`
- *Initial value* — `repeat`
- *Applies to* — All
- *Inherited* — No
- *Percentages* — N/A
- *Media groups* — Visual

border

- *Values* — `[ 'border-width' || 'border-style' || <color> ] | inherit`
- *Initial value* — See individual properties
- *Applies to* — All
- *Inherited* — No
- *Percentages* — N/A
- *Media groups* — Visual

border-collapse

- *Values* — `collapse | separate | inherit`
- *Initial value* — `collapse`
- *Applies to* — `table` and `inline-table` elements
- *Inherited* — Yes
- *Percentages* — N/A
- *Media groups* — Visual

border-color

- *Values* — `<color>{1,4} | transparent | inherit`
- *Initial value* — See individual properties
- *Applies to* — All
- *Inherited* — No
- *Percentages* — N/A
- *Media groups* — Visual

border-spacing

- *Values* — `<length> <length>? | inherit`
- *Initial value* — `0`

- *Applies to* — `table` and `inline-table` elements
- *Inherited* — Yes
- *Percentages* — N/A
- *Media groups* — Visual

border-style

- *Values* — `<border-style> {1,4} | inherit`
- *Initial value* — See individual properties
- *Applies to* — All
- *Inherited* — No
- *Percentages* — N/A
- *Media groups* — Visual

border-top, border-right, border-bottom, border-left

- *Values* — `[ 'border-top-width' || 'border-style' || <color> ] | inherit`
- *Initial value* — See individual properties
- *Applies to* — All
- *Inherited* — No
- *Percentages* — N/A
- *Media groups* — Visual

border-top-color, border-right-color, border-bottom-color, border-left-color

- *Values* — `<color> | inherit`
- *Initial value* — The value of the `color` property
- *Applies to* — All
- *Inherited* — No
- *Percentages* — N/A
- *Media groups* — Visual

border-top-style, border-right-style, border-bottom-style, border-left-style

- *Values* — `<border-style> | inherit`
- *Initial value* — `None`
- *Applies to* — All
- *Inherited* — No

- *Percentages* — N/A
- *Media groups* — Visual

border-top-width, border-right-width, border-bottom-width, border-left-width

- *Values* — `<border-width> | inherit`
- *Initial value* — `medium`
- *Applies to* — All
- *Inherited* — No
- *Percentages* — N/A
- *Media groups* — Visual

border-width

- *Values* — `<border-width> {1,4} | inherit`
- *Initial value* — See individual properties
- *Applies to* — All
- *Inherited* — No
- *Percentages* — N/A
- *Media groups* — Visual

bottom

- *Values* — `<length> | <percentage> | auto | inherit`
- *Initial value* — `auto`
- *Applies to* — Positioned elements
- *Inherited* — No
- *Percentages* — Refer to height of containing block
- *Media groups* — Visual

caption-side

- *Values* — `top | bottom | left | right | inherit`
- *Initial value* — `top`
- *Applies to* — `table-caption` elements
- *Inherited* — Yes
- *Percentages* — N/A
- *Media groups* — Visual

clear

- *Values* — `none | left | right | both | inherit`
- *Initial value* — `none`
- *Applies to* — Block-level elements
- *Inherited* — No
- *Percentages* — N/A
- *Media groups* — Visual

clip

- *Values* — `<shape> | auto | inherit`
- *Initial value* — `auto`
- *Applies to* — Block-level and replaced elements
- *Inherited* — No
- *Percentages* — N/A
- *Media groups* — Visual

color

- *Values* — `<color> | inherit`
- *Initial value* — Depends on user agent
- *Applies to* — All
- *Inherited* — Yes
- *Percentages* — N/A
- *Media groups* — Visual

content

- *Values* — `[ <string> | <uri> | <counter> | attr(X) | open-quote | close-quote | no-open-quote | no-close-quote ]+ | inherit`
- *Initial value* — Empty string
- *Applies to* — `:before` and `:after` pseudo-elements
- *Inherited* — No
- *Percentages* — N/A
- *Media groups* — All

counter-increment

- *Values* — `[ <identifier> <integer>?]+ | none | inherit`
- *Initial value* — `none`
- *Applies to* — All
- *Inherited* — No
- *Percentages* — N/A
- *Media groups* — All

counter-reset

- *Values* — `[ <identifier> <integer>?]+ | none | inherit`
- *Initial value* — `none`
- *Applies to* — All
- *Inherited* — No
- *Percentages* — N/A
- *Media groups* — All

cue

- *Values* — `[ 'cue-before' || 'cue-after' ] | inherit`
- *Initial value* — XX
- *Applies to* — All
- *Inherited* — No
- *Percentages* — N/A
- *Media groups* — Aural

cue-after

- *Values* — `<uri> | none | inherit`
- *Initial value* — `none`
- *Applies to* — All
- *Inherited* — No
- *Percentages* — N/A
- *Media groups* — Aural

cue-before

- *Values* — `<uri> | none | inherit`
- *Initial value* — `none`
- *Applies to* — All
- *Inherited* — No
- *Percentages* — N/A
- *Media groups* — Aural

cursor

- *Values* — `[ [<uri> ,]* [ auto | crosshair | default | pointer | move | e-resize | ne-resize | nw-resize | n-resize | se-resize | sw-resize | s-resize | w-resize| text | wait | help ] ] | inherit`
- *Initial value* — `auto`
- *Applies to* — All
- *Inherited* — Yes
- *Percentages* — N/A
- *Media groups* — Visual, interactive

direction

- *Values* — `ltr | rtl | inherit`
- *Initial value* — `ltr`
- *Applies to* — All elements, but see prose
- *Inherited* — Yes
- *Percentages* — N/A
- *Media groups* — Visual

The cautionary message, "but see prose," basically tells the author or user to ignore the properties in author and user stylesheets.

display

- *Values* — `inline | block | list-item | run-in | compact | marker | table | inline-table | table-row-group | table-header-group | table-footer-group | table-row | table-column-group | table-column | table-cell | table-caption | none | inherit`
- *Initial value* — `inline`
- *Applies to* — All

- *Inherited* — No
- *Percentages* — N/A
- *Media groups* — All

elevation

- *Values* — `<angle> | below | level | above | higher | lower | inherit`
- *Initial value* — `level`
- *Applies to* — All
- *Inherited* — Yes
- *Percentages* — N/A
- *Media groups* — Aural

empty-cells

- *Values* — `show | hide | inherit`
- *Initial value* — `show`
- *Applies to* — `table-cell` elements
- *Inherited* — Yes
- *Percentages* — N/A
- *Media groups* — Visual

float

- *Values* — `left | right | none | inherit`
- *Initial value* — `none`
- *Applies to* — All but positioned elements and generated content
- *Inherited* — No
- *Percentages* — N/A
- *Media groups* — Visual

font

- *Values* — `[ [ 'font-style' || 'font-variant' || 'font-weight' ]? 'font-size' [ / 'line-height' ]? 'font-family' ] | caption | icon | menu | message-box | small-caption | status-bar | inherit`
- *Initial value* — See individual properties
- *Applies to* — All

- *Inherited* — Yes
- *Percentages* — Allowed on `font-size` and `line-height`
- *Media groups* — Visual

font-family

- *Values* — `[[ <family-name> | <generic-family> ],]* [ <family-name> | <generic-family> ] | inherit`
- *Initial value* — Depends on user agent
- *Applies to* — All
- *Inherited* — Yes
- *Percentages* — N/A
- *Media groups* — Visual

font-size

- *Values* — `<absolute-size> | <relative-size> | <length> | <percentage> | inherit`
- *Initial value* — `medium`
- *Applies to* — All
- *Inherited* — Yes, the computed value is inherited
- *Percentages* — Refer to parent element's font size
- *Media groups* — Visual

font-size-adjust

- *Values* — `<number> | none | inherit`
- *Initial value* — `none`
- *Applies to* — All
- *Inherited* — Yes
- *Percentages* — N/A
- *Media groups* — Visual

font-stretch

- *Values* — `normal | wider | narrower | ultra-condensed | extra-condensed | condensed | semi-condensed | semi-expanded | expanded | extra-expanded | ultra-expanded | inherit`
- *Initial value* — `normal`
- *Applies to* — All

- *Inherited* — Yes
- *Percentages* — N/A
- *Media groups* — Visual

font-style

- *Values* — `normal | italic | oblique | inherit`
- *Initial value* — `normal`
- *Applies to* — All
- *Inherited* — Yes
- *Percentages* — N/A
- *Media groups* — Visual

font-variant

- *Values* — `normal | small-caps | inherit`
- *Initial value* — `normal`
- *Applies to* — All
- *Inherited* — Yes
- *Percentages* — N/A
- *Media groups* — Visual

font-weight

- *Values* — `normal | bold | bolder | lighter | 100 | 200 | 300 | 400 | 500 | 600 | 700 | 800 | 900 | inherit`
- *Initial value* — `normal`
- *Applies to* — All
- *Inherited* — Yes
- *Percentages* — N/A
- *Media groups* — Visual

height

- *Values* — `<length> | <percentage> | auto | inherit`
- *Initial value* — `auto`
- *Applies to* — All elements but nonreplaced inline elements, table columns, and column groups

- *Inherited* — No
- *Percentages* — See prose
- *Media groups* — Visual

NOTE **The cautionary message, "but see prose," basically tells the author or user to ignore the properties in author and user stylesheets.**

left

- *Values* — `<length> | <percentage> | auto | inherit`
- *Initial value* — `auto`
- *Applies to* — Positioned elements
- *Inherited* — No
- *Percentages* — Refer to width of containing block
- *Media groups* — Visual

letter-spacing

- *Values* — `normal | <length> | inherit`
- *Initial value* — `normal`
- *Applies to* — All
- *Inherited* — Yes
- *Percentages* — N/A
- *Media groups* — Visual

line-height

- *Values* — `normal | <number> | <length> | <percentage> | inherit`
- *Initial value* — `normal`
- *Applies to* — All
- *Inherited* — Yes
- *Percentages* — Refer to the font size of the element itself
- *Media groups* — Visual

list-style

- *Values* — `[ 'list-style-type' || 'list-style-position' || 'list-style-image' ] | inherit`
- *Initial value* — Not defined for shorthand properties

- *Applies to* — Elements with display: list-item
- *Inherited* — Yes
- *Percentages* — N/A
- *Media groups* — Visual

list-style-image

- *Values* — <uri> | none | inherit
- *Initial value* — none
- *Applies to* — Elements with display: list-item
- *Inherited* — Yes
- *Percentages* — N/A
- *Media groups* — Visual

list-style-position

- *Values* — inside | outside | inherit
- *Initial value* — outside
- *Applies to* — Elements with 'display: list-item'
- *Inherited* — Yes
- *Percentages* — N/A
- *Media groups* — Visual

list-style-type

- *Values* — disc | circle | square | decimal | decimal-leading-zero | lower-roman | upper-roman | lower-greek | lower-alpha | lower-latin | upper-alpha | upper-latin | hebrew | armenian | georgian | cjk-ideographic | hiragana | katakana | hiragana-iroha | katakana-iroha | none | inherit
- *Initial value* — disc
- *Applies to* — Elements with display: list-item
- *Inherited* — Yes
- *Percentages* — N/A
- *Media groups* — Visual

margin

- *Values* — `<margin-width> {1,4} | inherit`
- *Initial value* — Not defined for shorthand properties
- *Applies to* — All
- *Inherited* — No
- *Percentages* — Refer to width of containing block
- *Media groups* — Visual

margin-top, margin-right, margin-bottom, margin-left

- *Values* — `<margin-width> | inherit`
- *Initial value* — `0`
- *Applies to* — All
- *Inherited* — No
- *Percentages* — Refer to width of containing block
- *Media groups* — Visual

marker-offset

- *Values* — `<length> | auto | inherit`
- *Initial value* — `auto`
- *Applies to* — Elements with `display: marker`
- *Inherited* — No
- *Percentages* — N/A
- *Media groups* — Visual

marks

- *Values* — `[ crop || cross ] | none | inherit`
- *Initial value* — `none`
- *Applies to* — Page context
- *Inherited* — N/A
- *Percentages* — N/A
- *Media groups* — Visual, paged

max-height

- *Values* — `<length> | <percentage> | none | inherit`
- *Initial value* — `none`
- *Applies to* — All elements except nonreplaced inline elements and table elements
- *Inherited* — No
- *Percentages* — Refer to height of containing block
- *Media groups* — Visual

max-width

- *Values* — `<length> | <percentage> | none | inherit`
- *Initial value* — `none`
- *Applies to* — All elements except nonreplaced inline elements and table elements
- *Inherited* — No
- *Percentages* — Refer to width of containing block
- *Media groups* — Visual

min-height

- *Values* — `<length> | <percentage> | inherit`
- *Initial value* — `0`
- *Applies to* — All elements except nonreplaced inline elements and table elements
- *Inherited* — No
- *Percentages* — Refer to height of containing block
- *Media groups* — Visual

min-width

- *Values* — `<length> | <percentage> | inherit`
- *Initial value* — Depends on user agent
- *Applies to* — All elements except nonreplaced inline elements and table elements
- *Inherited* — No
- *Percentages* — Refer to width of containing block
- *Media groups* — Visual

orphans

- *Values* — `<integer> | inherit`
- *Initial value* — `2`
- *Applies to* — Block-level elements
- *Inherited* — Yes
- *Percentages* — N/A
- *Media groups* — Visual, paged

outline

- *Values* — `[ 'outline-color' || 'outline-style' || 'outline-width' ] | inherit`
- *Initial value* — See individual properties
- *Applies to* — All
- *Inherited* — No
- *Percentages* — N/A
- *Media groups* — Visual, interactive

outline-color

- *Values* — `<color> | invert | inherit`
- *Initial value* — `invert`
- *Applies to* — All
- *Inherited* — No
- *Percentages* — N/A
- *Media groups* — Visual, interactive

outline-style

- *Values* — `<border-style> | inherit`
- *Initial value* — `none`
- *Applies to* — All
- *Inherited* — No
- *Percentages* — N/A
- *Media groups* — Visual, interactive

outline-width

- *Values* — `<border-width> | inherit`
- *Initial value* — `medium`
- *Applies to* — All
- *Inherited* — No
- *Percentages* — N/A
- *Media groups* — Visual, interactive

overflow

- *Values* — `visible | hidden | scroll | auto | inherit`
- *Initial value* — `visible`
- *Applies to* — Block-level and replaced elements
- *Inherited* — No
- *Percentages* — N/A
- *Media groups* — Visual

padding

- *Values* — `<padding-width> {1,4} | inherit`
- *Initial value* — Not defined for shorthand properties
- *Applies to* — All
- *Inherited* — No
- *Percentages* — Refer to width of containing block
- *Media groups* — Visual

padding-top, padding-right, padding-bottom, padding-left

- *Values* — `<padding-width> | inherit`
- *Initial value* — `0`
- *Applies to* — All
- *Inherited* — No
- *Percentages* — Refer to width of containing block
- *Media groups* — Visual

page

- *Values* — `<identifier>` | `auto`
- *Initial value* — `auto`
- *Applies to* — Block-level elements
- *Inherited* — Yes
- *Percentages* — N/A
- *Media groups* — Visual, paged

page-break-after

- *Values* — `auto` | `always` | `avoid` | `left` | `right` | `inherit`
- *Initial value* — `auto`
- *Applies to* — Block-level elements
- *Inherited* — No
- *Percentages* — N/A
- *Media groups* — Visual, paged

page-break-before

- *Values* — `auto` | `always` | `avoid` | `left` | `right` | `inherit`
- *Initial value* — `auto`
- *Applies to* — Block-level elements
- *Inherited* — No
- *Percentages* — N/A
- *Media groups* — Visual, paged

page-break-inside

- *Values* — `avoid` | `auto` | `inherit`
- *Initial value* — `auto`
- *Applies to* — Block-level elements
- *Inherited* — Yes
- *Percentages* — N/A
- *Media groups* — Visual, paged

pause

- *Values* — `[ [<time> | <percentage>]{1,2} ] | inherit`
- *Initial value* — Depends on user agent
- *Applies to* — All
- *Inherited* — No
- *Percentages* — See descriptions of `pause-after` and `pause-before`
- *Media groups* — Aural

pause-after

- *Values* — `<time> | <percentage> | inherit`
- *Initial value* — Depends on user agent
- *Applies to* — All
- *Inherited* — No
- *Percentages* — See prose
- *Media groups* — Aural

The cautionary message, "but see prose," basically tells the author or user to ignore the properties in author and user stylesheets.

pause-before

- *Values* — `<time> | <percentage> | inherit`
- *Initial value* — Depends on user agent
- *Applies to* — All
- *Inherited* — No
- *Percentages* — See prose
- *Media groups* — Aural

pitch

- *Values* — `<frequency> | x-low | low | medium | high | x-high | inherit`
- *Initial value* — `medium`
- *Applies to* — All
- *Inherited* — Yes
- *Percentages* — N/A
- *Media groups* — Aural

pitch-range

- *Values* — `<number> | inherit`
- *Initial value* — `50`
- *Applies to* — All
- *Inherited* — Yes
- *Percentages* — N/A
- *Media groups* — Aural

play-during

- *Values* — `<uri> mix? repeat? | auto | none | inherit`
- *Initial value* — `Auto`
- *Applies to* — All
- *Inherited* — No
- *Percentages* — N/A
- *Media groups* — Aural

position

- *Values* — `static | relative | absolute | fixed | inherit`
- *Initial value* — `static`
- *Applies to* — All elements, but not to generated content
- *Inherited* — No
- *Percentages* — N/A
- *Media groups* — Visual

quotes

- *Values* — `[<string> <string>]+ | none | inherit`
- *Initial value* — Depends on user agent
- *Applies to* — All
- *Inherited* — Yes
- *Percentages* — N/A
- *Media groups* — Visual

richness

- *Values* — `<number> | inherit`
- *Initial value* — `50`
- *Applies to* — All
- *Inherited* — Yes
- *Percentages* — N/A
- *Media groups* — Aural

right

- *Values* — `<length> | <percentage> | auto | inherit`
- *Initial value* — `auto`
- *Applies to* — Positioned elements
- *Inherited* — No
- *Percentages* — Refer to width of containing block
- *Media groups* — Visual

size

- *Values* — `<length>{1,2} | auto | portrait | landscape | inherit`
- *Initial value* — `auto`
- *Applies to* — The page context
- *Inherited* — N/A
- *Percentages* — N/A
- *Media groups* — Visual, paged

speak

- *Values* — `normal | none | spell-out | inherit`
- *Initial value* — `normal`
- *Applies to* — All
- *Inherited* — Yes
- *Percentages* — N/A
- *Media groups* — Aural

speak-header

- *Values* — `once | always | inherit`
- *Initial value* — `once`
- *Applies to* — Elements that have table header information
- *Inherited* — Yes
- *Percentages* — N/A
- *Media groups* — Aural

speak-numeral

- *Values* — `digits | continuous | inherit`
- *Initial value* — `continuous`
- *Applies to* — All
- *Inherited* — Yes
- *Percentages* — N/A
- *Media groups* — Aural

speak-punctuation

- *Values* — `code | none | inherit`
- *Initial value* — `none`
- *Applies to* — All
- *Inherited* — Yes
- *Percentages* — N/A
- *Media groups* — Aural

speech-rate

- *Values* — `<number> | x-slow | slow | medium | fast | x-fast | faster | slower | inherit`
- *Initial value* — `medium`
- *Applies to* — All
- *Inherited* — Yes
- *Percentages* — N/A
- *Media groups* — Aural

stress

- *Values* — `<number> | inherit`
- *Initial value* — `50`
- *Applies to* — All
- *Inherited* — Yes
- *Percentages* — N/A
- *Media groups* — Aural

table-layout

- *Values* — `auto | fixed | inherit`
- *Initial value* — `auto`
- *Applies to* — `table` and `inline-table` elements
- *Inherited* — No
- *Percentages* — N/A
- *Media groups* — Visual

text-align

- *Values* — `left | right | center | justify | <string> | inherit`
- *Initial value* — Depends on user agent and writing direction
- *Applies to* — Block-level elements
- *Inherited* — Yes
- *Percentages* — N/A
- *Media groups* — Visual

text-decoration

- *Values* — `none | [ underline || overline || line-through || blink ] | inherit`
- *Initial value* — `none`
- *Applies to* — All
- *Inherited* — No (see prose)
- *Percentages* — N/A
- *Media groups* — Visual

NOTE The cautionary message, "see prose," refers to the distinction between inline and block level when using this feature. All descendants of element inherit specified text feature.

text-indent

- *Values* — `<length> | <percentage> | inherit`
- *Initial value* — `0`
- *Applies to* — Block-level elements
- *Inherited* — Yes
- *Percentages* — Refer to width of containing block
- *Media groups* — Visual

text-shadow

- *Values* — `none | [<color> || <length> <length> <length>? ,]* [<color> || <length> <length> <length>?] | inherit`
- *Initial value* — `none`
- *Applies to* — All
- *Inherited* — No (see prose)
- *Percentages* — N/A
- *Media groups* — Visual

NOTE The cautionary message, "see prose," refers to the distinction between inline and block level when using this feature. All descendants of element inherit specified text feature.

text-transform

- *Values* — `capitalize | uppercase | lowercase | none | inherit`
- *Initial value* — `none`
- *Applies to* — All
- *Inherited* — Yes
- *Percentages* — N/A
- *Media groups* — Visual

top

- *Values* — `<length> | <percentage> | auto | inherit`
- *Initial value* — `auto`

- *Applies to* — Positioned elements
- *Inherited* — No
- *Percentages* — Refer to height of containing block
- *Media groups* — Visual

unicode-bidi

- *Values* — `normal | embed | bidi-override | inherit`
- *Initial value* — `normal`
- *Applies to* — All elements, but see prose
- *Inherited* — No
- *Percentages* — N/A
- *Media groups* — Visual

NOTE **The cautionary message, "see prose," refers to the distinction between inline and block level when using this feature. All descendants of element inherit specified text feature.**

vertical-align

- *Values* — `baseline | sub | super | top | text-top | middle | bottom | text-bottom | <percentage> | <length> | inherit`
- *Initial value* — `baseline`
- *Applies to* — `inline-level` and `table-cell` elements
- *Inherited* — No
- *Percentages* — Refer to the `line-height` of the element itself
- *Media groups* — Visual

visibility

- *Values* — `visible | hidden | collapse | inherit`
- *Initial value* — `inherit`
- *Applies to* — All
- *Inherited* — No
- *Percentages* — N/A
- *Media groups* — Visual

voice-family

- *Values* — `[[ <specific-voice> | <generic-voice> ],]* [ <specific-voice> | <generic-voice> ] | inherit`
- *Initial value* — Depends on user agent
- *Applies to* — All
- *Inherited* — Yes
- *Percentages* — N/A
- *Media groups* — Aural

volume

- *Values* — `<number> | <percentage> | silent | x-soft | soft | medium | loud | x-loud | inherit`
- *Initial value* — `medium`
- *Applies to* — All
- *Inherited* — Yes
- *Percentages* — Refer to inherited value
- *Media groups* — Aural

white-space

- *Values* — `normal | pre | nowrap | inherit`
- *Initial value* — `normal`
- *Applies to* — Block-level elements
- *Inherited* — Yes
- *Percentages* — N/A
- *Media groups* — Visual

widows

- *Values* — `<integer> | inherit`
- *Initial value* — `2`
- *Applies to* — Block-level elements
- *Inherited* — Yes
- *Percentages* — N/A
- *Media groups* — Visual, paged

width

- *Values* — `<length> | <percentage> | auto | inherit`
- *Initial value* — `auto`
- *Applies to* — All elements but nonreplaced inline elements, table rows, and row groups
- *Inherited* — No
- *Percentages* — Refer to width of containing block
- *Media groups* — Visual

word-spacing

- *Values* — `normal | <length> | inherit`
- *Initial value* — `normal`
- *Applies to* — All
- *Inherited* — Yes
- *Percentages* — N/A
- *Media groups* — Visual

z-index

- *Values* — `auto | <integer> | inherit`
- *Initial value* — `auto`
- *Applies to* — Positioned elements
- *Inherited* — No
- *Percentages* — N/A
- *Media groups* — Visual

CSS3 specs are still a work in progress but the current status of development may be reviewed by visiting `www.w3.org/Style/CSS/current-work`.

Using Stylesheet-Creation Programs

No matter what approach you take to Web page creation — hardnosed hand-coding, WYSIWYG prototyping, or a combination of the two — you can always make life and work a little bit easier. Top-of-the-line Web page-creation programs such as Dreamweaver, GoLive, and Microsoft Expression Web have built-in capabilities for handling the creation of Cascading Style Sheets — both internal and external — as well as Web pages (see Figure 12-3).

FIGURE 12-3

Dreamweaver has a built-in capability to generate stylesheets.

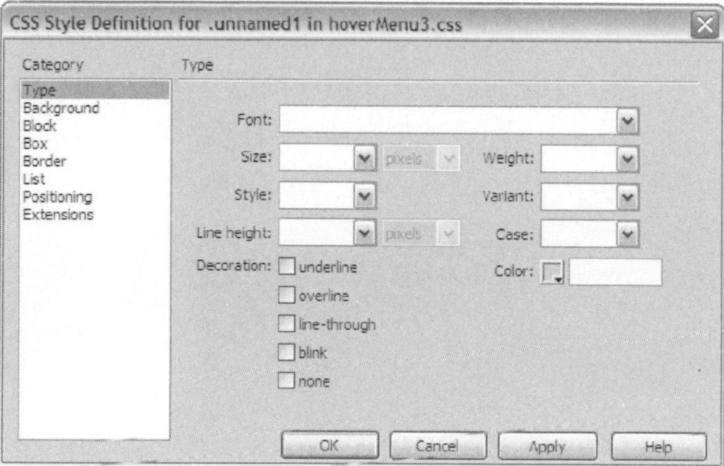

TABLE 12-2

Stylesheet Creation Programs

Name	Platform	Web Address
Style Master	Windows & Macintosh	`www.westciv.com/style_master`
Visual Studio Web Developer Express 2008	Windows	`http://www.microsoft.com/express/vwd/`

However, you can also find a number of specialized programs for making Cascading Style Sheets. Table 12-2 lists two of them you may want to try out.

Interesting CSS Sites

If you want to find out more about CSS, there are many good sites on Internet, as shown in Table 12-3.

TABLE 12-3

List of Useful CSS Sites

Website	URL
Complete CSS Guide	`www.westciv.com/style_master/academy/css_tutorial`
CSS Discuss	`css-discuss.incutio.com`
The Developer's Archive	`www.dev-archive.net`
CSS Tutorial	`www.w3schools.com/css`
CSS Vault	`cssvault.com`
CSS Zen Garden	`csszengarden.com`
Web Design Group	`www.htmlhelp.com/reference/css`
CSS support in Opera	`www.opera.com/docs/specs/opera9/css`

CSS Zen Garden (`www.csszengarden.com`) is a great site that uses different Cascading Style Sheets to transform the same HTML page in artistic ways. It shows the true potential of CSS to transform the same HTML into completely different visual formats. Also, there are some good links to CSS tricks and techniques.

The following sections discuss the relative and absolute positioning of images and block-level elements within the page. They discuss how to handle overflow of such elements through use of scroll bars and clipping. They also introduce the use of the division (`<div></div>`) and span (`<span></span>`) tags. The division tag is used to selectively highlight block sections for special formatting, while span tags are used to selectively highlight small sections of text for styling. As is pointed out, these techniques were developed by competing browsers during the browser wars of the mid- to late 1990s, so you will sometimes see the term *layers* used when discussing `<div>`.

Finally, we show how to set multiple layers in order using the `z-index` attribute within the `<div>` tag.

Adding Layers

In theory, any element on a Web page can be positioned on its own. In practice, however, you'll find that implementation of CSS properties is inconsistent, though most Web browsers in use today support positioning. To play it safe (like a man who wears both suspenders and a belt), you may encapsulate whatever you want to position within a layer defined by a `DIV` element.

NOTE **The `DIV` element is a generic block level element and is used to encapsulate into one element several disparate elements on a Web page. An example would be to encapsulate `<h3>`, `<p>`, and `<li>` all within a `DIV` element with the `id` of `sample`.**

```
<div id="sample">
<h3> content
<p>paragraph content
<ol> list content
</div>
```

NOTE **Netscape introduced a `layer` tag as an extension to HTML to position content. However, the tag was only supported by Netscape Navigator 4.x. The `layer` tag has since been replaced by the `<div>` tag in all modern browsers, but the original terminology stuck, so you will often hear `DIV`s referred to as layers.**

Using CSS positioning properties

The following HTML code positions a layer defined by a `DIV` element 20 pixels from the top of the Web page and 80 pixels from its left side, as shown in Figure 12-4:

```
<HTML>
<HEAD>
<TITLF>
Positioning a Layer
</TITLE>
</HEAD>
<BODY>
<DIV style="position:absolute;top:20;left:80;width:200;height:200;
background-color:blue;">
</DIV>
</BODY>
</HTML>
```

FIGURE 12-4

Absolute positioning allows full control over the placement of layers.

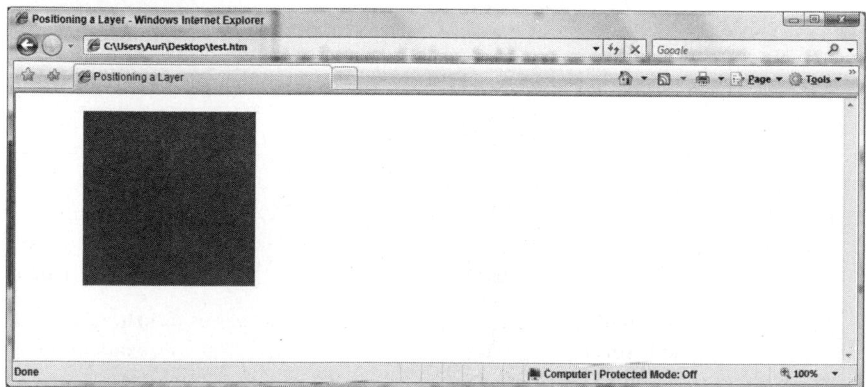

TIP **Giving layers negative values for the top and left attributes can move it off the screen. Of course, the values have to be at least as large as the height or width of the layer, or a portion of it will stick out from the edge into the visible area of the Web page.**

Going with the flow

To really understand the positions in HTML, you must understand that everything is formatted as if it were surrounded by a box. These boxes are then stacked side by side (*inline formatting*) or one beneath the other (*block formatting*). Elements are classed as inline or block. The elements `<span>`, `<u>`, `<b>`, and `<i>` are inline and are placed inline, while `<div>`, `<p>`, and `<img>` are block elements and are block-formatted.

CROSS-REF **See Chapter 4 for details of the formatting of HTML elements.**

For example, normal text is formatted inline, **bold text** as well, and ^{superscripts}, too. However, a paragraph is a block element and is placed below the preceding block. Notice that the elements flow across or down the page.

Normal flow is the position where the next element would be positioned by default. However, this can be changed by the use of positioning instructions. To complicate matters, a block can be nested inside a block — for example, an image inside a paragraph.

Choosing absolute or relative positioning

Absolute positioning is based on the upper-left corner of a parent block. *Relative positioning*, on the other hand, is based on the place where the element would have been placed by default, according to the normal flow. Also, absolutely positioned elements don't affect the normal flow. Consider the following HTML code:

```
<HTML>
<HEAD>
<TITLE>
Absolute versus Relative Positioning
</TITLE>
</HEAD>
<BODY style="margin: 0 0 0 0">
<DIV style="position:absolute;top:50;left:30;width:200;height:200;
background-color:green;">
</DIV>
<DIV style="position:relative;top:50;left:30;width:200;height:200;
background-color:blue;">
</DIV>
</BODY>
</HTML>
```

Notice in Figure 12-5 that the last block obscures the previous one. If the order is changed, then you will only see the green block.

FIGURE 12-5

Relative positioning is based on the place where the element would have been placed by default.

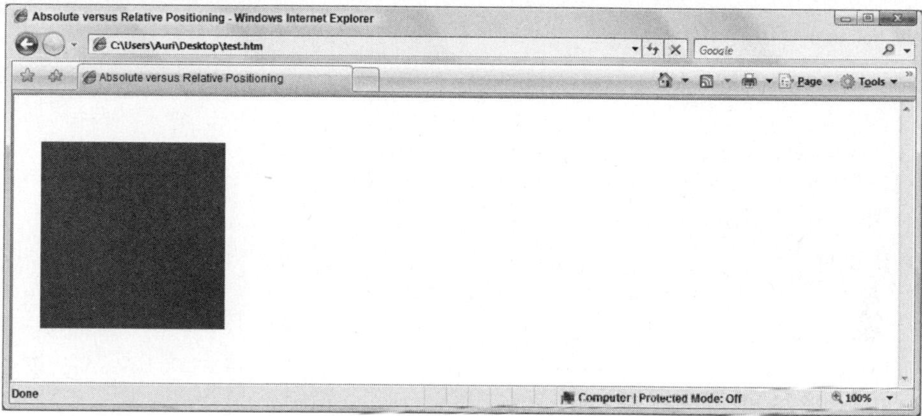

Note that the margin for the body has been set to zero. If the statement `style="margin: 0 0 0 0"` is removed, then we see something like Figure 12-6.

By default, the body element has a margin, so the normal flow of its first element, the blue square, will be offset. However, the position of the absolutely positioned green square is relative to the top left of the parent element; in this case, the parent is the body of the Web page, as shown in Figure 12-7.

FIGURE 12-6

Removing the margin settings reveals the other DIV.

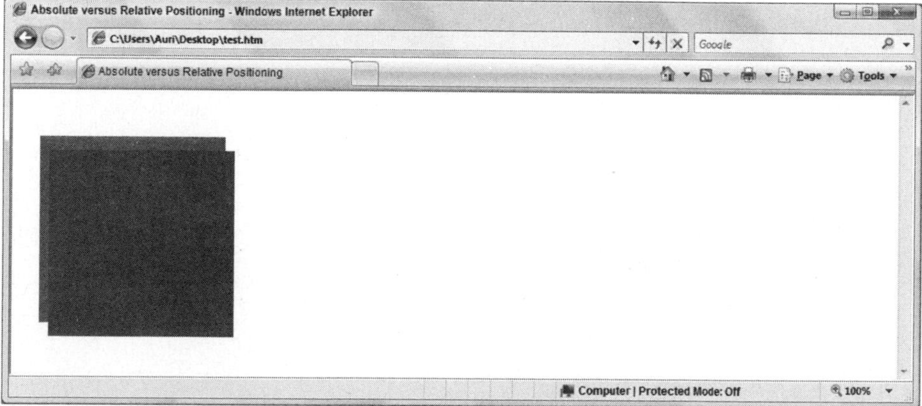

FIGURE 12-7

Adding text moves the relatively positioned block down.

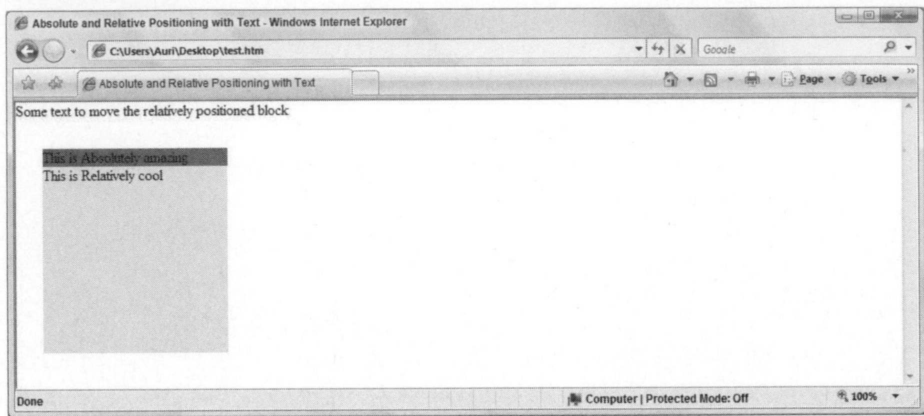

It might be a bit confusing that even absolutes are relative to something. It just goes to show that Einstein was right, and everything is relative.

To explain further let's see what happens when some text is inserted:

```
<html>
<head>
<title>Absolute and Relative Positioning with Text</title>
</head>
<body style="margin:0 0 0 0">
Some text to move the relatively positioned block
<div style="position:absolute; top:50; left:30;
  width:200; height:200; background-color:blue;">
This is Absolutely amazing
</div>
<div style="position:relative; top:50; left:30;
  width:200; height:200; background-color:yellow;">
This is Relatively cool
</div>
</body>
</html>
```

Nested elements

What happens if there is a box inside a box? Take a look at the following:

```
<html>
<head>
<title>Nested boxes Absolute and Relative Positioning</title>
```

```
</head>
<body style="margin:0 0 0 0">
<div style="position:absolute;top:50;left:30;width:200;height:200;
  background-color:blue;">
<span style="font-size: large; color: lime ">
This is Absolutely Relatively amazing</span>
<div style="position:relative;top:50;left:30;width:30;height:30;
  background-color:red;">
</div>
<div style="position:absolute;top:50;left:30;width:30;height:30;
  background-color:yellow;">
</div>
</div>
</body>
</html>
```

You can see in Figure 12-8 that the first large box has two boxes inside: a light gray relatively positioned box and a white absolute box. You can see that the yellow box is placed relative to the top left of the blue box, and the red box is shifted downward because of the text.

Overlapping Layers

Because layers can be positioned without regard to the location of other layers on the same Web page, as you have seen, they can occupy the same location on the page. This, obviously, can present problems seeing all the elements, because one of them can obscure another. However, it also opens up some intriguing possibilities in Web page design.

FIGURE 12-8

The white box is placed relative to the top left of the dark gray box, and the light gray box is shifted downward.

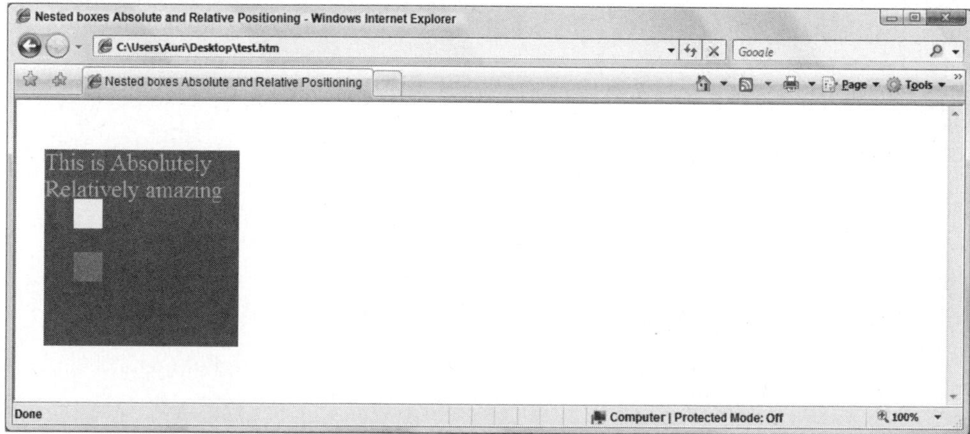

Stacking layers with z-order

The basic solution for handling overlapping layers is called *z-order* because there are three axes involved in positioning. If you think of the Web page as existing only on the screen of your monitor, the X axis runs across the screen from left to right. The Y axis runs from the top to the bottom of the screen. The Z axis, however, requires a little more imagination. It runs from the back of your monitor to the front of it.

The order of layers on the Z axis is specified via the `z-index` attribute. Any layer with a lower `z-index` value will be *underneath* another layer with a higher `z-index` value. Thus, in the following code sample, the first layer is on top of the second layer.

```
<DIV style="position:absolute; top:0; left:0; width:200;
            height:200; z-index:5">
</DIV>
<DIV style="position:absolute; top:0; left:0; width:200;
            height:200; z-index:4">
</DIV>
```

NOTE **If no `z-index` value is specified, it defaults to zero.**

If multiple layers have the same `z-index` value, the one that comes first in the code is the one that is beneath all the others, and the one that comes last is the one that is above all the others.

Using transparency and background color

While z-order is often used to make one layer cover another to hide it from view, the background color of the `DIV` element can be manipulated to create varying effects. If no background color is specified, then the layer is transparent and any underlying elements can show through.

In the following HTML code, the first layer completely covers the second one, and the background color of the second layer is still fully visible, as shown in Figure 12-9.

```
<HTML>
<HEAD>
<TITLE>
Using Background Color
</TITLE>
</HEAD>
<BODY>
<DIV style="position:absolute; top:0;left:0; width:200; height:200;
z-index:1; color:yellow; font-size:large;">Can you see me?
</DIV>
<DIV style="position:absolute; top:0; left:0; width:200; height:200;
  background-color:blue">
</DIV>
</BODY>
</HTML>
```

FIGURE 12-9

Backgrounds show through transparent layers.

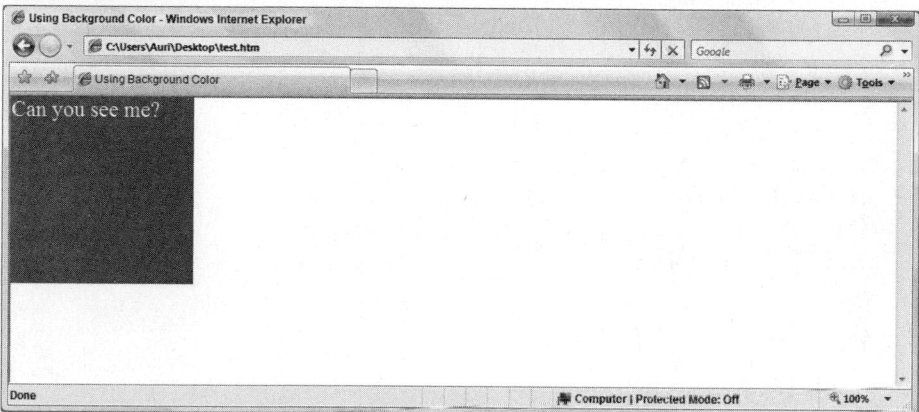

Clipping Layer Content

Clipping a layer is pretty much the same thing as cropping an image, with one exception — the remainder of the layer is still there but not visible. As with cropping, you are specifying a rectangular portion of the layer within which the visible portion of the element will appear.

The rectangle is set up with the `clip` property, and the values for it run as follows: `top`, `right`, `bottom`, and `left`. The following HTML code demonstrates how to set up a clipping region with a rectangle specified as `rect(20,80,100,10)` that has its top-left corner 20 pixels from the top, the right clip 80 pixels from the left side of the box, and the bottom clip 100 pixels from the top of the box and 10 pixels in from the left side. So, the clipped region is 80 – 10 = 70 pixels wide and 100 – 20 = 80 pixels high. The results are shown in Figure 12-10.

FIGURE 12-10

Clipping a layer is much like cropping an image.

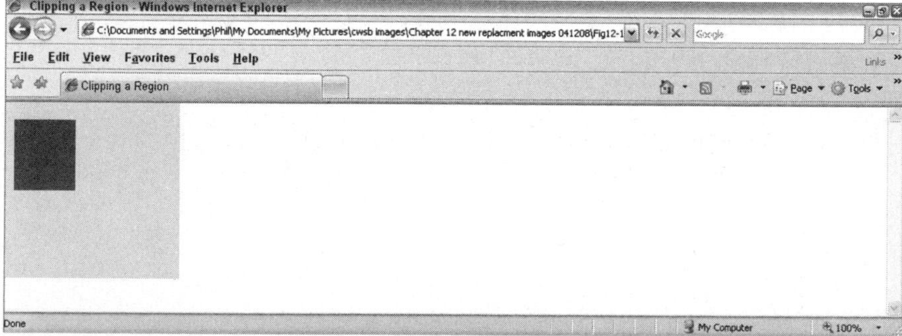

NOTE **If you have trouble remembering the sequence (top, right, bottom, and left), simply envision a clock with its hands at 12, 3, 6, and 9, respectively. In other words, the sequence is clockwise.**

```
<HTML>
<HEAD>
<TITLE>
Clipping a Region
</TITLE>
</HEAD>
<BODY>
<DIV style="position:absolute; top:0; left:0; width:200; height:200;
  background-color:yellow;">
<DIV style="position:absolute; top:0; left:0; width:200; height:200;
  clip:rect(20,80,100,10); background-color:blue;">
</DIV>
</BODY>
</HTML>
```

NOTE **A browser or two have still not fully implemented the CSS2 specification published by W3C. This states that the clip regions work in the same way as margins do — that is, the right side is measured from the right and the bottom is measured from the bottom.**

Visibility of layers

Not only can layers be positioned, but, like any HTML element, they can be set to be either visible or invisible. Obviously, an invisible layer isn't much use because no one can see it. The trick is to make it visible at some point to achieve a particular effect.

You can make a layer invisible by including the attribute `style="visibility: hidden"` And then set up a flag variable to determine visibility.

Handling Large Elements with Overflow Attributes

When an element is larger than the size of the layer that contains it, it is said to *overflow* the layer. There are various methods for handling this situation, ranging from letting the element's size override the layer size to adding scroll bars so the whole element can be viewed from within the layer's fixed size.

FIGURE 12-11

Overflowing content can be fully displayed despite the layer size.

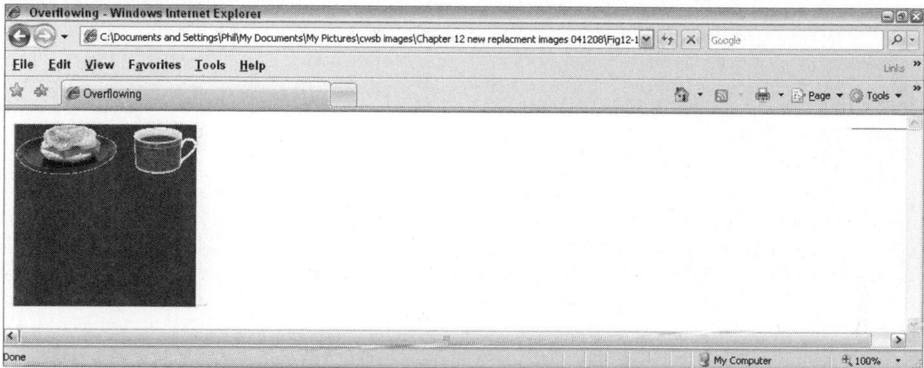

Visible overflow

When the `overflow` is set to `visible`, then the entire content becomes — you guessed it — visible, even if the layer that contains it is smaller than it is. The following HTML code illustrates how to accomplish this feat, and Figure 12-11 shows the results:

```
<HTML>
<HEAD>
<TITLE>
Showing Overflowing Content
</TITLE>
</HEAD>
<BODY>
<DIV style="position:absolute; top:0; left:0; width:200; height:200;
  overflow:visible; background-color:blue">
<IMG src="breakfast.gif">
</DIV>
</BODY>
</HTML>
```

Hidden overflow

Hiding the overflowing content of a layer may seem similar to clipping a region, but what you're really doing is simply not showing anything that falls outside the layer. The following HTML code

FIGURE 12-12

Content that overflows but is hidden is not visible outside of the layer.

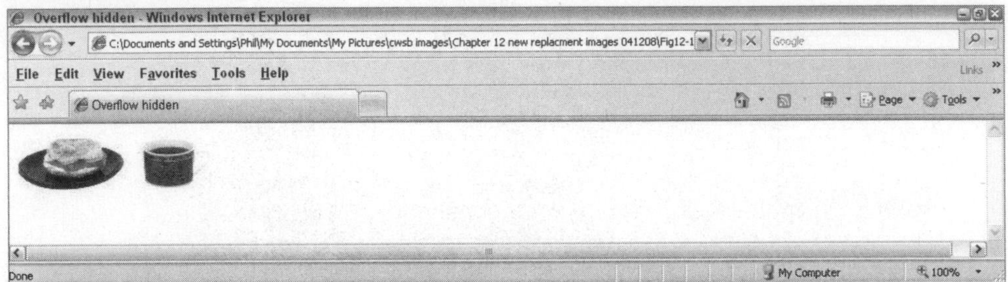

demonstrates how to set a layer so that only the portions of elements that are actually within its confines are displayed, and Figure 12-12 shows the results:

```
<HTML>
<HEAD>
<TITLE>
Hiding Overflowing Content
</TITLE>
</HEAD>
<BODY>
<DIV style="position:absolute; top:0; left:0; width:200; height:200;
  overflow:hidden">
<IMG src="breakfast.gif">
</DIV>
</BODY>
</HTML>
```

Scroll bars

As a compromise between full visibility and chopping off any overflowing content, CSS offers scroll bars. The following HTML code shows how to add scroll bars to your layers, and Figure 12-13 shows how they look:

```
<HTML>
<HEAD>
<TITLE>
</TITLE>
</HEAD>
<BODY>
<DIV style="position:absolute; top:0; left:0; width:200; height:200;
  overflow:scroll">
<IMG src="breakfast.gif">
</DIV>
</BODY>
</HTML>
```

FIGURE 12-13

You can make overflowing content fully visible within the confines of the layer by adding scroll bars.

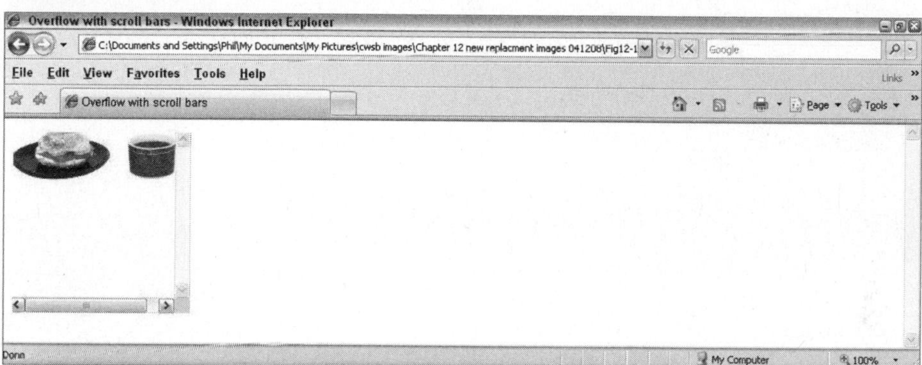

NOTE **You can also set** `overflow` **to** `auto`**, but there's not much point to that. The results are the same as not bothering to specify the** `overflow` **property at all.**

CSS and Layers Quick Reference

The following provides a quick reference for key items discussed in this chapter:

- *Inline* — Used to assign values to properties of a single element.
- *Embedded style* — Positioned in head of document to define style(s) for multiple elements (also known as selectors) within document.
- `DIV` — Used to define a generic block of elements just as span is used to define a generic group of inline elements
- `ID` — Used to define a single instance of an element
- `class` — Used to create a common identifier for a group of elements formatted in a stylesheet: `.classname{ property1:value1; property2:value2; property3: value3;...}`. Remember that a dot (.) precedes `class`.

Summary

Cascading Style Sheets (CSS) are one of the most powerful Web technologies in a Web designer's toolbox. CSS allows the Web designer to have a great deal of control over all the pages of a site, enabling him or her to configure numerous instances of an element through a single command in an external stylesheet, or to fine-tune multiple instances of an element (such as a list), or even to select a single element, through the use of embedded and inline styles.

In this chapter, you learned that style specifications "cascade" in importance, with the most important being the style closest to the element and the external stylesheet having the lowest priority. External stylesheets may be linked to several different Web pages simultaneously, thus creating overall stylistic control of an entire site.

You learned that the appearance of HTML elements can be redefined via CSS. Any element may become part of a CSS class, thus redefining specified attributes. Any element relationship may be specified via contextual selectors. Absolute positioning is relative to the top left of the parent element. Relative positioning is relative to where the element would normally be displayed.

This chapter discussed how the `z-index` value of an element determines which one is "on top" of another that occupies the same position on the Web page. The one with the lowest value is on the bottom. If two elements have the same `z-index`, the last one is displayed on top of the first.

Layers provide a good way to position elements on your Web pages. You learned that layers can be transparent or opaque. The content of a layer can be clipped or allowed to overflow the boundaries of the layer.

Chapter 13 introduces you to JavaScript.

Chapter 13

Making Dynamic Pages with JavaScript

IN THIS CHAPTER

Many people confuse JavaScript with Java. It's understandable, given the similarity in their names. But the two are not the same. Although some of JavaScript is somewhat similar to Java, Java is closer to C++ — all programming languages bear some degree of resemblance to one another. Java is a major language that is used for developing standalone programs, many of which are huge and extremely complex. JavaScript, on the other hand, is used to write short and simple programs that can run in Web browsers.

JavaScript's name came from Netscape licensing the Java name from Sun in order to capitalize on the Java craze at the time. JavaScript was originally called LiveScript.

Of course, you can use Java to write short and simple programs; many of the Java applets available to use on Web pages certainly fit this description. And you can also use JavaScript to create some incredibly intricate interactive programs on your Web pages. As with anything else on the Web, the limits are mainly up to you.

Trying Out JavaScript

Before we get into any of the details of how JavaScript works, let's see just how simple it can be. Type the following code into your HTML editor:

```
<HTML>
<HEAD>
<TITLE>JavaScript Is Great</TITLE>
</HEAD>
```

```
<BODY onLoad="alert('Welcome to the war, Robert!')"
onUnload="alert('Goodbye to all that')">

<P>Visit<A href="http://www.wiley.com/">www.wiley.com</A>.</P>

</BODY>
</HTML>
```

Save the file, and open it in a Web browser. The first thing you'll see is the popup message window shown in Figure 13-1. Click OK to make the popup go away. Then click the link. You'll get another popup message with the "So long" message shown in Figure 13-2. Click its OK button and the link is activated.

Simple, isn't it? Yet, in this short example, you've already *trapped* two *events*, used that fact to *invoke* the appropriate *event handlers*, and *called* on a *built-in method* of the *window object*, feeding it two different *parameters* to display two different *popup messages*. In plain English, you told the Web browser to display one message when the Web page is opened and another message when it went to another location.

NOTE **These italicized terms will be elucidated later in the chapter.**

FIGURE 13-1

A popup message window appears when you open the browser.

FIGURE 13-2

The "Goodbye to all that" Message appears.

Understanding JavaScript

JavaScript *isn't* Java, and it *isn't* HTML, either. JavaScript was built from the bottom up, however, to work together with HTML so that Web page designers could create programs to read and alter the values of HTML elements.

JavaScript is a language embedded within Web pages to provide interactivity and multimedia features within a static Web page. It provides dynamism through the use of events and event handlers. An event could be user input, such as clicking a mouse. That would be referred to as an `onclick` event. Events could also be `onload` (which does not require user intervention) or `onsubmit` (which could run validation checks on data input into a form once the form data has been submitted to a server for further processing). Events called functions (which is, for our purposes, the same as a method and is indistinguishable from a method in actual formatting) reside in the head portion of the HTML document. Functions, when called from the body by various events, execute the command blocks they contain, and then return control of the logic flow to the main program.

From time to time, people still ask if scripts are "really" programs. The answer is "yes." A *program* is a set of instructions to be carried out by a computer, and that's just what JavaScript creates. JavaScript, while a simpler language than many, is indeed a viable programming language in its own right.

Following are a few brief examples of features of JavaScript and associated programs to demonstrate the concepts.

NOTE **For more information, those who are just starting out with JavaScript might want to check out *Beginning JavaScript, 3rd Edition,* by Paul Wilton and Jeremy McPeak (Wrox, 2007).**

Working with variables, constants, and literals

Variables are the heart of programming. Without them, life would be much more difficult. A *variable* is an item that holds a value that is expected to change over time. The assignment operator is an old friend you've known since elementary school — the equal sign (=). If you want to assign the value `42` to the variable `answer`, for example, you simply write `answer=42`. This is an example of a *numeric variable*. A *character value* for a variable is surrounded by single quotes and a *string variable* value is enclosed in double quotation marks. This is done to signal to the program how it is to process the data. If it were numeric, then arithmetic operators would be applied. If it were string or character, logical operators would be applied.

Constant

A *constant* is a variable in which the associated value does not change. An illustration of a constant would be in an interest calculation program for a bank loan. While the amount of a loan and the duration would have variable inputs, the interest rate could be fixed (that is, constant) at some given percentage. An exception to that, however, would be where you were actually adding the underlying ASCII values of characters.

Note that, in the following example, we have used a fixed rate loan and not a variable rate loan.

The variable must always be on the left side of the assignment operator. The value to be assigned to it must always be on the right side of the assignment operator.

Declaring variables

Before it is actually used in a script, a variable should be *declared*, which means that you're giving the Web browser notice that it eventually has to deal with the variable. Variable declaration is done with the `var` keyword:

```
var answer;
```

This process is referred to as *declaring a variable*, or *variable declaration*.

You can kill two birds with one stone by assigning an initial value to the variable at the time of declaration:

```
var answer=42;
```

This process is referred to as *initializing a variable*, or *initialization of a variable*.

In JavaScript, if you declare a variable but do not initialize it, the variable is eventually purged from the system to reclaim memory. Other languages require an explicit *garbage collection* statement to reclaim memory.

Remember that a variable is actually a location in memory.

You do not, however, have to assign a value at declaration, nor do you *have* to use the `var` keyword. In fact, you often see JavaScript programs that have a line such as this in them:

```
textEntry = window.document.orderNow.visitorName.value;
```

In this case, the variable `textEntry` is both created and fed a value in one statement. It is, however, a good idea to explicitly declare the variable because, as time passes, you will forget why you created it.

Naming variables and constants

Although you have wide latitude in naming variables, the names should be descriptive of the kind of information they hold. For example, the current temperature might be expressed by the variables `currentTemperature`, `currTemp`, or even `cT`. If you wanted to specify that it was in Fahrenheit, you might invent the variables `degreesFahrenheit`, `degF`, or `dF`, instead. It's best to use descriptive, but not unnecessarily long, variable names.

It is customary (but not required) to start variables that consist of more than one word with a lowercase letter, and then to uppercase the first letter of each subsequent word. This helpful convention is referred to as *camel casing*. However, bear in mind that JavaScript is case-sensitive, so whatever capitalization you use must be consistent. If you call a variable `shirtSize` in one place and `ShirtSize` in another, don't expect your program to work properly.

JavaScript reserved words

The following table shows reserved words used in JavaScript.

Reserved Word	Reserved Word	Reserved Word
abstract	final	protected
as	finally	public
boolean	float	return
break	for	short
byte	function	static
case	goto	super
catch	if	switch
char	implements	synchronized
class	import	this
continue	in	throw
const	instanceof	throws
debugger	int	transient
default	interface	true
delete	is	try
do	long	typeof
double	namespace	use
else	native	var
enum	new	void
export	null	volatile
extends	package	while
false	private	with

There are a few restrictions on how you can name your variables. For example, you cannot give a variable the same name as any of the JavaScript reserved words (see the JavaScript Reference in sidebar for a list of reserved words). Your variable names cannot have any spaces in them, either. Finally, keep in mind that you cannot begin a variable name with anything but a letter or the underscore character (_). Table 13-1 shows examples of valid and invalid variable names.

TABLE 13-1

Valid and Invalid Variable Names

Valid Example	Invalid Example	Explanation
`Number1Choice`	`#1Choice`	The invalid example begins with something other than a letter or underscore.
	`1Choice`	
`moonPhase`	`moon Phase`	The invalid example has a space between the words.
`_switch`	`switch`	The invalid example is a reserved word. The valid one, even though technically legal, isn't a good idea either, because it's just too close to the reserved word for comfort. A simple typographical error could easily change `_switch` into `switch`.

As long as the name is legal, and you know what the variable name means, that's fine. But it's a good idea to bear in mind that you may have to come back to the script one day and revise it. And that day may be months or even years after you wrote it — months or years during which you've written many other scripts that all tend to blur together in your memory. It's always tempting to go for a very short and pithy variable name, but the more clearly it expresses its meaning, the easier it is for you to work with it over time.

Assigning different values

Once you've decided on a name for your variable, you can continue to assign different values to it forever. The `currentTemperature` variable may hold a value of `16` on a winter morning, `37` that same afternoon, or `105` in the depths of August. No matter what value is assigned to it, the variable itself remains the same, only its value changes. A *literal*, on the other hand, is a fixed value that never changes. You could set up a variable called `yardstick` that you assigned a value of `36` to, but there's no point in that because a yard is always 36 inches long. The value never changes, and the whole idea of variables is that they are a way to cope easily with changing values.

Value types

A value, whether literal or held in a variable, can be one of several types. The three most commonly used are numeric, string, and Boolean:

- *Numeric* — Just as it sounds — numbers, such as 8 or 37.
- *String* — Alphabetical characters or, to be more accurate, alphanumeric characters. Both "John ate a hot dog" and "78" are strings because the number 78 is enclosed in

quotation marks. If you intend to use numbers for calculation instead of using them as words in their own right, they should be numeric, not strings in quotation marks.

- *Boolean* — Logical values; the only two possibilities are *true* and *false*.

Affecting values with operators

You've already met one JavaScript operator, the assignment operator (=), earlier in this chapter in the section "Working with variables, constants, and literals." There are, however, many more, each of which performs a different task.

Comparison operators

The equality operator (which tests to see if two expressions are equal) is two equal signs (==). If you need to see if A is equal to B, and take different actions depending on the answer, you could use code such as the following example:

```
if (A==B) {
actionOne;
}
else {
actionTwo;
}
```

See the section, "Making choices with If and If . . . Else," later in this chapter for details on how the `if` statement works.

CAUTION **It's really, really easy to confuse the assignment operator (=) with the equality operator (==), even for professional programmers. After all, unless you learned programming in kindergarten, you were using "=" to mean "equals" long before you ever tried programming, and it's pure reflex to type it that way instead of "==". This is probably the single most common programming bug. If your script isn't working right, this is one of the first things to look for.**

The following example shows the right way to use both the equality operator and the assignment operator:

```
if (A==B) {
B=C;
}
else {
B=D;
}
```

The meaning of this example, step by step, is that the script looks first to see if variable A has the same value as variable B. If it does, B gets the value of C assigned to it. If not, B gets the value of D assigned to it. Whichever result you get for the equality comparison, the value of B changes. The values in the other two variables — C and D — remain unchanged because assignment is strictly a one-way street.

NOTE The assignment of a value always goes from right to left. Thus, the value in the variable on the left ends up the same as that in the variable on the right.

Also note that if you accidentally use = instead of ==, you'll get `true`, so the `if` case will always execute, (since `a=b` means `a` was successfully assigned the value of `b`, and thus `true`).

Other commonly used comparison operators include the following:

- `!=` — Not equal to
- `>` — Greater than
- `<` — Less than
- `>=` — Greater than or equal to
- `<=` — Less than or equal to

There is no single key to define less than or equal to, greater than or equal to, or not equal to for comparison operators. In each instance the *equal to* (=) is the second character of the string.

Arithmetic operators

The arithmetic operators used most often reflect, of course, the most common mathematical operations: addition, subtraction, multiplication, and division. Also, the unary negation operator and the increment and decrement operators come into play quite often.

- `+` — Addition. Adds two values together. When used with string values, it concatenates the strings — in other words, makes them into one string. In that case, it is known as the *concatenation operator*.
- `-` — Subtraction. Subtracts one value from another.
- `*` — Multiplication. Multiplies one value by another.
- `/` — Division. Divides one value by another.
- `-` — Unary negation. Although this uses the exact same sign as the subtraction operator, there is a subtle shade of difference. It is placed before a variable (literal numerical value) to reverse its current status. If the value is negative, the result becomes positive; if it is positive, the result becomes negative.
- `++` — Increment. Increases the value by 1. If placed before a variable (as in `++variable`), the value of that variable is returned, and then the increment takes place. If placed after a variable (as in `variable++`), the value of the variable after the increment takes place is returned. This only works with variables containing a number; otherwise, you'll get an error.
- `--` — Decrement. Decreases the value by 1. If placed before a variable (as in `--variable`), the value of that variable is returned, and then the decrement takes place. If placed after a variable (as in `variable--`), the value of the variable after the decrement

takes place is returned. This only works with variables containing a number; otherwise, you'll get an error.

CAUTION **The + operator (which is used either to add two numerical values or concatenate two string values) has a built-in solution for situations in which a JavaScript program tries to add a numerical value and a string value. It assumes that you mean the number to be interpreted as a string — as if it were within quotation marks — and converts it for you. Thus, if you try something such as `A = 78 + "modem"` you get "78modem" as the result. Also, `Y = "37" + 10` gets you "3710" instead of 47.**

There is a special kind of shorthand you can perform with the basic arithmetic operators to handle common situations such as the following one:

```
tax = tax - deductions;
```

Alternatively, this can be expressed in JavaScript shorthand like this:

```
tax -= deductions;
```

The addition, multiplication, and division operators can also be handled this way. `A += B` is the same as `A = A + B`, just as `A *= B` is the same as `A = A * B`, and `A /= B` is the same as `A = A / B`.

Note that when discussing arithmetic operators, you should keep in mind the following:

- A *binary* operator is one which requires operands both before and after the operator, as in 2 + 2, 10 – 5, 10 * 10, and 21 / 4.
- The `%` operator is called a *modulus*. The modulus returns the value of the remainder of an operator. Hence, if you were to take the division example, 21 / 4, and make it modulus, 21 % 4, the result would be 1. The remainder of 21 divided by 4 is 1.
- A *unary* operator simply requires an operand either before or after the operator. `++X` would be an example of a prefixed expression, and `X++` would be an example of a postfixed expression.

The following code shows an example of a prefix variable:

```
var x = 100;
var currentValue;
currentValue = ++x;    /* The currentValue would be 101 because x is
prefixed.  This means that 1 is added to X (100) and the result,
101, is then assigned to currentValue. */
```

The following code shows an example of a postfix variable:

```
var x = 100;
var currentValue;
currentValue = x++;    /* The currentValue would be 100 because x is
postfixed.  This means that  x (100) is assigned to currentValue and
then 1 is added to x. */
```

Logical operators

The three logical operators common to all programming languages are AND, OR, and NOT. When two values are compared with an AND operator, both of them must be true or the answer to the AND comparison is false.

When two values are compared with the OR operator, either one of them may be true and still return a value of true. Only if both of them evaluate to false is a return of false possible.

The logical NOT, on the other hand, is the logical equivalent of the arithmetic unary negation operator. If the value being evaluated is true, it returns false; if the value is false, it returns true. You would use a NOT statement to set a flag to indicate whether to enter a certain selection structure, for example.

Logical operators are expressed in JavaScript as follows:

- && — AND
- || — OR
- ! — NOT

Table 13-2 summarizes common JavaScript operator types.

Assignment operators

The assignment operator (=) is straightforward. Take the value on the right and assign it to the variable on the left, as shown here:

```
a = b
```

TABLE 13-2

Common JavaScript Operator Types

JavaScript Operator Types	Description of Operators
Comparison	<, >, <=, >=, =, !=
Arithmetic	Uses following binary operators: +, -, *, /, %
	Uses the following unary operators: ++, --, -
Logical	&&, ||, !
Assignment	=, +=, -=, *=, /=, %=
String	Multiple characters within quotation marks

If you use compound statements such as +=, the instruction is to take the operand on the left of +=, add it to the value on the right of the compound operator, and then assign that new value to the variable on the left of the compound assignment operator.

Consider the following example:

```
a = 25;
b = 125;
a += b;
```

The statement `a += b` is the equivalent of `a = b + a`. The result of this statement is `150`, since `a = (125 + 25)`. Hence, the value of `a` is now `150`, while the value of `b` is still `125`.

Similarly, using subtraction, you take the value of the operand on the left, subtract from it the value of the operand on the right, and assign the new value to the operand on the left. Consider the following example:

```
x = 99;
y = 22;
```

What will the result of the `y -= x` expression be? (Hint: The answer is -77.)

Compound multiplication (`*=`) and division (`/=`) assignment expressions work the same as += and `-=`.

Other compound assignment statements you may make might include `%=`, which will take the value of the left operand and divide it by the value of the right operand. The remainder will then be assigned to the left operand. Consider the following example:

```
x = 4;
y = 14;
y %= x;
```

The expression `y %= x` is equivalent to `y = y/x`. Then, `y = 2` because 2 is the remainder when you divide 14 by 4.

Strings

Finally, note that compound assignment statements can be made by combining separate string variables. This adding of separate strings into one longer string is called *concatenation*. It's a long word and a pain to pronounce, but all it means is adding variable values together.

Consider the following example:

```
beginString = "It is hotter than";
endString = "blazes in here!";
beginString += endString;
```

You could print it as follows:

```
document.writeln(beginString + "It's 103 with the air conditioning
on.");
```

The output would be:

```
It is hotter than blazes in here!It's 103 with the air conditioning
on.
```

We leave it to you to insert two spaces between the two sentences. You can also add string and non-string variables into one sentence.

Adding statements using event handlers

An *event* in JavaScript is an action that is taken by a visitor. A visitor may, for example, move his or mouse pointer over an image, enter data into a form, or click a link. An *event handler* is a script that you write to react to an event. Event handlers for particular events always begin with `on`, followed by the name of the event. A click event, for example, is processed by an `onClick` event handler.

Any time you use JavaScript to tell a browser to do one thing, you're making a *statement*. Each line in the following code is a separate statement:

```
document.write("This is being added to the page.");
alert("This is in a popup message window.");
globe = round;
```

NOTE **The `document.write()` is a basic method of JavaScript and, with trivial variations, several other object-oriented languages. If the three preceding lines of code were to actually be executed, the output for the first line would be the literal in double quotation marks enclosed within the parenthesis of the `document.write` method. For the second line, a message box would appear as shown in Figure 13-3 The third line just assigns the value in the right to the left variable.**

FIGURE 13-3

The message can appear in a popup window.

The three ways to put statements into your Web pages are:

- As attributes of an HTML element
- As plain statements in the contents of a `<SCRIPT>` tag
- As part of a function in the contents of a `<SCRIPT>` tag

HTML elements, of course, have various attributes. For example, the BODY element has a background color attribute, bgcolor. If you want to specify a value for that attribute, use this code:

```
<BODY bgcolor="blue">
```

In addition to the simple attributes you're used to, the elements also have some special attributes called *event handlers*. Event handler attributes are assigned values just as with any other attribute. You put the name of the attribute in, follow it with an equal sign, and then put the value within quotation marks. The following line from the opening example in this chapter shows how the process is identical to the way a background color is assigned. The only difference is the name of the attribute and the value that is assigned to it. The value, in this case, is a JavaScript statement.

```
<BODY onLoad="alert('Hi!')" onUnload="alert('So long - hurry
back!')">
```

See the section, "Using Events to Trigger Scripts," later in this chapter for more information on event handlers.

With event handler attributes, you can even specify multiple actions to be taken for a single attribute. Just separate each statement with a semicolon:

```
<BODY onLoad="alert('Hi!');alert('Welcome!')">
```

This causes the first statement — `alert("Hi!")` — to take place once the page is loaded, launching a popup window that contains the text `Hi!` When you've finished reading that statement and click OK, the next statement executes, launching the second popup message window as shown in Figure 13-4.

FIGURE 13-4

The second statement executes.

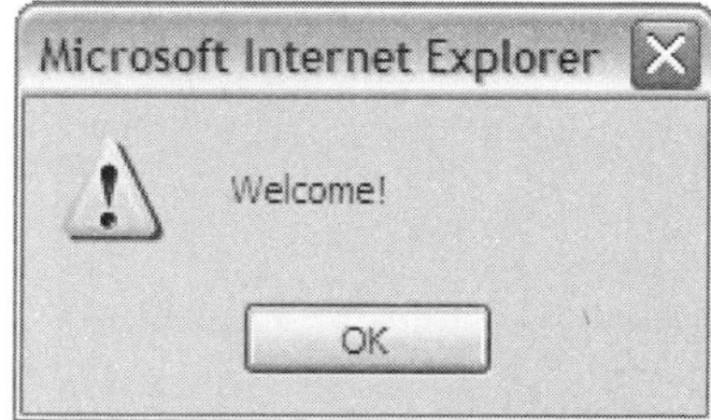

NOTE Statements that aren't contained in functions always execute in the order in which they appear.

NOTE You could also run the previous code by calling a function to execute the statements.

The eagle-eyed will have already noticed the use of two different kinds of quotation marks — double quotation marks (") to contain the attribute's value and single quotation marks (") within the statements themselves. This is a critical factor. If you tried the following line instead, you'd be creating trouble:

```
<BODY onLoad="alert("Hi!");alert("Welcome!")">
```

The problem here is that the Web browser knows that the first double quotation mark shows where the attribute's value begins, and the next one is where it ends. Thus, a Web browser reads this value as alert and comes to a screeching halt because it's a meaningless value. You can, if you want to, use single quotation marks to delimit the attribute's value, and double quotation marks inside the statements. The following code is perfectly valid:

```
<BODY onLoad='alert("Hi!");alert("Welcome!")'>
```

As long as you use a different kind of quotation mark to set off the attribute's value from the contents of the statements, you'll be fine.

Using the <SCRIPT> tag

Another way to add statements is within the <SCRIPT> tag:

```
<SCRIPT language="JavaScript">
document.write("This is the first line.<BR>");
document.write("This is the second line.<BR>");
document.write("This is the third line.<BR>");
document.write("This is the fourth line.");
</SCRIPT>
```

The first line opens with the <SCRIPT> tag to tell a Web browser that it's about to encounter a script, and it specifies JavaScript as the scripting language using the language attribute. If you do not specify a language, JavaScript is assumed to be the language used. However, no one can guarantee that this will always be the case, so it's best to go ahead and specify it.

The four statements simply add four separate sentences to a Web page, each one placed on a different line because there is a line break (BR element) included at the end of each of the first three sentences (Figure 13-5). Candidly, there are much better ways to achieve the same end, but it illustrates exactly how multiple statements have to be included.

The </SCRIPT> end tag specifies that there is no more script to follow.

FIGURE 13-5

Four statements are executed.

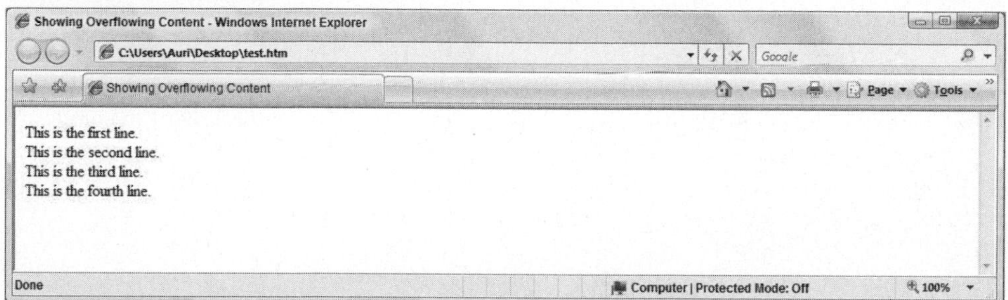

HTML comments are normally used to add notes on the meaning of the HTML code on a Web page. This helps both the original author and anyone else who works on the Web page later to grasp the meaning of any complex or unusual code. They have a special use when it comes to JavaScript, however. Because, in the past, several Web browsers did not support JavaScript, it became customary to wrap the material inside <SCRIPT> tags within HTML comments. These comments have a start tag of <!-- and an end tag of -->. The following shows how they were used:

```
<SCRIPT language="JavaScript">
<!-- Make this script invisible to old browsers.

document.write("This is the first line.<BR>");
document.write("This is the second line.<BR>");
document.write("This is the third line.<BR>");
document.write("This is the fourth line.");

// Back to normal. -->
</SCRIPT>
```

The reason this works is that a Web browser ignores anything within HTML comment tags. It also ignores any tags it encounters that it doesn't understand, which is why the <SCRIPT> and </SCRIPT> tags don't have to be inside the HTML comments. If a non-JavaScript browser encountered a script that wasn't inside comments, however, it would treat it as text to be displayed on the Web page.

Understanding the double slash (//) comment marker

But what about the double slash (//) at the beginning of the last line before the end tag? That's a comment marker, too, but it's a JavaScript comment this time, not an HTML comment. Take a moment to relax; it's okay if you're a bit confused at this point. Just remember that JavaScript isn't HTML, and HTML isn't JavaScript. If that last line just read `Back to normal` and ended in an HTML comment end tag, then the JavaScript interpreter wouldn't much like it. Although the interpreter would ignore the HTML comment end tag (just as it ignores the HTML comment start tag), it would see the "Back to normal" part as just plain text, neither HTML nor JavaScript.

Including comments

JavaScript comments are used for the same purpose as HTML comments — to add commentary to the Web page that won't be interpreted as any kind of actionable code. For example, the following bit of JavaScript includes a notation on its meaning:

```
alert("You have entered an invalid e-mail address.");
// Notifies the visitor that they need to go back and change the
// entry in the e-mail address text box.
```

The // method is one of two ways to add comments to JavaScript, and it has a simple limitation — it hides only one line. It doesn't matter how long that comment is, as long as you don't press your Enter key before you're finished with it. If you press your Enter key to add a line break, however, you begin typing on a new line — in the following example, everything after that is outside the comment:

```
alert("You have entered an invalid e-mail address.");
/* Notifies the visitor that they need to go back and
// change the entry in the e-mail address text box.*/
```

If you need to make long comments, there is an alternative method, which uses both a start and end tag. The start tag for JavaScript comments is /* and the end tag is */. The following code shows how they're used:

```
alert("You have entered an invalid e-mail address.");
/* This is the alert message that corresponds
to one of the new form entry checking algorithms
developed by XYZ Corporation. They were added to
our site in February. This one notifies the visitor
that they need to go back and change the entry in
the e-mail address text box. */
```

It is customary to put comments before the code, rather than after.

Processing statements

The <SCRIPT> tag can be placed anywhere on a Web page, either in the HEAD or the BODY elements. However, you must remember that statements are processed in the order they're found. This means that if you place a statement before the things it acts on, then you're asking for trouble. Consider the following bad example:

```
<HTML>
<HEAD>
<TITLE>Do Not Attempt This At Home</TITLE>
```

```
</HEAD>
<BODY>

<SCRIPT type="text/JavaScript">
<!-- Make this script invisible to old browsers.
document.write("The initial value was John.<BR>");
document.write("The current value is " +
window.document.formOne.firstName.value);
// Back to normal. -->
</SCRIPT>
<FORM id="formOne" name="formOne">
<P>Enter your first name: </P>
<INPUT type="text" id="firstName" name="firstName" value="John">
</FORM>

</BODY>
</HTML>
```

When you load this example into a Web browser, only the first `document.write` statement takes effect because the second one requires a value that hasn't been defined yet — the value in the text box named `firstName`, which is contained in the form named `formOne`. If the code is modified to place the `<SCRIPT>` tag and its contents after that form and text box are defined, however, it's a different story:

```
<HTML>
<HEAD>
<TITLE>This Time, It Works</TITLE>
</HEAD>
<BODY>

<FORM name="formOne" method="post">
<P>Enter your first name: </P>
<INPUT type="text" name="firstName" value="John">
</FORM>

<SCRIPT language="JavaScript">
<!-- Make this script invisible to old browsers.
document.write("The initial value was John.<BR>");
document.write("The current value is " +
window.document.formOne.firstName.value);
// Back to normal. -->
</SCRIPT>

<P>Enter a new name, then click on the "Refresh" or "Reload" button
at the top of your browser.</P>

</BODY>
</HTML>
```

Now, when the page opens, both `document.write` statements work. Because the initial value is still the same as the current value, both say the value is `John`, as is shown in Figure 13-6.

FIGURE 13-6

This figure illustrates identical values.

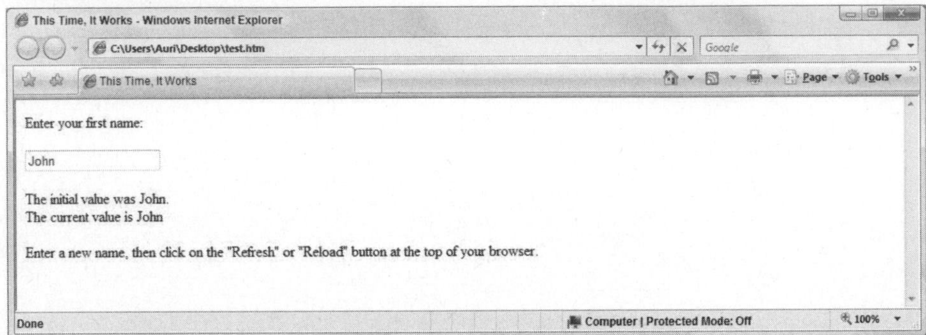

Resetting form value

This is probably as good a place as any to point out that Web browsers and JavaScript don't always do what you expect them to do. Generally, however, when you reload a Web page in a browser, everything is reset to its initial values.

Combining statements into functions

A *function* is a grouped series of statements that execute one after another. They are used to create more complex programming constructs than can be accomplished with simple statements alone. The basic layout isn't much different from any series of statements:

```
<SCRIPT>
function functionName(){
firstStatement;
secondStatement;
thirdStatement;
}
</SCRIPT>
```

The only differences are that a function is declared with the `function` keyword, which is followed by the name of the function, a closed pair of parentheses, and then an opening curly bracket. The statements are then listed as usual, and a closing curly bracket ends the function.

Calling a function

Remember that the statements that are inside of functions run only when called. The following example illustrates how this works: Functions exist with `<script> </script>` tags

```
<HTML>
<HEAD>
<TITLE>Reading and Displaying a Value</TITLE>
```

```
<SCRIPT>
function getTheName(){
var textEntry;
textEntry = window.document.orderNow.visitorName.value;
alert(textEntry);
}
</SCRIPT>

</HEAD>
<BODY>

<P>Enter your name, then click on the button.</P>

<FORM name="orderNow">
<label> Name</label>
<INPUT type="text" name="visitorName">
<INPUT type="button" value="Click Here to display name in the
message box." onClick="getTheName()">
</FORM>

</BODY>
</HTML>
```

Here's what happens in the code, step by step:

1. The function called `getTheName()` is declared. The Web browser reads it and stores all the information in it in memory, including the existence of the variable, `textEntry`. Although the function is ready to go whenever it is invoked, it does nothing at all at this time.
2. The visitor follows the instructions, makes an entry into the text box, and then clicks the button specified in the form.
3. The button's `onClick` event handler calls the `getTheName` function.
4. The current value of the text inside the text box is assigned to the variable `textEntry`.
5. The `alert()` method is triggered, with the `textEntry` value as its parameter. As a result, the value of the text inside the text box is displayed in a popup message box, as shown in Figure 13-7.

FIGURE 13-7

This figure shows the value in the message box.

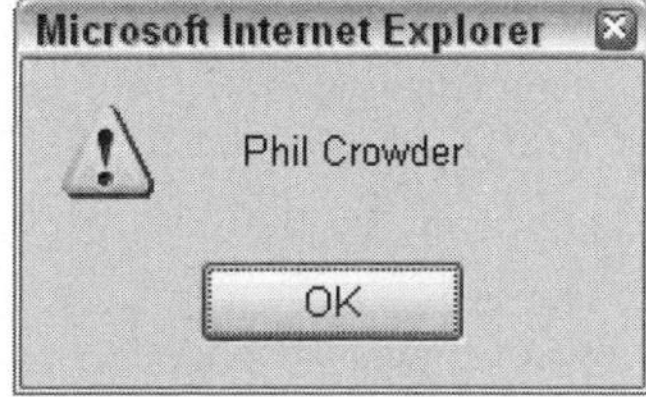

Calling a statement

A standalone statement or series of statements, however, runs automatically. Statements that are inside of functions run only when *called*. There's nothing mysterious about calling a statement. Just as you might call a friend's name to attract his or her attention, you call a function by using the function's name.

NOTE **The `alert()` method is a built-in method of the window object and can also be written as `window.alert()`. However, in most instances, the use of `window` in the path is unnecessary. It is assumed during the execution of the program.**

Understanding the scope of variables

The *scope* of a variable is the part of a Web page that it exists in. A variable that is declared before any functions are defined can be used in any function or by any statement that follows. A variable that is declared within a function, on the other hand, has scope only within that function.

This means that you can declare many different variables, all of which have the same name, without creating a conflict — *as long as those variables are declared within separate functions*. This is one of those capabilities that it's good to be leery of, however, because you might cause confusion.

Table 13-3 explains the types and ranges of variable scope.

A common example of this type of variable name duplication is the `count` variable that is normally used in loops. See the section, "Going in loops," later in this chapter.

Making choices with If and If . . . Else

A program, as mentioned earlier, is a series of instructions that are carried out in sequence. The sequence, however, doesn't have to be the same every time. The `if` statement and the slightly more complex `if...else` statement give a program the power to make decisions based on current conditions.

TABLE 13-3

Variable Scope

Variable Type	Scope (Range)
Global	Accessible to all functions. Declared at class level. For our purposes in this chapter, a class may be thought of as the same as the Web page.
Local	Accessible only to specific function where variable is declared

In plain English, an `if` statement says, "If the condition is true, then take this action. If it isn't true, then don't take any action." The JavaScript code version is as follows:

```
if (thisIsTrue) {
doThis;
}
```

The condition represented by `thisIsTrue` can be any kind of comparison test. The part that reads `doThis` would be replaced with any JavaScript statement or function. In the following example, we test to see if the value of the variable `x` is less than 3. If it is, then the variable `y` is assigned a value of `12` and the variable `z` is assigned a value of `53`:

```
if (x < 3) {
y = 12;
z = 53;
}
```

If `x` is equal to or greater than 3, however, nothing happens. The variables `y` and `z` are not changed, and the program flow simply continues on down to the next line of the code.

The `if...else` statement allows for a similar, but more complex, branching decision. This one might be expressed in English as, "If the condition is true, then take the first action. If it isn't true, then take the second action." The JavaScript version is as follows:

```
if (thisIsTrue) {
doThis;
}
else {
doThat;
}
```

The following example tests to see whether the value of the `season` variable is `"spring"`, `"summer"`, `"autumn"`, or `"winter"` and invokes different functions to display the appropriate seasonal observation:

```
if (season == "spring"){
  document.write("The Earth is like a child that knows poems.");
}
else {
if (season=="summer") {
  document.write ("To see the summer sky is poetry");
}
else {
if (season=="autumn"){
  document.write("Autumn is a second spring, where every leaf is a
flower.");
}
else {
```

```
      document.write("Every mile is two in winter.");
    }
  }
}
```

You will note that it is easy to make a mistake in coding, especially with the curly braces ({ }), so you may wish to simplify the coding by using a feature known as a *switch* (or *case*) structure. A switch structure allows you to check for multiple values of a single variable. In the earlier example, this variable was `season`.

Here is the same `if...else` structure rewritten as a case structure:

```
switch (season) {
case "spring":
  document.write("The Earth is like a child that knows poems.");
  break;
case "summer":
  document.write("To see the summer sky is poetry.");
  break;
case "autumn":
  document.write("Autumn is a second spring, where every leaf is a
flower.");
  break;
case "winter":
  document.write("Every mile is two in winter.");
  break;
}
```

You would really not necessarily deem this to be shorter than a selection structure, but you have neatly reduced the number of curly braces from 12 to 2. In other words, you have eliminated 10 possible sources of error.

You may have noticed the use of the `break` statement. This drops the execution of the program out of the case structure once the proper match has been made. If the `break` statement were absent, the case structure would still work, but the output would be different. In the first instance, let us say the value of `season` is `summer`. The output then would be: `"To see the summer sky is poetry."`

If the `break` statements were omitted, however, and the variable were still to be `summer`, the output would be:

```
To see the summer sky is poetry.
Autumn is a second spring where every leaf is a flower.
Every mile is two in winter.
```

Finally, you may, even more simply, put the multivalued variable, `season`, in an array.

```
var Season = new Array();
season[0] = "spring";
```

```
season[1] = "summer";
season[2] = "autumn";
season[3] = "winter";
```

However, the number of values is rather small for an array.

If you need to test for multiple conditions before deciding what action to take, `if` statements can be nested so that one condition is tested after another one is passed. This says, "If the first condition is true, then — and only then — check to see if the second condition is true. If the second one is true, too, then take an action." The following is the JavaScript version:

```
if (thisIsTrue) {
   if (thatIsTrue) {
     doThis;
   }
}
```

The following example tests first to see if a credit card number is correct, and then checks to see if the balance of available credit is enough to pay for the product. The credit limit is not checked unless the card number is a valid one. Only if both of these comparisons are true will the purchase be completed.

```
if (cardNumber == valid) {

   if (limit == highEnough) {
      completePurchase();
   }
}
```

You can also nest an `if` statement within an `if...else` statement, an `if... else` statement within an `if` statement, or an `if...else` statement within another `if...else` statement. The levels of complexity you can reach are truly mind-blowing, allowing for a practically infinite number of conditional decisions.

CAUTION **As with any other kind of power, it's best to exercise this in moderation. If you have 37 different `if...else` statements nested within 24 different `if` statements that are themselves nested within another dozen `if...else` statements, you'll never be able to untangle things if you need to modify the code later. When code appears to be too complex, rethink your approach.**

Going in loops

Most of us spend at least some time running around in circles. In JavaScript, you sometimes want to do this deliberately — a *loop*, in programming terms. If you've ever cooked a turkey on Thanksgiving, you already know all about loops. You open the oven and look at the meat thermometer to see if it's up to the "poultry" mark yet. If it isn't, you wait a little while, and then check again. You keep doing this until the thermometer shows the right reading, and then you break out of the loop and eat dinner.

The most commonly used loop is called a `for` loop, and in plain English, it could be articulated as, "For as long as a condition remains the same, I'll keep taking action. When it changes, I'll stop." Here's what it is in JavaScript:

```
for (initial expression ; condition ; increment expression) {
  statement or statements
}
```

The *`initial expression`* is simply where you declare a variable and assign a value to it. The variable name that is traditionally used here is `count` or `i` because the `for` loop counts over and over again (or you could say it *iterates*, if you want to get fancy about it).

The *`condition`* is anything using the comparison operators. You might, for example, establish a condition of `count==36`, a condition of `count<=100`, or just about any other comparison you want.

The *`increment expression`* is used to change the value of the variable established in the *`initial expression`* by adding 1 to it. It is poorly named because you can decrement the value as well, subtracting 1 from it. To add 1, you use `count++`; to subtract one, you use `count --`.

Let's say that you wanted to run through a loop that counted up from 1 to 10. Here's the JavaScript code you'd use:

```
for (var count = 1; count <= 10; count++) {
  statement or statements
}
```

We're being a little picky by including the `var` keyword. This is one of those situations in which you really don't need it, but it never hurts to specify that you're declaring the variable at this point. The variable `count` is assigned a value of `1`. Next, the looping condition is set so that the loop continues for as long as the value of `count` is less than or equal to `10`. Finally, the increment operator ensures that the value of `count` increases by one every time the loop comes around again.

When the loop begins, `count` is `1`. The statement or statements are executed. When they're all done, the loop starts over again and checks to see if the value of `count` is still less than or equal to 10. It isn't, so 1 is added to 1 to make it 2, and then the loop runs again. This goes on until the 10th time the loop completes. At that time, the condition is met because `count` finally holds a value of 10. The loop is finished at that point.

The following example shows this kind of count-up in action. It displays the numbers 1 through 5, each as an `H1` header:

```
<HTML>
<HEAD>
```

```
<TITLE>Looping Up</TITLE>
</HEAD>
<BODY>

<SCRIPT language="JavaScript">
<!-- Make this script invisible to old browsers.
  for (var count = 1; count <= 5; count++) {
    document.write("<H1>" + count + "</H1>");
  }
// Back to normal. -->
</SCRIPT>

</BODY>
</HTML>
```

Figure 13-8 shows the results.

FIGURE 13-8

Here is the result of printing a looping value.

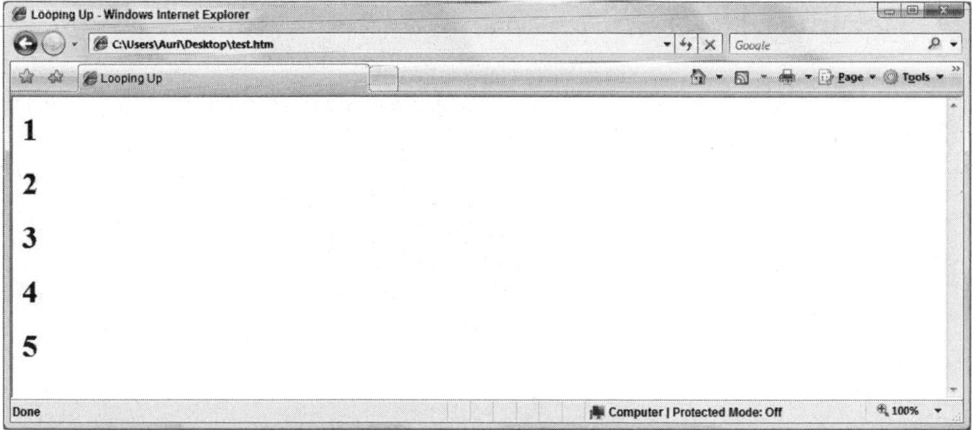

You can accomplish the reverse of this — counting down from 5 to 1 — by a slight variation in the code:

```
<HTML>
<HEAD>
<TITLE>Looping Down</TITLE>
</HEAD>
<BODY>

<SCRIPT language="JavaScript">
<!-- Make this script invisible to old browsers.
```

```
    for (var count = 5; count >= 1; count--) {
      document.write("<H1>" + count + "</H1>");
    }
    // Back to normal. -->
  </SCRIPT>

  </BODY>
  </HTML>
```

Here, the value of count is set to 5 to begin with and decremented by 1 with each pass through the loop. The condition that is tested for is whether or not the value in count is 1 or higher. Figure 13-9 shows the countdown page.

FIGURE 13-9

This figure shows the result of counting down with a decrement.

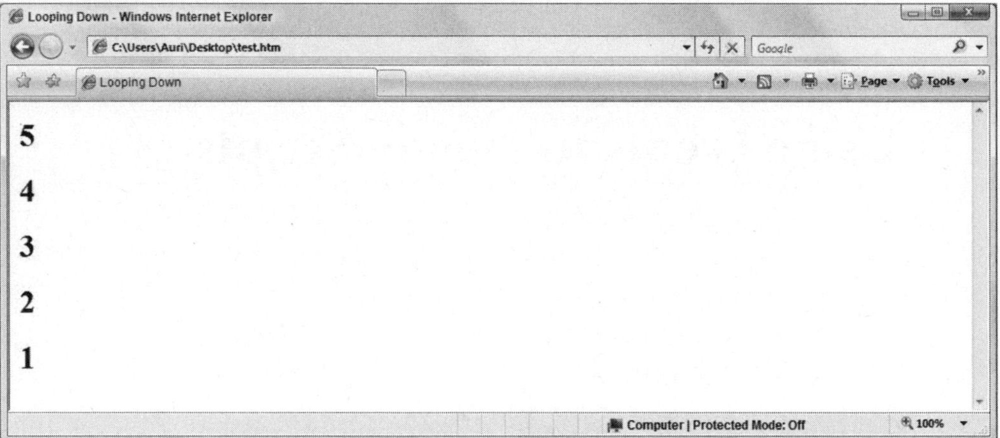

See the section, "Arithmetic operators," earlier in this chapter for an explanation of the -- (decrement) operator.

The for...next loop is but one of the looping structures available. The other common iterative structures are the do ... while and do...until. Each of these does the same thing as a for . . . next loop but each serves a different purpose. If you do not know the number of iterations in a loop, you would use a while statement. If you knew the number of times the program would execute the loop, then for...next is a reasonable choice.

Which JavaScript?

JavaScript was invented by Netscape and was originally called LiveScript. LiveScript was a wonderful idea that got a lot of Web designers interested in the possibilities, but it was pretty limited in what it could do. JavaScript has changed a lot since those early days and is currently in its fifth version. With each new revision, new capabilities are added. This means, of course, that older Web browsers can't interpret the latest changes because they don't even know they exist, and you can't teach an old browser new tricks.

Microsoft, as part of the browser wars, introduced a JavaScript variant called JScript. Although it is essentially identical to JavaScript, there are just enough differences to create problems for Web designers. The solution here is simple compared with other cross-browser compatibility issues, however. Internet Explorer supports only JScript variants, but JavaScript works on Internet Explorer. If you just stick with normal JavaScript, you're better off.

In an attempt to develop a standard version of JavaScript, the European Computer Manufacturers Association (ECMA), a European standards body, came up with ECMAScript. As you can guess if you have any experience with Web standards, this standard is way behind the times.

Using Events to Trigger Scripts

An *event* in JavaScript is an action that is taken by a visitor. A visitor may, for example, move his or her mouse pointer over an image, enter data into a form, or click a link. An *event handler* is a script that you write to react to an event. Event handlers for particular events always begin with `on`, followed by the name of the event. A click event, for example, is processed by an `onClick` event handler. Table 13-4 shows the event handlers that are common to Firefox, Internet Explorer, and all popular JavaScript-capable browsers.

NOTE **If you look at other JavaScript documentation, you find a great deal of confusion about events and event handlers. When a page loads into a Web browser, for example, this is a `Load` event. The event handler that reacts to that always begins with `onLoad=` and then some JavaScript code. However, you often find a `Load` event referred to as an `onLoad` event, even though `onLoad` is technically the event handler, not the event itself. The HTML standard even falls into this trap. It's best to just shrug this sort of thing off — as long as you know what's meant, that's all that's important.**

In addition to the common event handlers, specialized ones are particular to specific elements. The `FORM` element, for example, has `onSubmit` and `onReset` form handlers. Respectively, these mean that someone has clicked the Submit and Reset buttons.

TABLE 13-4

Alphabetical List of Event Handlers

Event	Meaning
`onAbort`	A user clicks the Stop button while an image is loading.
`onBlur`	An element loses focus.
`onChange`	An element changes.
`onClick`	The mouse button is pressed and released once.
`onDblClick`	The mouse button is pressed and released twice in rapid succession.
`onError`	An error occurs.
`onFocus`	An element receives focus.
`onKeyDown`	A key is pressed.
`onKeyPress`	A key is pressed and released.
`onKeyUp`	A pressed key is released.
`onLoad`	The Web page is loaded into the browser.
`onMouseDown`	The mouse button is pressed.
`onMouseMove`	The mouse pointer moves.
`onMouseOut`	The mouse pointer moves off the object.
`onMouseOver`	The mouse pointer moves over the object.
`onMouseUp`	The mouse button is released.
`onMove`	A window is moved.
`onReset`	A form is reset.
`onResize`	A window is resized.
`onSelect`	Text is selected in a text box or text area.
`onSubmit`	A form is submitted.
`onUnload`	The browser moves on to another page.

Triggering on page loads and unloads

When you go to a Web page, you cause a `Load` event. When you leave it, you cause an `Unload` event. A Web page is *loaded* when all the code for it has been transmitted from the Web server to the Web browser. A Web page is *unloaded* when a different Web page (or other file) is loaded into the browser. Unloading can occur in many ways — when a visitor clicks a link, uses the

Back or Forward buttons in the browser, manually enters an address in the address bar, or selects a page from his or her bookmarks (or Favorites) listing or the History listing.

One of the handiest things to do on a page load is to break your page out if it is contained within another Web site's frames. The following code shows one way to do it:

```
<HTML>
<HEAD>
<TITLE>Breaking Out Of Frames</TITLE>
<SCRIPT language="JavaScript">
<!-- Make this script invisible to old browsers.

  function frameBuster() {
    if (parent.location != window.location) {
      parent.location = window.location;
    }
  }
// Back to normal. -->
</SCRIPT>

</HEAD>

<BODY onLoad="frameBuster()">

<h1>Hahahahahahahahahaha! You can't keep me in your frame!</h1>
</BODY>
</HTML>
```

Figure 13-10 shows the Web page this code creates.

FIGURE 13-10

This figure shows the result of breaking out of frames.

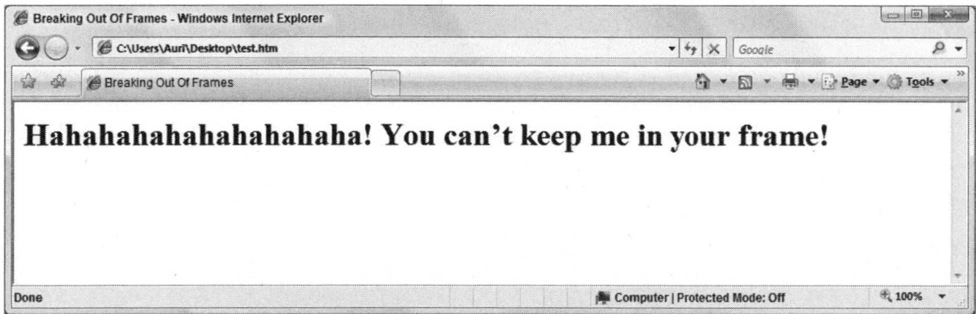

The function `frameBuster()` is called when the page is finished loading. It checks to see if the parent frame (`parent.location`) has the same URL as the Web page itself (`window.location`).

If the values of the two are not equal, they are made equal. The effect of this is to automatically detect the presence of a frame around your Web page and automatically ditch the frame.

CROSS-REF See Chapter 9 for information on frames and framesets.

Reacting to mouse movements

One of the most popular of all JavaScript techniques is the `onMouseOver` event handler (commonly called a *rollover*), which detects when the mouse pointer is over an element. Two related event handlers, `onMouseOut` and `onMouseMove`, are not as common, but are still a valuable part of your JavaScript armory.

The three event handlers are distinguished from one another by when they are detected. An `onMouseOver` event handler is triggered when the mouse pointer first crosses the edge of an element (usually an image, such as a navigation button), and remains active for as long as the pointer isn't moved off the element. An `onMouseOut` event handler is triggered when the mouse pointer is moved off the element. An `onMouseMove` event handler is triggered when the mouse pointer is over the object and is moved.

The following code demonstrates how these events work:

```
<HTML>
<HEAD>
<TITLE>Testing Mouseovers</TITLE>

<SCRIPT language="JavaScript">
<!-- Make this script invisible to old browsers.
  function showOver() {
    document.outputForm.readItHere.value = "Over";
  }

  function showOut() {
    document.outputForm.readItHere.value = "Out";
  }
// Back to normal. -->
</SCRIPT>

</HEAD>

<BODY>

>
<IMG src="female_student_relaxing_200.gif" width="200" height="177"
border="0" onMouseOver="showOver()" onMouseOut="showOut()">

<FORM id="outputForm" name="outputForm">
<INPUT type="text" id="readItHere" name="readItHere" value="Nada">
```

```
</FORM>

</BODY>
</HTML>
```

The two functions each write a word (Over or Out) into a text box depending on whether the MouseOver or MouseOut event is occurring, as shown in Figure 13-11.

FIGURE 13-11

This page uses a mouseover image.

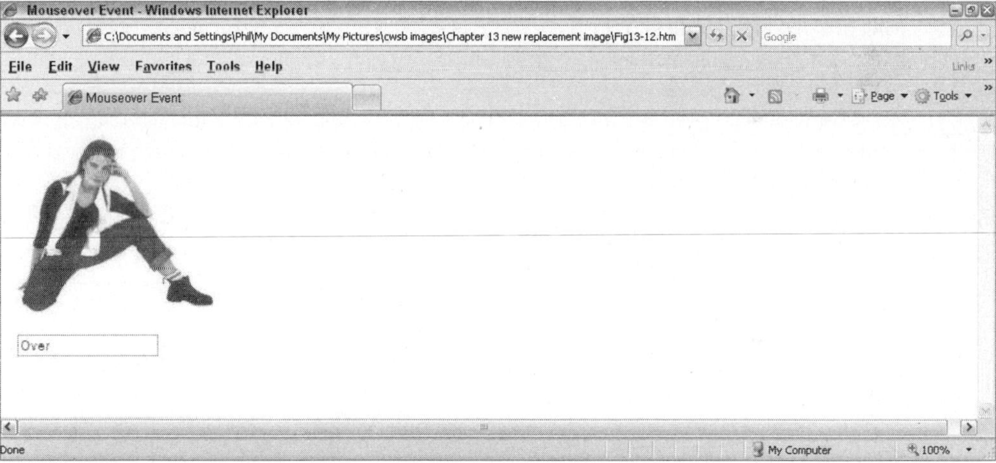

NOTE **It is strongly recommended that you use both the <id> tag and a <name> tag with identical values. The Document Object Model (DOM) uses the id attribute to identify elements, for example when using document.getElementById(). However, browsers use the name value to identify elements when using expressions like document.outputForm.readItHere.value. If you are going to send a form, you need to specify the name attribute. If you don't, the information won't even be sent to the server.**

Clicking and double-clicking

Every time you click with your mouse, you are causing three different events. Pressing the mouse button down is a MouseDown event, and releasing it causes a MouseUp event. The combination of these two is the third event, which is called an OnClick event.

CAUTION **Although you can assign all three events to a single element, it is not recommended that you assign both a MouseUp and an OnClick event to the same element because both are triggered when the mouse button is released.**

The following example creates a graphic demonstration in which the background color of the page changes in response to `MouseDown` and `MouseUp` events:

```
<HTML>
<HEAD>
<TITLE>Changing Background Colors</TITLE>

<SCRIPT language="JavaScript">
<!-- Make this script invisible to old browsers.

function makeBlue() {
  document.bgColor="blue";
}
function makeWhite() {
  document.bgColor="white";
}
// Back to normal. -->
</SCRIPT>

</HEAD>

<BODY>

<A href="#" onMouseDown="makeBlue()" onMouseUp="makeWhite()">Click
this to change the background color back and forth.</A>
</BODY>
</HTML>
```

Two functions are defined — one to set the document's background color to blue, and the other to return it to white. The first is triggered when the mouse button is pressed over the link, and the second when it is released. Figure 13-12 shows the Web page when the mouse button is down. The `# sign` is acting as a placeholder until the actual link is inserted.

FIGURE 13-12

You can change background colors with MouseDown and MouseUp events.

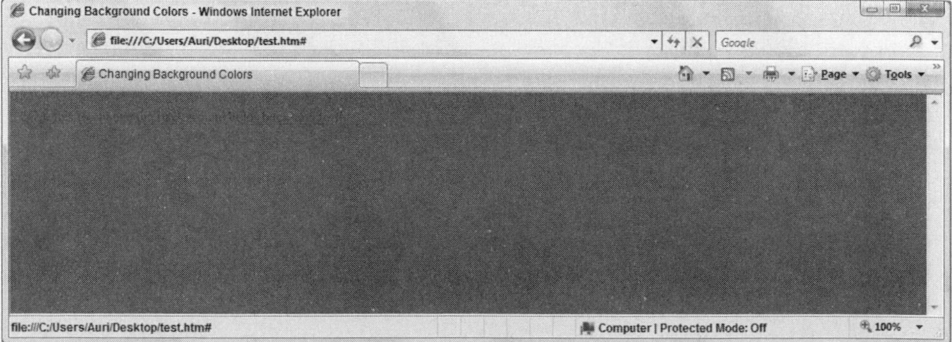

Pressing and releasing keys

Using your keyboard is pretty much the same thing as clicking a mouse button as far as JavaScript is concerned. Once again, what we normally think of as a single action — pressing a key — is broken down into three different events. When the key is pressed, but before it is released, it is causing a KeyDown event. Releasing the key causes a KeyUp event, and the combination of the two actions is a KeyPress event.

This works exactly as the mouse buttons, and the preceding example could be rewritten as follows:

```
<HTML>
<HEAD>
<TITLE>Changing Background Colors with Keys</TITLE>

<SCRIPT language="JavaScript">
<!-- Make this script invisible to old browsers.

function makeBlue() {
  document.bgColor="blue";
}
function makeWhite() {
  document.bgColor="white";
}
// Back to normal. -->
</SCRIPT>

</HEAD>

<BODY>
<FORM>
<INPUT type="text" onKeyDown="makeBlue()" onKeyUp="makeWhite()">
</FORM>

</BODY>
</HTML>
```

In this version, the background colors change in reaction to typing that takes place within a text box in a form. Each time a key is pressed, the background color changes to blue. Each time it is released, the background color reverts to white. This causes the screen to rapidly flash back and forth between the colors as you type.

Seeing Elements as Objects

Object-oriented programming sounds ominous at first, but it's simply a way of looking at things. Even if you've never done any programming at all, you're already familiar with the way it works, because it's simply an expression of the way the real world works. The book in your hands is an object. It contains other objects such as chapters, illustrations, example code, and so forth.

Similarly, a Web browser is an object that contains other objects that are represented by HTML elements.

When you're using JavaScript, a Web browser is called a *window object*. The Web page it contains is known as a *document object*. If there is an image in the Web page, it's an *image object*. You get the idea — it's all just another way of stating what's showing up in the browser and what's on the page. Objects are referenced from the top down, starting with the window object, and each object is separated from the next by a period. Thus, the Web page is referenced as `window.document`. If it contains an element named `sidePanel`, that form can be referenced as `window. document.sidePanel`. It's just as if you're going down a stairway one step at a time.

The Document Object Model (DOM) is a way of looking at a Web page that sees every element as an object and all of the element's attributes as properties of that object. Every object on a Web page is also a property of some object that is higher in the hierarchy than it is.

CAUTION **It's common practice among Web designers to skip the stage specifying the window object — because one Web browser is involved, you don't usually have to state that fact. Thus, many Web designers would simply write `document.sidePanel` instead of `window.document.sidePanel`. However, this approach can be hazardous, occasionally creating unforeseen results. Forms that are specified by name instead of position in the forms array, for example, can return a false error message if the entire object hierarchy leading to them is not used.**

Understanding properties

Every object has properties. For example, as an object, a coat has several properties, and some of these are the same for all coats — the number of sleeves, for example. Other coats have properties specific to that particular coat. The coat, as an object, has a size property. It has a color property. It has a lapel property, a pocket property, a lining property, and so on.

In JavaScript, properties are referenced by appending them to the object name. The two — object and property — are separated by a period, just as objects in the object tree are. For example, the size property would be expressed as `coat.size`.

To put it all together, if you want to get the text that a visitor typed into a text box named `myText` in the form named `formSeven`, you would express it as `document.formSeven .myText.value`. This flows down from the document object to the form object to the text box object, and finally to the value of that last object.

To get the value in a form that you can actually work with, you assign it to a variable, as in the following example:

```
wordsTyped = document.formSeven.myText.value;
```

From that point on, all you have to do is to work with the variable. The following example shows how this can be done in a form that allows a visitor to change the background color of the page:

```
<HTML>
<HEAD>
<TITLE>Working with Properties</TITLE>

<SCRIPT language="JavaScript">
<!-- Make this script invisible to old browsers.

function getColor(){
  colorChoice = document.pickAColor.visitorColor.options[document
.pickAColor.visitorColor.selectedIndex].value;
  document.bgColor = colorChoice;
}

// Back to normal. -->
</SCRIPT>

</HEAD>
<BODY bgcolor="Green">

<H1>Pick a color, any color.</H1>

<FORM id="pickAColor" name="pickAColor">
<SELECT id="visitorColor" name="visitorColor" onChange="getColor()">
<OPTION value="Aqua">Aqua</OPTION>
<OPTION value="Black">Black</OPTION>
<OPTION value="Blue">Blue</OPTION>
<OPTION value="Fuschia">Fuschia</OPTION>
<OPTION value="Gray">Gray</OPTION>
<OPTION value="Green">Green</OPTION>
<OPTION value="Lime">Lime</OPTION>
<OPTION value="Maroon">Maroon</OPTION>
<OPTION value="Navy">Navy</OPTION>
<OPTION value="Olive">Olive</OPTION>
<OPTION value="Purple">Purple</OPTION>
<OPTION value="Red">Red</OPTION>
<OPTION value="Silver">Silver</OPTION>
<OPTION value="Teal">Teal</OPTION>
<OPTION value="White">White</OPTION>
<OPTION value="Yellow">Yellow</OPTION>
</SELECT>
</FORM>

</BODY>
</HTML>
```

FIGURE 13-13

You can change colors using list properties.

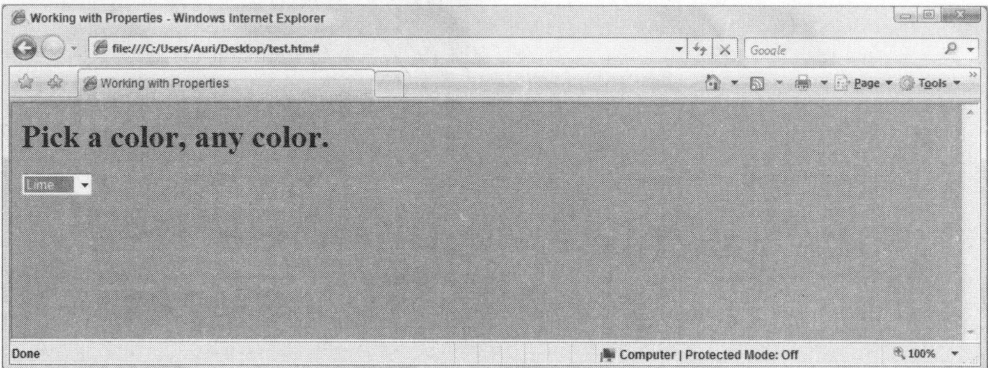

The results, as shown in Figure 13-13, are that the color that is chosen from the list sets the background color of the page.

Here's how it works, step by step:

1. The visitor chooses a color from the list.
2. The `onChange` event handler is triggered, which calls the function `getColor()`.
3. The function reads the value of the choice — the `selectedIndex` of the list — and assigns that value to a variable called `colorChoice`.
4. The value of that variable is assigned to the `document.bgColor` property, thus changing the color of the page.

Working with methods

A *method* is a capability of an object rather than a property of it. Think of a method as a built-in function that you don't have to bother with writing. For example, a refrigerator with an automatic ice maker has the capability to make ice, which is a method of the refrigerator object, and it is expressed as `refrigerator.makeIce()`.

The document object, for example, has a `write` method, which enables you to programmatically add new text to the Web page. It is expressed as `document.write()`. It's easy to confuse properties and methods at first, because both follow the object's name. Just remember that, as with functions, methods end with a closed set of parentheses.

The parentheses are there for a reason — the same reason they are there in functions. They are meant to hold parameters for the method to process. The parameters for the `document.write()`

method are the text or HTML code to be placed onto the Web page. To add the sentence, "Hey, I'm changing the page!" to the page, you would write the following:

```
document.write(Hey, I'm changing the page!);
```

Remember, you're not limited to adding only plain text — you can use HTML code as well. The following variation is just as valid as the original example:

```
document.write(Hey, I'm <I>changing</I> the page!);
```

Form Validation

One of the most common uses of JavaScript is to validate forms before they are submitted to the Web server.

The following code shows how to verify that the data in a form contains a name and an e-mail address. It uses regular expressions to perform the validation.

```
<html>
<head>
<title>Validating Forms</title>

<script language="JavaScript">
<!-- Make this script invisible to old browsers.

function check()
{
  if (document.form.name.value.length==0 )
  {
        alert ("You must enter your name");
        return false;
  };
  var nameRe=new RegExp("^[A-Za-z]+$");
  if (!nameRe.test(document.form.name.value))
  {
        alert ("You must enter your name only alphabetic characters
are allowed no spaces");
        return false;
  }
  var emailRe=new RegExp("^ [A-Za-z0-9]+@[A-Za-z0-9.]+$");
  if (!emailRe.test(document.form.email.value))
  {
        alert ("You must enter a valid email address eg: user@host
        .com");
        return false;
  }
  return true;
```

```
};
// Back to normal. -->
</script>

</head>

<body>

<form id="form" name="form" onSubmit="return check();">
First Name <INPUT type="text" id="name" name="name">
Email <INPUT type="text" id="email" name="email">
<input type="submit" value="Send">
</form>

</body>
</html>
```

In the form, we specify the `onSubmit` handler to call the function `check` before the form is submitted. If the event handler returns `false`, then the form is not submitted, so we say `return check()`. The `check` function validates the form and returns `true` if it is valid.

The following expression returns the number of characters in the string entered in the `name` text box. If it is zero then we ask the user to enter something.

```
document.form.name.value.length
```

Now for the complicated part — regular expressions. Regular expressions (REs) are used to search for matches of a particular character sequence in text. They are part of many programming languages — the Unix operating system uses them extensively in tools from the command line, and they have been included in JavaScript since version 1.1.

The following is brief (and simplified) explanation of REs.

You are probably familiar with wildcard characters such as ? (representing one character) and * (representing any number of characters) in the DOS and Unix command line. The regular expression for ? would be a period (`.`), followed by any character, or alternatively `[A-Za-z0-9]`, which means one character in the ranges of A to Z, a to z, and 0 to 9. If it is not in the given ranges, then it doesn't match. So, for *, it would be:

```
.*
```

or alternatively:

```
[A-Za-z0-9]*
```

The * at the end means zero or more of the preceding character or range of characters. It's a bit confusing that the RE for * has a * in it, but you have to bear in mind that they are different syntaxes. If we wanted one or more, we could write:

```
[A-Za-z0-9][A-Za-z0-9]*
```

But there is a better way:

```
[A-Za-z0-9]+
```

Here, + means one or more of the previous expression. In the preceding code, we checked the name with:

```
RegExp("^ [A-Za-z]+$")
```

This is because when the test method of the RE is called it returns `true` if the character sequence is found anywhere in the text. However, we want it to only return `true` if the whole text given corresponds to the RE. The ^ character specifies the start of the text and the $ specifies the end of the text.

So, `^[A-Za-z]+$` translates into English as a match for text that, from start to end, is composed of a sequence of one or more alphabetic characters. Now for the e-mail:

```
^ [A-Za-z0-9]+@[A-Za-z0-9.]+$
```

It starts with a sequence of one or more alphanumeric characters, has a @ in the middle, and then ends with a sequence of one or more alphanumeric characters. However, this isn't quite specific enough for a real e-mail address. If you really want to graduate in REs, take a look at the following:

```
^[A-Za-z0-9]+[-A-Za-z0-9._]*@([-A Za-z0-9]+\.)+[A-Za-z]{2,5}$
```

Table 13-5 takes you through this complex example of REs step by step.

TABLE 13-5

Complex Example of Regular Expressions

Part of the Regular Expression	Explanation
^	Starts with.
[A-Za-z0-9] +	A sequence of one or more alphanumeric characters.
[-A-Za-z0-9._]*	A sequence of zero or more alphanumeric characters or -, . or _. The - is specified as the first character because in this position it doesn't signify a range just the character itself.
([-A-Za-z0-9] + \.) +	The brackets turn a list of expressions into one group expression, so this really means one or more of the sequences alphanumeric character or - followed by a ., so this matched `abc.xyz`.

You can also check to see if check boxes, option buttons, or menu options are being selected. The following example shows how:

```
<html>
<head>
<title>Validating Forms</title>

<script language="JavaScript">
<!-- Make this script invisible to old browsers.

function check()
{
  if(! (document.form.football.checked && document.form
.swimming.checked))
  {
         alert("We only accept members who play football and swim so
you might as well select them both");
         return false;
  }
  if (document.form.gender[0].checked)
  {
         alert("You have to select your gender");
         return false;
  }
  if (document.form.language.selectedIndex==0)
  {
         alert("Please select a language");
         return false;   }

return true;

};
// Back to normal. -->
</script>
</head>

<body>
<h2>Club Membership</h2>
<form id="form" name="form" onSubmit="return check();">
First Name <INPUT type="text" id="name" name="name">
<br>
Gender
<input type="radio" name="gender" value="none" checked="checked">
<input type="radio" name="gender" value="male">
<input type="radio" name="gender" value="female">
<br>
Hobbies
<input type="checkbox" name="football">
<input type="checkbox" name="swimming">
```

```
<br>
Language <select name="language">
<option value="none">Please Select</option>
<option value="en">English</option>
<option value="de">German</option>
<option value="es">Spanish</option>
</select>
<br>
<input type="submit" value="Send">
</form>

</body>
</html>
```

Examining Browser Compatibility

That old bugaboo of Web designers, browser incompatibility, is nowhere more evident than when working with JavaScript. For example, the following code is perfectly valid JavaScript, yet it doesn't work in all browsers that have JavaScript support:

```
<HTML>
<HEAD>
<TITLE>Testing Mouseovers</TITLE>

<SCRIPT language="JavaScript">
<!-- Make this script invisible to old browsers.

function showOver() {
outputForm.readItHere.value = "Over";
}
function showOut() {
outputForm.readItHere.value = "Out";
}
// Back to normal. -->
</SCRIPT>

</HEAD>

<BODY>
<IMG src="female student relaxing_200.gif" width="200" height="177"
onMouseOver="showOver()" onMouseOut="showOut()">
<FORM id="outputForm" name="outputForm">
<INPUT type="text" id="readItHere" name="readItHere" value="Nada">
</FORM>
</BODY>
</HTML>
```

To make the same code work with other browsers, the reference to the text box's value must be changed from `outputForm.readItHere.value` to `document.outputForm.readItHere.value`. This is necessary, even though a form can only be a property of the document object.

The revised version (which works with Internet Explorer, Firefox, and Opera) is as follows:

```
<HTML>
<HEAD>
<TITLE>Testing Mouseovers</TITLE>

<SCRIPT language="JavaScript">
<!-- Make this script invisible to old browsers.

function showOver() {
document.outputForm.readItHere.value = "Over";
}
function showOut() {
document.outputForm.readItHere.value = "Out";
}
// Back to normal. -->
</SCRIPT>

</HEAD>

<BODY>
<A href="#" onMouseOver="showOver()" onMouseOut="showOut()">
<IMG src="female student relaxing_200.gif" width="200" height="177"
border="0">
</A>
<FORM id="outputForm" name="outputForm">
<INPUT type="text" id="readItHere" name="readItHere" value="Nada">
</FORM>
</BODY>
</HTML>
```

All modern browsers support `MouseOver` and `MouseOut` events for all elements.

You could become the world's greatest expert on JavaScript by designing complex code that works with both browsers. Believe us, some of the things you need to do to make the same function work on both browsers are incredibly complex. We've only scratched the surface. Other than that unpalatable alternative, though, what can you do about the differences? Many Web designers have adopted the technique of creating one Web site for each browser, making an entry page that determines the browser type and version. This page automatically redirects a visitor to the appropriate Web page.

Browser detection and redirection is done with the `navigator` object. Despite the name, it's present in Internet Explorer also. The browser name is found with the `navigator.appName` property and the browser version is detected with the `navigator.appVersion` property. The following code creates a Web page that displays these values for you:

```
<HTML>
<HEAD>
<TITLE>Reading and Displaying Browser Information</TITLE>
</HEAD>
<BODY>

<SCRIPT language="JavaScript">
<!-- Make this script invisible to old browsers.

document.writeln("Your browser is: " + navigator.appName + "<BR>");
document.writeln("The version is: " + navigator.appVersion + "<BR>");

// Back to normal. -->
</SCRIPT>

</BODY>
</HTML>
```

Figure 13-14 shows the results. This means that the browser used is MSIE version 4.0, it is compatible through MSIE 6.0, and can run in Windows NT 5.1

FIGURE 13-14

This figure shows the result of reading and displaying browser information.

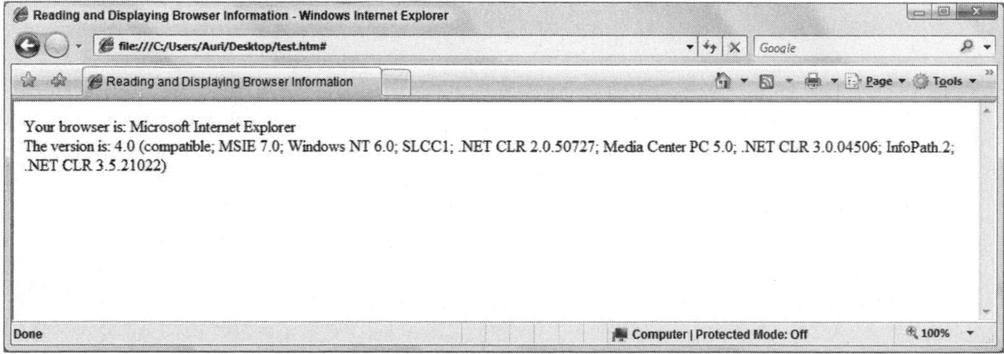

NOTE **The actual output, of course, depends upon which browser you are using.**

To apply this capability of sending visitors to an appropriate Web page for their browsers, you would use an `if` statement. Basically, you need to say "If the browser is Firefox, then go to the Firefox-enabled page. If it's Internet Explorer, then go to the Microsoft-enabled page instead." Of course, there are all sorts of variations, depending on your needs. You might want to take action only for Internet Explorer users, for example. The principles, however, are the same.

The following code tests to see if the browser is Internet Explorer. If not, it tests to see if it's Firefox. If it's either one, it sends the browser to the appropriate Web page. If it's neither, this Web page displays a message stating that the visitor is using a third kind of browser:

```
<!DOCTYPE HTML PUBLIC "-//W3C//DTD HTML 4.01 Transitional//EN">

<html>
<head>
<title>Finding Browser Type</title>
<script type="text/javascript">

function browserTesting()
{
  if (navigator.userAgent.indexOf("MSIE") != -1)
    {
    alert("You are running Microsoft Internet Explorer.");
  {
  window.location = "http://www.microsoft.com/windows/
products/winfamily/ie/default.mspx";
  }
  }
  else if (navigator.userAgent.indexOf("Firefox") != -1) {
    alert("You are running FireFox.");
  {
 window.location="http://www.mozilla.com/en-US/firefox/?utm_id=Q108
&utm_source=google&utm_medium=ppc&gclid=COTlyODi2pICFQEoPQod3FCGkg";
  }
  }

  else
    {
    alert("You are not using either Firefox or Internet Explorer.");
    }
}
```

```
</script>


</head>
<body>
<input type="button" value="Browser Type?"
onclick="browserTesting()"/>
</body>
</html>
```

If you were to check for Firefox, you would look for `navigator.userAgent="Firefox"`. For Opera, you would check for `window.opera="Opera"`. For Safari, it would be `navigator.vendor="Safari"`.

Although this technique of browser sniffing is very common on Web sites, there are several major problems. The first is that there is no real standard as to how browsers identify themselves in the app name, so you might not identify it correctly. Also, there are more than 30 browsers currently in use on the Web — Internet Explorer, Firefox, and Opera are among the most popular. Imagine the complex `if` statement required to support all of these. And what happens if a new super cool browser suddenly appears on the market and everyone starts using it? You would have to change all of your Web pages to support it.

If you want to use specific methods, the best way to handle browser detection is to test for capabilities. For example, you can test to see if the browser supports the DOM by checking for `getElementById`, or whether it is Internet Explorer by checking for `document.all`. The code is as follows:

```
if (document.getElementById)
{
  //Code that requires DOM support goes here.
}
else if (document.all)
{
  //Code specific to Internet Explorer goes here.
}
else
{
  //If it's none of the above should we kindly
  //ask the user to upgrade???
  //In fact it could be a braille browser
  //or some other custom browser.
}
```

JavaScript Quick Reference

The following provides a quick reference for key items discussed in this chapter:

- var — This is a location in memory.
- numeric — This variable is used in calculations. It does not have quotation marks around it.
- non-numeric — This variable has quotation marks around it and is used for strings, characters, and numeric values that are not used in calculations These are sometimes referred to as *literals*.
- =, -, *, /, % — These are arithmetic operators.
- <;, <=, >, >= — These are comparison operators.
- &&, ||, ! — These are logical operators.
- *Function* — This is a user-generated method called from the body of the program to execute its blocks of statements.
- if...else — This is a conditional statement determining which branch in the program the logic might flow to.
- for...next — This is a looping structure used when the number of repetitions is known in advance (preset).
- *Event* — This is an action taken by a visitor to your site.
- <onLoad> — This is an attribute that specifies command(s) for browser to execute while loading Web page.
- <onUnload> — This specifies actions to be taken by Web browser upon shedding a Web page.
- *Property* — This is a characteristic describing the object.
- *Method* — This is a capability of an object.

Summary

JavaScript is a programming language that works within a Web browser to give you greater control over the appearance and behavior of your Web pages.

In this chapter, you learned that JavaScript is used to create programs that read and alter the values of HTML elements. A *variable* is an item that holds a value that is expected to change over time. Any time you use JavaScript to tell a browser to do one thing, you're making a *statement*.

A *switch* structure is an iterative structure that simplifies coding. An *array* is a simple way to store multiple values in a single variable. A *function* is a grouped series of statements that execute one after another after being called to execute from within the program.

Each element on the Web page is a separate object.

Chapter 14 investigates ways to place the Web site you have designed on the Web, and discusses best practices for site placement.

Chapter 14

Putting It on the Web

Once you've created your Web site, you'll naturally want to put it online, right? Although you might have some Web space through your Internet service provider (ISP) or through a free Web service, a superior Web site deserves superior Web space. And picking that Web space involves just a little forethought, some planning, and even a little bit of fun.

In this chapter, you'll find a new home for your Web pages and move them in. Everything from picking your domain name to uploading your pages with an FTP program is covered here. Whether you just need a home for a personal home page or an expandable site for your e-commerce solution, you'll be ready to go when your Web site is finished.

IN THIS CHAPTER

Getting Your Domain Name

Your Web site's URL is the most visible part of your online identity. It's what you put on your business cards, in your advertisements, and on company T-shirts and letterhead. It's how people remember where you are on the Web, so an easily remembered URL is as important nowadays as an easily remembered company name.

Although you can use a URL offered by free Web space providers or your own ISP (such as `http://geocities.yahoo.com`), most businesses and many individuals buy their own domain names to make it easy for people to find them on the Web. If your online presence is `www.GoDaddy.com`, people can remember and find your site more quickly and easily. A domain name is generally a worthwhile and very affordable investment, once you're ready to get serious about your Web site and go beyond a simple personal page.

Choosing a domain name

Dot-com has become synonymous with *online business*. That's because the `.com` ending of many domain names stands for *commercial*. Originally, the domain name system was set up to categorize online entities by their types. The top-level domain names are the last part of a domain name (such as `.com`). Each top-level domain stands for a different category. Thus, there's `.com` (for commercial), `.org` (organization, usually nonprofit), `.net` (network services such as ISPs), `.gov` (government agencies only), `.edu` (educational), and `.mil` (military). Unless you're a public agency, you can't get a domain name in one of the last three top-level domains, but you can get them in `.com`, `.org`, and `.net`.

The Internet Corporation for Assigned Names and Numbers (ICANN) has also approved additional top-level domains: `.biz`, `.info`, `.name`, `.pro`, `.mobi`, `.aero`, and `.coop`.

As you think about possible domain names, you might want to follow these guidelines for making a decision:

- `.com`, `.pro`, `.aero`, or `.biz` — These are for a company or corporation.
- `.org` or `.info` — These are for a nonprofit organization.
- `.net` — These are for network service, but are usually used as a common alternative to .com, since many .com names are taken.
- `.name` or `.coop` — These are for personal Web site. You may also want to use a country-specific domain name.

You should also consider the following questions:

- Can I pronounce the name easily? Will people know how to spell it just by hearing it?
- Can I spell the name clearly? Many letters (especially "f" and "s") sound similar when spelled out over the phone.
- Is the name easy to remember? Does it have something to do with the content of my Web space, or the product or service I'm providing?

These days, most people realize that they're probably not going to get their first choice in domain names. Let's face it, most of the shorter domains are taken, and many of the longer ones are hard to pronounce or to type. So, when you go looking for a domain name, remember that it's hard to find a good domain — but not impossible. Have a list of at least 10 possible domains that would be acceptable, but don't go register them all. Domain "squatting" is one reason there just aren't enough domain names to go around anymore. Luckily, most domain name services will help you choose a domain name that's similar if your initial choice isn't available.

Once you have your list, the first thing to do is check out the WHOIS lookup at `http://netsol.com/whois`, shown in Figure 14-1. Type in the domain name you'd like and click Search. Don't include the `www` — that's not part of the domain name.

FIGURE 14-1

The WHOIS lookup at Network Solutions enables you to look up a domain name quickly and easily.

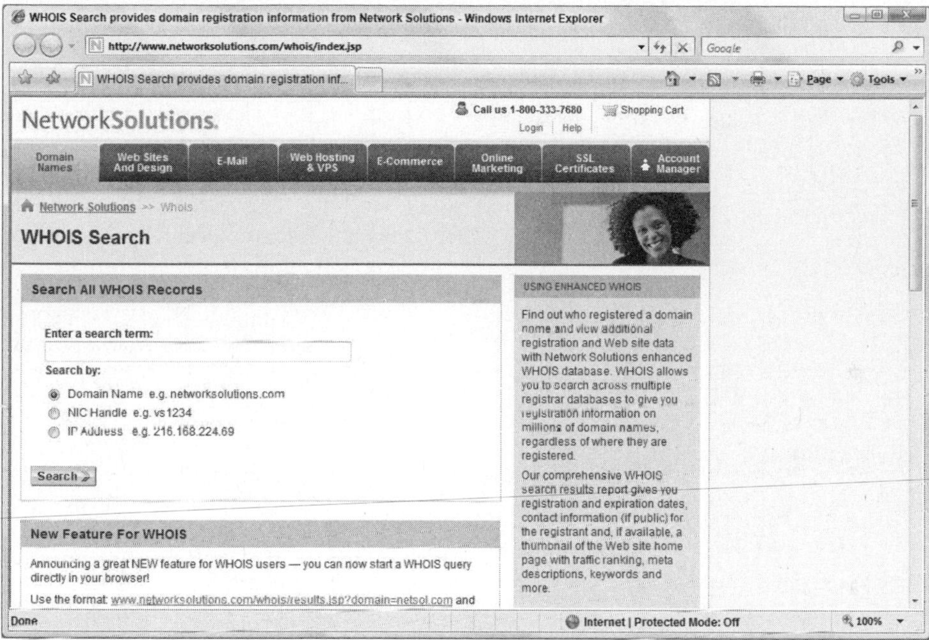

If the results look something like Figure 14-2, go back and try a different name. The domain that you wanted is already taken by someone else.

TIP **If you have some money to spend and you really want that domain name, you can always send a letter to the administrative contact offering to buy the domain. Popular domain names can run from a few thousand to a couple million dollars, so be sure to get your credit limit raised before you call!**

If the results of your domain name search come back empty, you'll get a response similar to Figure 14-3. Here's your chance to grab that domain! Click Add Selected Domain(s) to Order to register the domain using Network Solutions, or find a different registrar.

Picking a registrar

When you go to register your domain name, you'll need to find a registration company (also called a *registrar*) to register with. Registrars vary in price and services, ranging from about $7 a year to $80 a year, depending on the extension. Few registrars are more than $35 per year, although several of them are less. A good online guide to picking a registrar is at `www.register.com`.

FIGURE 14-2

WHOIS reveals the contact information for every domain name registered with Network Solutions.

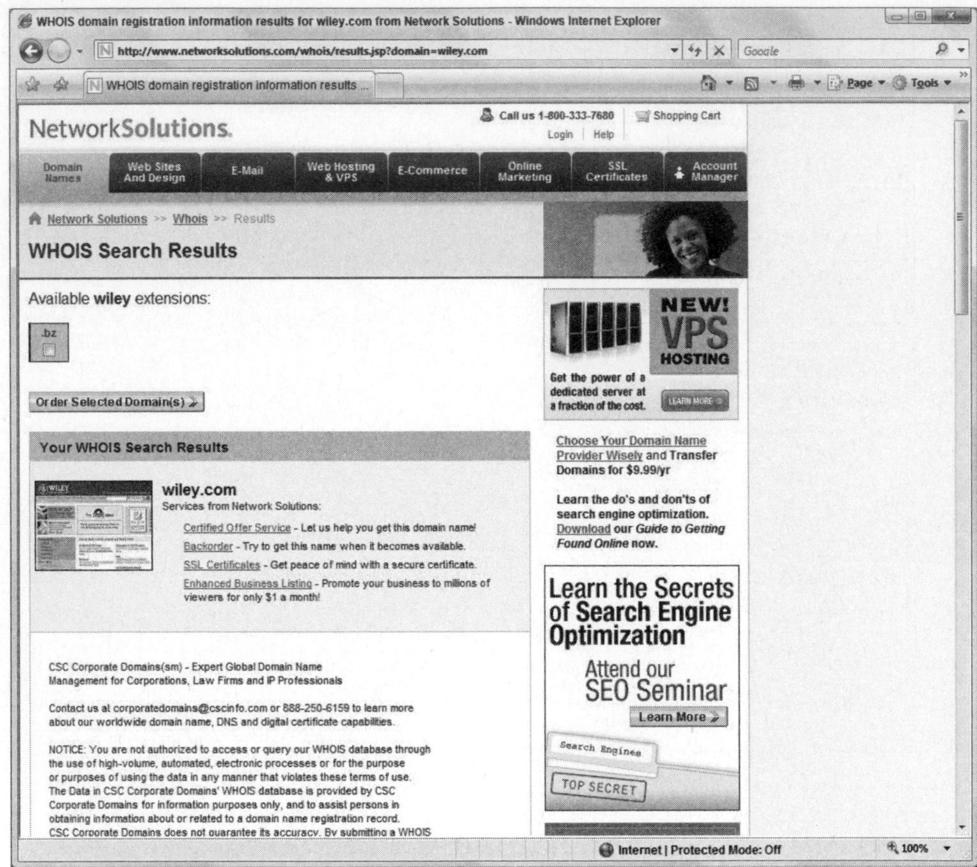

Some registrars require you to pay a fee if you want to transfer a domain name. Others don't. The transfer fee shouldn't be more than a year's worth of domain name registration. Also, you shouldn't have to pay a sign-up fee for registering your domain name, and you shouldn't sign up for more than two years at first. Be willing to sign up for those two years, though — a domain name is a commitment. Many registrars require you to create a Domain Name Service (DNS) server entry within a specific amount of time. This policy prevents name grabbing by companies and individuals who just want to "hold onto" a domain name and prevent others from getting or using it.

TIP **If you don't have a Web space provider or a domain name yet, hold off on registering your domain name. Most Web hosting companies offer reasonable domain name registration as part of their services.**

FIGURE 14-3

When a domain hasn't been registered yet, WHOIS lets you know.

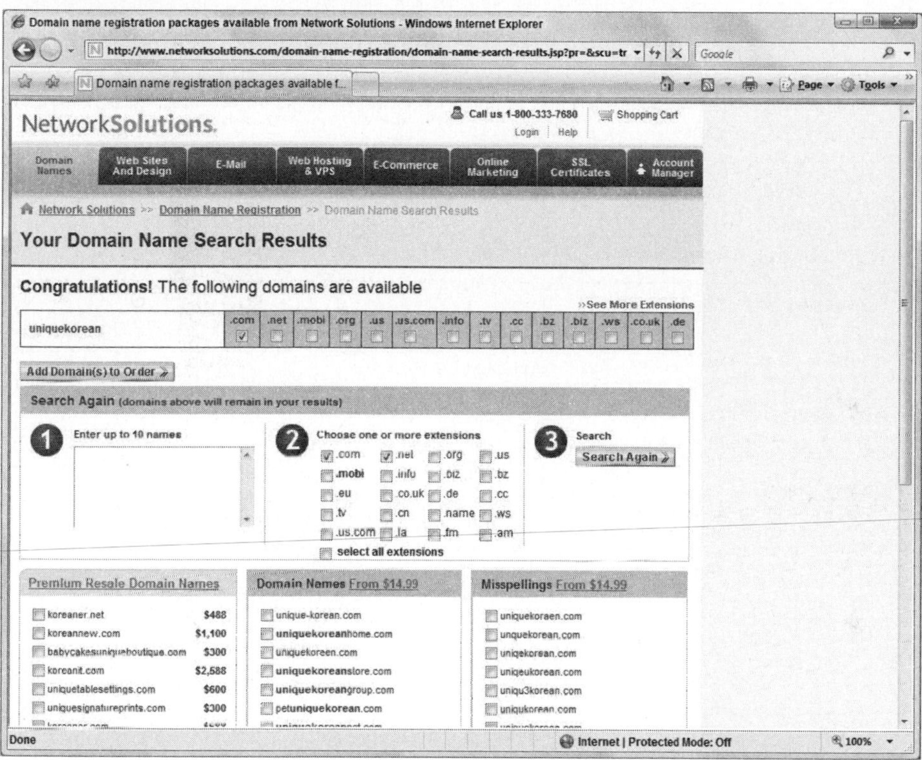

CAUTION **You would be well advised to be circumspect on accepting any offers of a free Web page site with domain name registration, however. It may be little more than an ad magnet. Those ads could be from your competitors, or on topics that you don't want but have no control over. It's best to use your own domain name and a hosting provider that doesn't add ads. Ask yourself, "What message am I sending to my customer?"**

There's another domain name registration option available to individuals, organizations, and many businesses. Although the registry is pretty much tapped out, the country-specific domains are not. Every country has its own rules on registering a domain. Many countries will let nonresidents register domain names for their country-specific codes. That's how all those `.tv` Web sites got their domain names — they registered with a domain registry at `www.tv` for Tuvalo, a small Pacific Island nation near Fiji.

The United States will let you register any `.us` domain, as long as you provide complete geographic information in your domain name.

For example, Wiley Publishing, the publisher of this book, could register wileypublishing.new-york.ny.us. While that might not be the easiest domain name to remember for a corporation, it works pretty well if you're an individual or organization and just want your own domain.

To register a domain name in the .us domain, go to www.nic.us. To register a domain name in another country, check the list at www.marcaria.com.

Coping with registration pitfalls

There aren't a lot of things that can go seriously wrong when registering your domain name, but there are a lot of little hang-ups that can happen when you register or transfer a domain name. Just remember that even though "Internet time" is a thousand times faster than the real world, there are still people behind the process of domain name registration. Be patient, and be wary.

Signing up for multiple years at a discount

Domain name registrars often offer a bulk discount if you sign up and prepay for several years' worth of service at the outset. Although this may seem like a good idea, be aware of how much time you're actually signing up for.

Other registrars might offer up to five years with some type of discount. In general, you should avoid being locked in to a registrar for more than two years. Domain name registrars may change the terms of service agreements in the middle of your contract. With a five-year contract, you could end up committed to new service terms that you don't agree with. In most cases, you can leave the registrar, but if you break your contract early, you probably can't get a refund.

CAUTION **Also keep in mind that many providers store your credit card information and automatically renew you when your original period expires. If you use a check card, make sure that you don't get bank fees. If you have a credit card and it expires, you may lose your domain name. Most registrars will notify you when they're about to renew you, or if your credit card has expired. However, remain aware of the status of your domains.**

Why does it take so long?

Some domain name registrars work very efficiently. They have an online sign-up system where you just enter in your information and credit card number, and everything goes very quickly and smoothly, automatically processed with a computer. Others are a little slower. If they're slow, it usually means that there's a human being somewhere holding up the process. Usually, that translates into more careful customer service.

Even in the fastest systems, there's a technological barrier to registering a domain name Even in Internet time, the whole process can take several days. During that time, your Web site might be available in one geographical area, but not in another as one server recognizes it ahead of the time when another does.

Finding a Web Hosting Provider

A Web hosting provider is like an ISP, except that it doesn't give *you* access to the Internet; it gives the Internet access to you. Specifically, the Web hosting provider makes your Web site available and visible to the public.

Web hosting providers fall into three categories:

- Virtual hosts
- Dedicated servers
- Co-located servers

These providers generally offer different amounts of Web space, allowable bandwidth use, customer support, and technological expertise. The server itself might run on a variety of software and hardware, some of which vary in reliability and ease of use. Naturally, more choices mean more prices; as you choose a Web hosting provider, be sure to pay attention to how much the service costs, compared to how much you're getting.

Picking the right Web server

A *Web server* is the combination of hardware and software that holds and displays your Web site to the Internet. Many people will try to connect to your server all at the same time, so the machine itself should have a powerful processor and lots of random access memory (RAM). Your server should also use a strong server software program to deliver your Web pages quickly and with few errors. For the same reason, your Web server should have a very fast connection to the Internet, at least a T1 line, or better a T3. You should put as much thought into your Web server as you do into your domain name. It's a key part of your Web site — without it, there's no site at all.

Finally, the Web server software should be secure enough that you don't have to worry about hackers getting in and changing your pages or hijacking your site without your permission. If you're going to be accepting or storing financial information (including credit card data), your server should use a high level of encryption. If you're inside the United States, use 128-bit for domestic connections and 40-bit for international connections (the higher the bit rate for encryption, the better the encoding is).

Although a Web server can generally run on almost any computer, most commercial Web servers will have a sufficient amount of RAM, hard drive space, and processor speed for a small- to medium-scale Web site. Any site holding more than 100MB of data or transferring more than 500MB a day should have its own dedicated server, either onsite or in a co-location facility. Dedicated servers and co-location are discussed later in this section.

Web servers run a variety of server software programs on all operating systems (OS). Some of the most common and reliable server combinations are the following:

- Sun Solaris OS with Apache as the Web server
- Linux (any flavor) with Apache as the Web server
- Windows Server with Internet Information Server (IIS) as the Web server

Other combinations include Macintosh with Netscape or another Mac OS Web server, BeOS, and even DOS. There are even tiny Web server programs available for the PDAs!

If you're shopping for a Web server combination, and you'd like to know what your competitors or partners use, go to the Netcraft Web site at `www.netcraft.com` and enter the Web site's domain name in the field. Click "What's that site running?" to see the results. You'll be given a short description of what OS, server, and extensions are installed on the server, as shown in Figure 14-4.

FIGURE 14-4

Find the OS, Web server, and server extensions and APIs (such as PHP) for any Web server on Netcraft.

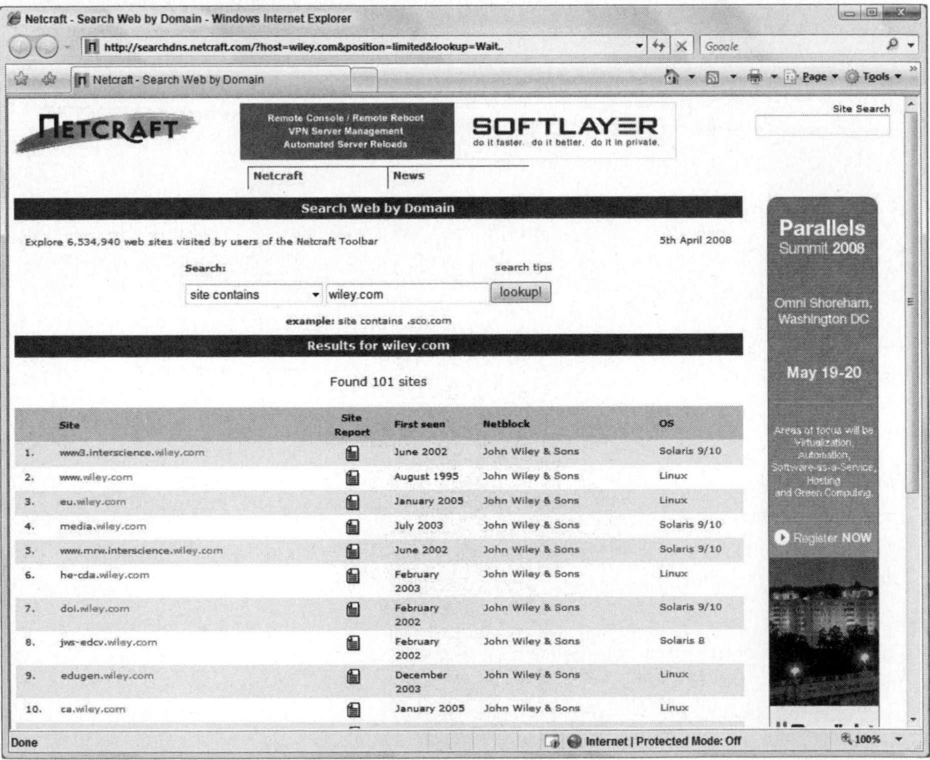

If the information is available, you can also see at a glance how long the server has been running, and when any data on it was last changed, as shown in Figure 14-5.

FIGURE 14-5

View uptime graphs and data quickly.

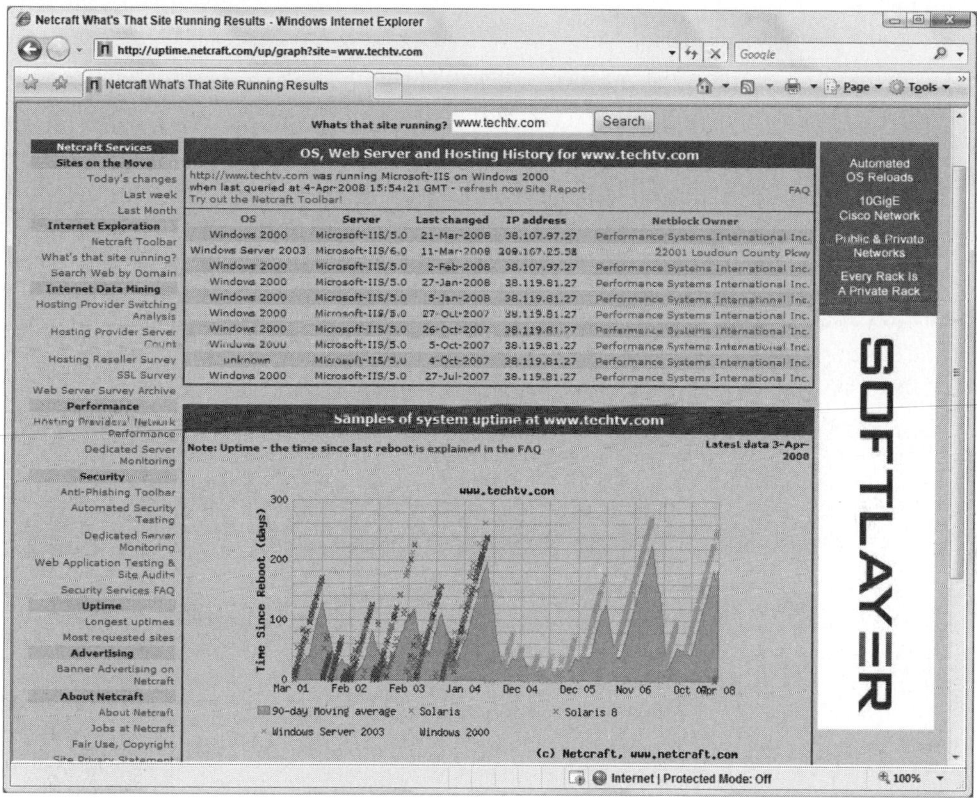

OS	Server	Last changed	IP address	Netblock Owner
Windows 2000	Microsoft-IIS/5.0	21-Mar-2008	38.107.97.27	Performance Systems International Inc.
Windows Server 2003	Microsoft-IIS/6.0	11-Mar-2008	208.167.25.38	22001 Loudoun County Pkwy
Windows 2000	Microsoft-IIS/5.0	2-Feb-2008	38.107.97.27	Performance Systems International Inc.
Windows 2000	Microsoft-IIS/5.0	27-Jan-2008	38.119.81.27	Performance Systems International Inc.
Windows 2000	Microsoft-IIS/5.0	5-Jan-2008	38.119.81.27	Performance Systems International Inc.
Windows 2000	Microsoft-IIS/5.0	27-Oct-2007	38.119.81.27	Performance Systems International Inc.
Windows 2000	Microsoft-IIS/5.0	26-Oct-2007	38.119.81.27	Performance Systems International Inc.
Windows 2000	Microsoft-IIS/5.0	5-Oct-2007	38.119.81.27	Performance Systems International Inc.
unknown	Microsoft-IIS/5.0	4-Oct-2007	38.119.81.27	Performance Systems International Inc.
Windows 2000	Microsoft-IIS/5.0	27-Jul-2007	38.119.81.27	Performance Systems International Inc.

One other thing you should look for are server extensions, APIs, and installed languages that enable you to install scripts to automate your site. An example of a Web server API is Microsoft API for Windows (MSAPI). Programmers can write scripts and programs to use MSAPI features and automate the site.

The free, open source options include Perl, a scripting language that has been used extensively on the Internet. In addition, PHP is a server-side HTML scripting language. It's probably the most effective way to create browser-independent dynamic Web pages, and it is an open source project, so no single company has control over its development.

Determining your space needs

The next question you'll probably be asking is "How much space do I need?" Well, that depends on a few things. First, are you just hosting a couple of HTML pages with a few graphics? Will you have a downloadable program on your site? Are you including audio files? Are you planning to serve Napster audio and video files?

The more complicated your media, the larger the files. The larger the files, the more space you'll need. As you know, HTML is just plain text, the simplest type of file. Compressed graphics such as GIFs and JPEGs are the next simplest type of file, followed by PDF files, audio files, and finally FLASH video. Executable programs can take up a little bit of space or a lot, depending on the size of the program. In general, however, you should plan for a lot of hard drive space if you want your users to be able to download programs and audio/video files from your site. Most Web hosting providers will provide much more than you need since storage is so cheap these days. Take the size of your site and multiply times five.

There is one other reason you might need more storage space. If you plan to run a database on your Web site, or to deliver database-driven content, you'll need to have a database available on your server. A database can be a simple Perl script and take up very little room on your hard drive, or it can be a full-blown relational database such as MySQL, Microsoft SQL Server, or Oracle, in which case you'd better invest in a multigigabyte dedicated drive. If you're doing database work (the discussion of which is out of the scope of this book), keep in mind that database space is not nearly as cheap when provided by the hosting service. However, it's usually much cheaper to pay for space from the host's database server, since you don't have to pay any of the database server licensing fees (which can be tremendous for an individual or small business).

Choosing a nonvirtual, virtual, dedicated, or co-located server

As you look at different Web hosting options, you'll notice that there is a very large variety of ways to put a Web site online. In order of technical complexity (and price), these are nonvirtual hosting, virtual hosting, dedicated servers, and co-located servers.

Nonvirtual hosting

The first option is *nonvirtual hosting*, which means that you don't have your own domain name. Instead, you either host your Web site on someone else's server (as in `www.theirdomain.com/myspace`), or you *park* your site on another domain (as in `www.myspace.theirdomain.com`). Sometimes these parked sites are also called *subdomains*. There are countless free Web space providers (such as Yahoo!, Geocities, Apple's .Mac, Tripod, TheGlobe, and others), and these usually offer nonvirtual hosting only.

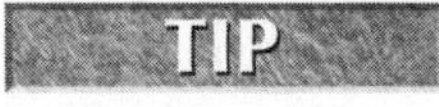

The 100 Best Free Web Space Services list at `http://100best-free-Web-space.com` is a good quick reference for choosing a free Web host.

Many ISPs offer Web space to their customers at no additional charge, and most Web hosting companies let you park your site on their domain at no additional charge. Because you don't have to pay for the domain name registration fees, the main advantage to this model is price. Sometimes domain availability is also a factor. If you can't find a domain name that suits you, you might find a Web hosting company with something similar where you can park your site and still have an easy-to-remember name. But remember, free parking may have unintended consequences.

Virtual Web hosting

The second option is called *virtual Web hosting*, or using a *virtual domain*. Here, you keep your Web pages and files on someone else's Web server, but you have your own domain name. People viewing your site don't know that your server isn't actually at your business or in a dedicated server. Depending on the size of your Web site, virtual hosting can cost anywhere from $5 per month to about $100 per month. If you have enough Web material that you need more space or bandwidth, you should consider a dedicated server.

Dedicated servers

Using a *dedicated server* involves leasing or providing your own Web server software and Internet connection, as well as the hard drive space. The hosting company maintains the Web server itself, so the hardware is maintained by someone else, and any software or technical problems are usually covered by the hosting company. These services generally cost $150 and up per month. They're good if you have a lot of files, a database, or if you're expecting a lot of hits to your site.

Co-located servers

Finally, you can purchase *co-located servers* for yourself. You own the hardware, the software, and everything in the box. You rent space on a rack in a specialized facility for computers. These facilities are generally climate-controlled for computers, have dry fire-suppression systems (so they won't fry your machine), onsite security ranging from someone who checks passes to special, locked rooms with bulletproof walls. Co-location facilities often offer technical support options. The most basic is the ability to request a technician to physically restart your machine if you're not able to go to the facility itself to fix a problem. If you choose to co-locate your server, you'll probably need to know a lot more about system administration than this book will cover, or hire someone who does.

Search for a co-location facility online at `http://www.nyi.net/colocation.html`.

When you select a co-location facility, make sure that it's close enough that you can reach it in an hour or so, in case of server trouble. Check their security and tech support options, and find out if they monitor their own network connection 24 hours a day. How quickly do they respond to network problems? Ask their current clients about their customer response and network response times. How fast is their network connection, and can they guarantee redundancy? Do they have more than one connection to the Internet in the building? Don't neglect the physical space, too. Is the room cool when you walk in? Are the aisles between the racks neat and free of clutter? Do you detect any dust when you look at their facility? Do they have a fire-suppression system that uses dry materials (such as gas) to put out fires? Dust, heat, and water are computer killers, so be picky about what you will and won't accept for these answers.

Balancing price-service ratios

As you can see, when it comes to Web space and service, you can get what you pay for, if you do a little research. Nonvirtual Web space should be free or included with your Internet service from your ISP. virtual Web space should cost from $5 per month to $100 per month, depending on how much bandwidth and storage space you get. A dedicated server is about $150 per month and up, and space in a co-location facility will cost anywhere from $300 per month to $1,000 per month and up.

But what does that $5 or $100 or $1,000 include? We've created a little table to help you understand what services are typically included or available in a virtual Web hosting package. Nonvirtual Web hosting companies usually offer the same services, unless they provide Web space for free. Free Web space companies offer a minimum of services, but you just can't beat the price. Because dedicated and co-location models put you in control of what's available on your server, we left those out of the table, too.

Typically, a Web hosting company offers two or three packages for your Web hosting needs. They might be called Silver, Gold, Platinum or Personal, Business, Executive, but they're basically three levels of Web services. Not all Web hosting companies offer the same package deals, of course, but the information from HostingMatters, Inc., shown in Table 14-1, gives you a quick look at what you might find in a typical package.

Ultimately, you want to have enough storage space, a reliable network connection, and enough user accounts to handle however many people will be working on your Web site or using your domain for e-mail or Web space. If you're the only one who will be working on the site, then you only need one FTP or telnet account. If you're one person on a ten-person team, you'll need more accounts.

NOTE **You may also wish to look at such sites as `land1.com` or `Brinkster.net` for inexpensive, reliable hosting services.**

If you're looking for a way to give accounts to Web users, ensure that you have CGI scripting, PHP, ASP.NET, Java, or a server module such as FrontPage or Expression Web available to create that kind of online community. Web user accounts aren't the same as Telnet, FTP, or e-mail accounts; they're a function of the Web site programming, not the server.

Investigating Web space providers

The best way to research Web space providers is to look at what you already have (through ISPs, work, school, or for free) and then hit the Internet. You want to look at as many Web hosting companies as possible before you make your final decision. One great resource for finding low-cost virtual and nonvirtual hosting companies is `www.budgetweb.com/budgetweb`.

Run a query to find a Web service provider that offers what you want for the price you're willing to pay, and look into them until you narrow your search down to two or three that offer similar packages at a good price.

Don't get locked into a yearly contract with your Web service provider. You should be able to leave any time you're not satisfied with their service.

TABLE 14-1

Web Hosting Plan Comparison

Service	Low-Level Plan	Mid-Level Plan	High-Level Plan
Disk Space (MB)	70	1050	2500
Data Transfer (MB)	20000	50000	100000
Sub Domains	1	35	100
FTP Accounts	1	15	50
MySQL Databases	1	9	20
E-mail Addresses	30	100	1000
Mailing Lists	—	10	40
Multi Domain Capable	1	35	100
Control Panel	Yes	Yes	Yes
FrontPage Extensions	Yes	Yes	Yes
Shell Access Available?	No	Yes	Yes
Raw Log Files	Yes	Yes	Yes
Subdomains Stats	Yes	Yes	Yes
Error Log	Yes	Yes	Yes
Perl	Yes	Yes	Yes
SSI	Yes	Yes	Yes
PHP	Yes	Yes	Yes
Monthly	$6.00	$16.00	$36.00
Quarterly	$18.00	$46.40	$99.60
Semiannually	$36.00	$86.40	$194.40
Annually	$72.00	$163.20	$367.20

Source: HostingMatters, Inc. (`www.hostmatters.com`).

Once you've picked two or three Web space providers, use the `traceroute` program to check how close to a network backbone the host company's servers are. In MS-DOS, type

tracert, followed by the domain name of the hosting company. In Linux, the program is called `traceroute` and works like this:

```
traceroute yahoo.com
```

The output is similar to this:

```
traceroute to yahoo.com (216.115.108.243), 30 hops max, 40
byte packets
 1 phoenix-nap.neta.com (206.124.164.1) 0.930 ms 0.607 ms 0.573 ms
 2 33.atm3-1-0.phnx-cust1.phnx.uswest.net (63.226.31.229) 3.934 ms
3.852 ms 3.686 ms
 3 gig2-0.phnx-gw2.phnx.uswest.net (206.80.192.251) 3.602 ms 3.702 ms
3.990 ms
 4 sl-gw15-ana-1-1.sprintlink.net (144.232.192.21) 11.339 ms
11.496 ms 11.467 ms
 5 sl-bb22-ana-5-0.sprintlink.net (144.232.1.109) 11.451 ms 11.927 ms
12.076 ms
 6 sl-bb20-ana-15-0.sprintlink.net (144.232.1.178) 11.505 ms
12.734 ms 12.016 ms
 7 sl-intsys-6-0-0.sprintlink.net (144.228.179.226) 61.808 ms
62.052 ms 61.629 ms
 8 pos4-0-622M.wr1.LAX1.gblx.net (206.132.112.85) 63.554 ms 63.292 ms
64.401 ms
 9 pos2-0-2488M.wr2.SFO1.gblx.net (206.132.110.85) 261.032 ms
274.364 ms *
10 so-6-0-0-2488M.wr2.SNV2.gblx.net (208.50.169.113) 258.041 ms
260.173 ms
```

Each line is a hop (or move from one machine to another) in the network connection. Essentially, it took 10 "hops" from `phoenix-nap.neta.com` (where the `tracert` connection started) to `yahoo.com`. It also took 260 milliseconds to reach `yahoo.com`.

You can also use `www.tracert.com/cgi-bin/trace.pl` to run `tracert` through the Web.

The `traceroute` originated through our service provider. The number of hops and server locations would be different if it started from your site.

Testing Responsiveness to Your Needs

In addition to the speed of the connection, you might want to check a few other ways that your Web hosting company can respond. The first is reliability. What's the uptime of the Web server and network connection? The Web server uptime can generally be obtained from Netcraft at `www.netcraft.com`. The network reliability is a little trickier. In general, you should go to the various online Web hosting company review sites and Usenet newsgroups, such as `alt.www.webmaster`, and check what's said about your host when you do a Web search on their name plus the word "review."

Obtaining customer service

The second thing you want to test is the customer service. If the Web hosting company doesn't have a phone number listed on its Web site, go with another company. If it does list one and it claims to offer 24-hour customer service, call the company at 1:00 in the morning to see if it's real. If you get voicemail or an answering service, you can expect that network problems won't be solved until the next morning, something you might not be able to afford. Also be sure to call during a peak time, around 5:00 in the evening. Time how long it takes to get connected to a live person. If you get a prerecorded message telling you to visit the company's Web site, hang up and walk away. If customer service is only available online, and a problem takes down their network, how are you supposed to ask them about it?

On the other hand you shouldn't expect network problems to be fixed immediately if you're paying very little. The level of service goes up with the type of service you have, which is somewhat directly related to the amount of money you pay.

Many Web hosting companies start out just fine in terms of customer service. They're fast, they answer the phone right away, and they provide continuous network connection on a very reliable basis. Alas, this kind of service does not usually last. As more people learn about the great customer service, new customers flock to the Web hosting company. Eventually, the company outgrows its customer service department. If they don't have a large enough customer base to justify a larger department, the quality of service suffers — and so do the customers.

It's an unfortunate fact online that few high-tech companies recognize the importance of customer satisfaction in making or breaking their businesses. In a matter of months, these companies may fail, simply because they did not help their customers in times of difficulty. Although it's okay to try out a newly established Web hosting company, be aware that in 9 to 12 months, the company may experience customer service growing pains. Watch for these, and jump ship if it starts adversely affecting your Web service.

Assessing technical support

Finally, call the company's technical support line to ask for help with installing a script or otherwise setting up your site. Ask them how much help they're willing to offer with these types of problems, and whether or not you'll have to pay for their technical expertise. In general, tech support should be willing to help you with questions directly relating to your account and setup, such as which e-mail servers to use when setting up your e-mail account. However, programming help and installing unsupported programs will probably cost a small fee, if it's available at all. If you think you'll be installing a lot of custom scripts, and you aren't a programmer yet, try to find a Web hosting company that offers that type of technical support, even for a fee. You'll have a much more positive experience with your Web service if technical support is available to you when you need it.

Avoiding Common Provider Scams

Although most Web hosting companies are legitimate businesses, some are run by unscrupulous people who are just trying to take advantage of customers. It's like any industry; you have to watch out for the bad guys when you're looking for the good ones. Naturally, you should stay away from any Web hosting company that sends you unsolicited e-mail about their services. By spamming you, such companies show no respect for your time and are unlikely to respect you as a customer.

As you research your Web hosting companies, log on to `http://groups.google.com` to read `alt.www.webmaster` (or use your newsgroup reader to check out the group instead) and ask about the specific company to see if anyone has had experience with it. This newsgroup is also a good resource for other Webmaster questions as you go through the process of creating the rest of your Web site.

For online reviews and rankings of Web hosting companies, visit `http://best-web-hosting-2008.com/` or `http://www.hostindex.com/voteresults.shtm.`.

Finally, be sure to read the Terms of Service before you agree to the Web hosting service. Not all Terms of Service agreements are identical. Some Web hosts reserve the right to change their Terms of Service agreements without notification, or to make major technical changes without notification. Changing IP addresses, though common, is a major technical change that should require that the Web hosting company notify you. Find out if they do before you sign on.

Thinking like a crook

As with any major investment, the adage *caveat emptor* (or "let the buyer beware") still holds true when choosing a Web hosting company. All Web hosting companies will tell you they're the fastest, best, most affordable deal in the world. Beware of fly-by-night operations that have only been in service a short time. Watch out for any signs that your Web hosting "professionals" are, in fact, a couple of unqualified high school kids. (Customer service that's only offered during after-school hours is a big tip-off!) If it looks too good to be true, it probably is.

As you go into the review forums and online, remember that some unscrupulous people will post positive reviews about their own companies without providing information about their own interest in the company. So, in some reviews, you might get someone claiming that this is the best Web hosting company in the world. Be sure you pick a Web hosting company that has more than one reviewer reviewing it, and check more than one hosting review site as well.

Suffering domain name theft

Domain name theft rarely happens, but when it does, it's serious. Because your domain name is registered through a registration service, it's hard for someone to outright hijack it without any legal recourse.

There are three main ways that someone can steal your domain name. First, they can hack into the DNS system and transfer your domain name entries to their site. Once detected, this kind of assault is easily remedied through your domain name registrar. The second method is to illegally convince the registrar to transfer the name. This is done through forged documents, faxes, and so on. If that happens, you may find that it's a bit more difficult to clear up. You'll have to prove that the transfer was fraudulent.

There is, however, one way for someone to steal your domain name and flat out get away with it. Most Web space providers are willing to handle your domain name registration for you, and most of them are scrupulously honest about handling the process. But you must be sure to read the fine print if you let someone else do it for you. Some providers will register the domain name to themselves instead of to you. If they do, you're out of luck.

The best solution for this is to do the registration yourself. It's not a difficult process — all you do is fill out an online form at any registrar. And you're covered that way.

Getting "unlimited" traffic or space

Unlimited traffic or Web space sounds like a great deal. And it is, if you frequently use a lot of bandwidth or have large files. For example, many adult Web sites have large files and high amounts of traffic, and there's only so much processor and network bandwidth to go around. If your Web hosting company offers unlimited traffic to you, they're also offering it to everyone. Because there is no foolproof way to get unlimited bandwidth to the Internet, this is an empty promise that will leave your Web site stranded. Frequent downtime and slower speeds may haunt your site, and you may soon find that users leave your site for greener (and faster) pastures.

The same goes for unlimited storage space. Although network speed isn't as much of a problem, unlimited storage space is an open invitation to anyone who makes large files available for download. They're also an open invite to anyone who wants to download those large files, which will ultimately lead to network slowdowns for you, too.

When it comes down to it, any Web hosting company that offers unlimited traffic or storage space isn't interested in providing customer satisfaction. Unlimited traffic and space are a setup for customer dissatisfaction. If you absolutely think you need to have unlimited bandwidth, find a Web hosting company that doesn't permit Napster-like file serving or adult content.

Rushing deadlines for special deals

"Order by tomorrow night and get $15 off!" "Order now for a free T-Shirt!" "Sign up now for cheaper long distance!" We've all heard these kinds of deals, and they can sometimes be a real bargain. When it comes to Web hosting, however, there are few deadline deals that can't be found elsewhere, later. There are so many thousands of Web hosting companies that you won't have a problem finding someone who will beat that deadline-based deal. The only time you should sign on with one of these limited-time offers is when the Web hosting company is one of the two or three that you've researched, it's beaten the `tracert` test, and you're satisfied with its Terms of Services agreement and customer service options. In other words, if you were probably going to sign up with them anyway, then go for it.

Exploring Bells and Whistles

Most bells and whistles you might be looking for are probably available on any standard virtual hosting account. Typically, you should receive the following services:

- One to five e-mail accounts
- Message redirection
- Autoresponders
- Web statistic program to help you track traffic to your site, and possibly provide information on your visitors
- Web-based control panel for you to use to manage your Web site and accounts

Getting extra e-mail accounts

Most Web hosting accounts come with an e-mail account, if not several. However, because e-mail accounts are fairly easy to set up, you can usually get additional e-mail accounts added to your account by contacting customer service for your Web hosting company. These extra e-mail accounts are not very expensive, usually incurring some small monthly fee per month for the extra service.

Redirecting messages

A *redirect address* is an e-mail address that forwards all mail sent to that address to another e-mail address. There are several advantages to redirecting e-mail. First, you can make your organization seem larger by having multiple e-mail addresses for user questions. For example, info@yourdomain.com, pricing@yourdomain.com, and techsupport@yourdomain.com can all go to yourname@yourdomain.com if you wear many hats in your organization.

A redirect address also helps you filter messages in your Inbox. In most e-mail programs, you can set a filter to move and file messages into specific directories automatically. Then, you just go to the directory to view mail that matches the filter criteria. For example, you could have a filter that says any mail sent to techsupport@yourdomain.com should be filed in a folder called `Technical Support`. When you read mail in that folder, you know the only questions you'll be asked are about technical support. And, you won't have tech support e-mail cluttering up your Inbox.

Many Web hosting companies have Web-based control panels to set up redirect addresses. If available, use these to set up as much of your site as possible.

If you don't have a Web-based control panel, but you do have a Telnet (or shell) account on a Unix or Linux server, you can often create redirect accounts in the shell program. Log in to your shell account using your username and password. Once logged in, at the prompt, type the following:

```
ls -a
```

This should produce a list of all files in your directory, including hidden files. Hidden files are usually system files. On Unix-flavor systems, their filenames start with a period. Thus, your directory listing might look something like Listing 14-1.

LISTING 14-1

Results of ls -a

```
awl:/home2/scottrell$ ls -a
./   .htgroup     .redirect anonftp@ maillists/
../  .htpasswd    .redirect.bkl* dead.letter mbox
.bash_history   .lynxrc      .redirect.bk3* du.dat    pass*
.bash_logout    .passwd/     .screenrc       infobots/ personal/
.bash_profile   .pine-debugl .wusage/        laptop/   www@
.bashrc   .pinerc       access-log@    mail/
```

There's only one thing you really need to pay attention to here. The `.redirect` file contains your forwarding addresses. You can edit this using a text editor, such as *vi* or *emacs* online, or download it with FTP, edit it in your text editor, and upload it again.

Adding or changing redirected addresses is fairly easy. Each line in the `.redirect` file is a new forwarding address. Enter the name of the address, without the domain information (`yourname`, not yourname@yourdomain.com). Put in a space, and then enter the full destination address. Listing 14-2 shows an example of a `.redirect` file.

LISTING 14-2

A .redirect File

```
voicemail sbryant@ekno.com
travelmail sbryant@ekno.com
phone mortaine@myvzw.com
chat scottrell@scottrell.com
steph scottrell@scottrell.com
webmaster scottrell@scottrell.com
speech scottrell@scottrell.com
default stephanie@Web-writer.net
biblebook scottrell@scottrell.com
```

The forwarding address in a `.redirect` is not a full e-mail address! It's just the username (for example, `Voicemail`, instead of voicemail@scottrell.com).

If you don't have control panels or a shell account, or you don't know how to use Telnet, contact your Web hosting company for help setting up redirect addresses.

It's possible the redirecting will bounce if you send to a domain not hosted by the service provider.

Using autoresponders to provide information

An *autoresponder* is similar to a redirect account in that it's not a full-fledged e-mail account on the system. However, unlike a redirect address, an autoresponder sends the contents of a file back to the original sender. A user on your Web site might click a button that says "Send Me More Info!" The user is directed to an e-mail address and sends a message to your info@yourdomain.com account. Although you could have this info address set up to redirect to your main account, you can also provide instant access to a standard information sheet using an autoresponder. When the visitor sends an e-mail to the address, he or she receives an automatic reply with the information requested.

You can usually set up an autoresponder to also forward the original message to a separate address. This is a good scheme for setting up a tech support address. You can set up an autoresponder with a link to the most commonly asked questions but also assure your clients that a more personal response will be coming.

Many Web hosts offer online forms for setting up and updating autoresponders on your Web site. The text of the autoresponder itself is usually saved as a file.

If you're using a telnet or shell account only and don't have a Web-based control panel, look again at the contents of your directory, using the `ls` command. There should be a directory called `autoresponder` or `infobots` or something similar. In Listing 14-1, the directory is called `infobots`. Go to that directory and view the files available. To add a new autoresponder, simply create a text file containing the information you wish to send as your response. Give it the same name as the autoresponder's address. So, if your autoresponder's address will be support@yourdomain.com, name the file `support`.

You can create this file using any text editor, including Notepad, but make sure that there is no file extension when you save the file. In Windows, that may be tricky — you might have to go into Windows Explorer and change the name to remove the file extension. If you create the file on a desktop machine, use FTP to upload it to your autoresponder directory.

NOTE **If you're using Telnet or a shell account to create an autoresponder, add an entry for the same e-mail address in your `.redirect` file to also forward a copy of the original message to a separate address.**

NOTE **Autoresponders can greatly increase your spam level by making your email addresses appear to be reaching "live" people.**

Getting visitor statistics

Any good Web hosting company will offer weekly server statistics telling you how many people visited your site, and when. These statistics may be as simple as a hit count, just telling you how many visitors you had. Or, they can be very extensive, including regional information on where your visitors come from, which pages they viewed and in what order, the times of day they visited, and any error messages they received. Data may be presented in tables, graphs, or charts. An example of a cumulative site report is shown in Figure 14-6.

FIGURE 14-6

Web usage software outputs useful information.

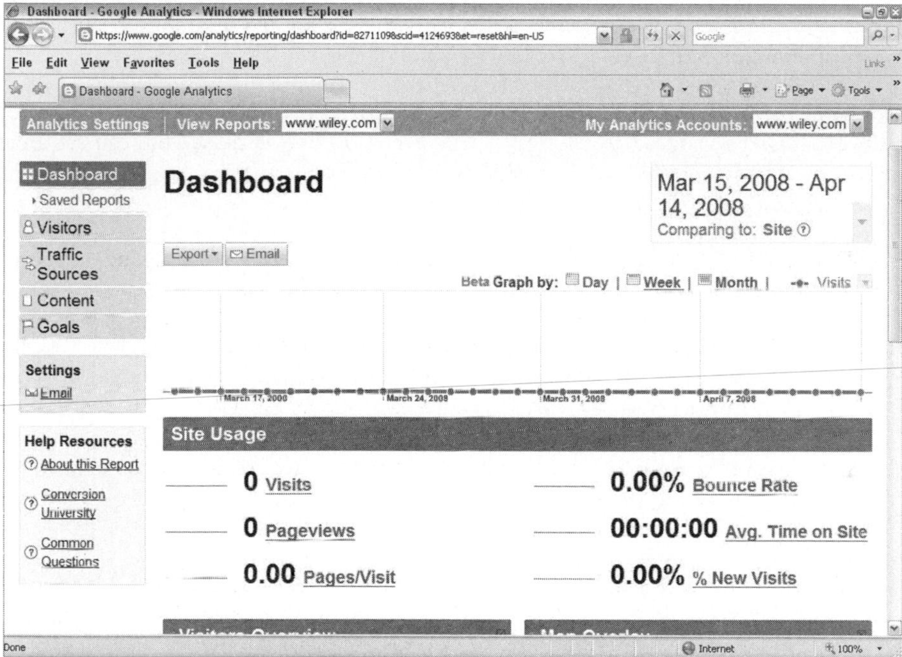

Most Web hosts also offer more advanced tables as well as weekly reports. These reports are a valuable way for you to track your Web site's development. Beware of any Web host that deletes reports after less than 6 months.

If you don't have a Web statistics program installed on your server, Google Analytics provides free Web statistics at `https://www.google.com/analytics/`**.**

Using control panels to set site options

Just as you can use control panels to set up e-mail options, you can also generally use control panels or shell commands to set up site options and permissions, including password-protected directories. On Windows Web servers, a *password-protected directory* means that you have to create a new Windows user account to access the files in that directory. In Unix and Linux, however, you can use Basic Authentication, the common method for setting new users, to set these up.

If you have a Web-based program to password-protect a directory, follow the instructions of your hosting provider. Although there will be individual variations in the process with different providers (see Figure 14-7), it essentially works like this:

1. Enter the directory you'd like to protect.
2. Type a username and a password for a user. Set a password that's easy to remember but difficult to guess. The user won't be able to change his or her own password after you create it, although you could change it if you want.
3. Click a button to add that username and password to your list.
4. Repeat Steps 2 and 3 for as many users as you want to add passwords for.

FIGURE 14-7

`Bravenet.com` uses a common form for adding authorized users.

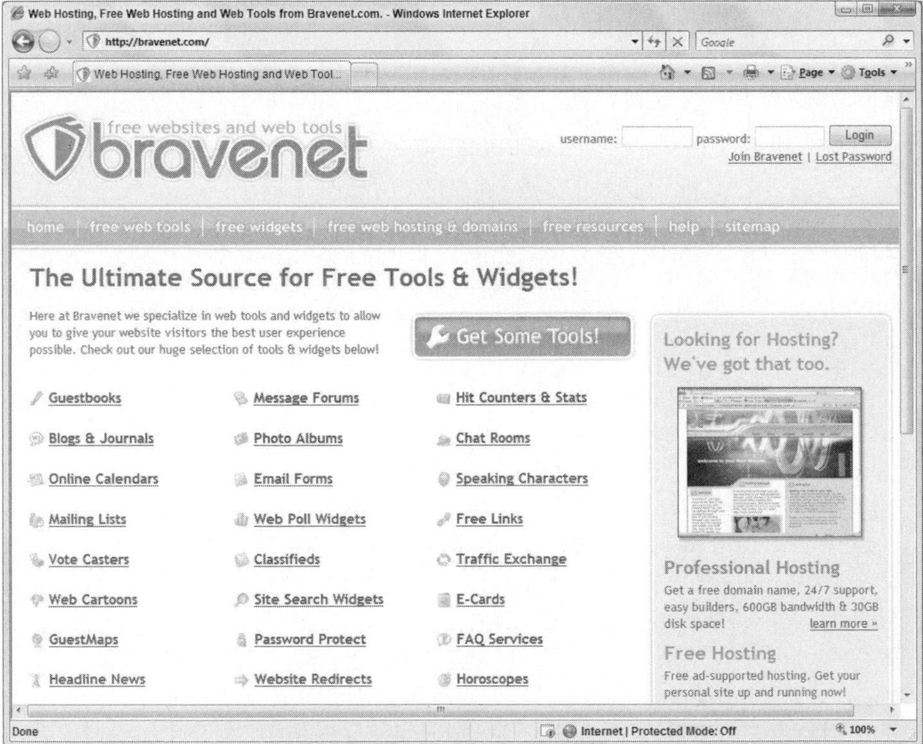

Of course, there's another option if you're a telnet or shell account user. If you have a shell account on a Linux- or Unix-based machine, you can set up a similar Basic Authentication scheme. First, log on to your account and go to your home directory.

Type **htpasswd -c .htpasswd username** to create a new username and password, as shown in Listing 14-3.

LISTING 14-3

Creating a Username and Password for Basic Authentication

```
awl:/home2/scottrell$ htpasswd .htpasswd MySelf
Adding user MySelf
New password: MyPassword
Re-type new password: MyPassword
```

NOTE **Note that the password itself (`MyPassword`) won't actually appear on screen as you type.**

Next, create or edit the `.htaccess` file in the directory you want to protect, as shown in Listing 14-4. Go to that directory, and put this file inside it. Replace the path `/home/` with the actual path to your home directory.

LISTING 14-4

Contents of .htaccess

```
AuthUserFile /home/.htpasswd
AuthGroupFile /home/.htgroup
AuthName Restricted_Area
AuthType Basic
<Limit GET>
require user personalaccess
</Limit>
```

The most important thing in this file is the `AuthUserFile` reference. This is a file containing the names and encrypted passwords of users. `AuthGroupFile` is optional — use it if you want to group your users so that they all have the same authorization.

`AuthName Restricted_Area` sets the name of this restricted area. We could have as easily named it `HalloweenPictures`. `AuthType` is basic — keep it that way.

The next bit of code limits the HTTP server from getting anything from the protected directory. In the `MySelf` example, you could add the following to the `.htaccess` file in the protected directory:

```
<Limit GET>
require user MySelf
</Limit>
```

If you don't have a Linux or Unix server, contact your Web hosting service about setting up password-protected directories.

Becoming a reseller

If you decide to resell your Web space, keep in mind the kinds of questions you asked your own Web hosting company before you signed on with it. Be ready to handle technical and network difficulties, many of which may be beyond your control. Be prepared to offer satisfactory customer service, competitive prices, and a meticulous payment tracking service. And of course, make sure your Web hosting Terms of Service permits you to resell your space.

Here's a checklist of things to do to become a Web space reseller:

- Make sure you're permitted to resell Web space through your Web host company. Some Web hosts offer a discount for signing up additional virtual domains.
- Decide on a Terms of Service agreement that is fair to both you and your clients.
- Set up a merchant account with a bank or credit card company so you can take payments by credit card.
- Install a secure Web server to protect your clients' credit card data when it's transferred online.
- Figure out how much it will cost you in costs and overhead, and set a competitive price that still covers your expenses.
- Set up a separate phone line for incoming customer support calls.
- Set up a blank account to serve as a template. Give it its own e-mail or shell account (or both), domain name (if you decide to offer virtual hosting), FTP account, and Web space. Put all the files you would ordinarily add to any new account (preinstalled CGI scripts, and so on) into this account.
- When you sign up new clients, copy the contents of your template account to the new client's account, changing filenames and paths as needed.
- Follow up with your clients. Send them a personal e-mail or call to make sure that the Web space is working out. A 5-minute phone call will go a long way toward customer loyalty!

Many resellers just have affiliate accounts and links, and everything's handled by the end ISP, while the affiliates get their cut.

Uploading Your Pages

The last step is to upload your Web pages to the server. After all, if you have all these great Web pages sitting on your hard drive at home, they're not doing anyone any good. So, you need to put them onto your Web server using FTP or HTTP.

Transferring with FTP

The most reliable way to transfer files originated more than 28 years ago, in the days of the Internet's infancy. File Transfer Protocol (FTP) was a very simple system by which one computer could send a file to another computer, regardless of what operating system or platform the two computers were using. It was one of the first cross-platform file transfer types, and it quickly became the most reliable.

Today, FTP is still the most stable, reliable way to move something from your computer to another computer. FTP programs are available in every platform and nearly every operating system, and many are even built into the operating system package. If you use a PC, you can open a DOS window and type **ftp** at the prompt. If you're connected to the Internet, you'll be able to connect to any FTP server in the world.

Putting your Web pages onto the server with FTP is fairly easy, and this section shows you how, using the shareware program WS_FTP.

The first step is to connect to your Web server. Open WS_FTP, and you'll see a dialog box asking you to choose a server, as shown in Figure 14-8.

WS_FTP comes with several preset FTP sites where you can find many files and programs available for free. However, you're not looking to download programs today. So, enter a new name for your Web server into the Profile Name text box. Type the host name, which is something like `ftp.yourdomain.com` or just `yourdomain.com`. You may need to ask your Web host provider for this information.

FIGURE 14-8

Pick a server from the Profile Name drop-down list box, or create a new one by typing in a new Profile Name.

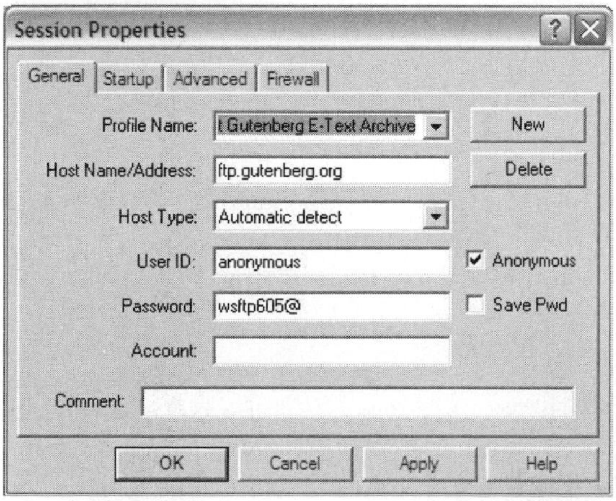

Leave the Host Type text box set to "Automatic detect," unless you have other instructions from your Web host company. Enter your account login name in the User ID text box, and your password. For security reasons, your password is not displayed on screen when you type it in.

Now, click the Startup tab to change your initial directory settings, as shown in Figure 14-9.

FIGURE 14-9

You can set the initial directories on the Startup tab.

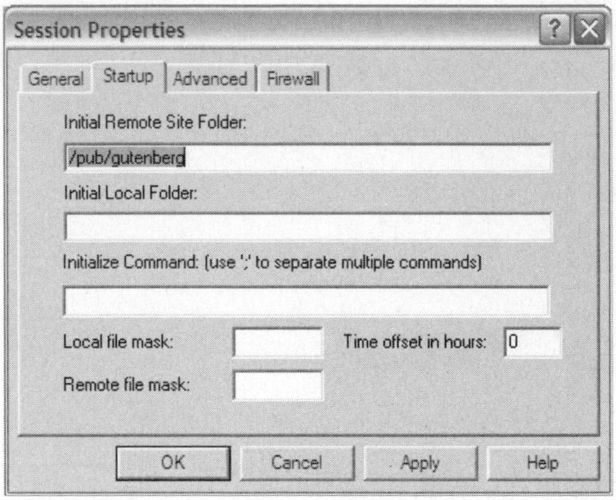

Enter the path (from your login home directory) to your Web space on the Web server's computer in the Initial Remote Site Folder directory text box. Enter the path to your local Web folder (on your hard drive) in the Initial Local Folder text box. Leave the rest of the fields blank; they're for advanced FTP programming and automation.

Next, select the Advanced tab, shown in Figure 14-10. Here, you can tell WS_FTP to keep trying to connect if you can't initially log on to your Web server. In addition, there's a network timeout option, so if there's no activity detected, WS_FTP will automatically close the connection.

The Remote Port is the port setting for FTP. Unless instructed otherwise by your Web hosting company, this value is always 21. Finally, passive transfers are required for certain network configurations, and are generally a good idea. A passive transfer prevents the FTP server from initiating contact during a connection — a little security feature to thwart hackers. Unless your Web hosting company is using an old version of FTP that doesn't support passive transfers, turn this option on by clicking the check box. If your connection to the server doesn't appear to be working, toggle this switch and see which works best.

Finally, click the Firewall tab (see Figure 14-11). You only need to specify these settings if you must go through a firewall to connect to the Internet. Most of the time, you won't need to modify this. Your system administrator (the person responsible for the firewall) will help you fill in the required information and get through the firewall.

FIGURE 14-10

The Advanced tab enables you to set timeout times and how many times to attempt the connection.

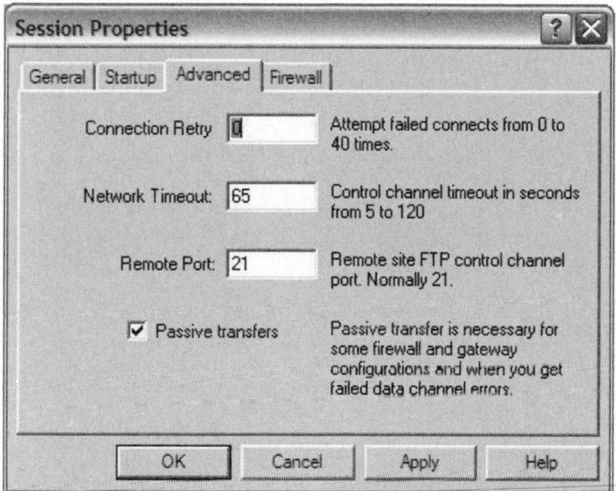

FIGURE 14-11

Select the Firewall tab if your Internet connection goes through a firewall server.

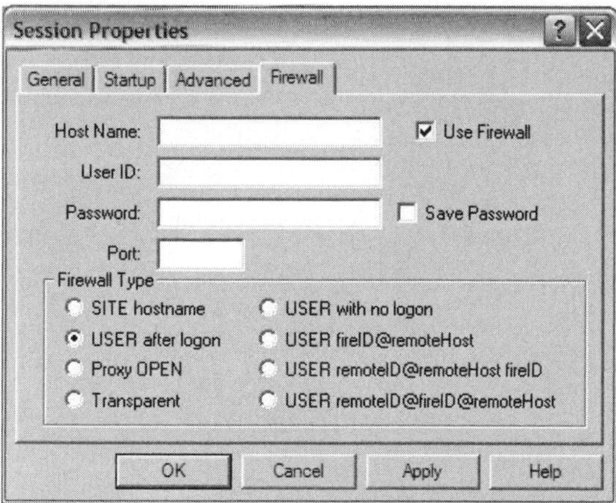

After you've filled in the fields and are ready to connect, click OK. As long as you've entered all the correct information, WS_FTP should connect you to your Web server and log you in. You'll be transferred to your initial directories, as shown in Figure 14-12.

FIGURE 14-12

Once you log in, you're transferred to the initial directories you set up.

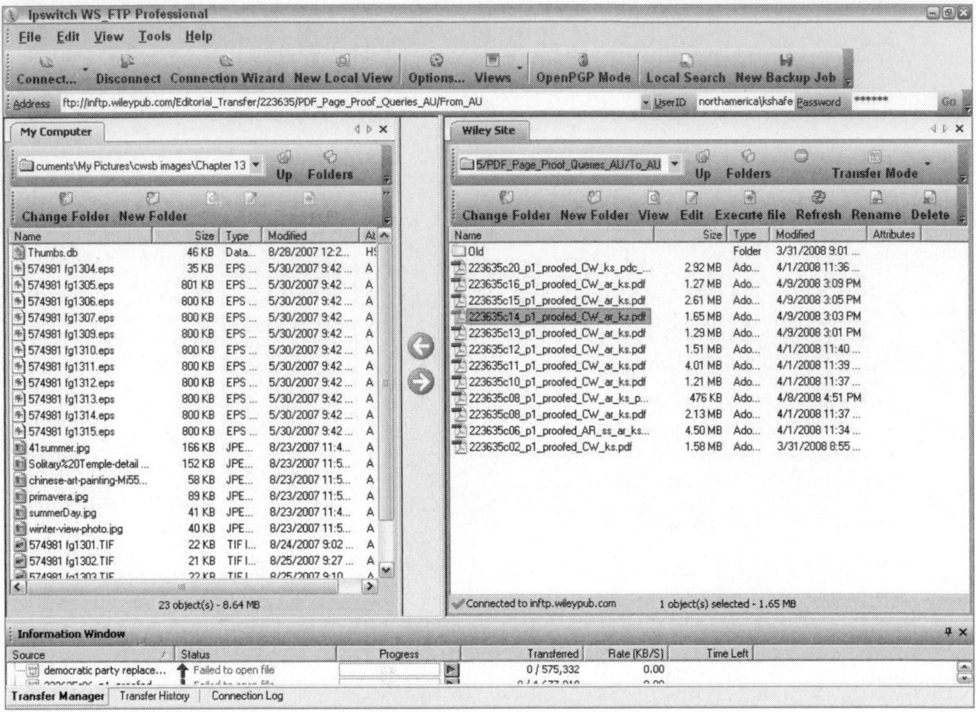

Look carefully at Figure 14-12. On the left-hand side is the Local System panel, which shows the contents of your hard drive. On the right-hand side is the Remote Site panel, which shows the contents of your Web server. The buttons next to each panel are explained in Table 14-2. There's also a blank field into which you can enter text.

There are two option buttons below these panels: ASCII and Binary. There's also a check box for Auto. In FTP terms, ASCII means any plain-text file, such as `.txt` and `.html` files. If you can open and edit it in NotePad or TextEdit, it's probably ASCII. Binary stands for all other files — graphics, programs, compressed archives (`.zip` or `.sit`), Word documents, and so on. Select the file type that you'll be transferring — ASCII for HTML files, or Binary if you're uploading graphics. Check Auto if you want to select and send more than one type of file at a time.

The ASCII versus Binary option is very important in FTP! If you upload a file and it doesn't seem to work, try transferring it in the correct type.

TABLE 14-2

Transferring via FTP

Button	Description
ChgDir	Prompts you to enter the directory you'd like to change to. You can also browse directories by double-clicking the folders, or by double-clicking the up arrow at the top of the panel to go up one directory.
MkDir	Prompts you to enter the name of the directory you'd like to create. Once you create a new directory, you can move to it through ChgDir or by double-clicking it.
View	Opens the selected file in whatever program you've selected for viewing files of that type.
Exec	Runs a program if you select a program file (an executable program, often ending in `.exe` on Windows machines).
Rename	Enables you to rename the selected file or directory.
Delete	Prompts you to erase the selected file or directory.
Refresh	Reloads the directory listing, reflecting any changes made to the files.
DirInfo	Produces a text file containing information about the current directory and its contents.

There are two buttons in the center, one pointing left and one pointing right. To upload a file, select it on the left side (the Local System side) and press the arrow pointing to the right. The file will be transferred to the server (see Figure 14-13).

TIP **You can also double-click the file to copy it from its current panel to the opposite panel (local to remote or vice versa).**

When you're finished transferring files, click Close to end your FTP session, and Exit to quit WS_FTP.

There are literally hundreds, if not thousands, of FTP programs available, however, so if you're not happy with WS_FTP, feel free to go online and find something better. For Mac users, the most popular by far is Fetch, which might already be installed on your Macintosh.

Uploading with Web browsers via HTTP

If your Web hosting company offers this service, you can also upload your files using an HTML form and HTTP. Many Web hosts provide a form for uploading files to the server, as shown in Figure 14-14.

FIGURE 14-13

Select the file and click the right arrow to upload it to the server.

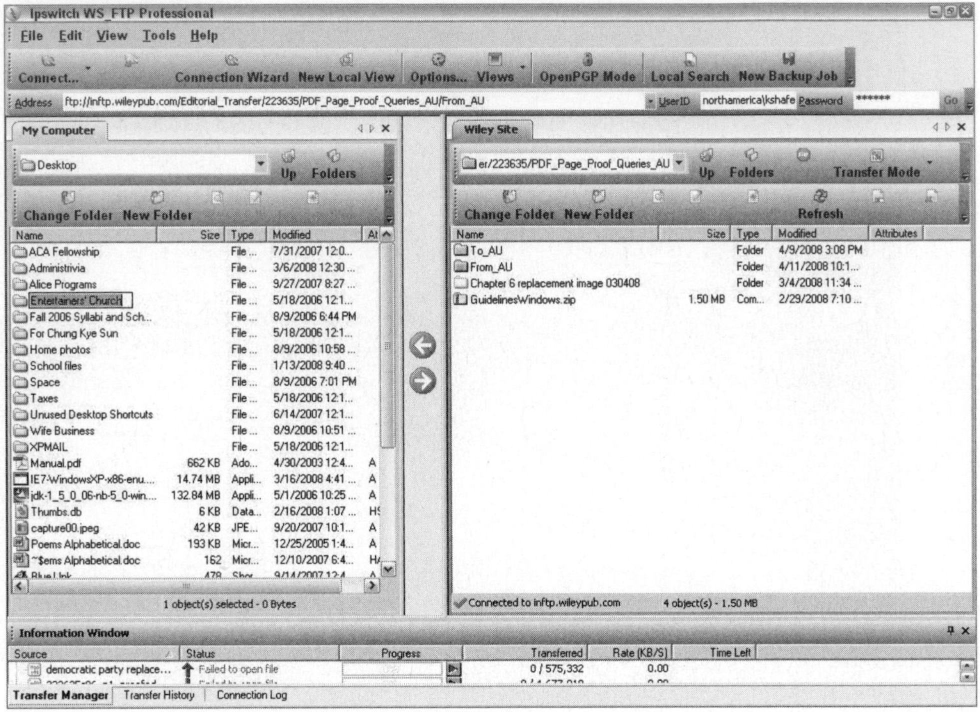

To upload a file, enter the path and filename, or click Browse to find it on your hard drive. After you find the file, click the Upload File now button for the form to upload it. The file is now available on your server in your Web space or through your control panels.

Web Posting Quick Reference

The following provides a quick reference for key items discussed in this chapter:

- *Domain name structure* — This categorizes entity by type (for example, .com, `.info`, `.mobi`, `.net`, `.org`, `.edu`).
- *WHOIS* — This is used to look up a domain name in a registry.

FIGURE 14-14

You can upload files for all client needs.

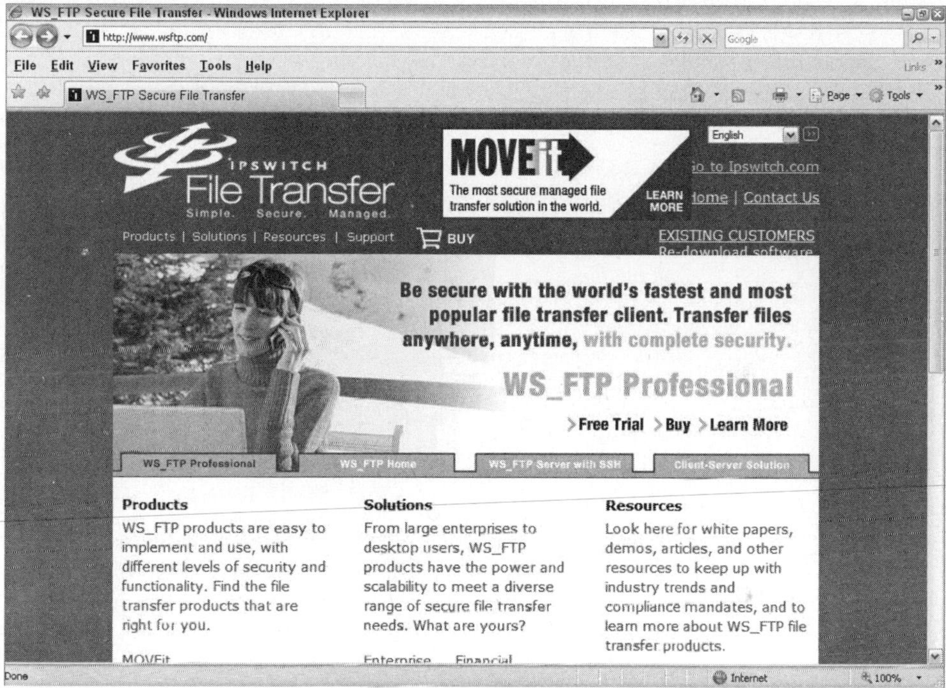

- `tracert` — This is a utility used to trace a route across the Internet from source to destination.
- *Redirect* — This is a small program that forwards all traffic from one address to another address.
- *Autoresponder — This* provides an automated response to e-mail sent to an address.
- *File Transfer Protocol (FTP)* — This is a Web program used to upload files to server.

Summary

As you can see, it's pretty easy to find a home for your Web pages and to put them there. You can make it more complicated, of course, but you don't have to. If you can use an online form, you can get set up with a Web server and domain name. If you can use a program such as WS_FTP, or if your Web hosting service has control panels to permit you to upload to your Web server, you can easily put your pages up on the Internet and become a published Web developer!

In this chapter, you learned how choosing an easily memorized domain name is one of the keys to online success. You may choose to use your own hardware, leased hardware, or even a software-only Web server solution. Whatever kind of Web server you choose should have plenty of extra space and transfer capability. Carefully research any Web space provider you plan to use. You can upload your Web pages via either FTP or HTTP, depending on your provider's capabilities.

Our sojourn continues with a jump from the marketing side to the more comfortable coding component as, in Chapter 15, we look into the future of HTML — XHTML.

Part V

Transitioning to the Future: XHTML, XML, and Ajax

IN THIS PART

Chapter 15

XHTML

IN THIS CHAPTER

There are hundreds of programming languages in dozens of families. They cannibalize, copy, contradict, and exterminate each other at a remarkable pace. There are procedural languages, functional languages, constraint languages, concurrent languages, object-oriented languages, query languages, logic languages, and on and on.

Though Standardized Generalized Markup Language (SGML) is viewed as the source of today's so-called markup languages, Generalized Markup Language (GML), which was created by IBM in the 1960s, is the origin of all markup languages. From the parent source and mostly through the vehicle of SGML, the children HTML, XHTML, XML, XSL, MathML, CML, and others have been derived, as well as such enhancements as frames, interactive forms, stylesheets, and scripts.

SGML is device-independent and is not tied to particular processor architecture. It is portable. It is extensible. It is scalable, and it can have design implementations for minimal essential features (as would be true of handheld devices). It can handle a wide variety of job implementations, even on a very large scale.

Microsoft is a big proponent of XHTML, although whether XHTML will take off and become something of an extension to HTML remains to be seen. Like any markup language, it is in a constant state of evolution and development because of the need to adapt to new technologies (primarily wireless handheld devices) and for improved integration with preexisting systems (HTML 4.01 and XML 1.0).

However, the constraint (tradeoff) of offering such a powerful and flexible system is complexity. And complexity equals time, and time equals money.

So, for the most of us, where time and money are daily challenges, we just use what we need of the vast SGML corpus. This is where HTML came from. In what will become a familiar refrain, this subset of SGML was designed to be smaller, faster, easier to design with, and focused on client needs. As you are aware, HTML allows the creation of Web pages that are device-independent, portable, and (as software and hardware advances have evolved) extensible.

A Quick Review of HTML

The first widely accepted version of HTML came about in the early 1990s as a joint contribution from Tim Berners-Lee and Dave Raggett. It was basically an instrument of text control, defining elements for paragraphs, lists, headings, inline formatting and inline images. In the mid-1990s, in response to new uses, HTML became more graphical and interactive. By the latter part of the decade, HTML had been "extended" by the inclusion of tables, forms, scripting, multimedia features, and international elements.

The driving force for all these innovations were the so-called "browser wars" between the primary contenders — dominant Netscape and late-starting Microsoft Internet Explorer (IE). While the benefits of the extensions were quickly obvious (such as greater options for site construction and organization, greater interactivity, and greater dynamism), the improvements paradoxically resulted in a fragmentation of the unitary goal of the Worldwide Web Consortium (W3C). Competing browsers brought forth slightly different versions of HTML, and, of course, their proprietary extensions nullified cross-browser compatibility.

In a sense, we were back to square one. We had a vastly improved technology, but in competing and mutually unintelligible versions. Plus, the plethora of browsers also made it difficult to determine what constituted valid code, and code could be incorrectly written but still successfully executed by the browser. Such errors were euphemistically referred to as the browser having forgiveness. This glossed over the inconsistency of element definitions for code as browser companies fiercely struggled to grow their market. It also tended to minimize the inherent confusion (and sloppiness) of Web page developers in using the various available HTML code extensions.

Such a situation created a ripe market for the greedy entrepreneurial Web guru wannabes. Those with the expertise were very, very limited, and very much in demand. They could command incomes roughly three times the level that were currently supported.

Enter XHTML

This all changed with the introduction of XHTML.

Officially, in 2001, XHTML 1.0 was introduced as a hybrid system containing the best of both worlds from HTML and XML. The best of HTML would be forms, enhanced tables, enhanced scripting capabilities, more multimedia features, and stylesheets — basically more dynamic features, and a basketful of increased layout options for the Web designer and Web developer.

Table 15-1 compares the features of HTML and XHTML.

TABLE 15-1

Features of HTML and XHTML

Type and Version	Introduced by W3C	Summary of Features
HTML 1.0	1990+	No actual standards existed, but so-called HTML v. 1.0 was an informal set of features not regularized until version 2.0 with significant inputs from Berners-Lee (who considered it an application of SGML), Cailliau, and Dave Raggett. It could include hypertext news, mail, documentation, and hypermedia; menus of options; database query results; simple structured documents with in-line graphics; and hypertext views of existing bodies of information.
HTML 2.0	1995	This was the first standardization of HTML. It had graphical browser support and included new interactive elements for forms. It is still the most widely supported standard on Web.
HTML 3.2	1997	There were earlier versions of version 3, but the pace of Internet developments and competing standards were rendered obsolete. This introduced support for scripts, as well as expanded elements for tables and forms. HTML 3.2 added widely deployed features such as tables, applets, and text flow around images.
HTML 4.0x	1999	This brought in capabilities to use stylesheets. It made this version more internationally flavored (such as use of foreign symbols in code rendering). It expanded features for tables, forms, scripting, and multimedia.
XHTML 1.0	2001	This is the most commonly used version today. It does not have universal browser support and will, perhaps, be superseded by XHTML 2.0 or (more likely) XML. It is really designed as a hybrid to bring uniformity, rigidity, and structure to HTML coding through standardization of elements and replacement of numerous attribute features with Cascading Style Sheets (CSS) equivalents. Minor revisions include the use of modules.
XHTML 2.0	200?	XHTML 2 is a general-purpose markup language designed for representing documents for a wide range of purposes across the World Wide Web. It does not attempt to be all things to all people, but rather supplies a generally useful set of elements. A key aspect is that it is likely designed not to be backward-compatible with earlier versions. This could mean a major reengineering of existing XHTML modules.

Remember that, as recently as five years ago, the most universally supported standard of HTML was HTML 2.0, developed in 1995.

In a good sense, this means that XHTML has provided needed rigor to Web page design and brought a great degree of cross-browser compatibility in the process. However, because XHTML does not use `attribute:value` pairs (with optional quotes) and requires you to close every element all the time, XHTML has removed some of the creative informality from HTML.

XHTML also can enforce code standardization, check the validity of a document (for content and structure), and review the syntax to ensure that it is well formed. This helps the coder to resolve bugs.

Transitioning to XHTML 1.0

On December 19, 2000, Tim Berners-Lee, creator of the World Wide Web and director of the W3C (`www.w3.org`), announced his support for XHTML 1.0. XHTML addresses the essential need of many developers — the creation of an HTML standard that is based on XML. XHTML 1.0 is the first major revision of HTML since 1997.

CROSS-REF **Chapter 16 provides more information on XML.**

Transitioning from HTML to XHTML involves making changes in document structure.

Document Type Definitions (DTDs)

All languages derived from SGML (and all versions of such languages) have a Document Type Definition (DTD). Broadly, DTDs define the syntax of the language. The acceptable values and properties are set. The structure of the elements, what the elements mean, and the relationships of the elements to the document (and to each other) are all defined within the DTD.

Therefore, when we use the expression, "x, y, and z elements are deprecated," we are saying that the syntax has been changed — new things have been added and some things have been taken away.

Table 15-2 shows deprecated elements and XHTML (CSS) equivalents.

TABLE 15-2

Deprecated Elements and XHTML (CSS) Equivalents

Name	XHTML (CSS) equivalent
`Attribute:value`	
`Applet`	`applet`
`Basefont`	`font-size: value`
`Center`	`text-align: center`
`Dir`	`dir: value`

TABLE 15-2 *(continued)*

Name	XHTML (CSS) equivalent
Font	font-family:value
	font-size: value
iFrame	
isindex	
menu	
s	text-decoration: line-through
u	text-decoration: underline

Table 15-3 shows deprecated HTML 4.01 attributes and the equivalent XHTML (CSS) elements.

TABLE 15-3

Deprecated HTML 4.01 Attributes and XHTML (CSS) Equivalents

Attribute	Prohibited Use in These Elements	XHTML (CSS) Equivalent Attribute:Value
Align	H1 - H6, paragraphs, images, lines (hr), captions, and tables	text-align:
background	Body	background-image:
bgcolor	table, tr, td, th, body	background-color: value
		background: value
border	img, object	border: value
compact	dl, ol, ul	line-height: value
height	td, th	line-height: value
hspace	img, object	padding: value
Links	body	link:
name	img, a, applet, form, frame, iframe, map	HTML attribute: id
size	hr	width: value
text	body	color :value
vspace	img, object	margin: value
width	hr, td, th, pre	width: value

The following is a simple illustration of the coding structure used for any DTD:

```
<!DOCTYPE ...>
<html>
<head>
<title> ... </title>
</head>
<body> ... </body>
</html>
```

You will note that the only difference between it and your absolutely standard HTML code is that the first line includes a DOCTYPE statement, which we will get to shortly.

To look to the future while accommodating the past, W3C settled upon three DTDs to go with the new look of XHTML:

- *Transitional* — This is a definition of XHTML that enables HTML 4.0 tags to be used within the syntax, enabling a transition from one language to the next. It was designed to function while incorporating most of the deprecated elements of HTML 4.01 that could be incorporated, upgrading attributes that could be upgraded, and dispensing with the inconvenient remainder by consigning them to future versions of XHTML.
- *Strict* — This is the implementation of XHTML as defined in the complete XHTML 1.0 standard.
- *Frames* — This is a version of the language that enables Netscape Frame elements to be used within XHTML-formatted Web pages.

Transitional

If you look at the metatags of most documents, you will probably find the document type to be Transitional. Look at the following code snippet from a well-known cutting-edge publishing company:

```
<!DOCTYPE HTML PUBLIC "-//W3C//DTD HTML 4.01 Transitional//EN"
       "http://www.w3.org/TR/html4/loose.dtd">
```

NOTE **The use of the word *document* simply refers to the Web page, and to *validate* simply means to check and see if the coding (in particular, the elements used in the coding) are in conformance with the standards of the DTD specified. Validation is also known as *checking for a "well-formed" document.***

This is referred to as a DOCTYPE declaration. It normally appears in the top of an XHTML document. Its purpose is to identify the type of DTD, as well as to reference for the XML parser the external location of the DTD file to be used to validate the document. A *parser*, like its linguistic cousin, is a program that is designed to verify that the grammar (syntax) is correct. Of course, it needs to know what kind of document it is parsing (Transitional, Strict, or Frame) before it can begin its long-nosed look. The previous code was an example of the Transitional DOCTYPE.

Let us do a bit of parsing ourselves as we decompose this declaration. The format of the generic DTD declaration is:

```
<!DOCTYPE root type "id" "url">
```

In this code, you can see that `root` will refer to HTML as the root element of the document, and it is indeed a given in XHTML that the root element *is* HTML — for it does encompass all of the other elements in the document tree.

Just as the `root` will always be HTML for XHTML documents, so shall the `type` always be `Public`. You will have different values assigned to the `id` and `url` attributes, depending upon the document type.

The reason for the existence of Transitional DTD is because of sheer numbers — millions upon millions of Web pages are written using the various previous versions of HTML. You can't just ignore them. Therefore, when you change into a system that is highly rationalized, you must still deal with the mishmash of order and looseness that is the absolute foundation.

Strict DTD

The generic form of the Strict `DOCTYPE` is as follows:

```
<!DOCTYPE html
PUBLIC "-//W3C//DTD XHTML 1.0 Strict//EN"
"http://www.w3.org/TR/xhtml1/DTD/xhtml1-strict.dtd">
```

Strict DTD does not support any deprecated features of the other two types of DTDs. It does not support frames in any way. It strictly conforms to the latest standards and is a logical predecessor to XHTML 2.0 (should that ever see the light of day), which may have *no* backward compatibility with earlier browsers (something that is being seriously considered).

Following are deprecated elements within Strict DTD:

- `a`
- `abbr`
- `acronym`
- `b`
- `bdo`
- `big`
- `br`
- `button`
- `cite`
- `code`
- `dfn`

- em
- I
- img
- input
- kdb
- label
- map
- object
- q
- samp
- select
- small
- span
- strong
- sub
- sup
- textarea
- tt
- var

Frameset

The generic format of the Frameset DOCTYPE is as follows:

```
<!DOCTYPE html
PUBLIC "-//W3C//DTD XHTML 1.0 Frameset//EN"
"http://www.w3.org/TR/xhtml1/DTD/xhtml1-frameset.dtd">
```

This DTD, is used to support frames and, as its name implies, supports frame-based documents. Like Transitional DTD, it also supports deprecated attributes and elements.

Following is some sample code using Frameset DTD:

```
<!DOCTYPE HTML PUBLIC "-//W3C//DTD HTML 4.01 Frameset//EN"
        "http://www.w3.org/TR/html4/frameset.dtd">
<html>
<head>
...
</head>
<frameset>
...
```

```
</frameset>
</html>
```

The following is an example of code used to create and render a Web page using Frameset DTD:

```
<!DOCTYPE HTML PUBLIC "-//W3C//DTD HTML 4.01 Frameset//EN"
          "http://www.w3.org/TR/html4/frameset.dtd">
<html>
<head>
</head>
   <frameset rows ="85,*">
         <frame src = "C:\Documents and Settings\Phil\My
         Documents\MyPictures\TheStorySingerHeader.jpg">
                <frameset cols="*,*, *">
                       <frame src="C:\Documents and
                       Settings\Phil\My Documents\My
                       Pictures\HuRim1.jpg">
                       <frame src="C:\Documents and
                       Settings\Phil\My Documents\My
                       Pictures\HuRim2.jpg">
                       <frame src="C:\Documents and
                       Settings\Phil\My Documents\My
                       Pictures\HuRim.jpg">
                </frameset>
    </frameset>
  </html>
```

This code renders as shown in Figure 15-1.

FIGURE 15-1

This is an example of coding using Frameset DTD.

DTD templates

The following list is a comprehensive set of templates for the correct forms for formatting all the DTD derivatives according to W3C (`www.w3.org/QA/2002/04/valid-dtd-list.html`):

- HTML 4.01 — Strict, Transitional, Frameset (and others):

```
<!DOCTYPE html PUBLIC "-//W3C//DTD HTML 4.01//EN"
   "http://www.w3.org/TR/html4/strict.dtd">

<!DOCTYPE html PUBLIC "-//W3C//DTD HTML 4.01 Transitional//EN"
   "http://www.w3.org/TR/html4/loose.dtd">

<!DOCTYPE html PUBLIC "-//W3C//DTD HTML 4.01 Frameset//EN"
   "http://www.w3.org/TR/html4/frameset.dtd">
```

- XHTML 1.0 — Strict, Transitional, Frameset:

```
<!DOCTYPE html PUBLIC "-//W3C//DTD XHTML 1.0 Strict//EN"
   "http://www.w3.org/TR/xhtml1/DTD/xhtml1-strict.dtd">

<!DOCTYPE html PUBLIC "-//W3C//DTD XHTML 1.0 Transitional//EN"
   "http://www.w3.org/TR/xhtml1/DTD/xhtml1-transitional.dtd">

<!DOCTYPE html PUBLIC "-//W3C//DTD XHTML 1.0 Frameset//EN"
   "http://www.w3.org/TR/xhtml1/DTD/xhtml1-frameset.dtd">
```

- XHTML 1.1 — DTD:

```
<!DOCTYPE html PUBLIC "-//W3C//DTD XHTML 1.1//EN"
   "http://www.w3.org/TR/xhtml11/DTD/xhtml11.dtd">
```

- XHTML Basic 1.0 — DTD:

```
<!DOCTYPE html PUBLIC "-//W3C//DTD XHTML Basic 1.0//EN"
    "http://www.w3.org/TR/xhtml-basic/xhtml-basic10.dtd">
```

- XHTML Basic 1.1 — DTD:

```
<!DOCTYPE html PUBLIC "-//W3C//DTD XHTML Basic 1.1//EN"
    "http://www.w3.org/TR/xhtml-basic/xhtml-basic11.dtd">
```

- HTML 2.0 — DTD:

```
<!DOCTYPE html PUBLIC "-//IETF//DTD HTML 2.0//EN">
```

- HTML 3.2 — DTD:

```
<!DOCTYPE html PUBLIC "-//W3C//DTD HTML 3.2 Final//EN">
```

- MathML 1.01 — DTD:

```
<!DOCTYPE math SYSTEM
    "http://www.w3.org/Math/DTD/mathml1/mathml.dtd">
```

- MathML 2.0 — DTD:

```
<!DOCTYPE math PUBLIC "-//W3C//DTD MathML 2.0//EN"
    "http://www.w3.org/TR/MathML2/dtd/mathml2.dtd">
```

- XHTML, MathML, SVG — DTD:

```
<!DOCTYPE html PUBLIC
    "-//W3C//DTD XHTML 1.1 plus MathML 2.0 plus SVG 1.1//EN"
    "http://www.w3.org/2002/04/xhtml-math-svg/xhtml-math-svg.dtd">
```

- SVG 1.0 — DTD:

```
<!DOCTYPE svg PUBLIC "-//W3C//DTD SVG 1.0//EN"
    "http://www.w3.org/TR/2001/REC-SVG-20010904/DTD/svg10.dtd">
```

- SVG 1.1 Full — DTD:

```
<!DOCTYPE svg PUBLIC "-//W3C//DTD SVG 1.1//EN"
    "http://www.w3.org/Graphics/SVG/1.1/DTD/svg11.dtd">
```

- SVG 1.1 Basic — DTD:

```
<!DOCTYPE svg PUBLIC "-//W3C//DTD SVG 1.1 Basic//EN"
    "http://www.w3.org/Graphics/SVG/1.1/DTD/svg11-basic.dtd">
```

- SVG 1.1 Tiny — DTD:

```
<!DOCTYPE svg PUBLIC "-//W3C//DTD SVG 1.1 Tiny//EN"
    "http://www.w3.org/Graphics/SVG/1.1/DTD/svg11-tiny.dtd">
```

- XHTML, MathML, SVG Profile (XHTML as the host language) — DTD:

```
<!DOCTYPE html PUBLIC
    "-//W3C//DTD XHTML 1.1 plus MathML 2.0 plus SVG 1.1//EN"
    "http://www.w3.org/2002/04/xhtml-math-svg/xhtml-math-svg.dtd">
```

- XHTML, MathML, SVG Profile (using SVG as the host) — DTD:

```
<!DOCTYPE svg:svg PUBLIC
    "-//W3C//DTD XHTML 1.1 plus MathML 2.0 plus SVG 1.1//EN"
    "http://www.w3.org/2002/04/xhtml-math-svg/xhtml-math-svg.dtd">
```

Making HTML compliant with XML

To make HTML compliant with XML and to make it modular, a number of syntactical rules must be adhered to, the same as for XHTML documents. The most important rule to follow is to properly manage tags. Browsers have very loosely supported strict HTML. The proper closure of tags such as the <h1> or the <p> tag is not always needed. The following script shows an HTML example that will be presented accurately in any current Web browser:

```
<html>
<body bgcolor="#FFFFFF" text="#000000">
```

```
<p><font face="Arial" size="4">The following text will be
displayed correctly in an HTML Web browser.
<p>Even though some of the tags are not correctly closed.<b>
```

Strict XHTML would not display this script. To begin with, the `<p>` and `<font>` tags are not correctly closed with a `</p>` and `</font>`. The strict nature of tag management within XML requires that all tags be correctly closed. In addition, the `<font>` is not supported in XHTML. Only CSS can be used to format the display of XHTML. Also missing from this document is the XML declaration at the top of the document identifying and defining the type of XML document, as well as the location of the DTD file to translate the XML tags.

To have the previous code work correctly as XHTML, it must resemble the following:

```
<?xml version="1.0"?>
<!DOCTYPE html PUBLIC "-//W3C//DTD XHTML 1.0 Strict//EN"
    "http://www.w3.org/TR/xhtml1/DTD/xhtml1-strict.dtd">
<html xmlns="http://www.w3.org/1999/xhtml">
<head>
<title>XHTML Page</title>
<style type="text/css" xml:space="preserve">
 body {
  background-color: #FFFFFF; //this is to say, white
  color: #000000; //this is to say, black
}
 P {
  Font-Family: Arial;
  Font-Size: 14pt;
}
</style>
</head>
<body>
<p>The following text will be displayed correctly in an XHTML
Web Browser.</p><p>As all of the tags are correctly
closed.<br />Ok</p>
</html>
```

As you can see, several new features have been added to the document. The first immediate change is the addition of the XML declaration at the top of the document. The insertion `<?xml version="1.0"?>` declares that the document is an XML document, and should be treated with the rules used with any XML document.

Following the XML declaration is a `DOCTYPE` declaration, which declares the DTD that is used. As the Strict translation of XHTML, the `DOCTYPE` is `"html PUBLIC "-//W3C//DTD XHTML 1.0 Strict//EN"`.

In the previous sample code, the line `http://www.w3.org/TR/xhtml1/DTD/xhtml1-strict.dtd` directs the browser to download the appropriate DTD file to translate the document.

The XHMTL namespace is defined within the <HTML> tag, identifying where the namespace is located on the Internet.

You cannot use the <font> and <body> tags to format in XHTML 1.0 with a strict DTD. A CSS replaces the tags in the first version of the document. The <body> background color and default text color are identified as white (#FFFFFF) and black (#000000), respectively. The presentation style for the <p> tag is defined as font Arial and size 14pt.

The rest of the document is presented as it would be in HTML, only without the formatting tags.

These are but a few of the number of changes that must be made to a document for it to be XHTML-compliant. Many tags that have been used by HTML designers have been removed For example, the <font> tag must be replaced with a CSS style. The same is true for the <center> tag, which also must now be a CSS style. The italics tag, <i>, must be replaced with the equivalent <em> tag, and the bold tag <b> must be replaced with <strong>.

A complete description of how to make a document compliant with XHTML is detailed at the W3C's Web site (www.w3.org/MarkUp). The site contains comprehensive documentation on the new standard, including links to tools that convert HTML 4.0 pages to XHTML.

The W3C provides a set of tools to prepare Web pages for XHTML. The tools can be located at the W3C HTML Validation Service (http://validator.w3.org) site. One particular tool, HTML Tidy, is very useful in converting poorly written HTML documents (such as those generated by Microsoft Word) and making them compliant with XHTML standards.

Contrasting XHTML with HTML 4.0

You should not overlook the fact that HTML 4.01 bears many similarities to XHTML 1.0 and may hardly be distinguished if the DTD is Transitional or Frameset. Both languages require the use of CSS for formatting, and both require the closure of tags for paragraphs. In many ways, XHMTL is a reformulation of HTML 4.0 in order to follow the rules of XML. By reproducing HTML 4.01 as an XML language, many of the extensions that are added to XHTML can be done successfully in a modular format (XHTML 1.1).

XHTML 1.0 enables the massive release of new Internet-accessing programs, such as personal desk accessories (PDAs), game consoles, and interactive TV boxes, which can be kept current with the latest Web page standards. All that is needed is a browser that understands XML and DTDs. A designer can still use text-editing tools to develop Web pages.

Table 15-4 shows the various types of XHTML.

Table 15-5 shows some commonly used event commands in HTML that are now used for well-formed documents under even Strict DTD for XHTML document types.

With the rapidly changing environment of the Internet, the inclusion of modules and extensible language, such as XHTML, is a natural fit.

TABLE 15-4

Types of XHTML

Language	Explanation
XHTML Basic	This was created in 2000 to answer the coding requirements of mobile Web users. It has a simplified version of modules. Being able to pick and choose the features allows smaller application sizes, resulting in faster download/upload times and faster execution of instructions by the processor.
XHTML 1.0	This was created in 2000. It has three DTDs (Transitional, Strict, and Frame). It is designed to combine the strong presentation features of HTML 4.01 with the data design advantages of XML.
XHTML 1.1	In this type, the provision of modules simplifies the coding process. Being able to pick and choose features allows smaller application sizes, resulting in faster download/upload times and faster execution of instructions by the processor.
XHTML 2.0	This type has been worked on since 2004. This is really so different that it may be considered a different language. Most presentation features currently allowed under Transitional and Frame DTDs have disappeared. Additionally, there is a possibility that it may be incompatible with earlier versions. Currently "a work in progress," its time of debut and final format are matters of some interest to the design/development community.

TABLE 15-5

Events Common to Both HTML and XHTML

Events	Results
`onclick`	A button was clicked.
`ondblclick`	A button was clicked twice.
`onmousedown`	A button was pressed down.
`onmouseup`	A button was released.
`onmousemove`	A pointer moved onto an element.
`onmouseout`	A pointer exited an element.
`onkeypress`	A key was pressed and released.
`onkeydown`	A key was pressed down.
`onkeyup`	A key was released.

Modules

After XHTML 1.0 came out, a minor revision was made to better provide for the extension of XHTML to the use of the ubiquitous Web: cell phones, PDAs (such as the Blueberry), pagers, and other handheld devices used for inventory or count purposes in business. The use of modules allows the development of applications that are specific to that device. For example, if you had a handheld device with text-only capability, it would use only the text module of XHTML and not have available such objects as images and maps. This modularization speeds up the sending and receiving of data because it takes up fewer CPU cycles and is less memory-intensive.

Table 15-6 provides a list of XHTML 1.1 and XHTML Basic modules as given by W3C (`www.w3.org/TR/2000/REC-xhtml-basic-20001219/xhtml-basic.txt`). Note that XHTML Basic was primarily devised to be used on mobile devices.

Other modules for XHTML 1.1 would include Frames (including iframes), some elements involving the appearance of fonts (big, small, super and subscripting), and stylesheets, which, when you think about it, is not currently a big issue with most text-messaging systems.

TABLE 15-6

Modules Used for XHTML 1.1 and XHTML Basic

Module	Function
`Structure Module`	`body, head, html, title`
`Text Module`	`abbr, acronym, address, blockquote, br, cite, code, dfn, div, em, h1, h2, h3, h4, h5, h6, kbd, p, pre, q, samp, span, strong, var`
`Hypertext Module`	`a`
`List Module`	`dl, dt, dd, ol, ul, li`
`Forms Module`	`form, input, label, select, option, textarea`
`Tables Module`	`caption, table, td, th, tr`
`Image Module`	`img`
`Object Module`	`object, param`
`Metainformation Module`	`meta`
`Link Module`	`link`
`Base Module`	`base`

Frowned-upon practices in older HTML syntax

In XHTML, the syntactic characteristics discussed here are no longer permitted, even though the results of such HTML foibles were often rendered correctly in several browsers:

- Empty elements (also called single-sided tags) such as <br>, <hr>, <img> must be terminated with a forward slash, /, preceded by a space such as <br /> or <hr />.
- You cannot use tags inconsistently. For example, if you mess up a header by coding <h3>Mary had a little lamb<h2>, some browsers will render it anyway, but XHTML-compliant browsers should not.
- You cannot mix and mismatch presentation elements. They must be in parallel sets. So, if you were to say, <p>This is an <i><u><b>example</b></i></u> of somebody stressing a word element and heavily overdoing it</p>, it would not be rendered correctly (or at all within a Strict DTD document).
- In the name of consistency, a document cannot be well formed unless it also has a closing tag for every opening one.
- All elements are lowercase in XHTML. You can't use <BR> or <H1> or <Li>, and certainly not something as inconsistent as <hTmL></HtMl> anymore. In particular, remember that attribute names must be lowercased, as in nowrap="nowrap", noresize="noresize", and bgcolor="red".

NOTE **With Strict DTD, everything — everything — must be just right. The syntax must be just right (well formed), and the content within the well-formed document must also conform to specifications (be valid). However, both Transitional and Frameset DTDs are designed to be backward compatible and fairly tolerant, and may still accept some of these.**

The following is also an example of using the strict DTD version of XHTML 1.0:

```
<!DOCTYPE html PUBLIC "-//W3C//DTD XHTML 1.0 Strict//EN"
"http://www.w3.org/TR/xhtml1/DTD/xhtml1-strict.dtd">
<html xmlns="http://www.w3.org/1999/xhtml">
<head>
<meta http-equiv="content-type" content="text/html;charset=utf-8"/>
<title>Illustration of Strict XHTML DTD Usage</title>

<script type="text/javascript" src="javascript/main.js"></script>
</head>
<body>
<h1>When Wind Does Blow</h1><br />
<pre>
<p> When wind does blow among the trees
And cool the earth with gentle breeze
How softly then my thoughts do go
To you my love in summer's glow.</p><br />
<pre>
For leaves are green on summer's day
And strong the limbs that slowly sway
In these sweet winds that never die
```

```
But time goes on and so must I

For summer now is turned to fall
As age does bend what once was tall
And gentle though the wind may blow
It still must cease to warm me so.

And I must leave thy golden breast
To seek the earth to find my rest
For softly though my dreams may go
My dreams are dust and time does flow.
</p></pre> <br />

<H3>The following excerpts also gives features of
deprecated elements and inline styles together in strict DTD</h3>
<h4 style="font-family:fantasy"> When one swims<h4>
<br />
<pre>

<h4 style="color:blue; font-family:Allegro BT"> When one
swims the sea of life
</h4>
<p>One may not build a moat
Nor firmly hold an anchor
And still expect to float.

Though anchor may seem steady
And firmly hold you down
If ye seek the air to breathe
By anchor you will drown

So swimmer of life's waters
Be careful what you dream
What you think you think you know</p></pre>
<pre>
 <style="font-family:Book Antiqua">( Is not as it would
<span style="font-size:150%; font-family:Book Antiqua">
<em><strong>seem</strong></em></span>)</style>


<p>And here's the story's moral
If I may sum it up: </P>
  <ul>
  <li>Always be what God made thee...</li>
  <li> and with him ye shall sup</li>
  <li><b>The End </li>
 </ul>
</pre>
</body>
</html>
```

NOTE In this program, note the use of deprecated presentation elements. Curiously, in this version, they still work, even though they should not, according to the W3C standards cited earlier in this chapter. This is not to suggest anything other than that is how it was rendered in the IDE we used, and it is, therefore, obvious that the document behaved as it did because the browser we used to render it was not yet sufficiently up to date to support Strict DTD.

Figure 15-2 shows how the coding renders the document using both styles and deprecated elements. Some of the deprecated elements demonstrated include an unordered list (as in the last example), as well as the use of formatting tags and other presentational features in the body of the document illustration.

NOTE In addition to the list of unsupported elements discussed earlier, some browser-specific elements such as the `marquee` element in IE are not valid under Strict DTD.

NOTE Strict DTD requires that all attributes have values. In many instances of Boolean statements, this results in pointless redundancy.

In Strict HTML, the checked attribute must be assigned a checked value. Table 15-7 shows a strict list of such required values.

TABLE 15-7

Attributes Requiring Values

HTML	XHTML
`checked`	`checked="checked"`
`compact`	`compact="compact"`
`declare`	`declare="declare"`
`defer`	`defer="defer"`
`disabled`	`disabled="disabled"`
`ismap`	`ismap="ismap"`
`multiple`	`multiple="multiple"`
`nohref`	`nohref="nohref"`
`noresize`	`noresize="noresize"`
`noshade`	`noshade="noshade"`
`nowrap`	`nowrap="nowrap"`
`readonly`	`readonly="readonly"`
`selected`	`selected="selected"`

FIGURE 15-2

The code creates this rendered page.

When wind does blow

When wind does blow among the trees
And cool the earth with gentle breeze
How softly then my thoughts do go
To you my love in summer's glow.

For leaves are green on summer's day
And strong the limbs that slowly sway
In these sweet winds that never die
But time goes on and so must I

For summer now is turned to fall
As age does bend what once was tall
And gentle though the wind may blow
It still must cease to warm me so.

And I must leave thy golden breast
To seek the earth to find my rest
For softly though my dreams may go
My dreams are dust and time does flow.

When one swims...

When one swims the sea of life

One may not build a most
Nor firmly hold an anchor
And still expect to float.

Though anchor may seem steady

And firmly hold you down
If ye seek the air to breathe
By anchor you will drown

So swimmer of life's waters
Be careful what you dream

What you think you think you know

Is not as it would ***seem***

And here's the story's moral

if I may sum it up

- always be what God made thee...
  - and with Him shall ye sup
    - **The End**

Creating an XHTML Document

According to W3C (`www.w3.org`), the following is the generalized template used for creating any XHTML `DOCTYPE`:

```
<?xml version="1.0" encoding="utf-8" standalone="no" ?>
<!DOCTYPE html PUBLIC "-//W3C//DTD XHTML 1.0 Strict//EN"
        "http://www.w3.org/TR/xhtml1/DTD/xhtml1-strict.dtd">
<html xmlns="http://www.w3.org/1999/xhtml" xml:lang="en" lang="en">

<head>
     <title>An XHTML 1.0 Strict standard template</title>
     <meta http-equiv="content-type"
          content="text/html;charset=utf-8" />
     <meta http-equiv="Content-Style-Type" content="text/css" />
</head>
<body>
     <p> ... Your HTML content here ... </p>
</body>
</html>
```

Note that the first line of the Strict DTD (and all types of XHTML documents) should be something very similar to `<?xml version="1.0" encoding="utf-8" standalone="no" ?>`. This is called the *XML declaration*, and while it is not a required line in the document, you should understand why it is there so that you can understand why you must always put it there, too.

Remember the XML parsers? They use this data in the declaration to determine both the encoding type and the content. All data is text or binary. You want to make clear to the parser what is what by specifying the encoding schema. Also, there are a few versions of XML out there, each with its own idiosyncratic features, so you might want to let the browser know which version you are talking about, and which encoding scheme. Otherwise, the browser may make a few assumptions or queries while rendering, which would slow down the system a bit — or crash it all together. Thus, if you do not give the parsers this information explicitly, they will make (intelligent) assumptions on rendering.

The XML declaration may be divided into three parts:

- The version of XML
- The encoding scheme
- The DTD location

These days, the XHTML version of the XML family most fully supported is XHTML 1.0 (although support for XHTML 1.1 is growing). As the differences between the two versions are not that significant, we would specify 1.0 to ensure that it is rendered to the greatest number of browsers. Hence, in the declaration, we have `?xml version="1.0"`.

The encoding tells the browser how to read the document. This is most likely going to be UTF-8 or UTF-16. If the encoding type is not specified, the browser defaults first to one and then to the other.

NOTE **UTF-8 is an encoding scheme that encodes characters in 8-bit blocks called *bytes*. UTF-16 is a character set that uses 16 bits (or 2 bytes) for encoding. Because there are thousands of possible characters for all the alphabets of the world, you can see why both encoding schemes are available. The encoding scheme will be either** `encoding="utf-8"`**or** `encoding="utf-16"`**.**

`Standalone` is a Boolean attribute with the values of only `"yes"`or `"no"`. For XHTML documents, you always want to put `"no"` because otherwise the browser will not go looking at the W3C site for the proper DTD for code validation. Hence, `standalone="no"`.

Namespace

A *namespace* is a way to uniquely identify duplicate elements with different values (called a *local namespace*) or combining languages from two or more sources into a single document (called a *default namespace*). Following is an example of a local namespace:

```
<html xmlns:prefix=namespace>
```

Let's suppose you had coding from two separate languages within one document. If the default coding of the document were to be XML, the standard declaration would be `<root xmlns="namespace">`, where `root` is HTML and the `namespace` is a unique ID. For reasons of clarity and consistency, the namespace referenced is typically shown as follows:

```
http://www.w3.org/1999/xhtml
```

When you look at this, you probably believe it is a URL. But it's not, really, even though you could use it to get to that location; it's just a unique identifier that everyone uses by convention.

If you were then to toss in a separate language (from the XML family) into the document, you would need to reference that language in the document as well for those element types. Let's choose MathML as the second language. This would be declared immediately below the default namespace declaration as follows:

```
<xml:ml=http://www.w3.org/1998/Math/MathML>
```

Every element in the document that comes from that local namespace would then be prefixed with `ml`, as in `<ml:tr></tr> <ml:td></td>`. Any tag not so prefixed would belong to the default namespace.

CDATA and PCDATA

Character data (CDATA) is all content of an XML document. It is not the markup for the document structure, and it is not parsed. The parts of a document that are treated as code are referred to as *parsed character data* (PCDATA). The difficulty arises because some of the same symbols that are used to delimit code elements (such as <> or &) can also be used within the content. Therefore, the data may be rendered incorrectly.

To remedy this situation within content, the character *code* and not the character itself is used. For example, the degree symbol would be `°`, as shown here:

```
<pre>&lt;person sex=&quot;female&quot;&gt;</pre>e &#176.
```

In this snippet of code, notice the use of character codes for the use of quotation marks " ".

NOTE **A similar difficulty arises in respect of use of quotes with strings and within strings in Java and JavaScript. This is resolved by alternating pairs of single and double quotation marks. This is also referred to as "escaping" characters.**

A complete copy of the ASCII code (courtesy of `www.asciitable.com`) is shown in Figure 15-3 and Figure 15-4.

FIGURE 15-3

The original ASCII had only 127 characters and was developed for teletype communication.

Dec	Hx	Oct	Char		Dec	Hx	Oct	Html	Chr	Dec	Hx	Oct	Html	Chr	Dec	Hx	Oct	Html	Chr
0	0	000	NUL	(null)	32	20	040		Space	64	40	100	@	@	96	60	140	`	`
1	1	001	SOH	(start of heading)	33	21	041	!	!	65	41	101	A	A	97	61	141	a	a
2	2	002	STX	(start of text)	34	22	042	"	"	66	42	102	B	B	98	62	142	b	b
3	3	003	ETX	(end of text)	35	23	043	#	#	67	43	103	C	C	99	63	143	c	c
4	4	004	EOT	(end of transmission)	36	24	044	$	$	68	44	104	D	D	100	64	144	d	d
5	5	005	ENQ	(enquiry)	37	25	045	%	%	69	45	105	E	E	101	65	145	e	e
6	6	006	ACK	(acknowledge)	38	26	046	&	&	70	46	106	F	F	102	66	146	f	f
7	7	007	BEL	(bell)	39	27	047	'	'	71	47	107	G	G	103	67	147	g	g
8	8	010	BS	(backspace)	40	28	050	(	(	72	48	110	H	H	104	68	150	h	h
9	9	011	TAB	(horizontal tab)	41	29	051	)	)	73	49	111	I	I	105	69	151	i	i
10	A	012	LF	(NL line feed, new line)	42	2A	052	*	*	74	4A	112	J	J	106	6A	152	j	j
11	B	013	VT	(vertical tab)	43	2B	053	+	+	75	4B	113	K	K	107	6B	153	k	k
12	C	014	FF	(NP form feed, new page)	44	2C	054	,	,	76	4C	114	L	L	108	6C	154	l	l
13	D	015	CR	(carriage return)	45	2D	055	-	-	77	4D	115	M	M	109	6D	155	m	m
14	E	016	SO	(shift out)	46	2E	056	.	.	78	4E	116	N	N	110	6E	156	n	n
15	F	017	SI	(shift in)	47	2F	057	/	/	79	4F	117	O	O	111	6F	157	o	o
16	10	020	DLE	(data link escape)	48	30	060	0	0	80	50	120	P	P	112	70	160	p	p
17	11	021	DC1	(device control 1)	49	31	061	1	1	81	51	121	Q	Q	113	71	161	q	q
18	12	022	DC2	(device control 2)	50	32	062	2	2	82	52	122	R	R	114	72	162	r	r
19	13	023	DC3	(device control 3)	51	33	063	3	3	83	53	123	S	S	115	73	163	s	s
20	14	024	DC4	(device control 4)	52	34	064	4	4	84	54	124	T	T	116	74	164	t	t
21	15	025	NAK	(negative acknowledge)	53	35	065	5	5	85	55	125	U	U	117	75	165	u	u
22	16	026	SYN	(synchronous idle)	54	36	066	6	6	86	56	126	V	V	118	76	166	v	v
23	17	027	ETB	(end of trans. block)	55	37	067	7	7	87	57	127	W	W	119	77	167	w	w
24	18	030	CAN	(cancel)	56	38	070	8	8	88	58	130	X	X	120	78	170	x	x
25	19	031	EM	(end of medium)	57	39	071	9	9	89	59	131	Y	Y	121	79	171	y	y
26	1A	032	SUB	(substitute)	58	3A	072	:	:	90	5A	132	Z	Z	122	7A	172	z	z
27	1B	033	ESC	(escape)	59	3B	073	;	;	91	5B	133	[	[	123	7B	173	{	{
28	1C	034	FS	(file separator)	60	3C	074	<	<	92	5C	134	\	\	124	7C	174			|
29	1D	035	GS	(group separator)	61	3D	075	=	=	93	5D	135	]	]	125	7D	175	}	}
30	1E	036	RS	(record separator)	62	3E	076	>	>	94	5E	136	^	^	126	7E	176	~	~
31	1F	037	US	(unit separator)	63	3F	077	?	?	95	5F	137	_	_	127	7F	177		DEL

FIGURE 15-4

The extended ASCII code was implemented to provide a character set for numerous other symbols that exceeded the limits of the original ASCII.

128	Ç	144	É	161	í	177	▒	193	┴	209	╤	225	ß	241	±
129	ü	145	æ	162	ó	178	▓	194	┬	210	╥	226	Γ	242	≥
130	é	146	Æ	163	ú	179	│	195	├	211	╙	227	π	243	≤
131	â	147	ô	164	ñ	180	┤	196	─	212	╘	228	Σ	244	⌠
132	ä	148	ö	165	Ñ	181	╡	197	┼	213	╒	229	σ	245	⌡
133	à	149	ò	166	ª	182	╢	198	╞	214	╓	230	µ	246	÷
134	å	150	û	167	º	183	╖	199	╟	215	╫	231	τ	247	≈
135	ç	151	ù	168	¿	184	╕	200	╚	216	╪	232	Φ	248	°
136	ê	152	_	169	_	185	╣	201	╔	217	┘	233	Θ	249	·
137	ë	153	Ö	170	¬	186	║	202	╩	218	┌	234	Ω	250	·
138	è	154	Ü	171	½	187	╗	203	╦	219	█	235	δ	251	√
139	ï	156	£	172	¼	188	╝	204	╠	220	▄	236	∞	252	_
140	î	157	¥	173	¡	189	╜	205	═	221	▌	237	φ	253	²
141	ì	158	_	174	«	190	╛	206	╬	222	▐	238	ε	254	■
142	Ä	159	ƒ	175	»	191	┐	207	╧	223	▀	239	∩	255	
143	Å	160	á	176	░	192	└	208	╨	224	α	240	≡		

In the event that data had embedded in it multiple instances of characters that could be misread by the browser as parsed rather than unparsed data (and cause a system crash), the data could be enclosed within a set of brackets that indicated the parser should ignore the data within the brackets. Occasionally, when using style commands, you may have data that would cause the system to render the page incorrectly, and this would be a good candidate to enclose within the brackets.

The formatting of a CDATA block is:

```
<![CDATA [
Enter the code you do not wish to be rendered here.
]]>
```

NOTE **You will automatically note that the one piece of code you cannot use in a CDATA block is the brackets because the parser, or Web browser, might read it.**

White space

After the CDATA and the PCDATA have been dealt with, pretty much all that remains is the white space. In HTML, the white space is automatically removed unless preserved by the use of the `<pre>`*`structured content`*`</pre>` element.

XHTML treats white space almost the same way, unless it is, say, within quotation marks. An example would be where you are appending a string variable to some other variable. For example, let's have the other variable be a decimal type with two positions to the right of the decimal and an implicit "$" symbol, as shown here:

```
document.write("The amount you owe is: " + decAmount + ".");
```

The output would be: *The amount you owe is: $12.95*. Note that there is a space after the colon (:) because you inserted it there. Also note that the period at the end of the sentence did not have a space entered into it.

Code Validation in an XHTML Document

After the document has been made and is well-formed according to typical standards of coding, you can then run it through a code validator (such as `validator.w3.org`) to see if it is in conformance with the W3C standards. Figure 15-5 shows the opening screen for the W3C validator, and Figure 15-6 shows the results of the validation.

FIGURE 15-5

This is the code validator screen of `validator.w3.org`.

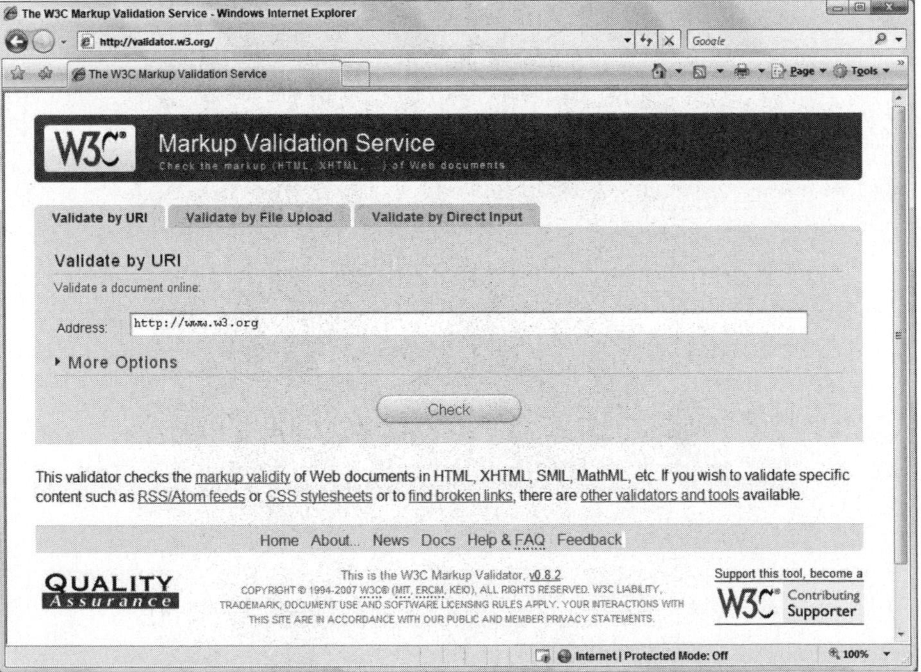

FIGURE 15-6

The results show that a site has successfully passed validation for Strict DTD.

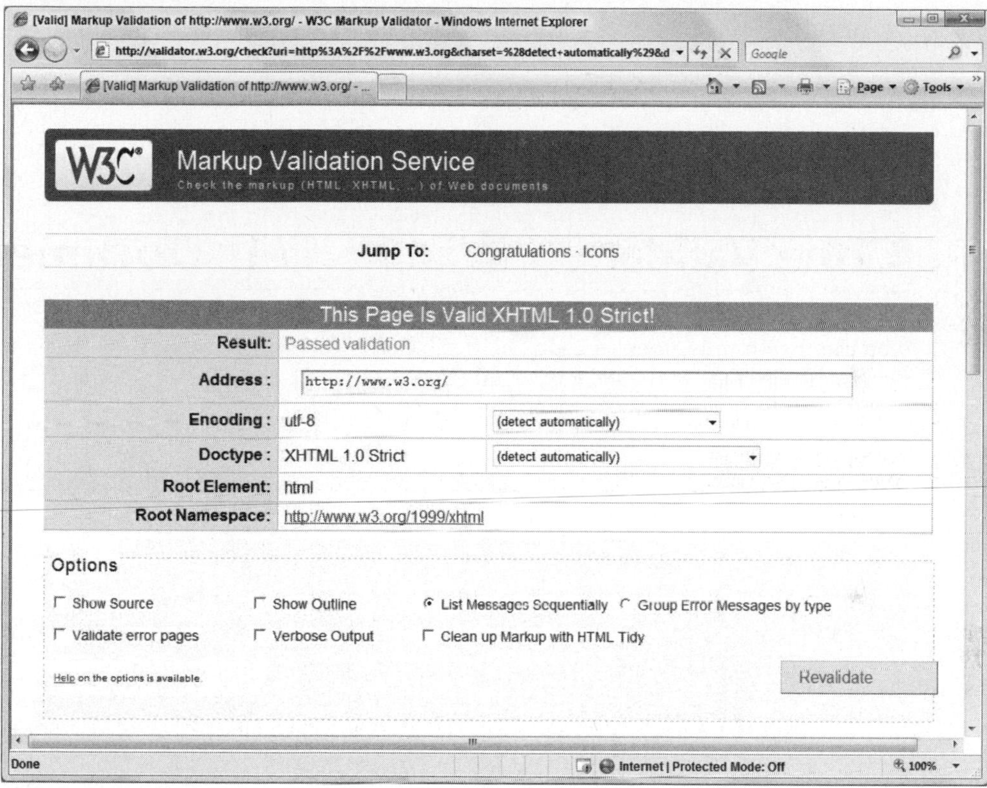

Once your site has passed validation, you may even add the following icon using the associated coding:

```
<p>
<a href="http://validator.w3.org/check?uri=referer"><img
        src="http://www.w3.org/Icons/valid-xhtml10"
        alt="Valid XHTML 1.0 Strict" height="31" width="88" /></a>
</p>
```

The address for the image is the W3C server where the image is located. To link to your local validation image, you must point the `img src` to it.

Last, if you have CSS on your site you may also validate that by linking to `http://jigsaw.w3.org/css-validator`.

Figure 15-7 shows a view of another site using code validator.

FIGURE 15-7

The institution that did more than almost any other government entity to bring into being the Information Age has failed validation with 42 errors.

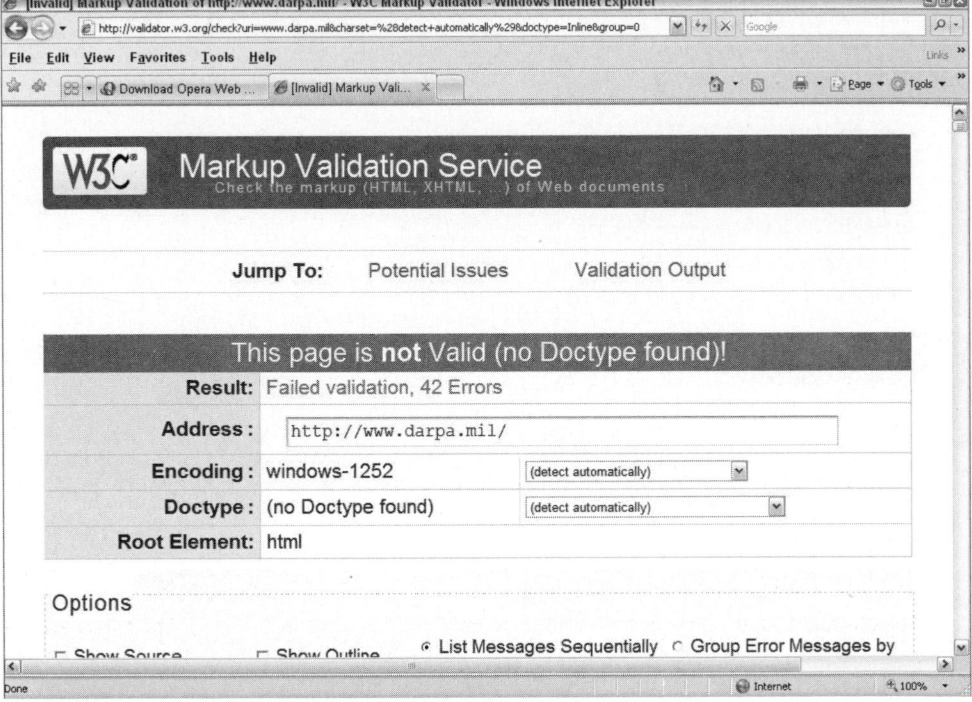

A typical thing to look for if your site is getting a failed score on validation would be to verify that you actually have an XML and or `DOCTYPE` declaration at the top of your coding. Especially take a look at how attributes are coded, and replace deprecated ones with the appropriate `styles` attributes. You should review the list of deprecated attributes and elements shown earlier in this chapter, but your best source for finding and fixing coding errors is at the validator site itself. Errors are specified and correct coding is offered. This degree of help greatly simplifies the validation process, reducing it to not much more than a cut and paste effort.

The attribute given here is required for an element that you've used, but you have omitted it. For example, in most HTML and XHTML document types, the `type` attribute is required on the `script` element and the `alt` attribute is required for the `img` element.

Table 15-8 shows some helpful sites for code validators.

TABLE 15-8

URLs for Code Validators and Compliance Tools

Source	URL
Tidy Little Code Checker and Validator Used For Both XML and XHTML	`http://tidy.sourceforge.net`
HTML Validator	`www.htmlvalidator.com`
Markup Validation Service	`http://validator.w3.org`
w3c Schools Site Validation	`www.w3schools.com/site/site_validate.asp`
Validome	`www.validome.org`

Table 15-9 shows some helpful sites that provide more information about XHTML.

TABLE 15-9

Helpful Web sites on XHTML

Sites	URLs
The Fish Tank Forum	`www.johncfish.com`
Website Tips for XHTML	`http://websitetips.com/xhtml`
eMacs Utilities for XHTML	`http://ourcomments.org/Emacs/nXhtml/doc/nxhtml.html`

Making Your Site Mobile with WAP/WML

As it stands right now, there are more mobile computing devices in use than desktop ones. And the trend is that the growth in the number of portable devices will increase even more rapidly. With the implementation of the Internet Protocol Version 6 (IPv6), approximately 2^128 or 340,282,366,920,938,463,463,374,607,431,768,211,456 devices will be able to be directly connected to the Internet.

Many cell phones and almost all personal digital assistants (PDAs) already have the capability to connect to Internet. And one of the problems faced by today's Web developers is that they are used to designing pages for desktop computers with screen sizes of 15 inches and up. The question that faces them is how to view the same information in a cell phone with a screen that could be little more than 1 inch in width. This is where Wireless Markup Language (WML) comes in.

What is WML?

WML is similar to XHTML. Think of it as a subset of XHTML, but with a few additions. WML is the file format used by most mobile phone browsers. Although the tags themselves are simpler, in some ways WML has more features than HTML. For example, with input text boxes in WML, you can supply the format of the data required and the browser automatically validates the data before sending the form. In HTML, you could achieve the same (but in a much more complicated fashion) with JavaScript. Many people speak of WAP-enabled phones and WAP pages. Really, the page is a WML page that you view in a WML browser on a WAP-enabled phone.

The Wireless Application Protocol (WAP) is to mobile phones what the HTTP is to desktop computer and laptops. It is the link between your mobile phone and Internet, and your Internet service provider (ISP), in this scenario, is the phone company. The ISP acts as a proxy or gateway by retrieving the WML pages you request, and then sends them via WAP to your phone. Any Web site can have WML pages without requiring any extra software.

The scripting language for mobile phones is called *WMLScript*. WMLScript is similar in function and syntax to JavaScript, which can be used on a standard Web page. However, as we have already mentioned, the most common uses of JavaScript (such as validating forms) are already incorporated into WML, so WMLScript doesn't play as big a role in the design of WML pages as JavaScript in HTML pages.

Now that you understand some of the basic terminology, we can turn to the design of WML pages.

Dealing with WML

WML is designed for devices with limited memory, a limited bandwidth wireless connection to the Internet, and a low screen resolution

In an attempt to overcome these problems, the designers of WML decided to break away from the way HTML works (where each HTML file represents a page on the screen). In WML, one file can contain several pages. The main file is called a *deck* and the pages inside are called *cards*.

The basic structure of a WML file is as follows:

```
<?xml version="1.0"?>
<!DOCTYPE wml PUBLIC "-//WAPFORUM//DTD WML 1.1//EN"
"http://www.wapforum.org/DTD/wml_1.1.xml">
<wml>
```

```
    <card title="Welcome to WML">
            <p>
                    <em>Emphasised Text!</em><br/>
                    <i>Italic Text!</i><br/>
                    <b>Bold Text!</b><br/>
                    <strong>Strong Text!</strong><br/>
                    <u>Underlined Text!</u><br/>
                    <small>Small Text!</small><br/>
             </p>
    </card>
</wml>
```

Note that this is an XML file, so the `<br>` tag, which has no content, is specified as `<br/>`.

To view the file, you have several choices. One is to put the file on any Web server and connect to it with a WAP-enabled mobile phone with Internet access. You could also use a browser that emulates a mobile phone and provides WML support — many are available on the Internet. Alternatively, you can use a normal desktop browser that supports WML. Opera is one of the few desktop browsers that is WML-compatible — a free version is available from `www.opera.com`. Figure 15-8 shows how Opera displays the previous WML file.

FIGURE 15-8

You can view a WML document in an Opera browser.

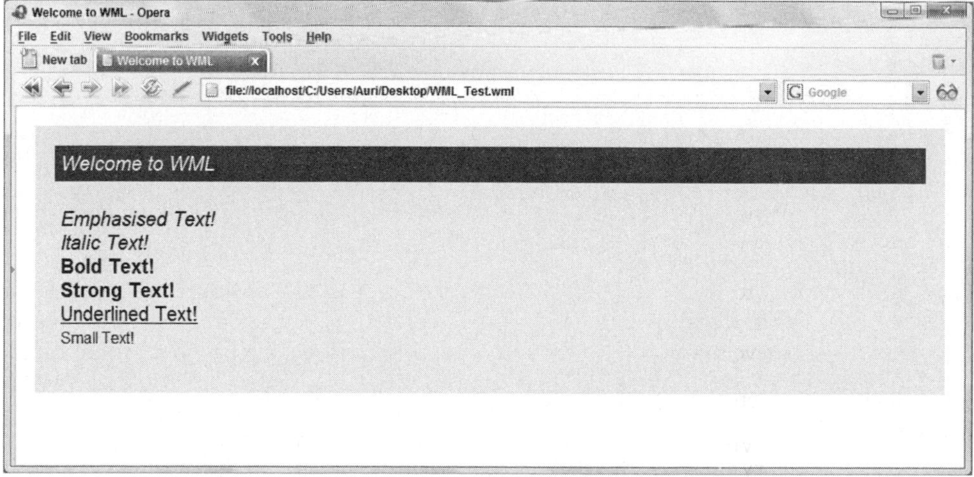

Let's go through the WML file step by step.

The first line is the declaration that specifies that the file is XML:

```
<?xml version="1.0"?>
```

The next line is the declaration of the DTD for WML 1.1:

```
<!DOCTYPE wml PUBLIC "-//WAPFORUM//DTD WML 1.1//EN"
"http://www.wapforum.org/DTD/wml_1.1.xml">
```

As shown in the following line, the `<wml>` tag is the equivalent of the `<HTML>` tag for an HTML file. It is the root element for a WML document.

```
<wml>
```

As shown here, a `card` element is equivalent to an HTML page. WML browsers only show one `card` element at a time.

```
<card title="Welcome to WML">
```

The following tags are identical to their HTML equivalents, with the exception of the `<small>` tag, which has the effect of displaying the text in a smaller font.

```
<p>

              <em>Emphasised Text!</em><br/>
              <i>Italic Text!</i><br/>
              <b>Bold Text!</b><br/>
              <strong>Strong Text!</strong><br/>
              <u>Underlined Text!</u><br/>
              <small>Small Text!</small><br/>
        </p>
  </card>
</wml>
```

CROSS-REF **See Chapter 4 for more information on the basic HTML elements.**

WML Tags

Most of the tags in WML are very similar to the tags in HTML. The major difference is that the number of attributes that they have is vastly reduced. Table 15-10 shows the set of WML tags in version 1.1.

TABLE 15-10

WML Tags in Version 1.1

WML Tag	Definition
a	Anchor or link*
anchor	Anchor or link (see a)
access	Used to define permissions
b	Bold*
big	Larger font*
br	Line break*
card	A unit of user interaction (a page)
do	A button for navigation or submitting a form
em	Emphasis*
fieldset	Groups a number of input controls together*
go	Used to display a given card
head	Head*
i	Italic*
img	Image*
input	Input control*
meta	Meta tag*
noop	No operation (used in event handlers)
p	Paragraph*
postfield	Used to specify a parameter and value to send to the server
pre	Preformatted text*
prev	Displays the previous page equivalent to history.go(-1) in JavaScript
onevent	Specifies an event handler
optgroup	Group options in submenu*
option	Option in a select menu*
refresh	Refreshes the page applying variable
select	Select menu*
small	Small text*

continued

TABLE 15-10 *(continued)*

WML Tag	Definition
strong	Bold*
table	Table*
template	A template for multiple cards
timer	Used to create a timer
td	Table data*
tr	Table row*
u	Underline*
setvar	Used to set a variable to a given value
wml	The root element of a WML page

*Similar to the <HTML> tag with the same name

Shuffling the cards

We have now seen one card in a deck, but there are many more cards available. Of course, we need to provide some means of navigating from one card to the others. One possibility is anchors.

Notice in the following WML file that each card has an `id` attribute. The relative URL for a card in WML is `#id`, where `id` refers to the `id` specified in the card you want to show.

The file `shuffle.wml` follows:

```
<?xml version="1.0"?> <!DOCTYPE wml PUBLIC "-
//WAPFORUM//DTD WML 1.1//EN"
"http://www.wapforum.org/DTD/wml_1.1.xml">
<wml>
        <card id="one" title="Welcome to WML">
                <p><big>A Big Welcome to WML</big></p>
                <a href="#two">Next</a>
        </card>
        <card id="two" title="Welcome to WML">
                <p>A Medium Welcome to WML</p>
                <a href="#one">Prev</a>
                <a href="#three">Next</a>
        </card>
        <card id="three" title="Welcome to WML">
                <p><small>A Small Welcome to WML</small></p>
                <a href="#two">Prev</a>
        </card>
</wml>
```

FIGURE 15-9

This WML document is composed of several cards with hyperlinks.

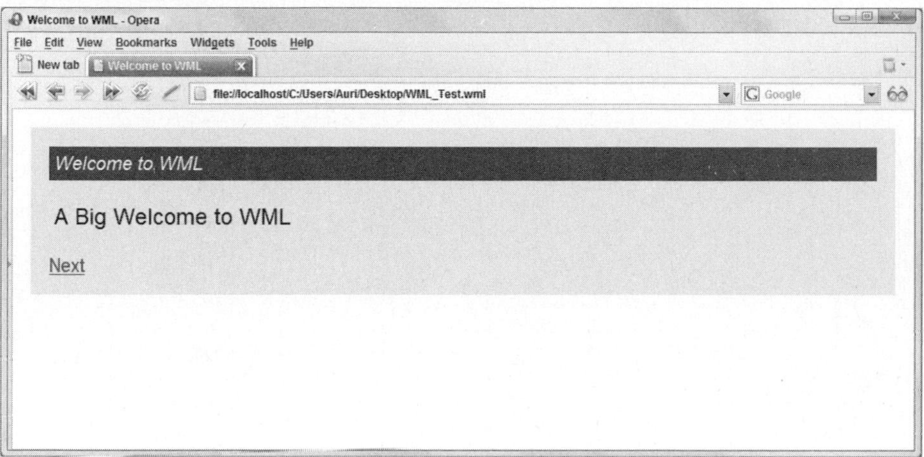

Figure 15-9 shows how this WML file is rendered.

Remember that, although there can be several cards in one deck, 52 is going a bit too far.

To go from one card to another, you use the URL of the deck (the WML file) plus # and the `id` of the card. You can, of course, jump from one deck to another. For example, if we wanted to show the second card in the previous file from another WML file in the same directory, we would use the relative URL `"shuffle.wml#two"`, as shown here:

```
<a href="shuffle.wml#two">Jump from one deck to another</a>
```

If you prefer buttons to hyperlinks, the last code changes to the following:

```
<?xml version="1.0"?>
<!DOCTYPE wml PUBLIC "-//WAPFORUM//DTD WML 1.1//EN"
"http://www.wapforum.org/DTD/wml_1.1.xml">
<wml>
        <card id="one" title="Shuffling Cards in WML">
                <p><big>A Big Welcome to WML</big></p>
                <do type="accept" label="Next">
                        <go href="#two"/>
                </do>
        </card>
        <card id="two" title="Shuffling Cards in WML">
                <p>A Medium Welcome to WML</p>
                <do type="accept" label="Prev">
                        <go href="#one"/>
```

```
                </do>
                <do type="accept" label="Next">
                        <go href="#three"/>
                </do>
        </card>
        <card id="three" title="Shuffling Cards in WML">
                <p><small>A Small Welcome to WML</small></p>
                <do type="accept" label="Prev">
                        <go href="#two"/>
                </do>
        </card>
</wml>
```

Figure 15-10 shows the second card in the Opera browser.

FIGURE 15-10

Here is the second of three cards with navigation buttons.

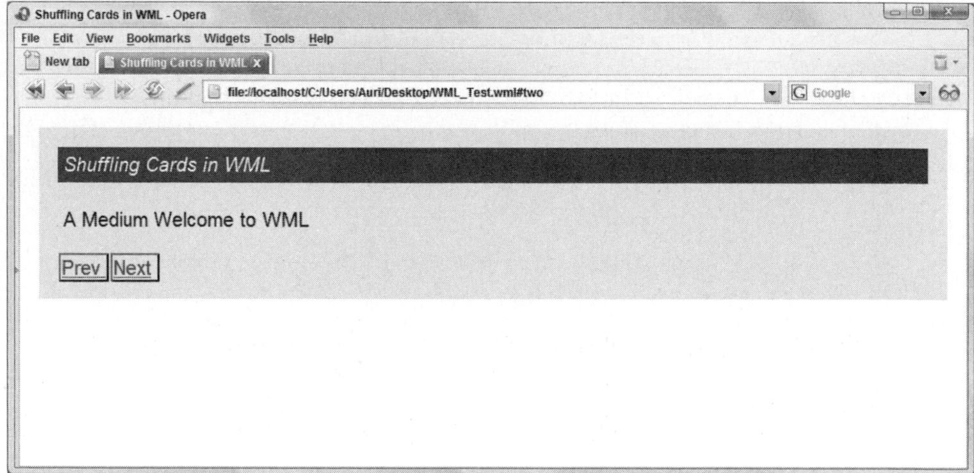

The equivalent in HTML would be to use the following:

```
<input type="button" onclick="window.location='next.html'"
value="Next">
```

CROSS-REF See Chapter 10 for information on buttons and Chapter 13 for details on JavaScript.

Interacting with Users

Up to now, we have seen the way to present information to the user. But most sites want to do more than that. After all, if someone wanted to navigate the Web, he or she would hardly choose a screen 1 inch by 1 inch to do so. The latest trend is mobile computing, where you can access the same sort of services available on the Web anytime, anyplace using a PDA, mobile phone, or an even smaller device. For example, many banks provide services such as consulting the account balance or making a transaction. There is no reason to stop anyone from providing services for mobile devices. However, to do so, you obviously need to solicit information from your users, even if it is just their login name and password.

Forms in WML

We have already seen in Chapter 10 how to use HTML forms to get input from users. In WML, the form elements are very similar. However, in WML, there is no `<form>` tag — all of the controls are directly in the card as if the card is already a form. WML has one-line text fields, multi-line text areas, and single-selection and multiselection lists. The processing of the form values on the server is much the same as for HTML forms.

The main difference between WML and HTML is that there are no option button or check box input types. The equivalent is to use single-selection lists instead of option buttons, and multiselection lists instead of check boxes. How a browser displays them depends on the browser implementation. It may display the options as a list or as option buttons or check boxes.

Here is an example of one-line input boxes:

```
<?xml version="1.0"?>
<!DOCTYPE wml PUBLIC "-//WAPFORUM//DTD WML 1.1//EN"
"http://www.wapforum.org/DTD/wml_1.1.xml">
<wml>
        <card id="one" title="User Interaction in WML">
                <p>Please enter your name</p>
                <input type="text" name="name"/>
                <do type="accept" label="Next">
                        <go href="#two"/>
                </do>
        </card>
        <card id="two" title="User Interaction in WML">
                <p>Hello $name</p>
                <do type="accept" label="Prev">
                        <go href="#one"/>
                </do>
        </card>
</wml>
```

Figure 15-11 and Figure 15-12 show how forms and variables function in WML.

FIGURE 15-11

This WML document shows the form to enter your name.

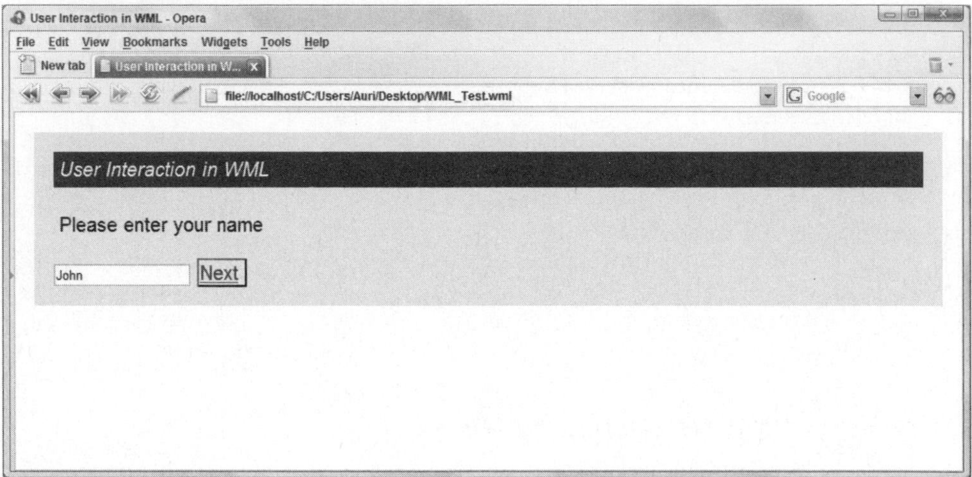

FIGURE 15-12

This WML document shows what happens when you click Next.

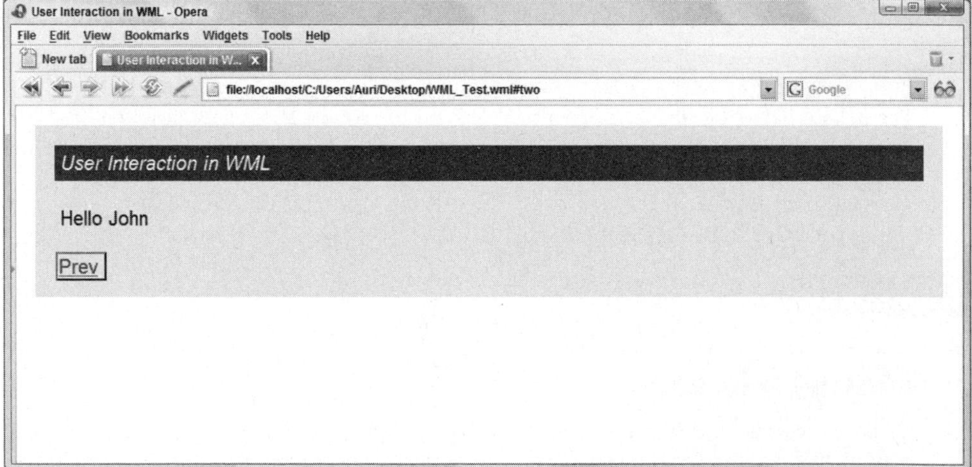

Specifying the format

One advantage of WML is that there are attributes for the `<input>` tag that specify the type of value a user must enter into a field before advancing to the next card, or whether a field can be left blank. To specify what format is required, you use the `format` attribute.

Specifying `format="*M"` means "any number of any characters." This is the default format. The asterisk represents zero or more times. If you want to specify one or more times, you could use `"M*M"`. This would mean one character plus zero or more characters, which adds up to one or more characters.

To restrict the input to only alphabetic characters, you would use `format="*A"` for uppercase and `format="*a"` for lowercase. If you wanted to only allow numerical characters (0–9), then you would use `format="*N"`.

You can specify how many digits or characters you want to accept by either repeating a format code a certain number of times, or by putting a digit before the previous codes. For example, to specify a maximum of five digits, you can either use `format="5N"` or `format="NNNNN"`.

Specifying required values

`emptyok` is the attribute for the input box that specifies, not surprisingly, whether the box can be left empty or not. The `emptyok` attribute works in conjunction with the `format` attribute to specify what values are acceptable.

The format mask by itself can be used to specify a required value. As mentioned earlier, `"M*M"` means one or more characters, so it's obviously a required field. However, in this case, you could accomplish the same result by just saying `emptyok="false"`. Remember that the default format value is `"*M"` — in other words, if the format mask says zero or more characters *and* `emptyok="false"`, meaning it cannot be zero characters, then it has to be one or more "M*M".

The default is `emptyok="true"` unless the format specifies otherwise. However, you can override what the format specification requires by explicitly including the `emptyok` attribute.

Although this approach is a little complicated at first sight, it is a great improvement on HTML, where you have to use a scripting language to validate every input field.

CROSS-REF **See Chapter 10 for information on text boxes and Chapter 13 on JavaScript.**

Menus à la card

It's an incredibly laborious task to enter text with a mobile phone. For those of you not familiar with mobile phones, you have to press a button anywhere from one to four times just to type in one letter. So, when designing a WML site, you should try to avoid using text boxes. One way of doing this is to use menus. As mentioned earlier, with WML, you can specify single-selection and multiple-selection lists. It's almost the same as HTML — the basics are very similar to the HTML lists seen in Chapter 10.

The following is a WML page showing a single-choice menu:

```
<?xml version="1.0"?>
<!DOCTYPE wml PUBLIC "-//WAPFORUM//DTD WML 1.1//EN"
"http://www.wapforum.org/DTD/wml_1.1.xml">
<wml>
  <card title="Menus in WML">
        <p><big>How about a menu</big></p>
        <select name="number">
                     <option value="1">One</option>
                     <option value="2">Two</option>
                     <option value="3">Three</option>
                     <option value="4">Four</option>
        </select>
        <do type="accept" label="ok">
               <go href="#next"/>
        </do>
 </card>
 <card id="next" title="Menus Choice">
        You chose $number
 </card>
</wml>
```

Multiple-choice menus

For multiple-choice menus, you must specify that the attribute `multiple` is `true`. After the user selects from the list, the value of the variable number will be a semicolon-separated list of the chosen options.

Here is an example of a multiple-choice menu:

```
<?xml version="1.0"?>
<!DOCTYPE wml PUBLIC "-//WAPFORUM//DTD WML 1.1//EN"
"http://www.wapforum.org/DTD/wml_1.1.xml">
<wml>
  <card title="Menus in WML">
         <p><big>How about a multiple choice menu</big></p>
         <select name="number" multiple="true">
                     <option value="1">One</option>
                     <option value="2">Two</option>
                     <option value="3">Three</option>
                     <option value="4">Four</option>
          </select>
```

```
                <do type="accept" label="ok">
                        <go href="#next"/>
        </do>
        </card>
         <card id="next" title="Menus Choice">
                You chose $number
         </card>
        </wml>
```

Figure 15-13 shows the multiple-choice menu in action.

FIGURE 15-13

Here is an example of a multiple-choice menu. In some browsers, it is presented as a set of check boxes.

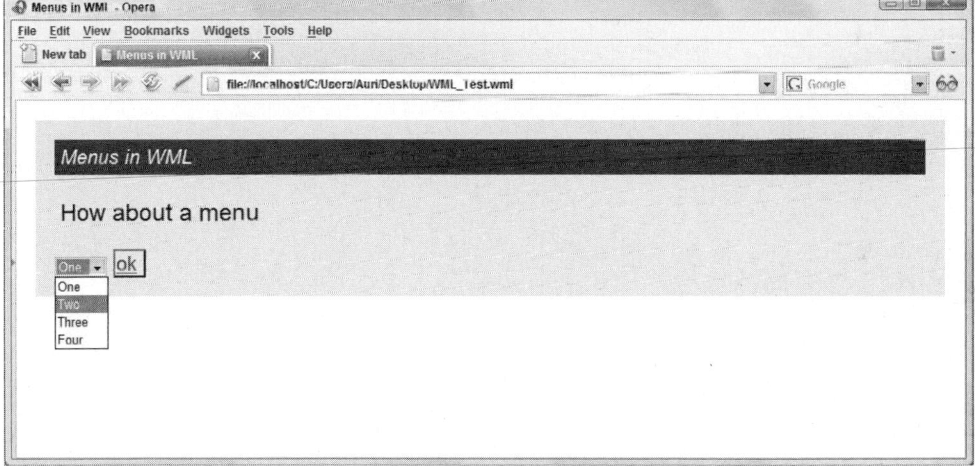

Differences between HTML lists and WML lists

The main difference between HTML lists and WML lists is that WML provides extra attributes for select tags: `value`, `iname`, and `ivalue`.

In HTML, if you want to specify that a certain option is selected, you must specify the selected attribute in the option or options. However, in WML, you just specify the variable name with the `name` attribute. If the variable is set, the corresponding option is automatically selected. If the variable is not set, then the default value is specified by the `value` attribute.

In WML, you can also work with the indexes instead of the values. The attribute `iname` specifies the name of a variable that holds the value of the index. If the variable is undefined, then `ivalue` specifies the selected index or indexes.

This may not seem like a huge benefit, but when you get down to server-side programming, you will appreciate that WML is much easier for this purpose.

See Chapter 10 for details on getting input with HTML forms.

Transforming XHTML into WML

You've probably been wondering what all of the fuss about XHTML and XSL was for. After reading this section, you'll understand why.

Previously, we talked about the challenge that Web developers face in designing sites that can be viewed by both a desktop machine and a mobile phone. Of course, you would not be able to see the same pages on both devices, but the content of each page should be essentially the same.

One solution is to have the content in one file, and separate templates that create the actual pages for each type of browser — for example, one template for a WML browser on cell phone with a minimal WML design, a second for an XHTML browser on a PDA only using basic XHTML, a third for a desktop machine with a resolution of 800 × 600, and yet another for a high-resolution graphical workstation with a broadband connection to the Internet. All this and more can be accomplished with XSL.

To demonstrate the principle, let's transform an example XHTML file into a WML file using a fairly simple XSL stylesheet.

The XHTML file is as follows:

```
<html>
<head>
<title>An example page</title>
</head>
<body>
<h2>This is an example page</h2>
<p>This is a paragraph</p>
<ul>
<li>List Item 1</li>
<li>List Item 2</li>
<li>List Item 3</li>
<li>List Item 4</li>
</ul>
<b>Bold</b>
<hr/>
<em>Emphasised</em>
</body>
</html>
```

Figure 15-14 shows the rendering of the XHTML file.

FIGURE 15-14

This is the XHTML file that will be transformed.

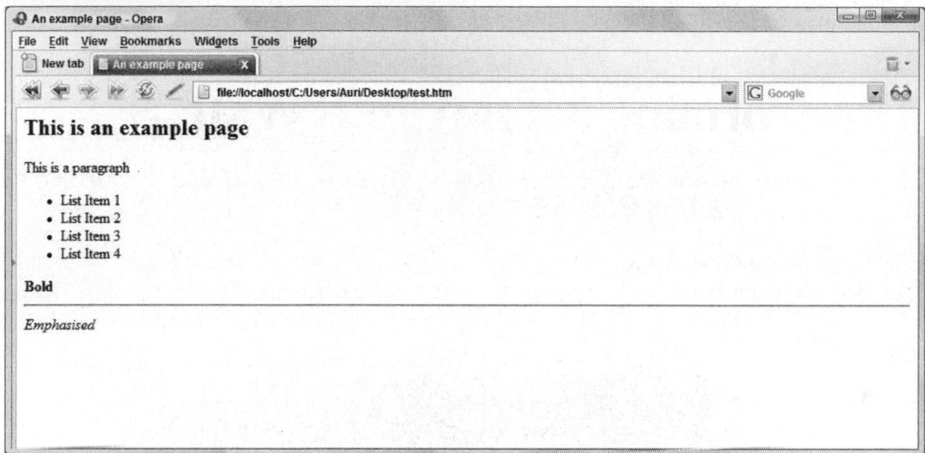

The XSL file is as follows:

```
<?xml version="1.0"?>
<xsl:stylesheet version="1.0"
xmlns:xsl="http://www.w3.org/1999/XSL/Transform">
<xsl:output method="xml"/>

<!- replace html with wml ->
<xsl:template match="html">
<wml>
<xsl:apply-templates match="@*|*|text()"/>
</wml>
</xsl:template>

<!- copy all html elements complete with attributes and
content. Except for the templates after this one ->
<xsl:template match="*"> <!- head|meta ->
<xsl:copy>
<xsl:apply-templates match="@*|*|text()"/>
</xsl:copy>
</xsl:template>
<!- replace headers with big text ->
<xsl:template match="h1|h2|h3|h4|h5|h6|h7|h8|h9">
<big>
<xsl:value-of select="."/>
</big>
</xsl:template>
```

```
<!- copy the following elements without copying attributes ->
<xsl:template match="table|tr|td">
<xsl:copy>
<xsl:apply-templates/>
</xsl:copy>
</xsl:template>

<!- change th to td ->
<xsl:template match="th">
<td class="th">
<xsl:apply-templates/>
</td>
</xsl:template>

<!- change body to card ->
<xsl:template match="body">
<card title="{/html/head/title}">
<xsl:apply-templates/>
</card>
</xsl:template>

<!- replace the following elements with their content and
a line break ->
<xsl:template match="li|dt|hr">
<xsl:apply-templates/>
<br/>
</xsl:template>

<!- replace the following elements with a paragraph ->
<xsl:template match="div|ul|ol|dl|blockquote|form">
<p>
<xsl:apply-templates/>
</p>
</xsl:template>

<!- ignore the following elements ->
<xsl:template match="title">
</xsl:template>

</xsl:stylesheet>
```

The resulting WML file after being processed by a program to apply XSLT transforms is as follows:

```
<?xml version="1.0"?>
<wml>
<head>
```

```
</head>
<card title="An example page">
<big>This is an example page</big>
<p>This is a paragraph.</p>
<p>
List Item 1<br/>
List Item 2<br/>
List Item 3<br/>
List Item 4<br/>
</p>
<b>Bold</b>
<br/>
<em>Emphasised</em>
</card>
</wml>
```

Figure 15-15 shows the rendering of the resulting WML file.

FIGURE 15-15

This is the result of our transformation.

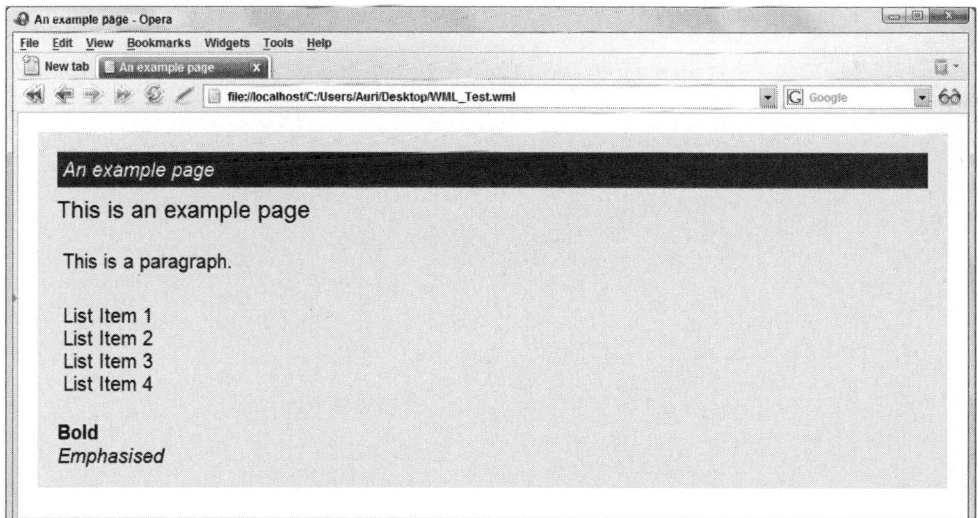

Explaining how this transformation works is beyond the scope of this book. For more information on XSL, see the XSL specifications at www.w3.org/Style/XSL. A quick search on the Internet also returns a long list of tutorials; for a good tutorial go to www.w3schools.com.

WML Web Sites

There are several interesting WAP sites on the Internet with in-depth information about WAP and WML, including the following:

- www.wapforum.org
- xml.coverpages.org/wap-wml.html
- www.w3schools.com/WAP/wap_forum.asp
- www.ust.hk/itsc/wap/emulators/nokia.html

Because the Nokia site is frequently updated, you would need to type WML or WAP in the search box to find the latest information.

Summary

This chapter began with a review of the history of HTML and its various iterations. This chapter also provided some background on XHTML, including the role that SGML played in the development of HTML, and noting that the latter was to be a simple subset of the former.

This chapter discussed in general terms the changes that would need to be made in transforming HTML to XHTML. These included an awareness of deprecated attributes and elements. Several tables of such deprecated features were provided.

The discussion examined `DOCTYPE` and the three DTDs. We gave the formatting of each and a coding illustration of each.

This chapter introduced a generic XHTML type document. We also went over in great detail the `DOCTYPE` declaration covering the XML version, the encoding and the use of `standalone` for DTD validation. We also looked at the two types of namespaces (default and local) with examples of each. We discussed and gave illustrations of PCDATA, CDATA and CDATA blocks. We also presented uses of white space.

This chapter also covered the rules of validation, noting, again, that the big areas of change were in depreciated atrributes and elements. We also introduced a code validator, `validator.w3.org`, to test for validity of the document.

You learned how WML is very similar to XHTML, but with the introduction of decks and cards. You learned how to format text in WML, how to use WML hyperlinks, how to introduce user interaction with text boxes, how to use single and multiple-choice menus, and how to transform XHTML into WML.

Chapter 16 examines XML in more detail.

Chapter 16

Designing with XML

IN THIS CHAPTER

Designing with XML

Schemas

XML Web sites

Web sites today must not only be prepared for rapidly changing content, they also must be prepared for rapidly changing technology. It has been true since the mid-1990s that a site must leverage HTML and JavaScript in its construction. More recently, HTML 4.01 with Cascading Style Sheets (CSS), scripts, and so on, has become the standard for coding components of your typical Web site. Most recently, the technologies required for building a site range from HTML 4.01 to Wireless Markup Language (WML) to Extensible Markup Language (XML) to XHTML to the dozens of XML-based languages/vocabularies. The new languages are necessitated because of the massive deluge of Internet appliances.

Designing with XML

A new era is dawning. The always evolving Web browser is undergoing another major metamorphosis. The lingua franca of the Web is now proclaimed to be XML.

The truth is that XML is an effort to simplify, systematize, and rationalize Web authoring through a set of easy-to-learn and easy-to-use markup commands. The new features are an effort to accommodate the changing face of the Web itself. HTML has always been designed as a markup language. By that we mean that HTML is concerned with providing a document with its structure. The content could be anything. There was no concern with being able to describe the content.

However, as the Internet evolved, the World Wide Web became not only a display medium but also a storage-and-search medium. HTML consistently provided the use of keywords in most all Web pages for the search engines to utilize. But the inclusion of keywords does not remotely approach the sophistication of being able to search within a document to find the content of a specific element and then to modify that content. XML purports to address the perceived limitation of millions of existing Web pages coded in HTML by eradicating a browser's support for only specific codes.

The probable scope of XML

XML, of course, is extensible. This means that it may be extended and modified to satisfy the needs of the Web developer. This extensibility is in contrast to HTML, which is not extensible, we are told. It uses add-ons. Scripts are add-ons. Frames are add-ons. Stylesheets are the latest add-ons. Never mind that they vastly improved the features available in HTML and opened the world of Web design to hundreds of thousands of new programmers while making the Web more indispensable. Never mind that HTML was the core. Add-ons complicated things, critics point out, which defeats the very advantage of using HTML in the first place. Now, XML is going to simplify things and make the Web pages responsive to the new demands and not only provide document structure but provide it in such a way that the document structure will tell about the document's content.

The truth of the matter is that XML is simple — if you do simple things with it. When you include features such as attributes and formatting of special characters, you also include local and default namespaces, external stylesheets, browser-specific elements, limited browser support for a number of features relating to its central function of data manipulation, multiple vocabularies, and so on — all making XML a far larger and more complex entity than many realize.

In short, if XML reaches close to its promises, we believe it is going to be one very complex system by the time it's over.

The structure of XML is very similar to HTML. Frankly, you could look at numerous XML documents and hardly tell the difference between languages unless you went right to the top and looked at the `DOCTYPE` declaration. The pages are formed of tagged content. The difference is that the tags are used to categorize the content. In other words, the tags encompassing data do not format the content. HTML tells about the document structure, not the content; XML provides a way to define and manipulate document content.

CSS and the Extensible Stylesheet Language (XSL) format tags on the page. The browser, independent of default standards, is forced to present the XML document as defined by the developer.

XML as applied to the Web is made up of the following features:

- Classified content
- CSS and XSL
- Namespaces

- Elements
- Document Type Definitions (DTDs)

CROSS-REF See Chapter 15 for more information on DTDs.

At this stage of its development, XML is the first language that can work on different operating systems, Internet devices, and products. A properly formatted XML document can display in a Web browser such as Safari, or on a cell phone (through WML), a Motorola pager, or a Palm PDA.

Note, however, that stylesheets must be coded differently for Internet Explorer (IE) browsers prior to Internet Explorer 7.

The objectives of XML may be summed up in three statements:

- XML must be easy to use, even for nonprogrammers.
- It must have all the beneficial features of HTML.
- It must be compatible for Internet use.

The overriding objective of XML development was to develop a language structure that could be used over the Internet, was simple to understand and use, and provided access to document content. The capability to author Web pages with XML made it seem a viable alternative to HTML.

XML Rules

Any XML document must adhere to a set of simple rules:

- The tags and attribute values are case-sensitive.
- There can only be one root element; all the rest of the tags must be inside the main element `<html></html>`.
- The document must be well formed, which means the following:
  - Nonempty elements must have closing tags (`<p></p>`).
  - Empty elements must use a special syntax (`<br />`).
  - Tags must be properly nested (`<p><a></a></p>`).
- Attribute values must always be quoted with matched double or single quotation marks (`<p class="test"></p>`).
- Attribute values cannot be omitted (`<dl compact="compact"></dl>`).

If you don't follow these rules, the browser will report an error and will not display the page. However, working with XML in and of itself is not that difficult. If you understand the way HTML tags work, then you are more than halfway to understanding XML. In fact, XHTML is HTML written according to the restrictions of XML.

CROSS-REF See Chapter 15 for information on XHTML.

Getting different XML vocabularies to work together – namespaces

The following list shows several of the derivative "vocabularies" (that is, "language lites") that have now been developed with the freedom inherent in XML:

- Channel Definition Format (CDF)
- Chemical Markup Language (CML)
- Math Markup Language (MathML)
- Musical Markup Language (MML)
- Open Financial Exchange (OFX)
- Synchronized Multimedia Integration Language (SMIL)
- Real Simple Syndication (RSS)
- Voice Markup Language (VoiceML)
- Extensible HTML (XHTML)

Many emerging XML vocabularies are already in mainstream use. These vocabularies can be used in the same XML file, or managed and displayed in a single Web page. The browser requires the correct DTD declaration in order to support the XML vocabulary used. Technically speaking, the vocabulary is called a *namespace*. The following example demonstrates four different XML namespaces declared in a single HTML page:

```
<html XMLns:v="urn:schemas-microsoft-com:vml"
XMLns:o="urn:schemas-microsoft-com:office:office"
XMLns:w="urn:schemas-microsoft-com:office:word"
XMLns="http://www.w3.org/TR/REC-html40">
```

In these examples, the programmer is declaring the XML schemas for HTML 4.0, Word 2000, Office 2000, and Vector Markup Language (VML). Such leverage enables richer and more informative content within any single Web page.

The tags within the document can specify which namespace they are in by prefixing the tag with the abbreviation for the namespace (for example `<v:path ...>`). The default namespace is the one that starts `XMLns=" "`; any tag that does not have a namespace defined is assumed to be from this vocabulary.

Here is another example from `w3.org` documentation of XML to show a local namespace declaration, which associates the namespace prefix `edi` with the namespace `name`.

```
 http://ecommerce.org/schema:
<x xmlns:edi='http://ecommerce.org/schema'>
  <!-- the "edi" prefix is bound to http://ecommerce.org/schema
       for the "x" element and contents -->
</x>
```

URN, URI, or URL?

The term *Uniform Resource Name* (*URN*) is a type of *Uniform Resource Identifier* (*URI*). You may remember that a *Uniform Resource Locator* (*URL*) is used to identify the location of a Web page (resource) on the Web. A URN names the resource.

The use of the URN is unusual, and appears to be automatically generated when a normal Word document is saved as an XML document. Most Web programmers use URIs.

Why are URLs so often used for URIs? Namespaces must be unique identifiers so that their vocabularies do not collide with each other in the event that they use the same tags and make the rendering of a document gibberish by the Web browser. URIs are built-in unique identifiers for namespaces.

Classifying content versus defining presentation

The content on an XML page is classified through the use of tags. The structure of a simple XML document is:

```
<?XML version="1.0"?>
<library>
  <Book>
     <Title>Creating Web Sites Bible</Title>
     <Author>David Crowder and Andrew Bailey</Author>
     <Category>Web Publishing </Category>
  </Book>
  <Book>
     <Title>Mastering Dreamweaver</Title>
     <Author>David Crowder</Author>
     <Category>Web Publishing </Category>
  </Book>
  <Book>
     <Title>Harry Potter and the Goblet of Fire</Title>
     <Author>J.K. Rowling</Author>
     <Category>Children/Adventure</Category>
  </Book>
</library>
```

The document declares itself as an XML document with the opening line `<?XML version="1.0"?>`. For any XML documents to be properly executed, this opening statement must be added.

The structure of XML appears to be very similar to HTML. The content is structured in an ordinary text-readable format, not machine code (binary). Each section is separated by what appears to be ordinary HTML tags. The reality, however, is that none of the tags are HTML tags. If this document were to be run through a browser, the browser would not know how to format the document. What most browsers do is to show the document as is, adding pluses or minuses next to each element to show or hide its children, as shown in Figure 16-1.

FIGURE 16-1

An XML document viewed in a browser with no stylesheet attached.

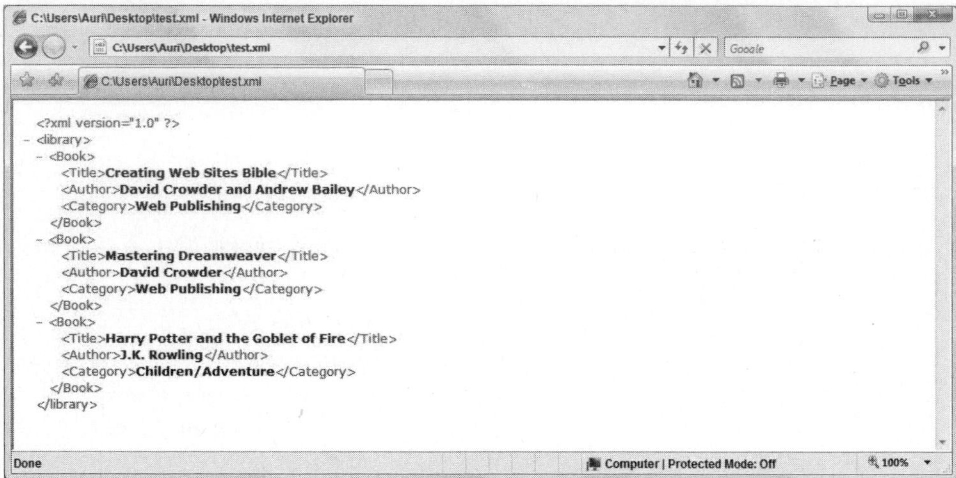

The power of the document is that *it does not format the data*. The tags can be managed and modified with scripting by either the server delivering the content, or through JavaScript and CSS on the Web browser. More recently, another tool has become available for separating style from content XML and HTML documents, and that is XSL. This newer technology is an advancement over CSS in that developers using XSL stylesheets can now have control over the way their Web documents are printed out, and they are also portable across different applications using Extensible Style Language Transformation X(SLT).

Specifying a CSS

Now, let's format the document in the previous example by using CSS technology. To do this, we insert the following line after the first line:

```
<?XML-stylesheet type="text/css" href="library.css"?>
```

The first three lines are now as follows:

```
<?XML version="1.0" encoding="UTF-8"?>
<?XML-stylesheet type="text/css" href="library.css"?>
<library>
....
```

Next, we must create the `library.css` reference file, which contains the style definitions that control the appearance of the individual content elements:

```
library { font-size: 14 pt; color: red; display: block; }
Book { font-size: 30pt; color: red; display: block;   margin: 1em;
background-color: yellow; }
Title { font-size: 30pt; color: blue; display: inline; }
Author { font-size: 20pt; font-weight: bold; color: red;
   display: inline; }
Category {font-size: 15pt; color: green; display: block;   margin:
0 0 0 1em}
```

CROSS-REF See Chapter 12 for information on CSS.

Figure 16-2 shows the result that the `library.css` file has on the XML document. It now looks like a normal HTML document.

We are restricted by CSS in that it only allows us to specify the format of text already present. We cannot add text, and we also cannot change the order of the content in the original document. To overcome this problem, the W3C invented XSL. The good news is that this also works like a CSS. The bad news is that because it is more powerful, it is also more complicated.

Specifying an XSL stylesheet

For this example, we change the second line of the previous XML file to the following:

```
<?XML-stylesheet type="text/xsl" href="library.xsl"?>
```

FIGURE 16-2

The XML document formatted with CSS now looks like a normal HTML document.

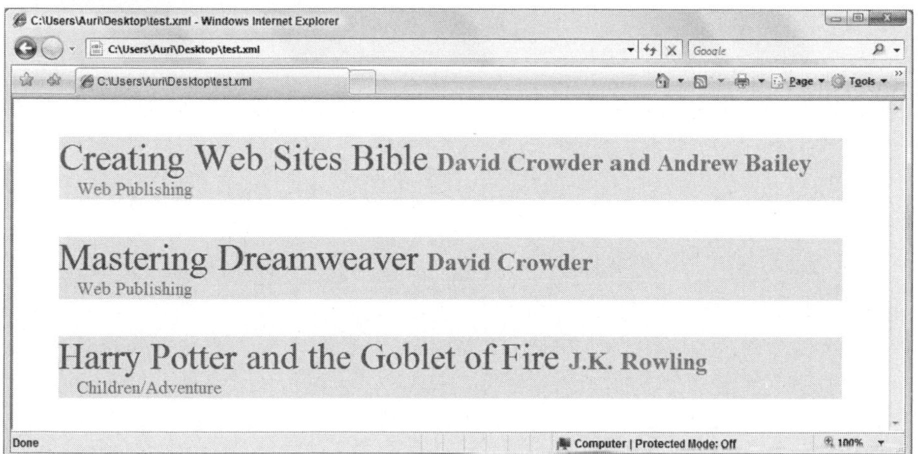

Now all that remains to do is to create the stylesheet `library.xsl`, as shown here:

```
<?xml version="1.0" encoding="ISO-8859-1"?>

<xsl:stylesheet version="1.0"
xmlns:xsl="http://www.w3.org/1999/XSL/Transform">
<xsl:template match="/">
 <html>
 <body>
   <h2>My Library</h2>
   <table border="1">
     <tr bgcolor="lime">
       <th>Title</th>
       <th>Author</th>
       <th>Category</th>
     </tr>
           <xsl:for-each select="library/book">
     <tr bgcolor="yellow">
      <td><xsl:value-of select="title"/></td>
      <td><xsl:value-of select="author"/></td>
      <td><xsl:value-of select="category"/></td>
     </tr>
           </xsl:for-each>
   </table>
 </body>
 </html>
</xsl:template>

</xsl:stylesheet>
```

Figure 16-3 shows the result of this XSL transformation.

FIGURE 16-3

You can use an XSL stylesheet to format an XML document.

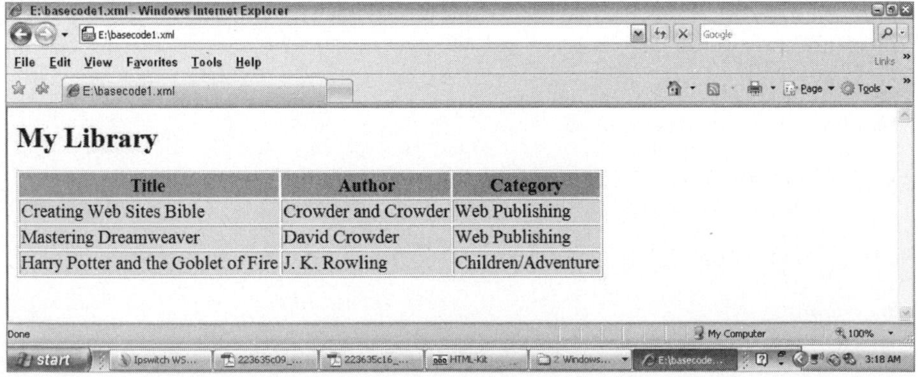

Note that now we have added three extra text elements: a title, a main heading, and column headings.

Let's go step by step through the stylesheet `library.xsl`. First is the instruction that denotes that this is an XML document:

```
<?XML version="1.0" encoding="ISO-8859-1"?>
```

The following is the root element of the document; the element's name is `stylesheet`. The `xsl:` prefix denotes that it is in the namespace `xsl`.

```
xmlns="http://www.w3.org/TR/REC-html40"
xmlns:xsl="http://www.w3.org/1999/XSL/Transform">
<xsl:stylesheet version="1.0"
xmlns:xsl="http://www.w3.org/1999/XSL/Transform">
```

Because anyone can define XML tag names, namespaces were invented to avoid collisions. In this document, we are mixing HTML with XSL. Collisions occur when two elements have the same tag name, but belong to a different context. To distinguish between two tags that have the same name (for example, the HTML `<title>` and the XSL `<title>`), all you have to do is specify the namespace for one of them (for example, `<xsl:title>`).

In this case, XSL doesn't have an element called `<title>`; it's just there to illustrate the point. The default namespace is declared by `XMLns="(where to find the definition on the Internet)"`. Other namespaces used are declared by `XMLns:prefixUsed="(definition)"`. Note that any prefix could be used, but it's best to use the standard one.

Note that the output is in the following. (Other valid output options are XML or text).

```
<xsl:output method="html"/>
```

Next, look at the following line:

```
<xsl:template match="/">
```

The forward slash `"/"` defines the document to be matched in its entirety. In this case it is the node element `<"library">`.

Every time you come across an element called `"library"`, apply the following template. Start with pure HTML to create the Web page:

```
<html><body>
<h2>My Library</h2>
```

Note that we also use CSS formatting:

```
<body>
<h2>My Library</h2>
<table border="1">
```

```
<tr bgcolor="lime">
<th>Title</th>
<th>Author</th>
<th>Category</th>
</tr>
<xsl:for-each select="library/book">
```

Remember that the library has three branches — the three books. For each child element that is a book, we do the following:

```
<tr>
<td><xsl:value-of select="title"/></td>
```

The XSL element `value-of` inserts the value of the expression defined in the select attribute (in this case, the text content of the `Title` element of the book). Translated into English, this means that it inserts the title. The next two lines are similar:

```
<td><xsl:value-of select="author"/></td>
<td><xsl:value-of select="category"/></td>
</tr>
</xsl:for-each>
```

And then you see the end of the loop:

```
</table>
</body>
</html>
</xsl:template>
```

The following is the end of the first and, in this case, only template. However, there can be any number of templates in an XSL document.

```
</xsl:stylesheet>
```

CAUTION **The following browser versions currently support `xsl` and `xslt`: IE 6.0 and later, Firefox 1.0.2 and later, and Opera 9.0 and later. Firefox can display XSL and CSS, and has XSLT implementation.**

Even if your browser doesn't support XSL transformations directly, you can use a tool to transform the XML content to HTML and then publish the result on the Web, or do it in real time with server-side processing. Many XSL transformation programs exist. Free ones include xsltproc (included in most Linux distributions), Saxon (available at `http://saxon.sourceforge.net`), or Xalan (`http://XML.apache.org/xalan-j`). Xalan is also included as part of the Java Development Kit (JDK) version 1.4 and later, freely available at `http://java.sun.com`. Both Xalan and Saxon are written in Java, and work on Windows, Mac OS, or Linux machines.

Microsoft's free Visual Web Developer Express may be of use as well.

Keeping the content separate enables the previous document to be delivered to a multitude of programs. The same XML file can be delivered to any browser.

Similarities to a programming language

XSL is very close to a programming language. It has `for` loops that repeat an action (or number of actions) for each element in the list, as shown here:

```
<xsl:for-each select="list of elements">
<!-- Actions --> </xsl:for-each>
```

It has `if` statements that execute one or more actions if the condition is true. The syntax is as follows:

```
<xsl:if test="condition">
<!-- Actions --> </xsl:if>
```

It also has a statement to choose one action from a set of actions, depending on the conditions specified for each action:

```
<xsl:choose>
  <xsl:when test="condition1">
  <!-- Action 1 -->
  </xsl:when>
  <xsl:when test="condition2">
  <!-- Action 2 -->
  </xsl:when>
  <xsl:otherwise>
  <!-- Default Action -->
  </xsl:otherwise>
</xsl:choose>
```

The conditions are evaluated in turn. If a condition is true, then the associated action is performed and then the next instruction after the `choose` statement is executed. If none of the conditions are true, then the default action inside the `otherwise` tag is carried out.

If you know a programming language, this is equivalent to a nested `if` statement. An example in C, VB, JavaScript, or Java would be as follows:

```
if (condition1) {
  //action 1
{ else if (condition2) {
  //action 2
} else {
  //default actions
}
```

However, the structure is more similar to a `switch` statement, as shown here:

```
Int gradeLevel;
gradeLevel=Integer.parseInt();
switch (gradeLevel)
```

```
     {
case 1: System.out.println("Go to the Gym");
     break;
case 2: System.out.println("Go to the Humanities Bldg.");
     break;
case 3: System.out.println("Go to Harrison-Jones");
     break;
case 4: System.out.println("Go to Science Hall");
     break;
     }
```

Following is the same document formatted in XML using Microsoft Word to create it and then saving the document as an XML document type. We have omitted monumental parts of it, but we just wanted to give you a better sense of the coding.

```
<html xmlns:v="urn:schemas-microsoft-com:vml"
xmlns:o="urn:schemas-microsoft-com:office:office"
xmlns:w="urn:schemas-microsoft-com:office:word"
xmlns="http://www.w3.org/TR/REC-html40">
<head>
<meta http-equiv=Content-Type content="text/html; charset=us-ascii">
<meta name=ProgId content=Word.Document>
<meta name=Generator content="Microsoft Word 11">
<meta name=Originator content="Microsoft Word 11">
<link rel=File-List href="DB5C578F_files/filelist.xml">
<link rel=Edit-Time-Data href="DB5C578F_files/editdata.mso">
<!--[if !mso]>
<style>
v\:* {behavior:url(#default#VML);}
o\:* {behavior:url(#default#VML);}
w\:* {behavior:url(#default#VML);}
.shape {behavior:url(#default#VML);}
</style>
<![endif]-->
<title>Sample case or switch structure</title>
<!--[if gte mso 9]><xml>
</o:shapelayout></xml><![endif]-->
</head>
```

Note that the preceding code completes the <head> structure. The <body> has several divisions <div> in it to distinguish the sections, and, of course, each section has the standard HTML block elements of <p> and other tag identifiers (such as span and class). In the following code, the <table> structure with multiple <tr> and <td> is also used:

```
<body lang=EN-US style='tab-interval:.5in'>
<div class=Section1>
<p class=MsoTitle>Sample case or switch structure</p>
<p class=MsoNormal><o:p> </o:p></p>
<p class=MsoNormal>Int gradeLevel;</p>
```

```
style='position:absolute;
 z-index:2' from="1in,1.85pt" to="1in,19.85pt">
 <v:stroke endarrow="block"/>
</v:line><![endif]--><![if !vml]><span style='mso-ignore:vglayout'>
<table cellpadding=0 cellspacing=0 align=left>
 <tr>
  <td width=90 height=1></td>
 </tr>
 <tr>
  <td></td>
  <td><img width=12 height=27 src="DB5C578F_files/image002.gif"
 v:shapes="_x0000_s1028"></td>
 </tr>
</table>
</span><![endif]><o:p> </o:p></p>
<br style='mso-ignore:vglayout' clear=ALL>
</div>
</body>
</html>
```

NOTE **You might remember that a big advantage of a case structure over a nested `if` structure is efficiency.**

XSL is very complicated at first sight, because it uses a different concept of programming. Taking a page from object-oriented programming (OOP), you might call this type of programming *template-oriented* programming.

To understand XSL, you must think of an XML document as an upside-down tree with the root at the top, as shown in Figure 16-4. The tree shown in Figure 16-4 represents the document structure and, although you cannot see the labels, the color coding represents the top-down document structure, showing the flow from `root: library` to the three branches of each book name (the second row). Derived from each of the three book names are the `Title`, `Author`, and `Category` of each book (the third row). Subordinate to those (the last row) is the content for each of the above document nodes.

Defining the structure of an XML document

For the stylesheet, `library.css`, we assumed that the library had books as child elements and that each book had `Title`, `Author`, and `Category` child elements. If this isn't the case, then the stylesheet won't produce an error — it will just do what it's instructed to do. For example, if the library has children that are shelves, which, in turn, contain the book elements, the previous stylesheet would not show any books, because we instructed it to match only books that are children of the library element.

How can we define the structure of the document to make sure it is valid? There are two solutions: a DTD or XML Schema. A DTD is much simpler but not as powerful as the XML Schema.

FIGURE 16-4

An XSL document has an upside-down tree structure.

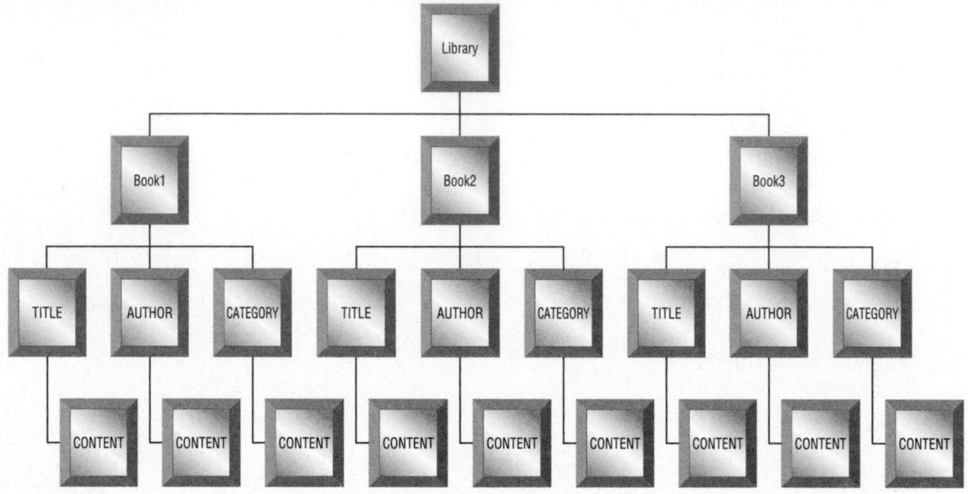

The DTD, as explained in Chapter 15, is a document that details how specific tags should be displayed, the type of content that can be entered in a given tag, as well as the method used to lay out tags. In many ways, it is the same as creating a custom HTML language that users can agree to.

Here is the file again, this time with a line specifying the structure:

```
<?XML version="1.0" encoding="UTF-8"?>
<!DOCTYPE library SYSTEM "library.dtd">
<library>
<Book>
<Title>Creating Web Pages Bible</Title>
<Author>David Crowder</Author>
<Category>Web Publishing </Category>
</Book>
<Book>
<Title>Mastering Dreamweaver</Title>
<Author>David Crowder</Author>
<Category>Web Publishing </Category>
</Book>
<Book>
<Title>Harry Potter and the Goblet of Fire</Title>
<Author>J.K. Rowling</Author>
<Category>Childrens/Adventure</Category>
</Book>
</library>
```

The second line of the file specifies that the root element of the XML document is `library` and that the structure is specified in the file on the local file system `library.dtd`.

The DTD (called `library.dtd`) referenced in the previous XML file is as follows:

```
<!ELEMENT library (Book)+>
<!ELEMENT Book (Title,Author,Category)>
<!ELEMENT Title (#PCDATA)>
<!ELEMENT Author (#PCDATA)>
<!ELEMENT Category (#PCDATA)>
```

Once again, let's go though this step by step:

The following line specifies that a library has one or more books as children. If we had wanted to allow a library with zero or more books, we could have said `(Book)*`. The brackets group an element or any number of elements. The + represents one or more of the previous, the * represents zero or more.

```
<!ELEMENT library (Book)+>
```

In the next line, you see that the book has a group of elements, `Title`, `Author`, and `Category`, in that order.

```
<!ELEMENT Book (Title,Author,Category)>
```

In the next three lines, `PCDATA` stands for "parsed character data," which means text. In English, a `Title` element has text content, and the same applies for the `Author` and `Category` elements.

```
<!ELEMENT Title (#PCDATA)>
<!ELEMENT Author (#PCDATA)>
<!ELEMENT Category (#PCDATA)>
```

Customizing tags

The "extensible" in XML is derived from the flexibility of the language. The previous example is XML displayed at its most simple: a declaration and some simple tags. The document can easily be extended. Richer information can be added by extending the document. In many ways, it is like categorizing content into different fields in a database table.

The following example shows how easily a brand-new tag, called `<Description>`, can be inserted into the file:

```
<?XML version="1.0"?>
<!DOCTYPE library SYSTEM "library.dtd">
<library>
<Book>
<Title>Web Sites Bible </Title>
<Author>David Crowder and Andrew Bailey</Author>
<Description>The Web Publishing Bible provides the designer with the
```

```
complete set of tools required to build, promote and manage a
Web site.
</Description>
<Category>Web Publishing </Category>
</Book>
<Book>
<Title>Mastering Dreamweaver</Title>
<Author>David Crowder</Author>
<Description>Mastering Dreamweaver takes the reader on a tour de
force examination of every feature in Macromedia's Dreamweaver.
</Description>
<Category>Web Publishing </Category>
</Book>
<Book>
<Title>Harry Potter and the Goblet of Fire</Title>
<Author>J.K. Rowling</Author>
<Description>Harry Potter is now in his fourth year at Hogwarts.
Prepare yourself for his most exciting adventures yet!
</Description>
<Category>Children/Adventure</Category>
</Book>
</library>
```

More on DTD

With XML, providing a freeform language is powerful. However, standard markup languages such as HTML have great strengths as well. With HTML, large groups of users can build Web sites and communicate, which is key.

As mentioned previously, the DTD is inserted into the top of an XML document. The content of the XML document is then validated in accordance with the rules of the DTD. The declaration that enables Web browser to interpret HTML 4.0 from a DTD is placed in the <HTML> tag at the top of the Web page:

```
<!DOCTYPE html PUBLIC "-//W3C//DTD XHTML 1.0 Strict//EN"
    "http://www.w3.org/TR/xhtml1/DTD/xhtml1-strict.dtd">
```

The !DOCTYPE provides the path the browser must take to find the DTD file that is used to interpret the XML tags on the page. An alternative method is to force the browser to locate a stored DTD within the browser program and execute that against the XML file. The following example is of Microsoft VML embedded within an HTML document. VML is a version of XML that, when translated with the correct DTD, takes the scripted VML tags and creates a vector image to display in IE. The DTD is stored within Microsoft IE and must be called from the browser:

```
<html XMLns:v="urn:schemas-microsoft-com:vml"
XMLns:o="urn:schemas-microsoft-com:office:office"
```

```
XMLns:w="urn:schemas-microsoft-com:office:word"
XMLns="http://www.w3.org/TR/REC-html40">
<head>
<link rel=File-List href="./Document2_files/filelist.XML">
<style>
v\:* {behavior:url(#default#VML); }
o\:* {behavior:url(#default#VML); }
w\:* {behavior:url(#default#VML); }
.shape {behavior:url(#default#VML); }
</style>
</head>
<body lang=EN-US style=`tab-interval:.5in´>
<div class=Section1>
<v:shapetype id="_x0000_t96" coordsize="21600,21600"
 o:spt="96" adj="17520"
path="m10800,0qx0,10800,10800,21600,21600,10800,10800,0xem7340,6445qx
6215,7570,7340,8695,8465,7570,7340,6445xnfem14260,6445qx13135,7570,14
260,8695,15385,7570,14260,6445xnfem4960@0c8853@3,12747@3,16640@0nfe">
 <v:formulas>
  <v:f eqn="sum 33030 0 #0"/>
  <v:f eqn="prod #0 4 3"/>
  <v:f eqn="prod @0 1 3"/>
  <v:f eqn="sum @1 0 @2"/>
 </v:formulas>
 <v:path o:extrusionok="f" gradientshapeok="t" o:connecttype="custom"

o:connectlocs="10800,0;3163,3163;0,10800;3163,18437;10800,21600;

18437,
18437;21600,10800;18437,3163"
  textboxrect="3163,3163,18437,18437"/>
 <v:handles>
  <v:h position="center,#0" yrange="15510,17520"/>
 </v:handles>
<o:complex v:ext="view"/>
</v:shapetype><v:shape id="_x0000_s1026" type="#_x0000_t96"
style='position:absolute;

 margin-left:112.05pt;margin-top:36.2pt;width:1in;height:1in;
z-index:1'/>
<table cellpadding=0 cellspacing=0 align=left>
 <tr>
  <td width=149 height=48></td>
</tr>
<tr>
 <td></td>
```

```
 <td><img width=97 height=97 src="./Document2_files/image001.gif"
v:shapes="_x0000_s1026"></td>
 </tr>
</table>
</span>
</body>
</html>
```

Web browsers do not recognize the VML tags unless they have the DTD for VML installed. The tags can only be displayed correctly with the inclusion of `XMLns:v="urn:schemas-microsoft-com:vml"` in the HTML tag. The tags are Microsoft-specific, and so only display correctly in IE. Beware of this when saving a Word document as a Web page.

NOTE **Recent Web developer tests have also shown VML to be compatible with Firefox 1.0.2 when exported with Word.**

DTDs provide programmers the flexibility to create their own tags and, through linking to the DTD, share the result with other users. This enables e-commerce between companies to greatly extend. No longer are expensive Electronic Data Interchange (EDI) solutions required to exchange information. The content in an XML document can be easily and efficiently shared between disparate systems.

NOTE **Further information on XML can be found at `www.XML.org`, `www.biztalk.org`, and `www.w3.org`. Each site provides a wealth of information on the latest DTDs, XML vocabularies, and supporting third-party products.**

DTDs are useful. They have been around pretty much as long as XML and have wide browser support. These are probably the reasons they are in process of being supplanted by an alternative Web page validation methodology called a *schema*. There are many schemas, of course.

Schemas

All schemas are referenced at the namespace `www.w3.org/2001/XMLSchema`. Schemas came about because of a limitation on the existing DTDs that was bound to be exacerbated with the relentless improvements to content on Web sites. Schemas support far more data types than do DTDs. (DTDs do not allow numeric data types, for example.) It is more difficult to develop mixed content with DTDs than with schemas, not to mention the fact that the DTD syntax is different than XML syntax. This means that a developer who also wishes to develop DTD must learn a new language. It should not surprise you to learn that any schema is an XML document. There are 44 built-in data types all together — 19 of them are so called *primitive* data types and the remaining 25 are *derived* data types from the primitive data types.

Table 16-1 shows a list of XML data types and their facets.

TABLE 16-1

XML Data Types

	Data Type	Ordered	Bounded	Cardinality	Numeric
	string	false	false	countably infinite	false
	boolean	false	false	finite	false
	float	partial	true	finite	true
	double	partial	true	finite	true
	decimal	total	false	countably infinite	true
	duration	partial	false	countably infinite	false
	dateTime	partial	false	countably infinite	false
	time	partial	false	countably infinite	false
	date	partial	false	countably infinite	false
Primitive	qYearMonth	partial	false	countably infinite	false
	qYear	partial	false	countably infinite	false
	qMonthDay	partial	false	countably infinite	false
	qDay	partial	false	countably infinite	false
	qMonth	partial	false	countably infinite	false
	hexBinary	false	false	countably infinite	false
	base64Binary	false	false	countably infinite	false
	anyURI	false	false	countably infinite	false
	QName	false	false	countably infinite	false
	NOTATION	false	false	countably infinite	false
Derived	normalizedString	false	false	countably infinite	false
	token	false	false	countably infinite	false
	language	false	false	countably infinite	false
	IDREFS	false	false	countably infinite	false
	ENTITIES	false	false	countably infinite	false

continued

TABLE 16-1 *(continued)*

Data Type	Ordered	Bounded	Cardinality	Numeric
`NMTOKEN`	`false`	`false`	`countably infinite`	`false`
`NMTOKENS`	`false`	`false`	`countably infinite`	`false`
`Name`	`false`	`false`	`countably infinite`	`false`
`NCNarne`	`false`	`false`	`countably infinite`	`false`
`ID`	`false`	`false`	`countably infinite`	`false`
`IDREF`	`false`	`false`	`countably infinite`	`false`
`ENTITY`	`false`	`false`	`countably infinite`	`false`
`integer`	`total`	`false`	`countably infinite`	`true`

Source: World Wide Web Consortium (W3C) at `www.w3.org/TR/xmlschema-2`

The most widely supported schema, XML Schema, is also the oldest.

Inclusive of primitive and derived data types, XML schemas have more than four times as many data types offered as DTDs. Categories where differences must be taken into account include `string`, `numeric`, and `date/time` data types.

string and numeric data types

It was realized that the type `string` had little definition attached to it, and so various `string` types were subsequently enumerated to fine-tune the control possible over the content. All `string` types have the following features:

- `length`
- `minLength`
- `maxLength`
- `pattern`
- `enumeration`
- `whitespace`

XLM has incorporated or constrained some of these features by defining the derived types shown in Table 16-2.

In plain terms, a *token* is any old text without formatting. Half the definitions in there are based on this definition of tokens.

Finally the numeric `integral`, `boolean`, and `float` data types are given with its subtypes.

TABLE 16-2

Derived Data Type Enumerated from string

Type	Description
ENTITY	An unparsed value in a DTD. An attribute type.
ENTITIES	A sequence of ENTITY values that have been declared to be unparsed in a DTD.
ID	Conceptually the same as an id in an HTML document, this is a single unique reference to a specific element within the XML document.
IDREF	Match the type of namespace specified in the local namespace. If this were identified as wazzit, then any element preceded by wazzit, as in wazzit:namespace, would be associated with that namespace.
IDREFS	Multiple IDREFs.
language	This is a so-called "natural language identifier." It is the alphabet, uppercase, and lowercase, and the set numbers 0–9.
Name	The base type of Name is derived from token.
NCName	This does not permit colon use within a string.
NMTOKEN	This is a string without spaces
NMTOKENS	This is a space-separated list of tokens. The base type is derived from token.
NormalizedString	This returns a new string that has the same text value, but binary representation is Unicode normalization form C.
token	This is the set of strings that does not contain the carriage return, line feed, nor tab characters, have no leading or trailing spaces, and that have no internal sequences of two or more spaces.

There are several data types in programming languages. A *data type* may be thought of as a class of data, and each of these data types has certain features associated with them. By analogy, if you were to consider books in a library, you could say that there is a general classification of books, and that within this general classification there are several types of books. One type of book would be fiction, one would be nonfiction, and then there could even be types of nonfiction such as science books, history books, biographies, and so on. There could even be something like an atlas, or a book without words (just pictures). Even though the content is very different, all of these fit the general classification of books.

In the same way, you have several different types of data. They all store data, but they all store the content in a different way. So, when the computer gets the data, it knows the proper way to display it on the screen — whole number as whole number, decimal numbers as decimals, and character as the correct letter, number, or special symbol.

If you have some data that is a number called an *integer*, you store it as an `integer` data type. This is a whole number. It does not have any decimal value associated with it. Because whole numbers can be anywhere from 1 to a very, very large number, they can be broken into more conveniently stored ranges. So, for example, a number may have a value of less than 255 would be stored using only a single byte of space. (This type of integer is called a `byte` or `short`.) Larger integers are called an `Integer` and even larger integers are called the `long` data type. Integers are used for counting whole objects or things, such as people or ornaments on a Christmas tree.

Of course, if you want to count parts as portions of the whole (such as slices of a pumpkin pie remaining after Thanksgiving dinner), you could use decimal values. For example, you might observe that the three pumpkin pies for Thanksgiving had been reduced to roughly 67 percent after dinner. You use two data types to talk about decimals. One is called a `float` data type and the other is `double`. This simply means that the value of the `float` is expressed to 6 or 7 places to the right of the decimal, while the value of the `double` is expressed out to 15 places to the right of the decimal. So, when the browser reads the variable and sees it is decimal data type, it displays the number with decimal positions to the right.

You also have a third numeric data type that you might not even realize is a number: the `char` (short for character) data type. Even though it displays uppercase and lowercase letters and special symbols, each individual number 0 to 9 it is considered to be in the number group because each of these are from the ASCII code and has a numeric value.

Examples of pre-XML `Integral` and `float` data types are shown in Table 16-3.

TABLE 16-3

General Numeric Data Types

Type	Length
`Integer`	4 bytes (value can range from -2147483648 to 2147483647)
`Long`	8 bytes (value can be a big number)
`Short`	2 bytes (value can be from -32768 to 32767)
`Byte`	1 byte (value can be up to 256)
`Char`	2 bytes (value can be from 0 to 65535)
`Float`	4 bytes
`Double`	8 bytes

Note that the range of values in bytes spans the range of positive and negative. So, the `Short Integral` type, 2 bytes, would have a range of -32768 to 32767. The only exception to this rule of the `Integrals` is, naturally enough, `char` (a shortened version of Character), also 2 bytes, which has a range of 0 to 65535. If you think about it a moment, it makes sense. Characters cannot be added or subtracted from each other, and no character is ever a negative.

XML allows its own class subtypes related to the types just shown. For the `Integer` data type, XML has four representations: `positiveInteger`, `negativeInteger`, `nonPositiveInteger`, and `nonNegativeinteger`. The distinctions between the first two, `positiveInteger` and `negativeInteger`, should be intuitive. `nonNegative` means a number greater than or equal to zero, and `nonPositive` means less than or equal to zero.

Finally, it also has `unsignedLong`, `unsignedInt`, `unsignedShort` and `unsignedByte` which as you have already inferred, share a common feature. Surprisingly, it is not related to positive or negative. The `unsigned` part refers to the presence of leading zeros. All four data types forbid them.

As shown in Table 16-1, there are two decimal values: `double` and `float`. There are two fundamental distinctions between the two types. One distinction, space allotted in memory, is shown in Table 16-3. The other distinction between the two is the number of places specified to the right of the decimal. There are six to seven spaces to the right for a `float` value, while a `double` type has 15.

`boolean` (included for form's sake) is actually a system that deals with logical values.

Date and time data types

Table 16-4 shows date and time types.

TABLE 16-4

Date and Time Types

4th Dimension	Format
`datetime`	yyyy-mm-dd:Thh:mm:ss
`time`	hh:mm:ss
`date`	yyyy-mm-dd
`gYearMonth`	yyyymm
`gYear`	yyyy
`gDay`	--dd
`gMonth`	--mm

Styles preceded with a "g" mean Gregorian format. Gregorian is a sequential numbering of the days of each year from first (1) to last (365).

The "T" in the datetime format represents "timezone"

Constraints on the month require that the entry be two-digit, and that no permissible value be greater than 31.

All times are 24-hour military style. (There is no such critter as 2400 hours.)

Primitive data types

The purpose of the many data types is to provide greater control over elements, and their attributes. After reviewing the original 19 data types, 25 more were added to give greater flexibility and control for the XML designer.

The following is a list of the 19 primitive data types.

- *Date/Time Group* — `dateTime`, `date`, `time`, `gYearMonth`, `gMonthDay`, `gYear`, `gMonth`, `gDay`, `duration`
- *Decimal Group* — `decimal`, `double`, `float`
- *Boolean Group* — `boolean`
- *Binary Group* — `base`, `base64`
- *Other Group* — `string`, `anyURI`, `notation`, `qName`

As you can see, the majority of primitive data types concerned time and date features, the standard Boolean, and some decimal data types.

Schema format

The general format of a schema is as follows:

```
<schema XMLns=http://www.w3.org/2001/XMLSchema>
</schema>
```

If you were defining more than one namespace, you naturally add a prefix for the namespace declaration. In this case, we would call the prefix `ex`.

```
<schema XMLns:ex=http://www.w3.org/2001/XMLSchema>
</ex:schema>
```

Schemas, again, go beyond what is available in DTDs, and can handle multiple content within an element. Such an element with multiple values is referred to as a *complex type*. The following album coding is a simple type.

A simple type contains only one value within the tag, as shown here:

```
<song>Story of a Star</song>
<song>Story of a Mermaid</song>
<song>Story of Mother</song>
<song>Tae Han Pal Kyung</song>
```

We can make it complex easily enough. As you can see in the following, a complex tag is one that has multiple attributes.

```
<song time="2:55">Story of a Star</song>
<song time="2:25">Story of a Mermaid</song>
<song time="3:12">Story of Mother</song>
<song time="3:27">Tae Han Pal Kyung</song>
```

Just to show you the versatility of the language you can also make tags all the following ways:

- As an empty element with two attributes:

  ```
  <song time="2:55" songName="Story of a Star" />
  ```

- All elements with no attributes:

  ```
  <song>
      <time>2:55</time>
      <songName>Story of a Star</songName>
  </song>
  ```

- A variation of these two using both elements and attributes:

  ```
  <song time="2.55">
      <songName>Story of a Star</songName>
  ```

Of course, to format them would require the use of a stylesheet, and, in the case of the previous example, using a stylesheet called `sf1.css`.

```
/*

   Filename: sf1.css
   This file contains styles used in the album.xml file.

*/

intro  {display: block;width:640px; color:black; text-align: center;
          font-size: 18pt; font-family:fantasy;border: 1;
          background-color: white;
}
```

```
singer  {display:block; font-size: 14pt; color:black;
          font-style:italic; font-weight:bold;
          font-family: Times New Roman; margin-left: 20px
}


songName {display:block; font-size: 16pt; color:blue;
           font-weight:bold; font-family: sans-serif;
              line-height:2
}



time {color:black; font-size: 12pt; font-weight: bold;
        font-family: Times New Roman; margin-left: 20px;

}
```

The output would be as shown in Figure 16-5

FIGURE 16-5

This shows the output of album.xml.

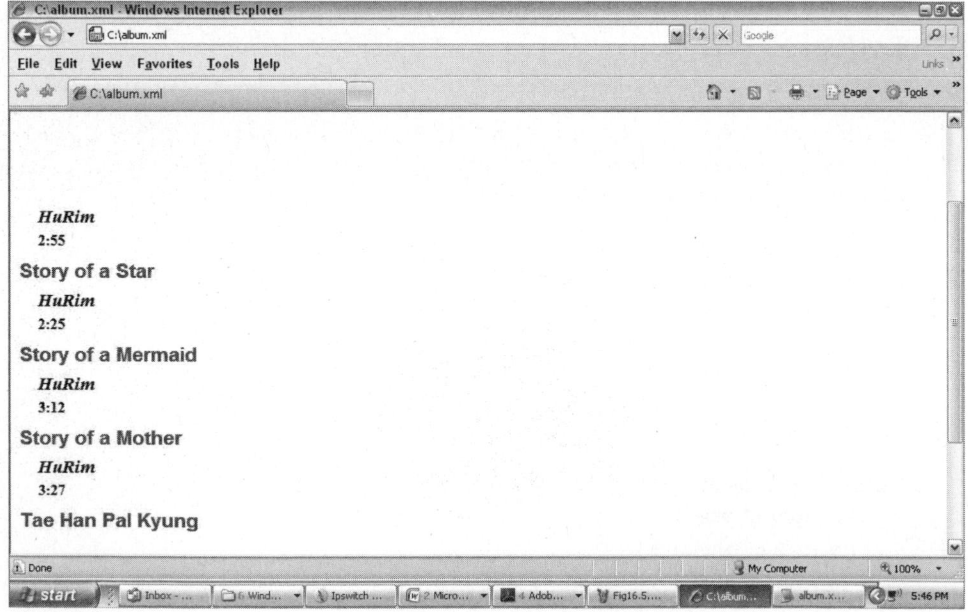

XML Web Sites

Following are some useful Web sites for information about XML:

- `www.w3.org/XML`
- `www.xml.org`
- `www.w3schools.com/xml/default.asp`
- `www.xml.com`
- `http://xml.coverpages.org/ni2002-01-09-a.html`
- `www.w3.org/TR/xmlschema-2`
- `www.w3.org/TR/2000/WD-xml-2e-20000814`
- `www.w3.org/TR/1999/REC-xml-names 19990114`
- `www.w3.org`

Summary

In this chapter, you learned about XML, the latest step in the evolution in Web page creation. It allows for the creation of extended element definitions and provides a way to define and manipulate document content. It has many derived languages (such as CML, Math ML, WML, XHTML, and others).

You learned how DTDs are used to define the structure of an XML document. DTDs detail how specific tags should be displayed, the type of content in defined tags, and the method used to lay out tags. DTDs ensure that document structure and content are in conformance with standards for being well formed and valid.

You learned how XSL is used to transform XML to another format. You saw how CSS is used to format multiple pages from a single location, and how namespaces define local and default vocabularies for same document.

Schemas provide improvements over DTDs. A schema offers many more data types than are available with DTDs. Additionally, since schemas are developed using XML, it is easier to write schemas for XML.

Chapter 17 looks at Ajax, a combination of technologies, that allows you to retrieve data rapidly without need of page refreshes.

Chapter 17

Ajax

Ajax is short for "Asynchronous JavaScript and XML." It is cross-platform. It is effectively open source. It is supported by these versions of the major browsers:

- Internet Explorer 5.0 and up
- Netscape 7 and up
- Firefox, Opera 8+
- Safari 1.2 and up

Chapter 13 discussed JavaScript and Chapter 16 discussed XML in detail. Ajax uses JavaScript to encode, call, transmit, and return small packets of data without requiring a screen reload.

Although it would be a stretch to call Ajax a new technology, and it is certainly not a programming language, it is an adaptive implementation of preexisting tools to provide an integrated, efficient new tool that can be used to make better, faster, more versatile Web applications.

As you may know, Ajax, which is a mix or reformulation of existing technologies, facilitates server interaction with elements of a Web page. This, in turn, results in a more responsive application with lower bandwidth usage, and, hence, lower costs, resulting in a win-win situation for all concerned. It is also these features that make it attractive to the so-called Web 2.0 crowd and, those who are involved in software design and development for mobile handheld devices. We will be looking at the future of Ajax in the Mobile Web later this the chapter.

IN THIS CHAPTER

Following are the major components of Ajax:

- JavaScript as the scripting language to call functions
- `XMLHttpRequest` is used for asynchronous data transfer from a server
- XHTML and Cascading Style Sheets (CSS) are used for uniform encoding and presentation cross-platform
- Document Object Model (DOM) is used for precise mapping and data display
- XML and XSLT (although, ironically, does not require use of XML for data fetch and transfer)

Ajax provides that slight margin of advantage to get ahead of the competition. But you must know when to use it, and then use it judiciously. You would tend to defeat one of its appealing features — fast, efficient downloads of small segments of data — if you repeatedly called for updates or refreshes of information. You would constantly be tying up system resources with repeated calls for new data, which may not be new at all (or necessary). Would you, for example, find it necessary to refresh the temperature field every 3 seconds on a weather page? It could be better done where a refresh of that field is only done when the new temperature does not equal the old temperature.

Async (asynchronous) just means that requests and data may be exchanged across the Internet from the client Web page to the server and back at any time. The JavaScript object used to do this is called `XMLHttpRequest`. However, there is no requirement that the asynchronous content be formatted in XML.

Let's take a bit of a deeper look into the `XMLHttpRequest` object.

XMLHttpRequest

`XMLHttpRequest` is an object that has properties (which have values) and methods (which have values to be passed or implemented). Following are some uses of `XMLHttpRequest` that illustrate its lightning speed:

- *Instant translation* — This is to the extent that a concept such as a word is synchronously defined among the thousands of existing human languages.
- *Smart shopping carts* — Allows the user to add, remove, or edit products instantly.
- *Immediate saving of data* — Why force the user to click "Submit" when this object allows direct saving of data?
- *Server/client side validation* — Allows you to validate data input on form controls as data is typed into each element.

TABLE 17-1

XMLHttpRequest Properties

Properties	Explanation
`onreadystatechange`	This property is invoked every time the `readyState` changes in response to Web server action. This property is actually assigned a function that holds the value of the change in state.
`readyState`	Represents the state of the `XMLHttpRequest` object. Holds the status of the server response. Following are possible values:
	0 — Unopened
	1 — Open
	2 — Sent request headers
	3 — Loading
	4 — `Loaded.xmit` complete
`responseText`	Response as string value.
`responseXML`	DOM representation of the response.
`status`	HTTP response status code.
`statusText`	String representation of HTTP status code of response.

NOTE **The biggest benefit of `XMLHttpRequest` is the elimination of roundtrips to the server. This makes the Web application work more like a desktop application, since the interface appears much more interactive and responsive than before.**

Table 17-1 shows a list of certain properties associated with the `XMLHttpRequest` object.

Table 17-2 shows a list of certain methods associated with the `XMLHttpRequest` object.

Because it is used to send and receive data to the server, the `XMLHttpRequest` object has three components or properties associated with each instance of it:

- `onreadystatechange`
- `readyState`
- `responseText`

The `onreadystatechange` property takes the value that has been returned by the server and stores it in the associated `function()`, which does the processing of the data returned by the server. This is a multistep process.

TABLE 17-2

Methods Associated with the XMLHttpRequest Object

Methods	Explanation
open(method, url, async, username, password)	method — HTTP method (GET, POST, HEAD, PUT, DELETE, or OPTIONS).
	url — The URL to request.
	async — Boolean to specify true or false condition.
	username — (Optional) Used for authenticating purposes.
	password — (Optional) Used for authenticating purposes.
setRequestHeader(name, value)	Specifies header-value pair to send.
send(content)	Sends request.
getResponseHeader(headerName)	Returns headerName.
abort()	Aborts the current request in response to invalid request or invalid format or user terminating the process.

The first step, the assignment of the function to the onreadystatechange property, follows the standard assignment format:

```
xmlHttp.onreadystatechange=function()
  {
         Executable statements
  }
Execute
```

The executable statements within the onreadystatechange property are contained within a selection structure that accepts one of five values from a server, each indicating a different state of the condition of the server in relation to the data request made. These returned values are stored within the readyState property. Each time the readyState property value changes, the onreadystatechange function() also executes. Those of you who are familiar with the OSI model might see a similarity to the request states and the analogous setup maintenance and teardown states of the Session Layer . . . or even Windowing.

Table 17-3 shows the five states that are transmitted back from the server to the readyState property within the onreadystatechange property.

The current state of the object is determined by value in the readyState attribute. When there is a change (in other words, when a state transition occurs), the value in this field changes as follows:

- The value of 0 would indicate that `XMLHttpRequest` object is in proper mode to be constructed.
- A value of 1 allows the send method to set up headers and send them to the server using the `send()` method.
- A value of 2 indicates that the request to the server has been sent.
- A value of 3 indicates the server is processing the request.
- A value of 4 indicates that the data request is complete. This does not necessarily mean that the data has been successfully received. It almost certainly has, but, in the event that the unexpected occurs, you will see a flagged message come up informing you of the failure.

With the data successfully transferred from server to requestor object, you can then invoke the third property of the `onreadystatechange` object, which is the `responseText` property.

When the `readyState == 4` control of the program shifts downward, the actual data sent back from the server can be retrieved by the following generic syntax:

```
Document.myForm.elementName=xmlHttp.responseText;
```

This is then sent on to the Web page element that requested it without reloading the entire document. The `responseText`, of course, would be the response from the server in a string value.

Figure 17-1 shows a flowchart illustrating the five conditions of `onreadystatechange`.

TABLE 17-3

The Five States of onreadystatechange Property

Variable Value (Constant)	State	Description	OSI Equivalents
0	Unsent	The request is not initialized.	Line idle.
1	Opened	The request has been set up.	Communications channel has been set up.
2	Headers Received	The request has been sent.	Sync and Ack.
3	Loading	The request is in process.	Data is being sent (Windowing).
4	Done	The request is complete.	Data transfer complete. Channel teardown.

FIGURE 17-1

Five conditions of onreadystatechange.

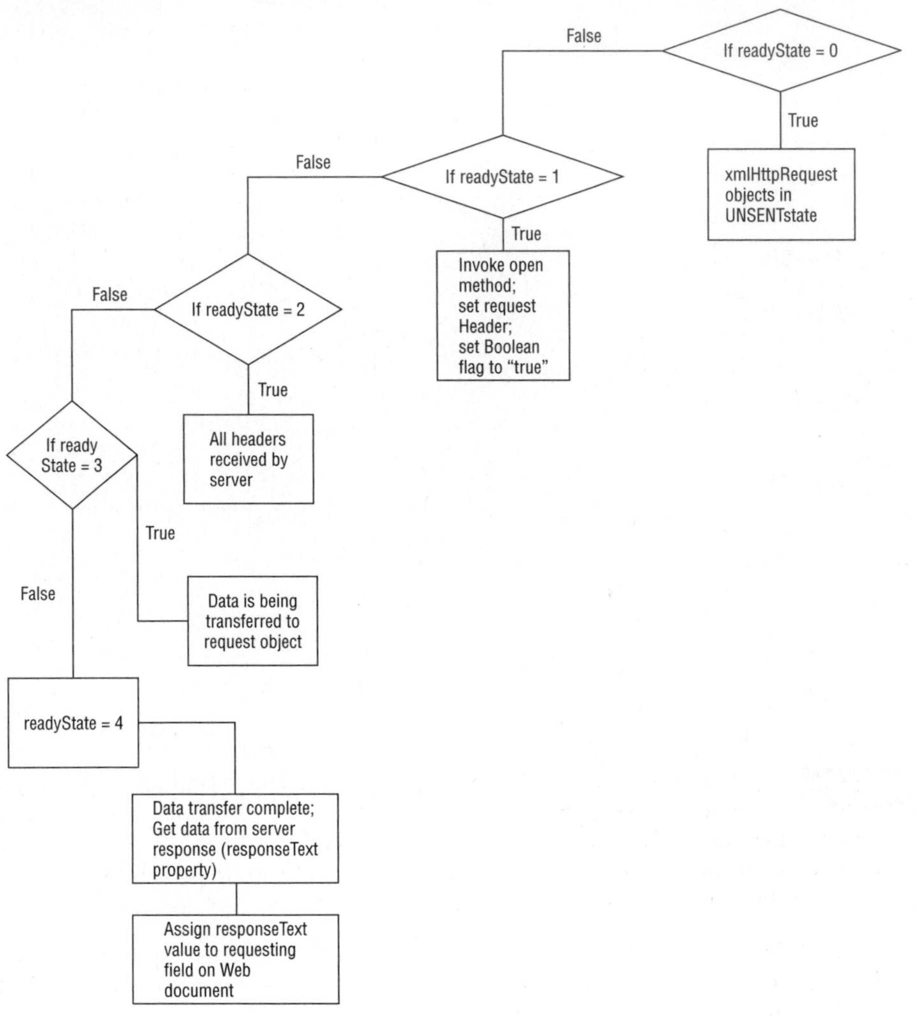

The coding at this stage of the `xmlHttpRequest` selection would look something like this:

```
If readyState = 0 the request has not been made
     Else if readyState = 1
          Invoke the open methodSet requestHeaders() using send()
```

```
                Set Boolean flag to "true"
                     Else If readyState =2
                          All headers received by server
                               Else if readyState=3
                                    Data is being transferred to request
object
                                         Else if readyState=4
                                              Data transfer complete get
data
                                                   from server response
                                                       (responseText
                                                         property) and
assign
                                                              to field on
web
                                                                 document.


                                              Error in data
                                                         Transfer Set
Boolean
                                                    Error Flag to "true"
                                         End If
                               End If
                     End If
          End If
     End If

Set xmlHttpRequest to default.
```

NOTE **This example is exaggerated just a bit to remind you of the importance of using white space to structure your coding — this is especially important when you have a series of nested statements, and you need to clearly associate each code block within a specific condition. If you have all columns flush to the left margin, you are likely to get sloppy and forget a closing comment, or become confused about which coding block goes with which selection.**

After the `xmlHttpRequest` object has been created, and its associated properties executed through the associated `js` file, the completed request is then returned to the originating file of the initial request (that is, the HTML file).

```
xmlReq.onreadystatechange = function();
{
  switch (xmlReq.readyState)
}
```

XMLRequest in Switch Format Case 0

In the following example, the request to the server by the `xmlRequest` object has not yet been made:

```
case 0: readyState = 0;
break;
```

XMLRequest in Switch Format Case 1

Consider the following code:

```
case 1: readyState = 1;
open();
```

Several actions take place with the open method and its parameters.

The parameters of the `open()` method are:

```
open(method, url, async, user, password)
```

The `method` parameter accepts the inputs of `GET`, `POST`, `HEAD`, `PUT`, `DELETE`, or `OPTIONS` and automatically converts them from lowercase to uppercase. Any other arguments will result in a `Syntax_Err` exception.

The `url` parameter will accept as an argument a valid uniform resource identifier (URL) that can be resolved relative to the base URL. This means, in plain terms, that you can reach the location of the target URL from your page. If you can't get there from here, you will get the error message, `SYNTAX_ERR`.

The `async` parameter will only be set to a Boolean `true` or `false`. The default value is `true`.

The `user` parameter will only accept user input that matched a stored user as valid, or that the program security scheme will accept. Other inputs will result in `SYNTAX_ERR` or `SECURITY_ERR` exceptions, and the program will be terminated.

The `password` parameter follows the same requirements as the `user` parameter. It does have a *stored password* and not a *stored user*, of course.

NOTE **The `user password` combination (or just `use`) is often omitted where these values have been stored or are not required by the security scheme. In a similar way, where the default value of `true` is expected, the `async` parameter is also omitted. In short, you could end up with a valid `open` method with just the parameters of `method` and `url`: `open(method, url)`, as in the following example:**

```
xmlReq.open('GET',myProgram.xml);
```

```
setRequestHeader();
```

Each request has a list of request headers with associated values. This method can be used to manipulate those values and set new request headers.

The parameters of the `setRequestHeader()` are:

```
setRequestHeader(header, value)
```

The `header` parameter must be in conformance with the standards of `field-name`. Where a header is an approved header, a value is appended to it. The following is an example:

```
client.setRequestHeader('X-Test', 'one');
```

In this case, the header would be `X-Test` and the associated value would be `one`. The `send()` method would then send the following header:

```
'X-Test, one'
```

There is a long list of potential problem headers. If any of the following appear in a header, the request is terminated for security reasons:

- `Accept-Charset`
- `Accept-Encoding`
- `Connection`
- `Content-Length`
- `Content-Transfer-Encoding`
- `Date`
- `Expect`
- `Host`
- `Keep-Alive`
- `Referer`
- `TE`
- `Trailer`
- `Transfer-Encoding`
- `Upgrade`
- `Via`

The request would also be terminated where the header = `proxy-` or for various instances of `null`.

XMLRequest in Switch Format Case 2

Consider the following:

```
Send()
```

The send() method would be used only when the setRequestHeader has been properly configured and the data in it is an acceptable not-null value. If the flag value is set to true, or if xmlRequestObject is not in the Opened state, you will get invalid error messages. Remember that the only argument of the send method is the data, which must be properly encoded according to DOM format. Once data is properly formatted and encoded according to the default UTF-8 or other encoding scheme as specified, it can be sent.

NOTE **DOM is discussed in more detail later in this chapter.**

XMLRequest in Switch Format Case 3

Once all HTTP headers have been received, the state of the object is changed to headers received, and an onreadystatechange call is made to go from that state to the next — Loading. Consider the following example:

```
case 3:
xml.readystate = 3;
```

The Loading state is the state of the object when the response entity body is being received. This state is represented by the Loading constant, with a value of 3.

XMLRequest in Switch Format Case 4

At the conclusion of Loading, the state changes to Done, Finished, or Complete. The async, if necessary, is reset and we go on to the next case. Consider the following example:

```
case 4:
xml.readyState = 4;
```

The Done state is the state of the object when either the data transfer has been completed, or something went wrong during the transfer. This state is represented by the Done constant, with a value of 4. The Done state has an associated error flag that can be either true or false. The initial value of the error flag is false.

In its entirety, the switch structure for determining the state of server response to the JavaScript object xmlHttpRequest is as follows:

```
xmlReq.onreadystatechange = function
{
switch (xmlReq.readyState)
{
```

```
case 0: xmlReq.readyState //executable statements
     break;
case 1: xmlReq.readyState //executable statements
     break;
case 2: xmlReq.readyState //executable statements
     break;
case 3: xmlReq.readyState //executable statements
     break;
case 4: document.testForm.textBox.value = xmlHttp.responseText; //
ready to send data back
     break;
default:
     break;
}
}
```

PHP code

Remember that this call to the sever takes places within a JavaScript program and that the data request and the data response are within that program. Once the response has been received, it is then returned to the requesting element on the original HTML page. Remember, too, that the `xmlRequest` need not be made to an XML document. In an example that we will be reviewing later, we will be looking at a request made to a PHP doc.

You can format a request to an ASP document, as well as PHP and XML document types. You will note that, in the beginning of the script within the HTML document, a test is performed on the browser to determine what kind of request to make. For example, you may need to know if the request should have the following form:

```
testReqVer = new XMLHttpRequest();
or
testReqVer = new ActiveXObject("Msxml12.XMLHTTP");
or
testReqVer= new ActiveXObject("Microsoft.XMLHTTP");
```

The coding within the HTML doc for this browser support check is as follows:

```
<HTML>
<BODY>
<SCRIPT type ="text/javascript">
function ajaxFunction()
{
var testReqVer;
try
  {
  testReqVer = new XMLHttpRequest(); //for Firefox, Opera, Safari
  }
catch (errID)
```

```
  {
     try
       {
       testReqVer = new ActiveXObject("Msxml12.XMLHTTP"); // for
IE 6.0
       }
     catch (errID)
       {
       try
         {
         testReqVer= new ActiveXObject("Microsoft.XMLHTTP"); //for
IE 5.5
         }
       catch (errID)
         {
alert("Your browswer does not support Ajax.");
return false;
         }
     }
  }
}
</SCRIPT>
<FORM name = "testForm">
<INPUT type = "text" name ="formfield1" />
<INPUT type = "text" name ="formfield2" />
</FORM>
</BODY>
</HTML>
```

Making an XMLHttpRequest

After you make the xmlHttpRequest object, you can now connect to the server using the open method.

```
xmlReq.open('POST', url, true);
xmlReq.send(' ');
```

The first argument specifies the HTTP request method to use (GET, POST, or HEAD, for example). The second argument is the URL to request. The third argument specifies if the request should be asynchronous, or, if processing should halt until a response is received. In most cases, you would want to set this to true.

To see what data the request object returned, you can use the responseText or response-Xml properties. The first is a string representation of the data returned from the server, and the second is a DOM-compatible version. Once you have made an XMLHttpRequest, you will need to update the Web page element based on the data retrieved. To do this, you can use the innerHTML property, as shown here:

```
document.getElementById('elementID').innerHTML = 'some text';
```

NOTE DOM will be discussed in more detail later in this chapter.

So, you combine these together and update the contents of an element to reflect the data returned by the server using the following code:

```
document.getElementById('someElement').innerHTML =
xmlHttp.responseText;
```

Taking all this together, you can write a simple Ajax application that consists of the following:

- A Web page that contains the Ajax-enabled link.
- When clicked, this link will make an Ajax request to the server. The server will retrieve some data and send it back to the device.
- When the device receives the data, it will update a page element with the data.
- If the device does not support Ajax, then it will automatically fall back to do a non-Ajax approach to fetch the data.

Following is an example of checking the server response to an xmlHttpRequest:

```
function test(data) {
 // taking care of data
}

function handler() {
 if(this.readyState == 4 && this.status == 200) {
  // so far so good
  if(this.responseXML != null &&
this.responseXML.getElementById('test').firstChild.data)
     // success!
   test(this.responseXML.getElementById('test').firstChild.data);
  else
   test(null);
 } else if (this.readyState == 4 && this.status != 200) {
  // fetched the wrong page or network error...
  test(null);
 }
}
```

```
var client = new XMLHttpRequest();
client.onreadystatechange = handler;
client.open("GET", "test.xml");
client.send();
```

Following is an example of logging a message on the server:

```
function log(message) {
 var client = new XMLHttpRequest();
 client.open("POST", "/log");
 client.setRequestHeader("Content-Type", "text/plain;charset=UTF-8");
 client.send(message);
}
```

Following is an example of checking document status on the server:

```
function fetchStatus(address) {
 var client = new XMLHttpRequest();
 client.onreadystatechange = function() {
  // in case of network errors this might not give reliable results
  if(this.readyState == 4)
   returnStatus(this.status);
 }
 client.open("HEAD", address);
 client.send();
}
```

DOM 3 Specifications for IDL Node Interface

As you learned in Chapter 10, the Document Object Model (DOM) can be represented as a tree-like structure having a root and trunk, many branches, and many trees. Figure 17-2 shows an overview of the DOM structure.

The segment in Figure 17-3 shows how the parent/child relationship functions to bring together values in two distinct (but logically adjacent) nodes of the parent node, Paragraph, `<p>`. Whereas both are direct descendants, the output would be the concatenated expression `Greensleeves`. However, where the nodes have a unique attribute identifying one of them, then, even where adjacency occurs, the output would be `sleeves` where the other element does not match in form.

Knowledge of how the DOM works will be important in tracking down some errors related to client-server exchanges using `xmlHttpRequest` but is beyond the purview of this chapter. More information on the DOM is contained in several Web sites easily accessible by any search engine, but we would suggest, as the "source of sources," `w3.org`.

FIGURE 17-2

Overview of the DOM architecture.

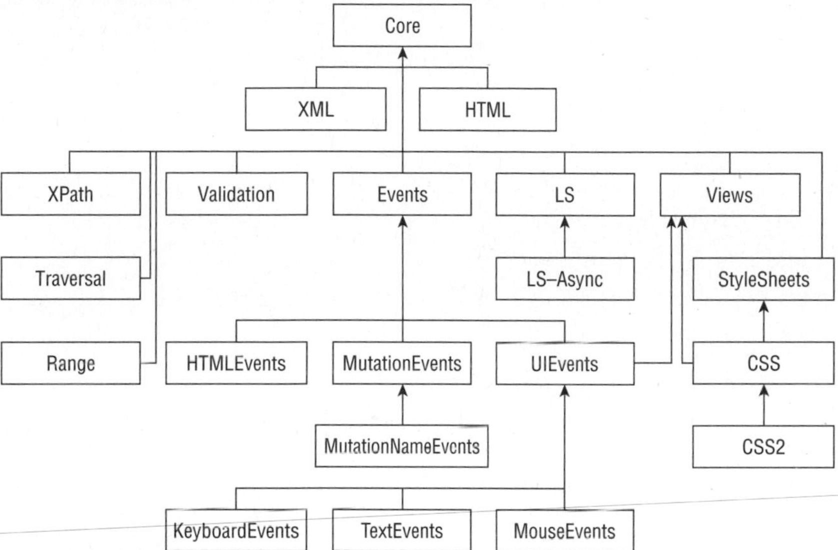

FIGURE 17-3

Parent/child relationship.

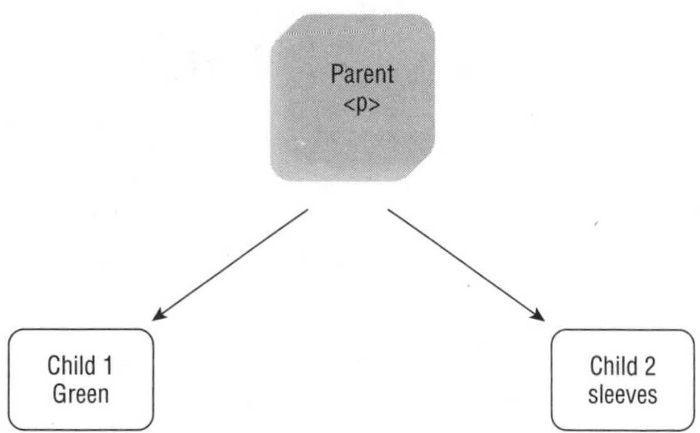

Ajax and the Mobile Web

Ajax may become a useful technology for mobile applications for the same reason that it is rapidly expanding in the more sedate market of desktop browsers: It is fast, efficient, bandwidth-friendly, and, because of this, will have cost benefits. Following is a list of browsers in the mobile market that support the basic Ajax components of the `XMLHttpRequest` object and basic JavaScript is generally current:

- Internet Explorer Mobile (also known as Pocket Internet Explorer)
- Safari Mobile (iPhone)
- Opera Mobile newer than v. 8.x, (but excludes Opera Mini)
- Minimo (Gecko-based)
- OpenWave newer than Mercury
- NetFront newer than v.3.4
- Blazer

This list is constantly shifting as new browser versions (and new and improved mobile devices) come out.

However appealing the features of Ajax might be to the mobile browser market, use alone will not drive the market. Applications developed for mobile devices would synergistically drive growth and would help Ajax achieve an unrivalled dominance in the Mobile Web-browsing experience.

There are advances in mobile devices that really minimize the bandwidth demands put on wireless browser communication. Using widgets (which are either the graphical interface on devices, or the slimmed-down application, including content, or a combination of both icon and application) that can be installed onto the mobile device via phone, this provides the focus and simplification required for ease of client use and ease of access to whichever applications are needed because so much of the content is preinstalled.

In short, mobile widgets often use components of Ajax, namely the asynchronous data transfer. Some observers prognosticate that, since widgets for mobile devices use one of the key features of Ajax (async data transfer) and since iPhone (which is very popular) also uses Ajax-based widgets, then usage is sure to grow.

Ajax Quick Reference

The following provides a quick reference for key items discussed in this chapter:

- Ajax is composed of the existing technologies of HTML, JavaScript, XML, CSS, and asynchronous data transfer.
- `XMLHttpRequest` allows a Web page to communicate directly with a server and update the page (page element) even after the page has been loaded.
- `onreadystatechange` property holds the latest value retrieved from the server's response to the `readystate` request sent out. These values can be `0` to `4`, and reflect various states of readiness for the data request sent.

- `xmlReq.open(Head, url, async, username, password)` is the generic request format.
- `xmlReq.send()` is the generic send format.
- `document.getElementById('someElement').innerHTML = xmlHttp.responseText;` is used to send retrieved data to a Web page element for which the request was originated.
- Different browsers have different versions of the `XMLHttpRequest` object.

Summary

This chapter provided a look at one of the Web's newest technologies that shows great promise for future expansion into both traditional Web sites and mobile sites because of its efficient use of bandwidth and high granularity.

This chapter began with a discussion of the basic features of Ajax, its origins, its main components, and how it functions to increase efficiency and decrease bandwidth for page refreshes. You learned about the components of the `xmlHttpRequest` object, including the methods, properties and values of each of the five possible values (0–4) of the change state. This chapter also explained the coding and technique for actually implementing an `XMLHttpRequest`.

This chapter looked at the DOM 3 specifications and the related IDL. We also illustrated the concepts of hierarchy and inheritance in the model.

This chapter also briefly looked at the expanding role Ajax may play in the mobile market.

Chapter 18 examines how to find, create, and enhance images on the Web.

Part VI

Images on the Web

IN THIS PART

Chapter 18

Finding, Creating, and Enhancing Images on the Web

When it comes to Web site content, words are perhaps the most important thing. However, no site is visually appealing unless it has some sort of graphical content as well. Unless you're a skilled artist, you need to look elsewhere for help. You need to know at least the basics of the image file types that work best on the Web. And you need to know where to find them, as well as how to stay out of trouble if you use them.

IN THIS CHAPTER

Exploring Graphics File Types

As you learned in Chapter 6, three graphics file types are in common use on the World Wide Web:

- GIF (Graphics Interchange Format)
- JPEG (Joint Photographic Experts Group)
- PNG (Portable Network Graphics)

Each provides its own advantages and disadvantages. With each file type, you must consider, of course, some technical details, but there are also some legal pitfalls to watch out for.

CROSS-REF **Chapter 6 provides more details on these graphics formats.**

GIF

GIF, the old standard, is a *lossless* file format, meaning that every single pixel in the image is always preserved when it is saved. There are tradeoffs with every method of saving images, and the drawbacks to GIFs are a fairly large file size for photographs and that the format is limited to a paltry 256 colors. Nonetheless, even though the GIF file format is pretty old, it remains one of the most common ones. Part of the reason for this, other than plain old inertia (it's supported by every graphics program), is that GIF provides a fast and easy method of adding animation to a Web site, and it is ideal for compressing text and solid shape, low-color images.

Back in 1989, the GIF format was beefed up to include the capability to hold more than one image in a single file, and to display those images in sequence. Voilà — instant cartoons. Although each new image in the file added to the size of the file, of course, it was still the smallest kind of animation file.

GIF leads to PNG

GIF may have inadvertently been the father of PNG. In brief, the compression algorithm for GIF was patented in 1983. This compression algorithm was named after its three co-inventors Zev, Lempel, and Wallace (LZW) The rights to this patent were granted to Unisys. It was a wildly popular compression technology and CompuServe chose it as their compression algorithm for their implementation of GIF (in 1987 and a revised version in 1989). In 1993, Unisys sought to enforce its legal rights by licensing agreements with several large commercial information service companies (such as CompuServe) at very reasonable rates. In addition, it was offered free for private and nonprofit organizations. Nonetheless, something of a grassroots rebellion began among Web developers who sought to develop and implement alternatives to GIF. This reaction against GIF (although not very successful) and the unjustified image of Unisys as a corporate bully going after the little guy did much to propel the subsequent growth of PNG.

JPEG

The JPEG format (commonly seen with the `.JPG` file extension) was an improvement in many ways over the GIF file format. In most cases, it allows for much smaller file sizes. The tradeoff is that there is some degree of information loss. However, JPEG images are generally much more than merely satisfactory, and the "loss" in most cases is only apparent in a mathematical formula. To the naked eye, the lossy image is as good as the original in almost every case.

PNG

One of the results of some legal difficulties with GIF licensing was the creation of a competing file format totally free of all legal complications. The PNG format was designed specifically to replace GIF images by a group of people who wanted to free the World Wide Web of the licensing problem.

While PNG files, in general, are competitive with GIFs, they do lack one major attribute — you cannot do animation with PNGs. However, a newer version known as Multiple Network Graphics (MNG) files is in the works that will include a GIF-like capability to include several images in a single file and play them back sequentially.

Comparing the three

JPG has compression and 16.7 million colors. GIF 89a has animation, transparency, and interweaving. It does not have compression but can be made to seem compressed by deleting certain colors from the image before transfer across Internet. PNG provides the best of both worlds in that it has everything GIF has and more — specifically multiple transparencies and the old JPG standby, compression. The only drawback to PNG is that it is not well supported by older browsers.

Choosing Image-Editing Tools

Unless you're going to totally abandon all pretense of having anything to do with Web page graphics and hand all that mysterious stuff over to someone else, you need to have some notion of what needs to be done to make your Web pages work. Even if you don't ever touch an image yourself, you'd better be aware of what is going on under the hood so that you have an idea of what can and can't be done.

It is impossible to do more than scratch the surface of such a complex topic in a single chapter. Thus, this is an overview.

There are three graphics programs that anyone seriously interested in Web design should be familiar with — Adobe Photoshop and Adobe Fireworks, Corel Suite (which includes Corel Painter and Corel Paint Shop Pro), the GNU Image Manipulation Program (GIMP), and an impressively fast graphics design suite, Xara Extreme. At least one of these (and perhaps all of them) belongs in your Web page creation toolkit.

CROSS-REF **Chapter 2 provides more details on Adobe's Creative Suite 3 (CS3), which includes Photoshop and Fireworks.**

Photoshop

Adobe Photoshop (see Figure 18-1) is the old, venerable workhorse of the graphics industry, familiar to every serious digital artist. Adobe Photoshop is important, not only because it has long been the industry standard but also because of the features it lacks — features that can be extended with plug-ins. When you get right down to it, all of the major graphics programs are fairly similar, and the choice of one over the other is largely a personal matter of user comfort. When it comes to adding features, however, you need to pay attention to whether or not the program you're using can handle Photoshop-compatible plug-ins. All four of the paint programs discussed here can handle these plug-ins.

You can download a trial version of Photoshop at `adobe.com/downloads`**.**

FIGURE 18-1

Photoshop is the most popular image-editing program.

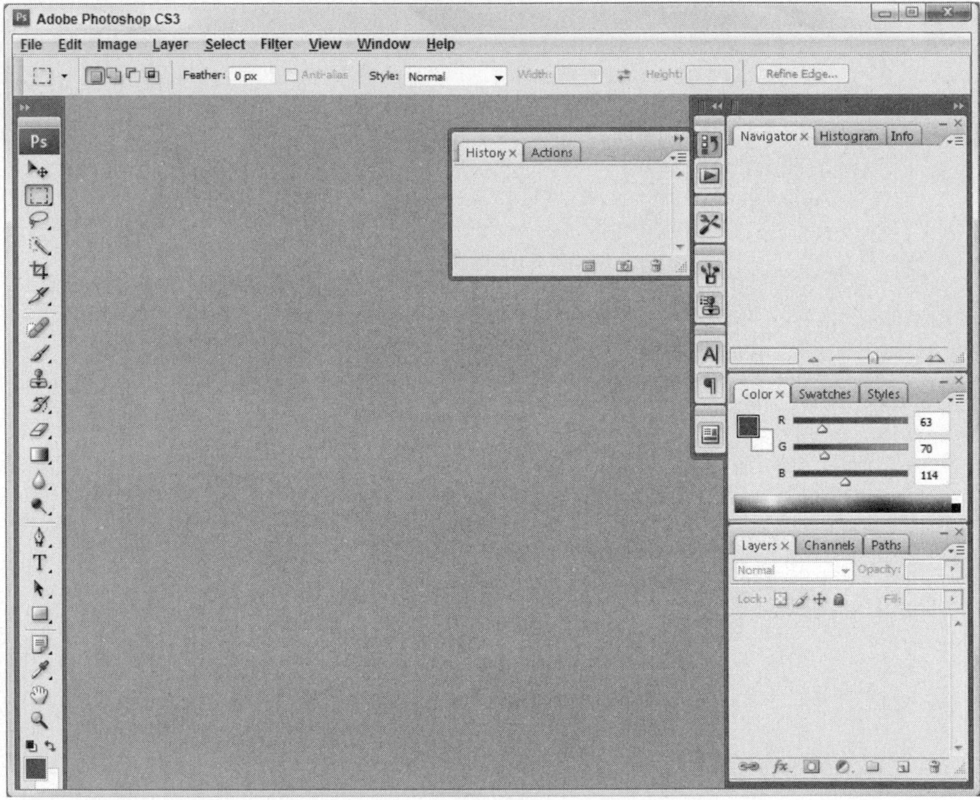

Fireworks

Adobe Fireworks (see Figure 18-2) is one of the most impressive programs we've ever used. It is similar to Photoshop in layout and function. Fireworks, however, is a child of the Web, and was deliberately designed for the purpose of making graphics for Web pages, rather than having such functionality tacked on as an afterthought. It was planned to be used in concert with its companion program, Dreamweaver, the premier Web page-creation tool, but it is also a perfect standalone graphics program.

CROSS-REF **Chapter 2 provides more details on Dreamweaver.**

FIGURE 18-2

Fireworks is designed for creating Web graphics.

Painter X

Corel Painter X (see Figure 18-3) gives you the feeling that you have gone into what is almost a case of virtual reality, rather than just another paint program. Working with it is like working on a real canvas with brushes so realistic that they almost drip paint onto your desk. You feel as if you need to keep a bottle of turpentine handy.

FIGURE 18-3

Corel Painter X is a full-featured painting and illustration program, and a good choice for those making the transition from traditional art to digital art.

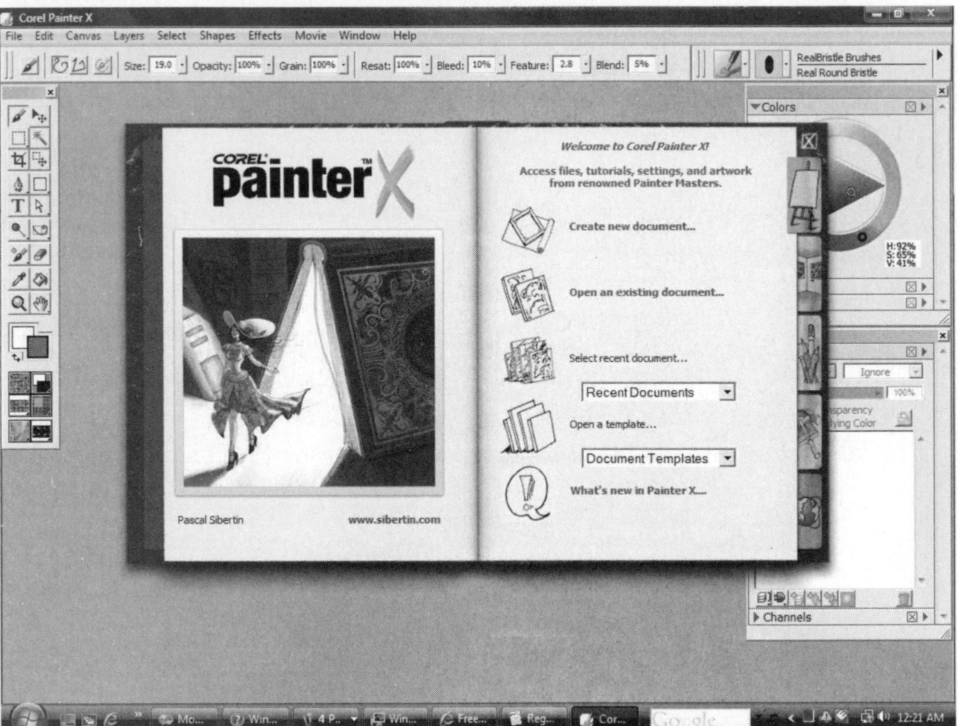

Paint Shop Pro

Corel Paint Shop Pro (see Figure 18-4) is an easy-to-use and powerful image editor. The newest edition as of the writing of this book, X2, has some plain-old fun features, such as the Time Machine (which gives photos a "period" look), in addition to enhanced cropping tools and sophisticated filter simulators. This is a program for both amateurs and pros. A personal plus for us is that it also offers reasonably priced academic editions.

FIGURE 18-4

Corel Paint Shop Pro, although shareware, is an excellent graphics program.

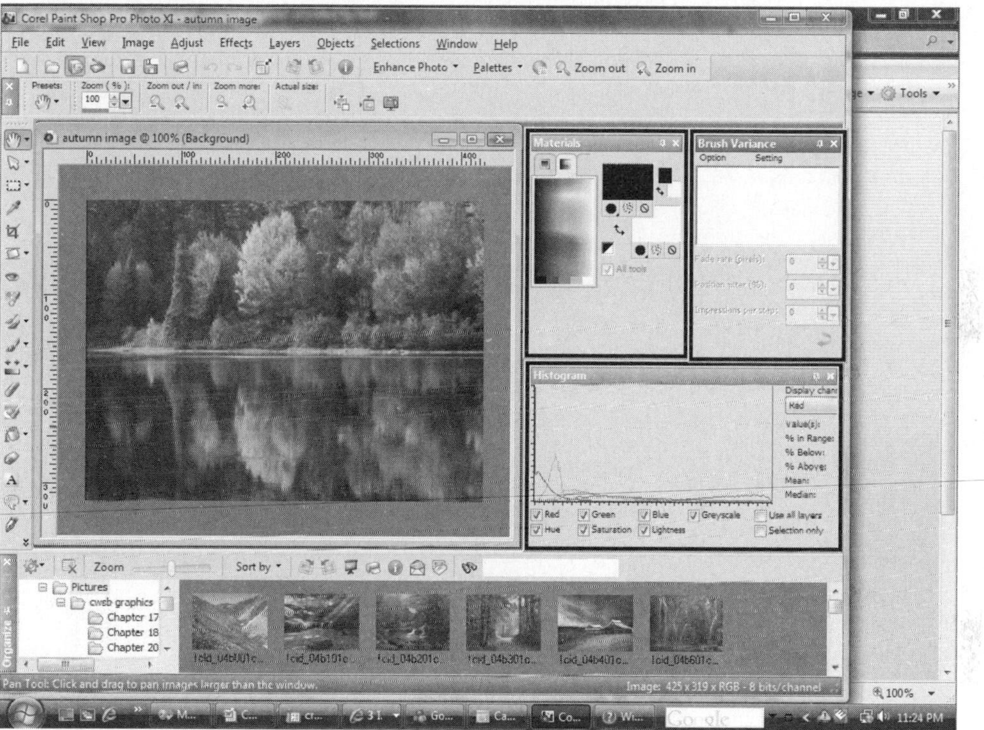

Xara

Xara Extreme Pro (see Figure 18-5) is a wonderful graphics program with extremely fast (as in Xara Extreme) vector graphics tools you can use for the designing and editing of images. It is very flexible, and you can create images ranging from the abstract (cartoons) to photorealistic images at speeds several times faster than Adobe Illustrator CS3. It has high levels of zoom and precision, has high onscreen quality, maintains a good work area, and, overall, is a bargain for serious illustrators.

Modifying Images

Most Web designers aren't good enough artists to draw their own images from scratch. This has led to a large market in clip art (that is, ready-to-use images, either photographs or drawings) that can just be dropped into your Web pages as needed.

FIGURE 18-5

This is a detailed vector graphic illustration created with Xara Extreme Pro.

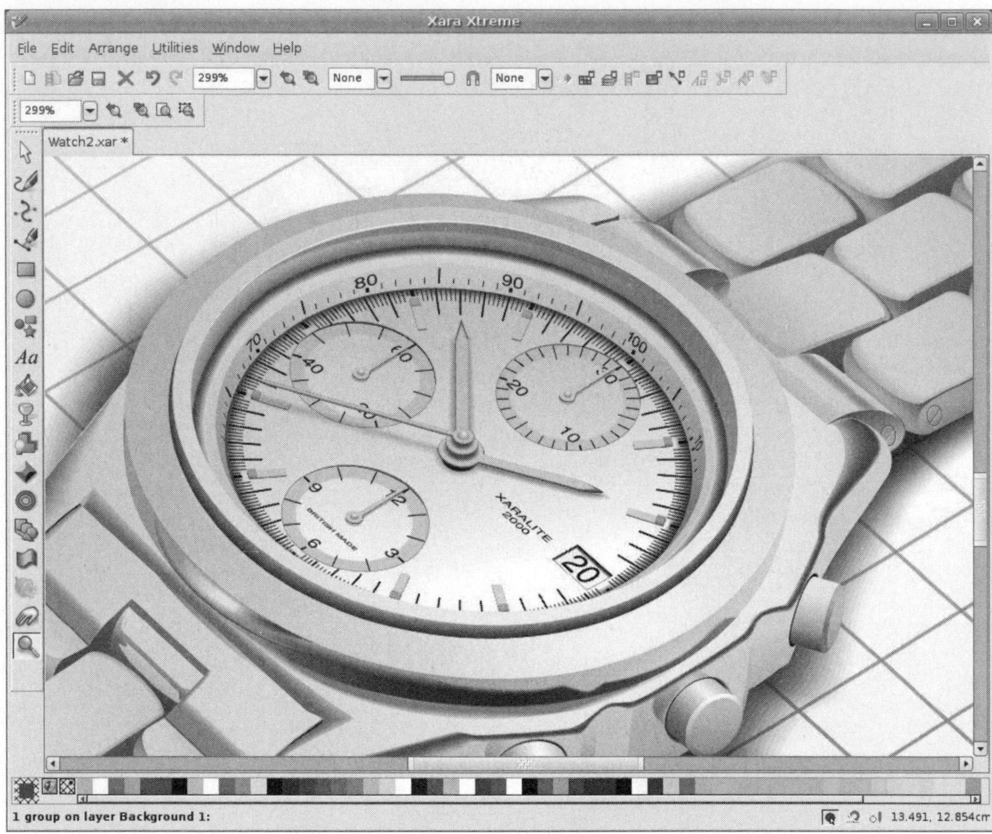

However, the needs of each site — indeed, the needs of each page within a site — vary, and there's often something about an image that makes it just not quite right. Perhaps it's too large, or too dark, or whatever. But with a little bit of tweaking, it can be made to work just fine.

Every graphics program has several methods of handling these situations. If you don't want to get deeply involved in learning the ins and outs of sophisticated graphics software just so you can use a few of the features once in a while, you might want to try a handy program called IrfanView (see Figure 18-6). It's a graphics viewer that includes some nice extras such as file type conversion and most of the capabilities discussed in this section.

NOTE **You can download IrfanView at** `http://www.download.com/IrfanView/3000-2192_4-10021962.html?tag=lst-1`.

FIGURE 18-6

IrfanView is a good program for making small, quick adjustments to images.

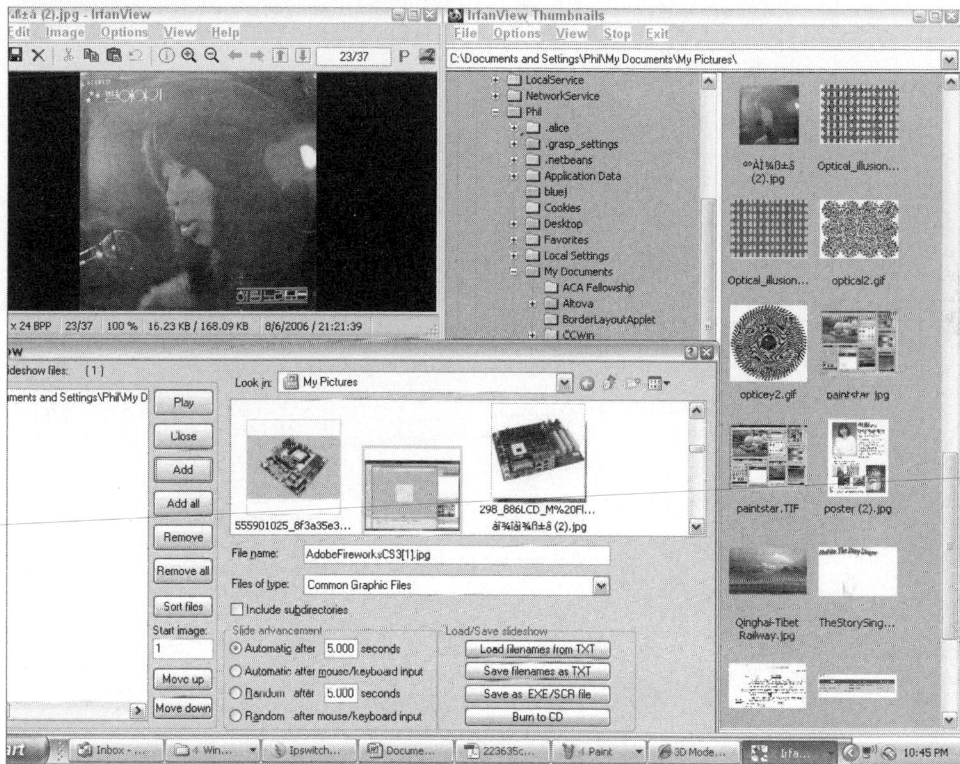

This section provides an overview of modifying images using the four most popular graphics programs — Photoshop, Fireworks, Painter, and Paint Shop Pro.

Cropping

Often, an image would be very useful, but in addition to things you want, there are also things in it you don't want. For example, you might have a picture of a bagel and a cup of coffee, but you only want to show the bagel. Cropping (which is eliminating all but a selected portion of an image) solves the problem. Figure 18-7 shows an original image of a bagel and cup of coffee and, underneath it, the cropped version.

The process is similar, but not identical, in each of the four major graphics programs. In each case, you use the Crop tool, usually represented by the icon shown in Figure 18-8. Three of the programs also offer a menu-based approach.

FIGURE 18-7

Cropping enables you to eliminate the undesired portions of an image.

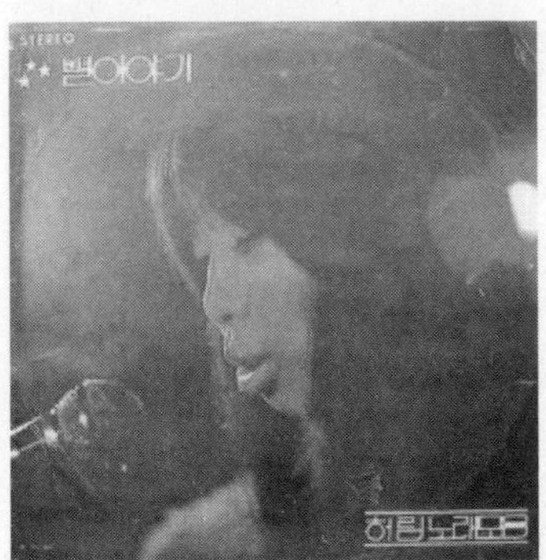

FIGURE 18-8

The Crop tool looks the same in all four programs.

Photoshop

To crop an image in Photoshop, click the Crop tool. Then, drag it to select the area you want to crop. When the area is selected, double-click within it. Alternatively, select the portion you want and choose Crop from the Image menu.

Fireworks

To crop an image in Fireworks, click the Crop tool. Then, drag it to select the area you want to crop. When the area is selected, double-click within it. You can also select the part to be cropped, then choose Crop Document from the Edit menu.

Painter

To crop an image in Painter, click the Crop tool. Then, drag it to select the area you want to crop. When the area is selected, click within it (the cursor changes to an animated pair of scissors when it is over the selected area) and you're done.

Paint Shop Pro

To crop an image in Paint Shop Pro, click the Crop tool. Then, drag it to select the area you want to crop. When the area is selected, double-click anywhere on the image. Alternatively, select the area, and then choose Image → Crop to Selection from the menu.

Resizing and resampling

One of the most common problems with images on Web pages is dealing with the physical size of the image. There's just a certain amount of real estate available on a computer screen, and a large image can quickly eat it up and overwhelm the rest of the Web page. While it's true that you can easily set the `height` and `width` attributes of a Web image, changing its apparent size on the Web page, this is not the ideal solution because you aren't actually changing anything but the way the image is displayed in a Web browser.

The original file is still the same size as it originally was, which means that its download time is still longer than it has to be. Also, Web browsers are not as sophisticated as graphics programs — you can get far better results by modifying the image in one of the graphics programs instead, like the one shown in Figure 18-9, which was resized in Fireworks.

When an image's size is altered, it runs into an information problem. Although you might not think about it very often, each pixel in an image is data. If the image is made smaller, there can't be as many pixels in it, meaning that some of that data has to go. If it's made larger, it has to have more pixels than it originally did, and that data has to come from somewhere. Both processes are handled by *resampling*, which is the process of figuring out what to do about the wayward pixels.

Making an image smaller is called *downsampling*. The reverse process is called *upsampling*.

Photoshop

To resize an image in Photoshop, follow these steps:

1. Choose Image → Image Size from the menu.
2. In the resulting Image Size dialog box (see Figure 18-10), enter the new figures for either the Width or Height. You can use pixels or percentages.

If the Constrain Proportions check box is selected, you only need to enter one of the figures. The other is automatically calculated to keep the image from being distorted.

FIGURE 18-9

Resizing in a graphics program produces better effects than simply resetting the width and height attributes in HTML.

FIGURE 18-10

This figure shows the Image Size dialog box in Photoshop.

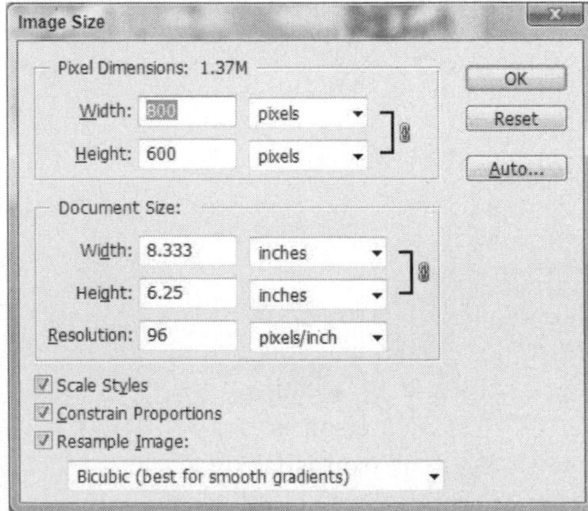

3. If desired, you can specify the type of resampling calculations to be performed by choosing one from the Resample Image drop-down list. The default is Bicubic sampling, which is the best.
4. Click the OK button.

Fireworks

In Fireworks, you resize an image exactly as you do in Photoshop, except that you choose Modify → Canvas → Image Size from the menu in Step 1.

Painter

Painter also follows the same routine as Photoshop, except that you choose Canvas → Resize from the menu in Step 1.

Paint Shop Pro

Paint Shop Pro's resizing works similarly, but the dialog box is quite different.

1. Choose Image → Resize from the menu.
2. In the Resize dialog box (see Figure 18-11), you can either enter the new figures for the Width or Height manually, or you can use the two arrows to the right of the input boxes to scroll up and down. The third, larger, arrow brings up a slider bar that you can use to more quickly change the size.

NOTE **You can set the size in either pixels or percentages.**

3. To keep the image's proportions intact, make sure that the "Lock aspect ratio" check box is checked.
4. Click OK.

Rotating and flipping

The orientation of an image can be altered by just about any graphics program. Some of them have only simple choices such as *flipping* an image (that is, creating a mirror image) horizontally or vertically. Thus, if you have a portrait in which the person is facing right and you flip it horizontally, you end up with an image in which the person is facing to the left. If you flip an image vertically, you are simply turning it upside down.

FIGURE 18-11

The Resize dialog box in Paint Shop Pro is different.

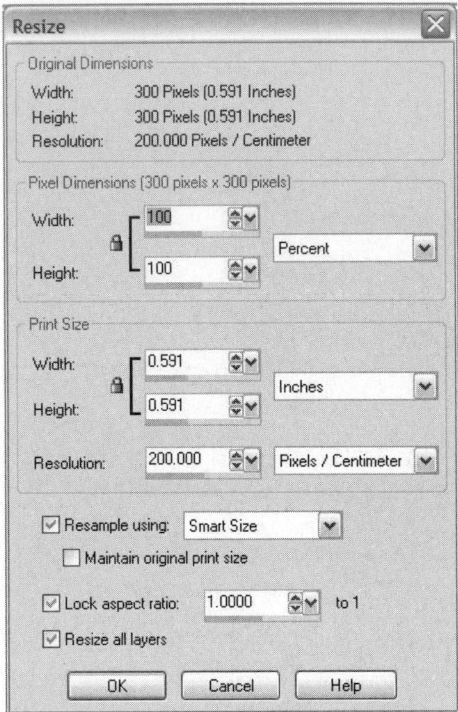

Rotation, on the other hand, can be done in either a simple or complex way. Most programs enable you to rotate by some fixed amount — usually in multiples of 90 degrees. The better ones, however, enable you to specify a particular degree of rotation — anywhere from 1 to 360 degrees. Figure 18-12 shows an image in its original orientation and rotated as well.

Photoshop

Photoshop enables both coarse and fine rotation. For coarse rotation, simply choose Image → Rotate Canvas from the menu, then choose 180, 90 CW, 90 CCW, Flip Canvas Horizontal, or Flip Canvas Vertical from the submenu.

For fine rotation, follow these steps:

1. Choose Image → Rotate Canvas → Arbitrary from the menu.
2. In the Rotate Canvas dialog box (see Figure 18-13), enter the number of degrees by which you want to rotate the image.

FIGURE 18-12

This figure shows a rotated image.

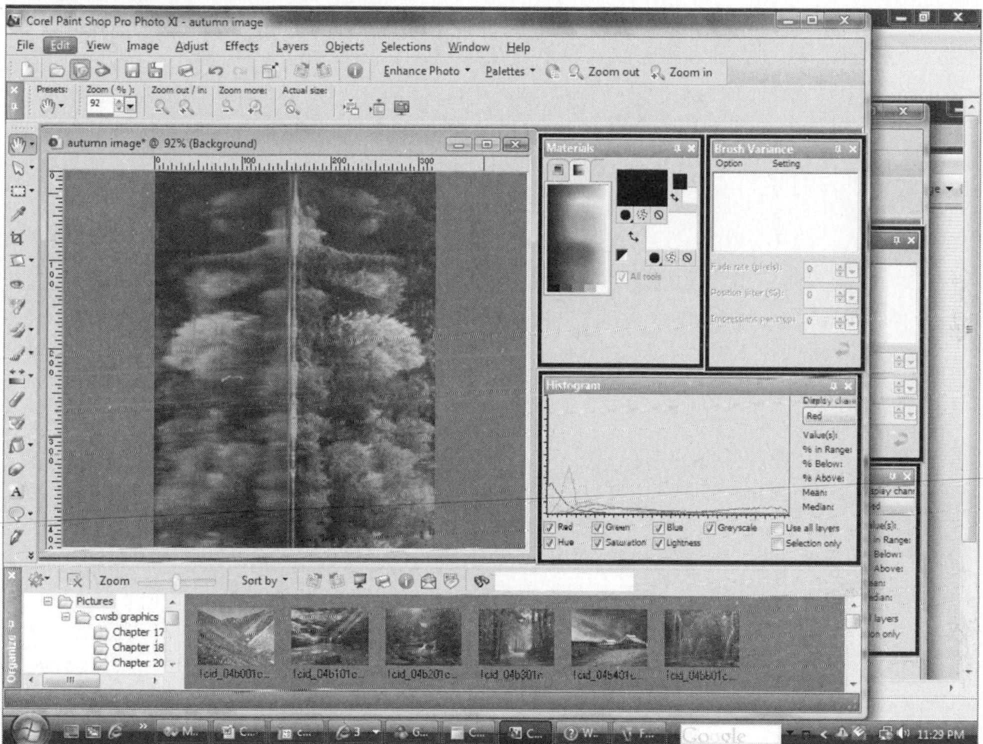

FIGURE 18-13

The Rotate Canvas dialog box speaks for itself.

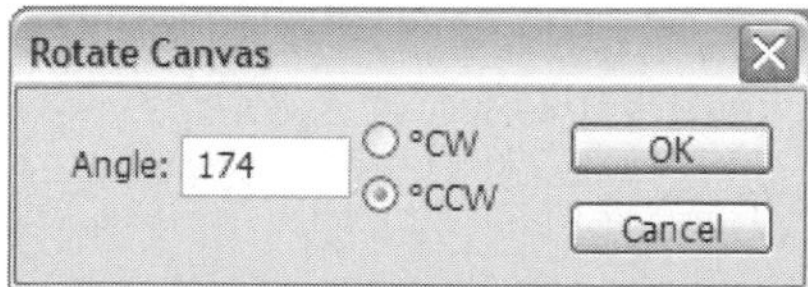

3. Click either the CW or CCW radio buttons to select clockwise (CW) or counterclockwise (CCW) rotation.
4. Click the OK button.

Fireworks

For simple 90-degree rotation and flipping in Fireworks, select Modify → Transform from the menu, then choose 180, 90 CW, 90 CCW, Flip Horizontal, or Flip Vertical from the submenu.

For finer rotation, the method isn't as obvious, because it isn't called "rotation." Here's how to do it:

1. Choose Modify → Transform → Skew from the menu.
2. Place the mouse pointer anywhere on the image (the pointer changes to a circular arrow). Hold down the left mouse button, and move the pointer in the direction in which you want the image to rotate.
3. When you are satisfied with the position of the image, release the mouse button.

Painter

1. Choose Effects → Orientation → Rotate from the menu.
2. In the Rotate Selection dialog box, enter the value for the number of degrees you want to rotate. This is the only option.

TIP **In Painter, all rotation is counterclockwise. To rotate clockwise, enter a negative number.**

3. Click the OK button.

Paint Shop Pro

To do a quick 90-degree rotation, choose Image → Rotate, then choose either Rotate Clockwise 90 or Rotate Counter-clockwise 90. For fine-tuned rotation, follow these steps:

1. Choose Image → Rotate from the menu.
2. In the Free Rotate dialog box (see Figure 18-14), click the Right or Left option buttons to set the direction of rotation.
3. To rotate by a fixed degree, click one of the three option buttons in the Degrees panel.

FIGURE 18-14

The Free Rotate dialog box allows you to perform fine-tuned rotation.

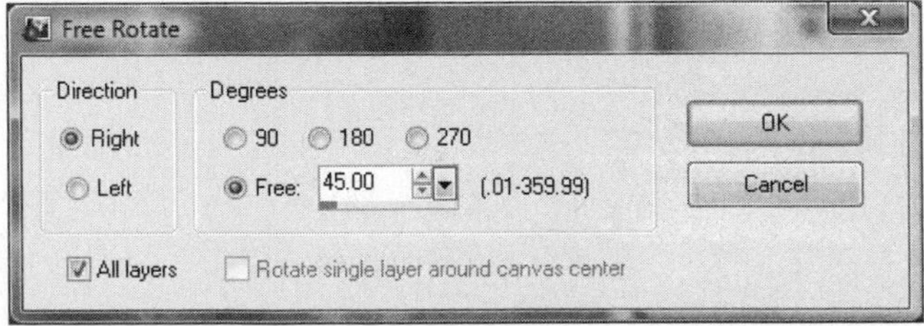

4. To rotate by a custom degree, click the Free option button and enter its value in the text box next to it.
5. Click the OK button.

Sharpening and blurring

It's difficult to repair a bad image, but sharpening can sometimes do it. If the image is a bit out of focus, applying a *sharpening* filter (in theory) makes it appear to be more focused. We're hedging so much in these comments because, with most images, sharpening doesn't do much to improve the appearance — it simply brings out more of the little flaws you didn't originally notice, but still leaves the important parts out of focus. It is, sadly, one of those things that sounds great, but just doesn't work well in practice much of the time.

Blurring, on the other hand, is the reverse — it takes a perfectly clear image and deliberately makes it out of focus. Despite how bizarre that may sound at first, there are often good reasons for doing this. Say, for example, that you were doing a Web site for an eyeglass manufacturer. You could use blurring for a before and after effect. The same technique could be used in any situation where a metaphor for achieving sight — or insight — would apply. Also, you don't have to apply a heavy amount of blur. A tiny amount of it results in a simple softening that can help disguise (or even eliminate) small flaws or graininess in an image.

It's also commonly used to make the product stand out from the background.

Blurring and sharpening work pretty much the same in all four programs, although there are minor differences in the menu options and layout.

Photoshop

In Photoshop, choose Filter → Blur or Filter → Sharpen from the menu. From the submenu, select the type of blur or sharpening you want to use.

Fireworks

In Fireworks, choose Filters → Blur, or Filters → Sharpen, from the menu. From the submenu, select the type of blur or sharpening you want to use.

Painter

In Painter, choose Effects → Focus from the menu. Then, select the kind of blur or sharpening you want to use from the submenu.

Paint Shop Pro

In Paint Shop Pro, choose Adjust → Blur, or Adjust → Sharpness, from the menu. Next, select the type of blur or sharpening you want to use.

Applying artistic effects filters

Plug-in filters, such as Kai's Power Tools (KPT), extend the capabilities of graphics programs. The standard for graphics filters is Photoshop compatibility — always check any graphics program you plan to use to ensure that it can use Photoshop filters. If it can't, you will find that your choices are rather limited. If it can, there are about 20 gazillion different options you can explore.

The basic kinds of filters that come with most image-editing programs (sharpen, gamma correction, and so on) are fairly common, and they are useful in a variety of situations. If you want to get really artistic (such as adding effects like metallic sheens, lightning, and so forth), you'll have to go for the plug-ins.

The exact method of operation depends on the individual plug-in filter, but in order to use them at all, you must make those filters available — that is, the program in which you're using them must be told where to find them.

Photoshop

Photoshop keeps plug-ins in its own dedicated folder. However, you may also indicate a second plug-in folder, as in the following:

1. Choose Edit → Preferences → Plug-Ins and Scratch Disks from the menu.
2. In the Preferences dialog box (see Figure 18-15), click the Additional Plug-Ins Folder check box.

FIGURE 18-15

You can set Photoshop preferences to locate plug-in filters.

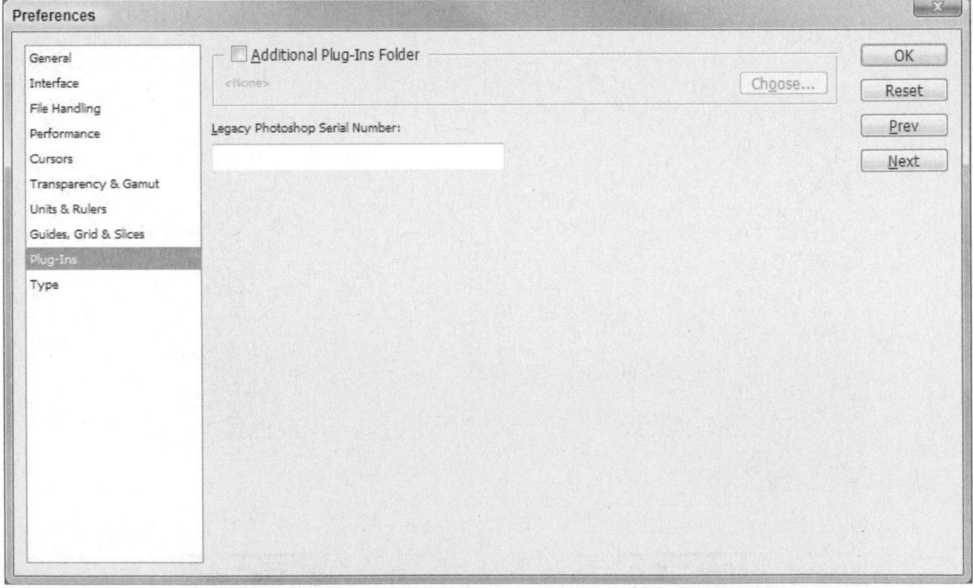

3. Click the Choose button and navigate to the folder that holds your plug-in filters. Then, select the filter and click the OK button to return to the Preferences dialog box.
4. Click the OK button to finish.

Fireworks

In Fireworks, the process is virtually identical:

1. Choose Edit → Preferences from the menu.
2. In the Preferences dialog box (see Figure 18-16), click the Folders tab.
3. Click the Photoshop Plug-Ins check box. Then, click the Browse button.
4. Navigate to the folder that holds your plug-in filters. Then, select it and click the OK button to return to the Preferences dialog box.
5. Click OK to finish.

FIGURE 18-16

You can set Fireworks preferences to locate plug-in filters.

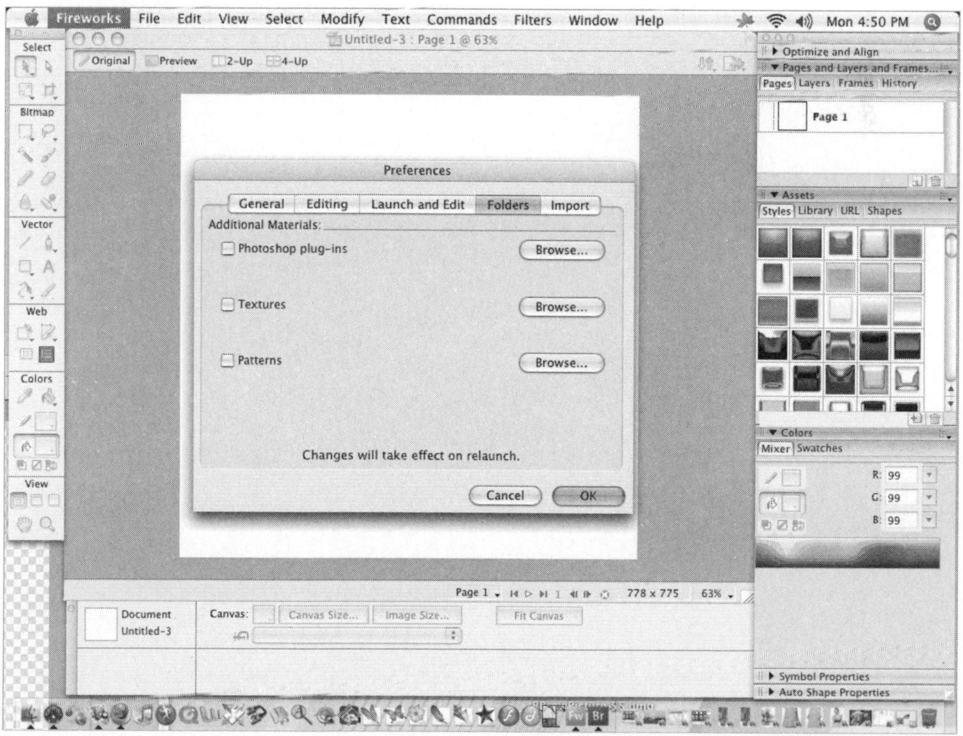

Painter

Painter has a comparatively laborious process. You must create a shortcut to the folder containing the plug-ins and add that shortcut to Painter's own plug-ins folder. In a typical Windows installation, this would be `C:\Program Files\Corel\Corel Painter 8\Plugins`. The way to avoid this is to simply install the plug-ins into that folder.

Paint Shop Pro

Paint Shop Pro allows multiple plug-in folders. To show the program where your plug-ins are located, follow these steps:

1. Choose File → Preferences → File Locations from the menu.
2. In the File Locations dialog box (see Figure 18-17), click the Plug-ins option in the list of file types.
3. Click the Add button, and then click the Browse button.
4. Navigate to the folder holding your plug-in filters and select it. Click the OK button to return to the Preferences dialog box.
5. Repeat Steps 3 and 4 until you have added all desired plug-in folders.
6. Click OK to finish.

FIGURE 18-17

You can set Paint Shop Pro preferences to locate plug-in filters.

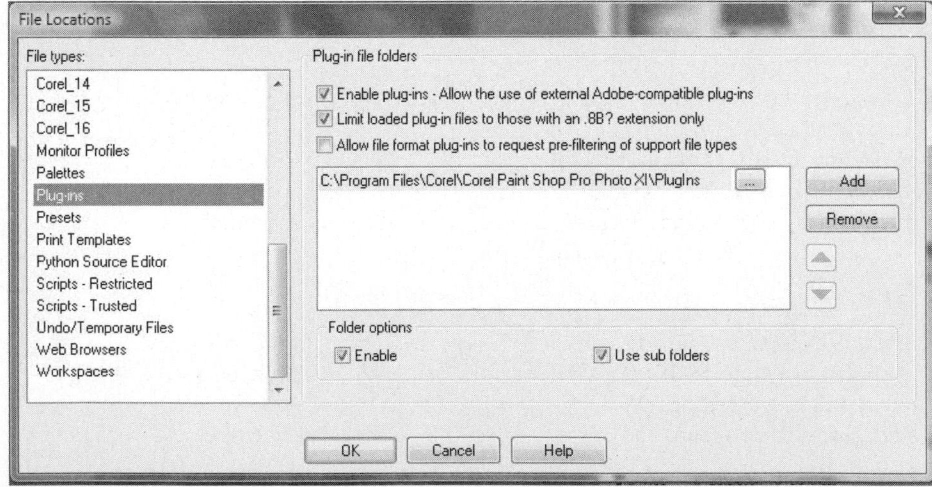

Using 3D Graphics Programs

While standard image-editing software is very useful — in fact, irreplaceable — most people do not have the artistic skill necessary to use it to its fullest. Art is, well, an art. And it takes a lifetime commitment to really do it well. Most Web designers are more skilled with computers (perhaps a bit more left-brain-oriented) than they are with artistic endeavors. Yet, graphics are a big part of the World Wide Web. It's difficult to imagine a serious Web site without graphics, and you can't always find just what you need ready-made and available for use.

Fortunately, there's a fabulous solution available. Graphics programs that are used to create three-dimensional (3D) scenes are geared toward exactly those people who are least comfortable with creating art in the traditional manner. Although some degree of visual awareness is required — you must be able to imagine what you want the finished product to look like, or you won't know where you want to go — no manual skill is needed. The 3D scenes can, when completed, be exported as normal two-dimensional (2D) graphics files, thus giving anyone the capability to create professional-looking images for their Web sites.

NOTE **All 3D programs are capable of both importing and exporting a variety of 3D file formats, which means that you can use objects that were created in one program in another one.**

Poser

Poser, from SmithMicro, solves one of the most pressing problems for non-artists: it allows the creation of stunning 3D human figures and animations through the use of its Simon and Sydney templates, and through the use of several exclusive third-party sources that allow the user to bring into startling realism new wildlife, as shown in Figure 18-18. Anime can be developed with Poser and it can be used to develop science-fiction and Fantasy themes, as well as using its tools to create photorealistic shots.

The human figure is one of the most difficult of all things to manage perfectly, and Poser does run into an occasional problem. First of all, it's pretty easy to do impossible things in Poser, such as moving an arm so that a hand is in the middle of someone's head. The program lacks rules that would prevent this. On the other hand (no pun intended), this also gives you total flexibility in character design — and Poser is often used to create nonhuman characters.

Bryce

Bryce, is a favorite of 3D artists because it's capable of quickly and easily creating realistic settings, as shown in Figure 18-19. It's also a favorite because it's capable of quickly and easily creating totally unrealistic settings. Whichever way your inclinations take you, Bryce happily generates land, sea, sky, stars, sun, and moon. It even throws in things like trees and comets if you instruct it to.

FIGURE 18-18

Poser enables you to easily create detailed and realistic human figures.

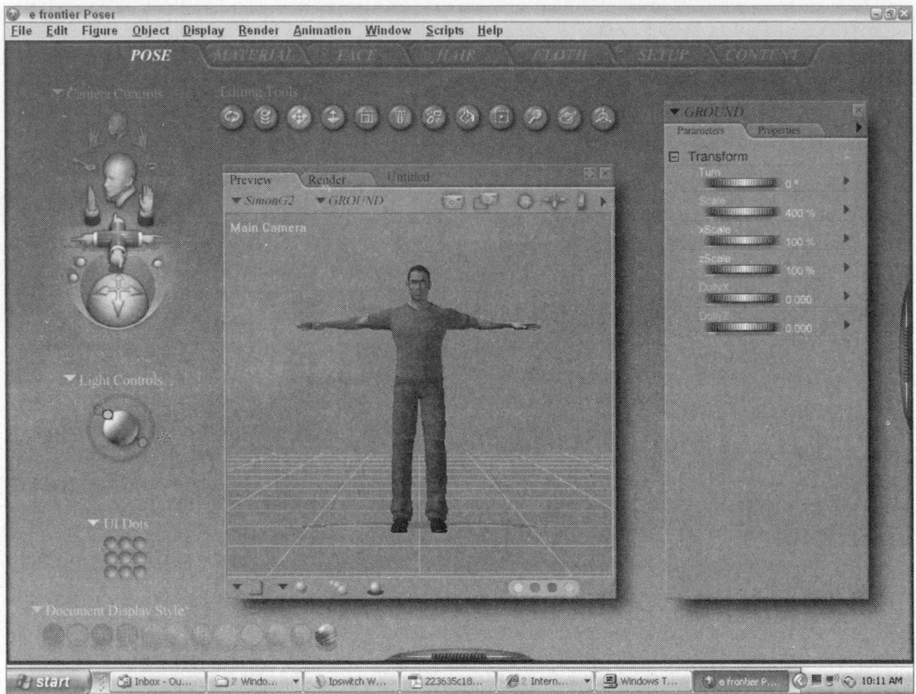

FIGURE 18-19

A seascape created in Bryce is an example of a realistic setting.

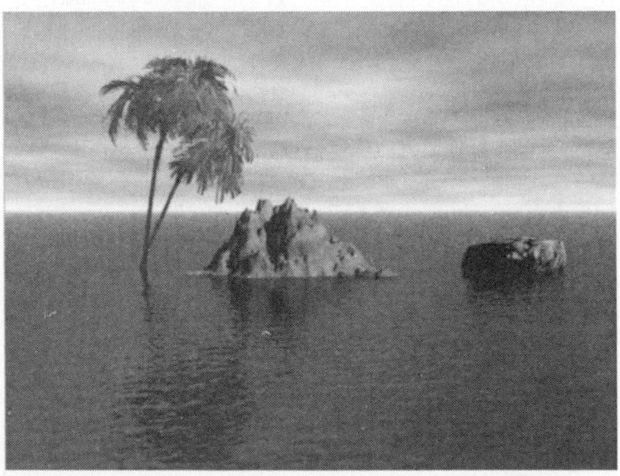

trueSpace

Caligari trueSpace (see Figure 18-20) is a heavy-duty 3D program, requiring a much steeper learning curve than Bryce or Poser. The interface alone is a serious challenge and, if you haven't cut your teeth on simpler 3D software, you might find this one a little bit intimidating. The old saying that anything worth doing takes some effort, however, is true here. trueSpace is more challenging because it is more flexible. Basically, if you can imagine it, you can make it in trueSpace.

FIGURE 18-20

trueSpace is a more powerful and flexible 3D program.

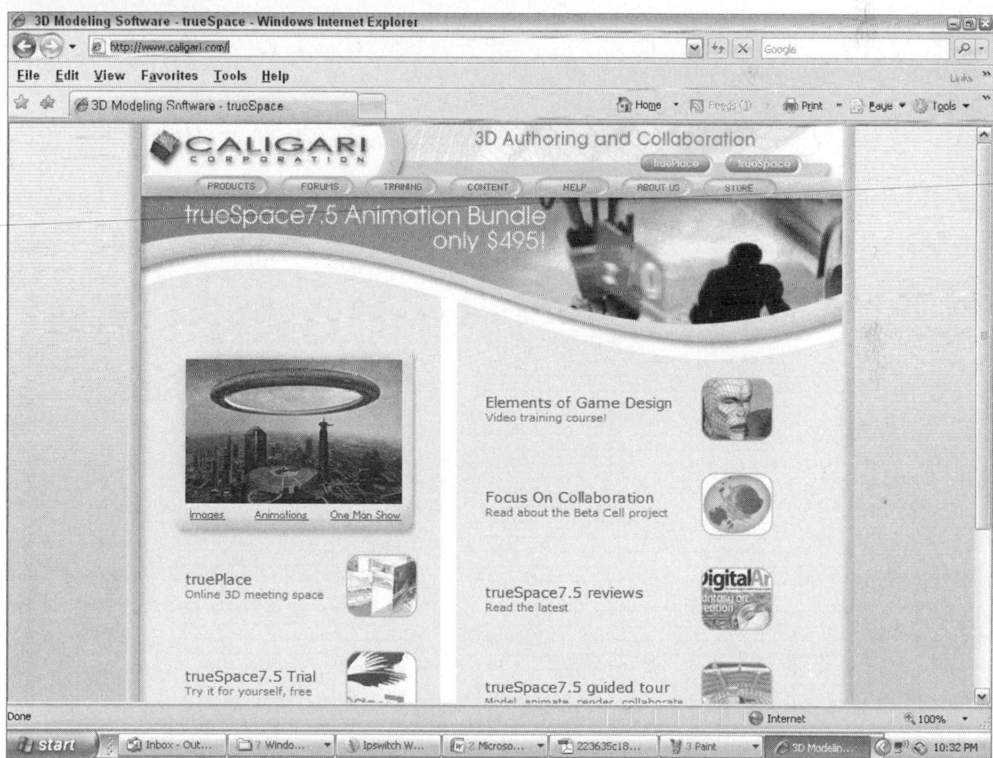

This program is, in our opinion, the best of the general 3D graphics programs. It is moderately priced, yet fully capable of holding its own with software costing much more. In fact, it offers a variety of features that are fabulously advanced. The best of these is that you can model in real time, operating directly on the various parts of your 3D creations.

Getting Free Images off the Web

There are so many different sources of free images on the World Wide Web that you could literally fill several volumes with nothing but listings of their URLs. We suggest that you pay careful attention to legal details (see the section, "Avoiding Legal Problems," later in this chapter), but other than that, there's such a cornucopia out there that you couldn't begin to tap it all, no matter how hard you tried.

Finding public domain photographs

The major source of public domain photographs (those pictures that are not protected by any copyright) is the United States government. As you're probably aware, there is a bewildering and complex assortment of different government agencies. You may not be aware, however, that any photographs taken by the employees of those agencies in the performance of their duties are public property.

CAUTION **Just because a photograph is in the public domain doesn't necessarily mean that you can use it any way you want to. For example, if there are identifiable individuals in the pictures, you cannot use them for advertising purposes without the permission of the people in question. When in doubt, ask a lawyer.**

Several agencies, such as NASA, have gone out of their way to make the vast array of such images easily available to the public, as shown in Figure 18-21. With other agencies, you may have to go to some trouble to get the images, and they may not be available in digital format, which means that you'll have to scan them on your own.

CROSS-REF **See the section, "Using copyrighted material," later in this chapter for more information on copyrights.**

Downloading free artwork

The Web is home to some of the most gifted artists the world has to offer. Many of them make some of their artwork available on the Web for the pleasant price of zero dollars, or a reasonable subscription fee, as shown in Figure 18-22. In most cases, such art is free only for noncommercial Web sites, but because the vast majority of sites fall into that category, that's not a bad deal. Even if you run a commercial site, you will be pleasantly surprised to find that you can generally purchase high-quality artwork with funds out of the petty cash drawer.

Finding suitable artists

There are so many artists, with so many varying styles, that the best way to find the one able to help your graphical image the most is — sorry to say — to spend a great deal of time browsing and looking at the wares. Before you start, it's best if you have a clear idea of the image you want to project on your site. Without that kind of preparation, you're going to waste a lot of time and effort. With it, you can usually tell with merely a glance at the first image whether or not it's worth your while to dig into the rest of the artist's offerings.

FIGURE 18-21

The NASA image archives are a prime source for free images.

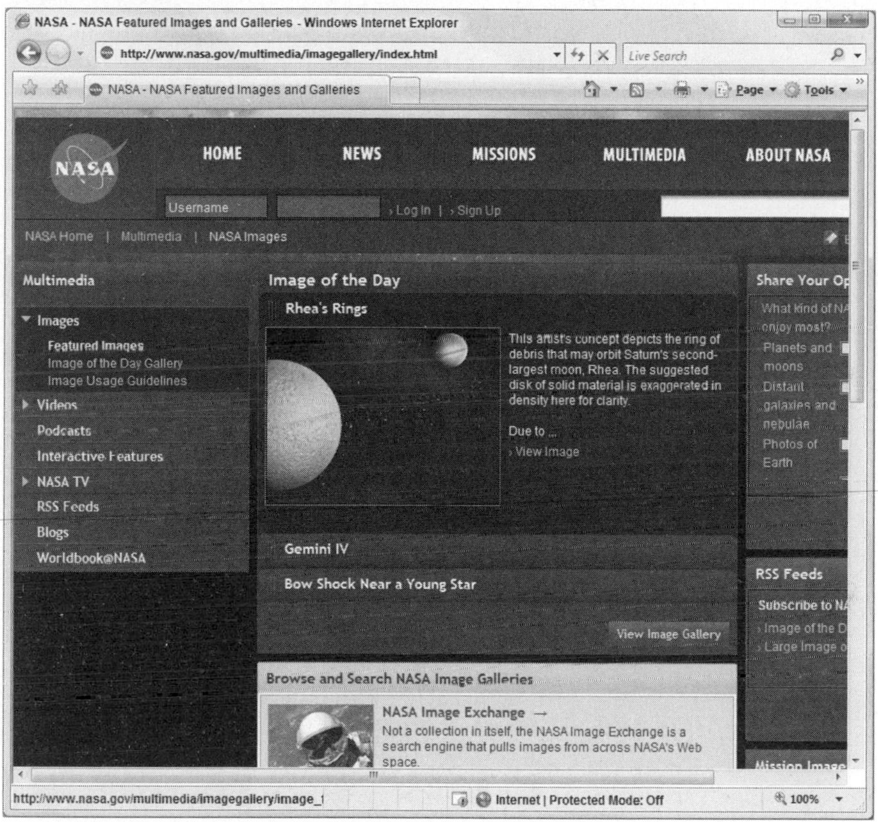

Having a high-speed connection to the Internet will spare you from spending a lot of time waiting for images to download.

Using stock photographs

You can lay your hands on millions upon millions of photographs of everything imaginable — easily and cheaply. And today, most of these photographs are available in digital format, either on CD-ROM or on the Web for immediate download. Stock photo agencies have long supplied the needs of print media, and they have now turned their attention to the World Wide Web, which has provided them with a bonanza like they've never known before. Stock photo agencies typically require payment for use of their images and may restrict usage, so read all legal notices carefully.

FIGURE 18-22

You can get tons of artwork with a subscription to Clipart.com.

Avoiding Legal Problems

Nothing can be easier than getting hold of or creating digital images. The Web is full of sites offering thousands upon thousands of image files. Practically every store that sells anything related to computers has CD-ROMs by the truckload that are filled with images, too.

The ability to get your hands on an image file, however, is not the same thing as the right to use it. There are all sorts of variations, ranging from limitations on the type of Web site that may use a particular image to the trickier nuances of licensing fine print.

Using copyrighted material

Copyright — the right to make copies — is usually vested in the individual who created the image. Whether that person is a digital artist or a photographer who later scans a print or transparency into a computer doesn't matter. The act of creation is what gives someone the copyright.

Modifying an existing image is not an act of creation. The resulting modified image is called a *derivative work* and is not considered to be original, no matter how major the modification is. This means that, if you use someone else's copyrighted material, it makes no difference what you do with it — it's still under their copyright.

There are few ways for the creator of an image to lose the copyright. One is for them to create the work under the terms of a contract that specifically states they are waiving their rights. This is called a *work-for-hire, (WFH)* contract. Another is for the creator to sell the copyright. Copyright is property — intellectual property, but property nonetheless, just as a car or house is — and can be bought or sold.

Often, however, the artist in question will license the rights instead of selling them. The artist retains the copyright while allowing others to use the image. There is, sadly, no such thing as a uniform license. Using existing artwork or photographs on your Web site is a wonderful way to solve the problem of adding good graphics. If you don't take the time to read and understand the fine print in the license, however, you can end up with a hassle on your hands instead.

This is especially true with "free" graphics. Many graphic images that are available at no cost cannot be used on a commercial Web site. The artists involved do not mind if someone uses the images on a private home page, or if a nonprofit organization uses them, but most artists take umbrage if someone is using their images in a money-making situation and not paying them for their work.

Sometimes, the licensing terms can leave you wondering exactly what you're supposed to do or not do. In more than one case we've seen, a license specifies that you're allowed to use the images on your Web site, but can't make the image files available for download. Maybe you can figure out some way to do both of those things, but we confess that it's beyond us.

We assume that the lawyers who wrote the license don't have the slightest grasp of how Web pages work. Or, perhaps it's just a question of intent. Maybe these licenses mean that you just can't suggest that people download their own copies of the images. Who knows? Considering that no Web page image can be displayed unless it's downloaded to a Web browser, and considering that browsers automatically cache a copy of the image on your visitors' hard drives, it hardly matters what you suggest.

There are two really good ways to handle a license like that. The first is to ask for clarification. If you get it, make a hard copy of the response and keep it where you can retrieve it if needed.

If you don't — or maybe even if you do, depending on the answer — then exercise the second good option. Don't use those images. It's just not worth it, even if they're the greatest pictures you've ever seen.

Respecting trademarks

Whether an image is an original you drew yourself or whether it comes from a collection, the subject matter of the image may be something to be concerned about. Let's say you're a talented artist and grew up in twentieth century America. You no doubt learned (and deliberately practiced) a good part of your artistic technique by carefully copying the work of established artists while you felt your way to your own approach. That means, simply, that you're probably pretty good at whipping out a perfectly recognizable Snoopy or Garfield.

These are normal stages in the growth of any artist — imitation is not only flattery, it is education. However, there's a big difference between studying an artistic technique and using someone else's trademarks on your Web site.

Summary

Images are the key to visually appealing Web pages. While it's possible to get by without them, no page looks as good without images as it does with them. The choice of the right tool for creating and altering images can be critical to your success. Although most drawing tools work in a similar way, each has its own quirks, and the choice is ultimately a personal one.

In this chapter, you learned that the three most common file formats on the Web are GIF, JPEG, and PNG. Fireworks, Photoshop, Painter, and Paint Shop Pro are the four most important image-editing programs. Existing images are often modified so that they fit the needs of a given Web page.

You have seen that all major graphics programs accept the addition of plug-in filters, which expand the programs' capabilities. 3D graphics programs can be used to quickly and easily create incredibly sophisticated scenes.

You have learned that public domain photographs and artwork do not have any copyright protection. Many images are available for free, even if they are copyrighted, as long as the copyright owner gives permission. Trademarked images cannot be used without permission even if you draw them yourself.

Chapter 19 begins a review of how to set up your Web site for commercial purposes.

Part VII

Cashing in on eCommerce

IN THIS PART

Chapter 19

Setting Up Your Store

eCommerce is not some big, mysterious new thing. The goals for e-businesses are the same as the goals of traditional business — the customer is simply reached through a new and different channel. You're selling either a product or a service to the same people you'd be selling to if there were no such thing as the Internet. Of course, with the worldwide reach of the Internet, you have access to many more potential customers or clients than ever before. And your customers can shop at your eCommerce store 24/7.

IN THIS CHAPTER

Choosing Your eCommerce Setup

Depending on what you're selling and how you want to market it, your storefront needs will fall into one of five categories:

- Single-product sites and specialty stores
- General stores
- Service sites
- Shopping malls
- Affiliate stores

Single-product sites and specialty stores

Single-product sales tend to be the province of the smallest kind of business — a single individual or small group of people. The product being sold is often a craft item or a book.

A specialty store is, at first glance, not very different from a single-product site. Both feature a very limited stock focused on one thing. A specialty store, however, carries more than one item, although those stores themselves fall into certain easy classifications:

- Bookstores
- Shoe stores
- Jewelers
- Automotive suppliers

Some stores fall into kind of a gray area between the two classifications. For example, as shown in Figure 19-1, the Web site for Jerry Stocking and Karen Bates (`www.achoiceexperience.org`) sells both books and tapes, but by a single author. Thus, we classify it as a single-product site instead of a specialty store.

FIGURE 19-1

achoiceexperience.org is a good example of a single-product Web site.

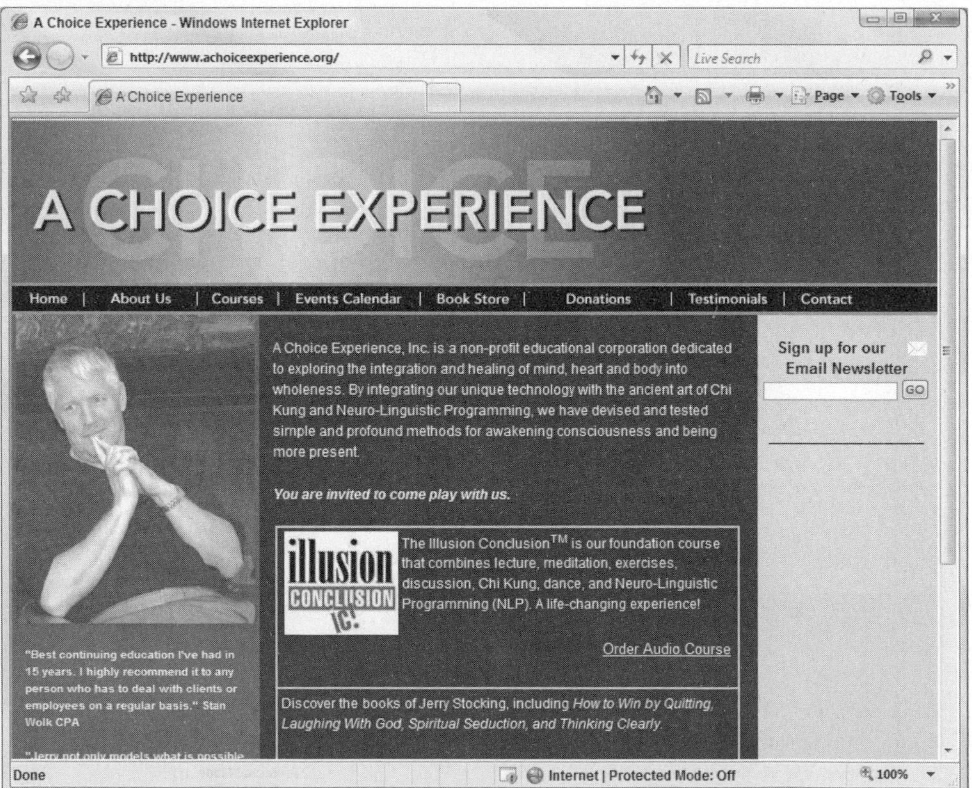

General stores

The era of the general store seemed to have pretty much passed many years ago, with the exception of a few large department stores. Even those have severely limited their stock, and if you want anything other than a few limited lines like clothing, jewelry, or perfume, you have to turn to their catalogs. Catalog sales, however, are practically tailor-made for the Internet. As a result, the new technology has brought about a return of the general store.

Even the big department stores like JCPenney offer more on their Web sites than they do in their typical stores (see Figure 19-2). Why? Because Web sites don't take up any physical space, which means that a huge site costs very little more than the simplest, one-page site does. When it comes to physical real estate, every square inch must be totally cost-effective. But a Web site can have several pages that don't draw much business without increasing the cost of the site.

FIGURE 19-2

You can find more at jcpenney.com than you can in most JCPenney physical stores.

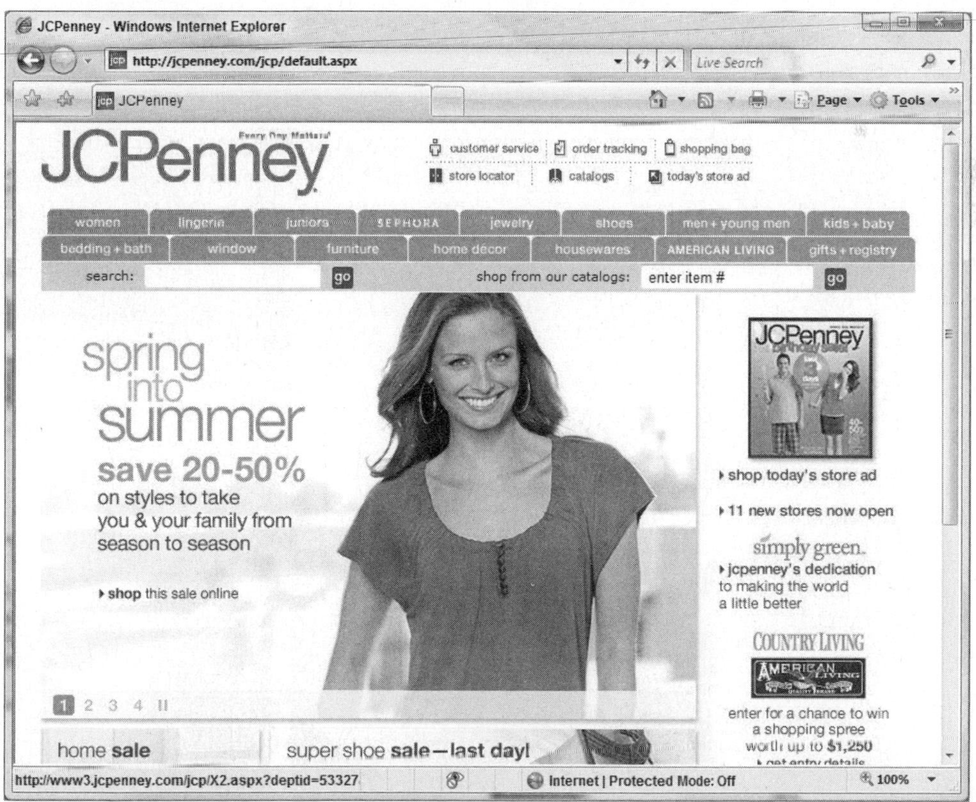

Take Amazon.com as an example. Jeff Bezos started selling books, without even having a "brick-and-mortar" store. Now Amazon sells everything from books to consumer electronics to sporting goods and more. Customers can choose just to search a particular "department" at Amazon, or search the entire "store" for almost anything they need.

Online superstores

Technology is advancing at an amazing pace. New gadgets, computer-related products, and other technologies are finding their way into many mainstream stores. Retailers such as Best Buy have devoted a large portion of their showroom to the latest digital technology: computers, camcorders, digital cameras, PDAs, MP3 players, and much more. In addition to being a thoroughly stocked retailer, Best Buy also maintains a huge online presence at www.bestbuy.com (see Figure 19-3). You can browse their entire inventory online, order products, and check local inventory.

FIGURE 19-3

You can find a wide variety of technology at bestbuy.com.

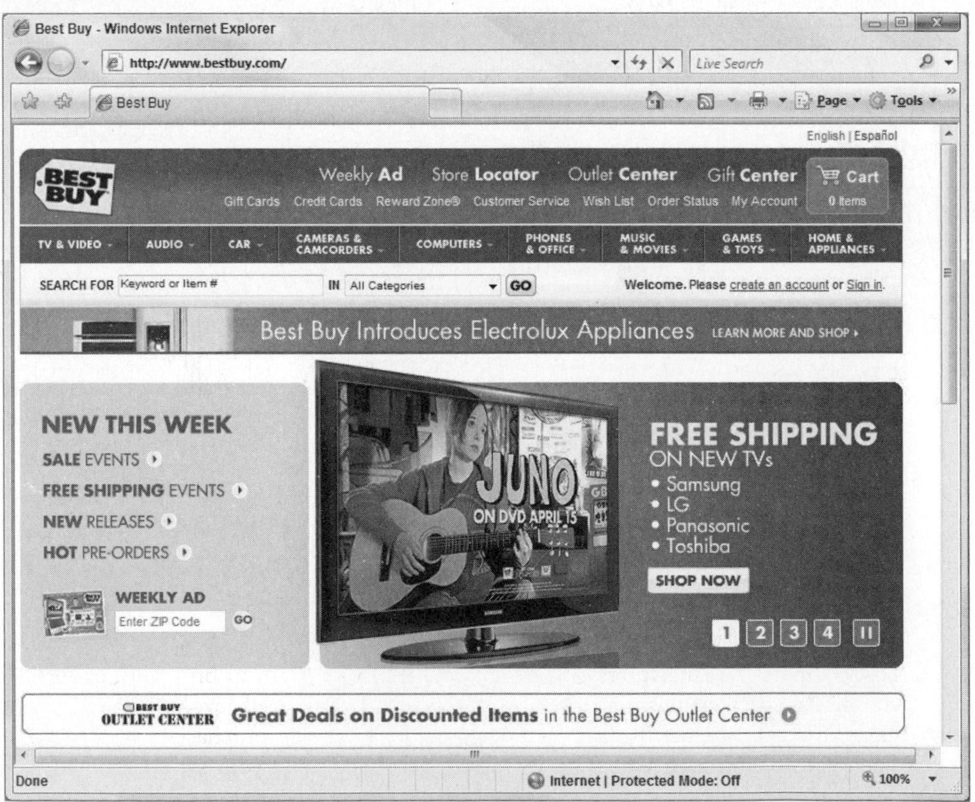

In addition to Best Buy, two other technology-based retailers can be found online: CompUSA (www.compusa.com) and Circuit City (www.circuitcity.com). Circuit City features detailed product descriptions, as well as product reviews on its Web site. The CompUSA site gives you the option of searching inventory in local stores, as well as ordering online for store pickup (see Figure 19-4).

FIGURE 19-4

You can reserve items for in-store pickup from the CompUSA Web site.

Online computer stores

Most computer manufacturers have their own Web sites. You can browse through their pages, read model specifications, and even order a system online. Dell revolutionized buying computers over the Internet. In fact, Dell computers can only be purchased through the Internet. When you visit the Dell Web site (see Figure 19-5), you build your system online and then place the order.

FIGURE 19-5

You can custom build your computer at the Dell Web site.

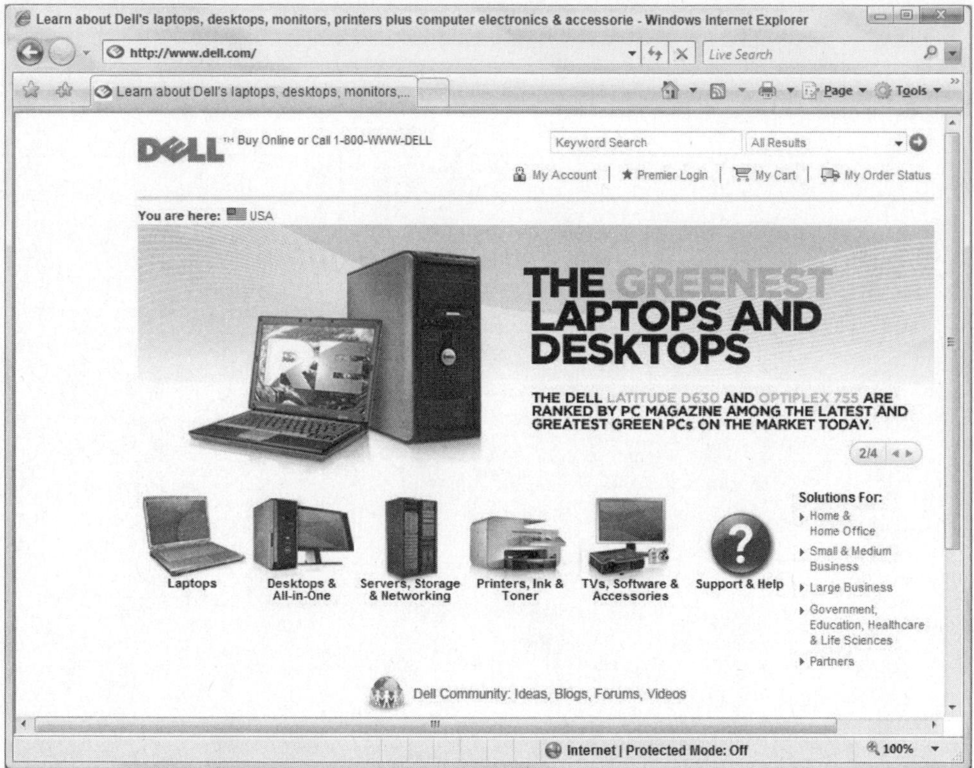

Service sites

The vast majority of people consider eCommerce to be the sale of some sort of product. However, the trend of the new economy — even before the advent of the Internet — has been largely toward services and information. In this regard, you'll find Web sites where you can purchase insurance, refinance your home, plan vacations, and so on. `Expedia.com` is an excellent example of this type of service (see Figure 19-6). From the company's Web site, you can check airfares and hotel accommodations, as well as rent cars.

Following are some common examples of service-based sites:

- Travel agencies
- Stock trading firms
- Insurance agencies

- Banks
- Auction houses
- Mortgage companies

FIGURE 19-6

Expedia.com is a good example of a service-based Web site.

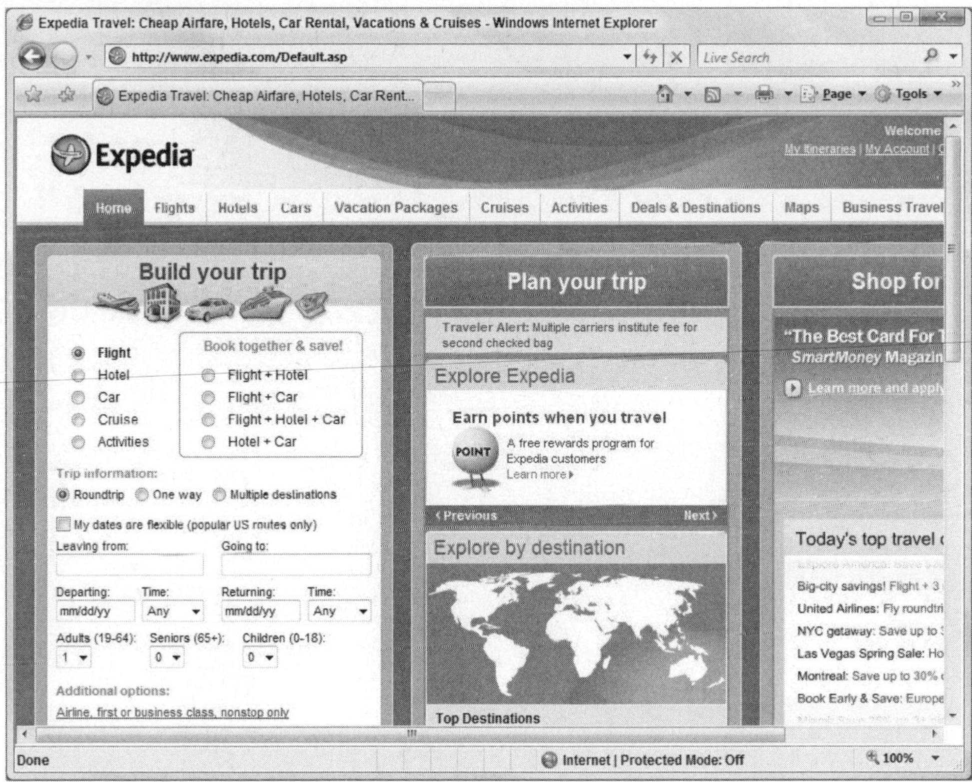

Service sites can offer visitors the opportunity to use — and purchase — the services on the spot, or they can be nothing but glorified advertisements for the brick-and-mortar version of the business.

Shopping malls

Running an online shopping mall requires an entirely different approach than opening any kind of store. If you're going to open a mall, you're not in the retail business, you're in the province of property management instead — virtual property, that is. In that case, you're in the B2B (business-to-business) market instead of the B2C (business-to-consumer) line. Shopping malls such as Excite (shopping.excite.com) provide a variety of services to their merchants, ranging from Web design assistance to payment processing (see Figure 19-7).

FIGURE 19-7

The Excite Web site is a major online shopping mall.

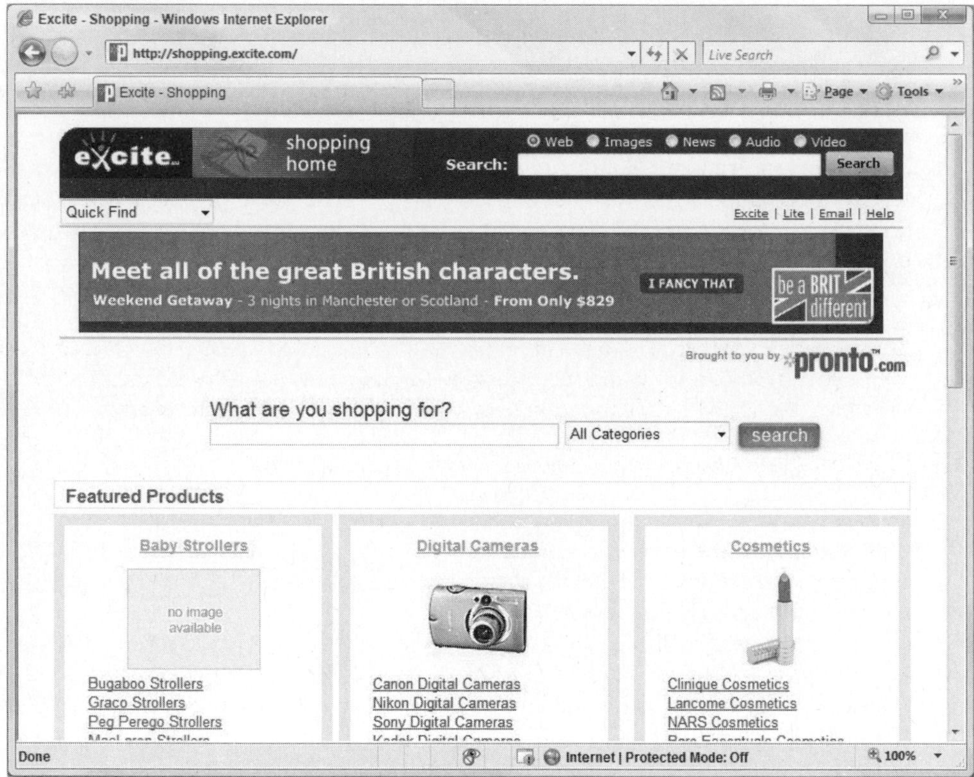

The majority of online shopping malls, however, are really not what you think they are. They are simply sites whose Webmasters have signed up for a vast number of affiliate programs. The "stores" in them are nothing but links to the companies they're affiliated with. So, oftentimes an Internet Mall is not where you would be especially interested in advertising yourself and your business.

Affiliate stores

If you own a Web site that provides information about a specific topic, and you're drawing a steady stream of traffic, an excellent way to augment your income is by setting up an affiliate store that sells products related to your Web site. When you set up an affiliate store, you create links to products at other Web sites. When a visitor from your site purchases a product, you get a percentage of the sale.

NOTE **Affiliate programs offered by retailers and major Web sites can offer you all the tools you need to check sales, market their products, and more. Link Synergy is an example of an aggregator of affiliate programs, and many sites have their own. This helps you make money, and helps the retailer gain recognition and, hopefully, popularity.**

Setting Up Shopping Carts

A *shopping cart* is an interface that enables your customers to choose which products they want to buy. The term is a good one because the analogy to an actual physical shopping cart is quite accurate. You wander up and down the aisles of a physical store, pick up items from the shelves, and drop them into a real shopping cart; then you take the cart to a checkout line and buy the items. Along the way, you may change your mind and remove some items from your cart.

Shopping cart programs work just like that, except that the purchaser is wandering around a Web site instead of a brick-and-mortar store. The shopping cart software uses a combination of Web page forms and a database to keep track of the items a site visitor wants.

CROSS-REF **See Chapter 10 for information on how forms work.**

After you choose the items you want to purchase, you proceed to the checkout. Most online shopping carts use some kind of secure server. This assures the purchaser that the credit card information they're entering online cannot be intercepted by a third party. Other online retailers use services such as PayPal (`www.paypal.com`). This cuts down on the retailer's investment, because the retailer doesn't need to be hosted by a secure server, nor does the retailer need to deal with a bank. PayPal is the secure server, and it takes a cut of the transaction for its services.

Addressing concerns about security

The heart of any transaction on the World Wide Web is security. Without that, your visitors won't want to purchase your product or service from your site. The security is provided, appropriately enough, by a *secure server*, which is simply a Web server that is capable of sending and receiving encrypted information between itself and a Web browser.

If the idea of *digital certificates* (a complex creation of coded information that identifies one entity as opposed to another) is a little intimidating to you, you'll be happy to know that you don't have to set it up yourself. VeriSign (see Figure 19-8) is the best-known issuer of digital certificates. DigiSign, Thawte, and GoDaddy are some other issuers of digital certificates. However, you don't have to arrange to set up your own digital certificate. That's one of those techie details that you can leave up to your Web hosting service. If your provider can't set it up for you, get a new one.

FIGURE 19-8

VeriSign takes care of most of the Web's digital certificates.

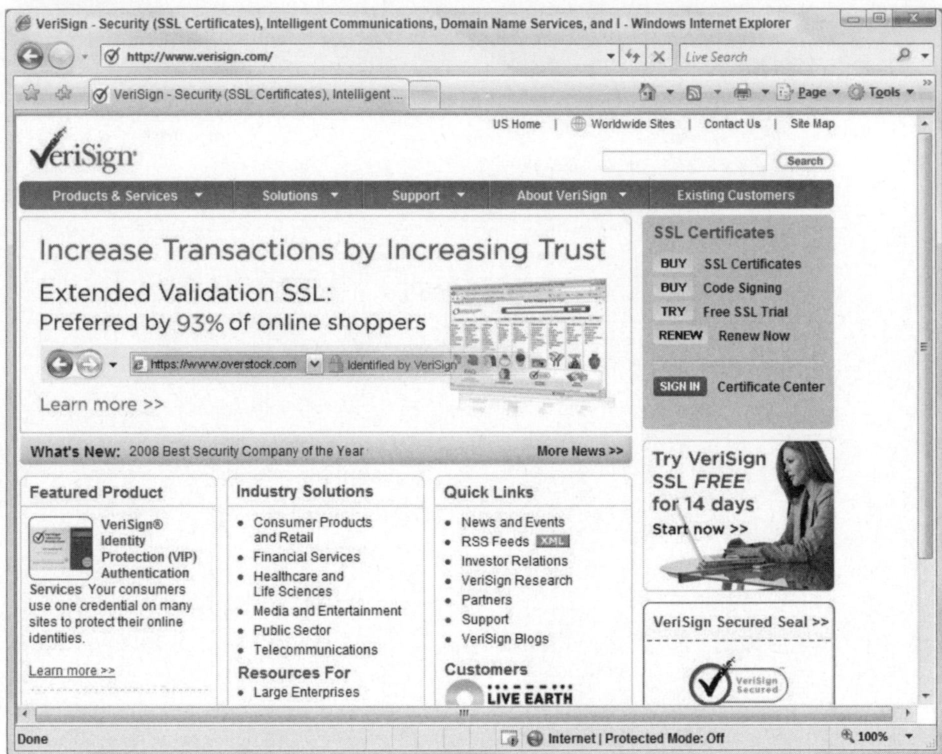

CAUTION **Just because you have a secure server doesn't mean a particular Web page is secure. Your Web site must be configured to use security. A secure connection is designated by the transfer protocol being identified with a URL beginning with HTTPS. The protocol used, Secure Sockets Layer (SSL), enables secure transmission of buyer data across the Internet from a client to a server.**

Joining mall-provided programs

The simplest way to get involved in eCommerce is to join an existing online shopping mall such as Yahoo! Small Business (see Figure 19-9). Each one will have its own software already in place, and all you have to do is upload your own Web pages to be in business. Of course, the mall will want something for its troubles, which means that it will cost you.

However, an online mall receives a lot of traffic — traffic you would have to generate if you set up your online store through your own Web site. Generating Web traffic is an art that online shopping malls have down to a science. If you decide to set up shop in an online shopping mall, you can be assured of getting some traffic.

FIGURE 19-9

Yahoo! Small Business is one of the fastest ways to get an online store up and running.

Check out the details of the agreement carefully. Some malls charge a percentage of sales, others a regular monthly rate. Which one you go for is largely a matter of personal preference, but ensure that you understand exactly what your own obligations are. If you pay a percentage, for example, is there a minimum amount per month? If so, you can find yourself with no sales one month, yet you still owe money for your online presence.

Table 19-1 provides the Internet addresses of several shopping malls.

Getting commercial programs

If you do want to go it alone and set up your own freestanding Web site, you still need a shopping cart. As you might expect, this is a growing market, and the more people become used to dealing with e-commerce, the more choices you're going to have.

Many Web hosting companies can set you up with a shopping cart program. The Web hosting business has become so competitive that companies need to offer additional services to stay in the marketplace, as shown in Figure 19-10.

TABLE 19-1

Online Shopping Malls

Mall	URL
ExciteStores	shopping.excite.com
Point & Shop	www.pointshop.com
MSN	shopping.msn.com
Shopzilla	www.shopzilla.com
Yahoo Shopping	http://shopping.yahoo.com

FIGURE 19-10

Web hosting companies can provide you with an online shopping cart system.

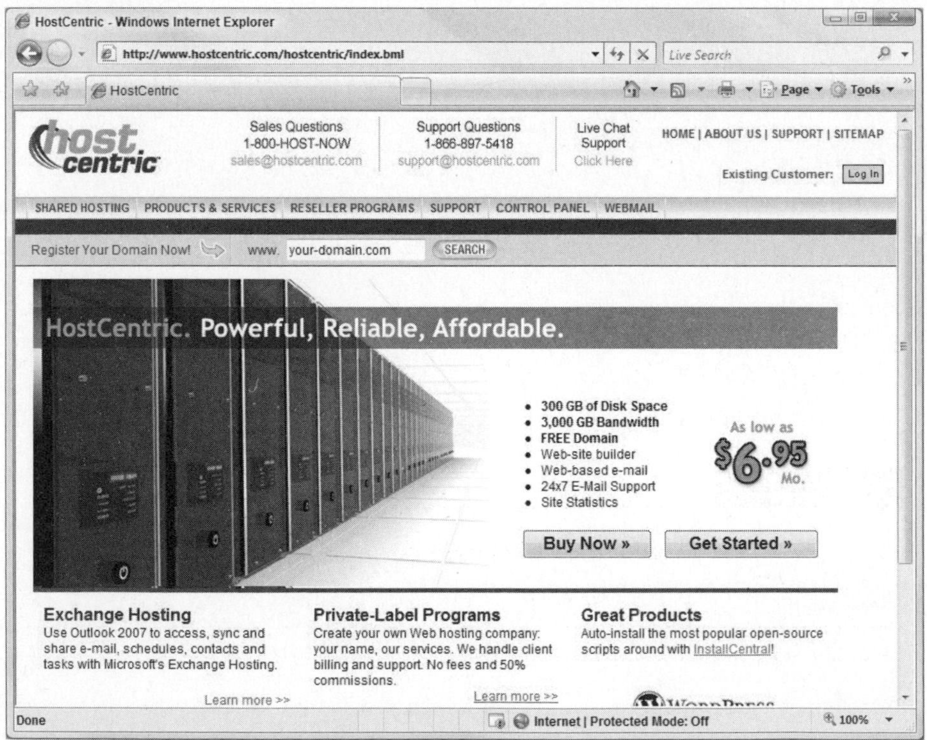

Or, if you prefer, you can get software to set up an online shopping cart at your existing Web site. Table 19-2 provides the URLs of companies that provide shopping cart software.

TABLE 19-2

Commercial Shopping Carts

Software	URL
Americart	www.cartserver.com/americart
Electronic Merchant Systems	www.emscorporate.com
Hypermart	hypermart.net
MerchandiZer eCommerce	merchandizer.com
Miva	miva.com/products
ShopCart	shopcart.com
ShopFactory	shopfactory.com
Yahoo! Small Business	http://smallbusiness.yahoo.com/ecommerce

Some of the companies also provide eCommerce Web hosting.

Using open source programs

Open source software is freely available and often comparable to — or even superior to — similar commercially available programs. Most often, open source programs run on Unix systems and are particularly common for Linux, the Unix-like operating system that is, itself, an open source project (see Figure 19-11).

Table 19-3 gives the addresses of some Web sites where you can find open source shopping carts.

TABLE 19-3

Open Source Shopping Carts

Software	URL
FishCart SQL	fishcart.org
Open Source Shopping Cart	javaboutique.internet.com/articles/shoppingcart
osCommerce	osCommerce.com

FIGURE 19-11

osCommerce is a fine Open Source eCommerce program.

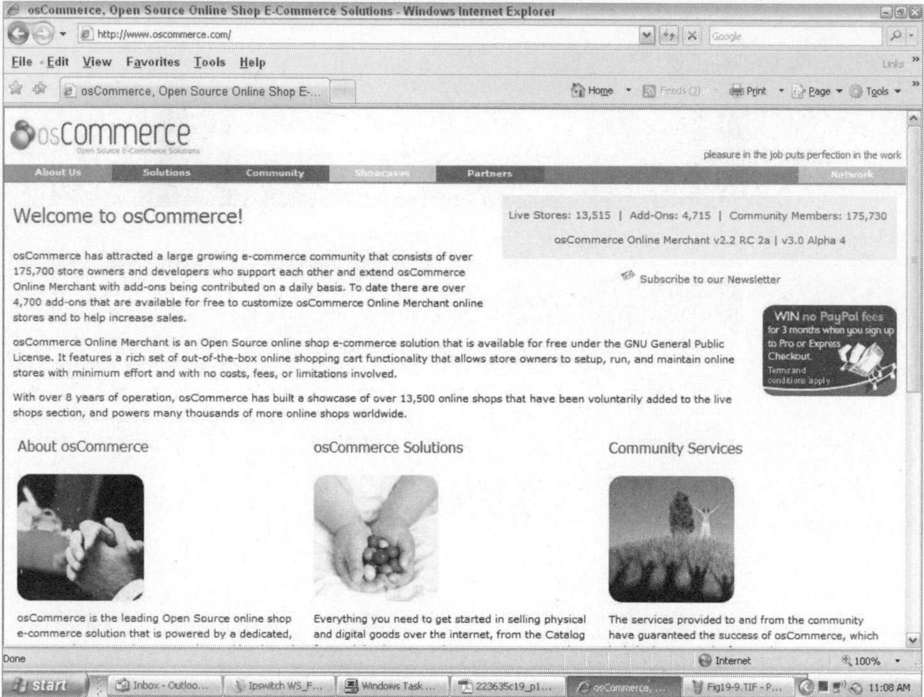

Taking Payments

The obvious difference between eCommerce and a brick-and-mortar store is that you cannot come face to face with your customers. There's just no way in the world that they can hand you cash for what they're buying, so you must have some way of accepting non-cash payments. There are three ways you can get paid: credit and debit cards, checks, and e-cash.

Credit and debit cards

The single most common way of purchasing products on the World Wide Web is with credit cards, as shown in Figure 19-12, although debit cards (the kind used to access ATMs) are gaining significant popularity as well and may soon exceed credit card use. No matter what kind of Web space provision you decide on, the odds are pretty good that the Web hosting service provides credit card acceptance. It's only the purely tech providers who are missing out on the opportunity to grab a few extra bucks by adding basic eCommerce services to their roster.

However, if your Web hosting service doesn't provide credit card acceptance, all you have to do is go to the source. Table 19-4 lists the URLs for the major credit card companies.

FIGURE 19-12

Credit cards are a necessity for any online business.

The sites in Table 19-4 will give you a lot of good information. You can't, however, get the credit card merchant account from the credit card companies themselves (except for American Express). Instead, they'll refer you to an outside company called a *merchant acquirer*, with whom you will actually sign your merchant agreement. Table 19-5 lists several such companies.

TABLE 19-4

Credit Card Companies

Company	URL
American Express	americanexpress.com
Discover Card	discovercard.com
MasterCard International	mastercard.com
VISA International	visa.com

TABLE 19-5

Merchant Account Acquirers

Company	URL
AMS Merchant Account Services	`www.merchant-accounts.com`
Best Payment Solutions	`www.best-payment.com`
Discover Business Services	`www.discoverbiz.com`
ePayment Solutions	`www.epaymentsolutions.com`
EZ Merchant Accounts	`www.ezmerchantaccounts.com`
MerchantAccount.com	`www.merchantaccount.com`
Merchant Systems	`www.merchant-systems.com`
Monster Merchant Account	`www.monstermerchantaccount.com`
PayPal	`www.PayPal.com`
Skipjack Merchant Services	`www.skipjack.com`
Total Merchant Services	`www.totalmerchantservices.com`

When you talk to these merchant acquirers, there are a few details you need to nail down. In a nutshell, they all come under the heading of "how much is this going to cost me?" The answer to that question, however, isn't as simple as you might think. Here are the points you need to cover:

- **Application fee** — Is there a charge for submitting the application form? If so, do you get your money back if the application is denied?
- **Setup fee** — Does it cost you anything for the account to be initiated once you are accepted? What does that fee include?
- **Statement fee** — What is the monthly charge for sending you a statement of your earnings and fees?
- **Discount rate** — This is one of the most important points. The discount is the percentage of your sales that the credit card company will take for its cut. The lower the discount rate is, the better. However, most Internet companies cannot get the kind of low discount rate that conventional companies can. This rate is usually based on your transaction volume.
- **Per-transaction fee** — Is there an additional flat fee that is charged for each transaction? If you sell high-ticket items like customized Ferraris, then the additional amount (maybe 30 to 50 cents) will mean nothing. But you understand why most stores don't

like taking credit cards for low-priced items. Generally, the more transactions you process per month, the lower the fee. The fee structure has to be negotiated, though, so shop around before choosing anyone, and ask any friends who own stores or sites that process credit cards to make sure you're not being scammed.

- **Monthly minimum fee** — If your sales don't take off as anticipated, you may have to pay the credit card company anyway. It's their way of making sure that, no matter what happens to your business, they always have a little something coming in.

NOTE **PayPal now offers a secure API for processing using `xmlHTTPRequest`. Further information on this interface can obtained at `www.paypal.com/IntegrationCenter/ic_nvp.html`.**

Watching out for chargebacks

Sooner or later, you're going to run into some situation in which your happiness over your credit card sale turns into anything from surprise to dismay as the sale goes sour. Your profit drops as you face a *chargeback* — the credit card company taking the money back from you.

There are many possible reasons for a credit card sale to fail; it can even happen if the whole approval process runs smoothly. A cranky customer who didn't read your return policy (or who did, but doesn't want to admit it) writes to MasterCard that you defrauded them and suddenly you have to defend your right to get paid. Another typed in the wrong credit card number and it was charged anyway. Stay in business for a while, and you can write your own list of problems easily enough.

Credit card fraud, however, is the one bugaboo that hits most companies the hardest. It's a multizillion dollar industry, and it's not going to go away. Your merchant account provider will doubtless be fully on your side in helping you to prevent it, but be sure to ask for specifics before you sign anything.

The most important item to have on your side is an *address verification system* (*AVS*). This is a service that compares the address your buyer gave on the order form with the address that the credit card company sends the bills to. If they're not the same, then the chances increase that the credit card is being used by someone other than its owner.

Of course, there are lots of cases where somebody legitimately wants to order something to be sent to a different address. The florist business, for example, would wither overnight if it insisted on delivering roses to your house instead of to your valentine's house. Nonetheless, if you are in a more common line of business, you should consider conflicting addresses to be a red flag. If you are willing to accept shipments to an address other than the billing address, then at least have separate address sections on your order form — one for the shipping address and one for the credit card billing address. That way, you can still run the AVS on the billing address. If it matches, then you may feel a bit easier about shipping to the other address.

Ensure that you follow up on chargebacks quickly. It's sometimes cheaper to give the money back than to challenge the chargeback. Many providers will charge you "extra" if you lose the chargeback claim, and the law is usually on the consumer's side. The extra charges can be $20 or more, so pay attention!

Checks

You can accept checks for your online business in two different ways. The first, of course, is the old-fashioned way: someone simply prints out an order form, fills it in, and mails it along with a paper check. The second possibility is for you to print the check and deposit it just as if it had been sent in the mail. Yes, it's legal — as long as you have the buyer's permission, that is.

If you're not familiar with this approach, take a look at the bottom of the next TV ad that's trying to sell you some fabulous gadget you just can't live without. Somewhere in the payment details, it'll doubtlessly say that you can pay with a check over the telephone. All you have to do is call them up and give them the information on the bottom of your check. This identifies two important things — your bank and the number of your checking account. Armed with that information, a check called a *paper draft* can be created. Checker (see Figure 19-13) is one company that offers software you can use to create paper drafts. Instant Check by EasyDesk Software and Smart Checker are other sources for paper draft software.

Table 19-6 lists sources for paper draft software.

FIGURE 19-13

Checker enables you to create paper drafts that work just like regular checks.

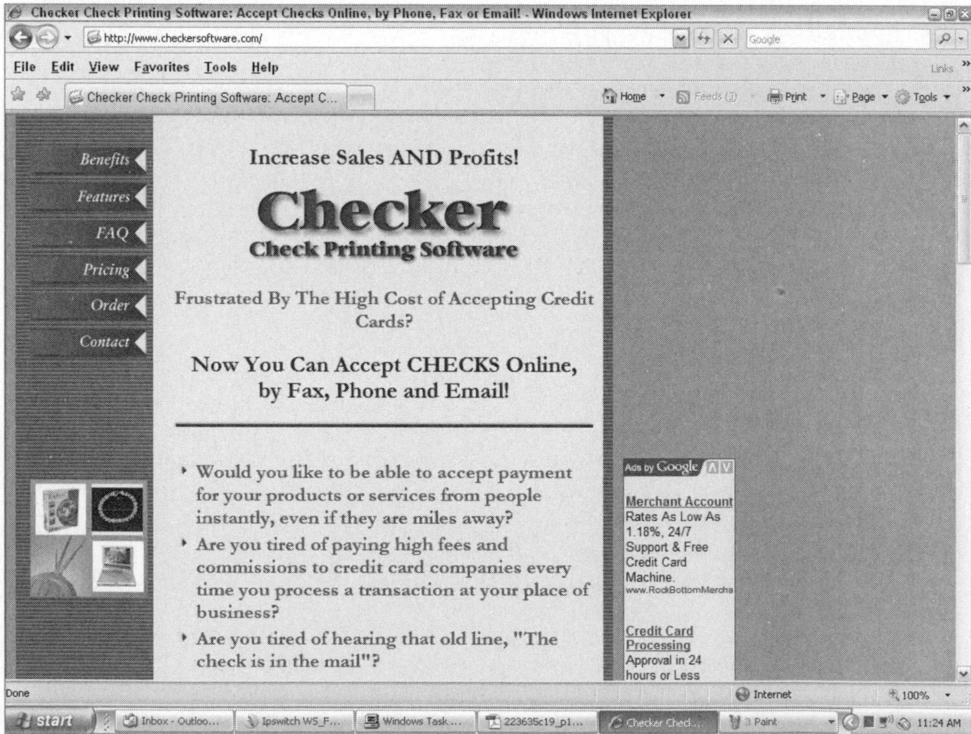

TABLE 19-6

Paper Draft Programs

Program	URL
Checker	www.checkersoftware.com
Draft Creator	www.advancemeants.com/draft
ChecksAndDrafts.com	http://checksanddrafts.zerman.com/
Smart-Checker	www.web-store.net/checker

This may sound scary to you — what's to keep them from whipping up as many checks as they want to and emptying your bank account? That's a good question, and you should carefully consider to whom you give that information. But everyone who ever wrote a check for anything already gave that information to everyone they ever gave or sent a check to. Remember, it's right there for anyone to read. You may want to point this out to your customers if they seem antsy about using the technique.

What's the real value of this capability? Simple — people who don't have credit cards can place an online order just as easily as if they had a wallet full of them.

Overall, though, you may likely not want to do business with people who won't use a credit card. Yes, you can save yourself the credit card processing fee. But that fee pales in comparison to bouncing the check and having to deal with banks and possibly attorneys to get paid. If you do decide to accept checks, it's best to have a policy that the check must clear before the item ships, and that you are allowed to charge the customer a fee if their check bounces. Each state varies when it comes to fees, but know the law and consider carefully your willingness to accept checks.

E-cash

E-cash is one of those ideas that sounds so good, you wonder why it hasn't taken off. In theory, it will one day be fully integrated with the online world. Some day, the visionaries say, your Web browser will interface with your bank account, and everything all along the line will be protected by the same kind of digital certificates that make secure Web servers work. When that day comes, all you will have to do to buy anything on the Web will be to say you want it. The money will be instantly debited, and the merchant will be instantly paid.

The concept, however, is far from a reality for a variety of reasons. First of all, no one can agree on an e-cash standard. In addition, the concept of digital certificates is difficult to get across to the public. Remember, many of the folks who will presumably one day use e-cash are still having trouble navigating a Web browser to the site they want.

Establishing return and refund policies

Before you ever ship your first order, you need to establish (and clearly post on your Web site) your policy regarding returns and refunds. Without it, you're asking for trouble from day one. As a credit card merchant, you have a few things you can do to protect yourself from losses, and this policy is one of the most important, yet often overlooked, ones.

Why? Because if you have a clearly stated (and obviously posted) refund-and-return policy, then the credit card company will abide by those posted rules in handling any complaints that your customers file with them. You can find a good example of a refund and return policy at `www.microcenter.com/how_to_shop/return_policy.html` (see Figure 19-14).

FIGURE 19-14

A clear return and refund policy is essential for a credit card merchant.

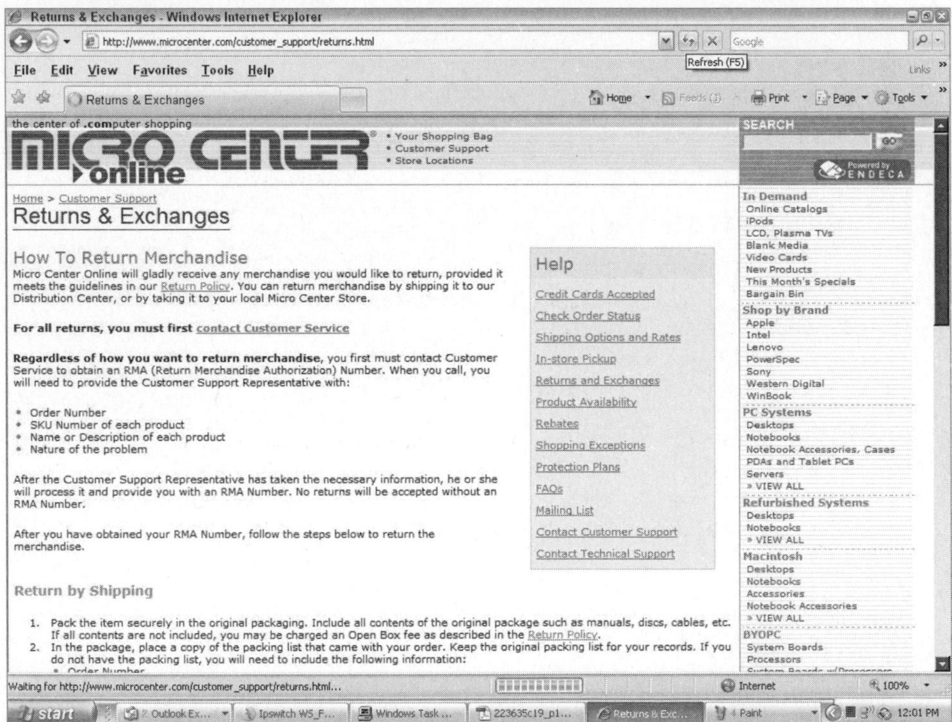

Here are some tips for what to keep in mind while creating your site's refund-and-return policy:

- **Time limits** — You should specify the length of time during which a product may be returned. Is it 30 days, 90 days, a year, a lifetime? Does the time limit vary for particular products or classes of products?

- **Valid reasons** — For what reasons will you accept a return or issue a refund? Are there any special conditions for different products? For example, do you need one policy for electronics and another for housewares?
- **Restocking fees** — Your customers should be aware that any open box may be subject to a restocking fee, often 15 percent. You should not allow returns of software or videos, since customers can buy, copy, and return. If you sell software downloads, you may restrict returns if you've already sent them a product key you can't revoke. Look to other sites, such as `BestBuy.com` and `Amazon.com` to see how they handle returns. They have good reasons behind their policies and are a good model upon which to base yours.
- **Return authorization** — Can your customers just send it back, or do they need to get an authorization form from you for the return? If the latter is the case, then you need to assign responsibility for handling the return approval process. Is it the job of customer service, technical support, accounting, or some other department?
- **Packaging** — If the item has been opened (and that is usually the case), does it have to be returned in its original packaging? What if the UPC code is missing from the box?
- **Documentation** — What proofs of purchase do you accept? If you're dealing solely online, you don't have a signed receipt. Any form of receipt you sent via e-mail, or that the buyer printed out from your Web site, can be easily forged. Therefore, you have to rely on your own sales records for your own protection.
- **Bricks and mortar** — If you operate a conventional, physical store in conjunction with your Web site, does the same policy apply to purchases from both? What about if someone tries to return a product at your store that was purchased from your Web site?
- **Shipping charges** — You need to factor shipping costs into your return calculations. Depending on your product, they may be a serious impediment to the return process. Be sure that you state who pays for what.

CAUTION **There may be specific limitations that apply to you, depending on where you live and what industry you are in. For example, you may find that you have to lengthen your time limit or make exceptions for residents in other states. Check with your lawyer to ensure that the policy you adopt does not violate applicable laws.**

Setting up an affiliate store

The amount of money you can earn with an affiliate store depends on the exact arrangement. Some affiliate programs track how many people visit them from your site and pay per click, just as with banner advertising. Others pay only if your referred visitor actually makes a purchase. Generally, a pay-per-click arrangement doesn't pay very much — pennies at the most. Commissions on purchases, however, can add up to a tidy sum.

How often you get paid also varies widely. Some companies pay monthly, but the vast majority pay quarterly, so you can only expect payment once every three months. And you may not receive a payment then either unless you pass the minimum threshold. Every such program has some minimum amount you must generate in order for them to bother with cutting and mailing a check. Usually, it's a pretty small amount, such as $10 or $20. And, if you're not making that much, you need to take a good, hard look at either the program or your own site, because something's wrong somewhere along the line.

Amazon (`www.amazon.com`) is an excellent example of online merchandise you can use for your affiliate store. To become an Amazon affiliate (see Figure 19-15), you fill out an online form. After your application is accepted, you have access to a section of Amazon's Web site where you set up your links, view traffic from your online store, and view your earning reports. Amazon even has storefronts you can build automatically — check out their aStores at `http://astore.amazon.com`.

FIGURE 19-15

You can become an Amazon Associate by filling out an online form.

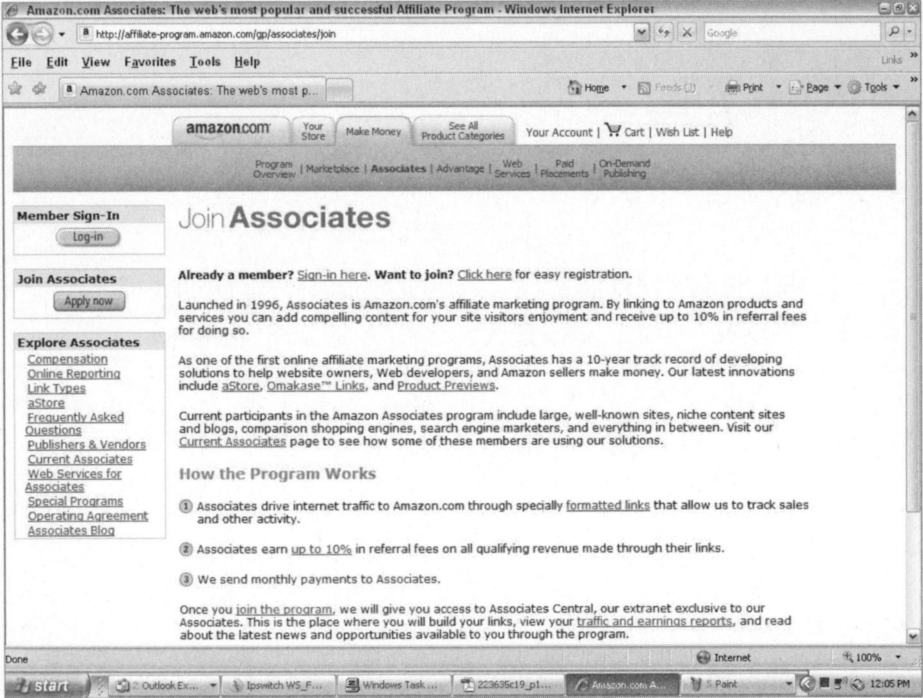

The best way to find out which affiliate program or programs are available is to check out some of the online guides that keep track of the current state of affairs in the affiliate world. Many of them have top 10 lists that tell you which programs are paying the best. Some also have reviews and commentary by people who have used the programs. Most of them also make money by referring you, so be sure to take a good look at several of them and don't just sign up right away with whichever any one site says is best. Table 19-7 lists the URLs of several different affiliate program directory sites.

TABLE 19-7

Affiliate Guides

Company	URL
AffiliateMatch.com	`affiliatematch.com`
ClickQuick.com	`clickquick.com`
ClicksLink.com	`clickslink.com`
Commission Junction	`cj.com`
LinkShare	`linkshare.com`
WebWorkers	`referralincome.com`

Utilizing Internet Buying Patterns

ECommerce began to be taken seriously in 1999, and all signs point to it being a major force in the economy of the twenty-first century. As surely as the sun rises and sets, as surely as spring follows winter, the calendar sets the peaks and valleys of Internet commerce.

Without question, the biggest buying spree on the Internet is during the December holiday season. A great many people leave their holiday shopping to the last minute, and the World Wide Web is the best place for them to get their shopping done. The increase in eCommerce makes it easy to find almost any product online. Buyers also find many unique gifts they could not purchase locally.

As shown in Figure 19-16, ClickZ Network (`www.clickz.com`) is one of the many online marketing firms dealing with eCommerce, and it has observed several interesting patterns developing over the past couple of years.

Table 19-8 shows ClickZ Networks analysis of eCommerce purchasing by quarter since 1999. Notice that online sales have steadily increased and the busiest buying period is the fourth quarter when people do their holiday shopping. In line with this, note that the biggest shopping day of the year is actually the day after Christmas — not Black Friday (the day after Thanksgiving).

It's important, however, to remember that nothing changes faster than the Internet. If you're going to be in business on it, you have to make it your business to keep up to date on the latest facts and figures.

Online purchasing trends as researched at `www.comscore.com` show surging growth in the online retail market with yearly increases of 25 percent through the end of 2005, and projected sales through the fourth quarter of 2007 to $30 billion, a 20 percent increase over the same period for 2006.

FIGURE 19-16

ClickZ Network is an online source of eCommerce data.

TABLE 19-8

Online Purchasing Trends

Sales Period	Total Retail Sales (in Billions)	eCommerce Sales (in Billions)	% of Retail Sales
Q4 1999	$787,212	$ 5,335	0.7%
Q1 2000	$714,561	$ 5,663	0.8%
Q2 2000	$774,677	$ 6,185	0.8%
Q3 2000	$768,139	$ 7,009	0.9%
Q4 2000	$812,809	$ 9,143	1.1%

TABLE 19-8 *(continued)*

Sales Period	Total Retail Sales (in Billions)	eCommerce Sales (in Billions)	% of Retail Sales
Q1 2001	$724,731	$ 7,893	1.1%
Q2 2001	$802,662	$ 7,794	1.0%
Q3 2001	$779,096	$ 7,821	1.0%
Q4 2001	$850,265	$10,755	1.3%
Q1 2002	$738,185	$ 9,549	1.3%
Q2 2002	$814,626	$10,005	1.2%
Q3 2002	$818,061	$10,734	1.3%
Q4 2002	$859,250	$13,999	1.6%
Q1 2003	$767,433	$12,115	1.6%
Q2 2003	$852,760	$12,718	1.5%
Q3 2003	$867,242	$13,651	1.6%
Q4 2003	$912,109	$17,512	1.9%

Updating Your Site

The immediacy of the Internet demands that a site be updated regularly. Creating, publishing, and publicizing a Web site are only the initial steps in the evolution of your site. When customers arrive at your site, they believe that the content is live, meaning that at any moment the site can change to reveal new and engaging content. This belief is impressed upon them by sites such as `CNN.com`, `CNET.com`, eBay, and the thousands of other sites that are driven by rapidly changing content.

Not only must Web sites be prepared for rapidly changing content, but they must also be prepared for rapidly changing technology. Not too long ago, a site would need to leverage HTML and JavaScript in its construction, whereas even more recently HTML 4.0 (HTML, Cascading Style Sheets, and Document Object Model Script) would have been the flavor of code required for the construction of a site. Today, the technologies required for building a site range from HTML 4.01 to Wireless Markup Language (WML) to Extensible Markup Language (XML) to Extensible HTML (XHTML) to the dozens of XML-based languages. The new languages are needed because of the massive deluge of Internet appliances.

Keeping Your Site Fresh

There are a number of ways to provide new and fresh content on a site. One simple approach is to set up a schedule for news releases. Updated material ignites communication between a company or another kind of organization and the customer. As an alternative, a Web site can freshen its content by developing encouraging ways for customers to communicate with each other from the site.

Using incremental uploads

It is better to have no Web site than to have a site that has not been updated. The Internet is littered with tens of thousands of sites that have not been updated for a year or more. Not updating a site for more than a week should be considered a cybercrime. For a high-traffic site, with perhaps a million page views a week, several changes to the front page of the site should be done each and every week.

CAUTION **This applies if your products change often. If you only sell a single product, it's best to ensure that your information is up to date and that it's easy to purchase the product. If you release a new version, yes, update the site. But "tried and true" is good, too. Don't change things just for the sake of change itself.**

Your customers' demands create the need for so many changes to a site. The single reason for the remarkable success of the Internet is that it offers immediate access to knowledge (hence the *information superhighway*). A site that does not provide a customer with the knowledge they are seeking — accurate and updated nearly up to the minute — will not keep that customer.

Information-rich sites, such as `Amazon.com` (`www.amazon.com`), Barnes & Noble (`www.bn.com`), and CNET (`www.cnet.com`), keep and retain loyal customers not because they necessarily offer the lowest prices but because they are able to provide the most information about a product. At `Amazon.com`, a user can read reviews of a book. Barnes & Noble provides free education on literature. CNET offers the most up-to-date information and resources for computer users and people in the computer industry.

The online magazine, Slate (`slate.msn.com`), discovered that the traffic to its site increased when the articles for a month were spread out over the course of a month. Customers could wait a day between fresh articles. But a whole month? It just doesn't work on the Internet. A site must be designed with the capability for easily and quickly inserting fresh content.

Establishing a schedule

An enormous amount of work goes into the creation of a Web site. That's why it's a crime when the owners of a site sit back on their laurels and expect the site to run forever without any changes.

Change is part of the Internet. Thus, change must be part of your site. But unlike change on the Internet as a whole, change on a Web site can be managed. The subject matter and content of a site determines the amount of change.

Often, the key to managing change is to produce a schedule for change. Humans are creatures of habit. If a user knows that a favorite Web site changes content on Monday, the user may make it part of their routine to check the site every Monday. Choosing a schedule is dependent on the type of content on a site; for example, a football site will want to synchronize its schedule with key football games.

In creating a schedule, consider the following questions:

- Do you publish a weekly magazine or newsletter? If you do, break the articles up and publish them to the site during the week.
- Do your customers expect information? Not every site requires daily updates. A company that manufactures zippers may only need to update monthly.
- Is your site linked to time-sensitive material? A site dedicated to a political candidate will host a considerable number of news releases prior to any voting.

Finding new material

With a schedule defined for delivering material, the next challenge is to find the content. Again, the material is going to be strongly defined by the type of site you have developed.

In creating new material, consider what you sell or otherwise provide on your site. Is your site for a manufacturing company, a medical business, or a financial concern? Each type of site has tools, products, and services unique to that business. Examine each product, tool, and service by defining the what, why, where, and how of each. If your company sells financial services, ask these questions for each service. When a customer's question is answered before it can even be asked, the customer's confidence with your product is increased.

A great feature for any site is a "Frequently Asked Questions" (FAQ) section. Ask any help desk or support center for the most popular questions asked by customers. Then, list the most popular questions and place them on the Web site. As the site grows, break down the FAQs for each service or product to increase the knowledge base of each of them.

Having your visitors provide material

Creating and generating new material is time-consuming and expensive. While new material is necessary, a site does not need to rely on itself alone for generating content. Unlike magazines and books, the Internet is computer-driven. With this in mind, savvy sites leverage this power to encourage e-customers to add their two cents to a site.

Companies such as `Amazon.com` and eBay learned early that enabling people to comment on products offered on their site empowers the customer. At `Amazon.com`, a customer doesn't have to rely on a professional book critic's review to judge a book. Amazon enables users to add their own comments to a book review. The customer is empowered to tell the world his or her likes and dislikes about a book. And this encourages other people to join the conversation. Before long, the product on sale is a talking point. Amazon capitalized on the Internet's ability to build a community.

Developing online communities that talk and interact with each is a vital part of the Internet. The single largest Internet activity is e-mail. Why? People want to communicate with each other. Community building can be done on any Web site.

Certainly, an excellent technique is to provide an opportunity for any product sold on the site to be not only a selling point but also a talking point. In many ways, acting as a talking point is a litmus test for any product. If the product really stands up to the sales and marketing, the comments posted will be positive and encourage sales. If the comments are negative, the feedback can be used to enhance the product.

FIGURE 19-17

The power of giving customers a "voice" has driven the success of iVillage.com.

Another way to encourage users to comment on the site is through online chat rooms and bulletin boards. This technology is nothing new and has been proven. Sites such as `iVillage.com`, the Women's Network, have built their entire business around enabling people to meet, talk, and find information on numerous subjects. The success of `iVillage.com` is largely because the categorization of content on its site, as shown in Figure 19-17. Content is not haphazard. Communities are grouped together. In turn, members are encouraged to stay focused on the subject of the specific community's content. For each community, a specific person is assigned as the site's gatekeeper. This person's role is to help keep the conversation moving if it has stalled, to encourage users to stick to the group's topic, and to police unwanted criticism (such as a user verbally attacking other users).

The iVillage technique is very successful and should be employed by other sites. Creating online chats where vice presidents and technologists talk to customers helps reinforce the company image. A customer who knows that he or she can talk directly to the company's president is more likely to be a patron.

Many companies wrestle with the idea of allowing anyone to add comments about its products on its Web sites. Let's face it — no one enjoys getting bad press. A site that manufactures water pumps would not like to see a user complaining that the pumps leak. The result of allowing customers to voice their feelings is generally positive. The value of building a community is only just beginning to be fully realized.

Adding Extra Value

These steps — adding articles to a site and enabling customers to add their own comments — are only the first toward increasing the amount of information a site has available to share with its customers. Successful sites are composed of a slew of tools that are employed to bring customers back to the site over and over again.

Producing newsletters and e-zines

Tools used by many companies, because they are relatively inexpensive, are newsletters and e-zines. Both of these products are essentially the same: information on products and services is sent to customers in an e-mail. While this may sound as if it's *spam* (the Internet equivalent of junk mail), it is not. The difference is that the customer requests the newsletter by filling out a check box on a form (the already notorious "check here to receive more information on our products" check box) or by registering with a site. A user is far more willing to receive e-mail from a company if they have requested it.

Newsletters and e-zines can take many forms. Rich HTML can be used to format the newsletter. But this should be done cautiously. Not all e-mail programs display HTML with images by default, such as Microsoft Outlook, so your e-mail can appear funky when received. The alternative is to use plain text, and although it's not as pretty, it does guarantee that everyone receiving the e-mail can read it. It's always a good idea to give your customers a choice to receive either format.

When creating a newsletter to be sent through e-mail, the only rule to bear in mind is to keep it brief. The average Internet customer receives 25 to 100 e-mails a day. No one has time to read through lengthy newsletters. Indeed, many readers may give up after the first few paragraphs, the first page as viewed on a normal computer screen. If you have important information, place it at the top of the letter.

Successful newsletters from companies such as DevX, RealNetworks, and BusinessWeek are used as tools to drive users back to the sites. The newsletter may contain news information, stock quotes, or press releases, but the intent is to get users to the sites to begin viewing advertisements or buying.

All articles in a newsletter should be very short — one to three paragraphs. If an article is longer than that, provide a link back to the main site for the full article. Important product news (such as a recall or news release) should be placed as the first article. The next article in the newsletter should be related to the main article, but with a twist. For example, the main article may be for a new car, whereas the second article can discuss the fuel savings of the new car. The third article should be part of some sort of series. For example, the third article for a car newsletter could be a series focused on maintenance.

The idea is to create a consistent format that customers come to expect. Creating newsletters that change format with each issue only frustrates the reader and drives them away from future newsletters.

Newsletters are a great way to get product information placed in your customer's Inbox. It also allows for the timely dissemination of information to customers, instead of relying on them to come to your site.

Writing product reviews

Whether it is a product or a service, the single driving need for almost every Web site is to sell, sell, sell.

The Web is unparalleled in its ability to reach and deliver to an enormously diverse range of customers. With this in mind, customers coming to your site expect to find product and service information that is fresh and up to date. Generally, customers search a company's site to obtain information on a product before making a purchase. This is particularly true of big-ticket items such as TVs, game systems, motorbikes, cars, and trucks. By providing timely, accurate, and concise information, they allow the customers to make an informed decision about a product before they enter the showroom. Indeed, when an informed customer arrives at a showroom to make a purchase, the sale is made much faster.

Perhaps nothing is more infuriating to a consumer than arriving at a site to find old, outdated information. This drives customers away. To ensure that a product is given proper visibility, work with a launch schedule, such as the following:

- Understand the product or service being launched.
- Create press releases for the new product.
- Leverage the content of the press release on the company Web site.
- Create a section on the site for the new product (the larger the product, the larger the section).
- Create a newsletter to be delivered through e-mail informing customers of the new product and providing a link directly to the site, where they can read additional information about the product.

By defining a new product launch schedule, a process is created whereby the Internet site is part and parcel of the whole advertising process.

Creating tutorials

Offering online education is an emerging technique being employed to keep customers coming back to a site. Today, many products (especially software) are complicated. Meanwhile, other products (such as books) are not necessarily complicated, but they still require interpretation. Online tutorials and classes are a great vehicle to further extend the customer relationship. In providing training, your company is extending a hand to your customers to enable them to become product specialists.

One company heavily involved in online training is Microsoft, which provides online tutorials and demos for its vast range of software products for its professional and home clientele. If you want to learn about an Office application (for example, Access), you can go to `office.microsoft.com/en-us/training`. Many other businesses provide training for their products online, and there are several organizations that exist primarily to only offer training online (one example being e-learning center).

This form of training or education is now being referred to as *edutainment*. The education is an extension of the site's traditional services. One goal of edutainment is to keep customers at the site longer so they have the opportunity to make additional purchases.

Summary

Many people see eCommerce as the most important aspect of the World Wide Web. It promises to revolutionize marketing. Your Web site needs updating in two ways. First, the content must be kept fresh. Second, the technology must keep pace.

In this chapter, you learned how the type of product or service you offer will determine the kind of Web site you need to present it. Shopping carts are software designed to enable your site's visitors to browse and purchase whatever you're selling.

You learned that Web hosting services can provide eCommerce solutions. Affiliate programs make it possible to sell products online without maintaining an inventory.

Credit cards are the most common form of payment on the World Wide Web. Paper drafts enable you to take checks instead of credit cards via your Web site.

This chapter showed how you need to establish a routine schedule for updating material such as product information and articles. Invite your visitors to participate in providing material. Opt-in e-zines are a great way to keep in touch with your site visitors and build community.

Chapter 20 discusses ways to incorporate advertising into your Web site.

Chapter 20

Using Advertising

IN THIS CHAPTER

- Advertising with Google and other search engines
- Working with advertisement agencies
- Promoting your site
- Exploiting search engines
- Working the Web directories
- Issuing press releases
- Setting up reciprocal links
- Evaluating banner exchanges
- Investigating alternative approaches

If you're serious about marketing online, you may want to consider advertising. When you advertise online, you reach out and contact more potential buyers or clients. You have various options for advertising online. You can pay a fee to search engines to boost your visibility when visitors search using keywords related to your product or service. In addition to advertising online, you can work with online marketing firms to enhance your visibility on the Net.

Advertising with Google and Other Search Engines

As of this writing, Google is undoubtedly the most widely used search engine. It's used by a wide variety of people from all over the world. The search engine is very user-friendly and delivers accurate results. As an Internet entrepreneur, you can significantly increase your chances of success by advertising with a search engine. In the following sections, you'll learn how to advertise your business using Google and other search engines.

Advertising with Google

When a user types a keyword or key phrase into the Google search engine, relevant results appear quickly. The top results (descriptions and URLs for Web pages) for the keyword or key phrase appear on the first search results page, and subsequent search results pages contain less relevant hits. As shown in Figure 20-1, the right border of Google's search engine results contains sponsored links from paid advertisers.

FIGURE 20-1

Paid advertisers appear on the right side of a Google search results page.

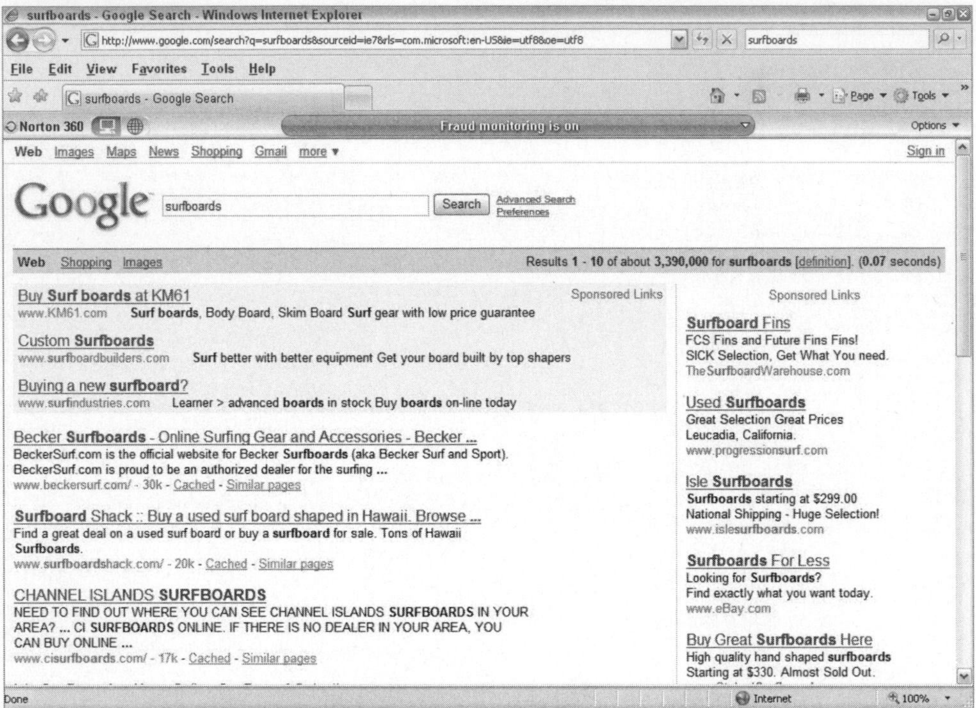

You can add your Web site to Google's sponsored links by using a service known as Google AdWords. When you use this service, you create your own ads and choose keywords to match your advertisement with potential buyers of your services or products.

The one-time activation fee for new advertisers to set up a Google AdWords account is $5.00. It takes approximately 15 minutes to set up a Google AdWords account. To set up a Google account with help from a guided tutorial, navigate to `https://adwords.google.com/select/login` and click the Start Now button, as shown in Figure 20-2. Clicking this button will take you to a dialog box that asks you to select either the Starter Edition or Standard Edition of AdWords. If you do not yet have a Web page created, or if you are new to Internet advertising, you should select the Starter Edition.

Should you elect to continue on from this screen, you will be brought to the first of several screens that will lead you through the many components of the process. This first screen will have several options that allow you to choose languages and currencies of your target customers.

However, we would strongly suggest that, before you go through all the steps of the sign-up process, you should first take a few minutes of your valuable time to view the sign-up demo at http://services.google.com/tutorial/awsignup/awsignup.html. It will be time well-spent.

FIGURE 20-2

The AdWords home page provides a link to a step-by-step sign-up tutorial.

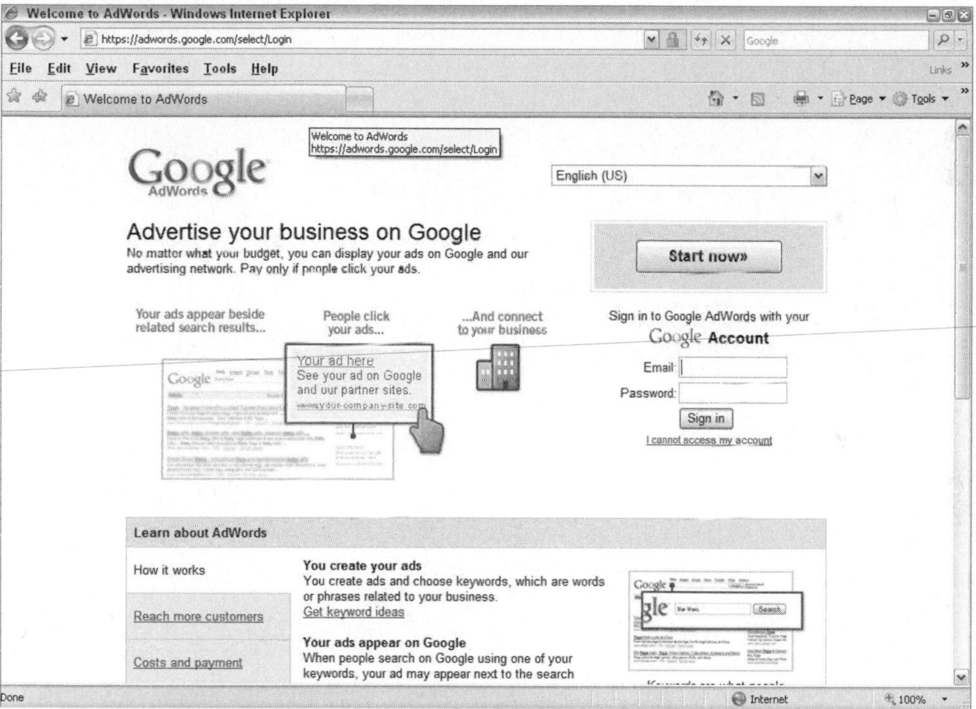

The sign-up process is explained in a series of four major steps, and Figure 20-3 shows this on the Sign-up Demo screen. Following are the four steps:

1. Choose target languages and countries.
2. Create ad groups.
3. Set your daily budget.
4. Create your account.

FIGURE 20-3

You can use the AdWords Guided Tour to sign up for an AdWords account.

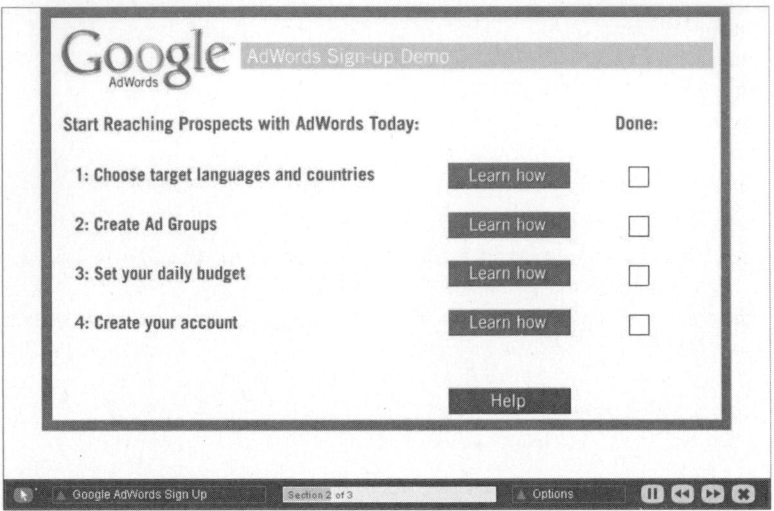

FIGURE 20-4

Your first step is to choose your target language and country.

The following explains the process in detail:

1. To begin the sign-up process, click the Learn How button for Step 1 to launch the Step 1 animated tutorial. (The lower portion of the screen is shown in Figure 20-4.) The tutorial explains all the intricacies of choosing the target language and country for your Google ad. During this step, you'll choose your target language and the country in which your Google advertisement will be displayed. If you're targeting multiple languages, you must create a different advertisement for each language, and the advertisement must be written in the language you are targeting. After the tutorial for the first step finishes, you'll be prompted to go to a URL (`https://adwords.google.com`), where you'll complete Step 1.
2. After selecting your target language and region, return to the tutorial and click the Learn How button for Step 2 to launch the Step 2 tutorial. In Step 2, you create your advertisement group and choose your keywords (Figure 20-5). When you name the advertisement group and create the ad, think outside of the box and consider what would make a potential customer click the link to view your Web site and potentially purchase your products. After viewing the tutorial, you're prompted to create your advertisement and to choose your keywords.

FIGURE 20-5

Your second step is to choose keywords.

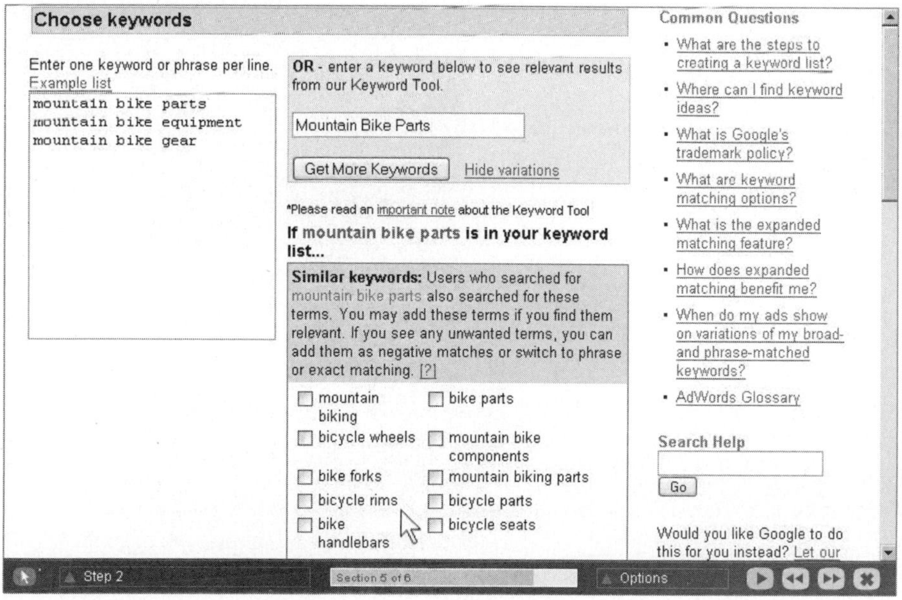

3. After choosing your keywords and maximum cost per click, return to the tutorial and click the Learn How button for Step 3 to launch the Step 3 tutorial. Step 3 is basically concerned with pricing issues and, in this step, you'll also learn how to set the maximum amount you want to spend, which helps you control your advertising budget. Google doesn't require a maximum or minimum advertising budget. You determine the amount you want to spend per month, divide it by 30, and enter that figure for your maximum daily budget (Figure 20-6). During this step, Google also makes a recommendation for a daily budget based upon estimated traffic. This budget is determined in part by the keywords you use to drive traffic to your site. If you decide to accept Google's recommended budget and find it isn't right for your business, you can change it (or a budget you specify) at any time. The purpose of the daily budget, whether you customize it or leave it largely in AdWords metaphoric hands, is to give you the immediate tools to gain and maintain control of your advertising costs. After finishing Step 3 of the Sign-up Demo, you establish your own pricing before returning to Step 4 of the tutorial.

FIGURE 20-6

Setting your AdWords budget is the third step in the process.

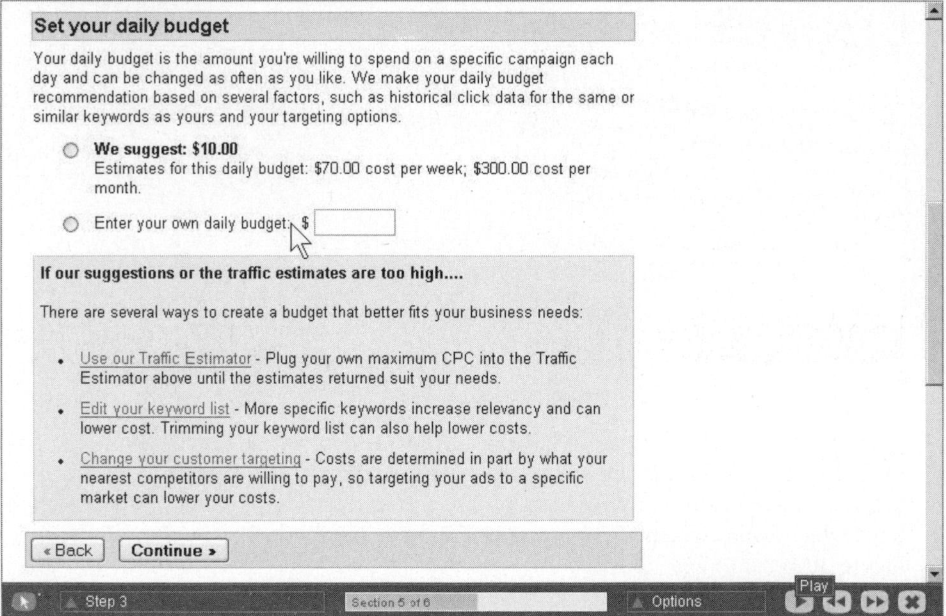

4. Click the Learn How button for Step 4 to launch the Step 4 tutorial. In Step 4, you review your settings before creating your account. You set up your e-mail account and verify your username and password (Figure 20-7). Ensure that you access e-mail often,

for you will use it to conduct business with your customers. After you have created your account, and have verified your email address, be sure to set up billing information for your clients who will soon be visiting your newly established AdWords account to make purchases.

That's all there is to it!

FIGURE 20-7

Create your AdWords account.

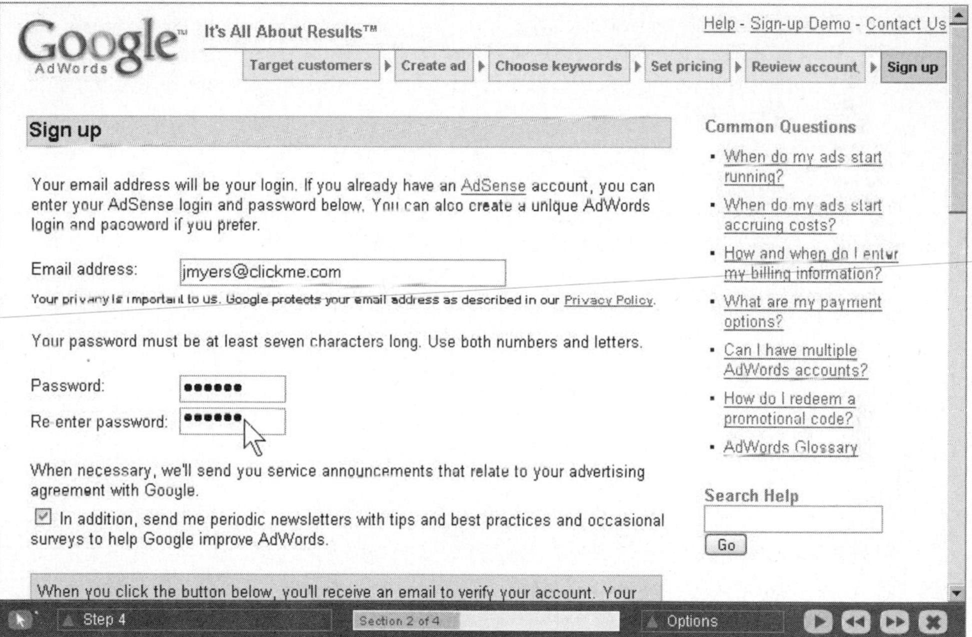

After setting up the AdWords account, Google will send you an e-mail asking you to confirm the account by clicking a link within the e-mail. After that step, your account is active and ready to reach thousands of potential buyers. At the end of the tutorial, you'll see a page that lists links which you can refer to for additional information and help on your AdWords account (see Figure 20-8).

After you set up a Google AdWords account, you can monitor the account to see how much the advertisement is actually costing you, how many click-throughs your advertisement is generating, cost per click, and so on. Figure 20-9 shows sample statistics for an account with three campaigns.

FIGURE 20-8

You can browse additional links for help on setting up and managing your AdWords account.

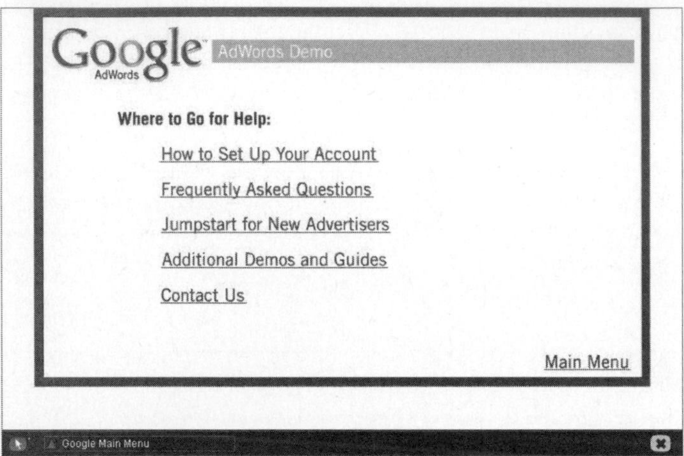

FIGURE 20-9

This figure shows a sample AdWords account with three campaigns.

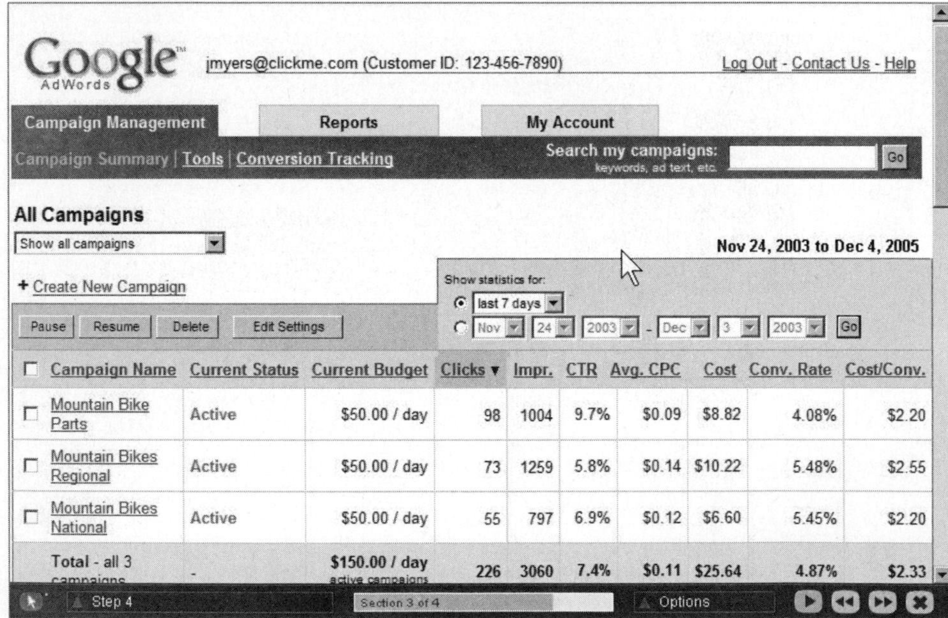

Advertising with other search engines

Google is not the only search engine where you can pay to have your site turn up in a search results page. Many major search engines offer this service. The majority of these are pay-per-click ads, and the sign-up process is similar to Google. Different search engines have different criteria for the manner in which they return results. If a search engine continually returns Web sites that feature services or products similar to those that you're marketing, it may be advisable for you to advertise with that search engine.

Yahoo (`www.yahoo.com`) is an example of a major search engine where you can advertise your site on a pay-per-click basis. To advertise with Yahoo, go to the search engine marketing site at `sem.smallbusiness.yahoo.com/searchenginemarketing` (as shown in Figure 20-10) and follow the prompts to set up an account.

FIGURE 20-10

You can set up pay-per-click advertising at the Yahoo Search Engine Marketing site.

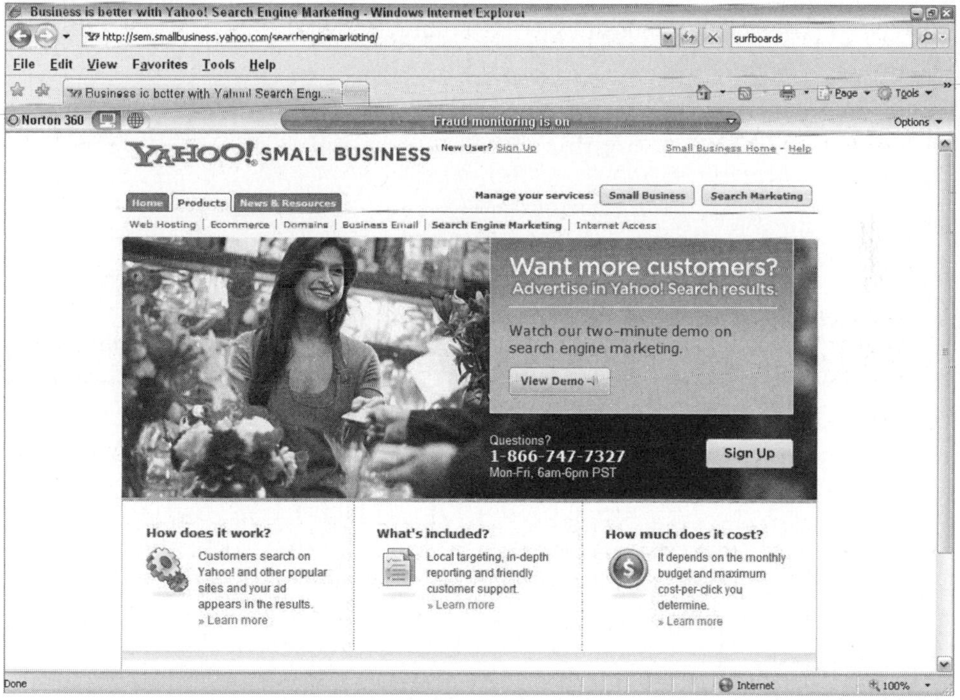

Table 20-1 provides an overview of major search engines that accept advertising. This is an area that changes with breathtaking speed. Overture and its resources and products have migrated to searchMarketing. Another great site is Microsoft Live Search (also listed in Table 20-1), which provides a variety of services for you to drive business to your content.

TABLE 20-1

Search Engines that Accept Advertising

Search Engine	URL
About	`www.about.com`
Ask	`www.ask.com`
Google	`www.google.com`
Search Europe	`www.searcheurope.com`
Yahoo!	`www.yahoo.com`
Microsoft Live Search	`www.live.com`
Search Marketing	`searchmarketing.yahoo.com`

Each search engine company has its own policy and requirements. You can find additional information by navigating to the home page of the search engine you're interested in advertising with, and clicking the site's Advertise link.

Advertising with banners

In addition to vaulting your Web site to a position of prominence by advertising with a search engine on a pay-per-click basis, you can also advertise with banners. You can advertise with a banner exchange (see Figure 20-11), a service where you agree to post banners from other Web sites on your Web site, and your banner is displayed on other Web sites within the exchange. This form of banner advertising can be effective. However, you are advised to check into any free banner exchange. Remember: "There are no free lunches."

If you opt to use a free banner exchange, you may find yourself promoting other people's services without getting much in return because the Web sites in the banner exchange don't get much traffic. When you research a banner exchange, consider the quality of the Web sites participating in the banner exchange and the products they offer. Also consider whether or not you really want to advertise the products offered by the other banner exchange participants. If possible, contact other banner exchange participants to see if they are satisfied with the service.

Other Web sites will require you to pay to display a banner on their sites. The cost of the banner depends on the prominence of the site and the page in the site on which you choose to display your banner. Frequency will also determine the cost of your banner ad. Many popular Web sites, such as `MSN.com`, are divided into sections by interest group. You can target a specific section of sites like this to maximize the impact of your banner ad.

FIGURE 20-11

You can promote your Web site by using a banner exchange.

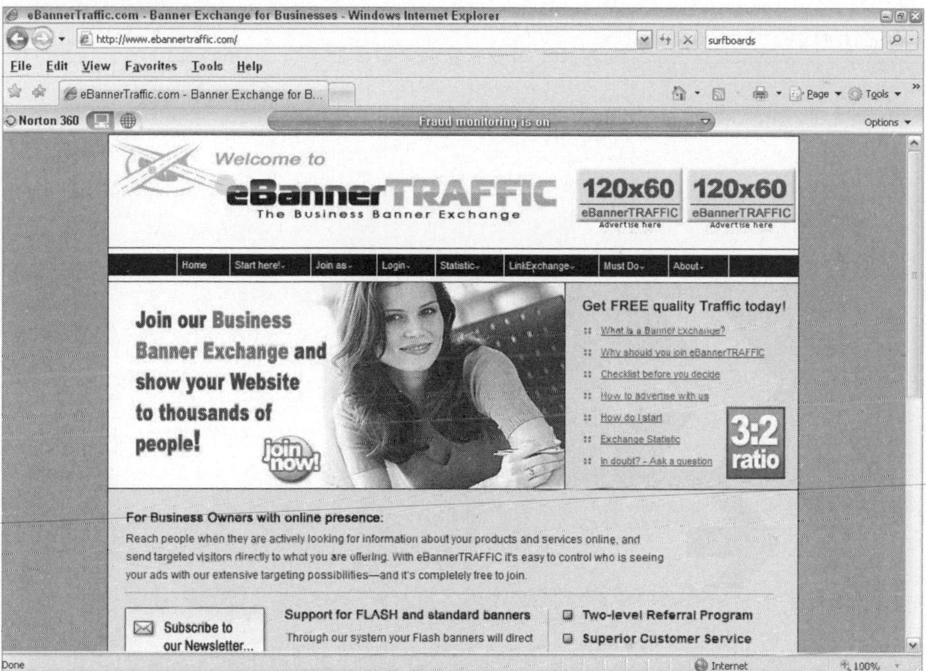

Working with Advertisement Agencies

An Internet business is no different than its brick-and-mortar equivalent. As such, you can grow your business by being a savvy marketer. However, when you're just beginning, or your business has grown to the point where you don't have time to concern yourself with marketing, it may be in your best interest to employ professionals — an advertisement agency that specializes in promoting Internet businesses.

Finding an Internet advertisement agency

The easiest way to find an Internet advertisement agency is to do a search in your favorite search engine. You'll find plenty of candidates from which to choose. In fact, the sheer quantity of returns you get from a search engine query may be quite intimidating — so many agencies and so little time.

The type of services offered by Internet advertisement agencies vary widely. You'll find agencies that do little more than optimize your site for a search engine and then submit it, as well as full-fledged agencies that will do the aforementioned and provide other services such as banner creation, banner advertisement serving, e-mail marketing, and more. Figure 20-12 shows a listing of Internet advertisement agencies at one Web site.

FIGURE 20-12

You'll find a wide variety of Internet advertisement agencies from which to choose.

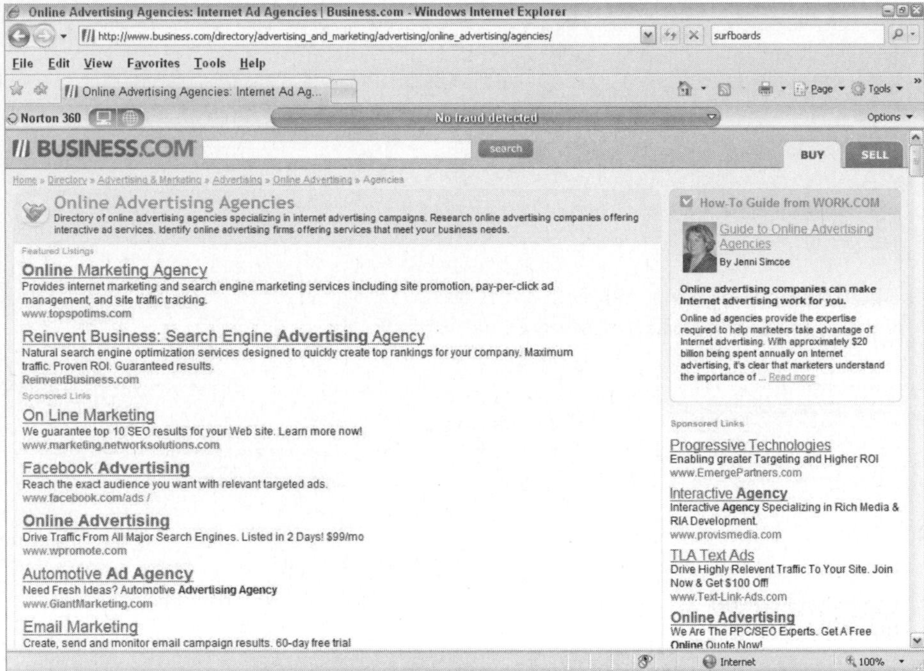

When you peruse the Web sites of online advertisement agencies, here are a few things to consider:

- Does the Web site look professional?
- What services does the agency offer?
- Does the agency list any case studies?
- Are there testimonials from satisfied clients? If so, does the agency provide links or contact information of the satisfied client? Can you contact the satisfied client?
- Does the site offer an FAQ page?

- Does the site list information about the representatives and key personnel? (This attention to detail is the sign of a professional agency.)
- Does the site have a contact page? If so, is the contact through e-mail only, or can you talk to a representative?

CAUTION **If an advertisement agency lists only e-mail contact information, proceed with caution. If you do contact an advertisement agency with e-mail-only contact, and you don't get a response within an hour or two, move on to another agency. We prefer phone contact because you can get immediate answers and size up the representative by his or her knowledge and tone of voice.**

Working with affiliates

Another alternative you may consider is *affiliate marketing*, which is the practice of sharing revenue among multiple Web sites. When you join a group of affiliates, you create links to the affiliate sites. The link coding tells the affiliate from which site the click-through came. Affiliates are paid on a per-click basis.

Another form of affiliate marketing is an online catalog where you feature merchandise that you do not inventory. When a visitor to your Web site orders a product, the product is shipped from the affiliate marketer and you get a percentage of the sale. `Amazon.com` is an example of an affiliate marketer. The coding in the link informs `Amazon.com` which affiliate merchant generated the sale. Payment for an affiliate marketer varies, depending on the company with whom you are affiliating. As a rule, payment is not issued until the affiliate has accrued a certain dollar amount. Payments are generally issued per quarter.

Table 20-2 shows the name and URLs of some Internet affiliate marketing companies.

TABLE 20-2

Internet Affiliate Marketing Companies

Marketing Company	Web site
BBL Internet Media	`www.bblmedia.com`
Affiliates World	`www.affiliates-world.com`
Affiliate Manager Guide	`www.affiliatemanager.net`
Leadhound Network	`www.leadhound.com`
Clix Galore	`www.clixgalore.com`
Share A Sale	`www.zyra.net/sharsal.htm`
Associate Programs	`www.associateprograms.com`

Before investing time and energy in any affiliate program, research the program thoroughly. Use the same criteria listed in the section, "Finding an Internet advertisement agency," earlier in this chapter to determine if the affiliate program suits your needs.

Promoting Your Site

So, you have developed a Web site that is rich in content, interactivity, and chock-full of information and ways to link like-minded people together. But no one is coming to your site. The Web has some 1 billion, 350 million sites. And all these sites are pushing their content hard. But what do you have to do to attract visitors? Do you have to heavily promote your site?

Savvy sites employ a multitude of popular services to drive users to their sites. From search engines to ad banners to e-mails, cleverly used services can drive customers to any site no matter how large or small.

The most popular service used is a search engine, such as Google, where a customer can search a term and bring up a list of sites that meet the criteria. Web directories, such as Yahoo!, are similar in concept to search engines.

E-mail is often a more focused method of distributing information. Though often lambasted in the press as *spam*, the door-to-door salesperson of the Internet, the clever use of e-mail can often yield higher traffic *click-throughs* (the term for driving a user to a site) than any other online marketing tool. Along with e-mail, an equally rich method for driving visitors to a site is the use of banners. Thoughtfully designed banners that work in conjunction with banner exchanges — large groups of users who share ad space with each other — can provide a cost-effective and statistically accurate vehicle for driving sales. In the last couple of years, online ads have matured. This has enabled the technology to increase its effectiveness.

As an old fortune cookie predicts, "The man who shouts from the top of the tree gets heard."

Exploiting Search Engines

Search engines have enjoyed a long history on the Internet. Search engines such as AOL, Lycos, WebCrawler, and DogPile have been part of the Internet since the mid-1990s, although MSN, Yahoo!, and Google have certainly come out on top.

A *search engine* is a site that enables a user to search for information by entering a term, clicking a button, and querying a database containing information on millions of Web sites to return a page of results in response to the query. Search engines immediately attract new Internet users for one simple reason: It is easy to find any Web site within a click or two.

Although Google is by far and away the largest with close to 50 percent market share (according to the latest Nielsen ratings of search engines), some of the earlier ones, such as Lycos (see Figure 20-13), Excite, and DogPile, are still, almost invisibly, on the market.

Lycos was one of the first search engines. The site now serves as a springboard to the Web.

FIGURE 20-13

Lycos search site is still in operation.

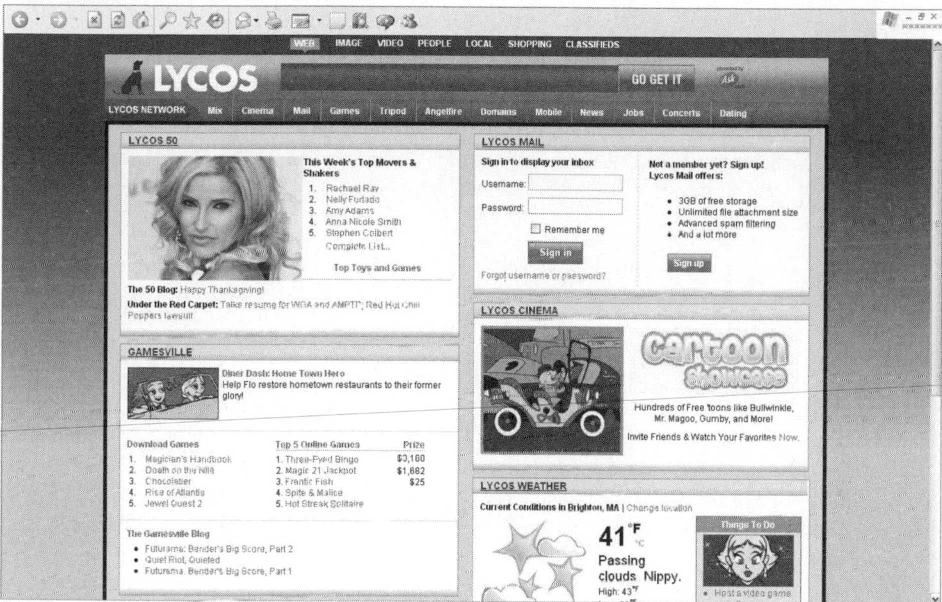

Search engines are designed to be central aggregations of content. Most users, looking for information, start with search engines. Users search topics ranging from "brain surgery" to "VCR repair" to "Ritz crackers" (yes, thousands of Web sites are dedicated to the noble cracker).

A search engine works by taking pieces of information on Web sites and storing them in a massive database. When a search is performed, the submitted search words are sent to the database which returns a set of records matching the user's request, and generates a results page.

The information in the search engine database is collected by software called *robots* and *spiders*. The robots and spiders move throughout the Web from hypertext links on Web pages and return formatted information from these sites to the main search engine. The end result of this sort of action is information like that shown in Figure 20-14.

NOTE **Typically, only 10 to 20 Web pages are listed on the initial results page for a search engine. The trick is to ensure that your site makes the initial results list!**

FIGURE 20-14

Lycos results page results from robots and spiders moving through the Web.

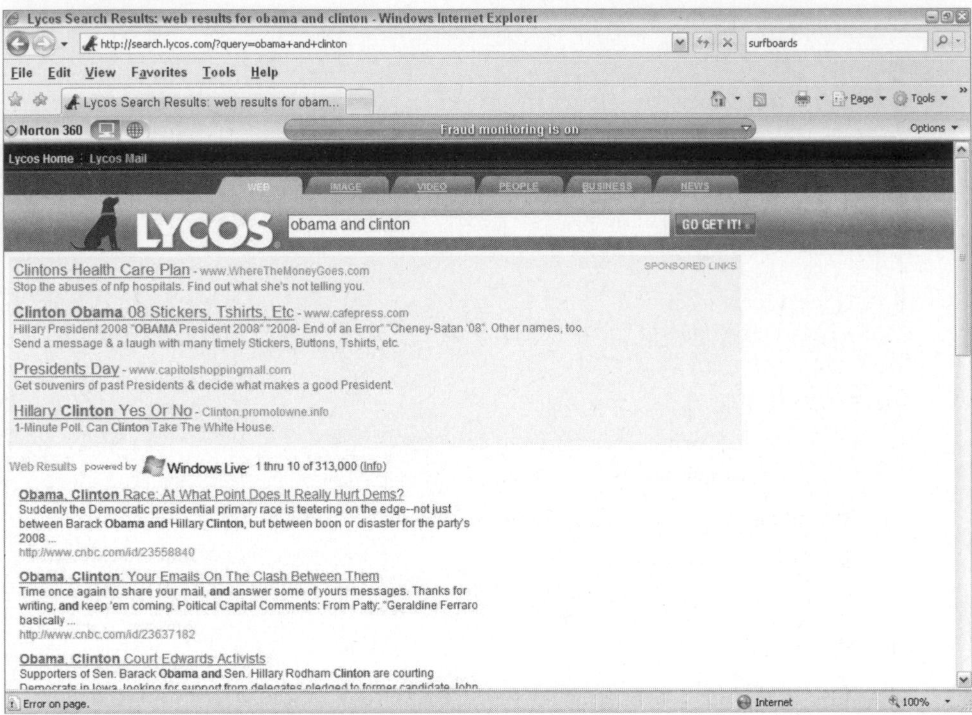

Search engines share these commonalities:

- A link to a Web site that contains the searched word
- A description of the site
- The full URL to the Web site that has been returned

In a sweeping glance, a user can look down the list of results and click the link that makes sense. Brief information is the key. If your site is listed but does not accurately define what your site is about, a customer may potentially pass over your listing.

Each piece of information that is delivered in the results page is critical. The link must be meaningful, the description must be detailed, and the name of the Web site must be easy to remember.

Understanding robots and spiders

A search engine works by cataloging information contained on Web sites throughout the entire World Wide Web. Search engines cannot catalog in detail all of the information on each and every site because of the massive amounts of data this would create. Search engines rely on software programs called *robots* or *spiders* that are launched onto the Web. Robots follow URLs from one Web page to another, cataloging key information about each page. This information is sent back to the main search database.

If a robot or spider has not investigated your site, you will not be in the search database. A robot can be forced to visit your site by completing a registration form with a search engine.

To determine whether your site has been visited by a search engine's robot, you will need to do some digging around. Each and every Web server maintains a set of records called *logs*, which provide rich data about the type of people visiting your site. You can ascertain what type of Web browser a user has, how long they stayed at your site, and where the user came from. Logs also show if a robot or spider has been to your site. Software such as WebTrends can analyze Web server logs to see if a robot has visited a Web site.

Robots are always searching Web sites. If a robot visits your site, many methods are available to ensure that a large amount of information about your site is exchanged with the robot.

Submitting your site

All search engines require that a form be completed before a search is done. Each search engine has its own form. The following is a list of links to some search engines:

- *All the Web* — `www.alltheweb.com/help/webmaster/submit_site`
- *Ineedhits* — `www.ineedhits.com/submission/submissionservices.aspx`
- *Excite* — `https://client.enhance.com/ols/index.do`
- *Google* — `www.google.com/addurl.html`
- *Search Europe* — `www.searcheurope.com/submit`
- *Gigablast* — `http://www.gigablast.com/index.php?page=about&subPage=addUrl`
- *Yahoo!* — `http://siteexplorer.search.yahoo.com/submit`
- *Microsoft* — `http://search.msn.com/docs/submit.aspx`

Going to each of these pages requires that a comprehensive registration form for each site be completed. This can be labor-intensive.

Keeping your site searchable

Robots search for key information about a Web site. The search engine uses this information to categorize your site, to determine how to display the site in the results page, and to seduce the customer into clicking through to the site.

Within the HTML on any Web site, you can add code to help make the site more search-friendly. The primary areas investigated by crawling robots and spiders are as follows:

- `<title>` tag
- `<meta>` tags
- `<alt>` tag

TITLE

In many ways, the most important tag on any page is the <title> tag that appears at the top of each page. This tag is located within the HEAD section of the HTML page. It appears like this:

```
<html>
<head>
<title>This is where the Title for the Web Page is placed.</title>
</head>
```

The <title> tag is very important because when a search engine displays a results page the text in the <title> tag is used as the link to your Web site. The link on the results page is underlined, which draws attention to it. Generally, a user glances down a list of highlighted links and chooses the most meaningful link.

When giving a page a title, consider the content on the page. If the page is the front page to a site, do not call it <title>Home</title>. Add more meaning to the title such as the following:

```
<TITLE>Company XYZ Home: Where you will find the best
plumbing</TITLE>
```

This title now tells the user about the company name, where the page is, and a little about what the company sells.

The title for a page does have some limitations. HTML cannot be used to format the text. Wrapping a company name with <b> tags to bold the text does not work. On the flip side of the coin, special characters such as ? (question mark), * (asterisk), # (pound), and ! (exclamation mark) can be used. Some sites go to great lengths to use these characters to differentiate their titles from other sites. For example, the following will work:

```
<title>^^^ --!STOP! CLICK THIS LINK FOR SUPER SALES! OR CALL MORTY @
555 1212-^^^</title>
```

Small amounts of extra information can make the difference between a user clicking through and ignoring the link.

META

<meta> tags are a great tool for fine-tuning how the results page will display a site. As with the <title> tag, <meta> tags are designed for multiple purposes, but their most common purpose is to provide information about a site.

<meta> tags are located at the top of a Web page within the <head> tag. There are two <meta> tags that are frequently used by search engines: keywords and description. The following code shows two <meta> tags in conjunction with the <title> tag and their placement on the Web page:

```
<html>
<head>
<meta name="keywords" content="book, bible, publishing, Wiley, Web,
HTML, promotion">
<meta name="description" content="The Web Publishing Bible
provides a user with the expertise to build, execute, and promote
```

```
a Web site.">
<title>This is the title.</title></head>
```

In this code, the keywords and description <meta> tags display slightly different information that is used by the search engine.

The <meta> tag keywords are used to categorize a site. Determining where to place a site depends on what words are used in the keywords <meta> tag. In the previous example, the keywords book, bible, publishing, Wiley, Web, <html>, and promotion are used. When a customer enters a search on any of these terms, this site will be presented. The more keywords you use to describe the content and theme of the site, the higher the probability of a site being retrieved by a search engine.

One caveat is that the keywords <meta> tag is limited to 255 separate words. Most robots and spiders ignore any more words. Too many words will hurt the position of your site in the search engines — they can only work with so many keywords.

The second <meta> tag, description, is an area enabling a description of the site to be filled out. In the previous example, the description explains that the site is about Web publishing.

The description <meta> tag is not limited to 250 words. As such, it should be used to provide a clear description of the site. However, many search engines ignore long descriptions, usually those greater than 64 characters.

ALT

The final tag that is often used by search engines is the <alt> tag. The <alt> tag is most commonly associated with the <img> tag. The following HTML code shows the <alt> tag being used in the <img> tag:

```
<img src="foo.jpg" width="417" height="163" alt="The alt tag is
similar to the Description meta tag and title tags">
```

The <alt> tag does a lot of double duty. For search engines, the <alt> tag is another method of extracting information from a page. This is important because graphic files cannot be searched by robots or spiders, but adding the <alt> tag enables a description to be associated with a graphic. The description can explain what the graphic file is and where it links to, as well as provide supplemental information about the content of the page. The search engine uses the <alt> tag to catalog the site.

Use of the <alt> tag is especially important for sites designed for aurally impaired Web surfers. Today, more 10 million people surf the Web with computers that are enhanced to "speak" Web pages. Clever use of the <alt> tag can provide rich information about a Web site.

The <alt> tag is not exclusively used by the <img> tag; *image maps*, placed on top of graphics to create hot spots, also leverage the <alt> tag. The following code shows a graphic with an image map:

```
<img src="foo.jpg" width="417" height="163" alt="The alt tag is
similar to the title tag." usemap="#Map" border="0">
<map name="Map">
  <area shape="rect" coords="47,45,97,92" href="home.htm" alt="This
link goes to the home page" title="This link goes to the home
page.">
 <area shape="circle" coords="187,69,55" href="contact.htm"
alt="Click here for further information on how to contact us. "
title="Click here for further information on how to contact us. ">
 <area shape="rect" coords="286,38,332,103" href="resources.htm"
alt="Click here for further information on the site " title="Click
here for further information on the site. ">
</map>
```

Each hot spot has its own link and <alt> tag. A unique description is now associated with each and every hot spot through the use of the <alt> tag. This information, in turn, is used to further categorize the site.

Extensive use of the ALT tag adds rich content on any given site.

Pulling it all together

The three sets of tags demonstrate how to add rich information to a site, but how does this translate to the search engine? Google clearly demonstrates the importance of meaningful information. Figure 20-15 demonstrates how all of this fits together.

Use of the <title>, <meta>, and <alt> tags combine to provide a meaningful results page.

The top of the page identifies the word "publishing" as the word being searched. The search has resulted in 12,300,000 entries, of which the top 1 to 10 are listed on this page. Following is how the results were obtained:

- The <title> tag is used to create the link to each page.
- The second "description" is extracted from a description <meta> tag.
- Textual content on the cataloged Web page and the <alt> tags is used to create the description of the site.
- Finally, the URL to the Web site is given along with the file size of the Web site.

Combined together, the user is presented with a rich set of information that will drive the decision on whether to click and view the site.

Ranking

Being listed or *ranked* among the top 10 results for any site is extremely important, especially when 8 million other sites are fighting for the same business. To a certain degree, this can be achieved through the use of <meta>, <title>, and <alt> tags.

A number of services (such as www.webposition.com) are available to let you know where your site is ranked.

FIGURE 20-15

The Google results page provides meaningful information.

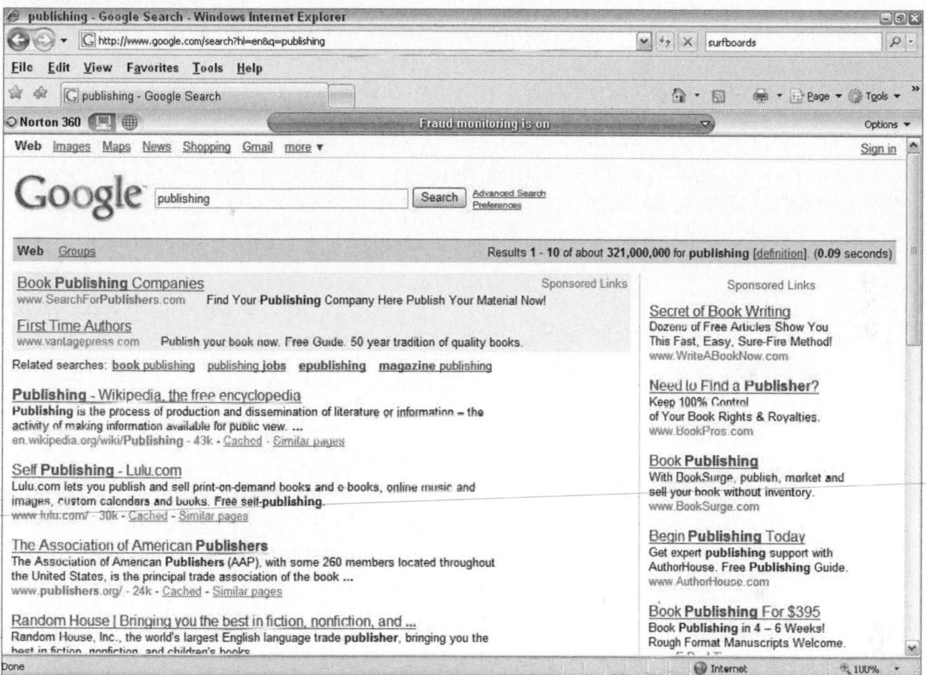

While search engines can change your site's ranking, most charge to increase the ranking. Paying for higher ranking may be worthwhile, if a search engine drives a huge number of users to sites.

Portals

Search engine sites are in the business of driving users to their service. In the past couple of years, many search engines (influenced by the massive numbers of users coming to their sites each day) have evolved to add additional tools and services such as e-mail, calendars, shopping, auctions, and online communities. The list of new services is ever-increasing. These new sites are evolving to become central aggregates of content or *portals*. The depth of the tools and services available at search or portal sites is demonstrated in Figure 20-16 by the Excite site. You will notice that the Excite home page surrounds its search engine with rich content.

Portals provide engaging content, driving users to the site. Once at the site, the primary service is the search engine.

By providing a rich set of tools and services, search engine portals are more likely to encourage users to keep coming back. For this reason, it's important that you strongly promote your Web site to search engine sites because, when the results page for a search is presented, you want to ensure that your site is there.

FIGURE 20-16

The Excite portal page surrounds its search engine field with content.

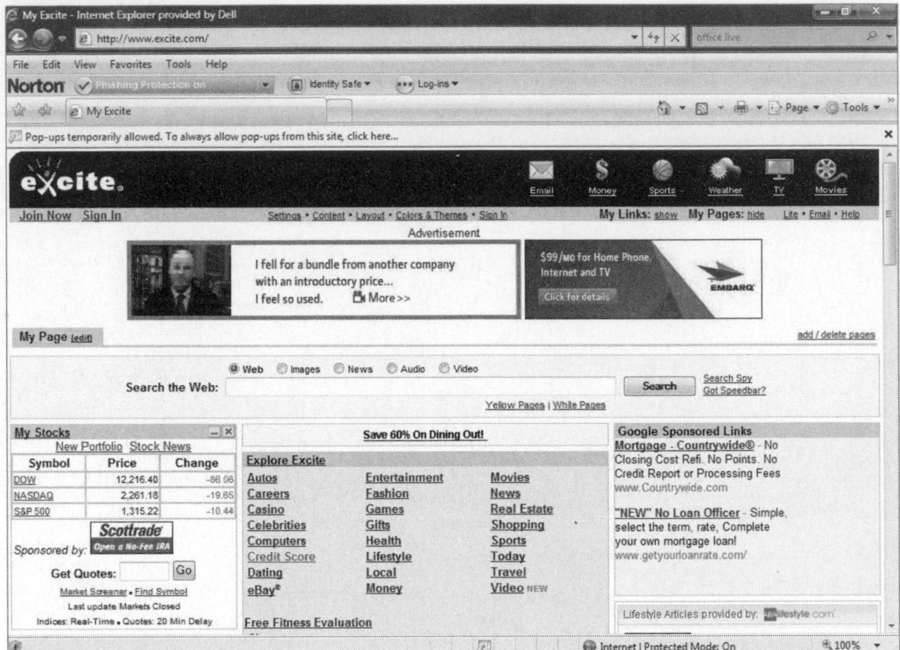

Blocking search engines

A robot or spider shouldn't be able to search for every Web page ever created. For one of a hundred reasons such as the content of the page, or based on a company decision, you may want to block a robot or spider.

While many ways are available to block spiders and robots, the easiest method to block is through the use of the ROBOTS <meta> tag. The tag is as follows:

```
<head>
<title>This page will not be indexed by a robot or spider.</title>
<meta name="robots" content="noindex">
</head>
```

Placing this line at the top of a Web page stops most search engines.

But not all search engines employ this method of blocking spiders and robots. Another method is to use the robots.txt file.

The robots.txt file is placed in the topmost directory for a site. When a search engine arrives at a site, it first looks to see if the robots.txt file is being used. In a Web browser, the link to the robots.txt file appears as follows:

```
http://www.companyname.com/robots.txt
```

The content within the robots.txt file determines how restrictive the search on the site will be. The following code prevents all robots from searching any part of the site:

```
User-agent: *
Disallow: /
```

In contrast, the robots.txt file can also enable any robot to search the entire site. This is done with the following code:

```
User-agent: *
Disallow:
```

Individual directories can be identified and blocked from robots:

```
User-agent: *
Disallow: /cgi-bin/
Disallow: /tmp/
Disallow: /private/
Disallow: /finance/results/
```

To fine-tune the robots.txt file, individual search engines can be excluded. In the following example, the Lycos spiders will not be able to search the site:

```
User-agent: Lycos
Disallow: /
```

The opposite would be to enable only the Lycos spiders to index the site, with no other search engines being allowed to do so:

```
User-agent: Lycos
Disallow:
User-agent: *
Disallow: /
```

The use of robots.txt is case-sensitive. It must be in lowercase. If you use ROBOTS.txt, it is simply ignored by any search engine.

Some of these web crawlers (or spiders or robots as they are also known) may be sophisticated enough to override the commands within the robots.txt file or other exclusions contained in the metatag headers.

Working the Web Directories

Often confused as search engines, Web directories are a must-have for any Web site promotion. A Web directory differs from a search engine in that it presents a customer with an ordered series of directories through which a Web site can be found. For example, a Web directory may present a customer with a series of high-level categories, such as hobbies, shopping, and computers. Each category, when selected, exposes another set of categories that further defines the main directory. If Hobbies is selected, a user could be presented with Fishing, Hunting, Sports, Reading, or Music. Selecting the category Music produces a results page similar to a search engine results page. The significant difference is the method by which the results page is found.

Let's assume that the most popular Web directory is Yahoo!. The most important feature on the page is the Web Site Directory. Directories, however, force users to take a number of steps to filter their results. In the case of Yahoo!, you might click the category News & Media. The linked page shows a set of categories within the broader scope of the Media.

The categorization style enables a user to fine-tune a Web site search.

It is not until you choose a subcategory that a set of links to actual Web sites is presented. By filtering through the categorized levels of the sites, a customer finds a Web site with arguably more accurate information. As Figure 20-17 demonstrates, the final results page may list only a handful of results. The benefit in the extra work is that each result holds information pertinent to the search.

FIGURE 20-17

The final Yahoo! results page only yields few examples in this case.

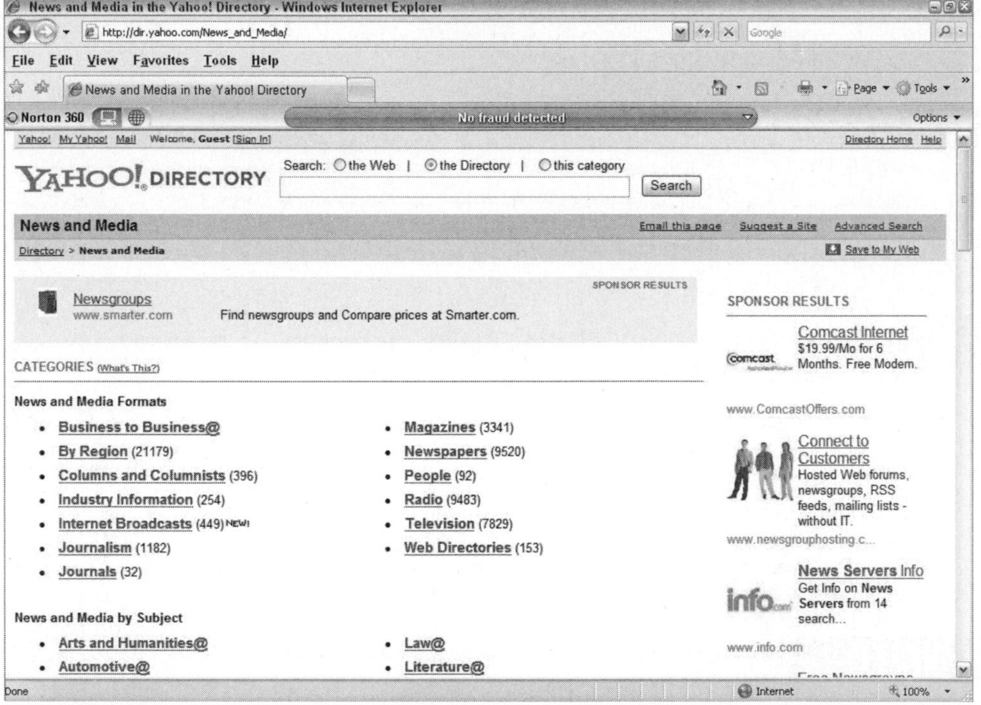

NOTE

A directory search yields more accurate links.

Ranking in a directory

Unlike search engines that rely on robots to find Web sites to populate a gargantuan database, directories rely on a human's touch. Each site that is submitted to a directory is initially categorized by the person submitting the site, and then, in the case of Yahoo!, it is inspected by a Yahoo! employee. When this process is completed, the submitted site is placed within the directory.

Where and when a site is placed and ranked within the directory is important in driving traffic to your site. Many directories charge a fee for raising the ranking of a site. With many surfers unwilling to dig too deeply for information from a search engine, it may be worthwhile to pay to increase your ranking.

Registering with the major sites

The registration process for a directory is slightly different from the process of registering with a search engine. The primary difference is that a site must be placed in a category. Often, two or three sets of categories are presented before a site can be fully categorized.

Yahoo! provides an excellent example on how to submit a site for registration to a directory. On each results page is a link to "Suggest a Site."

NOTE **If a directory is too broad, Yahoo! requests that it be further refined in order to place the site.**

Clicking the Suggest a Site button takes a user to Step One of the submission process.

Step One identifies the cost of partnering with Yahoo! if you run a business. This once free service now costs $299, although listings for private Web sites are still free.

NOTE **Yahoo! is the most popular location on the Web. Placement within its directory is crucial for promotion.**

With the largest Internet audience attracted to Yahoo!, a presence within its directory is critical for attracting business. In return, Yahoo! wants to guarantee that the level of content submitted to its site is rich and unique. By having a human analyze each site for content and originality, Yahoo! ensures that only elite sites are submitted.

The next form that a user must agree to lists terms and conditions specified by Yahoo! to all directory members.

NOTE **The terms and conditions enable Yahoo! to maintain a high level of quality for the content in its directory.**

When all terms and conditions are met, the submission form requests title information, URL, and a description. On submission, Yahoo! checks that the site is not currently in the Yahoo! directory and that it is a unique site. Yahoo! now asks for contact information and finalizes the contract and payment.

Other directory services are taking their cue from Yahoo! and are now charging for their services. With an ever-increasing number of users accessing the Internet, these types of fees are likely to appear on more and more sites.

Listing on free-for-all link pages

A slightly different version of a directory is a free-for-all (FFA) site, which collects links to specialty sites. Unlike commercial sites, such as Yahoo!, FFA directories are often run by hobbyists. Guests are encouraged to leave a link to other sites on the same topic as the hobbyist's site. This, in turn, begins building a database of links.

FFA directories are very cost-effective. They are free! The significant downfall comes with the return on investment. The traffic to your site from a link on a FFA directory may not be as heavy as a mainstream directory or a search engine.

Issuing Press Releases

Placement in search engines and directories is the first part of an online marketing campaign. As in the real world, some old standbys such as a press release can have Internet twists.

Saying the right thing

The site is built. It has been posted to all of the search engines and directories. Now, customers are starting to come to your site. As any salesperson will tell you, the hardest *sell* is to a customer who has already purchased from you. If you can persuade them to buy twice, then the third, fourth, and fifth sales are much easier.

In the computer-centric world of the Internet, making the repeat sale is no easy task. Selling often requires two people discussing a product — one selling the product, the other buying it. Because Internet customers do not have this human interaction, they can experience a sense of anxiety. Did I buy that book? Will the company charge my credit card correctly? Did my mom receive the flowers I sent?

By anticipating the anxiety and proactively working with customers, you can develop loyal relationships.

The most effective method of actively reducing customer anxiety is through the use of e-mail. Even though it's an old Internet tool, it is still the most effective and widely used Internet service. Every customer coming to purchase a product from your online store has an e-mail address. These addresses must be collected during the purchasing process. When a customer presses the Submit button to purchase products from a site, an e-mail must be immediately sent to the customer, telling the customer that the transaction has been successful, how much has been spent, and what has been purchased. If the product is to be shipped, an additional e-mail should be sent to let the customer know the day the product shipped. UPS, FedEx, and many package services have Web sites that can track packages as they move around the world. Generally, these services are free. Linking to these sites in any confirmation e-mail enables customers to track their own packages.

The key is to communicate with customers immediately. This reduces anxiety and increases consumer confidence. The customer is likely to return to make additional purchases in the future.

Finding e-mail addresses

It can't be denied that the strength and success of e-mail is its capability of penetrating directly into any user's Inbox. It is extremely easy to write an e-mail that can be instantly sent to millions of people. But how do you know whom to target with an e-mail?

Many companies supply e-mail distribution lists to millions of users for less than $1,000. Sending unsolicited e-mail to a large number of users is referred to as *spamming*. Spam, the official term for e-mail sent blindly to massive e-mail lists in the hopes of procuring sales, is not a good method for communicating with potential customers. Spam is the junk mail of the Internet, and most users rarely read it and seldom act on it.

NOTE **Spamming is illegal and fosters ill-will when received. See the Controlling the Assault of Non-Solicited Pornography and Marketing Act (CAN SPAM) Act of 2003 at** `www.ftc.gov/bcp/conline/pubs/buspubs/canspam.shtm` **for details.**

Meanwhile, e-mail can be effectively used when customers request it. For example, during registration, asks users to mark a check box next to a question that asks them whether or not they would like to receive additional information. Users who select this option expect to receive information. In this way, you can generate a list of loyal readers.

Formatting the e-mail – to use HTML or just plain text?

Today, e-mail offers much greater opportunities than ever before. Many companies are no longer just sending plain-text e-mail messages but rather are designing rich and engaging e-mail messages written in HTML. HTML-formatted e-mail is supported by most of the popular e-mail clients such as Microsoft Outlook and Eudora. Certainly, free e-mail services (such as Hotmail) support HTML-formatted messages as well. When sending e-mail, ensure that you include instructions at the bottom of the e-mail on how to unsubscribe from the mailing list. This provides users with the control over what e-mail is sent to them. If they do not want to receive the e-mail, they can unsubscribe.

Setting Up Reciprocal Links

Partnering is how businesses grow. The same happens on the Web. Web sites that offer similar or supporting services and products that complement your offering can help drive business to your site. The value of the two sites can be immediately increased by partnering, offering a link to the other site and, in return, having the site link to yours. For example, a customer buying software from a site that links to another site for training on the software is receiving a fuller and more gratifying shopping experience.

As with any partnership, understanding what you are getting into is the key to success. Before beginning any partnership, you must investigate the potential partnering site. Use a checklist, such as the following:

- Do the products or services enhance and support your current products or services?
- Are the same standards of design used on the site, and is the site similar in style to your own site? Using similar styles tells the customer that both sites have discussed and proactively agreed to work with each other.
- Is the customer service to the same standard as your own site?
- Does the potential partner site currently link with any sites that are considered competitors?

If all of the criteria match your needs, then begin by approaching someone at the company you want to partner with.

Evaluating Banner Exchanges

Web banners and ads are a mainstay of the Internet. Large entertainment sites are littered with banner ads. Why? Because they drive users to sites.

Today, banner ads appear on almost every site. The success of a banner is measured by a user clicking the ad, going to the advertised site, and making a successful purchase. This is known as the *click-through rate*. Most banners have a very low click-through rate of 0.04 percent. Depending on how many people hit a site determines how much to charge.

The following list demonstrates some of the typical monthly charges for online ads if the host guarantees 500,000 placements of the ad per month:

- *Search engines* — $20,000 to $50,000
- *Keyword advertising* — $40,000 to $70,000
- *City guides* — $20,000 to $80,000
- *Top 100 Web sites* — $25,000 to $100,000

With so much money riding on online advertising, the ad itself must sell.

Building the banner

What the banner looks like, how it is worded, and how it engages a user contribute to the final success of any banner.

To bring some standardization, the Internet Advertising Bureau (`www.iab.net`) has defined widths and heights for different styles of banners. The most common banner, the full banner, stretches across the top of the Web page and is 468 pixels wide by 60 pixels high.

Following are other sizes of banners that can be used:

- 392 × 72 pixels (full banner with vertical navigation bar)
- 234 × 60 pixels (half banner)
- 120 × 240 pixels (vertical banner)
- 120 × 90 pixels (button 1)
- 120 × 60 pixels (button 2)
- 125 × 125 pixels (square button)
- 88 × 31 pixels (micro-button)

Almost all Web sites that place banners on their sites conform to these standards. Nielsen// Netratings (`www.nielsennetratings.com`) tracks the success of different sizes of online ads, as shown in Figure 20-18.

FIGURE 20-18

Nielsen//Netratings track the success of online ads.

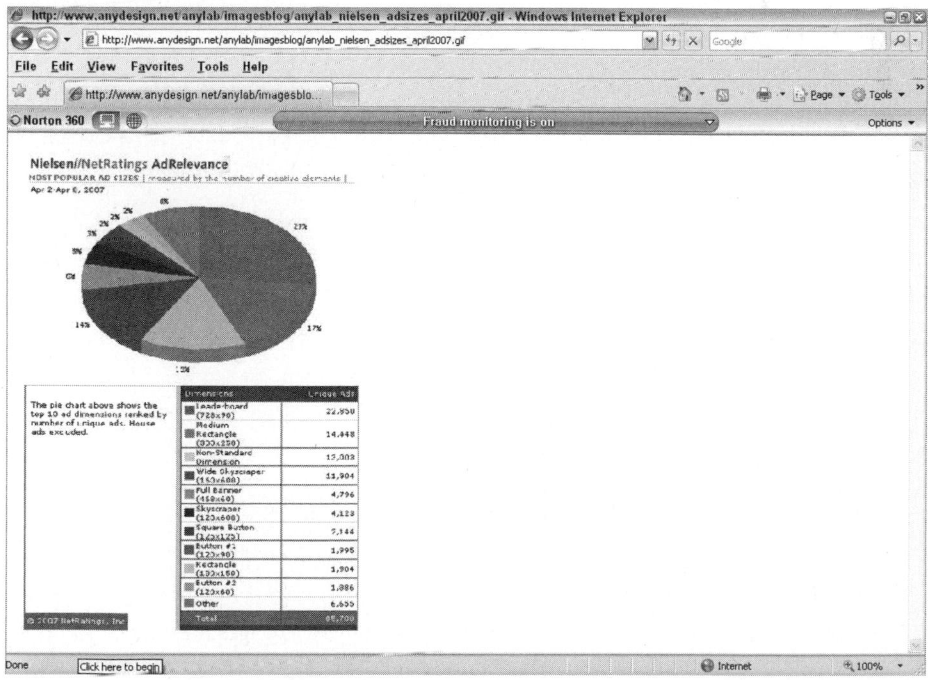

Design do's and don'ts

Creating the perfect banner size is one thing, but now the banner must be designed to be effective on the site.

The default graphic format for most banners is GIF. The format is limited in color depth (only 255 colors), but it makes up for this limitation with the ability to be animated. Though not elegant, several GIF images can be placed on top of each other to form a simple animation.

Another common feature on all banner ads is the inclusion of the words "click here." These words provide the consumer with an action to perform.

Multimedia ads

The days of the animated GIF image are numbered. More efficient and elegant media formats have matured over the last few years to increase the tools available to agencies for use.

The most interesting format to emerge is the Adobe Flash format. (Chapter 2 and Chapter 11 provide further information on Flash.) Flash is an animation format that can be scripted to interact with the user. Flash is engaging for several significant reasons. First, it is capable of bringing broadcast-quality animation over low-speed Internet modems. Second, its file sizes are smaller than animated GIFs (this enables the ad to start playing faster). And third, Flash can boast of having a significant portion of the entire Web-surfing population able to utilize it.

Other media formats, such as video and audio, are being constantly enhanced. Within a few short years, animated GIFs will become part of Internet history.

Banner exchanges

Where and how to place an ad on a page can be almost an art form. To help reduce this potential headache, a number of banner exchanges manage the placement of banners on millions of sites. An exchange places banners on sites that relate to the content of the banner (for example, a gardening site will receive banners on lawn equipment).

Each exchange functions similarly. A customer can buy advertising space by category and placement. Each exchange supplies statistics outlining the success of a banner. Future placement of the ad and the design of the ad should be influenced by this information.

Traditional advertising

With the increasing attention garnered by Internet and electronic advertising, it can be too easy to forget about more traditional means of advertising. Cable, magazine, and billboards can drive stunning results.

Unlike the Internet, more traditional forms of advertising do not have the exact empirical data online banners offer. There are no charts or graphs to measure click-through rates. This does not diminish the effectiveness of the advertising. Knowing who your audience is determines what type of ads to run. Running billboards, radio, and local cable ads may be a cost-effective method of reinforcing your brand name to offline users.

Yes, the Web store is, by nature, located online — a banner makes any Web site only one click away. However, other methods of advertising can help build brand equity and drive traffic to any site. A subtle mixture of both provides the greatest impact for the widest range of audiences.

Investigating Alternative Approaches

If you have an entrepreneurial spirit, you probably like to do for yourself, rather than to have others do things for you. In this regard, there are several things you can do to boost your Internet business and increase the visibility of yourself, your Web site, and your products. The upcoming sections show some proven methods for promoting yourself and your offerings.

E-mail advertising

E-mail advertising is a touchy business. These days, Internet users are barraged with huge quantities of junk e-mail (also known as *spam*) for every type of product or service imaginable. We're not suggesting that you resort to spam. If you send unwanted e-mail, it will actually harm your chances for success. However, a well-designed e-mail advertisement sent to buyers who have elected to receive information from your company can go a long way toward increasing your business. You can send a plain-Jane text e-mail advertisement or a full-fledged HTML advertisement, complete with images and hyperlinks to your Web site. Figure 20-19 shows an example of an HTML e-mail advertisement with images.

Amassing a mailing list

As mentioned in the previous section, we're firm opponents of delivering any form of unwanted e-mail. So, how do you get the e-mail addresses of qualified prospects who are interested in receiving information about your products or services?

One method you can use is to buy a mailing list. If you enter "e-mail mailing list" in your favorite search engine, you'll receive the URLs to many companies that specialize in selling mailing lists. However, this still involves the problem of unwanted e-mail. After you buy a mailing list and begin distributing your e-mail advertisements to names on the mailing list, you're going to get some nasty return e-mail messages telling you to cease and desist, while your other efforts will end up in your intended recipient's spam folder, never to be read. All in all, this is not a good return on your time or investment. So, if you do decide to purchase an e-mail mailing list, ensure that the people on the list are at least qualified prospects.

FIGURE 20-19

This figure shows a well-designed e-mail advertisement with images and hyperlinks.

NOTE **Many states have an anti-spam law. Before sending out mass e-mails, check your local laws to ensure that you're not violating them. Many anti-spam laws require qualified advertisers to put the abbreviation "ADV" in the subject line of a mass e-mail advertisement. Also, don't forget to review the requirements of the Controlling the Assault of Non-Solicited Pornography and Marketing Act (CAN SPAM) Act of 2003, which can be found at** `www.ftc.gov/bcp/conline/pubs/buspubs/canspam.shtm`**.**

A better method for building a list of qualified e-mail addresses is to collect them from your Web site. Many Web sites use a hover advertisement that drops in from the top of the home page when loaded, and asks the visitor to sign up for notification when the Web site is updated. The site Webmaster, or sole proprietor, then adds the e-mail address to a mail group in the address book of an e-mail application or to a database.

NOTE **Hover advertisements are created using software. You can find companies that sell hover advertisement software by doing an Internet search. You may be able to download a trial version of the software from some vendors.**

Another alternative for adding e-mail addresses to your address book or database is to give something away. For example, many Web sites that specialize in services such as promotion or marketing will give away an eBook. In order to download the free eBook, the visitor must provide his or her e-mail address. Clearly point out that the visitor will be receiving communication from you in the future, when new products or services are available.

TIP **You'll alleviate the fear of leaving an e-mail address at your Web site if you post a link to your privacy policy on the home page of your site and on any page that requests information from your Web site visitor.**

Sending newsletters

Even though you do an exemplary job of selling high-quality merchandise or services, and you follow up to make sure that your customers are satisfied after the sale, your efforts are quickly forgotten in the humdrum buzz of everyday life. A newsletter is one method many marketers use to keep their name and products in front of their customers.

You can ask Web site visitors to subscribe to your newsletter using one of the methods outlined in the previous section. If you do ask visitors to sign up for a newsletter, tell them how often you'll deliver the newsletter, and make sure that you adhere to the schedule. Sending a newsletter once a month is generally all it takes to keep your customers informed and interested in your products or services. Alternatively, you can assume that customers on your mailing list will welcome your newsletter and just send it to all recipients on your mailing list. Figure 20-20 shows an example of an HTML newsletter sent through e-mail.

FIGURE 20-20

An e-mail newsletter keeps your customers informed.

There are also e-mail-sending management companies, such as ExactTarget (`www.exacttarget.com`) that you can use.

Summary

In this chapter, you learned how you can promote your Internet business using various methods. You can draw buyers to your Web site using Google AdWords. You can advertise with major search engines on a pay-per-click basis. You can advertise your product or services using banners. You can promote your business using Internet advertisement agencies.

This chapter discussed how Internet affiliate marketing companies are available to aid in your marketing efforts. E-mail advertising is effective when directed to recipients who have requested information from you or your company. You can create an e-mail list of qualified prospects by requesting an e-mail address in exchange for a free eBook. E-mail newsletters are an effective way to keep your customers and prospects informed.

Chapter 21 is a catch-all chapter, which, as its title implies, covers all the bases.

Chapter 21

Covering All the Bases

IN THIS CHAPTER

- Using domain names and trademarks
- Soothing common fears
- Establishing policies for returns
- Investigating alternate approaches

Well, there just had to be a chapter where all the little, miscellaneous bits were covered, and this one is it. No matter what kind of Web site you're running (or contemplating running), there's something in this chapter that you'll need to take a look at.

From choosing a domain name that doesn't conflict with old-style business models and trademarks to figuring out how to fit the latest techniques of online advertising into your business model, we've got you covered.

Using Domain Names and Trademarks

A *domain name* is often thought to be the same thing as a company name. In most people's minds, a dot-com name is as much a corporate name as Nabisco, Ford, or Sears. But there's a tremendous difference in the legal sense.

CAUTION **We do not pretend to be lawyers, and this book does not offer legal advice, but rather merely presents a summary of situations that are of concern to Web developers. Always seek the advice of a qualified attorney with experience in matters pertaining to the Internet before making any decision or committing to any course of action relating to trademarks.**

A *trademark* is a symbol that indicates the source of a product or service. It has a tangible value because it establishes one brand as different from all others. A domain name is, legally speaking, an address on the Internet and nothing more. This may change over time as more judges become familiar with technical matters that are, so far, very new territory in law. But, as things stand right now, whether or not a domain name can be considered property is even disputed.

Why does such an esoteric question matter? According to the law, people and companies have property rights. What you own can't be appropriated by anyone else unless they break the law. No one can take your car or use your trademark, both of which are your property, without your permission. But, if you don't own your domain name, how can you have any rights to it?

Domain name disputes

Even if you find that a domain name isn't taken yet, that doesn't necessarily mean that you're home free. You can certainly register it in your name at one of the registrars, such as Network Solutions at `www.networksolutions.com` (see Figure 21-1), or the registrars listed at `icann.org/registrars/accreditation-qualified-list.html`. But there are some situations in which you may not be able to actually use it.

CROSS-REF **See Chapter 14 for information on getting a domain name.**

FIGURE 21-1

Network Solutions is one the best-known registrars.

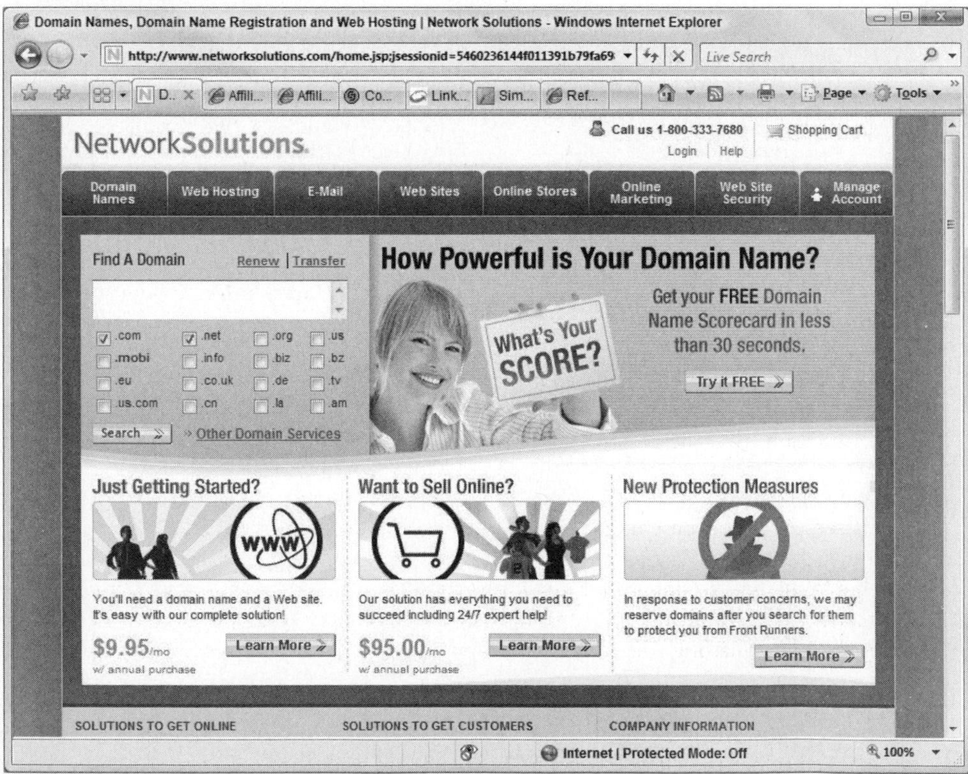

The most common dispute situation occurs when someone registers a domain name that is the same as or very similar to an existing trademarked name by another company. As soon as the company notices that your Web site is using that name, the trouble starts. Under current U.S. trademark laws, trademark owners *must* go after anyone using their trademarked names or likenesses without their permission. If they don't defend their right to the trademark, the law assumes that they're surrendering it.

All it takes to lose a trademark is for the company to not object loudly enough to its use as anything but a name for their product or service. Some examples of trademarks that died this way include aspirin, ping pong, tarmac, gunk, escalator, kerosene, and yo-yo. Since very few companies are willing to lose their trademarks, you can expect to receive a "cease-and-desist" order, commanding you to stop using the trademarked name online.

Under trademark law, they can't take the actual dot-com domain name away from you just because they own the trademark. But they can tell you to stop using it. You can, of course, fight the trademark owner. With the awesome power of the Internet, numerous campaigns have been waged against such situations. Many individuals have won the public opinion judgment, which is far more important to corporate PR departments.

The other recourse is to go to court and prove that you have a legitimate claim to your domain name — for example, if it's a variation on your own name, if it's a separate trademark for a company in a different industry, if it was registered before the trademark was registered, or if it's an `.org` registration. People owning `.org` domains have started to lose them to companies holding trademarks, but there are grounds for a fight.

Most importantly, however, if you get a *cease-and-desist* order that you plan to combat, contact your domain name registrar and ask them not to shut off service. Many domain name registrars shut off your domain name registry entries if they receive a copy of the cease-and-desist order, even though such an order is in no way a court order to the registrar. Read your terms of service agreement carefully to see if the registrar retains the right to halt or interrupt service in a trademark or domain name dispute.

Another sticky issue is using a celebrity's name as the basis for a domain name. While this will undoubtedly draw traffic to your site, as soon as the celebrity finds out, you're going to receive some attention from the celebrity's manager and attorney.

There are a couple of well-publicized cases where domain names using celebrity names have been purchased. A person purchased `juliaroberts.com` and put the domain name up for auction. Although the famous actress did not have her name registered as a trademark, the ruling cited that her name had secondary meaning and, therefore, the actress possessed "trademark rights" to her name. Administrative panels from the Uniform Domain Name Resolution Policy (UDRP) and the Anti-Cybersquatting Consumer Protection Act (ACPA) transferred ownership of the domain name to the actress.

Another case involving a celebrity name was `jimihendrix.com`. The estate of Jimi Hendrix complained under the UDRP that a Web site created by a supposed fan was actually being used to sell other celebrity domain names. The panel decided to transfer the domain name to the estate of the deceased rock star, because the "fan club" was not registered in the state in which the domain owner lived, and because the domain name was being used in bad faith.

Under the UDRP, when a domain name complaint is filed, the domain name owner is obligated to attend a mandatory hearing conducted by an administrative dispute resolution service approved by Internet Corporation for Assigned Names and Numbers (ICANN).

A complaint may result in action against the domain name holder if the resolution service finds that the domain name is identical or similar to a trademark name to which the plaintiff has rights, if the domain name owner has no rights or legitimate interest in the domain name, or if the domain name has been registered and is being used in bad faith. During the administrative hearing, the plaintiff must prove some of these elements (see note below).

NOTE **Because of the difficulty in proving "use in bad faith," this requirement has been changed from "mandatory" in conjunction with the two preceding conditions (the domain naming being identical or similar to a trademark name, as well as the domain name owner not having any rights or interest in the domain name) to "optional." In other words, you must prove the first two conditions *or* the third condition.**

Anti-Cybersquatting Consumer Protection Act

In November 1999, President Bill Clinton signed the ACPA into law. This law gives citizens the right to seek legal action if a trademark name or famous name is being used in bad faith. This act amends Section 43 of the Trademark law that prohibits bad faith registration or the use of a domain name that is identical to a registered trademark, is identical or disconcertingly similar to a distinctive mark (registered or not), or is misleadingly similar or damaging to a famous mark or name.

When a case is ruled in a plaintiff's favor, rewards issued under the Trademark Act are available. Alternatively, the plaintiff may elect an award of statutory damage between $1,000 and $100,000 per domain name (the amount is awarded at the discretion of the presiding judge). The plaintiff may also be awarded the transfer of the domain name. Under the ACPA, a trademark holder may file suit in federal court under an explicit provision of the act without having to resort to a traditional trademark infringement or dilution action.

Researching domain names online

When you decide to set up an online presence, the domain name you choose can bolster your Internet presence. Even if you choose a short domain name that fits the service or product you're intending to promote on the Internet, it's not the equivalent of an online trademark. Using a trendy domain name is fine, as long as you don't try to intentionally create a reasonable facsimile of an existing trademark, or use a celebrity's name. When choosing a domain name, it's a good idea to come up with a couple of derivatives of the domain name, and then research whether or not the name is available. You can research a domain name at Better-Whois.com (`www.betterwhois.com`), as shown in Figure 21-2.

FIGURE 21-2

You can find out if a domain name is available at Better-Whois.com.

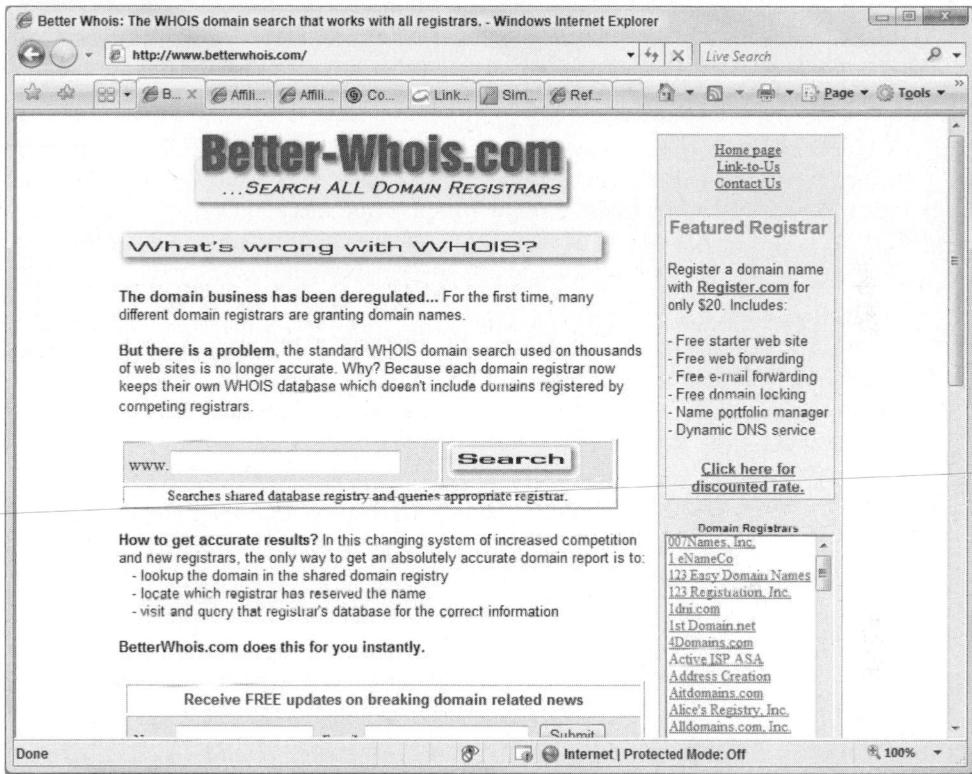

NOTE **Registering a domain name in no way signifies rights control over the mark. Contact the US Patent and Trademark Office for information** (`www.uspto.gov`).

Maintaining your domain name

You register a domain name for a given period of time, the shortest period being one year. After your registration expires, your domain name becomes available. Even if you don't set up a Web site with the domain name prior to the name expiring, it's a good idea to renew the registration, especially if it's a good domain name. If it's your company's identity it's a pain to re-educate all your customers. It's especially important to renew the domain name if you've been running a Web business under the domain and have temporarily taken the Web site down. It has been a common practice of Internet porn sites to scoop up domain names when they become available and point the domain name toward the server of their site. If your domain name lapses and so-called porn pirates purchase your domain, your previous customers will be in for a shock.

When you register a domain name, you may also want to consider registering derivatives of the name. If your site becomes popular, porn pirates can register derivatives or your domain. When people mistype your domain name, the porn site appears in their browser. And here's a funny story — this happened to the White House. Yes, `whitehouse.gov` pointed to the presidential quarters, while `whitehouse.com` pointed to, well, a very non-presidential destination.

Another common practice is to register the domain name with the other domain extensions. In addition to registering your site with the `.com` extension, you should consider registering it with a `.net` and `.biz` extension. You may also want to consider registering your domain name with the `.org` or `.info` extensions, depending on the type of business you're in.

Researching trademarks online

To avoid getting into a trademark/domain name dispute in the first place, you could hire a law firm specializing in trademark law to investigate all the possibilities for you. But that's an expensive proposition. It's far better to do the basic research yourself. Then, if you think you have a trademark-free domain name, have the lawyer confirm it — and trademark it for you, just to cover all the bases.

FIGURE 21-3

The U.S. Patent and Trademark Office Web site provides a variety of search options.

The first step in doing the trademark research is the most simple and obvious — go to any major search engine and punch in the name you want to use. If the search results show that someone is already using that name for their product or service, then it's back to the drawing board, unless your product or service is radically different, and that's a matter for a qualified attorney to decide.

If you can't find anyone already using the name, you're not out of the woods yet. You still need to check out the listings of current trademarks, such as the one at the U.S. Patent and Trademark Office (`www.uspto.gov`), as shown in Figure 21-3. Table 21-1 lists the addresses of several trademark databases, including official and international ones. While some are free, others are fee-based. Be sure to read all the fine print before committing to using any of them.

TABLE 21-1

Trademark Research Sites

Company	URL
Australian Trademark On-line Search System	`pericles.ipaustralia.gov.au/atmoss/falcon.application_start`
Canadian Trademark Database (English)	`http://strategis.ic.gc.ca/cipo/trademarks/search/tmSearch.do`
Canadian Trademark Database (French)	`strategis.ic.gc.ca/app/cipo/trademarks/search/tmSearch.do;jsessionid=0000YhYaYQ1EcJkmCi7HbBifdtV:1247nfca5?language=fre`
European Community Trademark Consultation Service	`http://oami.europa.eu/CTMOnline/RequestManager/en_SearchBasic`
Intellectual Property Office of New Zealand	`www.iponz.govt.nz/search/cad/dbssiten.main`
Japan Patent Office	`www.jpo.go.jp`
The American Trademark Company	`trademrk.com`
U.S. Patent and Trademark Office	`www.uspto.gov`

Soothing Common Fears

While you may be perfectly comfortable with computers, networks, and all the latest technological innovations, the Internet is a strange and scary place for many people. As more and more nontechnical people become Internet users, addressing this common fear is bound to become more of a factor than it is even today.

Publicizing your security

Except for the rare cases where a Webmaster is just plain crazy, all Internet sites have a fair degree of security. If you run your own Web server, you've doubtlessly seen to all the details yourself. If you're leasing space on a virtual server or other Web hosting service, presumably standard security measures are a part of the package. If not, move on to a better provider — you're not getting what you're paying for.

The general public, fed by Hollywood's "vision" of the Internet as a place where anyone who feels like it can break into any system, often doesn't understand that something as simple as encrypting an order in transit is all they need to be protected. Yes, there are plenty of talented hackers out there who can slip past just about any security setup. But most of them aren't malicious, and few of them are criminally inclined. They're far more likely to try to break into the United States government's computers just to prove they can do it than to try to find out who's ordering kippered herrings from an online grocery store.

Of course, the real fear that most people have is that someone will get their credit card information. Why this fear has become associated with the Internet is anyone's guess, because you give that information to strangers every time you use your credit card anywhere. Thousands of "someones" have access to your credit card information already, even without shopping online.

And you probably literally throw it away every time you take out the trash. Seriously. Take a good look at your receipts. Some of them are done up right, listing only partial information, just enough to identify the credit card — such as the last four digits — in case you need to make a return. Many others, however, give your full name, credit card number, and expiration date. When you wad up that shopping bag and toss it into the same trashcan you throw your junk mail into, you've given any trash raider all they need to buy anything they want — on your credit card. It's much more likely that criminals will go through your trash than intercept an online transaction or raid a database (this is not a joke — ask any detective who handles financial crimes).

TIP **Although this book's about the Internet, identity theft is a very real issue. To thwart the trash raiders, buy a paper shredder and shred anything that can be used to usurp your identity, including the endless barrage of credit card offers that appear in your mailbox.**

Nonetheless, as a Webmaster, you have to deal with the public perception, not the reality. And that means making a big deal about how secure your site is. Lay it on as thick as you honestly can. Display the logo of the company, such as VeriSign (`www.verisign.com`), that issues your digital certificate (see Figure 21-4). If your site uses 128-bit encryption, tell everyone that it's so good that the U.S. government won't allow it out of the country (it gets out anyway, of course, but that's another story). Make a special page with links to every technical report on encryption you can find — the more obtuse, the better. Your aim here is not technical education but consolation. Just let visitors know that they're as protected as it is possible to be. An up-and-coming certification site to also look at is Hacker Safe, which has been chosen by such companies as Hewlett-Packard, Sony, and Yahoo!.

FIGURE 21-4

VeriSign provides digital site identification.

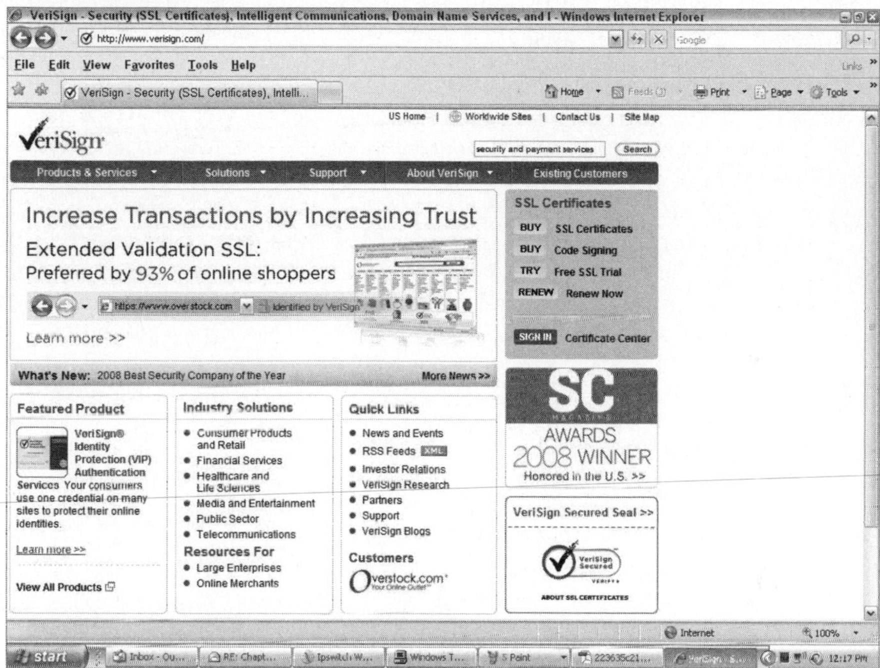

Creating a privacy policy

The first thing we look for before we give any personal information to any Web site is the site's privacy policy. Why? If the site doesn't specifically state that they keep your information confidential, you don't know who will end up with it.

We're hardly the only people with this attitude — Internet privacy is one of the hottest issues going. You're well advised to give serious consideration to your own site's privacy policy and to ensure that your visitors are well aware of it. Even if you don't run a commercial site, even if you don't sell anything to anyone, if you ask your visitors for any information at all, you need a publicly posted privacy policy.

TIP **Put two links to your privacy policy on every page where you ask for personal information — maybe even on every page in your entire site. Put one at the top of the page and the other at the bottom. That makes it easy for anyone to find one of them quickly.**

TIP **A Web pro we know brought up these additional pointers. Don't repeat links often. Privacy Policies are usually at the footer of Web sites or located in a menu somewhere, unless the site collects a lot of personal information. Such conditions would require telling people about the Privacy Policy by using a big ugly link or graphic.**

Why ask?

An astonishing number of Web sites ask their visitors to provide personal information when they have no legitimate use for it. Or, they require their visitors to register, selecting a username and password in order to access the site, even though the site is free.

Think long and hard before you do either of these things. Ask yourself, "What am I gaining by doing this?" Then ask yourself, "Is that worth putting my visitors through an extra hassle?" Everything that visitors must do that puts an unnecessary step between them and why they came to your site is a hassle.

TIP **Instead of creating your own privacy statement, you can save a lot of work by using the Direct Marketing Association's Privacy Policy Generator, which can be found at** `http://www.dmarwesponsibility.org/PPG` **(see Figure 21-5).**

Table 21-2 lists the Internet addresses for several privacy policies representing a variety of different companies and organizations.

FIGURE 21-5

The Direct Marketing Association helps you create a privacy policy.

TABLE 21-2

Example Privacy Policies

Company	Policy URL
Bloomberg.com	`www.bloomberg.com/notices/privacy.html`
Gibson Research Corporation	`grc.com/privacy.htm`
Marriott Rewards	`http://marriott.com/privacy.mi`
Red Hat Linux	`redhat.com/legal/privacy_statement.html`
The Free Garage Sale	`freegaragesale.net/privacy.htm`
The Internet Society	`isoc.org/help/privacy`
Tucows	`tucows.com/privacy.html`
United Parcel Service	`www.ups.com/about/privacy.html`

Establishing Policies for Returns

As mentioned in Chapter 19, if you run any kind of commercial site, you will, sooner or later, have to deal with some dissatisfied consumers. Whether you offer products or services, that ultimately means that you have to handle returns, exchanges, and/or refunds. If you have no policy in place for handling these situations, your bottom line could suffer, both because you may have to issue refunds you hadn't planned on and because many people will be reluctant to buy from you at all. You need to decide not only if you will accept returns but also details such as the following:

- *Type of settlement* — On returns, will you offer a full refund or store credit only? Do you want to charge a restocking fee? Will you only allow exchanges for identical products in the event of a defect? Will you charge a repackaging fee for opened items? What happens when you allow for return?
- *Time limits* — You probably don't want every sale to perpetually be a potential return. Set some kind of time limit on it, so that you don't have to maintain a large cash set-aside to cover returns long after the sale is made. Many merchants traditionally give 30 days for returns. Some go as high as 90 days, and only the most confident (and those with the deepest pockets) set no limits. Certain types of items that are particularly susceptible to return fraud are often given very short time limits. The number of camcorders people attempt to return right after graduation day, for example, is incredible. Unless you actually plan to run an equipment rental facility, set tight limits on anything that is vulnerable to use on a short-term basis. Also, things you yourself can't return should be excluded if the package is opened, such as software, DVDs, and CDs. The reason most stores don't accept returns on these items is that many customers buy them, copy them, and try to return them.

- *Shipping charges* — Are you going to "eat" the shipping charges for a returned item? Some companies, in the interest of maintaining good customer relations, make this a practice. Others, in the interest of keeping their bank accounts full, avoid it like the plague.
- *Authorization* — You don't want to be caught off-guard by returns. Most online companies only allow returns if the customer first contacts the company and explains the situation. Many times, any problem the customer has can be handled at this point, and the return avoided (minor details such as "Have you pressed the On button, sir?"). If the return is actually necessary, the company issues a Return Material Authorization (RMA) number. This number must be clearly written on the outside of the box when the customer returns it. Return departments automatically refuse to accept delivery of any item without an RMA number on it. And, of course, you'll want the customer to include a copy of the invoice with his or her return.

Whatever you decide to do in regard to your return policy, it should be prominently posted on your Web site. Presumably, most of your sales will be with credit card, and credit card companies automatically back up your return policy in the event of a complaint from the cardholder — but only if it is publicly available.

FIGURE 21-6

Yahoo! includes a Terms of Service policy.

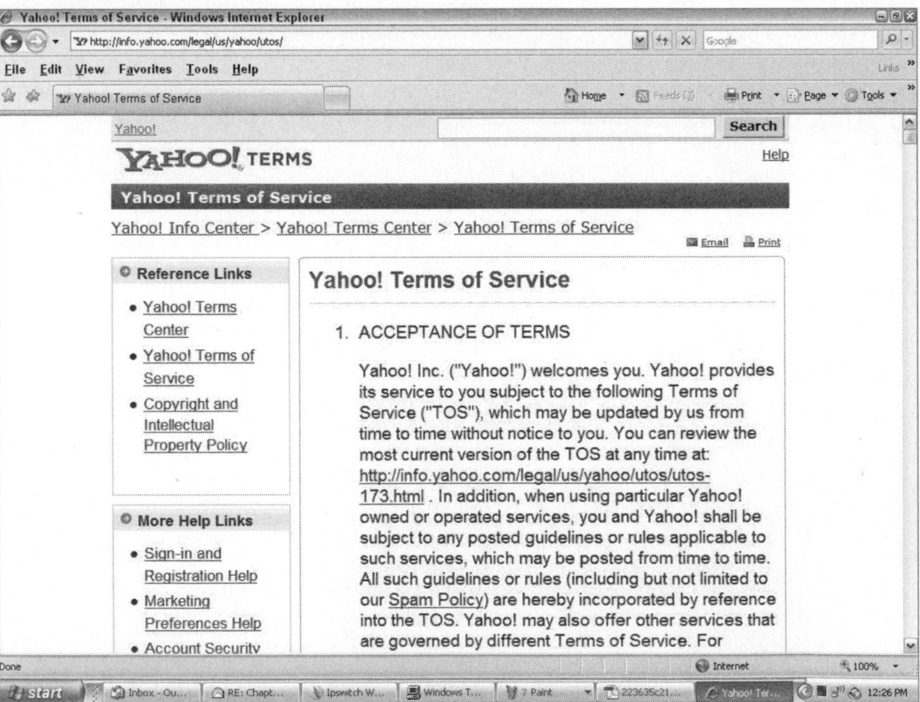

CAUTION **Ensure that you check out applicable state laws regarding returns. You may have to modify your return policy because of them.**

If you have decided to set up shop in an established mall such as Yahoo!, you'll have to accept the Yahoo! Terms of Service agreement (see Figure 21-6). Violation of a mall's requirements generally results in losing your membership, which effectively means shutting down your business. Some malls, however, allow each merchant to set individual policies. Check out all the details before you decide to open a store in a mall.

Table 21-3 lists the locations of a number of existing return policies that you can browse through for inspiration.

TABLE 21-3

Example Return Policies

Company	Policy URL
Bakery Equipment.com	`bakeryequipment.com/Customer-Service/Sales-Agreement.htm`
DreamRetail.com	`dreamretail.com/returns.html`
Hotel Supplies-Online	`hotelsupplies-online.com/returnpolicies.htm`

Investigating Alternative Approaches

If you don't intend to run a commercial site but still enjoy the idea of getting at least some money out of your Web site, you can take a couple of simple approaches. The first is to display advertising, making your site into a sort of online bus stop or billboard. The other is to refer your site's visitors to another company's products or services. Both are a type of advertising, of course, but they work slightly differently.

Accepting advertising

Banner advertising has long been an accepted part of the World Wide Web. Some banner advertising arrangements, called *exchanges*, are formed by groups of companies or even individual Webmasters, who agree to display small advertisements for each other's sites. The banners are rotated automatically, and the number of sites your banner is displayed on depends on the number of other members' banners you display on your own site.

Banner exchanges tend to have, by and large, pretty short lives and are of questionable usefulness. Too often, about all you end up doing is showing ads for the exchange itself.

You can, however, pay for banner ad arrangements, such as those provided by Advertising.com (see Figure 21-7), one of the most professionally run outfits in Internet advertising. They work both ends of the street, bringing together serious advertisers with both significant Web sites and opt-in e-newsletters.

FIGURE 21-7

Advertising.com provides a variety of services to Internet publishers and advertisers alike.

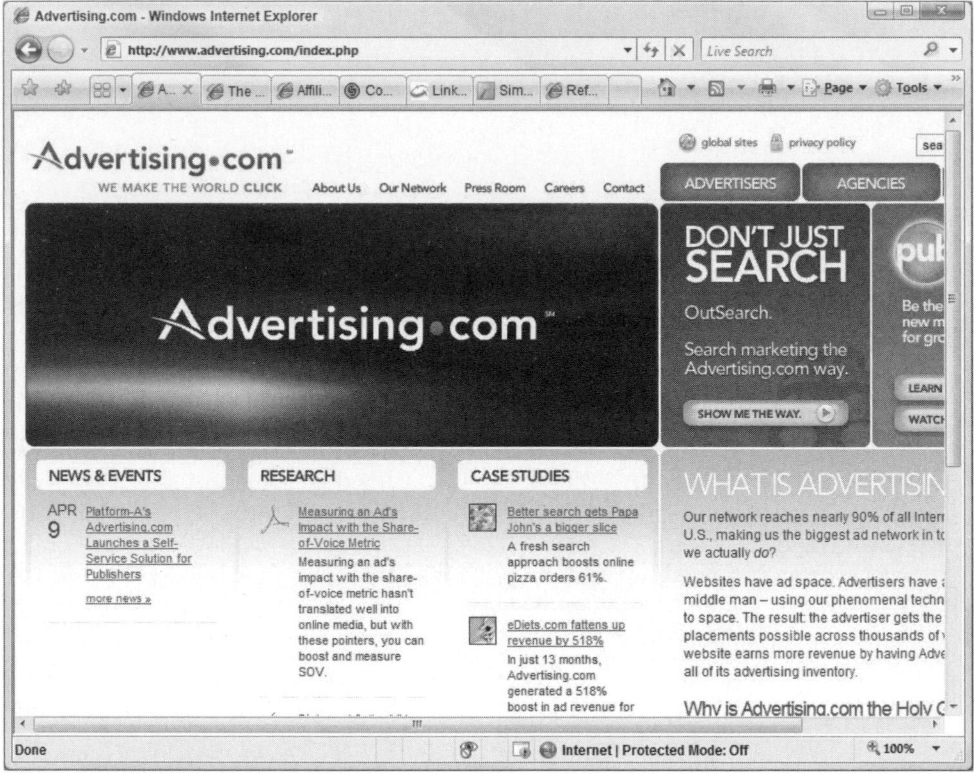

Companies such as this save you the trouble of finding advertisers who are interested in buying your space. These companies assist you in finding the right advertisers for your site's target audience. Usually, you have to demonstrate that you have a certain amount of steady traffic on your site in order to attract any kind of serious advertising. Just as a magazine must prove circulation figures, a Web site must be able to provide server logs upon request that show how many visitors come to the site each month. The number varies depending on the advertiser, but if you're not generating more than 50,000 visits a month, you're not even going to be close to making any money.

Table 21-4 lists several paying banner advertising resources for Webmasters.

TABLE 21-4

Banner Advertising Resources

Company	URL
Advertising.com	`Advertising.com`
AdDynamix	`Addynamix.com`
The Financial Ad Trader	`adtrader.com`
ValueClick	`valueclick.com`

Optimize your site for search engines

If you build it, they will come. Well, not quite. In order to ensure a steady stream of traffic to your Web site, you'll have to take certain steps. The obvious steps are to include the URL for your Web site in every piece of literature you mail, on your business cards, and in every e-mail you send. The other step you should consider taking is optimizing your Web site for search engines.

In the old days, Web developers resorted to all manner of chicanery to boost their Web sites as close as possible to the top of the first results page when a given keyword was entered into a search engine Search field. The methods were rather blatant, repeating the same keyword over and over on the home page and using a color that was so close to the background color, visitors couldn't see the keyword. But the search engine robots could, and, therefore, the Web page jumped to the top of the hit parade every time that keyword was entered in a search engine.

Times have changed, and search engine companies are wise to the tricks of the trade. Sites that resort to this type of chicanery can be booted from a search engine database or rank very low. So, how do you optimize your site for popular search engines?

You can purchase software to optimize your Web site. One popular search engine optimization tool is called WebPosition 4. You can download a trial version of the software at `www.webposition.com` (see Figure 21-8). The standard edition of WebPosition 4 supports up to five different Web sites and retails for $149.00. The professional edition supports unlimited domains and retails for $389.00.

Another great tool to look at is AddWeb, now in version 8.0. In the words of the company, AddWeb is "the most award-winning search engine optimization and promotion software," and has earned numerous coveted industry recognitions for its excellence and thoroughness of its program offerings.

If you don't like the idea of working with a piece of software, you can hire a company to optimize your Web site, and then submit it to the most popular search engines. The options vary depending on the company. Some will repeatedly submit your Web site to popular search engines, while others will offer tips for optimizing the keywords and home page text to boost your search engine rating.

FIGURE 21-8

You can download a trial version of WebPosition 4.

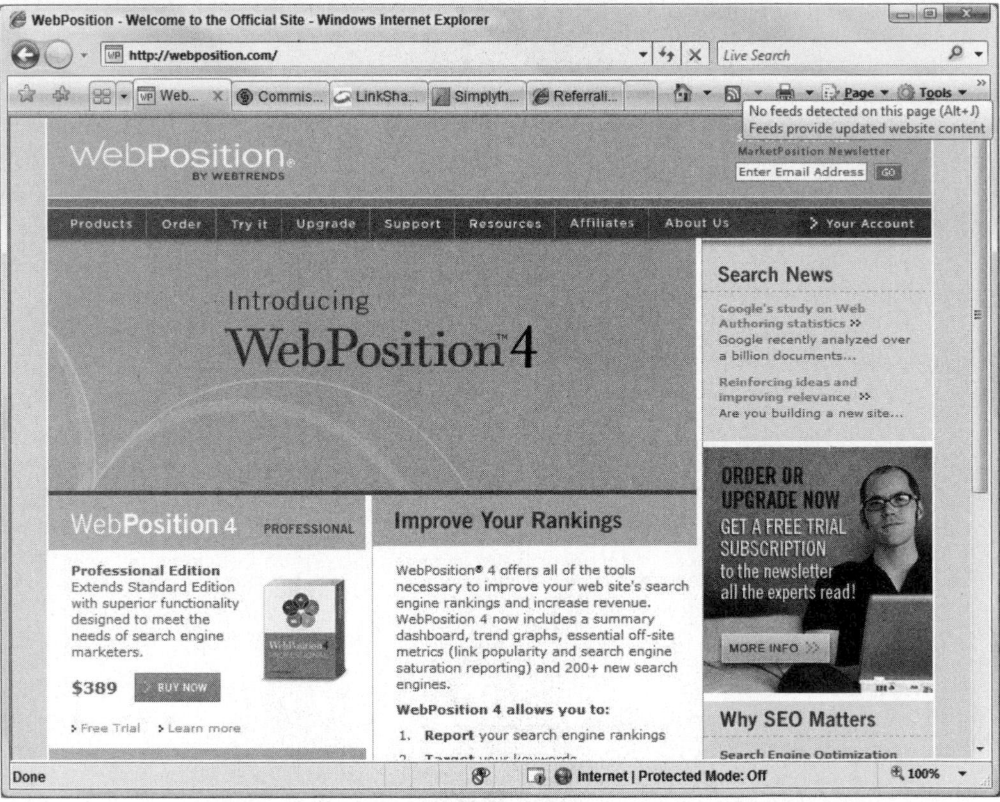

Table 21-5 lists some companies that provide search engine optimization services. The cost of submission and optimization services vary, depending on the number of search engines the site is submitted to. You can find submission services for as low as $39.00.

TIP **Before hiring any search optimization company, it's a good idea to ask the company for referrals before plunking down your hard-earned cash.**

TABLE 21-5

Search Engine Optimization Companies

Company	URL
360i.com	`www.360i.com`
dMedia	`www.dmediallc.com`
HighRankings.com	`www.highrankings.com`
Reinventbusiness.com	`reinventbusiness.com`
SEO	`www.seoinc.com`
Submit Express	`www.submitexpress.com`
SubmitToday.com	`www.submittoday.com`
WebPublicitee.com	`www.webpublicitee.com`
WPromote.com	`www.wpromote.com`

Summary

The new Web business model isn't something that's suddenly going to overwhelm the old one. It needs to fit into the existing one.

In this chapter, you learned that trademarks and domain names aren't the same thing. If you want to trademark your domain name, you'd better talk to an attorney who specializes in that sort of thing.

There are also a lot of good books and professional journals about trademarks and copyrights. A couple are *Patents, Copyrights and Trademarks for Dummies* by Henri Charmasson (Wiley, 2004) and *eBay PowerSeller Business Practices for Dummies* by Marsha Collier (Wiley, 2008).

You have seen how online security is a major concern with the majority of shoppers. If you offer online security but don't actively publicize it, you're making a major mistake. Make sure that you keep your visitors' private information private — and ensure that you tell them up front that you're going to do so.

Your return policies must be stated clearly and plainly, and they must be in accord with all the laws of the states you're doing business in.

You have seen how you can add to your site's revenues by accepting advertising — either direct or via affiliate programs. You can boost your site's ranking in search engines by using optimization software or by hiring online optimization companies.

Chapter 22 provides several ways to maintain your site and enable you to keep it up to date in terms of formatting and content presentation.

Part VIII

Keeping Your Site Fresh

IN THIS PART

Chapter 22

Maintaining Your Site

Even though the bulk of the work you perform on a typical Web development project deals with the actual creation of the site, a fair amount of time still needs to be devoted to site maintenance. In fact, it is the maintenance of a site that can often make or break it. This chapter focuses on ways to lengthen your site's functional life span through effective site maintenance.

IN THIS CHAPTER

Testing Your Site

Before uploading your site to a server and taking it *live* for all to see on the Internet, it is important to do some thorough testing. At this point, you want to determine that everything is working as you anticipated by ensuring the following:

- There are no broken links.
- The download times are acceptable for the targeted audience.
- All content is legible and functional in targeted browsers.

When you begin testing your site, it is helpful to have a table or spreadsheet containing information about your testing. For example, you can create a table that lists your targeted browsers across the top and targeted platforms down the left side. After you test each one, record your findings in the appropriate spaces. Table 22-1 gives you an idea of how this would look.

TABLE 22-1

Testing Spreadsheet

	Konqueror	Safari 3.x	Opera 9.24	IE 6.x	IE 7.0	Firefox	AOL	PocketPC Mobile Phone	iPhone
Windows 98									
Windows 2000									
Windows XP									
Windows Vista									
Mac OS 8									
Mac OS 9.x									
Mac OS 10.x									

Not all of the browsers and platforms listed in Table 22-1 will be appropriate for your testing situation. Ultimately, the browsers and platforms you test should be representative of your target audience. To help determine the most important browsers and platforms for your testing scheme, prioritize them according to which constitutes the widest portion of your audience.

CROSS-REF **For a review of Internet demographics, refer to Chapter 1.**

You may find that certain newer technologies fail to perform in older browsers. For example, while the use of Cascading Styles Sheets (CSS) provides more attractive pages in the newest browsers, you must also ensure that your pages "fail gracefully" in browsers that do not recognize or support CSS. If users of older browsers cannot see the newer technologies you're using, they should still be able to read and view the content in some form.

NOTE **Not sure how to test multiple platforms when you have only one or two computers? In the section, "Finding outside testers," later in this chapter, you'll learn ways around this.**

In addition to browsers and platforms, you must also test a variety of screen resolutions, as dictated by your target audience. At the very least, you should test your site under the following resolutions, using both Internet Explorer (IE) and Firebox.

- 800 × 600
- 1024 × 768
- 1280 × 800

Visit your site as a stranger

Chapter 1 discussed Internet demographics, specifically as they relate to knowing your target audience. When you test your site, you must do so with that target audience in mind.

Take a break from your site for a few days and go back to visit it as if you were seeing it for the first time. One way to make this task easier is to assign a role for yourself within the target audience, often referred to as a *user scenario* (see the sidebar "User scenario" for a typical example). For example, if you are creating a site for a toy company with a target audience that includes children ages 8 to 12, you might assign yourself the role of a 9-year-old child who is visiting the site in search of ideas for birthday presents.

There is one final test, which, from what we can tell, is infallible. Have your mother test it. This is, in Web design circles, known as the "Mom Test."

Friends and family, in general, can do a number on your site.

It can be quite useful (and even fun) to visit your Web site with the fresh perspective of a user scenario. By putting yourself in the shoes of a member of your target audience, you can identify elements that don't work as you intended, or sections that need to be better clarified. In our own work, we prefer to use several user scenarios, representing each major group in the target audience.

User scenario

Web Site: Toy Store

Role Name: Tommy Jones

Role Description: Tommy is a nine-year-old boy who is visiting the site for the first time. Tommy has used many similar Web sites, mostly with the help of his parents. For this particular after-school visit, Tommy is looking for things to put on his birthday wish list. He plans to share the wish list with his parents at dinner tonight.

Finding outside testers

Once you've performed your own testing, be sure to enlist the help of others. This can be accomplished through formal or informal user testing, depending on the size and complexity of your company and your Web site.

In formal user testing, you hire users from the target audience to perform certain tasks on the new Web site. So, in the toy store scenario, you may decide to hire several parent/child teams to test your site from both users' perspectives. A large number of testers are not required. A group of 5 to 10 people can provide realistic results or recommendations to greatly improve your site's usability.

Testers are typically paid somewhere between $25 to $50 for an hour or two of testing. You can usually find the best testers by advertising to your target audience. If your site is for a toy store, consider advertising at a local toy store or in the local newspaper, or simply ask friends and coworkers.

Prior to hiring the testers, create a list of key tasks, in order of importance, that you expect typical users to accomplish on your site. As your testers follow the key test list, observe them as they attempt to complete each task and record any relevant information. The sidebar "Record from user testing" gives a sample record from a user test performed on the fictional toy store Web site we've been using.

Keep a list of bugs you find. Don't add new features until you've fixed those bugs, and you'll find you have a better product at the end.

Record from user testing

Web Site: Toy Store

Tester: Tyler Hall, age 10

Task #1: Locate a pinball game for Nintendo 64 and add it to your shopping basket.

Observations: *From the home page (which was already loaded on the screen), Tyler quickly clicked the link for Video Games. After the Video Games page was loaded (it took 6 seconds), he read the page for 10 seconds before clicking a link for Nintendo 64. The Nintendo 64 page took 5 seconds to load. From here, Tyler couldn't decide where to go. He read the category titles but none matched "pinball." He also saw an alphabetical listing and finally decided to click "p" for pinball. When the "p" page was loaded, he read through all the titles listed (approximately 2 minutes) before giving up.* ***Observer note:*** *None of the pinball titles for Nintendo 64* ***begin*** *with the word "pinball," which is why they were not in the "p" section. Tyler could have found it by performing a search, but when asked why he hadn't done so, he replied "I didn't see the search box."*

To create the best situation, you should have the testers in the same room as your observers so that you can control the computer setups, interruptions, and environment. Even better is to have a testing room with a mirrored glass wall behind which observers can sit, so they don't distract the testers. You may be able to rent such a room in your area. In a more informal approach to user testing, you may simply ask a number of your friends or coworkers to test the site for you. This type of testing can be extremely helpful, particularly if you need to test your site under the AOL browser on a Mac, but you have only a PC, for example. You can also walk through the site with the person over the phone and record his or her comments in a similar fashion to that used in the formal testing.

Yet another way to use outside testers is through surveys or polls on your Web site. You may have seen something similar on other Web sites, particularly if you've done any shopping on the Web. Many online stores ask you to fill out an evaluation form, which is similar to comment cards you obtain at traditional stores.

One of the most popular evaluation systems for online stores is BizRate. Many stores use this company's services to gather feedback from shoppers. Then, potential shoppers can view the company's *rate card* at BizRate to determine whether or not to do business with it. A typical rate card at BizRate includes the following information from previous shoppers:

- Overall rating
- Ease of ordering
- Product selection
- Product information
- Price
- Web site performance
- On-time delivery
- Product representation
- Customer support
- Order tracking
- Shipping and handling

NOTE **For more information about BizRate, visit** `www.bizrate.com`**.**

If you decide to create your own online form for a similar purpose, consider asking the same type of questions of shoppers. If you ask specific questions, you're more likely to receive specific answers. In other words, it is more effective to post a form with questions such as, "How would you rate the download speed of our new site?" instead of "What do you think about our new site?"

If you're interested in asking a single question of your visitors, consider using a poll. If you don't have the experience to write a CGI script to process your poll or survey, plenty of free or inexpensive options are available online. For example, companies such as Sparklit or Alxnet offer free polls and surveys (among other types of scripts) that are easy to use and customize.

NOTE **For more information on Sparklit or Alxnet, visit** `www.sparklit.com` **or** `www.alxnet.com`**. Another great source for online polling and surveys is** `www.zoomerang.com`**.**

Evaluating input from testers and visitors

Once you've gathered information from testers and visitors, it's important to evaluate the findings and follow up with changes to your site as needed. The best way to prepare for an evaluation is to set up a series of success metrics prior to launching your test, poll, survey, or other feedback form.

Success metrics identify how you plan to gauge whether or not your site has achieved its goals. To determine the success metrics for your site, first review the goals for your site to identify the intended purpose. The following list shows a few examples of success metrics for Web sites:

- Improve consumer awareness of the company among 18- to 24-year-old female Internet users to at least 50 percent, as measured by independent surveys of customers.
- Register 250 paying members within the first three months of the launch.
- Generate online sales of merchandise totaling $500,000 after six months of operation.
- Enhance satisfactory customer support for shoppers, as measured through independent surveys of customers.

Once you've identified what you consider to be successful for your site, you can evaluate any feedback you receive. For example, if you have not met your targeted goal of $500,000 in sales after 6 months, you can ask your users why they didn't make purchases. In many similar situations, customer satisfaction surveys show that 68 percent of customers feel the ordering process is too difficult. After companies listen to users and alter the ordering process, sales are more likely to reach their targeted levels.

Another key point in evaluating feedback is to set a specific time frame in which you will gather the feedback, and another time frame for evaluating it. If you evaluate responses one by one, it is more difficult to get a clear picture of the results than if you evaluate all of the feedback together. In other words, consider evaluating your site feedback on a weekly or monthly basis, instead of daily.

Finally, don't consider having an e-mail address on your Web site as your only form of gathering visitor feedback. While you may indeed get some feedback through a simple `mailto` link on your site, you're likely to receive more complaints than constructive feedback. The best way to effectively gather and evaluate feedback is by asking direct questions of targeted users.

NOTE **Don't forget about your site's server logs! They may also be a source of feedback because they identify concerns, such as how many people received errors when visiting your site, how long typical visitors spent on your site, and where they came from.**

Coping with Visitors Changing Your Site

One common frustration among Web designers is that visitors to a site have the ultimate authority on how it is displayed. In other designed media such as print advertising, every viewer sees the same advertisement, at the same size, with the same colors, and with the same layout.

The opposite is true for Web design because a single Web page can be interpreted in many different ways, according to the viewer's settings and preferences.

Browser preference settings

Most browsers give viewers the option to adjust preferences related to the display of Web pages. For example, Firefox enables users to specify in which font faces, sizes, and colors in which they want to view Web sites. Figure 22-1 shows how Firefox handles these preferences.

FIGURE 22-1

Users of Firefox can customize font and color settings.

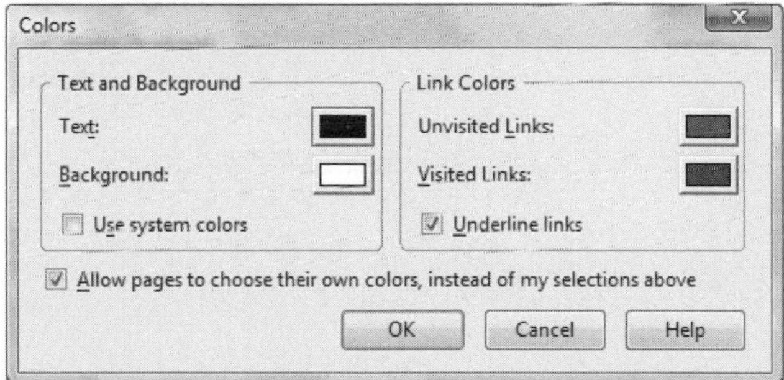

IE users can also customize their browsers, although in a slightly different way than Firefox users. Figure 22-2 and Figure 22-3 show some examples of the IE preferences in Internet Explorer 7 on the PC.

IE users can also set up their own personal style sheets to manage options such as the font size, style, and color of the displayed text content.

Our impression is that the majority of Internet users do not customize their browsers in a way that greatly affects the display of your pages. Perhaps the most commonly adjusted setting in the browser is the font size, making it easier for visitors to see pages according to their own needs. As a result, it is probably worthwhile to test your site under several different font settings to ensure that all text is still legible.

FIGURE 22-2

Users of Internet Explorer 7 can customize color settings.

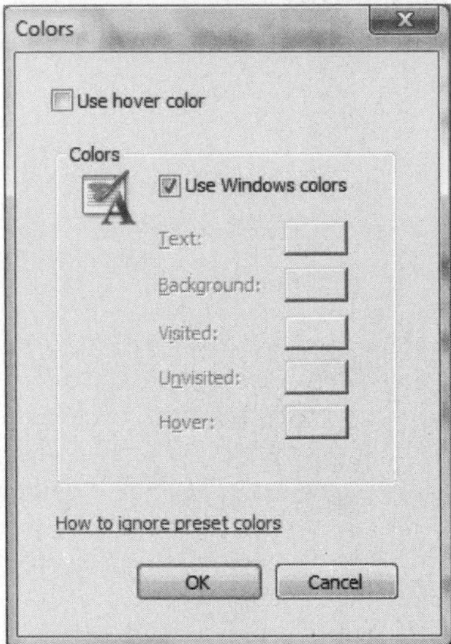

FIGURE 22-3

Users of Internet Explorer 7 can customize these language settings.

Maintaining Consistency on Your Site

One of the beauties of the Web is the ease with which things can be changed. Although it may be tempting to change your site each time you learn of a new tool, technology, or feature, this approach may not necessarily benefit your visitors.

Visitor comfort

A constantly changing Web site cuts into your visitors' comfort level with the site. Maintaining the comfort level on your site is important for two reasons.

First, you don't want to adopt any new Web technologies so early that no one knows how to use or comprehend them. And second, you don't want to change the elements of your site so quickly that your visitors never really learn how to use them. For example, if your local grocery store switched the locations of your favorite foods weekly or monthly, you'd probably find shopping there quite frustrating. The same is true of Web sites that change structure and layout too often.

For these reasons, it is worthwhile to limit major upgrades to the structure and layout of your site to once or twice a year. In the interim, focus on the actual content of your site, ensuring that it is user-friendly and timely. Gradually updating the content of your site over time and fixing minor problems as you encounter them is called *site maintenance*.

Common maintenance tasks

The following list provides an overview of some common maintenance tasks:

- Update product information and sales
- Archive or update news/press releases
- Update job listings
- Update contact information (such as e-mail addresses, mailing addresses, and phone and fax numbers)
- Revise home page copy (such as a daily/weekly/monthly feature or article)
- Publicize events (perhaps on a calendar)
- Add new links
- Verify existing links
- Remove outdated links
- Promote new services/features (within the Web site)
- Update photos
- Promote the Web site (on the Internet)

The question of whose responsibility it is to perform maintenance on a Web site is not easily answered. Large companies often subcontract the work to consultants or other firms. Smaller companies sometimes add this task to an existing employee's responsibilities. However, you can hire a company that focuses specifically on Web site maintenance tasks.

Site improvement tools

If you decide to perform your own site maintenance, many tools are available to assist you. To make changes to your HTML, you'll need some type of HTML editor. Many HTML editors offer specific site maintenance tools such as link and HTML validators, so be sure you check for those before looking for (and possibly paying for) other tools. In addition, don't forget to check with your host company — many of these companies offer maintenance tools with hosting packages.

Services in the improvement category of maintenance tools include a full range of tools from link validators to traffic analyzers.

Several companies offer such services. Here's a list of some of the more popular ones:

- editCom (`edit.com`)
- LinkAlarm (`www.linkalarm.com`)
- Net Mechanic (`www.netmechanic.com`)

So far, the tools we've listed are run online. However, you can purchase several high-quality products to install on your own system. Typically, products such as the following are used by Webmasters who want to manage their own site maintenance:

- NetIQ (`www.netiq.com`)
- AppScan QA by Watchfire (`www.watchfire.com/products/appscan/`)
- WebMaster Resources. (`www.google.com/webmasters/`)
- Google Analytics (`www.google.com/analytics`)
- CyberSpyder by Aman Software (`www.cyberspyder.com`)

Server monitors

A relatively new breed of online maintenance tools relates to third-party server monitoring. Companies such as @Watch (`www.atwatch.com`) monitor your Web server, checking at regular intervals to ensure that everything is working correctly. If they detect an outage, you are notified within five minutes.

One of the biggest advantages of these services is the independent nature of the monitors. Because the monitoring company is not the hosting company, you may be more likely to be notified in a timely manner about lapses in service.

Summary

It's not enough to just whip up a good-looking site and walk away from it. You need to thoroughly test and maintain it, too.

In this chapter, you learned that broken links are one of the most common and irritating problems with Web sites. Test your site with every available computer platform and browser. Ask outsiders to test your site and provide you with feedback. Keep your site consistent and fresh.

Chapter 23 introduces you to the world of RSS.

Chapter 23

RSS

RSS (Really Simple Syndication) is an easy way to distribute Web content (for example, newsfeeds, sports events, weather, other subjects of personal interest) from one Web site to multiple others. A user must subscribe to a syndicated feed. RSS files can be automatically updated. Content should be written in XML.

The simplicity of RSS (that is, the size of the data transfer and speed of transfer) makes it a very useful application to have for mobile devices (podcasts). You can easily imagine getting live feeds from the stock exchange when values of a selected portfolio of stocks change. You may, as well, look into space shuttle activities or our future trips to Mars and beyond. It is easier to have these feeds keep you abreast of what interests you in the happenings of the world, rather than your having to visit a few dozen sites several times a day.

Modern operating systems have RSS built in. For example, Windows Vista has an RSS reader as part of its SideBar utility, and there's an RSS database engine built into the operating system. Mac OS X 10.4 and later also has RSS built in as a screen saver and widget. RSS is a great way for your customers, employees, clients, and yourself to get up-to-date information as it's released. Keep this in mind when marketing your RSS feed.

IN THIS CHAPTER

Origin of RSS

The background of the origin and development of RSS is a reminder that, even with the best of intentions, smart people with sound ambition and good technology can still go astray in the confusing morass of copyrights and property rights. The origin of RSS goes way back in the almost mystical 1990s when Internet startups were almost as common as acne on a teen, and dot-com millionaires were popping up like toads in spring.

It was Apple, of course, that led the way. One man in particular at Apple, R. V. Guha, continued his development of the syndication technology with another flagship of innovation and savvy, Netscape.

As part of Apple's Advanced Technology Group, Guha created a Meta Content Framework (MCF), which, as its name implies, specified formatting for metadata for Web sites. This is the foundation on which his subsequent development of the Resource Description Framework (RDF) took place at Netscape. RDF has a structure that translates easily into an object-oriented format — attribute and values — such that the statement "These autumn hills are of variegated colors" — could be decomposed into `autumnalHills.color(variegated)`. These specifications became part of the RDF framework under the aegis of W3C, and further information on it can be found at the W3C site (`www.w3.org/RDF`).

Indeed, RDF is so widely adaptable that it has been the modeling milieu for quite a number of syntax formats. In the late 1990s, versions of RSS (called RSS .9 and RSS .91) came out based on the RDF specs.

RSS .9 was a syndication feed initially developed for only Netscape feeds through its portal `My.Netscape.com`. Subsequent developments removed RDF elements and replaced them with another syndication format produced by Dave Winer. This version was known as RSS 0.94. In the meantime, mergers and acquisitions killed off this promising new technology for Netscape for a number of years, during which time it continued to be developed by Winer at another company, UserLand.

Depending upon which working group you follow, RSS could mean "Rich Site Summary," or "RDF Site Summary," as well as other interpretations. Despite identical acronyms, they were pretty dissimilar: one had a DTD component, and another didn't; one provided syndication in the way we would understand it today, and another simply summarized site contents. And, as to be expected with competing groups working not necessarily in harmony with each other, you had incompatible versions being produced.

Most versions are backward compatible, but, because RSS was almost two separate formats incidentally named, even that is not as useful as it might otherwise be. For those interested in the specifics, refer to the Web site at `http://diveintomark.org/archives/2004/02/04/incompatible-rss`.

UserLand Software failed to obtain trademark rights to RSS. But that did not stop development of RSS by UserLand and other groups. RSS 1.0 (through the combined efforts of Guha within the RSS-Dev working group) came out in 2000, adding support for XML namespaces, and brought back support for RDF.

RSS 2.0 came out in 2002, but it was legally unclear as to who owned the rights (as well as what was open source, what was proprietary, and what was Netscape's role) to it. So, another syndication version, Atom, came out in 2003. It was then adopted as the official syndication standard by Internet Engineering Task Force (IETF).

FIGURE 23-1

The RSS icon was accepted by Microsoft.

FIGURE 23-2

The RSS XML icon also is a standard.

XML RSS 2.0

What appears to have solidified support and the future direction of RSS was Microsoft's announcement in 2005 that it was using the standard RSS icon for syndication feeds, as shown in Figure 23-1. Figure 23-2 shows the RSS XML icon that is standard.

NASA Page with Links to RSS Feeds

Now let us take a look at a sample Web page with multiple links to a variety of RSS feeds. The Web page shown in Figure 23-3. is from the National Aeronautical and Space Administration, and has multiple links shown in the middle of the page.

The following illustrates the process of making a link to an RSS feed on the NASA Web site.

- The XML declaration defines the XML version as 1.0 and the encoding scheme as UTF-8:

  ```
  <?xml version="1.0" encoding="UTF-8"?>
  ```

- The following defines the location of the stylesheet to be used. XML stylesheets have an XML extension and allow Web designers great elasticity in the way Web docs are presented. This allows XML documents to have cross-platform support.

  ```
  <?xml-stylesheet href="/externalflash/NASA_Detail/NASA_Detail.xsl"
  type="text/xsl"?>
  ```

- This defines the RSS version:

  ```
  <rss version="2.0">
  ```

FIGURE 23-3

The NASA RSS Feeds page provides links to the various RSS channels.

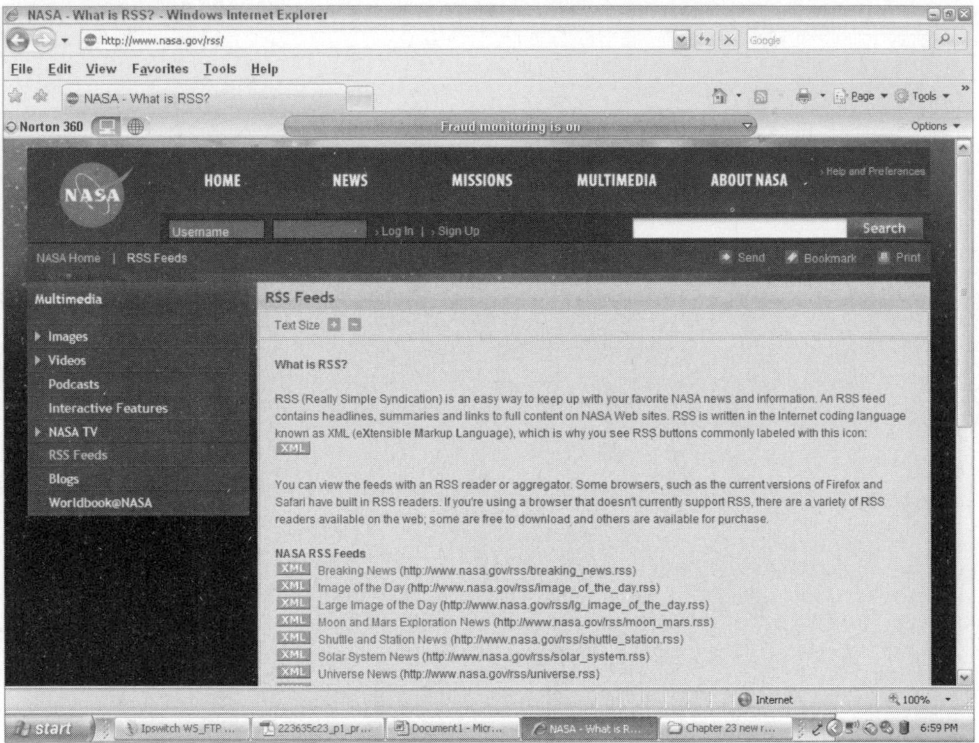

Now, consider the following code:

```
*/
<channel>
<title>NASA Breaking News</title>
<link>http://www.nasa.gov/audience/formedia/features/
index.html</link>
<description>A RSS news feed containing the latest NASA news
articles and press releases.</description>
<language>en-us</language>
<docs>http://blogs.harvard.edu/tech/rss</docs>
<managingEditor>cenger@nasa.gov</managingEditor>
<webMaster>brian.dunbar@nasa.gov</webMaster>
```

```
<item>
<title xmlns:java_code="xalan://gov.nasa.build.Utils1">NASA
Selects 38 Partnerships to Advance Key Technologies</title>
<link xmlns:java_code="xalan://gov.nasa.build.Utils1">http://www.nasa
.gov/home/hqnews/2007/oct/HQ_07232_IPP_Seed_Fund.html</link>
 <guid xmlns:java_code="xalan://gov.nasa.build.Utils1">http://www
.nasa.gov/home/hqnews/2007/oct/HQ_07232_IPP_Seed_Fund.html</guid>
 <description xmlns:java_code="xalan://gov.nasa.build.Utils1">
On Wednesday, NASA's Innovative Partnerships Program Seed
Fund announced the selection of 38 partnerships that will advance key
technologies to meet critical needs for NASA's mission.</description>
 <pubDate xmlns:java_code="xalan://gov.nasa.build.Utils1">Wed,
31 Oct 2007 00:00:00 EDT</pubDate>
.
.
.

</item>
</channel>
</rss>
```

Let's take a look at what is going on in this code:

- `<channel>` — This would be a specific RSS feed, such as a Christian Broadcast Network (CBN) channel or a Fox News Channel (FNC) channel. The channel element is used to describe the feed and has three sub-elements (or child elements, if you consider channel as the parent node.): `<title>`, `<link>`, and `<description>`. A channel must also have one or more `<item>` elements. Each `<item>` element also has three required child elements: `<title>`, `<link>`, and `<description>`.
- `<title>` — This refers to the title of the channel. In the example code, the title for the channel is "NASA Breaking News."
- `<link>` — This is the URL to the channel. The following is the link in this example:

  ```
  <link>http://www.nasa.gov/audience/formedia/features/index
  .html</link>
  ```
- `<description>` — This describes the nature of the channel.
- `<language>` — This simply identifies the encoding scheme for that specific feed.
- `<item>` — This has the same three required elements as the `<channel>` element previously discussed, and they are used in the same way, but instead of defining on the channel level, they define the specific feed level.
- `<guid>` — This element (short for *Globally Unique Identifier*) is a unique 128-bit number that is produced by a Windows operating system or a Windows program to identify

a particular component, application, file, and/or user. As a matter of fact, it is such a good unique identifier that some database administrators use the guid as a primary key.

Figure 23-4 shows the hierarchy of channel elements.

Following are other elements not shown in this example:

- <image> — This allows images to be displayed. It also has three elements: <url> (which defines the path to the image), <title> (which acts as text backup or alt tag while the image is being loaded for display), and <link> (which defines the hypertext link to the RSS channel).
- <category> — This is used as a metatag to allow grouping of like domains by RSS aggregators.
- <copyright> — This contains copyright information.

Figure 23-5 shows the sub-elements of <item>.

Table 23-1 shows a more comprehensive list of the optional elements.

FIGURE 23-4

This hierarchy of channel elements in an RSS feed shows the required children of <channel> and required children of <item>.

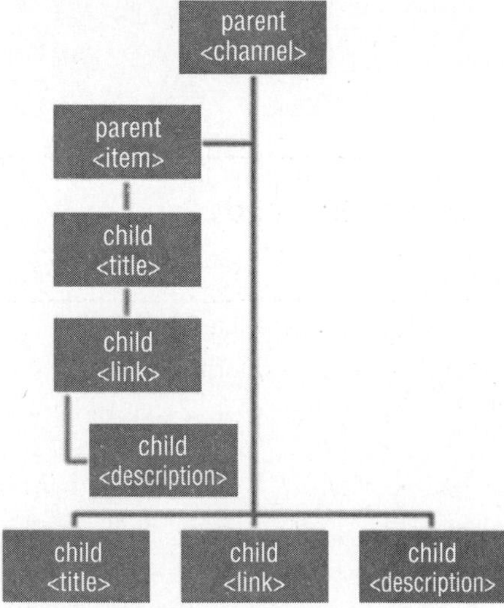

FIGURE 23-5

In this diagram, you can see the optional sub-elements of `<item>`.

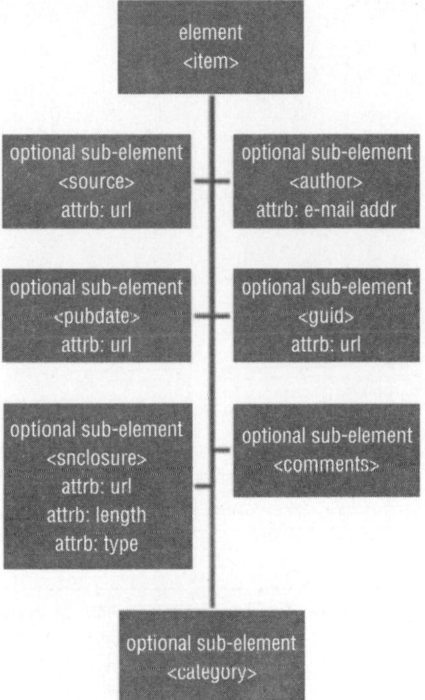

TABLE 23-1

Optional Elements for RSS Feeds

Element	Description	Example
`language`	The language the channel is written in. This allows aggregators to group all Italian language sites, for example, on a single page. You may also use values defined by the W3C.	`en-us`
`copyright`	Copyright notice for content in the channel.	`Copyright 2008, Wiley and Sons`
`managingEditor`	E-mail address for person responsible for editorial content.	`www.wiley.com` (Chris Webb)

continued

TABLE 23-1 *(continued)*

Element	Description	Example
webMaster	E-mail address for person responsible for technical issues relating to channel.	Auri@technorati.mobi
pubDate	The publication date for the content in the channel. For example, the *New York Times* publishes on a daily basis, the publication date flips once every 24 hours. That's when the pubDate of the channel changes. All date-times in RSS conform to the Date and Time Specification of RFC 822, with the exception that the year may be expressed with two characters or four characters (four preferred).	Sat, 07 Sep 2007 12:12:00 EST
lastBuildDate	The last time the content of the channel changed.	Sat, 29 Feb 2008 9:42:31 EST
category	Specify one or more categories that the channel belongs to. Follows the same rules as the <item>-level category element.	<category>Newspapers</category>
generator	A string indicating the program used to generate the channel.	MightyInHouse Content System v2.3
docs	A URL that points to the documentation for the format used in the RSS file. It's probably a pointer to this page. It's for people who might stumble across an RSS file on a Web server 25 years from now and wonder what it is.	http://backend.userland.com/rss
cloud	Allows processes to register with a cloud to be notified of updates to the channel, implementing a lightweight publish-subscribe protocol for RSS feeds.	<cloud domain = "rpc.sys.com" port = "80" path = "/RPC2" registerProcedure = "pingMe" protocol = "soap"/>
ttl	ttl stands for "time to live." It's a number of minutes that indicates how long a channel can be cached before refreshing from the source.	<ttl>60</ttl>
image	Specifies a GIF, JPEG, or PNG image that can be displayed with the channel.	
textInput	Specifies a text input box that can be displayed with the channel.	

TABLE 23-1 *(continued)*

Element	Description	Example
`skipHours`	A hint for aggregators telling them which hours they can skip.	
`skipDays`	A hint for aggregators telling them which days they can skip.	

Source: `www.w3.org`

Figure 23-6 shows a sample of an RSS Feed page generated from the NASA Web site.

FIGURE 23-6

This is an illustration of a NASA RSS feed page.

Here is the full XML version of the example RSS Feeds page shown in Figure 23-6:

```
<?xml version="1.0" encoding="UTF-8"?>
<?xml-stylesheet href="/externalflash/NASA_Detail/NASA_Detail.xsl"
type="text/xsl"?>
<rss version="2.0"><channel> <title>NASA Breaking News</title>

<link>http://www.nasa.gov/audience/formedia/features/
index.html</link>

<description>A RSS news feed containing the latest NASA news
articles and pressreleases.</description>

<language>ens</language>

<docs>http://blogs.harvard.edu/tech/rss</docs><managingEditor>
cenger@nasa.gov</managingEditor><webMaster>brian.dunbar@nasa
.gov</webMaster><item> <title xmlns:java_code="xalan://gov
.nasa.build.Utils1">NASA Selects 38 Partnerships to Advance Key
Technologies</title> <link xmlns:java_code="xalan://gov.nasa.build
.Utils1">http://www.nasa.gov/home/hqnews/2007/oct/HQ_07232_IPP_
Seed_Fund.html</link> <guid xmlns:java_code="xalan://gov.nasa.build
.Utils1">http://www.nasa.gov/home/hqnews/2007/oct/HQ_07232_IPP_
Seed_Fund.html</guid> <description xmlns:java_code="xalan://gov
.nasa.build.Utils1">On Wednesday, NASA's Innovative Partnerships
Program Seed Fund announced the selection of 38 partnerships
that will advance key technologies to meet critical needs for NASA's
mission.</description><pubDate xmlns:java_code="xalan://gov.nasa
.build.Utils1">Wed, 31 Oct 2007 00:00:00 EDT</pubDate> </item> <item>
<title xmlns:java_code="xalan://gov.nasa.build.Utils1">NASA to
Establish Nationwide Lunar Science Institute</title> <link xmlns:
java_code="xalan://gov.nasa.build.Utils1">http://www.nasa.gov/
home/hqnews/2007/oct/HQ_07233_ARC_Lunar_Institute.html</link>
<guid xmlns:java_code="xalan://gov.nasa.build.Utils1">http://www.nasa
.gov/home/hqnews/2007/oct/HQ_07233_ARC_Lunar_Institute
.html</guid> <description xmlns:java_code="xalan://gov
.nasa.build.Utils1">NASA has announced its intent to establish a new
lunar science institute.</description> <pubDate xmlns:java_code=
"xalan://gov.nasa.build.Utils1">Tue, 30 Oct 2007 00:00:00
EDT</pubDate> </item> <item><title xmlns:java_code="xalan://gov
.nasa.build.Utils1">New Center Assignments for Moon Exploration
</title> <link xmlns:java_code="xalan://gov.nasa.build.Utils1">
http://www.nasa.gov/home/hqnews/2007/oct/HQ_07234_ESMD_
Work_Assignments.html</link> <guid xmlns:java_code="xalan://gov.nasa
.build.Utils1">http://www.nasa.gov/home/hqnews/2007/oct/HQ_
07234_ESMD_Work_Assignments.html</guid> <description xmlns:java_code=
```

```
"xalan://gov.nasa.build.Utils1">NASA announced Tuesday which agency
centers will take responsibility for specific work to enable
astronauts to explore the moon.</description> <pubDate xmlns:java_
code="xalan://gov.nasa.build.Utils1">Tue, 30 Oct 2007 00:00:00
EDT</pubDate> </item> <item><title xmlns:java_code="xalan://gov
.nasa.build.Utils1">NASA Awards Environmental Management, Safety
Service Contract</title> <link xmlns:java_code="xalan://gov.nasa
.build.Utils1">http://www.nasa.gov/home/hqnews/2007/oct/HQ_
C07053_GRC_Envir_Mgmt_and_Safety.html</link>
<guid xmlns:java_code="xalan://gov.nasa.build.Utils1">http://www
.nasa.gov/home/hqnews/2007/oct/HQ_C07053_GRC_Envir_
Mgmt_and_Safety.html</guid> <description xmlns:java_code=
"xalan://gov.nasa.build.Utils1">NASA has selected SAIC to
provide environmental management and safety office support at NASA's
Glenn Research Center, Cleveland.</description> <pubDate xmlns:java_
code="xalan://gov.nasa.build.Utils1">Mon, 29 Oct 2007 00:00:00
EDT</pubDate> </item> <item><title xmlns:java_code="xalan://gov
.nasa.build.Utils1">NASA to Announce Work Assignments to Enable
Lunar Exploration</title> <link xmlns:java_code="xalan://gov
.nasa.build.Utils1">http://www.nasa.gov/home/hqnews/2007/oct/HQ_
M07149_ESMD_Workforce_Telecon_Advisory.html</link>
<guid xmlns:java_code="xalan://gov.nasa.build.Utils1">http://www.nasa
.gov/home/hqnews/2007/oct/HQ_M07149_ESMD_Workforce_Telecon_
Advisory.html</guid> <description xmlns:java_code="xalan://gov.nasa
.build.Utils1">On Tuesday, Oct. 30, NASA will take another important
step toward returning astronauts to the moon by assigning key future
Constellation Program work to its field centers.</description>
<pubDate xmlns:java_code="xalan://gov.nasa.build.Utils1">Tue,
30 Oct 2007 00:00:00 EDT</pubDate> </item> <item><title
xmlns:java_code="xalan://gov.nasa.build.Utils1">Discovery, Space
Station Crew News Conference</title> <link xmlns:java_code=
"xalan://gov.nasa.build.Utils1">http://www.nasa.gov/home/hqnews/
2007/oct/HQ_M07150_Crew_News_Conference.html</link> <guid xmlns:java_
code="xalan://gov.nasa.build.Utils1">http://www.nasa.gov/home/hqnews/
2007/oct/HQ_M07150_Crew_News_Conference.html</guid> <description
xmlns:java_code="xalan://gov.nasa.build.Utils1">The 10 crew members
flying aboard Discovery and the International Space Station will hold
a news conference at 6:48 a.m. CDT on Oct. 31.</description>
<pubDate xmlns:java_code="xalan://gov.nasa.build.Utils1">Mon,
29 Oct 2007 00:00:00 EDT</pubDate> </item> <item><title
xmlns:java_code="xalan://gov.nasa.build.Utils1">NASA Showcases
Next International Space Station Component</title> <link xmlns:java_
code="xalan://gov.nasa.build.Utils1">http://www.nasa.gov/home/hqnews/
2007/oct/HQ_M07148_STS-122_Columbus_Media_Event.html</link>
<guid xmlns:java_code="xalan://gov.nasa.build.Utils1">http://www.nasa
.gov/home/hqnews/2007/oct/HQ_M07148_STS-122_Columbus_Media_Event
```

```
.html</guid> <description xmlns:java_code="xalan://gov.nasa.build
.Utils1">NASA's Kennedy Space Center will hold a media event
at 2 p.m. EDT Wednesday, Oct. 31, to highlight the next pressurized
element to be launched to the International Space Station
.</description> <pubDate xmlns:java_code="xalan://gov.nasa
.build.Utils1">Thu, 25 Oct 2007 00:00:00 EDT</pubDate> </item>
<item><title xmlns:java_code="xalan://gov.nasa.build.Utils1">Media
Accreditation Deadlines for Next Shuttle Mission</title> <link
xmlns:java_code="xalan://gov.nasa.build.Utils1">http://www.nasa
.gov/home/hqnews/2007/oct/HQ_M07147_STS-122_Media_Credentials
.html</link> <guid xmlns:java_code="xalan://gov.nasa.build.Utils1">
http://www.nasa.gov/home/hqnews/2007/oct/HQ_M07147_STS-122_
Media_Credentials.html</guid> <description xmlns:java_code=
"xalan://gov.nasa.build.Utils1">NASA has set media accreditation
deadlines for the upcoming space shuttle mission, STS-122. Shuttle
Atlantis is targeted to launch Dec. 6.</description> <pubDate
xmlns:java_code="xalan://gov.nasa.build.Utils1">Wed,
24 Oct 2007 00:00:00 EDT</pubDate> </item> <item><title
xmlns:java_code="xalan://gov.nasa.build.Utils1">NASA Offers
$2 Million Lunar Lander Competition Prize</title> <link
xmlns:java_code="xalan://gov.nasa.build.Utils1">http://www.nasa
.gov/home/hqnews/2007/oct/HQ_M07146_x_prize_Lunar.html</link>
<guid xmlns:java_code="xalan://gov.nasa.build.Utils1">http://www.nasa
.gov/home/hqnews/2007/oct/HQ_M07146_x_prize_Lunar.html</guid>
<description xmlns:java_code="xalan://gov.nasa.build.Utils1">The
purpose of the lunar lander challenge is to accelerate technology
development leading to a commercial vehicle that could one day
be capable of ferrying cargo or humans back and forth between
lunar orbit and the moon's surface.</description> <pubDate xmlns:
java_code="xalan://gov.nasa.build.Utils1">Wed, 24 Oct 2007 00:00:00
EDT</pubDate> </item> <item><title xmlns:java_code="xalan://gov
.nasa.build.Utils1">New Satellite Images Show Vast Size of Wildfires
</title> <link xmlns:java_code="xalan://gov.nasa.build.Utils1">
http://www.nasa.gov/home/hqnews/2007/oct/HQ_M07145_Fires_
Image_Advisory.html</link> <guid xmlns:java_code="xalan://gov
.nasa.build.Utils1">http://www.nasa.gov/home/hqnews/2007/oct/HQ_
M07145_Fires_Image_Advisory.html</guid> <description
xmlns:java_code="xalan://gov.nasa.build.Utils1">NASA satellites have
obtained new images of the California wildfires, illustrating the
scale of the blazes. The National Interagency Fire Center reports
that 12 uncontained fires have burned more than 335,000 acres.
</description> <pubDate xmlns:java_code="xalan://gov.nasa
.build.Utils1">Wed, 24 Oct 2007 00:00:00 EDT</pubDate>
</item></channel></rss>
```

Figure 23-7 shows the NASA Breaking News RSS page.

FIGURE 23-7

This is a NASA Web page channel feed.

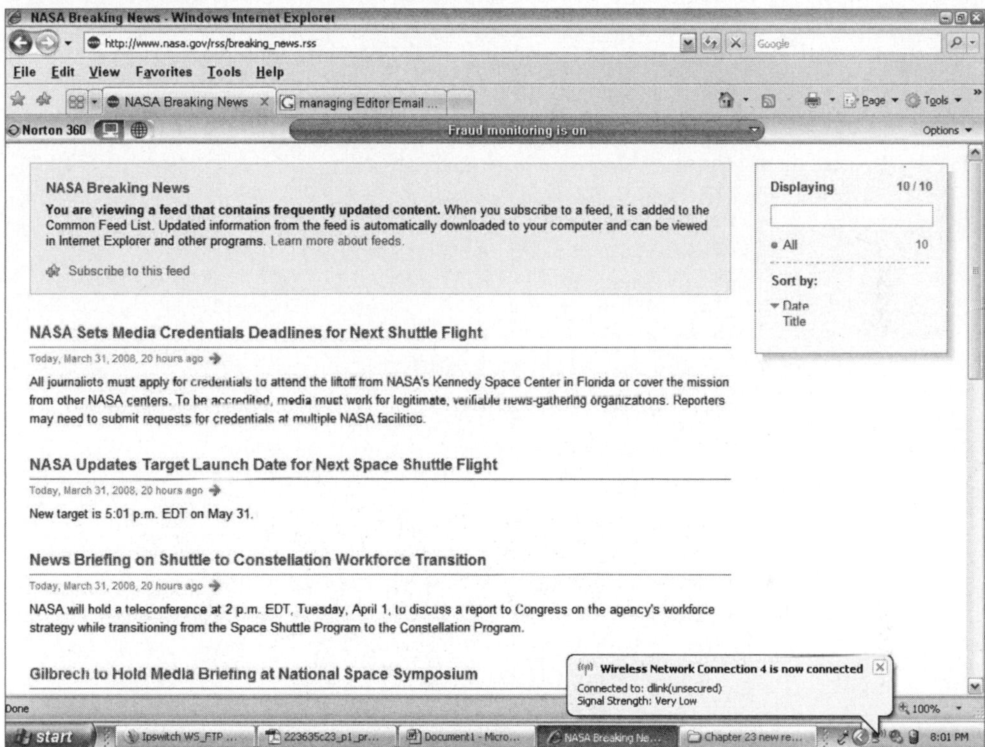

Following is the code from the page shown in Figure 23-7. Notice that this is an XML document. Each <item> element consists of four sub-elements that describe, respectfully, the source of the link: the URL for the channel (<link>), a string that uniquely identifies the item (<guid>, a brief description of the channel (<description>), and, finally, when the item was published (<pubDate>).

```
<?xml version="1.0" encoding="UTF-8"?>

<?xml-stylesheet href="/externalflash/NASA_Detail/NASA_Detail.xsl"
type="text/xsl"?>
<rss version="2.0"><channel><title>NASA Breaking News</title>
<link>http://www.nasa.gov/audience/formedia/features/index.html
</link><description>
```

```
A RSS news feed containing the latest NASA news articles and press
releases.</description><language>en-
us</language><docs>http://blogs.harvard.edu/tech/rss</docs>
<managingEditor>cenger@nasa.gov</managingEditor><webMaster>
brian.dunbar@nasa.gov</webMaster>

<item><title xmlns:java_code="xalan://gov.nasa.build.Utils1">NASA
Sets Media Credentials Deadlines for Next Shuttle Flight</title>
<link xmlns:java_code="xalan://gov.nasa.build.Utils1">
http://www.nasa.gov/home/hqnews/2008/mar/HQ_M08070_STS-124_
credentials.html</link>
<guid xmlns:java_code="xalan://gov.nasa.build.Utils1">
http://www.nasa.gov/home/hqnews/2008/mar/HQ_M08070_STS-124_
credentials.html</guid>

 <description xmlns:java_code="xalan://gov.nasa.build.Utils1">All
journalists must apply for credentials to attend the liftoff from
NASA's Kennedy Space Center in Florida or cover the mission from
other NASA centers. To be accredited, media must work for legitimate,
 verifiable news-gathering organizations. Reporters may need to
submit requests for credentials at multiple NASA facilities.
</description>

<pubDate xmlns:java_code="xalan://gov.nasa.build.Utils1">
Mon, 31 Mar 2008 00:00:00 EDT</pubDate> </item>

<item><title xmlns:java_code="xalan://gov.nasa.build.Utils1">NASA
Updates Target Launch Date for Next Space Shuttle Flight</title>
<link xmlns:java_code="xalan://gov.nasa.build.Utils1">
http://www.nasa.gov/home/hqnews/2008/mar/HQ_M08069_STS-124_
launch_date.html</link>

 <guid xmlns:java_code="xalan://gov.nasa.build.Utils1">
http://www.nasa.gov/home/hqnews/2008/mar/HQ_M08069_STS-124_
launch_date.html</guid>

<description xmlns:java_code="xalan://gov.nasa.build.Utils1">New
target  is 5:01 p.m. EDT on May 31.</description>

<pubDate xmlns:java_code="xalan://gov.nasa.build.Utils1">Mon,
31 Mar 2008 00:00:00 EDT</pubDate> </item>

<item><title xmlns:java_code="xalan://gov.nasa.build.Utils1">News
Briefing on Shuttle to Constellation Workforce Transition</title>

<link xmlns:java_code="xalan://gov.nasa.build.Utils1">
http://www.nasa.gov/home/hqnews/2008/mar/HQ_M08072_workforce_
transistion.html</link>
```

```
<guid xmlns:java_code="xalan://gov.nasa.build.Utils1">
http://www.nasa.gov/home/hqnews/2008/mar/HQ_M08072_workforce_
transistion.html</guid>

<description xmlns:java_code="xalan://gov.nasa.build.Utils1">NASA
will hold a teleconference at 2 p.m. EDT, Tuesday, April 1, to
discuss a report to Congress on the agency's workforce strategy
while transitioning from the Space Shuttle Program to the
Constellation Program.</description>
```

RSS Quick Reference

The following provides a quick reference for key items discussed in this chapter:

- `<item>` — An element within the RSS feed. Analogous to a program on a television channel.
- `<category>` — Used as a metatag to allow grouping of like domains.
- `<comments>` — Explanations of purpose of each Web feed. It is nonexecutable.
- `<image>` — A graphic, such as a photo or drawing that is sometimes part of the Web feed.
- `<channel>` — Content from an associated Web site that is fed into a host page frequently. Because it is a source of a specific RSS feed, it may be thought of as a particular channel on a television set that provides a specific type of program. (These programs, of course, may be thought of as items of the channel.)
- `<title>` — The name of the feed.
- `<link>` — A link to the source of a Web feed.
- `<guid>` — This is a Globally Unique Identifier, which is a unique identifier used to identify a component, application, file, or user.
- `<description>` — Another HTML tag that provides a concise statement of the contents of the feed. It would be analogous to a newspaper headline.

Summary

This chapter has discussed the origins of RSS and explained the reasoning leading to the development of Atom as an alternative syndication format. It provided examples of RSS feeds from NASA sites and presented a breakdown of the elements involved in creating links to sites used in the RSS feeds.

Chapter 24 provides an overview of blogs and other communications for a Web site.

Chapter 24

Blogging

A *blog* (short for *Web log*) is an online diary. From a high-level point of view, a blog is simply a Web page that is updated every day or so with new thoughts, comments, and links to interesting Web content. But blogs have taken on a life of their own and can be seen as an art form, a creative outlet, and a whole new way of looking at the Web — or even at the world.

Blogging solves the biggest problem people have after they get their initial Web site up, that is, wondering what do I do now? A regular Web site can seem rather complete and finished and leave you (and the user) wondering where new, fresh content goes. With a blog, new, fresh content is the whole reason for the site — and all you have to do to keep the site alive is update it regularly.

The World of Blogging

Blogs came to many people's attention through politics. The abortive presidential campaign of Howard Dean, Democratic candidate for president of the United States, reached a peak of popularity and hype in late 2003 and early 2004. At the center of the campaign's success in attracting money and volunteers was the Internet — and at the center of the campaign's Internet strategy was the candidate's blog. The 2004 Dean campaign itself became its own Internet "bubble." Many of Howard Dean's advisers went from eyeing office space in the West Wing to looking for another campaign to join in a few short weeks in early 2004. But blogging continued to grow, having shown what a powerful tool it can be for getting people's attention.

NOTE In this presidential cycle of 2008 there is a definite generational gap in the use of the Internet as a source of politicial activity and news gathering according to a survey of Internet usage during the 2008 campaign by the Pew Research Center. While 24% of the population overall learns something about the campaign off the Internet, almost half of young people ages 18 to 29 (42%) said they regularly got such information from the Internet. Both figures represent a doubling of use over January 2004. 27% of young people under 30 (and 37% of those under 24) cite the social networking sites of YouTube and Facebook as sources for their election and campaign news.

Only 8% of the population admit to having actually visited a candidate's Web site. This is the same percent as those who visit sites satirizing the campaign.

Blogs already have their own subculture and vocabulary. *Blogging* is maintaining your blog by adding new content to it; the *blogosphere* is the wonderful world of blogs, which tend to be extensively linked to each other. (Some of the most popular blogs are simply updates about the latest postings on other blogs.) Many people spend several hours a day cruising their favorite blogs and adding new content to their own.

But you don't have to devote your life to blogging to get a lot out of it. Even major news outlets post updates (in lively areas such as politics) in blog form, and many Web site creators have added a blog to their existing sites.

One way to use a blog is as a tool for adding news (and new interest) to existing Web or even printed content. Figure 24-1 shows the blog for a textbook, *Fundamentals of Building Construction: Materials and Methods* by Edward Allen and Joseph Iano (Wiley, 2003).

The blog is hosted on Typepad, a popular tool. The blog takes what might seem a rather dry subject and brings it to life with frequent updates.

NOTE If you need more information about blogs after reading this chapter, there's a wealth of information online. There are also several good books about blogging. Some books we can recommend are *Blogging for Dummies, 2nd Edition* by Susannah Gardner and Shane Birley (Wiley, 2008), *Blogging Heroes: Interviews with 30 of the World's Top Bloggers* by Michael A. Banks (Wiley, 2007), *The IT Girl's Guide to Blogging with Moxie* by Joelle Reeder and Katherine Scoleri (Wiley, 2007), and *ProBlogger: Secrets for Blogging Your Way to a Six-Figure Income* by D. Rowse (Wiley, 2008).

This chapter starts by introducing Blogger — the first widely popular tool for blogging. It then introduces other top tools and describes how to add blogging to an existing site, just as the construction example shown in Figure 24-1 does. Use the tools described in this chapter to put a toe in the water of blogging — or to dive all the way in.

Using Blogger

For several years now, the Number One tool for blogging has been a Web site with an easy name to remember: Blogger (`www.blogger.com`). Blogger makes it very easy to create your own Web site based around a blog of your own.

FIGURE 24-1

A blog can be used to bring a textbook to life.

Blogger is a great way to get started with blogging — or even to make your initial foray into Web publishing. That's because blogging keeps you focused on providing new content — and Blogger makes it very easy to create an initial site and to keep it updated.

A brief history of Blogger

Blogger was started several years ago by Pyra Labs, an energetic small company that recognized the potential of blogging early on. Blogger was begun as an easy-to-use, entry-level tool for creating blogs. It quickly became extremely popular, gaining more than a million registered users.

Being this popular, however, created challenges. Being the most popular brand in the blogosphere meant that hundreds of new users a day came to Blogger to get started — but these new users wanted a very easy-to-use tool with a lot of support. The experienced users wanted the tool to have depth so they could take their blogs further. Creating tools that can meet such a wide range of needs is expensive. So, Blogger itself needed some support.

Along came Google. As the most popular search engine on the Web, Google was a natural fit for the most popular blogging tool on the Web. Google needed to get better at helping its users search blogs — and Blogger needed Google's resources to keep improving what it offered.

In 2003, Google acquired Pyra Labs, its six employees, and its 1 million-plus registered users. Shortly afterward, the tool was improved with a spellchecker, increased stability, user-friendliness, and other new features — and it continues to be upgraded and improved.

As with many other free Web services, Blogger hosts advertising on your pages — and keeps the revenue for itself. It's not a bad tradeoff for what you get, and you can always move to an alternative service that doesn't include advertising — although you'll probably have to pay for the privilege. Radio Userland (`www.userland.com`) is one alternative paid service to consider if you want an ad-free site. It is also possible that your hosting provider has blogging tools available.

TIP **The setup process described here will put your blog on `blogspot.com`, with a name something like `yourname.blogspot.com`. To have your site hosted elsewhere, use the advanced blog setup at `www.blogger.com/adv-create-blog.g`, described at the end of this chapter. To use the advanced setup, you'll need details such as the FTP server to use; ask for help from your site's host if you need it.**

Setting up your blog on Blogger

Since the acquisition of Blogger by Google, many more resources have become available that make the service easier to use. Blogger recently updated its interface to make it even easier to create a blog.

However, though the steps are easier, it's still worth taking the time to create your blog carefully. If you like blogging, you may be living with the choices you make here for a long time!

Entering initial information into Blogger

Start by creating your blog by going to `www.blogger.com` (see Figure 24-2).

NOTE **If you look closely at the Blogger home page, you'll see a link to BlogThis, a quick way to comment on any Web page. Don't worry about this for now — we'll describe it later in this chapter. The link, not shown in the figure, is at the bottom of the Home page.**

From the home page, click the orange arrow with the words, "Create your blog now." You'll then see the "Create a Google Account" page, as shown in Figure 24-3.

Unfortunately, what you're about to do next looks a little simpler than it is. You have to understand all of these steps to end up with a setup for your blog that you like. Read this section before you actually enter anything, so you can see how each step affects the whole.

First, enter your e-mail address. If you already have an existing Google e-mail address, you must first sign in before you can proceed with creating and registering a blog. If you do not have an

FIGURE 24-2

Blogger greets you with a simple starting page.

existing Google account, just proceed with completing the form. This is your sign-on name for Blogger; it will never be shared with others without your permission.

TIP **Blogger is so popular that many of the choices you might think of (such as your first name followed by your last name, or "blogmaster," or something similar) are likely to be already taken. Choose something that's easy to remember but that's likely to be unique.**

Next, enter and retype your password. Be sure to make it difficult to guess but easy for you to remember, and keep it secret. Anyone with your username and password in hand could post content to your blog, which could be quite embarrassing to you.

The next step is where things get interesting. It's time to enter your display name. This name will show up when you post on Blogger, so don't make it too silly. Also, don't choose a display name that gives away your real name. You want to preserve your anonymity, except when you specifically choose to reveal who you are.

You also might want your display name to relate in some way to two things you enter on the next screen: your blog title and blog address.

FIGURE 24-3

Blogger asks for a bit of info to set up your account.

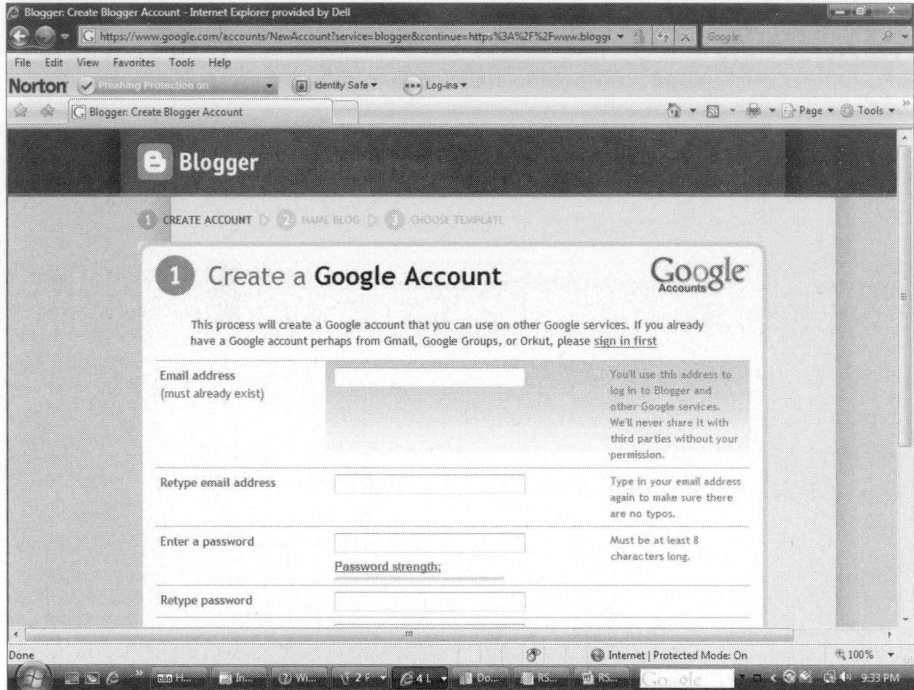

Next do the word verification check. This to verify that a real person is applying to start a blog. Sometimes the word is hard to read, but if you make a mistake (or two), you'll be given another chance to get it right.

Next, take a moment to read the Terms of Service agreement. Click the link to read them. They pop up in a new window, so don't worry about losing track of the data you've already entered. After you've read the Terms of Service agreement, click the check box to accept the terms.

NOTE **It's worth reading the Terms of Service agreement; you'll be entering a lot of personal data into your blog, and it's worthwhile to know what Blogger and Google believe they have the rights to do with it.**

Now double-check your choices; you won't get a chance to change them before creating your blog. Then click the Continue arrow.

If you're unlucky, the same screen will reappear, along with an error message that says there's a problem with something you entered. Most likely, your username is a duplicate of one that's already in use. Try a different one and click Continue again.

When you're fortunate enough to have all the data right, the next screen will appear.

Choosing your title and blog address

After you get all the data right on the first screen and click Continue, you get the "Name your blog" page shown in Figure 24-4.

FIGURE 24-4

Play the name game with your blog.

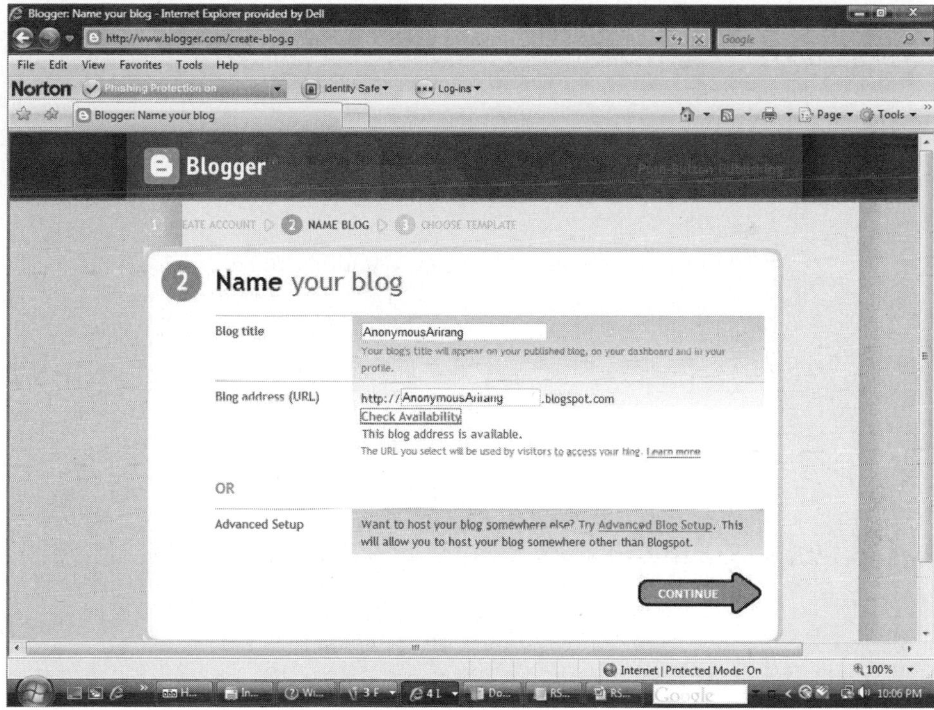

Enter the title for your blog. Give this some thought. Ideally, the title should stand out, should describe something special about your blog, should relate to your display name (as mentioned previously), and should relate to the blog address you'll enter next, which must be unique.

Once you have the title right, enter the blog address, the first part of the URL for your blog. The blog address will be added to the domain name `blogspot.com` to form the URL for your blog. (A computer programmer would say the domain name is *prepended by* your blog address.) For example, if you enter *frogwatcher* as your blog address, and it's accepted as unique, your URL will be `frogwatcher.blogspot.com`.

Your blog address, like your username, must be unique — there's no way two sites can be allowed to have the same URL. A great many desirable names are already taken. So, think carefully about a display name, blog title, and blog address that work together and are unique, so as to pass muster.

NOTE **Google can help you search for interesting blogs on `blogspot.com`, including blogs related to what you want to do. Use the search string "site:`blogspot.com` *topic*", entering the topic you're interested in. Google will return results with suitable pages. The results won't be perfect — it's difficult for Google, or any search engine, to keep up with bloggers! But you're likely to find some interesting reading.**

Once you have everything as you want it, check it over. You won't get another chance to change these options. Then, click the Continue arrow. As with the first screen, if you're unlucky, the same screen will reappear, along with an error message saying that there's a problem with something you entered — probably a duplicate blog address. Try a different one and click Continue again. Eventually, you'll hit on something unique, and the next screen will appear.

Use a template for your blog's look

Once your second screen of data is accepted, you'll get the "Choose a template" page shown in Figure 24-5. Scroll down to see all the template choices.

FIGURE 24-5

Get the look you want.

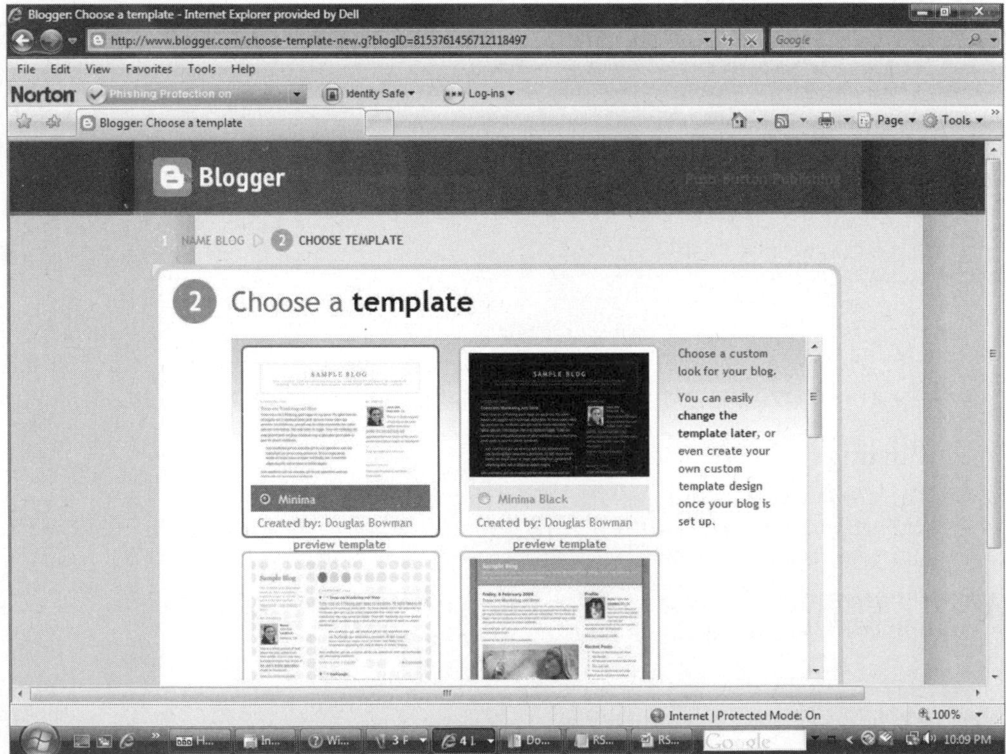

Choosing a template is not quite as easy as it first appears. Look at the small template images (called *thumbnails*) to determine which might suit you. To see a preview, mouse over the thumbnail image — your cursor will appear as a pointing finger. Next, click to see a popup window with a somewhat larger preview.

To select a template as your choice for the appearance of your blog, click near the option button. But be careful. Once you make a choice, your blog will be created instantly; you won't have a chance to review your choices or change anything first.

NOTE **You can always change your template later — either in part (by editing the page's HTML) or completely (by choosing a different template). Blogger will move your data, intact. But the results of changing your template can be frustrating, so take a bit of extra time in choosing a template initially so as to do all you can to make a good choice.**

When you're content with your choice of template, and are ready to create your blog, click Continue. Your blog will be created.

Now's a good time to take one more step. Click the Start Blogging arrow to open your blog so that you can start adding content to it. When your blog appears, save the URL in your Web browser's Favorites list. (In Internet Explorer and Firefox, you can click Ctrl+D to add the current page to your Favorites.)

Adding to your blog

Although you have to think about the steps, creating a blog is pretty easy. It's keeping it updated regularly with new content that's difficult. Yet, keeping your blog up to date is what enables you to truly claim the title of blogger.

Once you've created your blog in Blogger — try saying "blog in Blogger" three times fast! — you can let it sit, empty, for as long as you'd like. But we recommend that you dive right in and start entering content.

As you do so, you have a lot of options about how to enter text, how to set up options for your blog, and more. This section describes each of the screens you use to update and manage your blog, so you and the people who visit can get the most out of your blog from the beginning.

Posting

You create the posts that appear in your blog using the Posting page shown in Figure 24-6. Though you can edit, delete, or rearrange posts later, your blogging life will be easier if you use this page to get your posts right the first time (at least most times).

TIP **If you find yourself at your site's Dashboard and want to post, click the link to your page and then click the Create link.**

When you enter text on the Posting page, it shows up as plain text, with no formatting. You can cause the text that actually appears as your posting on the Web to be formatted or linked using four options.

FIGURE 24-6

Posting is the whole point of blogging.

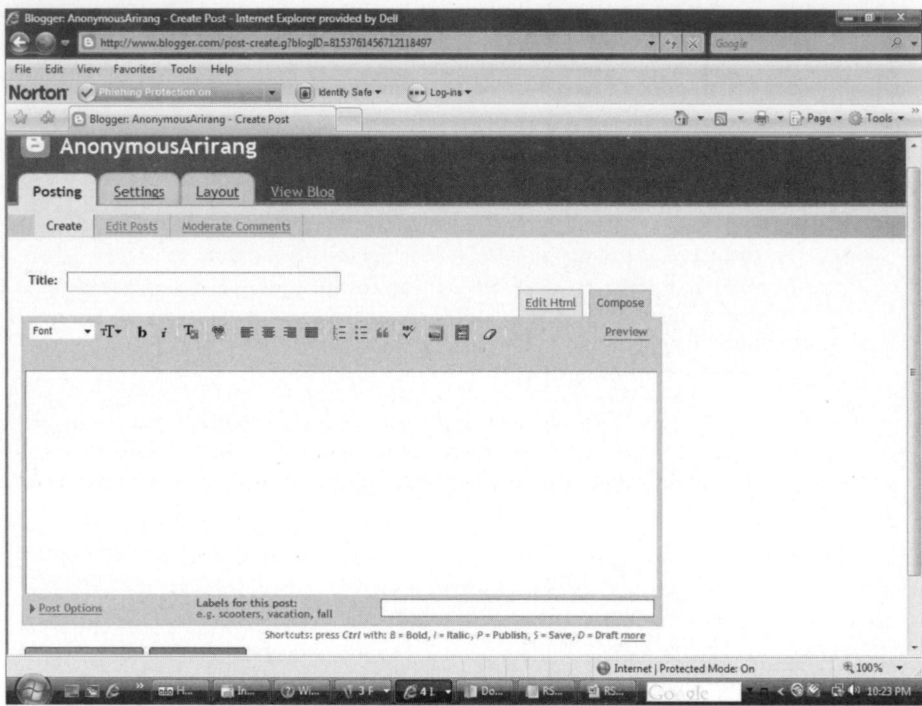

The first option is bold. This makes the text you select appear as bold text in the user's browser. First, highlight some text to select it, then choose the bold option. The HTML tags <B> and </B> will surround the text, and the surrounded text will appear bold.

Don't overuse bolding — it makes it appear as if you're yelling at your readers. For each phrase that you put in bold, consider whether you can reduce the bolding to a word or two. For each word (or two) that you put in bold, consider whether you can use clearer writing to remove the need for bolding altogether.

The next option is italics. This works like bolding, but the text appears italic (of course). Select the text you want, then choose the italics option. The HTML tags <I> and </I> surround the text, showing where italics will begin and end.

Unlike printed italic text, italic text on screen actually grabs the reader's eye less than plain text, because italics make the text more difficult to read on screen. So, as with bolding, use italic text sparingly, and keep in mind that some of your readers may have trouble reading it.

The third option is to link. To link text, highlight the stretch of text that you want to make into a link, then click the globe-and-chain icon. You'll have the opportunity to enter the Web address that you want to link to. To get rid of the link, delete the linked text.

Much of the point of blogging is to provide links to interesting content on the Web — sometimes within a main focus of interest for your blog, sometimes just a personal or a whimsical choice. So, link a lot. As with using bold and italic text, it's good to keep the text that you link brief and to the point. (Although it's overused, having the phrase "click here" as a link does tend to get readers to click.) But sure that the linked text, in combination with the text around it, lets the readers know what they're likely to see on the other end of the link — unless part of the point of your blog is to surprise people!

The final option is the blockquote. Text that you make into a blockquote is indented and displayed in a different font. It's usually used to highlight quoted text.

Don't use unending paragraphs of blockquoted text. You may end up with copyright problems if you quote too much, for one thing. Consider using a blockquote in lieu of a link. If there's an interesting few lines of text somewhere, consider blockquoting it, and providing a link to the source so that most of your blog visitors can see what you're talking about without necessarily having to follow the link.

CAUTION **Be careful about quoting song lyrics. They're copyrighted, and quoting more than a line or two of them may bring you unwanted attention. Other people post song lyrics on their sites, but there's no reason for you to push — or just plain exceed — the limits of copyright law. (Several sites that contain song lyrics have had to remove them under legal pressure.)**

You also have the option of spellchecking your content — a capability added since Google purchased Blogger, and for which those of us with bad spelling can be grateful.

Other Blogger options

Since it's the area where you add new content and keep your blog up to date, you're likely to spend most of your time editing your Blogger site in the Posting area (hopefully anyway). But Blogger has a lot of other options.

One option you should use a lot is View Blog. All it does is pop up a new window with your blog in it. This is very nice for checking what you currently have.

Don't simply use View Blog to view your site after you make changes. You may also want to use this option to see what's currently on your site as you're writing new posts.

The Settings area is nerd heaven. You can change dozens of options on separate pages with Basic, Publishing, Formatting, Comments, Archiving, Site Feed, Email, and Members options.

You should spend time getting to know these options. With them, you can do really cool things like sending e-mail that automatically is posted as an addition to your blog. However, don't spend all your time messing with the settings — a blog is there for you to post to!

With the Template area, you can see the HTML code for your template. This may or may not useful to you. You need real HTML and design skill to make useful changes to your template, but if you have that skill (or know someone who does), this may be a good area for you to spend time on.

You can also choose a different preexisting template in this area. This doesn't take any special skill — your whole blog just automatically appears the way you want it.

FIGURE 24-7

The Dashboard is a control panel for your blog.

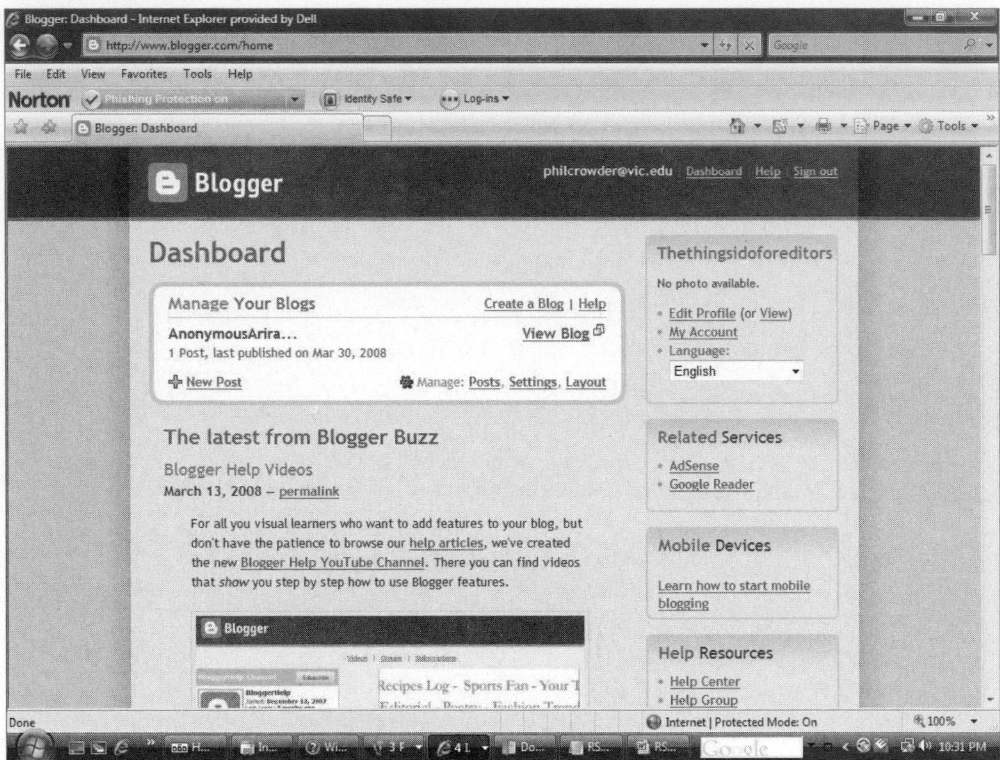

The Dashboard is the screen you'll typically see when you first sign in to Blogger. From the Dashboard, you can manage your entire blog. Figure 24-7 shows how the Dashboard appeared for one of the authors' blogs.

The BlogThis! option on the context menu is a particularly powerful one. It enables you to put a new icon in the toolbar of your Web browser, which you can use to quickly add a post to your blog that links to the site you're visiting at that moment. This is a great tool for bulking up your blog quickly with interesting content.

There's a lot you can do with your blog. You can allow other people to add comments to it, for example. Enjoy your blog — and keep adding to it. It's the gradual accumulation of comments and links over time that makes a blog worthwhile.

As soon as you've set up your blog and chosen your basic settings, tell people about it. You can form a whole new online community around your very own blog.

Alternative Blogging Tools

Blogger is not the only tool out there. In fact, as you spend time in the blogosphere and note where various blogs are hosted, you'll run into a variety of different sites that host blogs. You'll also run into many "roll your own" blogs, created with a tool or simply with pure HTML, that live on individual users' domains.

It's worth knowing something about the various blogging tools and add-ons that are out there so you can make an informed choice of the best way to get started with blogging. Perhaps you can even make a different choice for the best tool to use once you've achieved some momentum as a blogger.

NOTE **If you want your blog to automatically include content from other blogs — or to serve as a source that publishes automatically to others — check out the description of RSS and Atom in the section "Radio Userland" later in this chapter.**

There's a wide variety of blogging tools out there. Each has its own advantages and disadvantages, as well as its own thriving community of users. You may wish to check out Technorati and RSS Pings as a few examples. Technorati, in particular, has a coterie of Web developers who are dedicated to the principles of open source software.

AOL's Hometown

If you know anything about AOL (which has always focused on users), it may not surprise you to know that AOL includes a strong blogging feature. What might surprise you is to find out that the tool, hosted at AOL's Hometown Web-building site, is free to AOL members — that is, no charge beyond your AOL membership.

AOL calls a blog a "journal," as shown in Figure 24-8. AOL blogs are very easy to use and fairly capable — and, if you're already an AOL user, an AOL blog might be just about an automatic first choice for you.

AOL enables you to add posts directly to your journal or to send them in using instant messaging. AOLbyPhone is another way to add posts — you just call your post in by phone, and it appears as an audio clip.

You can make it easy for people to add comments — even non-AOL members. And you can make your journal public or private. AOL Alerts let you know when someone comments, or lets readers of your journal know when you've posted.

There are certainly limits on AOL Journals — older posts disappear from the screen fairly quickly, for example. But you can get around these limits by using other AOL capabilities, or combining your blog with a Hometown Web page or the "You've Got Photos" feature. These capabilities, and the support (from other users, and from AOL itself) that AOL is known for, may keep you an AOL Journals user for a long time.

FIGURE 24-8

AOL offers a Hometown for blogs — and Web pages.

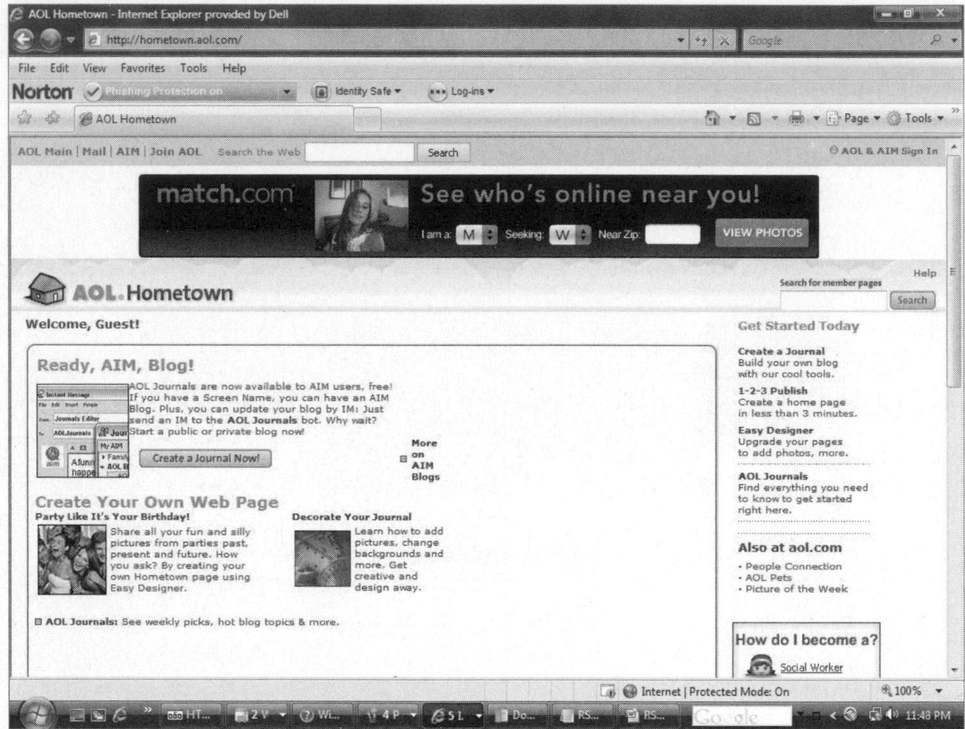

blogs.com and TypePad

`Blogs.com` is home to the TypePad Weblogging service (see Figure 24-9). TypePad is a hosted service, much like Blogger but without the ads — and with a set of features that may lead you to prefer it to rivals.

Cost is an issue. You may get a certain amount of introductory time free, but in mid-2007, charges for the service ranged from $4.95 a month for basic service to $29.95 for premium. (See `http://www.typepad.com/pricing/` for current figures and associated features.) The charges aren't bad if you're serious about your blog, but if you only post once in a blue moon, or want to save your money for other purposes, a free service may be a better choice.

For simply adding posts to your blog, TypePad is quite capable. You can allow or disallow comments on each individual post you make, and you can have comments wait in a queue for you to approve or disapprove them. (The first time someone comments on one of your posts with a string of obscenities, you may run, not walk, to turn on this feature.)

FIGURE 24-9

You'll see some great blogs at Typepad.

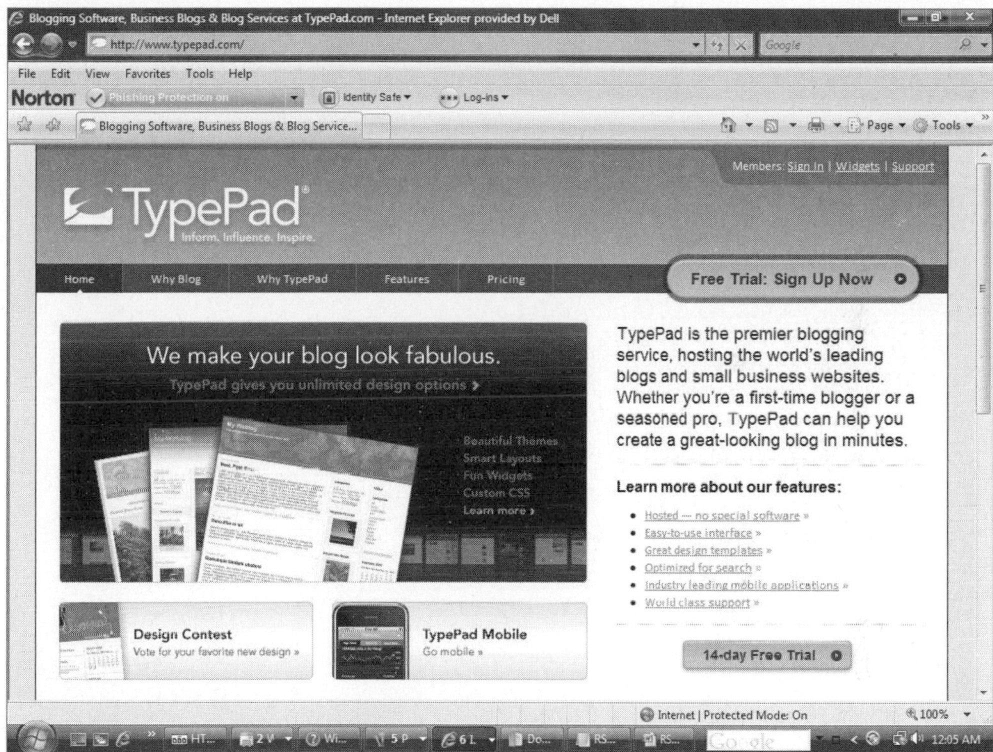

TypePad is also good for hosting photographs. You can add photo albums to your blog, with photo thumbnails, and display built-in pages. Links to `Amazon.com` for books or music are generated automatically within a list that appears alongside your posts.

Keeping your blog up to date is easy, too. You can post using a browser, e-mail, or a Wireless Access Protocol (WAP) enabled phone.

You need to know a little HTML to get the most out of TypePad, but it's easy to pick up the little bit that's needed. And TypePad will produce a nice-looking blog that you'll be proud to have people link to.

NOTE **If you are technically savvy, or know someone who is, Movable Type may be for you. Movable Type is the engine behind TypePad, and you can install it on your own site. If you know Perl (the scripting language widely used within Web sites), or know someone who does, check out Movable Type at** `www.movabletype.com`**.**

LiveJournal

Want to join more than half a million people in an exciting online community based around blogging? LiveJournal (www.livejournal.com) may be the place for you to do it (see Figure 24-10).

FIGURE 24-10

LiveJournal is a strong blogging community.

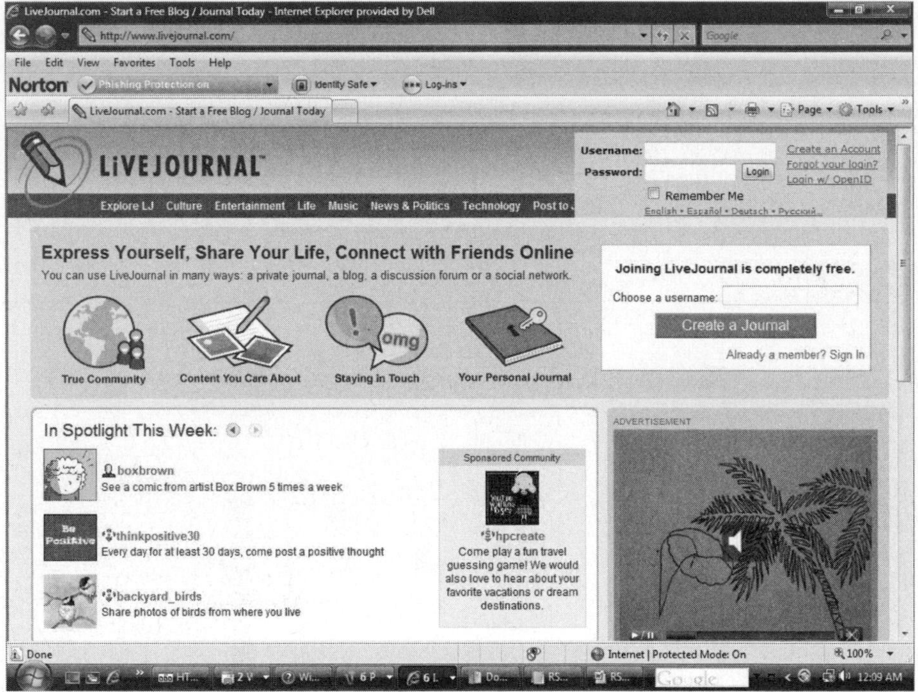

LiveJournal is very community-oriented. In fact, when we tried the service, the only way to get a free account was to have a current member invite you — an invitation you may want to take, if you get one. Otherwise, the service recently charged a reasonable $25 a year for its Basic package.

Comments on posts are as much a part of the LiveJournal scene as posts themselves. There's a strong discussion board capability built in, and you can get an e-mail notice sent to you when someone responds to your comment. It's easy for bloggers to link their blogs to one another, and you can add polls to your blog to get quick feedback.

You can post using a browser or a simple tool, although photos weren't supported when we checked the site out recently. (You can always post photos on another service and link to them from your blog.) But LiveJournal continues to grow in activity and popularity.

Radio UserLand

Userland is a powerful tool well suited to creating a serious blog — one that includes other users' content through an automatic stream, and that can easily be streamed into other sites. Figure 24-11 shows the Radio UserLand site.

You need some technical knowledge to get the most out of UserLand — and a little dough. A UserLand blog costs just under $40 a year ($39.95). As for technical knowledge, the higher-end capabilities of UserLand are based on RSS, a specification for using Web site content as a *syndication source* or *feed* into other Web sites. If this sounds like fun to you, then UserLand may be your best choice. If not, you may want to start with a simpler service.

To create your UserLand blog, you use desktop Web server software so that you can edit your blog while disconnected from the Internet. Once online, you *upstream* your additions to the Web, leaving you with a local copy of your site's content. You also have the option of posting from a browser or via e-mail, and you can post pictures as well as text. You can allow visitors to your site to add comments on your post.

FIGURE 24-11

Radio UserLand makes you a blogging broadcaster.

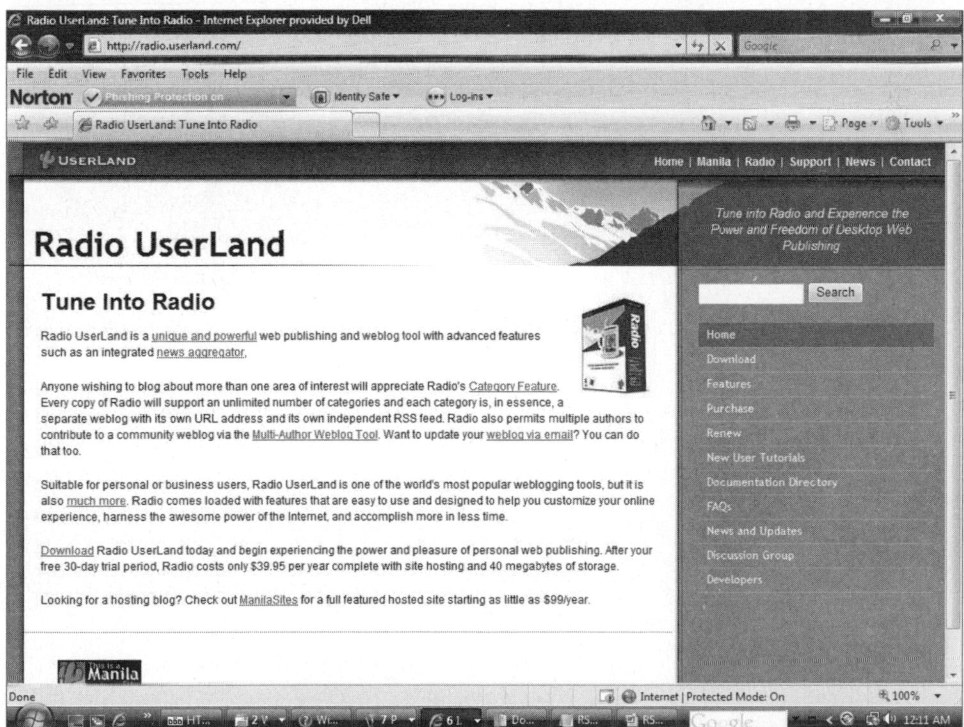

The real power of UserLand kicks in if you use RSS. UserLand manages the RSS 2.0 specification, and you can automatically take in other RSS content as a feed to your site and enable others to take your own site as a feed to theirs. If you want to have all the latest content on a topic, or if you have a lot of people who want to republish what you say, RSS and UserLand may be the way to go.

However, all of this is not simple. Even the acronym is controversial. Some say that RSS means Really Simple Syndication; others, Rich Site Summary. In any event, RSS may be replaced soon by an updated specification called Atom.

CROSS-REF RSS is discussed in Chapter 23

But the specifics of RSS may not be a problem for you. Increasingly, this kind of capability is being built into hosted sites, or made available through easy-to-use tools. So, you may be able to take advantages of the capabilities of RSS without worrying about what the acronym means.

Check out Microsoft Live Spaces (`http://home.services.spaces.live.com`), which is also integrated into Windows, so you can blog from many of the free Microsoft Live applications, such as Photo Gallery and the free Live Writer application.

Blogging add-ons

There's a tremendous range of blogging add-ons for everything from adding capabilities to your blog, to keeping up with new posts, to contributing to the latest and greatest technical specifications underlying blogging.

Following are a trio of the best resources for blogging add-ons:

- `http:windowslivewriter.spaces.live.com/blog/`
- `www.bloggersblog.com/widgetlinks`
- `www.writerswrite.com/blogging/software.htm`

Each of these sources has dozens of resources. Perhaps a brief profile of a few of them will encourage you to go check out the range of what's available:

- *Bloggers Blog* — Bloggers Blog is a tool that enables you, as a blognatic, to do almost anything, or add almost anything, bloggish to your own blog site. Its blogging categories run from A to W and cover more topics than we, with our combined minds, would ever be able to conceive. Bloggers Blog is full of widgets and fun. Check it out at `http://www.bloggersblog.com`. Figure 24-12 shows the home page.
- *blogBuddy* — blogBuddy is a tool that enables you to access the capabilities found in the Blogger API. The idea is that you can get access to added capabilities, before they're implemented in Blogger or elsewhere. The blogBuddy news page (which you can visit at `http://blogbuddy.sourceforge.net`) hasn't been updated for a while, but if you're technically oriented, this might be a good place to find out something about what's possible with blogs.

- *blogdex* — Calling itself "the Weblog diffusion index," blogdex tracks the most-quoted stories in the blogosphere. The contents don't always reflect well on the blogging community, and sometimes cover controversial topics, but they do tell you what's going on out there. Visit `http://blogdex.net` to see for yourself. Bloggist beware, however. No one quite knows the current state of blogdex because, as the Web site delicately explains, it is being "rethought."

FIGURE 24-12

Bloggers Blog is just one of the scores of tools out there.

Integrating Blogging

Integrating blog content into a regular, non-blog Web site is not that difficult and can add life and interest to a site that might otherwise become stale. There are several ways to do this, from the easy to the complicated, but any of them can bring the power of blogging to a Web site near you.

Blogging as a writing style

Many mainstream news sites (such as `msnbc.com`) use blogging as a style of writing. Just add a new header and a few paragraphs of text to the top of your Web page every so often, commenting on whatever's happened recently, and link to relevant resources. Presto — instant blog!

You can have one or several such blogs on a Web site. If you don't mind cranking up your HTML-editing program, or using a Web site host's tools for each update, this is a very easy way to make your site more lively and interesting.

Integration by reference

You can create a blog using any of the tools described in this chapter (or others) and then link to it from your Web site. For example, you can create a full blog in Blogger (described previously), posting everything you can think of in it and inviting comment from all and sundry.

Then, copy and paste the "best of Blogger" from your blog into your regular Web site. Link to the whole thing for those who just can't get enough. Using this approach, you might end up with the best of both worlds — a very good blog and a very good Web site.

Full integration

You can fully integrate a Web log into your site through several different means. For example, Blogger includes an option called Advanced Blog Setup (see Figure 24-13) that enables you to put a fully capable Blogger blog right onto a page of your Web site.

FIGURE 24-13

Blogger offers one way to integrate a blog.

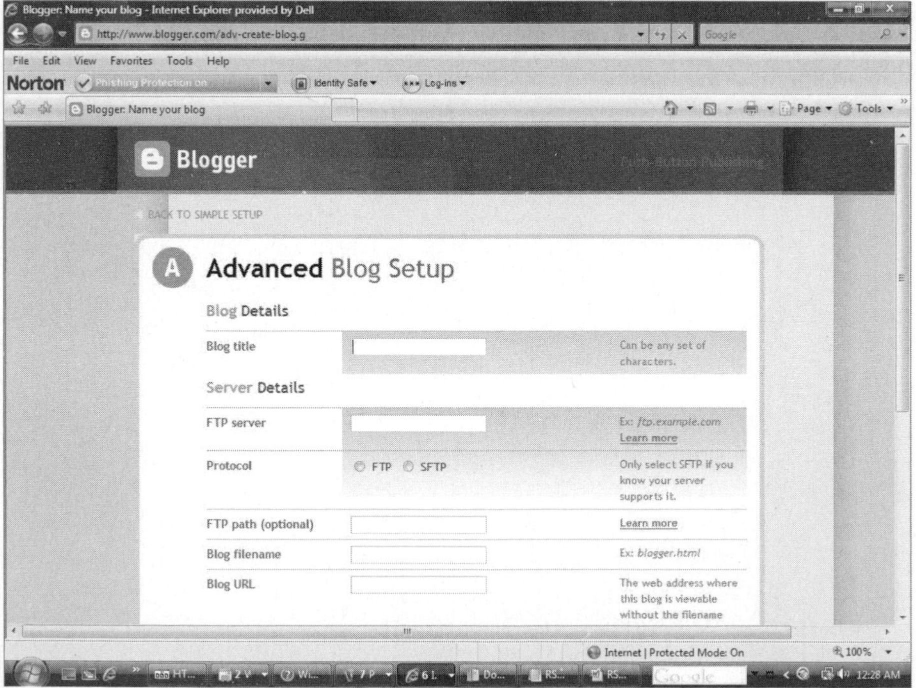

NOTE **You may also use iframes.**

You'll need FTP access to your Web site and a few details of where Blogger needs to send updates. Ask your Web host for help if you need it. But, with this capability, you end up with all the power of Blogger, right in the middle of a Web site over which you have full control.

RSS is another way to integrate your blog into your site into your blog, or just about anything else you want to do. See the earlier section "Radio Userland" for details.

CROSS-REF **RSS is discussed in Chapter 23.**

Summary

Blogging is a breakthrough in keeping a Web site up to date and interesting. There are many ways to create your own blog or to add a blog to an existing site. You can even use a blog as a stream of data into your own site, or others' sites.

In this chapter, you learned that blogging makes it easy for anyone to be heard on the Web. Blogger, now owned by Google, is one popular way to start your own blog. Providers ranging from AOL to Microsoft to Radio UserLand and beyond provide a wide variety of tools for blogging. One of the most current and exciting open source web tool is Wordpress (codex.wordpress.org /Main_Page). It's easy to integrate a blog into your existing site.

Index

Symbols and Numbers

A

B

C

D

E

F

G

I

K

L

M

N

O

P

Q

R

S

T

U

W

X

Y

Z